OPPOSITE ATTRACTION

ALSO BY JULIE GILBERT

Ferber:

The Biography of Edna Ferber and Her Circle

Umbrella Steps

OPPOSITE ATTRACTION

*The Lives of Erich Maria Remarque
and Paulette Goddard*

JULIE GILBERT

P A N T H E O N   B O O K S
N E W   Y O R K

Permissions acknowledgments are on pages 507–510.
Illustration credits are on pages 510–13.

Library of Congress Cataloging-in-Publication Data

Gilbert, Julie Goldsmith.
Opposite attraction: the lives of Erich Maria Remarque and
Paulette Goddard / Julie Gilbert.
p.   cm.
Includes index.
ISBN 0-679-41535-1
1. Remarque, Erich Maria, 1898–1970—Marriage.   2. Goddard,
Paulette—Marriage.   3. Authors, German—20th century—Biography.
4. Motion picture actors and actresses—United States—Biography.
I. Title.
PT2635.E68Z67 1995
833' .912—dc20
[B]

Book design by Deborah Kerner

Manufactured in the United States of America

First Edition
2 4 6 8 9 7 5 3 1

This book is for my parents, Janet and Henry Goldsmith,
who understand "the process" so well, with a special
thank-you to my father,
who contributed his considerable knowledge, translating
skills, and compassion.

It is for my husband, Francis Daniel,
who cheered me on through many an anxious day and night.
And it is for my agents, Robert Lantz and Joy Harris,
who believed that it should, could, and would be written.

It is in memory of Harriet Pilpel,
who was always an inspiration to me,
and finally, it is in memory of Dan Seymour,
who would often say in his succinct way when I dawdled,
"Write your book."

CONTENTS

FOREWORD

THERE ARE CERTAIN PEOPLE it is hard to imagine as ever having undergone infancy, unsure steps, formative years. Erich Maria Remarque and Paulette Goddard seem to have been born iconoclastic, good-looking, and successful. He, having been a world-renowned novelist beginning with his antiwar classic, *All Quiet on the Western Front*, and she, beguiling, shrewd, beautiful, and always the center of attention, capturing whatever she desired. Both were free spirits, playing the game of life with complete expertise. Had they not eventually found each other, it would have been most unusual.

It was more than a decade ago that a wise and brilliant lawyer and friend of mine named Harriet Pilpel became enthusiastic about the idea of my writing a biography of Remarque.

In 1990, Paulette Goddard died at the variously reported ages of seventy-five, eighty, and eighty-one. Her obituary in the *New York Times* was as dazzling as her fabled jewelry collection.

Shortly afterward, I was in the office of Harriet Pilpel and told her that I was intrigued by even the small report of her life in the *Times* obituary, and wanted to write a biography of Paulette Goddard instead. Harriet Pilpel looked aghast. "But you certainly can't do a book on Paulette without doing a book on Erich!" she said.

My thanks to all those who collaborated with me to make this book possible. My special gratitude goes to Richard Kay, co-executor of the Paulette Goddard Remarque Estate, who gave me all the keys to this particular kingdom; to Frank Walker, former head of the Fales Library (which houses the Erich Maria Remarque Collection) in the Elmer Holmes Bobst Library at New York University, who was ever courtly in assisting me in my quest; to New York University, for permissions and access to the estate; to Monika Anderson and Gerdi Eller, my hard-working translators of Remarque's diaries written in German and of most of the correspondence and articles in German, who cheerfully dedicated themselves to my deadlines; to Lois Granato, for her insightful knowledge of the Widow Remarque; to Andrea Miller, who diligently and intelligently transcribed my tapes; to Caroline Shookhoff, for retyping the entire manuscript in record time; to Alain Bourgeois, for his invaluable counsel and care; to Thomas Schneider, for his unstinting help and support; and to my editor, Shelley Wanger, for her astute advice, patience, sense of humor, and genuine caring.

I also thank the following: Marvin Taylor and Maxime la Fantasie at the Fales Library of New York University; Ann Harris, Coordinator of the Film Studies Program at the Tisch School of the Arts at New York University; Robert Noto, Head Counsel of New York University; S. Andrew Schaffer, General Counsel for New York University; Judge Alain M. Bourgeois (ret.); Mary Corliss and Terry Geesken at the Museum of Modern Art Film Stills Archive; Janet Lorenz at the Margaret Herrick Library of the Academy of Motion Picture Arts and Sciences; Ron Mandelbaum and Howard Mandelbaum of Photofest; Francicka Safran, Curator of the Stefan Zweig Collection in the Reed Library at the State University of New York College at Fredonia; Valerie Vlasaty and Elizabeth Rioux at Sotheby's Jewelry Department; Frederick Hughes, executor of the estate of Andy Warhol; Lan Nguyen, Kate Westerbeck, Kate Rowe, Kathy Schulz, Anthony F. Holmes, Bob Consenza, Tom Grochowski, Melissa Kozlowski, Vicki Gibson, Alyce Mott, Steven Bach, Peter Riva, Billy Wilder, Michael Hall, Bob Colacello, Rod Steiger, Celestine Wallis, Luise Rainer, Ruth Albu Morgenroth, Ruth Marton, John and Romana Parkes, Mary Wickes, Doris Scharnberg, John Gavin, Bob Hope, Lillian Gish, Kim Guggenheim, Irene Heyman, Antonietta Bellosta, Paola Bellosta, Regina Gfeller, Ruth Fantoni, Barbara Wiese, Budy Keibel, Helen Murray, James Frazier, Rolf Gerard, Licci Habe, Warren Alpert, Jean Tailer, Jinx Falkenburg McCrary, Steven Aronson, Ellen Dunham, John Johnstone, Charles Silver, Curtis Riess, Leonard Nimoy, Burgess Meredith, Patricia Roc Reif, Lady Dojean and Sir Peter Smithers, Peter Stone, Roz Starr, Anita Seltzer, Charlotte Elk Zernik,

Victoria Wolff, Luciana Reffiori Cariboni, Daniel Selznick, Margaret Horlitz, Douglas Fairbanks, Jr., Gardner McKay, Lew Ayres, Macdonald Carey, Fritzy Weiner, Robert Lantz, Sheila Siegmer, Dr. Joseph Bissig, Diana Edkins, Iris Roseveare, Sara Barrett, Richard Horst, Penny Proddow, Marion Fasel, Duane Michals, Joseph Mankiewitz, Robert Pilpel, Bob Ulman, Carlton Rochell, Bruce Miyagishima, Ristorante Al Pontile and Ristorante Al Porto (in Ascona, Switzerland), the Powell Library Film Department at the University of California, the Library of Congress, and the Federal Bureau of Investigation.

Last, but certainly not least, I salute Prof. Dr. Tilman Westphalen, Dr. Phil. Thomas Schneider, Claudia Glunz, M.A., Annegret Tietzeck, Dieter Voigt, and Michael Fisher: the archive team that is a shining jewel in the Remarque crown. Working at the Erich-Maria-Remarque Archiv/ Forschungsstelle Krieg und Literatur at Osnabrück University in Osnabrück, Germany, Dr. Westphalen, head of the archive, Dr. Schneider, and all the others helped me to understand and appreciate the political value of Remarque, the man, and his work yesterday, today, and tomorrow. I smile slightly ruefully at them now, for I have shared Remarque's story with Paulette's, as I told them I must. My best hope is that Erich Maria Remarque and Paulette Goddard will continue to intrigue and entertain.

JULIE GILBERT, November 1994

OPPOSITE ATTRACTION

CHAPTER ONE

A GERMAN YOUTH

1898–1922

ERICH MARIA REMARQUE once said about himself that he was abundantly Cancerian because he was a crab with razor-sharp claws. Born Erich Paul Remark on June 22, 1898, in the Provinzil Hebammen Lehr- und Entbindungsanstalt (Provincial Midwife and Maternity Hospital), he was the second son and as such was positioned for a combative role against his older brother, Theodor Arthur, who was the favorite.

The Remarques had French roots. Johann Adam Remarque had been born in Aachen, near the French frontier, in 1789, and was a master nail-smith by trade, but moved with his German wife, Anna Elizabeth Franken, to Kaiserwerth on the Rhine in Germany. There, either by design or by clerical error, the spelling of their surname was changed to Remark. Their one son, Peter Aloys Remark, followed in his father's footsteps as a nailsmith and married a seamstress, Adelheid Baumer; in 1867, she gave birth to a son, Peter Franz, who broke family tradition by training as a bookbinder and joining the merchant marine. When Peter Franz married Anna Maria Stallknecht in 1895, he moved to the Westphalian town of Osnabrück in Lower Saxony, where his four children were born—one of whom would not belong within this strict Catholic, working-class, unimaginative family and would eventually reclaim the French spelling of his great-grandfather's name.

In the early days of Erich's parents' marriage, his father put in long hours as a bookbinder at a firm known as Prelle's on Hakenstrasse. Among his fellow workers he was not popular: "His dry and unfriendly nature contributed little towards making a pleasant working environment," said one co-worker. At home he was equally taciturn, prompting his awkward but attractive young wife to give all her attention to her new son, Theo. Lonely and isolated, Anna Maria had the baby as her only solace.

Birth control was not practiced by the Roman Catholic Remarks, and the arrival of two daughters soon followed the boys. Erna was born on September 6, 1900, and Elfriede three years later, on March 25. The slightly older Erich looked fondly upon his sisters, both of whom were fair, sweet, and docile. Though Theo died of influenza in 1901 at the age of six, his mother continued to honor the memory of him as the favorite son.

Erich's mother, Anna Maria, did not take three-year-old Erich to the funeral, but when it was over she came home, took him aside, and said, "Now you have to be the best one." Erich, hating the idea of being an understudy, of winning the part by default, hit his mother in the face. Decades later, he recalled the traumatic moment to the journalist Victoria Wolff, a trusted friend: "I still suffer from that stupid reaction of mine. And I really hit her hard. But somewhere I must have decided that I would be the best one."

There was another factor that might have added to young Erich's feelings of rejection and emotional dislocation. The Remarks were constantly moving: they lived at Jahnstrasse 15 when Erich was born, then up the street at Jahnstrasse 21 from 1900 through 1901, then onward to Schinkelerstrasse in 1902. For the next fourteen years there were seven more moves, until 1915, when they settled in Hakenstrasse 3. This was an attic apartment in a house owned by the Prelle firm, which employed Peter Franz, who in later years worked there as a master machinist. But it was probably less the Remarks' roving spirit than a canny pragmatism on Peter Franz's part that caused the moves. The real reason, according to Hanns-Gerd Rabe, an Osnabrück colleague and Remarque expert, is that a lower rent was charged for each of these newly built, or "wet," houses; when the plaster dried and the house settled, the rent escalated.

Despite a dour and rigid atmosphere at home, Rabe confirmed that Erich was able to abandon himself to a fairly normal childhood:

LEFT: *Peter Franz Remark and his son Erich, age one, in 1899.*

ABOVE: *Anna Maria Remark with her daughters, Erna and Elfriede, in 1915.*

ABOVE: *Elfriede, flanked by Erna and Erich, ca. 1909 .*

The different homes on Jahnstrasse held the key to the child's paradise, with the "snat path," the "poplar ditch" and the then still unpopulated "desert," which was so dry during hot summers that the smell of fire, started by children, attracted the curiosity of others, among them Erich. Unforgettable times were spent in the "poplar ditch," which used to swell during the rainy season and flood the gardens. The magic, stemming from the solitude of the quiet landscape, the spring with its abundance of flowers, the paradise created by a wealth of birds and other wildlife, encouraged the young Erich to collect plants and butterflies.

Erich had a fairly serious butterfly collection as well as a makeshift aquarium of fish in jars. He also collected stamps and worked at magic and hypnotism. For a time, he became intrigued with the ancient Greek Games and threw himself into gymnastics, becoming, in 1911, a member of the Osnabrück Gymnastics Club. But although he might have had an aura of being well-rounded and happy, he felt more isolated than his performance conveyed. In an interview in 1929, he commented plaintively on his past: "I never felt that anyone at home or at school understood my tendency to dream, my desire for far-away worlds. I never received guidance with my reading."

At the age of six, Erich began elementary school, and from 1904 until 1908 he was a somewhat unruly pupil of the Domschule (Cathedral School). But a maverick intelligence was already in evidence by the time he was twelve. One teacher, reading aloud Erich's essay describing a previous summer's vacation, came to the line "Proud and prominent traverses the white sailboat, *The Albatross*, the gleaming surge of the open sea." He approached Erich's chair, yanked him up from his seat, hit him several times, and demanded to know from which book he had copied the fancy language. Erich, bewildered by his teacher's question and rough treatment, didn't answer, which only enraged the teacher more. He struck Erich over and over until he finally answered, "It was like that at the seashore where I spent my vacation—four full weeks. I simply had to describe it that way."

In 1908 the Remarks pulled up stakes again, moving to Jahnstrasse 29 in the south part of the city, where Erich entered the Johannisschule, remaining there until 1912. Because Erich was considered of the artisan class, his formal education was to end with this second school. He was to be educated in the basics under the auspices of the Catholic church for only eight years. He would never have the benefit of attending a Mittelschule, intermediate school, or its alternative, the German Gymnasium, where upper-class students learned French, Latin, English, and the humanities. These courses, from which Erich was barred, were the very ones that his active mind craved.

Erich both suffered from these limitations and overcame them. A classmate in the Johannisschule reported, "I shared my schooldays with Remarque. He always was easy on himself. Luckily, he was bright enough and didn't need to study at home. The only subject he truly liked was history of literature. He was always the best in class, rather outspoken, and therefore often got into arguments with the teachers."

Young Erich tried to fit in as much as he could without compromising a darker, more solitary, unique side of his personality. When his ambitions were curtailed by the reality of life in an industrial town as well as his family's economic situation, he naturally turned inward and reinvented his aspirations as fantasy. Eventually a writer emerged, but his life could have gone another way. A 1929 entry from *In the Twenties*, the published diaries of Harry Kessler, a German diplomat and social chronicler, depicts Remarque reflecting upon his early self: "He told me his story in great detail and almost without a pause for breath. As a boy from a lower-middle-class home in Osnabrück, he was very unhappy at the lack of any intellectual mentor. At fifteen, he sweated his way through the *Critique of Pure Reason* [Kant], though without much appreciation. It always seemed to him extraordinary that he should exist at all. He spent a disconsolate youth interspersed with thoughts of suicide."

Remarque often drew a rather Dickensian picture of his youth. It was probably his overactive imagination and his love of books, drawing, and music that saved him. From an early age Erich had an ability—a talent, in fact—for finding romance and adventure in the mundane. As is evident in all his writing, colors, textures, sounds, and smells were palpable, verging on the anthropomorphic. And although he had no encouragement, he read voraciously and had very specific literary tastes by the time he was thirteen. The works of Herman Hesse, Stefan Zweig, Dostoevsky, Thomas Mann, Goethe, and Proust became his lifetime companions. His passionate interest in music began when he sang in the choir at the Johannis school. "I wanted to become a musician, a pianist, or perhaps a painter," he said wistfully, years later. "However," he continued, reiterating his iconoclasm, "neither at home nor at school did I find understanding for my dreams or support for my trials." In fact, Remarque would always feel he had suffered a lack of love because of his older brother. His self-pity also took the form of feeling he wasn't understood or supported in his desire for an artistic life. Life looked bleak. There seemed to be only three realistic futures for him: postmaster, teacher, or pharmacist.

By the time he was twelve, his best friend was Kristen Kranzbuehler, who would later become a featured character as Kemmerich in *All Quiet on the Western Front*. Along with boyish capers in the company of Kranzbuehler, his copious collections of butterflies, rocks, stamps, and goldfish served as his great escape prior to entering the Präparande, the three-year Catholic preparatory school that paved the way for him to enter a Catholic teachers' training college.

There, from 1912 to 1915, Erich received the education that would enable him to teach. The Präparande, behind Old Saint Mary's church, was staid and quiet and had a bucolic air. Although under the auspices of the Catholic church, this "prep" school was not run solely by clerics. The staff of lay teachers could be guided by the local priest and yet not practice exactly what he preached.

Erich was not rebellious in the conventional sense. In that day, in that country, and coming from his station, it would have taken a truly aberrant streak to create disorder. His best revenge would eventually be to depict the narrow-mindedness of some of the staff members from the Präparande in his early published novels. A case in point was a teacher named Konschorek, who became Roman Kantorek in *All Quiet on the Western Front*: "Kantorek had been our schoolmaster, a stern little man in a grey tail-coat, with a face like a shrew mouse. . . . It is very queer that the unhappiness of the world is so often brought on by small men. . . . They are mostly confounded little martinets."

Joseph Witt, a classmate of Erich's who moved with him from the prep school to the Präparande, recalled that he had an aptitude for literary history and read avidly from the works of Jack London, Rilke, Franz Werfel, Schopenhauer, and Nietzsche. He was an average student who followed his studies dutifully, and was, on the whole, popular with the other boys.

Erich lived at home all during his schooling, and although not much is documented about this time with his family, it is clear from his fiction that he felt more sympathy toward his mother than toward his father. He resembled her physically, with large bones on a medium frame, the same wide, fair brow, clear blue eyes, and sensuous mouth. Anna Maria's love of music—particularly piano concertos—most likely inspired his early love of music and piano. The Remark home was not so humble that they did not have a piano in the parlor, fairly typical of German homes at the turn of the

*Erich at age thirteen with Wolf,
his German shepherd, 1912.*

Erich (bottom row, third from right) with his Präparande classmates, ca. 1913.

century. Erich, perhaps in the beginning to gain his mother's favor, practiced playing the piano, but soon developed a real passion for it and began to compose his own scores. He knew this was not a career open to him, but it did not stop him: "I wanted to become a musician, a pianist . . . if I hadn't been wounded on my hand in the war," he said years later, still seeming to lament the twist of fate that had led him to literary concertos.

From his father he inherited a taste for the mysterious, the metaphysical; yet, unlike his father, he never developed a lifelong fascination with magic tricks. Johannes Spratte, a co-worker of Peter Franz Remark's, provided this view of Peter's darker leanings: "Peter Remark liked to concern himself with occult things. I can still see him attempting with his pocket watch to conjure up things which are between heaven and earth. If one showed him a photograph of a person whom he did not know he allowed his pocket watch to swing over this photograph and then said, often surprisingly correctly, who was dead or was still living."

Erich, in the years to come, would also show an interest in the unknowable, becoming increasingly dependent on astrological readings and charts. He would not travel, marry, or sign a contract on a certain date if the stars were not auspicious. In retrospect, Peter Remark and his pocket watch seemed quite quaint.

At the end of 1915, after three years of prep school, Erich's final report card read, "Attentiveness and eagerness: GOOD. Obtained results: In general GOOD." He was getting by gracefully, performing well but not exceptionally. He was cheerfully meeting his parents' expectations, but still managed to express his individuality. He gave piano lessons to earn pocket money in order to further polish his already elegant good looks. He liked fancy ties and wore cologne on his clean-shaven face and neck, whereas most of his peers wore the nicks of a clumsy razor blade. He metamorphosed from a bookworm into a rather flamboyant adolescent, ready to embrace the events that, beginning in 1916, would transform his destiny.

Erich moved on to the Catholic Seminary for Teachers, which, as Hanns-Gerd Rabe explained, "appeared isolated from the academic life of the city, because it had been under the auspices of the bishop until 1907, when it was put under government control." And it was at this time that Erich found another means of expression to help him break away from the strict and provincial life of being a grammar school teacher.

He began to write little essays and verses. Several circumstances bolstered this pursuit. There was the burgeoning youth movement in Germany that came to be called Wandervögel, which translates as "bird of passage." It was a nature-proselytizing group that was fervently embraced and supported by Osnabrück's Protestant factions. Erich rejected this movement, and in doing so spurned a highly prescribed portion of the supposedly liberal education of imperial Germany. It was not long before he was caught playing truant and forced to join the Osnabrück Youth Corps—a requisite for all youths who were not members of Wandervögel. Erich could not have been that reluctant a member of this Youth Corps, for in June of 1916 his first words to appear in print were published in their journal, *Heimatfreund*. The essay was titled "From the Homeland: Of the Pleasures and Troubles of the Youth Corps." It won him a prize of thirty deutsche marks. The prose, which describes a day in the Youth Army, is as young as its seventeen-year-old author and has the kind of intensity and nationalistic rapture that signaled a certain militaristic fervor:

The sun appeared through gray, ragged clouds and shone on the white, freezing earth. We had assembled in front of the sports hall, according to rank. It was bitter cold and our breath rose like steam in the air. We were supposed to have a battle with another company. This one had destroyed train tracks and occupied a nearby forest. While they took up their position, we marched to "Netterheide," a large, flat troop-training ground, to exercise for a while.

The marching colony has assembled quickly and the company marches to the battleground. Step by step we creep forward, listening again and again, and stop. Finally, it becomes lighter ahead of us; we have reached the edge of the forest. . . . Two, three men come across the meadow to our hiding place. Did they see us? Nonsense! Get back, guys, get back quietly, we can take these three youngsters as our prisoners. There they come. Five more steps, 3, 2—"Stop!" We jump up and get them. How surprised they are! That was a good catch. But now we must go back. At 6 o'clock we should be back with the troops. Carefully back! Triumphantly, we are taking the prisoners with us. . . . All our impatience and suspense reappear and dissolve into a truly cruel scream, as we race across the meadow. Whoops. My foot gets stuck in the moor. . . . Storm! Everybody races forward screaming, shooting, applauding. A deafening noise erupts, the old forest giants shake their tops. "Assemble!" Hot and breathing heavily, we line up in the meadow. Our critic praises our goodwill, but reprimands us for our wild advance. A soldier must be patient. Then we return to the country road. . . . Yes, it was wonderful. All believe that. "Let us sing a song! Yes, yes, of the birds of the forest!"

We are marching home in the dark. High in the sky the silver light sails along in the eternal space. The moon surrounds the dark clouds with silver trimming and casts his light over the sleeping, rustling trees and the distant hills, covered with a soft, silvery mist. From a distance, one can hear the soldiers sing on their way home and a quiet echo is heard: "The birds in the forest sang so beautifully. At home, at home, we will see each other again!"

Erich Remark, Osnabrück

This essay does reveal chauvinistic as well as personal sensibilities and idiosyncrasies that would surface in Remarque's classic *All Quiet on the Western Front* and other works from then on. There are the beginnings of recurring images such as the moon, whose silver light is generously described in many other books. This piece, with its sense of action, duty, drama, poetry, and irony, is a harbinger of the masterpiece that he would write ten years later, when he was twenty-seven.

In the early part of 1916, Erich met up with a group of true soulmates who shared his passion for literature and art. Calling themselves the Circle of the Traumbude, the Dream Circle, they were young and as bohemian as one dared in imperial Germany. They met to read aloud, discuss, and encourage one another's works, as well as to dissect and rebuke "the sad state of parental, academic, and governmental authority."

The leader of this pack of idealists was a painter and poet named Fritz Hörstemeier, who was probably the single most important and uplifting influence in young Erich Remark's life. The group gathered almost daily at Liebigstrasse 31, in the attic of the house where Hörstemeier lived. Hörstemeier, who was thirty-three when Erich met him, had brown silky curls, a mustache and goatee, a dancer's body, and a romantic and elegant approach to life. This older man became an idol for Erich, standing for everything that his father wasn't. Hörstemeier had been a house painter, and led a nomadic life, wandering through Berlin, Dresden, Munich, and even as far as Italy. To an Osnabrück boy, he was a true cosmopolitan. He had left his profession to become an artist, following his heart and managing to eke out a modest living. Owing to a serious angina condition, he rarely went outdoors—although he understood and extolled nature. He was limited to his garden hut and to the immediate countryside, which, at that time, was still gloomy and romantic. He painted still lifes, flowers, portraits, and interiors in oil, tempera, and pen-and-ink. His diaries—from 1904 through 1917— were dense with philosophical observations, love paeans to nature and humanity; they expressed a thirst for beauty and a bedrock belief in God's

Remarque's mentor, Fritz Hörstemeier, in his "dream attic," ca. 1915.

A meeting of the Traumbude Circle with Fritz Hörstemeier, left, and Remarque right, ca. 1915.

eminence. The simple, reflective tone of the diaries is reminiscent of Nietzsche. In addition to his other gentle pursuits, he played several instruments, and was a vegetarian, but he did reveal a militant side in leaving the Catholic church and requesting cremation.

Erich blindly followed and practiced everything that his "darling Fritz" (as he would refer to him in his own diaries) espoused. The Hörstemeier credo was peaceful and almost childlike: a youth-oriented search for Art and Beauty. The members of the circle posed questions about art, music, love, and literature. They celebrated the answers. They attempted to transpose reality into a transcendental emotional world of beauty, one inhabited by lofty beings of a pure character. But along with this idealization of life, there were some strange, Teutonic ideas. The Dream Circle was committed to nudity as the only fully realized state of being, and in keeping with that, honored sexual freedom and liberation. The magazine that was their bible, *Die Schönheit*, specialized in nude features advocating the benefits of health, sports, and sunshine. A note from the Osnabrück archive regarding Hörstemeier says, "He delighted in the pleasure of the naked, undisturbed human being during sports activities . . . and took nude photos in the woods."

The second odd, yet rather touching, note in the ethos of the Traumbudekreis was their determination to transform dun-colored Osnabrück into one of the cultural capitals, rivaling Munich, Dresden, or even Berlin.

By all existing accounts, Hörstemeier, although eccentric, was neither delusional nor despotic but exceedingly decent, with the highest of hopes for a better society. And for Erich, who had railed against being trapped in an emotionally, intellectually, and aesthetically impoverished world, Hörstemeier was a god.

"What does one think about at seventeen?" asked Remarque in a 1930 interview with the French journalist Frédéric Lefevre, and then he went on about the harsh events that crashed his "dream circle." "For my part I was dreaming that I should become a composer, and behold, I found myself thrown into barracks and then, a few weeks later, I was sent to the front. My life had changed the moment when I began to organize it freely in accordance with my dreams."

As early as 1915, there were classmates of Erich's who were signing up to serve in the Great War. But Erich resisted as long as he could. Through Hörstemeier and the Dream Circle he had gained creative inspiration. He knew by the time he was eighteen years old that he had to either be a composer or a writer. He also knew that as a seeker of truth and beauty, although patriotic, he was not militaristic. He was naturally a pacifist, and in that sense alienated from the Teutonic mentality. Also, at this time, his mother was diagnosed with cancer, which would eventually metastasize. Her agonizing bouts with the disease severely debilitated the family.

As a counterpoint to his mother's illness, Erich fell in love for the first time. Her name was Erika Haase and she was a member of the Dream Circle. Nothing is known about her feelings, but according to his diary, which Erich began to keep in 1918, the relationship was platonic (beginning with this diary of 1918 and in the years to come, Erich was erratic in dating his diary entries as well as his correspondence): "On my table there stands a picture of Erika as a springtime fairy. There's a deep, sincere friendship between Erika and myself. We are related, and aware of the fact. I will always picture her, at the Kottmans', sitting on the arm of the sofa in the lamplight, singing songs for the lute in her clear voice. What a marvelous figure, hair flowing down her back, her fine head, and those brown eyes! What pretty songs she sang! They still run through my head."

Throughout his life, Erich's relationships with women would divide into ones either of brotherly affection or of grand passion. Though this first relationship seemed to be about gentle affection, Erich tended to gravitate toward difficult and tortuous passions. How much his unsatisfactory relationship with his mother had to do with it we will never know.

On November 21, 1916, Erich was drafted. Recruit training was in Osnabrück in a camp called Kaprivi-Kaserne. The course that Erich and some of his classmates were put through was strict but physically endurable. Erich found he had more tolerance for it than for the petty power plays of the military bureaucracy. Prussian training drills were conducted by Corporal Himmelreich, later to become the loathsome villain Himmelstoss in *All Quiet on the Western Front*:

> I went to No. 9 platoon under Corporal Himmelstoss.
>
> He had the reputation of being the strictest disciplinarian in the camp, and was proud of it. He was a small undersized fellow with a foxy, waxed moustache, who had seen twelve years' service and was in civil life a postman. He had a special dislike of . . . me, because he sensed a quiet defiance.
>
> I have remade his bed fourteen times in one morning. Each time he had some fault to find and pulled it to pieces.

Hanns-Gerd Rabe puts it well when he says, "The most difficult time to describe in R.'s life is his time as a soldier, because reality and fiction in his

novel *All Quiet* . . . often overlap, despite the fact that the novel does not portray R.'s war experiences; however, he does use the reality of war in its brutality."

Among the recruits in Erich's unit were classmates from the Seminary for
Teachers, who became material for many of his future novels. Troske, Georg
Middendorf, Katchinsky, and Seppel Oelfe were boys only days before, who
nicknamed Erich "Schottenpaut" and "Schmieren" (referring to his messy
handwriting). Now they were all on the front line. But along with the fear
and rigor of suddenly having to fulfill the requirements of being grown men
was the cheek and swagger of recently bygone days:

> One Sunday as Kropp [based on Georg Middendorf] and I were lugging
> a latrine-bucket on a pole across the barrack-yard, Himmelstoss came by, all
> polished up and ready to go out. He planted himself in front of us and asked
> how we liked the job. In spite of ourselves we tripped and emptied the
> bucket over his legs. He raved, but the limit had been reached.
>
> "That means clink," he yelled.
>
> But Kropp had had enough. "There'll be an inquiry first," he said, "and
> then we'll unload."
>
> "Mind how you speak to a non-commissioned officer!" bawled
> Himmelstoss. "Have you lost your senses? You wait till you're spoken to.
> What will you do, anyway?"
>
> "Show you up, Corporal," said Kropp, his thumbs in line with the seams
> of his trousers.

On July 25, 1917, Troske, one of Erich's comrades, was struck down by
shell fragments. Erich heroically carried him to safety, but he died anyway.
In *All Quiet*, Remarque transposes the real Troske into the character of Kat,
whose name was taken from Katchinsky. Erich, a great name-scrambler, was
also fond of pseudonyms; his fiction constantly kept friends and lovers guess-
ing. The following passage is probably close to what happened on that summer day:

> The going is more difficult. Often a shell whistles across. I go as quickly
> as I can, for the blood from Kat's wound is dripping on the ground. We can-
> not shelter ourselves properly from the explosions; before we can take cover
> the danger is all over.
>
> We lie down in a small hole to wait till the shelling is over. I give Kat some

As a young teacher, Erich stayed in this house in Lohne for nine long months, 1919-1920.

LEFT: *Erich wearing his controversial lieutenant's uniform, with his dog Wolf at his side, 1918.*

During World War I, Remarque, second from right, seated with fellow soldiers, 1918.

tea from my water bottle. We smoke a cigarette. "Well, Kat," I say gloomily, "we are going to be separated at last."

He is silent and looks at me.

"Do you remember, Kat, how we commandeered the goose? And how you brought me out of the barrage when I was still a young recruit and was wounded for the first time? I cried then, Kat, that was almost three years ago."

During his three years in the army, Erich never fought, though he was close to the front. Six days after he dragged Troske away from enemy fire, he was wounded in three places by shrapnel from English long-range shells. It was at the start of the English offensive on July 31, 1917, when he was hit behind the lines. He was wounded above the knee, above the right wrist, and in the neck. Although the wounds were not life threatening, they were severe enough to take him out of the war and into the hospital. He was initially brought to Field Hospital 309 in Thourot, and then, in mid-August, to Saint Vincenz's hospital in Duisburg. It was there that Erich Maria Remarque began to emerge, turning from the rookie soldier into a distinctive civilian.

Everyone noticed Erich. He was extremely handsome and charming. He made his substantial convalescence work in his favor, laying plans for a projected stay and taking a position as clerk in the Secretariat.

On September 26, 1917, Erich went back briefly to Osnabrück, but not to rejoin his battalion. He went to attend his mother's funeral, and years later, in an interview in 1929, he reflected on the loss: "I was without aim, unhappy, disappointed, and lonely. My mother had died in the meantime, and what is a family without a mother?"

The most poignant evocation of his feeling for her, and for himself as her son the soldier, came through the character of Paul Bäumer, the first-person protagonist of *All Quiet*:

> The room is dark. I hear my mother's breathing, and the ticking of the clock. Outside the window the wind blows and the chestnut trees rustle. . . .
>
> Out there I was indifferent and often hopeless—I will never be able to be so again. I was a soldier, and now I am nothing but an agony for myself, for my mother, for everything that is so comfortless and without end. . . .
>
> Ah! Mother, Mother! . . . why can I not put my head in your lap and weep? Why have I always to be strong and self-controlled? I would like to weep and be comforted too, indeed I am little more than a child; in the wardrobe still hang short, boy's trousers—it is such a little time ago, why is it over?

Remarque was far more bitter in his actual musings about his mother and the war. He mockingly said that he was glad to have been placed in the midst of battle: "If my mother had spoiled me, then I would have noticed the difference between war and peace even more."

Erich took some time off in Osnabrück. It was good to be home. In fact, it was especially sweet because he still belonged to the war effort, and who knew after his wounds healed if he would come home again alive or in a box? As he wrote to his old friend Rabe in 1957, no city was as close to his heart as Osnabrück, which he admitted was the background for all his books. And he would always write of it lovingly—gossiping, judging, feeling possessive. To his friend Middendorf, whom he had nicknamed "Dopp" for no discernible reason, he reported chattily about Osnabrück and its wake of war wounded and dead:

Dear Dopp! Please excuse my long silence. My mother died, and I was on vacation in Osnabrück and did not think about writing. I have much to tell you. Anyway, Kohlrautz, who was shot in the stomach, died a few days after. And think: Theo Troske did not only get shot in his heel, but also had three shots in the head. The poor guy died a few days later. I met Wiemann in Osnabrück. A fragment that hit him in the thigh penetrated into his stomach ... Kranzbuhler lost his leg up to the knee ... Butcher Tobar walks with two canes. This was a wonderful reunion! You don't know this yet: I have received a shot in my neck. Otherwise everything in Osnabrück is as it always was. . . . It will take some time with my wounds; they don't heal so well. Doesn't matter! I am not sorry. And how are you, beloved Dopp? . . . If you can write me the addresses of all comrades, please do so.

As concerned as he was about his comrades, he was also uneasy about returning to the war. One of his most traumatic memories was that of lying in the trenches on the front during fire attacks. Years later he found some relief from the experience by actually re-creating it in the garden of a friend. Victoria Wolff, his neighbor in Ascona—the town on the Swiss-Italian border where he would eventually settle—indulged him in this bizarre fantasy during a visit to her house when he was already in his mid-thirties: "It was early evening and he said, 'Now I will make my dream come true. You wait. Just wait.' So we made a trench in my garden. And he had brought everything to supply the trench: bottles, glasses, pillows, blankets, and flashlights. Whatever he wanted. That's what he was dreaming of when he dreamt about the war. 'I want to have a trench in the garden, and somebody who listens to me. You have to listen to me!' And I would listen to him as he told me stories of the war and after the war."

For a German youth to not celebrate the glory of fighting, to hate watching comrades slain, to avoid being sent back into the fray, meant being wounded pretty badly. Perhaps Erich somewhat prolonged his sufferings, for he remained in the hospital until October 3, 1918. His tone, however, is buoyant and playful, and he makes his life sound extremely busy as he writes to his favorite friend, Dopp. The letter shows his gleeful intent upon staying safe:

> Dear Dopp, Scoundrel, dearly beloved! . . . My wounds have not yet healed. I have made preparations to stay longer in the hospital. I am flirting with the daughter of the hospital director, and I am helping out as a clerk at the Secretariat. Thus, I am thinking that if I don't get hit with a slate from the roof or any other kind of infamous action, then I intend to spend the freezing cold winter here.
>
> I can go for walks, flirt with the girls (from the Rhineland), give piano concerts, be happy, and be spoiled by the Red Cross nurses and go home with them. I'm a beloved man by all.

And then there is this postscript: "Write about life, as I am doing now. And I hope you take great interest when I tell you that I am writing a novel!"

All Quiet on the Western Front, or in the German, *Im Westen nichts Neues*, was not the first novel by Erich Maria Remarque. The very first novel, *Die Traumbude (The Dream Room)*, was written by Erich Remark while he was still in the hospital. Blatantly and romantically autobiographical, it depicts a world not unlike the one created by Hörstemeier and his Dream Circle. The writing of this novel overlaps with the beginning of Erich's fascinating diaries, which he would continue to keep—with some extended lapses—up until 1965.

In June of 1918, Fritz Hörstemeier died at the age of thirty-six and was cremated in the nearby city of Bremen, since Osnabrück was not equipped to carry out cremations. Erich was released from the hospital in order to attend and play the organ at the service of his dear departed friend. The loss propelled him into a flurry of writing rather juvenile, ardent prose and verse, as well as dispatching letters to various artistic idols in the worlds of art, literature, and music.

Erich was also beginning to exert a powerful attraction over various women. By the time he was seventeen, he was either quite experienced in love or he was caught up in a boastful fantasy. In addition to the many passages about women, the diary of 1918 is especially valuable to the Remarque canon, since one never again sees such overarticulated candor. These pages reveal the emerging writer: his vulnerable traits and musings; a combination of probing self-analysis, political polemic, humanistic conscience, and a Cyrano-like sensibility.

There is also a surprisingly romantic lament for Fritz Hörstemeier:

> The pain of losing you is still burning, Fritz, the wound is still bleeding. Your golden-brown eyes, filled with wonder, now only exist in my memory, and your soft voice only lives on in the rustling of ashes in some far-off urn . . . Fritz, the only one to whom I could bare the deceptions of my soul! The only one who pondered with me the riddles of my being! . . . I wish I were two years in the past, back in Fritz's fairy-tale retreat, his brown room. How snug and cozy that always was; the golden-brown coloring of the room, gently highlighted by the reddish lamp, with youth, beauty, and happiness there too, and yet overlaid with a melancholy hint of the parting to come. . . . The never-ending longing for you is welling up in me again, Fritz. In the last two years I scarcely saw you for five days—and then I was still borne down by the loss of my mother. And how I would like to give you all the love and goodness that is your due—now that I've grown up.

During his extended hospital stay in Duisburg, the mature personality of Erich began to emerge. Being noticed meant a great deal to him, as did being compassionate, as did being in love. He deliberately alienated himself at times, yet had an overwhelming need to communicate. He was also becoming rigorously antisociety and antiwar in a country that prided itself on both. If the government had gotten hold of some of the entries in his early diary, he would have been in dire straits long before his eventual necessary exile. One particular entry, dated August 24, 1918, reveals impassioned youth, but also a warrior's disillusionment. It is a precursor to his particular blend of pacifism and patriotism in *All Quiet on the Western Front*. It is also an example of the hyperbolic idealism he espoused in his first novel, *Die Traumbude*.

> We, the young, who have served a difficult apprenticeship to manhood . . . we, who have become true to ourselves through death and danger, who have sought and found our true souls, should revolt against the laws and the arts. We demand life and art which is worthy of us! And if we don't get it,

then we'll smash the old and create for ourselves a mold into which we fit! Let's go, this is it! . . .

One good thing may come out of this war, and that is my prayer: may it allow the youth of Germany to find itself!

Music had always been an important part of Erich's life. Because of his wounded hand, however, he had given up any thought of becoming a concert pianist, though he took great pleasure in giving piano lessons as well as in composing and listening. Only three years later and not so very far away, in Berlin, the young Marlene Dietrich would grapple with her inability, because of injury—said to be either a strained finger ligament or a wrist ganglion—to realize her chosen musical career. In less than two decades, the two would be famously linked.

In the fall of 1918, Erich was busy with life at the hospital. He composed music to the poetry of Ludwig Bate, whose disability made him dependent on hospital care and with whom he often met in Room 77, the common room of the hospital. Erich wrote Bate a fan letter in which he attempts to describe poetry: "I always think that a poem is like a painting. Just as a painting is a harmony of line and color, and should not contain any disturbing colors and must select very carefully, the same is true of a poem. The colors are the words and the lines are the sounds."

And it was in the hospital in Duisburg that his music, painting, and poetry all fused to form his writer's eye, which he began to record in his diary:

> I walked quietly, slowly along the Promenade in the twilight, thoughtlessly enjoying all the gaiety. . . . Of course, I mustn't fall into one of my critical or ironic moods, otherwise everything becomes repulsive and a torment to me. Strolling along, looking in a book shop window here, enjoying a picture or two there, admiring the golden color of someone's hair or a fine horse, seeing a petal-red mouth, trying to read the character behind an interesting face here, eyeing an elegant girl there . . . this is relaxing and calming.

In early October, Erich saw an end to his recovery-sojourn. He would have to return to the field and stand at an icy post in the trenches. He was just bemoaning his fate when, he records, "We're at peace! People aren't exactly overjoyed at the fact. I suppose we'd got used to the war. It was a cause of death like any other sickness. A bit more serious than T.B. I'm not really happy about it, either. I'd already had the idea that I was going back into the field. Now it irritates me that there's nothing doing. Well, who knows, perhaps it will work out after all. Then, I'll look forward to peacetime again. And at the same time I'm apprehensive about it. Everything's changed, with Fritz dead, no real relationship to anyone—everything misfired, postponed, smashed. I have to make a fresh start of a life I left so bright and cheerful. Now, I'm alone and broken. Everything is gray and dull." In fact, the armistice had not been signed and Erich would, only a few weeks later, find himself about to return to the front.

Erich was sent back to Osnabrück on October 31, 1918. He was deemed fit to return to active duty, but he never got near the front again. Less than two weeks later, on November 11, 1918, the armistice ended the war in the wake of Germany's collapse.

The ramifications of peace by default were severe. Erich and his comrades were faced with an aborted mission, a lapsed heroism, and a depressed, belligerent country that did not want to readmit what it considered to be impotent soldiers as honored or even respected civilians. Hanns-Gerd Rabe captures the shameful treatment: "I had just handed over my plane to the English and arrived at the train station in Osnabrück. The properly attired station attendant demanded that I surrender my travel ticket. I begged his forgiveness for having returned home alive from the war. Unfortunately, no train tickets were sold during the war, only one-way tickets for a hero's death."

The Remarque historian Harley U. Taylor, Jr., conveys the impact of Germany's attitude upon Erich and his future creative psyche:

> It was to a volatile and vitriolic situation that Remarque and his comrades returned. . . . Remarque, who placed a very high value on comradeship, was appalled by the sight of his former comrades who had survived the horrors of war now opposing each other in combat. This important concern is expressed in *Der Weg zurück* (*The Road Back*), his first novel after *All Quiet on the Western Front*, which makes just as important a statement about the postwar problems of the returned soldier as *All Quiet on the Western Front* made about the soldier in combat. Adjustment to civilian life was not easy for Remarque and his friends.

Around this time Erich began to exhibit behavior that was generally considered peculiar. Rabe recalls one example: "These unquiet times, with revolution in the air, tempted him to strange and inexplicable behavior at times. He was seen wearing war decorations he had never received; a photograph of the time shows him in fully decorated uniform with a horse whip in one hand while leading with the other a beautiful German shepherd."

The shepherd was the family dog, Wolf, the uniform was that of a lieutenant, and among the decorations was the highly prized Iron Cross. Everything was in question in terms of validity except the dog. A photo exists of Erich in his new, full regalia, wearing not only one Iron Cross First Class but an Iron Cross Second Class, and, as Harley Taylor cites, "a badge worn by German soldiers to indicate war wounds."

Erich wrote a letter to Erika Haase, his early love from the Dream Circle days, indicating that the wearing of his uniform and medals was becoming a way of life: "I had to overcome a spiritual catastrophe—fate has hard fists. But on Sunday, I threw everything behind me and raised my head with pride, tied a funny bow around the neck of my dog, and in the sunshine I placed a willow-catkin into my Iron Cross, wore my lieutenant's armband (that's what I am now), and paraded around, full of pride and elegance, so that the eyes of the Philistines widened. This is me!"

Rabe, among many others, felt that there was not enough proof or motive for the citation. After all, many a soldier had helped drag a wounded comrade away from the action. Even Erich's dear "Dopp," Georg Middendorf, upbraided him for wearing "false medals," to which Erich countered by producing a document from the Arbeiter- und Soldatenrat (Council for Workers and Soldiers) substantiating their validity. There is no record, however, of his being given the document. Rabe's viewpoint was that it amounted to "Remarque's tendency to be an impostor, by calling himself a lieutenant when, in fact, he never went beyond private." Rabe also explained that there had been a hearing carried out by the government of Osnabrück in which Remarque "had to admit that he unrightfully wore the uniform of an officer and the Iron Cross, which resulted in a serious, written reprimand, as evidenced by his personal file."

The idea that Erich would disgrace himself through such a deliberate fabrication is still not totally accepted; however, his need for recognition is well documented. Dr. Thomas Schneider of the Erich-Maria-Remarque Archiv in Osnabrück, and one of the leading authorities on Remarque, feels he had documents for the medals but that the rest of his behavior was justified by what he had been through:

> The rumors were that he was wearing the medal without any documents, which is definitely not true; however, he was wearing the lieutenant's uniform illegally. . . . He was very young and he'd lost everything—his

mother, his mentor—so he had to find a place again in the society. He had
no bright vision of his future at that time, so he needed a symbol, and perhaps tried to find his identity by these acts, or by this "acting." He also wore
a monocle. And the people in the small town of Osnabrück would say,
"Look, there is that Remark kid. He's really foolish." But they would talk
about him; they'd give him recognition, which he badly needed. . . . So, he
got himself an image in a way.

Erich did feel enormous guilt for never having fought at the front, even
though he was stationed there, and for enjoying and even capitalizing on his
long hospitalization and for not electing to go "once more into the breach."
When he finally heightened his war experience in *All Quiet on the Western
Front*, he made his protagonist and alter ego, Paul Bäumer, die in the war.

In 1919, Erich, along with Georg Middendorf and other soldier comrades,
returned to the Catholic Seminary for Teachers to complete the studies that
would enable him to teach. This was a disturbing period for the men, who,
on one hand, were eased back into the system through the benevolence of the
Fatherland, yet once situated, were treated poorly. They were not given any
special recognition or compassion. Everybody wanted to forget about the
war, including those who had not brought about a German victory. The ex-
soldiers had a very difficult time, which Remarque made clear in his fourth
published novel, *The Road Back (Der Weg zurück)*, which was blatantly autobiographical in its concern for his and others' problems of displacement,
adjustment, and the future. Remarque's protagonist, Ernst Birkholtz, is a
schoolteacher who takes his final exams at the Seminary for Teachers, but
decides to give up his teaching position in the hopes of a more exciting life.
By taking this stand, Birkholtz, by the grace of God, fared better than his
comrades. He could have gone the way of a character named Willy
Hohmeyer, who gave up everything to teach, not even in but near
Osnabrück. Ernst Birkholtz can be thought of as a Paul Bäumer whom
Remarque allowed to survive.

He says as much in a 1929 interview: "In my next book, which I am now
writing, I describe the way back to life; how a young man like myself—and
Paul Bäumer—experienced war as a youth, who still carries its scars, and
who was then grabbed up by the chaos of the postwar period. He finally finds
his way back into life's harmonies."

Erich, finding himself back in school and working toward his teacher's degree, began to write prolifically—if not magnificently—and was
published quite frequently in the magazine *Die Schönheit (Beauty)*. Fritz

Hörstemeier, whose poetry had been favored by the magazine, had passed Erich on to them as his protégé. In one of Erich's early poems, titled "You and I," he walks with the dead Hörstemeier:

> Once my path will be done too
> Once the dead night will disappear,
> roses will bloom below my foot,
> graced by your golden greeting!
> Once, all longing will be quiet,
> and all desires are quiet!
> The great happiness, the deep dream
> once will become true;
> One, You and I.

Even though he was a self-proclaimed loner, Erich was never alone for long. Aside from his attraction to good-looking women, who were equally drawn to him, he found immense satisfaction in male friendships. Though he never hero-worshiped another man again as he had Hörstemeier, his friendship with Hanns-Gerd Rabe, whom he met at the Catholic Seminary for Teachers, became one of the most enduring of his life. Bonded by the insufferable situation at the school, where the teachers did not treat them with the dignity due returning soldiers, Erich and Rabe shared a state of mind. No longer naive or boyishly rebellious, but rather hardened by war experience, they could no longer be regarded as juveniles. From *The Road Back*, Ernst Birkholtz speaks for them: "There they stand now and propose to teach us again. But we expect them to set aside some of their dignity. For, after all, what can they teach us? We know life now better than they; we have gained another knowledge—harsh, bloody, cruel, inexorable."

The increasingly bitter situation pitting faculty against students was led, in fact, by the director of the Seminary for Teachers, a man named Wess. He guided the faculty in blocking the demands for a reformed curriculum. He was contemptuous of the seminarians' insistence upon respectful treatment. Two student factions formed in protest. Erich led the Catholic faction; Hanns-Gerd Rabe, who was enrolled in the Evangelical Training Seminary, led the Protestant faction. Rabe was a man of the world compared to Erich. He had been a commander on the Western Front, an officer on a general's staff, and a pilot-observer in the air corps—making combat flights. Mature, with a keen grasp of reality, he offered the same kind of support as had Hörstemeier. Rabe's worldly experience and Erich's naive and passionate sense of injustice complemented each other.

The two leaders, sponsored by the student body, were sent to Hannover to air grievances before a provincial school council. They eloquently pleaded their case for certain reforms and acceptance as studying soldiers, not students. The one issue that was not settled was determining the length of the program before they got their certificates. Erich and Rabe sought higher counsel in Berlin. The two young men went before the minister of education, argued their case, and were victorious: guidelines were set in consideration for the soldiers. As a result of this heroic mission, Erich was made president of the Student Union for Veterans. He also gained an enemy in Director Wess, who began an act of vengeance that would have ramifications before the year was out.

Rabe observed Erich fondly yet critically over the next couple of months: "[He] demonstrated a rather nonchalant attitude toward the pursuit of the required studies. He was more concerned with the development of his own interests, especially through reading, theater, and concerts. He dressed well, and was known to have said to his fellow students, 'If you want to get on in life, you need to take care of your appearance.' After he had donated his household keep to his father, the money he earned giving piano lessons and selling his poetry and essays went mainly toward personal finery. Erich created the ideal bohemian atmosphere in the garret of the family house, surrounded by his books, his own paintings, and a piano. He was reading voraciously, concentrating on Thomas and Heinrich Mann, Werfel, Hofmannsthal, Poe, Stendhal, Schopenhauer, Nietzsche, Rilke, Balzac, Flaubert, Proust, and Jack London."

At twenty, Erich was undergoing constant mood swings. On February 18, 1919, he writes a rather bizarre letter to a Miss Mimi, who seems to have been one of the Hörstemeier clan. He is alternately downhearted, defensive, maudlin, self-deprecating, sulky, mournful, rhapsodic, philosophical, melodramatic, and nostalgic. The most interesting part of the letter is the way he views himself:

People have become very distrustful of me, but you believe me, that I know! That's because you see a human in me, while the others see in me satan, experimenter, cold-hearted egotist. But believe this too: Maybe there is no bigger egotist among us than me! This sounds pompous, and praising oneself smells terrible, but still I assert it! This has been my battle over the past two years: I have been away from the I! I have lived too much for others, and was too careless toward me. . . . Never once did anyone offer me help. I always had to help them. No one asks about me, but that's all right. I will continue to help because it's my proof of friendship. Perhaps that sounds strange coming from this scoundrel, this beast of a fellow, but I owe it to Fritz. As much of a human being as I am, I owe to him—the only person whom I've ever truly loved. I have spoken for the last time to you from my soul, and will be lost to all of you.

He signs the letter, "Adventurer/Erich Remark." Remarque was ready to say good-bye to his old life much sooner than the possibilities offered. The "adventure" that lay ahead was a substitute teaching post in the remote village of Lohne, and the only way he could get from the hamlet of Lohne to the not much larger town of Lingen was by bicycle or on foot. From August 1, 1919, until March 31, 1920, he was an unhappy grammar school teacher. In retrospect, Osnabrück seemed like a mecca to which he couldn't escape, even on weekends, because of the obligatory Sunday church services. No matter how discontented he was, however, he was storing up material. Erich always stood out and people were naturally drawn to him. He made a friend of the son of the headmaster, Dr. G. Woste, and visited the family frequently, entertaining them by playing operettas on the piano. He had sold his piano in order to help underwrite printing costs for the publication of his first novel, *The Dream Room*. The publishing house of the magazine *Die Schönheit*, Verlag der Schönheit, brought out the book in 1920.

"A dreadful book! If I hadn't written something better later on, this book would be reason enough to commit suicide," Remarque said later about his first novel, which upon publication received less than enormous fanfare. Its opulently romantic, embroidered style gave no indication of the trenchant, linear fiction that was to come. Upon the publication of *All Quiet on the Western Front* in 1928, Remarque's publisher, Ullstein, with the author's full cooperation, bought up every copy of *The Dream Room* they could find.

During this time, Erich lived with a family named Schomaker, kept company with a girlfriend, a Fräulein Diederichs, and managed to maintain his enthusiasm for Truth, Love, Art, and Beauty. All this was disturbed by the reemergence of Wess, the director of the Catholic Seminary for Teachers, who later had many villainous fictional incarnations in Remarque's work. He had filed a complaint with the Osnabrück government against Erich's supposed political affiliation and activities with the Leftist Sparticist's wing (which was denounced by Erich, but this was never proved one way or the other), as well as the wearing of a bogus uniform. The government then registered this complaint with the district school director in Lingen.

According to Rabe, Erich put a disclaimer on the whole issue and got off with only a warning. However, friends in high places helped. Woste, the headmaster's son, vouched for Erich's character and competence as a teacher. The matter was dropped, but the fictional postscript would live on.

Trouble followed Erich from the first teaching position to the next one. This time he was stationed in an even more remote locale, in Klein Berssen, Hummling, a small village whose school held about fifty students at eight grade levels. Erich again was a substitute, for a teacher named Nieberg, who, although on sick leave, lived with his family and Erich right above the school. It was an awkward situation, leaving Erich little privacy.

The school was next to a church presided over by another villainous character, Deacon Brand. This priest sought to make Erich's life as difficult as possible. He demanded that the school adhere to the dictum of the Roman Catholic church. Erich balked; even as a substitute teacher, he insisted on control of his domain. He also knew that Brand had given Nieberg a hard time, and so automatically sided with a potential comrade. Brand took advantage of a note from the village mayor describing Erich as "one who has problems adjusting to his surroundings." He ridiculed Erich about his dress, his writing, and his artistic temperament. He wrote Erich long, threatening letters. He sought to cut Erich's salary, and at one point withheld it. He was the kind of bully to whom many young teachers would succumb, but not Erich. Like a skillful duelist, he parried Brand's thrusts—advancing and lunging at just the right moments. The acrimonious confrontations were in the form of a two-month correspondence. Only Erich's letters are legible; in fact, Brand's illegible hand became a large part of the squabbling. In one letter, Erich writes, "Regarding your comment whether I can read your handwriting now, I would like to reply with commendation that you have much improved and if you continue to practice, you could achieve many nice things."

Because of his reputation for being outspoken, Erich was not left alone. The correspondence was sent to the government of Osnabrück for investigation, whereupon Erich was called upon by a council to submit a written defense, which he did with belligerent eloquence:

> The information submitted by Priest Brand is Not True! . . . During my
> initial interview with the Deacon, I said that I would supervise the children

daily in the church. Despite that, the Deacon released the children, even though I was present. I asked him twice to leave that to me and he agreed to do so. But he did not do that and I sat there like a dumb boy, so that the community even gossiped about it. I know that the man is a product of his environment, but he went too far—especially by attacking me and my colleague. I am a peaceful person and I am tolerant, but if someone hits me on my right cheek for no reason, then I will hit back with full force.

He resigned from his second teaching job at the end of July. He requested that the government place him in a third position, nearer to Osnabrück, which it did, and from August until November of 1920, he was a substitute teacher in the village of Nahne. He completed this period uneventfully, at which time he asked to be dismissed from all teaching duties and left the government service without any explanation. Erich went on to lead a hand-to-mouth existence in the postwar Weimar Republic, working as everything from clothes salesman to tombstone salesman to organist in an insane asylum.

This coming of age in his sometimes beloved, always benighted hometown of Osnabrück was deceptively significant. More than three decades later, he created a searing facsimile of those few years in the novel *The Black Obelisk*.

For Erich, 1920 was a prolific year, and although he didn't get the recognition he sought, he was in print much of the time. Most of his other work reflected the purple prose of *The Dream Room*. However, his poem "Evening Song" brought him brief glory when one of his heroes and a leading poet and lyricist of the day, Karl Henkel, wrote rather extravagantly, "It's one of the most moving love songs I ever read." The small poem foretells the time to come when a more jaded Remarque craved the hedonistic possibilities of the evening.

EVENING SONG

And although the day was wild and distressing,
gnawed away by irony and scorn and sorrow—
a kiss from you—the fragrance of your hair
made me forget my pain by evening.

Although the relentless fire of the day
robbed me of my belief of life,
it needed only the stroke of your hand,
that I believed again in the evening.

And even if everything that I experienced
was a useless fight from beginning to end,
it was still good and beautiful—because
over it rested the blessing of your tender hands.

Erich was also trying to develop a critical eye, but his judgments tended to be overly harsh, reflecting his youth and lack of any knowledge of art history, as in an excerpt from his article "Art and Nature," published in *Die Schönheit*: "The model for 'Europe': one notices the hanging breasts, the unattractive arm, the poor line of the crossed leg and the somewhat bored and coquettish look in the face. . . . All models lack the resolve, the liveliness, life, urgency which lift the sculptures from the casualness of the model to a work of art."

And he was experimenting with various forms: verse, sketch, review, profile, and short story. Many of the pieces were published in the *Osnabrücker Tageblatt*, which, although the only daily newspaper in town, still had a standard to uphold. The publishers saw in Remarque not only an agile mind with great powers of observation, but spirit and a precociousness verging on sophistication.

In between selling tombstones and bolts of fabric, writing, dreaming, and planning, Erich did not neglect his love life. Courting actresses was an early habit; he basked in their beauty and reveled in their passionate personalities. All of this is evident in a piece titled "Oooh, la la Theatreball": "In the checkroom, one can hear soft violin sounds through the cracks in the door, peachy shoulders of girls gently shake under the fleece of the coats. Pale, tender hands touch the buttons and pull on the veils. Small feet in silk stockings and dull, gray leather boots, transparent silks, and delicate lacquered shoes shine like the backs of sacred scarabs."

He had also fallen for an actress, known only as Lolott. Appearing on stages throughout Germany, she seemed worldly compared with her predecessor, a local Osnabrück actress called Lucia. Erich liked women who were passionate, vain, neurotic, and dependent upon him for a certain amount of intense time. In her letter, Lolott is possessive yet self-involved: "Erich, days of alternating torment, questioning, joy, and sorrow lie behind me, yet I was always in your hands. Painfully, I often felt you were near me—often called out your name as I walked through the streets. . . . But soon I shall again be at your side."

The only recorded correspondence of Erich's comes four months later:

"Lolott, beloved—I tighten my clamps of steel around your beloved being and hold you tight! . . . You are tied to my life! I love you!"

Erich knew enough about himself to admit to being at a standstill in late 1921. He had no work, his novel had not been heralded, and his prospects looked dim. He needed a mentor, and so attempted to appoint the greatly respected Austrian writer Stefan Zweig to the task. His letter to Zweig represents Everyman's creative soul begging to be acknowledged and thereby justified and set free. It goes so far out on a limb that one can only imagine Zweig's reaction upon receiving it.

Mr. Stefan Zweig,

I am writing to you with the right that exists for every creative person! I am 23 years old, was the "Prugeljunge" brat of my parents; I am a wanderer, shepherd, worker, soldier, I am self-taught, I am a teacher and a writer. At the moment I am experiencing the predicament of fate. I am having a terrible fight with my work (because for me, creating is not a literary and academic matter, but a bloody one which always deals with life and death) and I need people who can help me. I don't know anyone else, or better to turn to than you! You have the finest touch, sympathy and understanding of anyone that I have found. . . . Here is the situation: I want you to tell me now whether the road I am on is the right one! I would like to send you some pieces of my writings, which in my fight with my work have crystallized, and I would like your judgment. Please excuse me if I neglect to be polite, but this means everything to me; it is my only hope of a way out. It is life and death to me. . . . I come to you Mr. Zweig and ask you as human to human: Write me whether I may send you a few poems which have crystallized from the wild fight for the great work, and which you will examine. I cannot abstain from enclosing a few now. And please remember, this means everything to me! Feverish and painful will be the hours awaiting your reply. It would be easy for the stretched bow of my being to break. Please answer me as soon as possible.

His signature for the first time reads, "Erich Maria Remark." It's not clear whether he took the "Maria" in honor of a much admired writer, Rainer Maria Rilke, or if he inserted his mother's middle name as a talisman. However, in the town's official register of 1922, he still appears as "Erich Remark, Writer."

Stefan Zweig did prove helpful in opening a few key doors for Remarque, but in 1942, he (age sixty) and his young wife (thirty-three) were found in bed, holding hands in a double suicide, in Petropolis, outside Rio de Janeiro. Zweig was a pacifist, a humanist, a Jew, and a man without a country who had lost one of his close friends, the writer Joseph Roth, to suicide. As if part of some strange ritual, he and his wife took part in the frenzy of Carnival just before they died.

While playing the organ on Sundays in the Osnabrück insane asylum, Erich cemented a friendship with Pastor Biedendieck, who had been his confessor before the war. As partial compensation for his job as organist, the pastor gave him free meals and wine and reported that Remarque was a frequent guest in his house, where they indulged in discussions about music, theater, concerts, art, and literature lasting into the wee hours.

"We shared the dream to be writers," he recalled long after Remarque had accomplished it. "We both worked as concert and theater critics. I must say I keep this time in dearest memory, even though I was far from being a real critic." Erich was not cut out to be a real critic either. His reviews in the early twenties tended to be too philosophical and verbose, yet when he was acute, his opinions were constructive and playful. "I ignore the slight errors, such as the grotesque clouds with the colorful angels, the archangel Michael who wore a silver bracelet and the costume of an old Germanic hero."

Pastor Biedendieck, who was not a very spiritual priest but rather worldly, with a fondness for good food and drink, helped point the way toward Erich's emerging sensuality. Pastor Biedendieck was to receive two substantial roles in his fiction: he was to go under the name of Bodendiek in *The Black Obelisk* and under his own name in *A Time to Love and a Time to Die*. Remarque always looked out for his positive early influences, treating them gently, lovingly, and with good humor in his novels. But woe to Deacon Brand and the like. He was ruthless in depicting their fate.

In the beginning of 1922 Erich began work as a tombstone salesman for the Vogt Brothers—in particular, a man named Karl Vogt, with whom he became fast friends. In a time of soaring unemployment, the job was, to quote Erich, "A godsend." He also said of his time there, "We designed and sold atrocities depicting lions with toothaches or bronze eagles bereft of wings, whenever possible with golden crowns. . . . I really was worth my money; with famous innocence I even sold the oldest stone left over from the time of Art Nouveau." With all the bravado of a good salesman, Erich threw himself into this job, perhaps due to some foresight that these were to be his final days in his beloved yet stifling Osnabrück.

The events that Erich lived through during this time, he mirrored in his novel *The Black Obelisk*, which he was not to start work on until 1943:

The narrator and hero is Ludwig Bodmer, a salesman and an advertising and office manager in the Kroll Brothers' tombstone business in the town of Werdenbrück. The story takes place between April and October 1923, the height of the inflation in Germany. It is a time when workers are paid twice a day and high rollers become rich. The poor, particularly the war-disabled and old people who depend on pensions, are starving because their pension increases can in no way keep up with inflation. At the end of the novel, things turn for the better; the value of the German mark is reestablished, and Bodner leaves Werdenbrück for a job with a newspaper in Berlin.

In October 1922, Erich left Osnabrück for Hannover and a full-time job writing articles for the magazine *Echo-Continental* (owned by the Continental Rubber Company), for which he had already done some advertising copy and editorial work. When the Osnabrück government officials invited him to return to his senses and teaching, he responded on February 11, 1922, with imperious brevity: "I am now Publicity Manager and Chief Editor for the Continental Company in Hannover."

Little is known about how Erich's father and his sisters felt about him prior to his becoming a household name, but once he did they expressed their respect for his wealth and humbled themselves before him. The many moves, the mother's illness and premature death, the father's taciturn nature, and Erich's demand for privacy in their always cramped quarters put a severe strain on family relations. Erich had never been close to his father, and after he remarried Erich kept even more of a distance. The date of the remarriage is unclear, because many of the town records—along with much of the town of Osnabrück—were destroyed by bombs during the Second World War. Peter Remark's second wife was called Maria, but there is no information concerning her background. What is known is that she committed suicide sometime around 1943.

One might speculate that it was not a terrible wrench for Erich to take leave of his family. Clearly, he was eager to get ahead and the opportunity had arisen. In October he moved to Nikolaistrasse 11 in Hannover and began a shorter climb to where he thought he should be.

His writing took a different bent. He was paid to write technical pieces—slogans, advertising copy—to sell a product. Contrary to what might have been expected, given his need for personal expression, he thrived in the job. His sense of humor came to the fore while writing about rubber, as in a slogan for bathing caps:

*Remarque's drawing of his mother, Anna Maria Remark, on her
deathbed, 1917.*

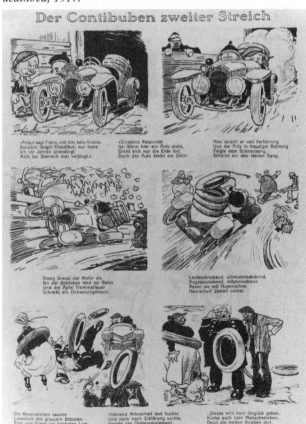

*Remarque's popular
feature in
Echo-Continental:
"The Captain Hein
Priemke," for which he
wrote the captions, 1922.*

Then Hein cries out in wild horror,
"Friederike, it's all over!"
Then he swore to himself on the spot:
You will remain a bachelor forever!
Just think: if the old frump
Had had a Conti bathing cap,
This sort of thing would never
Have happened to her.

The character of Hein (Captain Hein Priemke) was the cartoon hero of a popular series he developed, and became the symbol of Continental Rubber, the umbrella company of the magazine. Erich could say anything with Hein as his spokesman. There were sixteen episodes in the series, but only a few were salvaged.

In October of 1922, Erich wrote a watershed piece for the literary supplement of the *Hannover Kurier* titled "Fall Rain"—the contents of which were nothing unusual; he used his trademark anthropomorphic metaphors concerning nature: "The leaves of the chestnuts hang down to earth; rain nails the length of the church tower; fall hammers the coffin of summer shut." The new element was the byline: "Erich Maria Remarque." It was the beginning.

CHAPTER TWO

MARION GODDARD LEVY, AKA . . .

1910–1936

In 1846, Daniel Gozard emigrated from England to America and settled in Hartford, Connecticut. Five subsequent generations of his family lived and worked as farmers in Hartford County. The name Gozard eventually became Goddard. By the 1880s, Daniel's descendants had relocated to South Dakota, where, in Watertown, on October 23, 1887, his great-great-great-grandson Leslie's Illinois-born wife, Nellie Hatch, gave birth to their first child, Alta Mae Goddard, a pretty child who was very flirtatious from an early age. Although the Goddards were Episcopalian, not Mormon, they chose to move to Salt Lake City. It was just becoming a boomtown with the completion of the transcontinental railroad, which meant many new job opportunities and a substantial increase in population.

Leslie and Nellie Hatch Goddard's second child, Helen, was born on April 9, 1898, in Salt Lake City. Alta, who now had a sister eleven years her junior, was enrolled at Rowland Hall, an exclusive Episcopalian girls' school. All evidence is that Leslie Goddard was doing very well for himself, and his family considered itself prosperous. Leslie had started as a bookkeeper, but by 1900 had opened—in the very desirable Walker Brothers Bank Building—his own real estate company, the Goddard Investment Company, in order to take advantage of the city's recent prosperity. His company, which was especially active in the Avenues district, bought real estate lots and built homes on them with spectacular views of the city and the valley below.

But in 1903, Leslie Goddard's family was in ruins. His wife, Nellie, had deserted; Leslie gave up his own home and moved in with his father, Louis; and then, in May of that year, he married his secretary, Louise E. (for Effie) Stalter. Leslie was forty-two, Effie was twenty-six. According to one distant family source, when her mother left, Alta, who was then fifteen or sixteen, went to live with her father, stepmother, and sister. In 1905, she entered the Salt Lake Collegiate Institute, and the next year she changed to St. Mary's Academy. Among her classmates there was Dollie Levy, the sister of her future husband.

The picture of Alta as a well-adjusted coed, living at home with her new stepmother, ten or eleven years her senior, and her sister, eleven years her junior, was refuted by Helen Murray, Alta's niece: "At the time of the divorce, when Alta was perhaps fifteen or sixteen, my mother's sister, Alta, went to live with her father, and my mother was reclaimed by Nellie. Aunt Alta, as we used to call her, left home very young. My mother told me that she ran off with a circus, though since Mother wasn't there at the time and had a tendency to get wrong ideas about things once in a while, that could be a misapprehension."

It seems more likely that Alta had run off to some kind of traveling show. She was striking, with her dark hair, very fair skin, and green eyes. It would not have been surprising if she had been drawn to show business, with her dramatic looks, her bewitching, vagabond mother, and, not least, her rich Uncle Charlie.

Leslie's brother, Charles Goddard, was living in New York City in 1903. He had just started the American Druggists Syndicate, a company akin to Palmolive or Colgate, which manufactured drug and toilet articles. "Uncle Charlie" was living at the Hotel Chatsworth, 344 West Seventy-second Street, and in 1908, registered at the same hotel was Leslie's daughter Alta, who had last been in Salt Lake City's *Polk Directory* in 1906. On December 28, 1908, she had married another Salt Lake citizen, Joseph Russell Levy, in an Episcopal ceremony at the Hotel Chatsworth. She gave her age as twenty on the license; Levy is listed as twenty-eight.

J. R. (as he was known) Levy was the son of Sam Levy, one of the first cigar manufacturers in Salt Lake City. The logo of his company was "Sam Levy's Famous Cigar—the Pioneer Brand," advertised with a sketch of a rather robust woman in a corset, smoking a cigar. His office was in a prime location downtown on Main Street, and he was apparently quite prosperous. J. R. attended the Salt Lake Business Institute, after which he was employed by his father as a clerk and bookkeeper, until the death of Sam in 1904, where-upon there were various skirmishes with his brothers about what to call the business. First it was Sam Levy Cigar Manufacturing Company; then Levy Brothers; then, in 1907, J. R. Levy & Bros.; and finally, in 1909, Sam Levy's Sons.

J. R. might have brought Alta back to Salt Lake City for the one year he was running the company. In 1908, his mother, Marie, was listed as having moved to New York, but by 1909, the three had moved back to Salt Lake City, where J. R. tried to head the family business and failed. By 1910, J. R. Levy was gone from Salt Lake City.

Marion Goddard Levy, as her name appears on her birth certificate, Alta and J. R.'s only child, was born on June 3, 1910, in either Great Neck, Long Island, or Whitestone Landing, Queens. Years later, her second husband, Charlie Chaplin, said that she was born in Brooklyn, and she was quoted in Earl Wilson's column as saying, "I was really born at 100th and Amsterdam in Manhattan." No one knows when or why she started calling herself Pauline (the name in every biographical report) and despite the birth certifi-cate date of 1910, the years 1905 and 1915 appear on one passport and vari-ous legal documents. Pauline Marion Levy—whose father later spelled it LeVee or LeeVee—was half Jewish. She was most likely named after her paternal grandmother, Pauline Levy, and the name Marion was in honor of J. R.'s mother, Marie. Pauline developed quickly, and by the time she was six, it was clear she was going to be a great beauty.

Little is known about her childhood, but because of a suit that J. R. Levy brought against his daughter in later years, the court records are revealing about the family between 1911 and 1926. Pauline always said that her father walked out on her mother and her very early on, but Levy saw it quite dif-ferently. He testified that "he supported and educated [Paulette] and even borrowed money to prepare her for her professional career." He also made an allegation of kidnapping in his testimony: "Levy testified yesterday that his wife 'disappeared' with their daughter while the child was young. He said he found them living in Iola, Kansas, and that he brought the child back to New York, but she was 'taken away' from his apartment while he was absent."

A Paramount Studio release presented her early years in the following way: "When she was very young, her parents separated, and she went with her mother. They moved a lot and she got her education in quick doses at numerous schools, among them Mount St. Dominic's, which was a convent in New Jersey." "I was about eight or nine," she recalled years later: "I went for two years. It was Dominican. The sisters were lovely. But it was a very inexpensive convent. That's why I was there. It was forty dollars a month for everything. I hated the way it smelled, but I prayed to the windows—the vitrines—with all the symbols on them." She also attended Ursuline Academy in Pittsburgh. As early on as grammar school, Pauline wanted to be an actress and she persuaded her mother to give her lessons in dramatics, dancing, and singing.

Pauline and Alta were survivors. Pragmatic and lively, they looked alike, but Pauline was much smarter than her mother. A shrewd and strong-minded child, she always had a plan. She and her mother were forced to travel frequently in order to avoid a custody battle, and Pauline learned early to trust no man unless he was well off, like Uncle Charlie, and ultimately to depend on nobody but herself.

The two went as far as Canada for a while, but there are no records of any schooling for Pauline while they were there. If they were on the lam, as is indicated by Levy's statements under oath during his efforts to regain his daughter, then proper stakes and schooling would have been too easy to trace.

There are stories about Pauline's formative years. There was even one year, 1918, when Alta and Pauline seemed to have disappeared entirely. There are many rumors, about Alta and Pauline being cardsharks on cruise boats along the St. Lawrence River, that Pauline began to model before she was ten, and that Pauline, during her only year of high school, was labeled the fastest girl the school had ever known.

By 1923, when Pauline was twelve, she and Alta were back in New York; years later, she recalled that summer to the Hollywood columnist Hedda Hopper: "Mother and I used to spend our summers with my uncle, Charles Goddard, at Great Neck, L.I. He had a beautiful house on the edge of the grounds of a country club, of which he was president (the Soundview). In front of the house was a permanent dance floor; and each Saturday night meant a party to which were invited the biggest theatrical stars of that time: Marilyn Miller, Jack Hazzard, Jack Donohue, the Dolly sisters, Harry Pilzer, the Frank Cravens, the Arthur Hopkinses, and occasionally a Barrymore. . . . I made up my mind then that I was going to be a great star, and that I'd be more famous than anybody out there. It just had to be. I watched the biggest ones—how they walked, danced, dressed, behaved. And I kept saying, 'I can do it much better. And someday I'll prove it to the world.'"

Uncle Charlie provided stepping-stones for dreams, but not money. As a preteen, Pauline modeled children's fashions at Saks Fifth Avenue. "By the

*Pauline as a precocious and
beguiling child in 1917 or 1919. (The
date seems to have been doctored.)*

*Pauline with her mother,
Alta Goddard Levy,
ca. 1910.*

*Pauline with her
uncle Charlie.*

time I was thirteen," she is quoted as saying, "I discovered things weren't coming to me on a silver platter. I wanted to attend Ned Wayburn's school of dancing. But that cost ten dollars a week—and it took all the money Mother and I had to run our little apartment on Ninety-fifth and Broadway. So I had to earn my tuition. I did it by quitting school in the first year of high and modeling. We had nothing. Twenty dollars a week. That's very little to live on. Bread and butter and lettuce and that was it."

Pauline's cousin Helen never understood the reality of their penury: "There was Uncle Charlie, who had children. He had four of them, all told. And there was my grandmother, and I think there were seven or eight brothers and sisters. Three of them never married. So, you know, they were the only second-generation children . . . you'd think that Alta could have asked her father to help her. He was not a wealthy man, but he was reasonably successful, a real estate person. But I'm sure he could have helped if she were desperate."

Even though what lay ahead for Pauline was the top of the heap, she never lost a deep need for acquisitions, counterbalanced by a stringent frugality. "I think a background of poverty is good," she once said in an interview. "You can always go back to living on twenty dollars a week." By the time she was thirteen, she was earning fifty dollars a week modeling at the fashionable women's store Hattie Carnegie. At fourteen, Pauline began modeling in the garment district on Seventh Avenue. At fifteen, her earning power increased enormously when she became employed by one of the biggest names in show business, Florenz Ziegfeld, to whom she was introduced by Uncle Charlie. Thanks to one major influence in her life, her childhood hardships were about to end.

Uncle Charlie knew everybody and had a warm spot for his prettiest niece. He recognized in her something of his own enormous drive. Years later, when Alfred Hitchcock made a movie called *Shadow of a Doubt*, depicting an intimate relationship between an Uncle Charlie and his favorite niece that sours when she finds out he is a murderer, Paulette made the comment, "That was Uncle Charlie and me before he murdered anyone." In reality, Paulette was indebted to Uncle Charlie for the rest of his life.

In fact, although Alta and young Pauline were scraping by during those years, family and friends were around. According to Tom Vitelli and Michele Swaner (a distant cousin of the Goddards), "Paulette must have known her grandfather, Leslie, from the age of seven. [What she remembered, Paulette once said, was, "He was handsome, smelled good, and wore knickers."] Alta's stepmother, Effie, was in New York, as was Alta's sister,

Helen. . . . And of course there was Uncle Charlie and his family, plus Aunt May and Aunt Minnie."

When Leslie moved to New York in 1918, he was employed by his younger brother Charlie's real estate firm, Estates Realty Company, with offices at 342 Madison Avenue. "Life in those days, for Uncle Charlie at least, was a pleasant season of good friends and profitable work. The Goddards spent the week in the city and the weekends on Long Island."

For Pauline, 1926 was a watershed year. Still technically deemed a child in May—when Alta's divorce became final and she gained custody of her daughter—Pauline, at sixteen, became a true working woman the next month, when she was hired for Ziegfeld's summer review, *No Foolin'*, originally titled *Palm Beach Girl*. Pauline made several changes. She dyed her hair blond and bobbed it, and while she was in Palm Beach, Florida, with the revue, she gave herself the new Frenchified name of Paulette Goddard. Paulette caught the eye of the Palm Beach press, perhaps because, as the actress Constance Collier used to say, "She was a natural born honey pot."

Paulette's interviews had an unreal air about them: "At first Mother wouldn't let me come, but she finally relented. And the first persons I saw in Palm Beach were my uncle and aunt, Mrs. C. H. Goddard, whom I haven't seen in four years. We're all in love with this place. I'm crazy about swimming and horseback riding. I brought a new riding habit with me and then learned there were no horses here. Well, maybe I can use it when I go bicycling."

Paulette instinctively knew how to promote herself and beguile the press. She deftly bent the truth for print. It is highly unlikely Alta would have put up any resistance at all to the "Great Ziegfeld." It is also hard to believe that the mother and daughter, in such arduous pursuit of the good life, would have stayed away from Uncle Charlie's estate for four years. It is true that in 1926 Charles sold his Soundview estate—keeping the cottage in Great Neck—and moved his wife, Grace, and their two children, Livingston and Elizabeth, to the town of Menton on the French Riviera. But he did keep a yacht down in Palm Beach that Paulette could use, and his move coincided perfectly with the launching of her career. She no longer needed his Long Island estate and what it represented.

During her first stay in Palm Beach, Paulette enjoyed being thought of as the new golden girl. Paulette may have had a bit part in *Palm Beach Girl*, but she already knew the secret of the game: she behaved like a star. And Palm Beach—just emerging as the queen of winter resorts—was the ideal backdrop for her. The eastern rich were flocking there to build their grand show-case houses, to attend endless rounds of parties, where they would flaunt their jewels and finery by night and by day, to shop, and to golf. There was plenty of gambling and, for those interested in the more exotic, easy access to Cuba.

Ziegfeld spared no expense in commissioning an elaborate theater, with all the most up-to-date details, to be built from an old assembly hall especially for his revues and tryouts. It even had a sliding glass roof so that his well-heeled patrons could be entertained beneath the stars. He called it the Montmartre, and it was *the* spot to go to in Palm Beach during Paulette's the-atrical debut. "The musical numbers were lavish and one in particular had the chorus girls rise up as if out of the ocean. The costumes were designed so the damsels looked dripping wet, and the girls wore huge floor-length head-dresses made of feathers that gave the effect of foamy waves on the ocean." The audiences were as illustrious as the production. Opening night "includ-ed Ziegfeld's pals Edward F. Hutton [heiress Barbara Hutton's father] and millionaire Leonard Replogle. . . . Millionaire playboys eagerly awaited each fresh crop of gorgeous showgirls."

Amid all this glamour, Paulette's head turned—of all places—toward school. She and a friend from the chorus, Mary Jane, enrolled in the local high school of West Palm Beach. The press loved it, calling them the pearls of the Ziegfeld troupe and pursuing them for interviews, which they happi-ly gave: "Just because we are dancing here now is no reason why we should deny ourselves the advantages of a proper education," Mary Jane said. Paulette added, "You really don't know how anxious we are to get started in school. After having wasted so much time here and really accomplishing nothing, school looks like a pleasing prospect."

Paulette's diplomatic skills might have slipped that day, but she was equally capable of blunt statements, and she later on made it a habit to throw in something unexpected during interviews. She did something else in this interview that she continued all her life: she withheld her age. "Both of the girls are of school age. Mary Jane is just sixteen. Paulette will not admit to how old she is." It was probably the one time Paulette wanted to hide how young she was—as well as to protect her mother from any harsh criticism of sending a minor to work.

The plan for their schooling was impressive: Latin, French, home eco-nomics, English, history, and mathematics. They were to appear at school on Monday at eight-thirty sharp. They were supposed to study between perfor-mances and then head straight home after the theater. Paulette's "home" was highly luxurious, since she was staying with Uncle Charlie and his wife on their yacht.

They never did make it to school that Monday. The revue, under the new name of *No Foolin'*, was moved to Broadway. It opened at the Globe Theatre on June 24, 1926, and ran for 108 performances. Perhaps the most memorable aspect of the run for Mr. Ziegfeld was the threatened strike that was commandeered by Paulette:

This is the first time New York has ever looked a blonde striker in the eyes. Three flaxen-haired lovelies of the Blonde Choristers Union visited the New York offices of Florenz Ziegfeld today and threw down the silken gauntlet. They will walk out Wednesday after the matinee of *No Foolin'* at the Globe Theatre, they told the press, unless the said Florenz retracts his words. The words spoken recently at one of the Ziegfeld interviews for the press were to the effect that he preferred brunettes. "Retract or suffer," was the ultimatum delivered by Paulette Goddard of the Blonde Strike Committee, which continued with "Everybody knows that gentlemen prefer blondes. If Mr. Ziegfeld prefers brunettes, it is a sign that he is no gent. If he does not retract his cruel words by Wednesday afternoon, every blonde in the company will walk out and leave the drama flat on its behind." Nearly 75 percent of the Ziegfeld choristers are blonde, natural or otherwise, and a walkout would leave the house practically dark. If the retraction is not published in the newspapers before the zero hour, the strikers will put on their clothes and march, leaving nothing but a brunette outlook for the tired businessman.

The irony of Paulette's defiant stand was that she was the "otherwise" among the blondes. She wittily countered this fact by stating, "We consider them blondes if they are on our side. Blondeness is a state of mind."

The great Florenz Ziegfeld rebutted with bluster: "I have never said anything against blondes. . . . Beautiful brunettes are the rare article. I am trying to organize a chorus of only brunettes for my next show, in South America. Plenty of beautiful blondes come and offer to become beautiful brunettes for the season, but that doesn't interest me. I don't like synthetic blondes or brunettes. There's nothing worse than a synthetic blonde. If they want to strike, let 'em strike! Anybody that wants to strike during this weather is welcome."

It was the middle of July. The girls decided to drop the strike in exchange for some publicity pictures.

This episode was not unlike young Erich Remark's railing against Deacon Brand and fighting for what he believed, no matter what the consequences. Neither one was fired for coming up against an employer, and in Paulette's case—synthetic blonde regardless—she was rehired by Ziegfeld for his next show, *Rio Rita*, which was to open February 2, 1927, at the Ziegfeld Theatre in New York.

During this time, Paulette and her mother, Alta, used to being nomads, were staying at Uncle Charlie's cottage in Great Neck and commuting into the city. There were no romantic entanglements for either mother or daughter. In fact, life was entirely about Paulette for both of them. It took all their energy to keep her launched and cutting more of a swath each day. On her opening night of *Rio Rita*, Paulette received flowers and a note from her mother that read, "Dance 'hot' darling!"

The show, a typical Ziegfeld extravaganza, starring comedians Bert Wheeler and Robert Woolsey, was a great success, and Paulette, in a glorified bit part, got noticed. Along with the featured players Charles King and Polly Walker, she sang, "Honey, Be Mine." She sang and danced a number known as the "dance hot." A reviewer wrote, "Irving Fisher and Paulette Goddard make you forget Chicago winter with 'Florida, the Moon, and You.'" The cast termed her "the perfect sitter," because in the number she sat with very little on in the arc of a prop moon while being crooned at by Fisher.

In fact, Albert Vargas, whom Ziegfeld commissioned to do a series of paintings for the lobby of the Globe Theatre, chose Paulette to christen the project. And, of course, it received publicity: "Mr. Vargas considers Miss Goddard one of the foremost beauties of the connoisseur Florenz Ziegfeld."

Paulette had been noticed. Just after the opening of *Rio Rita*, the Broadway producer Archie Selwyn approached Paulette with an offer to star in his latest Broadway-bound venture, *The Unconquerable Male*. She accepted, pulled out of *Rio Rita* after only three weeks, and went into rehearsal with the new play. It tried out in Atlantic City, ran for three days, and closed in Atlantic City. "I thought I was something wonderful," Paulette said, "when they put me in a play. They said, 'She looks beautiful.' They hadn't bothered to ask me about my acting ability. Of course the play folded in a week."

Two weeks later, Paulette met the man who was to be her first husband, Edgar William James, through Uncle Charlie. James, who had just broken off a serious relationship with the young and dazzling Tallulah Bankhead, came complete with patrician good looks and background. As president of the Southern States Lumber Company of North Carolina in Asheville, he was an authentic magnate, or, as Paulette preferred to call him, "Baron

*Paulette with her first husband,
Edgar James, in Cannes, 1927.*

LEFT TO RIGHT: *On the honeymoon: Alta in Europe with the newlywed
Edgar James, 1927. Paulette as Mrs. Edgar James with her horse in Asheville,
North Carolina, ca. 1928.*

Lumber." He was also, unknown to Paulette at that time, a heavy gambler.

This might not have been a great passion, but Paulette deeply enjoyed what was good for her, and Edgar James was good for her—and her mother. They had scraped by long enough and were ready for a much needed vacation from hardship. Paulette later described the courtship and marriage:

Our courtship was one of those whirlwind affairs which wound up with an elopement. We were married June 28, 1927, in Rye, New York, at four o'clock in the morning after routing the license clerk and minister out of bed. The marriage didn't work after a while, though, and as I was under age, we considered having it annulled. However, I continued living with Edgar until after I became of age, which meant that divorce would be necessary. He suggested an extended trip to Europe, probably thinking that such a journey would bring us closer together. We were gone nearly a year and a half, but the benefits from the marital standpoint were only temporary. Our chief trouble was having nothing in common. The two years before going to Europe we spent most of our time at Edgar's country estate in Asheville. He loved sports of all kinds, particularly fox hunting. I didn't care for those things, and there was nothing for me to do except play golf, swim, hunt and attend social affairs. I was bored to death and when I saw upon our return from Europe that I was faced with the prospect of resuming this sort of life, we decided to call it quits.

It was not quite as simple as all that. She was sixteen years old when she married a man twice her age. They had one need in common: she needed to be taken care of, and he needed to take care of a child bride. She seems to have provided enough excitement for him not to have been the one to walk out. And at one point, there had been talk of a child—not their own, but one that Paulette would recruit for appearances. Paulette's cousin Helen recalls the rationale: "Paulette offered to adopt my brother Michael, who was a darling little kid with curly red hair and freckles. Mother said the offer was made mostly because Paulette was tired of people thinking she was her husband's daughter and thought it might make her look a little older to have a child. I don't know if Paulette was serious, though my mother always believed she meant it and that the offer was made partly to help her out."

There are several theories regarding Paulette's rather sudden decision to marry at such a tender age. One is that she did it for entirely mercenary reasons and that it was her mother's doing, or at least partly for her mother's benefit. Following Alta and Joseph's divorce on May 4, 1926, the court ordered Mr. Levy to pay Mrs. Levy ten dollars a week for support of Paulette, still a minor. He refused, and in a deposition years later involving a suit that he waged against his own daughter, he testified that he had been ill, unable to support himself, and that his sixteen-year-old, stage-faring daughter was capable of paying him fifty dollars a week! His refusal to pay child support coincided with Edgar James's courtship, leading to the conclusion that Paulette and her mother exchanged a rotten, broke father (and husband) for a refined, flush one.

Paulette's cousin Helen remembers hearing about Paulette, when she had just become a Follies Girl, visiting Uncle Charlie in Great Neck and sitting on his lap during much of the visit. Her measurements at the time were 34-23-35. She was a conspicuously ripe teenager, who dressed in revealing clothes and had already been taken under the wing of Flo Ziegfeld, an expert in pulchritude. Out of necessity, she knew her way around rich men. And in those days, rich men were mostly older. So, she played the daughter-woman—deceptively young, deceptively knowing, and because she was so physically lovely, the combination presented itself as irresistible. Her composure and astonishing maturity put these men at their ease and sanctified their impulses.

Paulette had vivid memories of a never-innocent childhood that she described to her secretary Lois Granato. When she was small, her father managed a chain of Warner Brothers movie theaters, which meant that he was frequently on the road. He wanted his glamorous young wife—who carried the nickname of "Legs" Goddard—to be with him, but decided that a child would be an encumbrance and so, more often than not, left Paulette with one grandparent or another. No young child, not even one as resourceful as Paulette, could be impervious to the cold shoulder of being left behind. Paulette's way of licking her wounds was to invent a marketing game—the item being herself. When it rained, she would stand on a corner holding a large umbrella. Then she would pick a man whose looks she liked—well dressed and without face whiskers—and would approach him, hips swaying, eyelashes batting: "If you give me a dime, I'll cover you with my umbrella," she would say, "and if you give me a quarter, I'll let you look under my skirt."

Edgar James was her best customer ever. She didn't have to make any bargains with him. And Alta liked him. It was always critical that Alta not merely approved of, but practically fell for, the men that her daughter married. It was an ongoing ritual. In all of their marriages—four for Paulette and three for Alta, the setup was the same: an adult male, an adult female, and a precocious, beguiling child.

Paulette's marriage to James provided her with her first legitimate starring role. "I breathed; he watched," she recalled to her last husband, Erich Maria Remarque, of the union with James. And indeed, for a brief time, James appeared to be completely taken with his child bride. However, regardless of how much pleasure her husband offered, Paulette saw the marriage as a matter of basic survival for her and her mother. "I am what I am—because of my mother . . . because my mother left me alone. . . . It made me very independent. I got married when I was fifteen because I had no place else to live." (Here she has changed her age; she tended to alter the facts to suit her mood.)

James gave her a house on an elegant estate and an identity as his very rich, indolent wife. She talked about the life with easy disdain. "He was from North Carolina and we went there to live. In Biltmore Forest. That's where I learned to hunt and jump and so forth. I was sixteen when we were married. And we had a *beautiful* house there and I—didn't know how to live that way. It was suburban but with corn whiskey, you know, for breakfast. They'd give you a big shot before you got on the horse, you know? It's supposed to be elegant and chic to do that, but I didn't get it at all. I couldn't live that way."

Contrary to her breezy dismissal of the marriage to the press, it was James who said he had tired of her, saying she was both "too much and not enough" when he wrote to his lawyer in preparing the case for divorce. He had taken her mother in, traveled with Paulette on an extended trip throughout Europe, introduced her to hunt-club society, couture clothes, and gastronomic delights—and finally, he needed his "creation" to be a wife. Paulette was not, nor would ever be, that.

In her divorce testimony in 1929, Paulette accused James of cruelty, claiming he was often mean—threatening and screaming at her and capable of behaving in an uncivilized manner, as in this one instance: "He picked me up by the ears from a chair and then would plop me down on the floor."

James, although represented by top Asheville attorney C. T. Pugh, offered no subsequent testimony. What he did offer the eighteen-year-old Paulette was a divorce settlement of $375,000. "My husband had given me enough money so that 'You'll never have to do anything you don't want to do.' He gave me cash!" Paulette crowed in a recollection years later.

Paulette seemed to have landed at the top of the heap before she was twenty. In the summer of 1930, the local press in Reno reported she had come back for the second time, to get her final papers. "Now I can hardly wait to be free," said Paulette, "and I'm having a marvelous time meanwhile. I adore Reno and my mother is going to buy a ranch here so I can come back and visit."

Hollywood beckoned, but the road to recognition was not to be as smooth as Paulette's new seal coat. When she left Reno, she was given a farewell party by Alta, who was billing herself as Mrs. Al Goddard of the Riverside Hotel. The two would be parted for the first time since Paulette had been a small child. While Paulette pursued her career to no avail in Los Angeles, Alta sat on "their" fortune. Paulette soon returned to Reno to get her mother (who never did buy property there) and head for a dude ranch in Arizona, where they stayed until they had hatched a more concrete plan of how to succeed in Tinseltown. No more posing in front of some beauty queen's speedboat; no more back-door or second-rate anything. Paulette decided to go abroad instead. That was what rich young women did to recover.

Touring Europe was like a second honeymoon for Paulette, and a first one for Alta, who probably never in her wildest dreams had seen herself taking the baths at Baden-Baden, browsing the couture houses in Paris, or visiting the sights of London. It was on that trip that they began a luxurious and shrewd collusion. Wealthy, beautiful, charming, often taken for sisters, they reveled in knowing the value of it all. They remained close in the years to follow, talking or corresponding about everything from men, money, and career to what kind of new buttons to put on an old Schiaparelli coat.

They returned to the States, heading for the dude ranch in Arizona again and staying long enough for Paulette to recover from minor injuries suffered in a car accident there. Paulette and Alta would use the dude ranch as a sanctuary several more times. They liked the rugged, polite men, the spectacular big skies, the outdoor life, and the simply prepared, amply proportioned food. They were both good eaters. It was in this wholesome environment that they finally hit upon the "crash Hollywood" plan that would eventually work. Paulette would not be one of thousands shown more couches than scripts. She would present herself in her latest incarnation: a woman of independent means. She would have no past. And no more extra work. The first time she had been in Hollywood, in 1929, she had done two extra stints: a Laurel and Hardy short called *Berth Marks* and *The Locked Door*, produced by United Artists, directed by George Fitzmaurice, and starring Barbara Stanwyck.

In late 1930, in the midst of the Great Depression, Paulette was in Hollywood again, accompanied by a $19,000 Duesenberg, a Paris wardrobe,

CLOCKWISE: *Paulette, eighth from the right, in* The Girl Habit, *1931. As the Ziegfeld blonde, in 1926, and left, as an extra in* The Kid from Spain, *with Eddie Cantor, 1931.*

and her mother. They found a pretty bungalow high in the Hollywood Hills that they lived in a for a couple of years. But Paulette would descend from the hills—like any other actress—in search of parts.

She called them "bits" or "walk-ons," but they were "extras" nonetheless, if one measured. She appeared in a Paramount picture called *The Girl Habit*, starring Charlie Ruggles and Margaret Dumont, in 1931, and in 1932 was in *Pack Up Your Trunks* and Warner Brothers' *The Mouthpiece*. She also managed to fit in a "bit" of schooling in 1931 during a stay in New York. She enrolled at the American Academy of Dramatic Arts, where she attended classes for two weeks.

After two years of eking out a vocation, 1932 turned out to be a banner year. She was signed to a contract with Samuel Goldwyn to make *The Kid from Spain*, starring Eddie Cantor, and in the chorus alongside her were other longing aspirants—Lucille Ball, Betty Grable, Anita Louise among them. The director was the prestigious Leo McCarey, and the choreographer, the equally prestigious Busby Berkeley. Paulette was not impressed, did not get along with Goldwyn, and was reputedly fired and rehired four times before she was tapped, socially, by Henry Ginsberg, who happened to run Hal Roach's studio for him. Ginsberg hankered for Paulette, thinking she had something for him and probably for the movies, waltzed her around, and then signed her to a contract—prior to her even meeting Hal Roach. Roach didn't seem to mind, and in fact, accepted this by putting a degree of momentum behind her.

According to Goddard's biographers Joe Morella and Edward Z. Epstein, Roach ran a small operation near MGM. He usually made shorts but occasionally produced a full-length feature. Paulette had gone with him even though he wasn't known for making stars, because she had been promised a lot of attention. And soon "The blonde starlet's picture began appearing in newspapers, and she was publicized as 'a brand-new find' whom Roach was going to develop into a star."

Paulette recalled this period with her usual insouciance, skipping over two years of effort and frustration: "So I arrived in Hollywood and I had my own Duesenberg and open Lancia for sunny days. And the boss of the studio said to me, 'Paulette, please don't come in those cars! You're driving the other actresses crazy! You're working here for two hundred dollars a week and you've got them all bugs. Thelma Todd is going to kill herself.' So I ran into this fellow who was a car maniac and that's what we had in common, because I adored cars. His name was Craney Darts. He *was* the Crane Plumbing Company. And he had nothing on his mind but redoing cars. So he took a Chevy and souped it up so it was worth about ten thou so that I could go into the Hal Roach Studio and nobody would hate me."

Paulette was busy appearing in comedy shorts such as *Show Business*, starring the "queen," Thelma Todd, and comedienne Zasu Pitts, and then playing opposite Charles Chase in the two-reelers *Young Ironsides* and *Girl Grief*. Her participation called for cheesecake topped with an antic sense of humor. She carried off this combination with aplomb. Also with aplomb, she began to dodge all pointed questions about herself. When Roach's publicity department asked, "How old?" she replied, "Oscar Wilde and Goddard say that 'Any woman who tells her age tells anything.'" She was also partial to telling anyone who asked her that her father was an industrialist named J. R. Goddard. She had always made herself special, and continued to hone the practice as if divining that the payoff would arrive. It did, and each version of it became part of Hollywood history.

Through Henry Ginsberg, Paulette had caught the eye of and become friendly with Joseph Schenck, who at that time, in 1932, was head of United Artists Studio. She was invited to a party aboard his yacht, where Charlie Chaplin was also a guest. Chaplin, a melancholy loner, was deeply attracted to Paulette's combination of beauty and brains. They discussed a potential investment of hers, which he dissuaded her from making, and they discussed hair color—he persuaded her to dye her hair back to its natural chestnut. By the time they disembarked, they were planning their life together.

In 1933, the journalist Edwin Shallert wrote about their romance as follows:

> That he [Chaplin] was originally caught by her personality at the time she appeared in the Cantor picture is in some ways remarkable, for despite the fact that she attracted much individual attention, she was not the unusual type that she is today. . . . In the movie colony it [blonde hair] is supposed to soften the face, but in Paulette's case it had exactly the opposite effect. Since she has permitted her hair to become its more natural brunette shade, she is infinitely less flaunting and brittle-looking than formerly. . . . The colony never felt then that she had a future professionally. Once more, therefore, Charlie appears as the discoverer.

Charles Spencer Chaplin's reputation preceded him. Comic genius, womanizer, anarchist, socialist, Communist, legendary lover, millionaire, purveyor of nymphets. When at forty-three he found twenty-one-year-old

Paulette, he had already been married twice—the first time to a sixteen-year-old actress named Mildred Harris, who said she was pregnant, admitted it was a lie after they'd wed, and then did become pregnant, though the child died in infancy. When Chaplin and Mildred divorced, she received an enormous settlement. His next wife was his pregnant (by him) leading lady from *The Gold Rush*, sixteen-year-old Lita Grey, with whom he had two sons, Charlie Jr. and Sydney. The marriage fell apart shortly after Sydney's birth. As reported by Morella and Epstein, "The ensuing divorce was hostile, headline-making and scandalous. 'When Lita Grey divorced him, she put out vile rumors that he had a depraved passion for little girls,' recalled Louise Brooks, with whom Chaplin had had an affair. 'He didn't give a damn, even though people said his career would be wrecked. It still infuriates me that he never defended himself against any of those ugly lies, but the truth is that he existed on a plane above pride, jealousy or hate. He lived totally without fear.'"

An element of blackmail made Lita Grey's settlement unusually large: $625,000. Lita Grey had threatened to expose in court the names of the five women Chaplin had affairs with during the marriage—the most prominent being Marion Davies, the mistress of William Randolph Hearst. Lita Grey got the money as well as custody of the boys, who were allowed to visit their father on alternate weekends.

Chaplin's latest silent picture, *City Lights*, had been released in 1931 and had presented his new protégée and temporary passion, the winsome blonde Virginia Cherrill. Up to this point, all Chaplin's leading ladies—Edna Purviance, Lita Grey, Virginia Cherrill, and Georgia Hale—had ended up doing only one picture for him; their careers were finished after they had starred for him. So, when Chaplin discovered Paulette, everyone was fascinated but few took her very seriously. Lita Grey did. It was Christmas and she was staying at the Ambassador Hotel in New York. She had just returned from a vaudeville tour and, to make up for her absence, decided to fuss over the boys and throw a holiday bash and, despite the acrimonious divorce, to even invite their father. Chaplin accepted and arrived stating that he could not stay long because Paulette was waiting downstairs.

Lita Grey insisted that he bring her up for a proper introduction: "Paulette entered the suite, a dark-haired, buoyantly alive vision in black velvet. I liked her instantly, liked the aura of vitality and genuineness about her, and we hit it off together right away. . . . She informed me she was plain Pauline Levy from Long Island. I informed her I was plain Lillita McMurray from Los

Angeles. . . . [She] was disarming, a wonderful, wonderful girl with a good sense of humor. I'll never forget how beautiful she looked. . . . She had class. She put me at ease by ignoring herself, bypassing mention of Charlie and telling me what a colossal performer I was."

Paulette always instinctually knew how to play a scene perfectly. It was one of the secrets of her enduring success—especially with men. Paulette actually disliked black and wore it only when a dramatic, emotionally packed moment was at hand. She also used Pauline Levy extremely sparingly. She was not immediately cozy with most other women—unless they were not a physical or psychological threat. The last thing she said to Lita Grey was "I like you, plain little Lillita McMurray from Los Angeles. I'd love to see you again."

Paulette never saw the ex–Mrs. Charlie Chaplin again. She didn't have to. She was on her way.

At the start of the "Chaplin years," Paulette got enormous publicity. And she was expert at keeping it that way. She never quenched speculation with candor, and as a result, the press was her servant: "There is no biographical data on Miss Goddard. She seems as mysterious as Greta Garbo herself. Here are a few notations. She drives to the studio in a Hispano-Suiza, she wears lounging pajamas trimmed in blue fox on the set, and a pearl necklace with a diamond clasp. A large diamond clasp."

Although there were Pygmalion-like features to the relationship, financially Paulette was independent. Chaplin did not have to worry that she might be just another sponger. "You have no idea what a sensible girl she is," he remarked to one of Paulette's few women friends, the writer Anita Loos. "She is very canny, she has her own money, and she takes excellent care of it."

Paulette, however, had always had the habit of accepting expensive gifts. She also knew how to solicit them with psychological finesse. Anita Loos understood her aspirations: "When she began to earn a living at fourteen by modeling dresses for a Seventh Avenue wholesale house, her daydreams were of diamonds from Van Cleef & Arpels, Balenciaga dresses, Revillon furs, Renoir paintings, Dom Pérignon champagne, and Persian caviar. She always seemed to bypass the labor which would bring them about."

Jewelry—particularly diamonds and rubies—was her passion. Paulette felt she had always been attracted to precious stones. She traced the origin of her fondness: "I've always loved stones. I've had them ever since my mother had her first date when I was four years old. Her date bought me a box of candy and inside were all these lousy little stones from Woolworth's and I wore them and I just loved it."

It was thought that Anita Loos based the character of Lorelei Lee in *How to Marry a Millionaire* on Paulette, her first marriage, and her escape from it with glorious booty. Among her possessions immediately following her first divorce were expensive automobiles—a Rolls-Royce and a Duesenberg— and two diamond bracelets valued at $85,000 each.

At fourteen, Paulette had already understood that her looks could dictate her destiny. At fifteen she had met her first millionaire, William Rhinelander Stewart: "Will Stewart. He was my first engagement. I have a star sapphire engagement ring from him. But I was sitting on his lap one day and we were making plans, and I said, 'You know, Will, I really think I should tell you I'm fifteen.' Well, he dropped me on the floor! And that was the end of my romance."

By her own admission, Paulette was, though she had tried, not properly focused on her career before she met Chaplin: "I started very young in the career thing. I wanted to go to parties on yachts. I didn't know what I was doing the first five years. I was yachting and this and that and the whole thing. Palm Beach, and I was brought up in El Morocco. . . . It was hard when I was a kid of sixteen, because I was with all these glamorous people— I would have to take a gin before I could go into a room. Or two, or three. And I was an alcoholic at eighteen! And thank God I met Charlie. He said, 'Your hair's turning gray. What are you doing?!?' I said, 'I'm so shy, believe it or not. So painfully shy.'"

Pre-Paulette, Chaplin had been lonely and had taken to wandering down Sunset Boulevard at night, gazing pensively into store windows. Distraught over his lack of family life and saddened by the marital breakup of his dear friends and business partners, Douglas Fairbanks, Sr., and Mary Pickford, he felt he was careening into middle age. After he had met Paulette, he said, "The bond between Paulette and me was loneliness."

Within the first year of their being together, she gave him the companionship he needed, and he instilled in her the discipline to back up any talent that she had. Their mutual admiration and support was enhanced by how much Chaplin liked Alta, who was just about his age. The configuration of a happy threesome was repeated again, but this time the stakes were enormous.

No matter what kind of excitement Paulette must have been feeling, she played it close to the chest. In late 1932, she decided to put some distance between her and Chaplin, and headed for New York to visit old haunts and her mother, who had moved back to the city for a while to be among her relatives. She also wanted to give the affair "room to bloom," as she put it in a card covered with roses that she'd sent to Alta.

Chaplin drove Paulette to the airport and kissed her good-bye, which set off a furor among Hollywood's tongue-wags. Columnist Dorothy Kilgallen scooped the story with the headline "CHAPLIN KISS NO BETROTHAL," DECLARES SHY PAULETTE. "'I'm not going to marry Mr. Chaplin,' said the young lady decidedly, squelching all rumors with a petulant toss of her golden bangs: 'Mr. Chaplin just saw me off. Of course he did kiss me goodbye, but my goodness,' she said girlishly, 'that doesn't mean I'm going to marry him. . . . I kissed a dozen or so as I was leaving. Leslie Howard was one. I can't even remember them.'"

She certainly grew bolder in her interviews, letting it be known that she was her own woman, with definite plans and opinions regarding her complex situation: "It isn't so much that she'd object to being a man's third wife, she explained, but she's only just recuperating from matrimony herself and thinks she's entitled to a vacation. Miss Goddard has heard all about the little Geisha girl who created a mild sensation when Chaplin announced he was bringing her from Japan. If Chaplin decides to make a picture with Japanese locale, he will use that trick to good advantage. Miss Goddard will have just a week in New York in which to settle her affairs and return to the contracts awaiting in Hollywood."

The "contracts" were not copious. She had turned down an offer for the title part in *The Perils of Pauline* and refused a term contract with J. I. Schnitzer. *The Kid from Spain* had been released, plus all the shorts she had made for Hal Roach. Her career lay at the mercy of Chaplin, who bought her contract from Roach, making her part of the repertory company at the Charles Chaplin Studios. But there was yet to be any role for her. He had a vague idea. "Paulette struck me as being somewhat of a gamine. This would be a wonderful quality for me to get on the screen . . . the tramp and the gamine."

Being away from Chaplin helped to solidify Paulette's commitment to him. The romantic and social aspects of the first year had been heady. They were chronic tennis match watchers (in those days a novel and smart thing to do); they went to the openings of plays, lunched at Ciro's, dined at the Brown Derby and Levy's, a popular Hollywood café; they danced at the Coconut Grove; they frequently made a foursome with the great silent screen actor John Gilbert and his fourth wife, actress Virginia Bruce, and they had a car accident together. Neither was seriously hurt, and each was reported in various accounts to have been at the wheel.

Chaplin was about to wield enormous professional power over her; he already had intellectual, emotional, and sexual leverage. Chaplin had a reputation for his amazing anatomy and sexual appetite. Lita Grey concurred, recalling a Chaplin statement cum threat that "he was a stallion and she'd better resign herself to it." In a letter to her mother, Paulette wrote, "Charlie takes everything out of me." However, it was Chaplin who eventually did not want to sleep with Paulette, because he felt that she stole his precious energy during the night.

One of the strongest bonds in their relationship was Paulette's passion for Chaplin's boys and vice versa. Charlie Jr., who decades later was asked by a Paulette-in-between-marriages to be her escort around town, remembered his first glimpse of her: "He [Chaplin] helped a beautiful platinum blonde out of the car. Syd and I were so thunderstruck we could only stare. Her pale, shining hair framed a piquant, heart-shaped face alive with sparkling green eyes. . . . We lost our hearts at once."

Paulette clearly had a way with little boys. When she moved into Chaplin's mansion in Bel-Air, at the end of 1932, among their several illustrious neighbors was the David O. Selznick family, which lived directly across the street. Young Daniel was smitten. "I saw them all the time because I was constantly bringing the tennis balls back that they batted across the street into our garden. . . . what I want to say about her is that she was so infectious. Her personality was like champagne. She was adorable, flirtatious, so alive and so responsive to me as a child, as a male child, and I frankly knew or had met a great many film stars as a child . . . but I don't remember a film star with that kind of vivaciousness. And her freckles were wonderful. A lot of women try and have them removed, but on Paulette, they gave a kind of animation to her face. I mean, God! . . . I later realized how sexy she was, but as a child I didn't know that it was sexiness."

Chaplin was thinking hard about his next picture, whose working title was *Production Number 5*. It would introduce Paulette in a starring role opposite "The Tramp." But only when she was ready. Under his tutelage she studied drama with Samuel Kayzer, and took dancing, singing, and voice (elocution) lessons several times a week. She was a rapt and apt student, absorbing everything. And of course Chaplin, her Svengali, was always there, giving her the most invaluable lessons.

Paulette recalled, "He told me you can't be clever. If you just be your own self, it comes through more than anything. And then they're kind to you. They love you. One thing I learned from Charlie—I learned many things, but when I was first learning to act he said, 'Baby, don't be afraid to make a mistake. Because when you make a mistake, they love you." And they did! I didn't know what I was doing. I was crawling around in circles. And he said, 'Forget it. Don't criticize. Don't analyze. Be it and if you're wrong, they will love you.' And that's the secret of performance. You cannot be clever. People hate cleverness. They despise it. And irony and—all of it. But if you make a mistake, they say, 'Oh, isn't she real!'"

While Paulette was pursuing acting under Chaplin's guidance, she felt anxious and beholden. She recounted the tumult of emotions: "Wanting to act gave me an added tiny fear in the back of my head that I had all the time. Acting is anxiety. . . . You wouldn't be there unless you wanted to do your best. . . . And everybody cares. No matter what they say."

Chaplin was a taskmaster during weekdays, subject to bouts of tense, manic activity, often followed by depression and withdrawal. At night, he was capable of exhibiting a dual personality—either being distant and formal, demanding evening clothes and punctuality at dinner, which would be ceremonial and solemn, or he could be charming, generous, and benevolent, giving Paulette for Mother's Day the biggest, purest diamond she ever received or presenting her with a yacht.

Before he knew Paulette, Chaplin owned a yacht called the *Edna P.*, after his first leading lady, Edna Purviance. He sold it, embracing tennis and golf as hobbies instead, and enjoyed the pleasures of his friends' yachts—such as Joseph Schenck's. Paulette had developed quite a taste for such West Coast resorts as Catalina, Santa Cruz, and Santa Barbara and the yachts that could ferry her to them. Paulette wanted her own yacht and was very open about it. Many of the poshest yachts were docked in San Pedro, and one Sunday, Paulette and Chaplin—who normally took a Sunday excursion together— motored to the dock, where Paulette lost her heart. There was a fifty-five- foot cabin cruiser that could sleep six and a crew of two. It was a sister ship to the *Runaway*, which belonged to the director King Vidor, a friend of Chaplin's. They visited the boat three times that week. Finally, the next Sunday, when Chaplin headed the car in the direction of San Pedro, Paulette squirmed, saying that she really couldn't browse the boat one more time, that it would be rude. Chaplin insisted that for that kind of money it wasn't rude and continued to head for San Pedro. Paulette refused to get out of the car when they arrived. Chaplin could bother those nice people again, but she would wait in the car until he was done and could take her to a late big

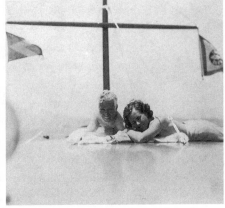

Happy at sea on the Panacea, *1935.*

Chaplin clowning with Paulette.

The Panacea, *the yacht Chaplin bought for Paulette, 1932.*

breakfast. Chaplin insisted that she take one more look. As they were ascending the gangplank, she smelled something very much like coffee and eggs and toast. Chaplin had already bought the yacht and had sent his cook to prepare Paulette's big breakfast. Chaplin was in charge of naming the boat and considered calling it the *Edna P. II*, but instead decided upon *Panacea*, which was a tribute to Paulette.

It was approximately four years between the time Chaplin and Paulette met and the premiere of *Modern Times*, which evolved from *Production Number 5*. Paulette was in serious training for two of those years, worked on the film for nearly a year, and then waited for its distribution. Never out of the public eye, she was one of the most famous unknowns in the world. The big question was whether she and Chaplin were married or simply living "in sin." Couples with Hollywood careers did not do that in those days. Studios were known to sever contracts over lesser scandals. That a young German actress named Marlene Dietrich, who was being discovered in a big way in America, was nefarious regardless of gender didn't matter. She was married and had a young child. If Paulette and Chaplin were not married, then he was even more of an iconoclast and anarchist than already billed, and she was a slut. However, nothing could be proved; there were rumors that they'd wed and that they had not. They continued to excite interest without igniting the press and public sentiment.

Fawning articles such as this were common: "Paulette Goddard is the most extravagantly gowned, luxurious-looking girl in Hollywood. She has poise and charm, which so many Hollywood beauties haven't. Recently it was reported by the tax assessor that Chaplin, the London slum boy, was the wealthiest motion picture star, having more than $7 million worth of taxable securities, surely enough to support a wife. His 50-room house in Beverly Hills is a lonely spot for the small, gray-haired comedian, who seldom emerges into Hollywood society. Does marriage tempt him again?"

After the premiere of *The Kid from Spain*, at which Paulette (who was only an extra) was escorted by Chaplin along with Mary Pickford, Gary Cooper, Norma Shearer, and Irving Thalberg, she made almost unheard-of leaps. Although she wouldn't commit to any talk about their marital status, in every other outward way her behavior toward Chaplin was wifely. She slowly began to redo the house, his social life, and the familial environment. She saw to it that they entertained on a large scale, and she acted as the perfect hostess (in the beginning), filling his house and yacht with illustrious guests. Some of them would fall for Paulette, such as H. G. Wells, Aldous Huxley, George Gershwin, Harry Hopkins, Howard Hughes, writer Hugh

Walpole, tennis player Tim Durant, and two women who became lifelong friends—Constance Collier (with whom she later took acting lessons) and Anita Loos, who said about Paulette's handling of would-be lovers, "Many ladies knew how to say no, but to do so without offending or making an enemy was a definite talent."

She seemed dedicated to the life and art of Chaplin. Friends noticed a change in both of them. Paulette stopped wearing makeup. Her days were full of lessons and rehearsals in preparation for her starring role. When she had a break, she would go to a yarn shop, buy lots of multicolored wool, and knit sweaters for Chaplin. She even became part of Charlie Jr. and Sydney's interests by being athletic with them, taking them sailing, snorkeling, fishing, and up to Lake Arrowhead for skiing—just the three of them.

"Most people in Hollywood couldn't comprehend Paulette's genuine interest in Chaplin's children," said Anita Loos, "but that facet of her personality was what made Paulette truly unique . . . when Paulette moved in, she adopted the boys, not as Mama but as someone much more fun; the French term 'copain' is a better description of their relationship than that cold, sexless term of 'pal.'"

Paulette was determined to enroll in an English course at UCLA, and the head of the department, Margaret B. Ringanalda, was impressed to the point of being captivated: "She . . . told me how she had been educated in a convent and wished to go on being educated, particularly in English literature and writing: 'I write little poems and things now,' she explained with a deprecatory gesture. . . . Much to her regret and mine, it was impossible for her to enter the university as she had planned, because in a few months' time Mr. Chaplin was to begin work on the picture in which she is to play opposite him. If she could not attend classes, she would have the courses brought to her. She was the rarest of students, the type who wanted to know for the sake of knowing."

If Anita Loos had to sum up in one word what Paulette Goddard had, she would say "allure." Constance Collier called her a "natural honey pot." Was she also a natural poseur? Was she really intellectually curious? Was she aesthetically inclined, domestically capable, maternally oriented? Or was she at the right place at the right time with an appetite so voracious that it put her into high gear, perfectly adaptable to any situation at any time? Brilliant opportunist or true acolyte? Lois Granato, her secretary for the last fifteen years of Paulette's life, never saw her read a book unless it was "junk, something sensational or about something deviant." Paulette admitted herself that she couldn't cook—"How can you cook caviar?"—and although she was a

At the races with her new diamond ring, a gift from Chaplin, ca. 1935.

Franklin Ardelle, Norma Shearer, Paulette, and Chaplin on Joe Schenck's yacht,
Invader, *1934, off Santa Catalina Island.*

good knitter, it had gone by the wayside by the time she was in her thirties. As for having children, "I never deeply wanted them," was what she said. But beginning in 1932 was her moment when all of her powers were working for her. If she could get this lucky, she was determined not to blow it, not to let anything slip.

The training period became more intense. In between getting the picture ready, Chaplin and Paulette kept dodging marital sightings: it was thought they were married June 1, 1933, or in the middle of 1935, aboard the yacht off Catalina Island. Douglas Fairbanks, Sr. and Jr., knew as much as anyone. Douglas Sr. had just married Sylvia Ashley, a cool social beauty, whom Paulette admired for "her poise bred in the bone" and who was to have a rather minor affair five years hence with Erich Maria Remarque. She and Douglas Sr., who were frequently being entertained by Chaplin and Paulette, passed down some sense of the situation to Douglas Jr., who in 1938 was to costar with Paulette in David O. Selznick's *Young in Heart*: "I always assumed they were married. But maybe they weren't. Maybe they were just shacking up together. I knew Charlie very well from the time I was a little boy, because he was a great friend of my father's. So I would see a fair amount of Charlie. Whether there was a common-law marriage or a real religious marriage or a civil marriage—nobody knew. But they were married as far as their social life was concerned."

Paulette recalled the parties in the house on Summit Drive and the days that predated Sylvia Ashley, the days when she was still being shaped by Chaplin:

> We had seven servants. All you had to do was ring a bell. There was no servant problem. They were all Oriental. The house was right next to Pickfair. We went up once or twice. But Charlie hated to go. It was so stuffy. I mean, they'd come in arm in arm, Douglas and Mary, hating each other. He was fooling around and she had somebody, but they'd come arm in arm. We'd go once in a while when they had somebody snakey or terribly interesting like Mountbatten. *Snakey* was the word we used in those days for a glamorous person. . . . Charlie hated Mary anyway because of United Artists. She was a little tyrant. Always trying to take 50 percent instead of her 20 percent or something. A friend of mine went to interview Mary Pickford recently, and she said she wouldn't see him but she'd talk to him on the telephone. So he went to Pickfair and he's in one room and she's right in the next room and they talked on the telephone. That was always the way

she was. It was all behavior. . . . But Hollywood back then was real. It was heaven. People giving a new piece of jewelry every night. No bunk about it.

Paulette always knew how to flirt and be given things, but Chaplin taught her to flirt intellectually. He devised a plan to abet her absorption, which she practiced until perfect. It became the secret of her success with the literary, artistic, and political circles she found herself in through Chaplin, and then later sought out herself.

"Charlie was a great talker. He loved an audience and would hold forth on every subject in the world. We used to play 'pass the evening,' doing little three-minute speeches. He trained me so I was able to speak for three minutes on any subject. But not four. Not one minute longer. Any subject. He just threw it at me. It is a lovely game. And that's the way I learned everything I know."

Those who were close to Chaplin denied that his politics were too radical and socialist. In fact, his ideas came from his belief in equality and his mischievous desire to play the devil's advocate and stir up a little controversy. Paulette felt that his political views could not be defined.

Anarchy was to him a very romantic thing. He loved all the men whose lives were sacrificed to get shorter hours of labor. . . . And during the Chicago riots, he was trying to write for the rights of the people and that showed in his work. . . . But he wasn't a Leftist. He was just a great talker. . . . But sometimes I'd get sort of bored with it, and I'd take everyone ice skating after dinner. That's how I got the name Little Lord Fauntleroy. I'd go in my shorts . . . but that's what Charlie liked to do . . . talk, talk, talk . . . but, of course, with great charm. But most people would come expecting to be highly entertained—like Harry Bridges, who was the head of the dock workers in San Francisco—and he'd come with four or five economists from NYU, young men, and I'd take them aside and say, "We're having champagne and caviar." And I thought they were Communists and was afraid they'd think I was very pretentious, so I'd whisper it and they'd boom out, "That's just great!" And Charlie would hold forth to them about economics. And they'd sit there and sort of teeter off into drowsy-world because they'd want to go skating with me. Or do just anything. . . . Because they wanted to see him do his marvelous things. Which he could do, but didn't. He'd talk. Physically, mentally, he was—anything, everything. But he never went ice skating with me. He never went out for games. Except tennis. . . . And it's laughable to think of him as a Communist because he was a number one capitalist, as everyone who was involved with him knew. People resented the fact that he had acquired so much money . . . tremendously!

For Paulette, the years 1934–1936 were golden ones. In Hollywood, with Chaplin, she met everyone there was to meet. "It was the glamour of the world. All of the artists of the world were there—international artists. Huxley, Isherwood, Schoenberg. Anyone you could wish for in politics. They'd either be coming from Japan or the Orient, or they'd be on missions, or they'd be coming from Europe. And Stravinsky. And Horowitz would come to play the piano after dinner. And Einstein would bring a string quartet to the house. He'd say, 'I can come for lunch if I can bring the other three.' . . . And play. Not for any audience. And not for *names*."

This period provided Paulette with some of her most vivid experiences. There was the time that Gertrude Stein and Alice B. Toklas visited the set of *Modern Times*. Paulette was instantly taken with both of them. Stein did not charm Chaplin, however. While on the set, she had an idea for him that she thought would enhance his film. Before she could offer it he said, "I can't use it, Madame." Stein sat there like a stone for a while and then said, "What you need is a dog to come in and pee right away onscreen." Chaplin gave her an extremely wintery smile. "It won't work," he said. Chaplin had dismissed Gertrude Stein from their life. Paulette said simply, "He didn't like her. She was too special."

Chaplin spent $1.5 million on *Modern Times*. Production began in early October 1934, and Chaplin didn't stop fiddling with it until early 1936. Every day in between Paulette was treated like "a rag and like royalty," in her recollection of a period that she recalled as the most vivid, important, and rewarding of her life. It was also "the best picture I ever made," she always said.

I was about to start the picture of *Modern Times*. I'd been a showgirl and I'd been a model and all those things were wrong with me. The way of walking and everything. And I walk in and I'm wearing a Valentina—you know, the Russian dressmaker. A plain little dress but *so* expensive! It cost five hundred dollars then! You know, a day dress. And I had my hair done to be beautiful and eyelashes on and came walking in—the Goddard Walk. I've lost it, thank God. I had to. I had to unlearn it to play this part. I'll tell you what he did to me that absolutely cured me—you see, working with Charlie was the greatest school for acting that *anyone* could *ever, ever* have.

I mean, he knew it *all*. But anyway, this day that I walked in he said, "That isn't it, baby." And he took a bucket of water and he threw it on me and that's how I got my hairstyle in *Modern Times*. It broke my heart. And I cried and cried and cried. And he said, "Cry, damn it, *cry*! Camera!" And he called Rolley Totheroh over, who loved me so much—you could tell by the camera. He'd bring it like a kiss, a caress. And he was just a plain cameraman but such a dear man. And Charlie'd say, "Rolley, get the camera in here! *CRY*, God damn it, get down on your knees and look up at me!" And the tears were running and it was the best shot I ever had! And that's how my hairstyle came. It was never set after that.

Catherine Hunter was Chaplin's efficient, diplomatic, and seemingly divine press secretary. It was her job to see that everything was exclusive and protected, and, if promoted, it had to be in the most fairy-tale-like way. She wrote a release describing the working environment of the Chaplin studios at La Brea and Sunset:

> As for Paulette's dressing room, its color motif is peach and white. She has a lovely tiled bath and shower and a huge outer room that but for its huge white three-mirrored dressing room table resembles a sitting room. A peach carpet entirely covers the floor and her big white combination clock-radio, chaise longue, chairs, tables, etc. all carry out the same color motif. Walt Disney personally sketched several of his famous characters for her and duly autographed, they are framed in white on the walls.
> A spirit of friendliness prevails. Every person who has ever visited the Chaplin lot speaks of this immediately. From our general manager, Alfred Reeves, down to Bebe, the telephone operator—not forgetting Teddy, the dog of uncertain origin but very definite appeal, and Topaze (just a cat), incidentally a prime favorite with Mr. Chaplin—the place exudes an atmosphere that is definitely not Hollywood or a studio in the generally accepted sense. Courtesy, consideration, a fine feeling of cooperation and good-will are prevalent.

On February 5, 1936, *Modern Times*, or as Paulette always referred to it, "My School for Acting," opened at the Rivoli Theatre in New York. Paulette's reviews supported her transition from unknown to star, in a role that, as James Robert Parish pointed out, "was a difficult role in which to be 'introduced' to the filmgoing public. . . . Paulette demonstrated that she responded to painstaking direction well and could perform the typically

LEFT: *Paulette in her first big film,* Modern Times, *1936.*

Paulette did most sports, including skiing—here at Lake Arrowhead.

over-rehearsed Chaplin scene with delightful spontaneity." Frank S. Nugent, in the *New York Times*, endorsed her as "a winsome waif and a fitting recipient of the great Charlot's championship." Although in its initial release the black-and-white movie was only moderately successful in box-office receipts, critics across the board hailed Paulette as Hollywood's top new personality.

"Whatever Chaplin touched in her," said the actor Burgess Meredith, who was to become Paulette's third husband, "made her absolutely marvelous. And she never quite achieved that again, did she?"

BONI

1 9 2 2 – 1 9 3 3

As PUBLICITY MANAGER and editor of the Continental Rubber Company's magazine, *Echo-Continental*, Remarque was required to do a lot of traveling. He was sent to the Balkans, England, Switzerland, Italy, and Turkey to promote Continental's rubber products as well as to write special feature articles. His writer's eye and voice began to take on a new sophistication. The influence of his idealistic mentor, Fritz Hörstemeier, receded into the background as Remarque began to gather some experience of his own.

As a single man on the road, he succumbed to two temptations: drinking and prostitutes. Friends and colleagues had begun to notice the drinking. He was also getting a reputation at certain bars, street corners, and houses in a number of cities in Europe. He had a genuine tenderness for "women of the night." He found their reduced circumstance, which they attempted to disguise and embellish, touching and profoundly human. He often refrained from having sex with them, but discovered a deep eroticism just being in their company. He liked to talk with them until the early hours of the morning, buying them Calvados, cigarettes, or a snack, watching them indulge and relax. He treated them with respect, which must have bemused them, since he was so attractive and available. With his thick, silky fair hair, penetrating blue eyes, handsome physique always impeccably dressed, and aloof yet charismatic air, he was very seductive.

Remarque had a girlfriend during this time whose name was Brigitte Neuner. The relationship might have started during the Dream Circle period, but the earliest evidence of its existence is a chain letter Remarque sent her in 1920. In the correspondence, which lasted over ten years, Remarque's tone toward Brigitte was uncharacteristically jocular and randy. In these letters he begins to form a system of nicknaming, pseudo-naming, game playing, and anagrams. He starts a letter to her with "Heinrich, how are you? I think that you have stripes like a zebra and are peeling like a plantana," and signs with an elusive "B.," which stands for Boris, sometimes, or for Boni— short for Saint Boniface. Brigitte was a departure from the tormenting women usually around him: with her he could joust, complain, and at times even play the lout. All the letters are addressed to her in Berlin—significant in that Berlin, the German mecca, was his goal, and that he already had her as a welcoming mistress there. However, he patiently served two more years of his apprenticeship in Hannover before arriving in Berlin.

In June of 1923, Remarque became editor in chief at *Echo-Continental*, and took great pride in announcing it to everyone. He was now in charge of advertising, publicity, and all editorial matters. He wrote to Karl Vogt, the monument mason in Osnabrück for whom he had worked, informing him of his new position but also making it clear that he wanted to keep a toehold in Osnabrück. Remarque had always loved cars, and with the Hannover job he could assign himself to cover and write about all things pertaining to cars—a perk of working for a company that manufactured rubber parts and tires. Vogt, as well as other friends, preyed on him for favors, which he tried to fulfill:

Dear Karl, This evening I am driving to the "Rennaufsicht" [race supervision] in Brussels. . . . I can get only one tire and one tube every six months— also they will be more expensive—I will see—be patient—you will receive them. . . . Give Helm my regards, he should write to me more often. When I see both of you, I will tell you all about Indians, Americans, and Negroes, etc. with whom I deal daily.

What is interesting about the relationship with Vogt is that their positions somewhat reversed themselves. When Remarque was down and out, Vogt supplied him with a decent job and restored his confidence. In Hannover, having moved on and up, Remarque took the tone of a mentor with Vogt, who sought his advice about cutting loose and taking chances. Remarque offered shrewd inspiration:

> You are right, it is the uncertainties in life that have a special attraction. To wait for accidental happenings lends to one's existence often a strange mood. However, one must have a certain amount of self-assurance to make the right decision at the right time. Try to adapt this approach into every-thing you do, of course with certain limits; one should not merely live into the day and leave everything up to God. And then one more thing: only rely on yourself, never on others. Always try to have the reins in your hands. You won't believe how easy it is to lead other people. The one who says I can and I will always succeeds; because almost all always wait only for the moment that someone will go ahead of them.

He signed the letter "EMR," a signature he began to affix to articles and letters during this time. He also used *Que*, the last three letters of the new spelling of his last name, on advertising essays for the trade. Special, stylish effects seemed to reflect his need to be different and important.

In 1923 Hannover was a willowy twenty-two-year-old actress-dancer named Jutta Ilse Ingeborg Ellen Zambona. Jutta was a ravishing, cool, lan-guid, natural blonde, a divorcée who had been married at an early age to an industrialist named Winkelhoff. Her beauty and style were somewhat oth-erworldly. Tall, angular, and very thin, with long arms and legs, she always dressed extremely stylishly in white or beige. Her huge eyes were deeply set under lids that had a natural lavender tinge, her small, perfect bow mouth was painted a deep red, and she had a very feminine, delicate air. With her small, heart-shaped face, she looked like a doomed princess out of a Grimm's fairy tale. Indeed, she had had tuberculosis as a result of malnutrition suf-fered during World War I and she controlled it by regular sojourns to a sana-torium in Davos, Switzerland. Outwardly fragile, she wrapped steel bands around Remarque. He was instantly and deeply moved by her. Their rela-tionship was a powerful symbiosis on which the years had little effect and which neither really understood. More than a decade after they had met, been married, and divorced, Remarque was able to fictionalize her in his fifth novel, *Three Comrades*: "Her hair was brown and silky and in the lamp-light had an amber sheen. Her shoulders were very straight but inclined a lit-tle forward, her hands were slender, a bit long, and bony rather than soft. Her face was narrow and pale, but the large eyes gave it an almost passionate strength. She looked very good, I decided . . . like a slim young Amazon, cool, radiant, sure, and unapproachable."

Once, late in his life, when asked about himself, Remarque snapped, "I dislike everything autobiographical as well as biographical. It appears to me an overestimation of one's own importance and therefore indirectly egotism, trimmed with vanity . . . every writer has to deal with what he feels. Some like to talk about themselves and their life, others prefer to have their work speak for itself. That's the group I belong to. . . . Whatever I learned in life I have used in my books anyway and the rest is private and has no relation to my work, and that's the way I would like to keep it."

Remarque generally portrayed Jutta in a favorable light. In *Flotsam*, she appears as the German refugee Ruth Holland, an enigmatic, sensitive, and sickly heroine who flees to Vienna and overcomes her past through love. In *Heaven Has No Favorites*, she appears as Lillian Dunkerque, the rich but doomed heroine, who is deceptive and seductive, yet compassionate. In life, Jutta was a less tragic heroine and a far more complicated woman (and a chronic thorn in Remarque's side) than the way she is depicted in Remarque's fiction. Hans Wagener in his *Understanding Erich Maria Remarque* notes how Remarque allowed for Pat Hollman's demise from an incurable disease in *Three Comrades*: "It is futile, however, to speculate why Remarque deviated from his autobiographical model—whether or not, for example, he put 'a symbolic end to the most significant love of his life.' The reason for Pat's death within the context of the novel is clear: love and happiness cannot exist in such perilous times." The perilous times were Berlin during the Weimar era.

Jutta Zambona was born in Hildesheim, Germany, on August 28, 1901, the daughter of Heinrich Emil and Antonie Ida Wilhelmine Zambona. (Though she was also called Jeanne, by those who knew her after she had left Germany, in his diaries and letters to her, Remarque referred to her mostly as Jutta or Peter or Johannes.) She had a sister, Edith, and a half sister, Hertha; Edith married the brother of Hermann Göring, a doctor who was very much against Göring, the Nazis, and Hitler. The family origins were Italian and Danish. Jutta loved languages and spoke German, French, Italian, and English.

Like the character Pat Hollman, Jutta "typified Remarque's feminine ideal: an attractive, compassionate woman who could be both lover and comrade." Unlike Pat, Jutta could also be treacherous, and had frequent lovers during her time with Remarque. But in the beginning of the relationship she and Remarque were extremely in love, emotionally and physically. And for Remarque to experience a grand passion, in contrast to his many liaisons with prostitutes, he had to be totally involved emotionally and intellectually, since he had a Calvinist streak that made him feel that carnality was contemptible.

Jutta noted to an old friend, Charlotte Elk Zernik, that Remarque was, in fact, mostly impotent during their marriage. He did continue his relationship with Brigitte Neuner during his courtship (however sporadically) and the early part of his marriage to Jutta, but the very things that excited him— the chase, the elusiveness, the foreplay, the promise—could not be part of any marriage.

The struggle between love and desire can be seen in a piece that he wrote called "Decadence of Love":

> You smile, dear lady, but believe me: the most wonderful thing about love is not the result, but the preliminary activities. Everything before, the touching, caressing, pushing, denying—this silent, cat-like striving, this hidden battle of both participants, that is the highest. . . . We are primarily onlookers, and less participants. Tender, shimmering, and exotic moods, are more important to us than feelings. . . . A year ago I met a woman who attracted my attention, because she had such delicate ankles, which is always a sign of good breeding. . . . She was blonde, almost as blonde as you, Madame. I met her often for tea, and soon I felt this shower of excitement. Then, fireworks started. Our war of words started. I already was ahead. Whenever she tried to retort, I was ready to confuse her, then she tried to confuse me, but ultimately she let me win. When I then would see her again the following day, her brain sharpened into the tip of her head. I let her have a few moments to relax and then I retorted again with clever remarks and left her speechless. The woman was beautiful. Her legs could be noticed under her gown. This woman wore gowns, not dresses. She had beautiful white hands. My blood began to sing.

"It was apparently a leitmotif in his life. Always women, women, women," Charlotte Elk Zernik has said in recalling what Jutta must have perceived; "according to what she [Jutta] said, Goddard, finally, sexually was the right one." He also might have slowed down a bit by then, since he was fifty-nine when he married for the last time.

At *Echo-Continental* Remarque was making a name for himself as a journalist and editor. His sports articles were considered quite original, for he

LEFT: *Remarque at his desk in Berlin, sporting his trademark monocle, ca. 1923.*

Remarque's athletic and agile girlfriend, Brigitte Neuner, at the Dutch resort Nordwijk aan Zee, ca. 1922.

LEFT: *Edith Doerry, who helped Remarque get his job at* Sport im Bild.

would cleverly link rubber, his company's concern, with such overlooked pastimes as bicycle riding, or put a new spin on boating by writing about it as a popular and romantic sport. His articles also broke new ground, espousing such novel ideas as improving physical health or sponsoring an atmosphere of competition, which the Germans took to with relish. His pieces about cars and racing led to his receiving endorsements. He was on the cusp of another rise.

Dr. Thomas Schneider, a Remarque historian and Osnabrück archivist, has related a slightly circuitous set of circumstances that provided both career and relationship opportunities for Remarque. It began with the appearance of another woman: "On New Year's Eve in 1923, a discussion took place between Kurt Doerry, a leading sports journalist in the Weimar Republic who founded the first German sports magazine, *Sport im Bild* [*Illustrated Sport*], and the representative of the Continental Rubber Company in Hannover, a Mr. Holtzheuer. The conversation shifted to the journalistic ambitions of Doerry's daughter, Edith, and on January 19, 1924, Edith Doerry was asked by Remarque to submit an article to the *Echo-Continental*":

Dear Miss:

Per discussion with Mr. Holtzheuer, I have to thank him for your address and request that you send me an article about tennis, hockey, maybe also swimming, written with your father, since I have few of such articles for the *Echo-Continental* at this time. . . .

It would be appreciated, if you could send some photos, too; you participated in some sporting event and you could send some interesting pictures to enliven the article.

I hope to receive your reply soon, and remain, Cordially, Erich Maria Remarque.

Excruciatingly correct and polite, his correspondence remained in this vein for a while. However, as if it were a persistent courtship of an extremely shy person, he deftly begins to inject some warmth—personal, yet never overwhelming. In a subtle way, Remarque was seducing Edith Doerry. He tells her they will use her article on hockey and asks for one on tennis, says they have sent the fee of 50 DM and asks her to "pass the enclosed article along to your father for his approval for *Sport im Bild*. . . . I thank you for your assistance and please forward my best wishes to your father." Schneider has summarized the success of this venture for everyone involved: "Edith Doerry's articles [primarily on sports themes] appeared regularly after an introductory article written by her father for *Echo-Continental*. Remarque then had the opportunity to publish his articles and short stories in *Sport im Bild*." In the summer of 1924, after still more requests for articles, he began to mix business with personal chitchat. What made this careful movement forward all the more interesting is that he had yet to lay eyes on Edith Doerry, though he was about to.

Remarque and Edith Doerry met on October 7 at the offices of Continental to "take care of business matters," as Remarque put it in a letter prior to the meeting, adding, then "we can go somewhere to talk for an hour." Clearly, they hit it off. Fair and slender, Edith Doerry had a sweet, shy prettiness, not unlike the looks of his sister Erna. Remarque must have understood their attraction to be about both convenience and pleasure. Ten days later, after Edith had arranged for him to get his toe in the door at *Sport im Bild* in Berlin, he wrote her again: "You were so kind to arrange a meeting for me at *Sport im Bild* and in addition were such a good guide through Berlin that I am embarrassed to ask for your assistance, while thanking you for your kindness. Please write me another 2–3 essays in the next 2 months for the *Echo*. Although you are already considered to be a regular contributor for the next year, I would like to place these articles personally. Do I have your approval? I am very much indebted to you, with best regards."

A little more than a month later, in early November, Edith Doerry was helping Remarque look for an apartment in Berlin. He had been made an editor at *Sport im Bild* and was to begin his duties in January of 1925. He was very specific about what he was looking for in an apartment, and in this letter he writes to Edith Doerry with enormous grace and ease:

> I would like to have a nice, furnished 2–3 room apartment, with morning sunshine or sunny in general, private, with bath and kitchen. I would prefer 3rd floor or penthouse, possibly with an elevator. Price to 200–250 DM all right.
>
> I would be very happy if you would investigate for me, but don't trouble yourself too much—but one never knows, an opportunity might present itself. Can I count on you?
>
> ... Your article has time till the 10th of the month. Please take your time writing it. ... Unhappy me, I alone shall write 8 articles on cars for the exhibition—And other things—I hope to hear from you again soon.

Although feminism was not rampant in the Weimar Republic, Remarque, as an editor, had the women's readership very much in mind—as is evidenced in his suggestions to Edith about possible articles in his letter of December 4, 1924:

If you like football [soccer], volleyball, or water ball, then write something about that. Or: the educational value of easy athletic activities, or about the sport itself—or: influence of gymnastics on modern illnesses (tuberculosis, neurasthenia, etc.)—or a tennis theme—or: womanly or unwomanly sports (football played by women in England or America), hockey and competition, should women participate in these sports more for exercise (yes) or in competition—and which type of sports activities? Rugby and its technique and tricks—The lady as driver of cars (clothes, what should she take along, supplies, weapons, what should she know about the motor, how should she drive?)—I hope you can use some of these.

It would be difficult to prove whether Remarque and Edith Doerry had an affair, although during the next few years of a limited correspondence, there are references to a certain kind of intimacy. Remarque obviously cared for her, but it seemed that she was in love with him. So much so, in fact, that her mother, either sensing that it might be futile or that a young editor was an inadequate spouse for her daughter, whisked Edith off to Capri for several months. While she was "in exile" and Remarque was settling into his job at *Sport im Bild*, something changed between them. His letters convey a new intimacy: "Dear Edith, the days fly and fly and one morning a letter arrives. . . . I have received your letter and your card and thank you for both, especially the letter. You will understand that I always wait at least an hour, because I do not want to write just any letter—but I have so much work and there's pressure to earn money for others."

This is the first hint of the complications of his life. At some point Jutta arrived in Berlin to live with Remarque. That relationship had not been on a back burner, although he was also involved with Edith, who, after all, was the boss's daughter. Edith's mother, trying to save her daughter from Remarque, inadvertently put more romance into the situation than there had initially been. Edith no doubt was in some emotional crisis and was writing to Remarque, longing for communication. He was in a sticky spot—in love with one and wanting to requite another. In a letter dated March 31, 1925, his tone is delicate; he tries to relate to her as a kindred spirit while not giving her too much hope—not dashing all hope either.

> I am telling you in detail about this, because today as your letter arrived, I was aroused by the thought that so much time has passed during which I have not even noticed the routine. Part of this is my fault because I don't write to many people—the written word does not really say everything I would like to say. Letters and words on paper are so easily misunderstood.
>
> But I have often thought about you. And I already had the feeling, as if the warmth of Capri and the sea, Naples, the gold-dusted southern sky would make everything that has passed unimportant; the spirits are still hovering around, but these do not have any power anymore. . . .
>
> I believe that in this most difficult of all situations, nothing is as consoling as the elements—sun, water, distance, and wind. That's why I am so hopeful that you will return, flexible and free.

By April 1925, Remarque had found an apartment at Kaiserdamm 114 in the Berlin suburb of Charlottenburg. It was sunny and spacious enough for two. Edith's correspondence continued—and steamed up. She nervously sent him some photographs of herself most likely in the nude, judging from Remarque's response:

> Dear Edith, how beautiful your pictures are—who should find it shocking?—I am very happy that you sent these to me. How tanned you must be by now.
>
> I have been in a crisis too—a strange one—but lasting. . . . We will have much to talk about after your return and I am looking forward to it. . . . We are not sensitive enough in our literary expression to write long letters—return and then we will talk, talk, talk of the heavens, people, earth, and all those things that are never ending. Always yours, E. Maria.

The next record of any correspondence was a congratulatory telegram that Remarque sent to Edith Doerry upon her marriage to an Englishman named Leslie Roseveare, whom she had met on Capri. Approximately a month later, on October 17, 1925, Remarque married Jutta Ilse Ingeborg Ellen Zambona.

According to Dr. Thomas Schneider, "The experience on Capri, as seen from Edith Doerry's memory, is presented as a plot by her mother, who desired that her oldest daughter should marry an Englishman." In a letter to

Edith, Remarque gives a sense of his marriage, which might have been on the rebound. His hurt and resigned tone does not reflect a happy nuptial state, and his regard for his new wife seems one more of duty than ardor. It is difficult to know what the reference to Edith's anger means:

> Dear Edith, I have postponed my reply to your best wishes telegram from day to day, in order to have a quiet hour, because everyday matters seem to overshadow everything. The apartment, furniture, money, and other silly things steal time away from important things. . . . I thank you for your congratulatory telegram. . . . Marriage has not changed anything. I have a person to whom I mean much, perhaps everything. . . . I will try to make this person happy, because I cannot become happy myself. . . . I am not any different now than from the time you marched, angry, into the editorial offices, but I am honest in all things and for this reason have few disappointments. . . . Best regards to your husband.

Edith Doerry Roseveare, reflecting back, wrote in 1980, "In this situation, he behaved very well, and did not stop our friendship. Only a little later, in the unfortunately lost short story, 'Quasi una Fantasia' [published in *Sport im Bild* in 1925], did he vent his frustration and called me a heartless child of wonders and sports, while the elegant, luxurious woman, Ilse Jutta Zambona, showed herself to be dependable and faithful."

As an editor of the famous Scherl Verlag's weekly magazine, *Sport im Bild*, Remarque dealt mainly with sports and sports figures, although fairly quickly, along with Konrad Elert, he began to change the magazine into one with an authentic literary reputation. His world, however, was also about amusement, competition, and celebrity. One of his dashing friends was Rudolf Caracciola, a celebrated racing-car driver known throughout Europe, whom he often accompanied on motor-racing trips and who enabled Remarque to cover races with inside knowledge. For the past five years Remarque had been writing, and was continuing to write, "lots of articles about rubber tires, cars, collapsible canoes, engines, and goodness knows what, simply because I had to make a living from it." His offhand assurance of business as usual could not belie the fact that his fantasy had become a reality. Harley Taylor depicts this time in Berlin as one of great vitality, with a "wide range of intellectual, cultural, and sensual activities." Berlin at that time was an important artistic center, against which success could be fairly measured.

Remarque easily became a part of the aggressive and cliquish world of Berlin journalists. Aside from the hard work, the camaraderie was strong. Long "editorial" meetings took place in such Berlin cafés as the Café Jadicke on Kochstrasse. Remarque—wearing natty clothes and often sporting a monocle—was everywhere—at Das Romanische Café, at the Viktor Schwannecke Café on Rankestrasse, at the Film Club. In the evenings he took his wife to concerts, balls, opera, theater; if the event was gala, they were there. A few lines in an article from *Die Literatur* describes Jutta Remarque's effect: "The judges of the nightly beauty competition unanimously awarded the first prize to the charming Mrs. Remarque, who was the center of attention in a particularly striking backless dress."

Ruth Albu, a young actress who at about that time was appearing in plays along with another young actress, named Marlene Dietrich, remembers "Johannes" Remarque as being not unlike a striking sculpture. "She was a decorative object because he had a great sense for decorative objects. His absolute yearning for glamour had something to do with it. She was like a Della Robbia. A very beautiful acquisition."

Remarque was also working hard—even more so than he had done at *Echo-Continental*, because there was more pressure to dazzle in Berlin. All his articles were written longhand with a pencil, in German, a practice he would continue all his life. As a middle-aged man living in America, he reflected, "Although I have lived in this country for over twenty years, I still write in German and have someone else translate. . . . I never learned to type. . . . When I was an editor in Germany, inflation had wiped out everyone's earnings and labor was cheap. I swore I would never have a job in which I had to do my own typing."

His own fiction would take a backseat to the magazine writing until late 1927. Most of his articles had to do with cars: "The Politeness of Car Drivers: Behavior on the Road," and an odd, surreal little piece called "Melchior Sirr's Transformation," about a man who became as much of a machine as his car. The name Melchior Sirr reverberated many years later, in his marriage to Paulette Goddard. He used it as a pseudonym for a screenplay called *L'Americana* that he was supposed to have collaborated on with Paulette.

Some of the work that he was doing for *Sport im Bild* was prophetic—an experiment with material that eventually became thematic. He was already writing about Jutta and would continue to do so for years. One could argue that she was his most important female muse, starting with a character he called Lilian Dunquerke in a short story for *Sport im Bild* titled "Vandervelde's Race."

One portion of this early work, with auto racing as its subject, is as telling about Remarque's character and his humanist credo as anything he was to write later. The hero of the story is a racer named Vandervelde, who was superstitious and never raced without his beloved dog by his side, and who has been promised by the infamous Lilian Dunquerke that if he wins a big race, he can win her. Vandervelde is suddenly in the lead, having bypassed the American and the Italian:

> A thousand thunderous screams could be heard. Two hundred meters in front of the goal, a flame shot up from the car; with a burning car, Vandervelde raced on, toward the goal. Then something unexpected happened. Apparently, when the car was refilled hastily, some gasoline had been dripped onto the car, and a tongue of flame licked along the car. This was not very dangerous in itself and Vandervelde could have reached the finish line without problems; but the dog next to him was apparently touched by the flames, because he howled terribly.
>
> Vandervelde, victory almost at hand, fifty meters in front of the finish line, stopped the car to see what had happened to the dog. That same moment, the Italian approached and finished first.
>
> Vandervelde did not care. He caressed his dog and walked past the crowd, which bombarded him with questions. They shook their heads over this bizarre situation, to lose a race because of a dog.
>
> Liliane Dunquerke stood in front of Vandervelde. She was pale. They drove to the hotel without saying a word. There, Vandervelde treated his dog, who had a minor burn wound. He looked up and said: "It's nothing serious, in a few days he will be well again. I could have gone on, but I did not know how bad the injuries were and how painful."
>
> This was the minute in which Vandervelde had won Liliane Dunquerke.

This contains three of Remarque's passions: beautiful women, fast cars, and not least important, dogs. He had many throughout his life. Shortly after his marriage to Jutta, they got an Irish terrier whom they named Billy. Not unlike Nick and Nora Charles's Asta in *The Thin Man*, Billy went everywhere with the sleek, good-looking, social Remarques. Later, they owned more dogs, but Billy remained the favorite. Remarque later acquired cats— many were strays he took in—because they fascinated him in their sensuality and disloyalty. (He referred to Marlene Dietrich as "Puma" throughout their relationship.) But dogs were his mascots.

———

Being a part of the social whirl drove Remarque, in 1926, to an act as bizarre as the one when he postured in the lieutenant's uniform and military decorations back in Osnabrück. Feeling perhaps that his accomplishments were inadequate, or that his marriage fell short of a state of grace, or that in general he was still second best, he bought himself a title. For five hundred marks, he made an arrangement to be "adopted" by a Baron von Buchwaldt, an aging cavalry captain down on his luck. Until his breakthrough with the publication of *All Quiet on the Western Front*, Remarque was registered in Berlin as Erich, Freiherr (Baron) von Buchwaldt. He carried a calling card to that effect, which showed a five-pronged, pearl-tipped crown, indicative of nobility prior to 1800. On the police station register, his full title was "Ehemann [married man] Erich Freiherr von Buchwaldt gen. [named] Remark." So, even with the snobbish title, he could not shake little Erich Remark in the eyes of the officials.

This was one of Germany's great moments artistically and economically. The country was prosperous, with foreign capitalists, particularly Americans, investing in its future. Wages for workers were high, and many Germans were feeling rich. "Germans were riding the crest of an economic boom, though the 'recovery' was a false one. . . . In 1925, the musician Schoenberg left Vienna to settle in Berlin and established the city as a center of German music." (Years later he emigrated to the States and graced the home of Charlie Chaplin and Paulette Goddard.)

Rich Germans could afford to be social, but there was one Berlin woman whose invitation to her salon meant more than most. "Betty Stern was a friend of the famous or the famous-to-be. She was the wife of a buyer for a Berlin textile firm . . . they lived in an unpretentious two-room apartment in the Barbarossa Strasse. . . . She was starstruck. She loved knowing stars or stars-to-be, knowing their hopes, their fears, their loves, their secrets, and bringing them together. In her modest surroundings she created a salon, a halfway house for those climbing ladders of the theater, movies, journalism, and publishing. . . . The more established salons of Berlin were like Rudolf Nelson's elegant Sunday afternoons or evenings . . . attended by Heinrich Mann or Arnold Schoenberg or Max Reinhardt." Rudolf Nelson was an impresario who produced stylish revues and owned his own theater on the Kurfürstendamm, for which he wrote and composed his own shows. Nelson's son, Herbert, viewed Stern and his late father not so much as competitors as co-hosts: "If you had already made it, you got invited to my father's. If you didn't get invited to Betty Stern's, you weren't going to make it."

Remarque went to Betty Stern's. In fact, he was one of her favorites, but there is no evidence that he mingled with another habitué, Marlene Dietrich, though chances are they were in the same salon at the same time. Since there was a hierarchy of creativity in Berlin—as anywhere else—and Dietrich's star was more in the ascendant than Remarque's at that time, perhaps she didn't deign to notice him. And with his sometimes secure, sometimes insecure ego, perhaps he steered clear of his future "Puma," who could eclipse anybody in the room. In 1930, she wrote from Hollywood to her husband, Rudolf Sieber: "We saw *All Quiet on the Western Front*. It's a tremendous success here. Fascinating that it's the same Remarque I used to see at Mutzbauer's. Please send me the book. I want to read it in German the way he wrote it."

A death knell was sounded for the Weimar period when Adolf Hitler was released from prison after his participation in the failed putsch in Munich in 1923. A few years later Hitler came very close to Remarque's journalistic world through Remarque's "big boss," Alfred Hugenberg, owner of the Scherl Verlag, which published *Sport im Bild*. Given that Remarque seemed almost apolitical for the first few years at *Sport im Bild*, and that in less than a decade he would come to be regarded as a German enemy and outlaw, it is interesting to note that Hitler nearly did some business with his company:

> The irony of Remarque's being employed by one of Germany's most typical Weimar Capitalists should not be lost. Hugenberg's opposition to the liberal Weimar Republic existed openly in his position of leadership within the Nationalist Party. He had served as a financial director of the Krupp armament empire. Besides owning a large portion of UFA, which in the 1920s meant the German film industry, Hugenberg made the Scherl Verlag a vital part of his financial holdings. . . . He used his access to German banking houses to obtain funds for the publication of nationalist literature. This included an ill-fated attempt to join forces with a forty-year-old Adolf Hitler in a common effort to end reparations to the Allies for the defeat suffered in World War I.

Remarque's second novel, *Station am Horizont* (*Station on the Horizon*), was serialized in three issues of *Sport im Bild* in 1927 and four issues in early 1928. It is a novel set in the world of racing drivers and the beautiful people surrounding them. The hero is a driver named Clerfayt; the heroine, the second version of Liliane Dunkirk (with an improved spelling). According to the Remarque scholar A. Antkowiak, it is a fluent piece of storytelling, but houses the "creed of a snob": "The heroes move in a mundane tinsel-world, where waiters in evening dress serve select meals, and where flirtation and motor-racing are the substitute for real life. . . . Platitudes are served up as profound thoughts." Generally considered a literary feather at the time, the work was passed off by one of Remarque's friends, Christian Kruger, as an "unpretentious novel with first-class radiators and beautiful women."

Actually, the work was the basis for two novels. The first, *Three Comrades*, was close to being his most successful after *All Quiet*, and the movie, starring Margaret Sullavan and Robert Taylor, was a big hit. The other novel was *Heaven Has No Favorites*, made into the film *Bobby Deerfield*, starring Al Pacino as the racer who was originally called Clerfayt.

Remarque was completely self-deprecatory regarding *Heaven Has No Favorites*: "I had experimented . . . in order to find a style. But everything remained dull and colorless and I was never satisfied. Probably because I was on entirely the wrong track." Toward the end of 1927, he sat down to work on the most important book he would ever write. It took him six weeks to complete *All Quiet on the Western Front*. He explains how his "intentional analysis" came about:

Formerly, I had never thought of writing about the war. . . . I was busy with work of a different kind. I was employed as a "picture editor" of a periodical. The evenings I devoted to a variety of things. Thus, for instance, I made a number of attempts to write a play, but I was never successful in that I suffered from rather violent attacks of despair and my mind reverted to my experiences during the war. I was able to observe quite similar phenomena in my acquaintances and friends. We all were, and still are to the present day, the victims of restlessness. . . . The shadows of the war oppressed us, and particularly so when we did not think of it at all. On that very day on which these ideas swept over me, I began to write, without lengthy reflection. This was continued for six weeks—every evening when I returned from the office—and by that time the book had been completed. . . . I had no confidence whatsoever in my work as a literary product, because it was the first time I had written in such a style.

Remarque put the completed manuscript in his desk drawer for six months before he submitted it to his employer, Scherl Verlag, for possible publication.

Not knowing he had written a masterpiece—in fact, thinking quite the opposite—he was left with the dilemma of whether to pursue writing fiction. He continued with his daily grind at *Sport im Bild*, and at night went out drinking with friends. He often drank himself into a stupor, and more than occasionally ended up in a room of a brothel. But the next morning he would appear, perfectly dressed and clean shaven, in the office as always; after these "benders," it is difficult to imagine how he functioned at his job.

Remarque never drank anything just to get drunk. He chose his spirits as a connoisseur—only the best wines, champagnes, and brandies. In fact, recommendations for certain wines and brandies run through his novels. Mention of a fine bottle is always given in his diary. Robert Lantz, who was one of Remarque's agents during the forties, fifties, and sixties, explains, "Erich certainly only drank wine and brandy. He didn't drink six scotches and so on. None of that. It's also very un-German. Erich would not tolerate bad stuff."

Late in 1927, Remarque, in print, began the rhapsody of a lifetime addiction with his "Ode to the Cocktail," which appeared in *Sport im Bild* to popular acclaim. The sybaritic prose verges on parody; this is the last example of his opulent writing style.

Warmed apricot with ice-dust added at the last moment, then Pruenelli, ginger, pomerance, and a drop of lemon followed by whipped cream to which two drops of curaçao have been quickly added. Crystallization in the mixer starts; after about three minutes, one can see how it is streaming down from the edges. It stops slowly and a ray of trickles starts from the center. The mature crystals hang in the glass like honeycombs. Fresh pineapple juice is added and the mixture is ladled into a round crystal bottle, sealed airtight, slowly heated and stays in water for one hour and is cooled down to an icy temperature again. In seven full-moon nights, the bottle rests in the light of the moon and then is stored in a dark place. Sun may never hit it. After one year, the bottle may be opened; this mixture is the basic essence of the blue hour. . . .

One should start mixing with at least thirty different liqueurs. Training is an absolute necessity. The cocktail wants to feel the hand of the master.

At the same time that he was detailing a lively "Peppermint Absinthe Rondo" for his cocktail piece, Remarque was adding an introductory statement to *All Quiet on the Western Front* that leaves no doubt about the transmogrification of Remarque from lightweight to moral chronicler: "This book is to be neither an accusation nor a confession, and least of all an adventure, for death is not an adventure to those who stand face to face with it. It will try simply to tell of a generation of men who, even though they may have escaped its shells, were destroyed by the war."

Even though this book would change Remarque's life, he was fond of pretending he was a simple, retiring man who just wanted to stay away from the bright lights and live quietly in the country: "As for what they call fame, I don't want it. It comes between a man and reality. As soon as you become a celebrity you've lost touch with humanity, this life. That is why I live so quietly and keep out of the limelight. I must keep in touch, otherwise I cannot write simply and directly for the minds and hearts of ordinary men and women. I want to have a little place in the country and breed dogs." Is this the same man who longed for recognition, calling attention to himself throughout his childhood and young adult life? Shunning the limelight, yet appearing at all the places to be seen; wanting a simple life, yet drawn to expensive cars and complicated women; desiring to appeal to the hearts and minds of ordinary men and women, yet keeping a good distance from his unsophisticated father and sisters. He said that he suffered bouts of spiritual depression until he returned to his own truths, which freed him to write The Book.

Yet, according to certain sources, he seemed difficult and aloof, and knew exactly where he was headed at all times: "Remarque pleaded innocence. He maintained that he really did not understand how the book got written, that it seemed to have taken on a life of its own and been created all by itself. He would come back in the afternoon from his office and get to work on the book without making any corrections. In the original manuscript there were almost no deletions or changes, and those that exist were insignificant. Although he had written before, he did not consider himself literate, and so when he finished the book, he regarded it with a certain amount of mistrust."

Remarque's wife, Jutta, felt that she herself was the inspiration for his discipline and hence lightning-quick output. Every morning, before he went to work, he read her what he had written the night before, and every morning she told him that it was good, very good, but not great yet. It seemed to have goaded him into just the right kind of frenzy.

Curt Riess, a journalist and colleague of Remarque's during that time, assessed him coolly:

We were always conscious of the fact that this enormously attractive man really had very few true friends. Before he became famous in the Berlin of the late twenties, we didn't care for him. We were sports journalists—he was one of them. We considered him a pompous ass, a fellow who was always immaculately turned out, gave himself airs as though he was better than anybody, and, as the crowning insult, wore a monocle. He was marvelously good-looking, but that was really more a question for the ladies, of whom it was said he consumed many. . . . When he told me that he had offered his book to several publishers, but that it had been turned down frequently, I told him, "Who, today, ten years after the end of the war, wants to know anything about the war? I would tear up the manuscript, throw it away, and forget about it."

The film director Billy Wilder, who was then living and working in Berlin, offered another version of the same advice:

I knew Remarque quite well. He was the editor of a magazine which was sort of the equivalent of *Vogue* magazine here. He had the plushest, most esteemed job you could have gotten in German journalism. I was a reporter and writer back then. We had lunch here and there, and one day at one of those lunches, he told me that incredible idea of his. He was going to quit his job and finish his novel. And I thought he was just absolutely out of his mind. "Who wants to quit this job? I mean, you can't go any higher!" He said, "Well, my wife insisted I finish the book." I said: "What is it about?" He said: "It's about World War I." And I said: "My God, now!?! This is 1928. Who is interested in the world war?" We didn't know that it was one or two. We did not number them yet. . . . And I'm sure that other friends of his—colleagues—had tried to talk him out of taking that—what we then thought suicidal move of giving up a great career.

The even greater future career cost him. In many ways he forfeited his freedom—to grow as an artist, to live in his own country, to maintain privacy. There were several claims as to how *All Quiet* came about.

Leni Riefenstahl, later known for her closeness to Hitler and her films *Triumph of the Will* and *Olympia*, was at that time an ex-hoofer and an out-of-work actress. Remarque was a friend of hers, and a good enough friend, she maintained, that he escaped to her apartment to write a major portion of the novel.

Remarque described the writing of the book as a kind of catharsis:

The truth was, there was something on my mind—the weight of horror and suffering I had seen during the war years. It was still there, unexpressed and chaotic, robbing one of peace of mind, making it impossible to settle down to ordinary avocations of civilian life. . . . The idea for my book came as a sort of safety valve. I came home one night from my work and started to write it. For obvious reasons I adopted the fiction form, but what I put down was the truth. I was not writing for any wide audience; my object was to see clearly the experience I had been through and therefore I wrote with the utmost simplicity and integrity as though I were telling the story to my intimate friends. I avoided all panegyric and let the terrible facts speak for themselves.

After the book was finally published in 1929, it ran to forty-three separate printings, for a total of more than one million and a half books in the original German. There were book-club editions in every country in the world. There were translations ranging from Afrikaans to Zulu and at least seven separate editions in India and many in English. The book appeared in Afrikaans, Bulgarian, Catalan, Chinese, Croat, Czech, Danish, Dutch, Esperanto, Estonian, Finnish, French, Greek, Hebrew in Tel Aviv, Hebrew in Warsaw, Hungarian, Icelandic, Italian, Japanese, Korean, Latvian, Lithuanian, Macedonian, Norwegian, Polish, Portuguese, Romanian, Russian, Spanish, Swedish, Tamil, Turkish, Ukrainian, Urdu, Vietnamese, Yiddish (believed to have been translated by Isaac Bashevis Singer), and Zulu.

The enormous impact of the book is captured in a letter in January 1929, from Remarque's British editor at Putnam, Herbert Read:

Dear Herr Remarque,

I was very glad to get your letter of Jan. 12th. I enclose on a separate sheet a few queries that have arisen so far in the course of the translation. As a matter of fact, several of our difficulties have been solved by the discovery at the War Museum of a German dictionary of soldiers' slang ("Schwere Brocken"). But there are still a few passages that puzzle us.

Before receiving your letter, Mr. Wheen and I had a discussion about the English title, and we came to the conclusion that "All Quiet on the Western Front" was not so bad after all. Messrs. Putnam agree, and now I have had a letter from the Verlag Ullstein saying that they too approve of this title. So I think we may regard that as settled. I still think it is not so good as the German title, because it is not so neat and incisive. But it is a familiar phrase, and has all the ironic implication of the German title.

. . . With closer acquaintance, my admiration for your book only grows. It seems to include everything, absolutely everything, that we experienced out there, "im Westen." And it holds good and true for the English soldier just as for the German soldier.

Remarque originally submitted his manuscript to Samuel Fischer Verlag, which was part of Fischer Verlag, a leading publishing house in Germany. He sent it there because Ullstein, another publishing giant, had acquired the rights to *Station on the Horizon* and had sunk it into oblivion, just as they had done with *The Dream Room*. But Fischer Verlag turned down the manuscript with sentiments similar to Billy Wilder's: nobody wanted to read about a war ten years later. Remarque then offered it to Fritz Ross at Ullstein, who recommended it to his superior, Paul Wiegler. Wiegler decided to publish it, but to serialize it in a newspaper first. It ran from November 19 to December 9 in *Die Vossische Zeitung*, and proved to be such a big hit that the newspaper sold out each day. The book was officially published on January 31, 1929, and by the year's end had sold more than a million and a half copies. Remarque had tapped into something much bigger than anyone realized, astounding himself along with the entire publishing industry.

The Remarque archivist Dr. Thomas Schneider felt it was also a case of clever marketing:

> Remarque started to write *All Quiet on the Western Front* as a biographical report on his war experiences in winter/spring 1928. In August 1928 he finished the novel, which was at the time an explicit pacifist novel. In late August 1928 Ullstein publishers, to whom the novel was sold, presumably forced Remarque to change the pacifist passages into more moderate statements. By an advertising campaign for the novel starting in November 1928 Ullstein created a new image of the author Remarque. . . . The *Vossische Zeitung* announced the advanced serialization scheduled to start running the next day as follows: "Erich Maria Remarque, not a professional author, a young man in his early thirties, has suddenly, just a few months ago, found the need, the urge to put into words that which befell him and his school friends, an entire class of young, life-loving men of whom not a single one survived."

Schneider suggests that Remarque might have planned the book for many years prior to writing it—that he was thinking about it as early as when he was in the hospital in Duisburg and wrote to his pal "Dopp" Middendorf to fill him in on "front-line" events, saying, "much interested, am writing a novel."

Apparently, years before, Remarque had started collecting eyewitness war reports. Though there had never been any mention of a title, early on he had made an allusion to an official army bulletin following a bloody battle that said, "No news on the Western Front." Remarque had thought all along that *All Quiet* would be a prequel to *The Road Back*, which dealt with soldiers returning in defeat, and which he had begun work on as early as October 1928. Before the publication of *All Quiet*, he had sold the rights to *The Road Back* to Ullstein, who had shrewdly and quickly bought up the remainders of *The Dream Room*, as well as making *Station on the Horizon* all but obsolete. In order to enlarge his readership, Ullstein went so far as to publish a letter from the wife of a veteran: "My husband who had been in the field and twice wounded had never told me of any of his front-line experiences. Now he always pushes this book in my hands, saying, 'Here, you can read a truthful description of life at war.'"

According to Schneider, the Ullstein contract, dated August 6, 1928, stated that Remarque would receive two thirds of all revenues derived from the publisher's rights. Ullstein would have rights of first refusal to a planned but not yet named sequel and all other Remarque works created prior to the end of 1930.

Angelika Howind, a former leading archivist in the Remarque archive in Osnabrück, has written that Ullstein ran a very tough, contrived, and shrewd campaign to market *All Quiet*:

> In 1929 alone there were over two hundred German essays and articles reflecting the angry debates *All Quiet* set in motion. After the purchase of the manuscript by Ullstein . . . they used all their tricks of advance marketing to overcome the strong German militaristic tendencies. They created an artificial EMR—intending to separate his book from other war novels. By falsifying data, they created the illusion that *All Quiet* was an autobiographical document written by an inexperienced, untutored representative of all front-line soldiers. They wrote that his diary had been a catharsis. That it reposed in his desk and it would have remained there had not his friends increasingly urged him to have it published. This is at odds with the real EMR, who took an active part in the book's promotion. . . . He dreamed of an author's life and, in poems and short fiction, he spoke of far countries, beautiful women, upright men. . . . It becomes clear that the book's gestation came from the renewal of the German myths about the heroes, the emerging discussions of the causes for the loss of the war, and his reviewing a

number of postwar novels. His book was constructed, laid out, written and rewritten in different shapes until the final manuscript was considered worthy of publication. The book was intended to turn into a trilogy—The Front, Return Home, Reintegration; two and three are compressed into his fourth novel, *The Road Back*. He needed and used the war as a backdrop; little was really autobiographical since his own front-line experience was limited to one and a half months. . . . In hindsight, it is clear that Ullstein was not at all convinced it had a winner and some of the clauses in the contract were to be for the publisher's protection.

But there had to be a pro-Remarque lobby at Ullstein because only two and a half months after signing came the prepublication serialization in their money-losing, liberal newspaper, which announced the book using the Unknown Soldier hype and even carried the non-pro writer bit far enough to make EMR older in order to maintain the autobiographical comparison to Paul Bäumer, the *All Quiet* hero.

The first printing of 30,000 was spoken for by pub date, and a second run of 20,000 was ordered immediately. The drums were being beaten; bookstores received complete window decoration layouts. The 5/21/29 issue of a publication called *Börseblatt für den Deutschen Buchhandel* [equivalent to the American *Publishers Weekly*] carried a twenty-page promotional segment showing worldwide pro and con reactions and listing open and closed translation rights. Pröpylaean put out a special pamphlet—*Der Kampf um Remarque* [*The Battle Around Remarque*], again giving the heated pros and cons gathering steam and, in the process, let it be known that the book had passed the 650,000 mark in sales. In six months, more than a half million sold—a success never before achieved by a German novel. . . . There is little doubt that Ullstein contributed immeasurably to the success of *All Quiet*, and also that Remarque contributed the right book at the right time. Ullstein took the privilege of contouring the text in different editions for different audiences, in an attempt to avoid an excess of controversy.

In 1929, Remarque was to undergo the first great watershed of his adult life. His marriage to Jutta was over. He was still fond of her, always addressing her with the hoydenish nickname of Peter, but their marriage had unraveled, exhausted by endless infidelities on both sides. He had resumed or continued his affair with Brigitte Neuner, as well as trying to keep in touch with Edith Doerry Roseveare, to whom he wrote on December 22, 1928: "It is strange, Edith, that people who love each other can create such

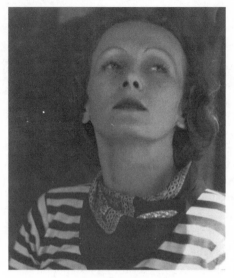

Remarque's first wife, Jutta Ilsa Ingeborg Ellen Zambona, 1923.

RIGHT: *Remarque and Jutta in Berlin, 1927 or 1928.*

Remarque and Jutta enjoying the German nightlife, ca. 1929.

misunderstanding. You are one of the few people to whom I am as close as I know, and if we would not hear from each other for years, we would only have to be together for one hour to restore the old relationship again."

Jutta, who considered herself an artist but never showed or sold any of her art, was painting wild and sad women and, in between tubercular bouts and visits to the sanatorium, was in love with a man named Franz Schulz. Before Schulz, there had been many others. It's thought that she was unfaithful first and that he, wounded by his wandering, beautiful wife, fell back into his old and familiar ways. In a sense they were perfectly matched, never became enemies, and after being married and divorced twice, still felt a certain love and respect for each other. They mourned their failed relationship all their lives.

Axel Eggebrecht, a journalist friend of Remarque's, felt that they had drifted early on in their five-year first marriage:

> I used to hang about at the Toppkeller on the Schweriner Strasse, a sort of low-class bar where everybody from the West Side of Berlin would congregate. . . . The chief attraction and challenge was a beam into which anyone was invited to drive a nail with a single blow. If you could do it, you got a free glass of brandy. . . . I tried it once just to show off before a sexy young girl. Afterwards I sat down with her and her husband, who introduced himself as an editor on the staff of Hugenberg's magazine, *Sport im Bild*. . . . He liked being a snob, left the bar with a cane and greatcoat, and had a Fiat. I was invited to come home with both of them. We had drinks and looked at his aquarium. . . . He wasn't at all disturbed that I was actually making a pass at his wife. . . . Thus I began a month's liaison with Jeanne, the wife of Erich Maria Remarque. . . . I soon found out he himself was having an affair with another woman. . . . I took trips with Jeanne into the Lusatian Alps. . . . He saw us off on the train. . . . She was sharp, but very indolent. . . . She told me that she had fallen in love with a friend of mine, Franz Schulz. . . . In the meanwhile, *All Quiet on the Western Front* had appeared in the *Vossische Zeitung*, then in book form. . . . Remarque became well off. . . . He was now driving an expensive sports car and I bought his little car.

The Remarques had taken an apartment in a house at 5 Wittelsbacherstrasse in a fashionable section of Berlin. It was on the third floor (there was a lift) and was not large but decorated in the latest style. Her colors of beiges, whites, and soft grays predominated. There was a large aquarium with atypical tropical fish, a fancy, lacquered Victrola, and several small African sculptures. Soon, Remarque would begin to collect seriously: paintings (mainly Impressionist), fifteenth- and sixteenth-century Persian and Spanish carpets, Chinese bronzes, Etruscan sculpture—but in 1928–1930 Jutta Remarque's elegant, cool, anemic taste prevailed. In contrast, her hot-toned "wild women paintings," as Victoria Wolff called them, decorated her bedroom. They had separate bedrooms—as Remarque did later with Paulette. He liked to maintain a certain mystery and distance.

In the first flush of success, Remarque fought against but capitulated a good deal of the time to being Ullstein's best promotional tool. He traveled, appearing at various book functions, and gave interviews. He also made sure he had the right wardrobe. He cared very much about the way he looked and was finally able to buy the best—cashmere sweaters and jackets, silk shirts, camel's-hair coats. He dressed casually but impeccably, although his one flaw was that, at five feet ten inches, he fell short of physical perfection.

During this period Jutta, who was still pursuing her liaison with Franz Schulz, "felt poorly" most of the time. In later years Remarque said that her various afflictions were probably exaggerated if not fictitious. Her maladies included painful menstruation and chronic fatigue, tendon inflammation, chronic biting of her inner cheek (causing swelling and discoloration), and migraines.

In early spring of 1929, Remarque took a leave from celebrity, setting off on a driving trip through France, and stopping at luxurious inns in Normandy, Brittany, Limoges, and the Pyrenees. He had planned for Jutta to rendezvous with him in Limoges and accompany him the rest of the way. "Dear Daddy [she wrote from Berlin], I hope it's okay with you that I leave here on Thursday afternoon, before it will be too difficult because I have my period very heavily and should stay for two or three days in bed. I have difficulties being up, I get dizzy easily and don't have much strength. I think it is wiser to wait another day, than to fear being bothered by this nonsense for another two weeks—as happened the last time. Don't be angry or impatient. I certainly would come earlier if it were possible."

Axel Eggebrecht saw a change in both of them later that spring. *All Quiet* had created a furor in the Weimar Republic. Up to that time nothing had been as popular yet controversial. Because it was embraced by a vast reading public, it was regarded by ultra-nationalists as subversive. Its antiwar and antimilitaristic themes inflamed the National Socialist party.

Axel Eggebrecht has written, "He [Remarque] was terribly pessimistic. . . . But eventually, whether he liked it or not, Remarque became a promoter of democratic and humanistic ideas. . . . I suppose I should never have given him another thought if it had not been for one memory of him that colored my feelings toward him. . . . After Remarque made a fortune, he became terribly conventional. He demanded faithfulness and obedience from Jutta. He had her shadowed during her liaison with Franz Schulz. After that, she submitted to this tyranny."

Victoria Wolff has spoken with candor about the two of them:

> Jutta was extremely beautiful. Much more beautiful than Paulette. She was very simply but very magnificently dressed. White pants or gray pants and a sweater. Nothing else. Not like Paulette. I don't think she was tubercular. She was very healthy. She acted. She acted sick. Wife who needs support. Remarque always said to me, "She only comes to me when she wants something from me." They finally got a divorce, but she wanted to remarry him to get a passport. He was good to her. He stopped loving her. He hated her, but he was good to her. Much, much earlier, he loved her and got violently jealous—this pacifist. One day, in Berlin, she had an affair with an ugly, ugly film producer—and Remarque knew about it. We all met in a café and Remarque boxed him down without any warning. Just threw him on the floor and left. Later, he said, "If she would have cheated on me with someone I respected, I wouldn't say a thing. But with such dreck—with such a dirty, dirty guy!"

It gives another face to their story to think that Jutta, who, after all, had been an actress, was acting out imaginary illnesses. But she seems to have caused him quite a time emotionally and financially. She must have felt well enough when she took up with a couple of indolent spendthrifts from good families. The golden Weimar era spawned a particular breed of spoiled young men who never worked and who sponged on their parents' wealth. They were perfect candidates for the encroaching Gestapo—the first real cause to come along in their lives.

Victoria Wolff remembers the two that Jutta fancied: "No decent woman would want to be around them. They were very loud, running around on motorcycles and in fast cars, having a no-good reputation and nothing to say. But Jutta, in order to hurt Boni, made a play out of it. And wherever she went, she took the two along, which did hurt him."

Jutta would die in 1975, five years after Remarque, but he lovingly killed her off in his fifth novel, *Three Comrades*, which he began in 1932 but did not complete to his satisfaction until 1937. There was nothing subtle about his feelings for Pat Hollman, nor her feelings for his stand-in, Robby Lohkamp:

> She rested her head on my shoulder. "If you want to live still, then there must be something you love. It's harder, but it's easier, too. You see, I had to die; and now I'm just thankful I have had you. I might easily have been alone and unhappy. Then I would have been glad to die."
> Then suddenly everything went very swiftly. The flesh of the dear face melted. The cheekbones protruded and at the temple, the bone showed through. Her arms were thin as a child's arms, the ribs stretched taut under the skin and the fever raged in ever fresh bouts through the frail body.

Remarque remarried Jutta in 1938, a year after the novel was published. As they took their vows for the second time, Margaret Sullavan was dying exquisitely in the screen version of *Three Comrades*.

Although Remarque had craved recognition, he was not prepared for the kind of fame that confronted him. It was one thing—and rare at that—for a German writer to be celebrated by his country, but Remarque achieved worldwide acclaim with just one book. He was paradoxically also vilified for it. The suffering and deaths of a group of young soldiers were seen as a demand for pacifism and antimilitarism. With Hitler's Nazi party on the ascent, these concerns were not politically popular. Though Remarque was loved by the public, he was seen as an enemy by the government. An example of one of the Nazi propaganda smears against him claimed that he was born a French Jew with the surname Kramer; he had simply reversed this name, replacing the *k* with *que*:

> Little Kramer, the child of modest parents . . . was quick to deny his past as a soldier after he returned from the first world war. He liked himself in the role of the pacifist in the decadent company of war-winners and Jewish intellectuals. Not a worker but a dilettante, he tried to be a village school-teacher, theater critic, advertising consultant . . . amateur race-car driver, editor at a Berlin sports paper. *Im Westen Nichts Neues* was the result of a dirty fantasy that no one wanted to publish, until the Jew Ullstein, certain of the destructive effect on honor and respect, used Remarque to set him off against the national conscience. During the subsequent war, he survived safely in California where he, an immigrant, wrote about concentration camp cruelties and winter in Russia, none of which he experienced himself.

Remarque's version of the way the rumor got dispelled was through a lucky fluke. A Nazi agent who was tracking him called up asking to speak with Mr. Kramer. The gardener got on the phone: "Yes, this is Kramer, the gardener of Mr. Remarque here." Rosa and Karl, the couple that Remarque was to employ to care for his Swiss villa a couple of years hence, served their master well by having the last name of Kramer. The rumor, however, did linger until even after his death—with mention of it in several of his obituaries.

As a reward for the strong book sales, his publisher, Ullstein, gave Remarque a Lancia, the car of his dreams. It was an undeniable status symbol, representing to him something sleek yet temperamental. He called the pearl-gray car his Puma. The Lancia became Puma I, and when he became involved with Marlene Dietrich, she was his golden Puma.

The car came just in time to transport Remarque out of Berlin and away from what he came to regard as his tormentors. Asked once why he never spoke up during the intense debates surrounding The Book, he replied, "Because I didn't and don't consider it necessary. . . . Once a work is finished, the author has nothing further to say about it, even if there is a risk of being misunderstood. If this is the case, then his work has not succeeded, and talking about it serves no purpose. But I am of the opinion that I was only misunderstood where people went out of their way to misunderstand me.

By the spring of 1929, Remarque had resumed his relationship with Brigitte Neuner. She was leggy, pert, very sexy, and also married. Their affair was hardly clandestine, as they arranged to meet at various alpine resorts and spas, even Baden-Baden, and their correspondence—certainly on Remarque's part—was substantial and openly flirtatious. Her dog, Mac, and Remarque's Billy would travel with them when they met.

During the early thirties, their relationship took on a certain robust domesticity. While he traveled extensively, savoring his newfound wealth, she acted as a quasi-business adviser–assistant–secretary, seeing to such financial transactions as liquidating 1,000 marks or dunning Ullstein for a royalty payment. She also forwarded his mail and probably chortled at his demanding, often facetious instructions: "You should write more often, best would be a daily report. . . . Be good, Heinrich; during this time of separation darn all stockings, check all dresses, check to see whether every piece of laundry has tags, knit, do embroidery, be virtuous—spring stands outside the door, be a smart virgin!"

She brought out a buoyant, chatty, playful quality in him that would forever disappear after they stopped seeing each other. He would sign his letters

"Your faithful father," "Christian," "Kuno," "Your Julius," "Ferdinand," "Edward," and "Boni." These aliases became a protective trend. They coincided with his sister Erna's making a large profit for herself on the sale of his war diaries and letters—waiting, of course, until the success of The Book. Betrayed by his own sister, from then on he saw to it that no one would take advantage of private letters that carried his signature.

There were many aftershocks from The Book that bewildered him. He was on the defensive a lot, and for good reason. *Der Kampf um Remarque* (*The Battle Around Remarque*) was a pamphlet that Ullstein issued, explaining—from the right and left—the upheaval that the book was causing. In it was a letter from a soldier blinded in the Great War who hailed the book as the sole true account of what had really happened to the German soldiers. Remarque singled this man out and commended him, for, irreversibly scarred by the war, he was the very kind of hero the book extolled. But for every bit of honor or praise experienced by Remarque, there was also an attack or even a charge of plagiarism.

In one of many defending arguments and explanations that Remarque wrote during this embattled time, he said, "That opposition to my works does not always come from neutral places is demonstrated by an amusing incident that took place in connection to my book. The leading national-socialistic paper published an article written by a soldier who fought for four years in the trenches. . . . The article, which was five pages long and which was copied word for word from my book, was cited as being an authentic report, not a 'Remarque invention.'"

Remarque's portrait of the German soldier as being heroic just because he fought, even though he died and even though the war was lost, was pointed to by conservative publications as dangerous to German youths. This feeling was echoed in articles written by such esteemed figures as Thomas Mann, Stefan Zweig, and Fritz von Unruh. The Austrian dramatist Carl Zuckmayer, who was later a friend of Remarque's, wrote a positive review, and gave credence to a sentiment that came out of the progressive factions of the Weimar Republic: Remarque had written the war novel that could bring the entity of war to a halt. How then, after such a major antiwar document, could war be defended? Ironically, Zuckmayer, an admirer, had served to fan the flames of the right even higher.

Thomas Mann would not be seen on the same street as Remarque for fear that his popularity would suffer. In 1933, when Remarque was already in exile from Nazi Germany and had moved to Ascona, Switzerland—which was to be regarded as a haven for artistic émigrés—he was dogged by their mutual antipathy, and spoke bitterly about it. "In 1933 he didn't want to be seen on the street with me in Ascona because he would have to lose his public in Germany. Mann also was never banned. It only became too much for him when he, the non-Gymnasium graduate, had his honorary doctorate from Bonn revoked."

Their feud carried over to Hollywood in the late thirties and early forties, where many exiles, fleeing from Hitler, were able to form a community and make a living. Some, like Billy Wilder, Fritz Lang, Marlene Dietrich, Elizabeth Bergner, Lilli Palmer, Otto Preminger, Erich von Stroheim, Oscar Homolka, Alexander Korda, and Luise Rainer, managed to rise to the top, despite having been uprooted emotionally, intellectually, and culturally. Thomas Mann, who, according to Remarque, was the self-appointed leader of Hollywood's exiled intelligentsia, continued to shun his best-selling colleague. According to Mann, Remarque was a lightweight who had written a book that showed him to be a one-trick pony, while he, Mann, every day before breakfast wrote a thousand words—no more, no less—for his entire life. Mann and his coterie, which included such writers as his brother Heinrich, Franz Werfel, Stefan Zweig, Bertolt Brecht, and Anna Seghers, had no use for what they considered was Remarque's famous popularity, lack of literary follow-up, and absence of political activity. Brecht and Seghers were particularly vociferous in protesting against the Nazis, as well as advocating Communism. Brecht must have caught Mann's attitude toward the soigné Remarque, for he commented, "There is something missing in his face, probably a monocle." And in continuing their bullying of Remarque, they termed his work a "success factory" and found it "trivial." They turned up their noses when he established a friendship with the fellow émigré and writer Lion Feuchtwanger, dismissing them both as mining similar literary veins.

And as for Stefan Zweig, to whom Remarque had written imploringly for appraisal and guidance of his writing ten years prior to *All Quiet*, Remarque wrote to him again in late 1929: "You probably don't even remember me. But I continued my life, and it was difficult because I could not deal with it so well, but finally, I wrote a book anyway. Only now, do I have the courage to send it to you, because I always doubted that it was good enough." He sent Zweig a signed copy of the book. "I would be really happy if you would consider this book as a beginning." Despite the charming presentation, Zweig denounced the book.

Another German writer called Zweig, Arnold Zweig, who had written *Der Streit um den Sergeanten Grischa* in 1927, and who was a leading figure among the literati, took real umbrage at Remarque's success, calling the book "slapdash" and saying, "Remarque is a good amateur and he could even have turned his book into a great novel. His amateurism lies precisely in having failed to see the angle from which he should have tackled his subject. He lit on it, but passed it blindly by. There, where he describes the farmer's lad who can't stand the war anymore when he sees the trees in blossom and thereupon runs away. That is where I would have started the story and centered everything else on this boy. Then it would have become a great book."

No matter how great a hue and cry the book caused among Fascist and rightist factions, the first hardcover edition of the German version was never altered. To Germany's credit, "no attempt was ever made to ostracize it, rewrite it, or integrate it with the Nazi political view." That changed with the 1929 British edition published by Putnam and translated by A. W. Wheen—the first of many English editions. According to one writer, Claude Owen, this edition, which was expurgated, was the only one available in English. It had sold 300,000 copies by the end of 1929, more than twenty times the number of its closest rival wartime novel, *Her Privates We*, by Peter Davies.

With translations, the author may never know how he is being misrepresented. For many years, Remarque spoke no English, and even when he did, he was not really fluent. He could think only in German, so he was very dependent on his translators. In the case of *All Quiet*, experts find some of the editions printed from the original English translation misleading and woebegone. Owen has detailed some of what Little, Brown and Company did when it published what became known as the "U.S. Kindergarten edition" in 1929: "Little, Brown had acquired the rights to and published the Wheen translation, following the British Putnam edition, deleting the following major sections." He goes on to illustrate a passage where Remarque writes about soldiers overcoming any bashfulness about bodily functions that says, "To the soldier, his stomach and his digestion are more thoroughly known topics than to other people. Three-quarters of his vocabulary is derived from them." "The publishers—not the censors—," says Owen, "considered [this] 'too robust' for their readers."

In honor of the blue laws of Boston, there was another omission in Little, Brown's edition. Owen writes, "The most significant suppression is the hospital scene in which the injured and crippled Lewandowski finally has his wife visit him while the rest of his comrades leave the room in order to give the two a chance to turn the hospital room into a nuptial chamber. Here we have a severely wounded soldier whose physical injuries are further aggravated by his doubts of ever living a normal life again—including that of a father and a husband. Nothing could be more natural, more normal, and the only perversion rests with those who saw fit to erase this portion from the text."

Despite the book's financial success, there has been only one English-language translation of *All Quiet on the Western Front* in over sixty years. The initial response to the work in German was on a level that the English-speaking world will perhaps never understand. There are multiple dissertations on the phenomenon of *All Quiet*, on the components that added up to the perfect and seemingly indestructible work, but Curt Riess, a journalist and colleague of Remarque's during that halcyon time, puts it simply and powerfully: "What created the great success of the book? Certainly it was about the war, although one had already read enough about it. But now, for the first time, people learned what it was really like, that there was nothing heroic about being there, that it was dirty and hateful. Remarque pictured this without any romanticizing. . . ."

It seems that Remarque went out of his way to graphically depict the violence of war:

A naked soldier is squatting in the fork of a tree, he still has his helmet on, otherwise he is entirely unclad. There is only half of him sitting up there, the top half, the legs are missing.

"What can that mean?" I ask.

"He's been blown out of his clothes," mutters Tjaden.

"It's funny," says Kat, "we've seen that several times now. If a mortar gets you it blows you clean out of your clothes. It's the concussion that does it."

I search around. And so it is. Here hang bits of uniform, and somewhere else is plastered a bloody mess that was once a human limb. Over there lies a body with nothing but a piece of the underpants on one leg and the collar of the tunic around its neck. Otherwise it is naked and the clothes are hanging up in the tree. Both arms are missing as though they had been pulled out. I discover one of them twenty yards off in a shrub.

Remarque would never be able to repeat the success of *All Quiet*. But he tried, and late in 1929 he returned to working on *The Road Back*, which he had begun and then dropped in 1928 prior to his cathartic experience with *All Quiet*. *The Road Back* was meant as a sequel, was difficult when he started it, and continued to be so. The divine sensation of "automatic writing granted through inspiration" would happen to him only once in his lifetime.

was always difficult for Remarque, and the great success at age
did not make it easier. All through his diaries of the thirties, for-
ñfties, he makes comments such as "Must stop this and get back to
' "Work eludes me," "Sharpened pencils, what should I write—a
novel or a play?" "Working badly, but pleasant, calm mood all day—as
always after an evening's drinking."

Remarque began to suffer a good many minor ailments, just like the wife
he was about to divorce. Before the ailments became larger and truly
obstructive, he used them to help fend off working: "A writer's backside
must be in good condition," he writes in a diary entry in June 1936.
"Lumbago isn't a very good stimulus. In most cases fame is achieved by the
seat of your pants. For the others it's either good luck or a swindle—with a
couple of exceptions. Oh, Muse!"

His relationship with Jutta was so rocky at the end of 1929 that he felt he
couldn't work at home, so he placed an ad in the Osnabrück daily paper for
some quiet rooms. He believed he could go home again and reclaim his peace
of mind. The ad was anonymous, for he was beginning to be disturbed by his
fame. What finally moved him to get away was not the catty articles, reports,
and even a book debunking his fame, but a blockage by the German Officers'
League of a chance for him to be awarded the Nobel Prize in Literature. A
letter was written to the Nobel Prize committee protesting any forward
motion toward rewarding him.

A Frau Maria Hoberg answered the ad and welcomed him to the upstairs
of her house on Johannisstrasse, which was opposite his old friend and
former employer, Karl Vogt and the Vogt Brothers Masonry. He worked
poorly there for a month. Concerned about his dying marriage and about
Jutta's increased spending, tormented that his "second" book was not getting
written, and upset about his chaotic reputation as celebrity/charlatan/
traitor/playboy, he was about to have—in fact, almost longed for—a nervous
breakdown. He grappled with the chaos in a letter in 1930 to Putnam, his
London publisher, who had sent him a pile of clippings, reviews, and interviews with assorted misinformation:

When I see what the rainbow presses and the ones who are eternally caught
up in yesterday make of me, I sometimes feel like a monster. My age varies
between 22 and 55 years and I cannot keep ahead of the various different
names I supposedly have, or how many different regiments, brigades, and
divisions I had belonged to, or did not belong to. Then, in the same breath
they assert that I stole my manuscript from a dead comrade, or copied it

from other war books and wrote it at the request of *Entente*. The newest information about me changes from day to day. All that I can say to this is that I wish that these people would be right in at least one item: that I was never a soldier. Then I could really believe that I am a good writer, of which I still have to convince myself. Besides, I believe that an author should have said his last word regarding his book with the last word he wrote. If it is good, then it can withstand tough critics, otherwise any justification would be superfluous.

Wounded vanity would be the main reason for replying to such personal attacks. Self-love is only permissible after one has reached the 70th year and has completed one's life-work. But I am still young and I only just started. I would find it ridiculous to consider myself a good writer, after having written only one book. I have to evaluate my abilities first; and I am working toward this goal. Working—not speaking and fighting. I am less inclined to speak, because all that nonsense and gossip is stupid and dumb and above all so mean-spirited and crazy that they are shaking their heads in Germany!

It is interesting that Remarque portrays Germany as sympathetic toward him when in fact Germany had turned against him and would eventually disown him. Also interesting is how vociferous he was while claiming peace and silence. And all the while unable to do the one thing that would save him: work well. However, he kept at it, every day trying to force something. If he didn't write, he thought about it, talked about it, dreamt about it.

Curt Riess, who was with him as a young journalist in Berlin, knew his habits: "He worked slowly . . . he often worked until late at night, but then, he had days when he did nothing. He wrote with a pencil, and an eraser was always near at hand, so that one always had the feeling that what he had just written might not necessarily be permanent and might have to be erased. What distinguished him from other authors that I was familiar with was that he really didn't like to work and was happy to be interrupted. When one called him on the telephone and asked whether it was inconvenient, he always said: 'No! On the contrary.' He was glad to talk. . . . Letters were always answered immediately. Any excuse would do which took him away from actual work."

All during 1930, his relationship with Brigitte Neuner seemed to sustain him. It was the year of his divorce, for the first time, from Jutta, and because he was traveling a lot—often accompanied by his newly divorced wife—he relied on Brigitte's common sense and earthy sexuality. In most of his letters to her he calls her "Brave Heinrich," and mentions money: "If you want, go ahead and pay the rent"; business and money: "Putnam is pushing Ullstein because of the corrections. Send them everything . . . every day they print earlier means more money"; asking for advice: "Here, the mark fell from 123 to 122, one should be careful, what do you think, Heinrich?"; giving advice: "My delightful one, I wish with all my heart that your apartment will be finished soon, that you spend money and that you are feeling well. . . . Keep your ears up in this turbulent life, Heinrich, stretch your fingers out and hold tight!"

They slipped away to the Dutch resort of Nordwijk aan Zee; they ordered the Lancia together and made plans for road trips, which would include some racing driving. Remarque hooked up with his racing friend Rudolf Caracciola, with whom he entered some semipro contests. When he writes to Brigitte about the Lancia, one sees his passion for cars: "In the back, it should not go too low, otherwise it will look as if the cooling line rises. . . . Do you really want lights next to the windshield? What color? Bright red? Or a radiant blue? Or almost white?"

As long as there were obstacles, they ached to be together. Remarque was spending time at the Davos sanatorium with his supposedly ailing wife, whom he was about to divorce, while Brigitte was attending to his business matters, driving his new Lancia, and planning their future. Both, although unhappily married and on the verge of divorce, were not yet free. But it was as though Brigitte was already in training to be Jutta's successor: "Oh, Heinrich, as soon as we have finished our dirty business, then? You see, we will both be ready at the same time—the worst will be over by the end of next month." And he was already talking to her in an intimate, mock-sexist manner: "Thus, Heinrich, don't only drive around in the car, but remember that you have duties!"

In between divorce proceedings, involvement with Brigitte, constantly defending his right to be a writer, the encroaching deadline for the ever-elusive second novel that could cement his reputation, he was dealing with his first taste of Hollywood. The president of Universal Pictures, Carl Laemmle, had flown over to Berlin to woo Remarque and purchase the film rights to *All Quiet*. Ullstein sold him the rights, but Remarque turned down Laemmle's offer to play Paul Bäumer in the movie, though he tried to write his own screenplay—grumbling about it to Brigitte: "I am sitting here and trying to write poetry for the American Laemmle. It's difficult if one knows the man personally." Then later, from Paris, where he went to escape Jutta

Remarque with his art dealer, Walter Feilchenfeldt, who helped him form his celebrated collections.

Remarque discussing the film version of All Quiet *with producer Carl Laemmle, Mrs. Laemmle, and Carl Laemmle, Jr., 1930.*

and the pressures by mainly drinking: "Unfortunately, I still have to come up with a new title for my book and a film manuscript for Laemmle. There are a few dark clouds, but only small ones."

The plan was to meet Brigitte in Paris immediately following her divorce, and though it is not certain this meeting took place, one cannot help but feel that they deserved to savor their freedom together. They had been through a lot together, not the least of which was the bizarre instance of Jutta's running up a debt and receiving a court summons for it, which Brigitte took care of paying. They deserved a fuller relationship than either of them had been having. And they certainly seemed to have shared a lively, if not Teutonic, physical life. Remarque's jocular verbal threats imply a certain heat: "I miss your letters, write, otherwise I will hit you!" . . . "Allow me to quickly pinch your bottom." . . . "Just to caution you, I have enclosed clippings from the *Hamburger Freudenblatt*! [paper devoted to sexual activities]. As soon as I return, I will use a BB gun to shoot holes into your behind so that it will look like a sieve." . . . "You will get many slaps, because you did not do things the way they should have been done." For all the talk that would come later about Remarque's impotence, his feelings for and activities with Brigitte Neuner seemed to belie that state.

Their relationship ended in late 1930, when the newly divorced Remarque met someone else, more complicated and less attainable. Her name was Ruth Albu; she was an actress and would feature brightly in his increasingly turbulent life.

A writer of Remarque's sudden stature had to have an agent. He had met the right one through Betty Stern, but at the time only thought he had found a flattering friend in Otto Klement, an elegant character with several flourishing careers. Klement functioned as a publisher, theater producer, play broker, and literary agent. When he approached his friend Remarque in a business capacity, Remarque felt he had fallen into the best of both worlds—here was someone capable whom he could trust for business matters, and who would also drink with him and get him home if necessary. As Remarque's fame increased, so did his benders. It was not uncommon for him to be surprised to find himself safe in his own bed in the morning, having to piece together the puzzle of what had happened and who had rescued him. When he went out with Klement, he could really relax. The German-born Klement spoke fluent English and was especially useful to Remarque during the early Hollywood negotiations when Remarque's English amounted to "How do you do?; I love you; Forgive me; Forget me; Ham and eggs, please."

It was Klement who advised him not to write the screenplay for *All Quiet* but instead to concentrate on finishing *The Road Back* so that they could cash in on it with a movie sale. Dutifully, Remarque returned to the Hoberg house in Osnabrück for eight weeks of work in order to finish the novel. He had had quite a year. Although he had been divorced, he was still living and traveling with Jutta; he had been in a car accident in his new Bugatti en route to a race track in Berlin and had broken his beautiful matinee-idol nose. He bemoaned this, but with a touch of humor, in a letter to Brigitte in 1930: "My nose is really broken. I visited Prof. Joseph, who set my nose straight again. Now, my nose must heal, but most important, it must be straight again. I was told that Prof. Joseph is actually more suited to treat inflammations and tumors."

In early 1930, the new minister of education, a Dr. Frick, who belonged to the Nazi party, chillingly presaged things to come when he announced that *All Quiet* had been banned as "pacifist, Marxist propaganda" in all the schools in Thuringia, a large region in central Germany. At this time, the royalties on the American sales of the book amounted to $90,000, and in addition there was money from the film sale, plus Remarque's advance for *The Road Back*. Little did he know when he took sanctuary in Osnabrück that summer of 1930 that it would be the last time he would see the hometown of his childhood intact; and that he would not finish a book for more than seven years.

"In my next book," he announced to reporters before heading to his Osnabrück retreat, "which I am now writing, I describe the way back to life, how a young man like myself—and Paul Bäumer—experienced war as a youth, who still carries its scars, and who was then grabbed up by the chaos of the postwar period. He finally found his way back into life's harmonies."

The team that Carl Laemmle assembled to make the movie of *All Quiet* was a winning one; it launched some careers and enhanced others. His son, Carl Laemmle, Jr., was to serve as producer; Lewis Milestone was to direct; Maxwell Anderson—best known as a playwright (*High Tor*, *Winterset*)— would do the screen adaptation; and George Abbott (the venerable director) would write the screen story. Both Anderson and Abbott worked on the dialogue. When the final credits rolled, Anderson's name for the adaptation was joined with that of Del Andrews, a friend of the director's. Milestone had acted quickly in strengthening Anderson's adaptation, which Milestone, upon being handed the first half of the script, couldn't believe was "so horrible, so pedestrian and sentimental, so far removed from the spirit of the novel."

Everyone agreed that the film's trump lay in the casting of Paul Bäumer. "The role of a lifetime," says Lew Ayres, who won the role at the age of twenty when he was unknown by the kind of quirky default that provides the cutthroat business with its sentimentality. Ayres, in his eighties, still tells the story as if he savors every moment:

> I had tried before to get a test for the picture. All the young chaps I ran into were trying. Well, due to [Paul] Bern's influence, I was tested. But Milestone didn't want me. He wanted Douglas Fairbanks, Jr., and was waiting for permission from Fairbanks's studio to make an exchange. While waiting, they had run six months of back-up tests for this particular role. Well, the day after I had made the test, Milestone found out that it was impossible to get Fairbanks, so instead of going through six months of back tests, he requested to view the ones starting with the day before. And there I was. It was a godsend.

The filming of *All Quiet* lasted for five months. It was shot on a thousand-acre ranch in southern California, upon which a facsimile of a military camp was constructed: "Twenty acres were dynamited to make an authentic-looking no-man's-land and a network of trenches was constructed under the direction of military veterans. In fact, there were two thousand film soldiers, largely ex-service men of several countries, who lived under military regulations during the filming."

Harley Taylor, Jr., continues the report of this rigorous filming:

> Battleground realism was achieved by the use of more than twenty thousand pounds of black powder and tons of dynamite. Six thousand land mines were planted and detonated. Twelve flamethrowers were used, as well as twenty German howitzers that had been captured by the American Army.... A French village which covered ten acres was built in order to be destroyed in one of the movie's bombardment scenes.... The battle scenes ... involved two thousand men and extended over a mile.... Six assistant directors rehearsed the big scenes with the aid of telephones, sirens, pistol shots, and whistles. Former army sergeants were put in charge of individual groups and rehearsed many of the scenes a dozen times before the shooting ... a 280-ton crane, which carried cameras and sound equipment, was used to achieve maximum realism by getting as close as possible to the action.

Upon meeting Remarque in New York several years later, Lillian Gish, who had been through the lavish and perilous production of D. W. Griffith's *Birth of a Nation*, recalled her sense of déjà vu when viewing *All Quiet*.

"Believe me, I had déjà vu, too," Remarque replied with a twinkle. "First in the writing, then on the screen. It was enough."

Lew Ayres recalled the whole experience like a first love—overwhelming, clumsy, unforgettable: "We started in November of '29 and finished up in the spring of '30. They took a couple of weeks to work with the young folk. We all learned to be German military men. We had to be drilled; we even had a German director especially brought in to bark at us. We learned how to wear the uniforms, to polish the boots—all very Prussian."

Universal, which had planned on a blockbuster, got one. The reviews were raves; the careers of Lew Ayres and Lewis Milestone were launched, with Milestone winning an Oscar as best director. America wanted to see this film; the response was an inspired one, as toward a film of the highest merit.

The film of *All Quiet* was an international success—except in Germany. On December 4, 1930, it was to be presented (dubbed in German) at the posh Mozarthalle in Berlin. There were rumblings that many Germans were not pleased. In the pre-Hitlerian atmosphere, the film was regarded as an attack on German nationalism.

Joseph Goebbels was head of the Nazi party in Berlin at the time, and also in charge of the Brown Shirts in the city. He could have probably written an article execrating Remarque, but not everybody would read it. It wasn't special enough. What he devised did the trick of stopping the film "dead on arrival." He ordered his men to attend the first showing of the picture, and when the lights had been dimmed and the initial credits barely over, they released a flock of white mice and stink bombs, and hurled beer bottles accompanied by shouts of "Germany Awake!" The audience panicked. The projector shut down. The management tried to capture all the white mice, which obviously took some time. A portion of the audience remained, the house went dark again, mice were released again, another melee, and finally the evening's event was canceled. Later, there was an attempt to show it again, but too much damage had been done and eventually the film was a forbidden fruit throughout Germany.

Probably the wisest and most influential relationship that Remarque ever had was with the young German actress Ruth Albu. As with most of his serious attachments, this one, even when romantically over, would remain in his life.

"The truth was that I loved him more than he loved me," Ruth Albu says simply, looking back on their complicated time together.

Small, perfectly proportioned, with reddish-blond hair and an insouciant quality, Ruth had the beginning of an important career in Germany but did not have enough time to become a star there. Born in 1908, she was discovered by the composer and musician Friedrich Hollander, who wrote many popular lyrics, such as "Falling in Love Again" for *The Blue Angel*. At seventeen she played in his clever, sharp, satirical revues. She had an attention-getting role in Carl Zuckmayer's *Schinderhannes*, and in the transplanted American hit *Broadway*, by Philip Dunning and directed by George Abbott, she was one of six highly prominent chorus girls, dancing alongside her peer Marlene Dietrich, who would become her successor in Remarque's affections. Ruth's career flourished until Hitler rose to power, and then, at the age of twenty-four, she left the German stage, went to Austria, and, in her words, "did a few things there."

At the age of nineteen, Ruth got married to Heinrich Schnitzler, the son of Arthur Schnitzler. It was with him one evening that she went to a dinner party and met "her fate"—the newly divorced man-about-town whom everyone knew as "Boni."

"He was a displaced person," she reflects. "He never had—and rued not having had—an upper-class background, and so he turned himself into a glamorous bon vivant." But at twenty-one, all she knew was that he was the toast of the town as the author of the phenomenally successful *All Quiet*. She was dazzled by him—as was her husband. When they got home, it was all they could discuss.

"And then Erich called me the next day, and soon after it wasn't hard to leave my husband for him. Boni was smashing-looking, maybe a little short for a man—certainly by today's standards—and he was canny, with eyes like a fox. And he loved and respected humor and intelligence. He was the love of my life back then. I was convinced that I could never love again. He spent his life trying to obscure himself, though, not wanting to let anyone in where he couldn't control things. He was deeply attached to his loneliness. He wrapped it around himself like his beautiful cashmere sweaters."

They were basically worlds apart. She had breeding and education, and was Jewish. All of that made him feel like a poseur—even the Jewish part. "I'm just a spy," he would say. Ruth made connections for him, and with his success, he began to indulge himself in material pleasures that had long been just a fantasy. He began to buy old Oriental carpets, which he stacked one on top of the other because he bought so many that there was no room for them all to be laid out.

"Why do you do that?" Ruth asked.

"I want to be near them," he would say.

Ruth was the practical one. She felt that he should go on buying whatever pleased him, but that there should be some method to it, so she introduced him to one of the most famous art dealers in Berlin, Dr. Walter Feilchenfeldt. They struck up a friendship immediately, and with the casual air of an expert, Feilchenfeldt introduced Remarque to great paintings that were available. After his first acquisition, for 80,000 DM, of van Gogh's *Passage inférieur du chemin de fer* (*Train Crossing*), he rarely turned anything down. Suddenly, he was the owner of a sizable collection, from which each of the pictures, four decades later, would be worth millions of dollars. When he was buying his most valuable art, a Renoir or a Manet went for between 80,000 and 100,000 DM, which was approximately $20,000 U.S. dollars at that time. He purchased masterpieces by Toulouse-Lautrec, Daumier, Renoir, Pissarro, and Degas. He owned three oils and twenty watercolors by Cézanne, who was his personal favorite. Among these was the painting *Paysage en Provence*, which had formerly belonged to Harry Kessler, who had attempted to be somewhat of a mentor to Remarque during his early literary career in Berlin. But Remarque preferred to leave his German origins behind when it came to art. As Richard Arthur Firda comments, "Remarque refused to show primary allegiance to Germanic art and culture. In his aesthetic tastes, he remained true to his Gallic ancestry."

Although Ruth was ready to share a life with Remarque, she saw that it would not be that simple. He seemed to need her, yet pushed her away. "I didn't have the glamour quotient that he craved," she reflects philosophically. But back then, she was caught in a spell and it was impossible to be self-protective. There were warnings, but she couldn't act on them.

He used to read to her from his new work, but she suspected that he needed a sounding board and didn't really care what she thought. He told her that Jutta was the one who understood his work best. During the time that Ruth knew Remarque in Berlin, Jutta retained the apartment while Remarque lived at the Hotel Majestic on Brandenburgerstrasse, which was where he wrote.

Remarque's work was torturing him, and Ruth found herself absorbing all his tension and frustration. In addition, he was drinking and womanizing rather heavily. "I'm off to the club," he would announce at unexpected times during the afternoon or evening when she thought he was just settling down to work, or when she thought they were about to go out together. He was a member of a famous lesbian club in Berlin called Mali, where he would often go to eat, drink, and relax in relative anonymity. Ruth had heard that the atmosphere there was like "a comfortable family café." Sometimes he would go to El Dorado, where, as Dietrich's biographer Steven Bach puts it, "There was something for everyone: boys, girls, dog fanciers."

Remarque's passion, although an increasingly dark one, was his work, where Ruth felt one of his best qualities was "his painting of scenes and essences." After a good day's work, his passion was exhausted, and after a lousy day's work, his passion was invested in drinking. "Erich never had a lot of passion for the act itself," Ruth says, and then, matter-of-factly, "He was usually too drunk."

Ruth kept her own apartment in Berlin, and then later moved to Vienna for a while, but she traveled with him and considered herself his girlfriend for about three years. While he was leading the high life, she predicted that the end in Germany was near. She understood that the nationalist-oriented Germans did not like Remarque; he was a pacifist and therefore a traitor. Sooner or later he would be an endangered citizen. She suggested that Switzerland was just the haven he needed, and fortuitously on one of their trips, they found a spacious—though not immense—villa in Porto Ronco, a small village above Ascona in the Italian part of Switzerland. The villa, perched over Lake Maggiore with a spectacular view, was called Casa Monte Tabor and had originally been owned by the nineteenth-century artist Arnold Böcklin. In 1931, Remarque, brilliantly guided by Ruth, bought it for 80,000 DM, moved in his art and his rugs, and lived there—off and on—for the rest of his life.

Remarque, Ruth, and Jutta all contributed to its decoration. Jutta was still very much on the scene. She had an insidious way of being especially endearing just when she had to go away to Davos or Arosa for her health spa treatments: mineral baths and extremely attentive, extremely expensive doctors, most of whom also happened to be attractive. Gossip would spread quickly in the small community when there were flirtations involving the former Frau Remarque. Her letters to Remarque, such as the following, were typical of her continued involvement with him:

Dear, dear Boni, I just called one more time to wish you a good morning after our disagreement last night toward the end of our phone call. I beg you not to get excited or crazy by the gossip of some women. Please think of

Casa Remarque, the villa in Porto Ronco that Remarque bought in 1931.

Remarque probably took this picture of Jutta on the dock below the villa.

yourself and your health and your nerves. Whatever has been between us is now past, due to the divorce; and whatever will become of us shouldn't be affected by the gossip of some nasty folks. You know all about me now, and I think you dug even deeper, but I am not responsible for the gossip people spread, and I am not able to correct it from here, because I don't know what's true and what's invented.

My dear goo, get away from all the muddle of the city and come up here into the good, clean air. I understand that you don't want to be with me, and that's all right, but you have to understand that I would be happy to talk to you and to see you. You must know how much I wait for a sign from you. Just a small note like: "Well, you old rascal, you are some piece of work, but I haven't quite forgotten you; I'm still here and ready to pluck your feathers. Now, babushka, remember how well we got along when I was still secretly entering that first apartment, and think of the time, seven years ago, when I visited you at Oblischka's rooms."

My sweet, tell me whatever you like, tell me or write to me that it will be this or that way in the near future, tell me the painful things, but tell me something! Believe me, it's also a difficult and painful time for me now. Often I'm awake for hours, lying on the balcony and crying. I'm so tired, you can't imagine. The quiet and depressing valley without sun forces one to think, only it's not very reviving. My love, I will write to you again tomorrow; cannot go on now.

Ruth Albu didn't buy any of it. "She was tough," she says, "and she outlived him by five years. She wasn't so sick. But he just loved her beauty, always. He loved beautiful things."

Marlene Dietrich fit perfectly into the category of "beautiful things." By consensus of opinion of both sexes, Marlene Dietrich was an object of great desire.

Ruth Albu had been in a play with her and remembers thinking, "She was just a very nice German girl who happened to have glamour." Ruth did not think she was particularly sensual: "I think that Marlene could not have cared less about sex, that it wasn't a big deal with men or with women, that she wasn't particularly sexy, but it came out when she acted it for the camera. She looked like a glamorous star. Always. When she was first discovered in my show, there was this old actor who said, 'This is going to be a great star.' We were all special girls. Each one of us at the beginning of a career. And she was one of us. But she dressed differently. She had stage-door johnnies. We all had admirers, but it was knee-deep with her. When she left the theater, all these guys were standing there. Nobody knew who she was. She didn't have more to do than most of us. But she was—for the guys—what one called a Haremartico, which means the men's department in a department store. They called her 'penis eyes.' "

Contrary to the general opinion that Remarque officially met Dietrich on the Lido in Venice in 1937, Ruth Albu sets the "magnetic moment" considerably earlier, and she most likely would have remembered the meeting that altered her destiny: "We were still in Berlin, and I was having a meal with Erich when Marlene passed our table, and because she knew me from the theater said, 'Well, hello there, Ruth, it's great to see you.' I introduced her to Erich and she sailed on. I felt it was at that moment that I lost him."

This checks out with an entry from Remarque's diary of 1938: "Alone with Puma later [they were in Paris], who by the way wrote me her first letter during the meal, and she said she felt as she had that time in the Eden Hotel eight years ago, when we first caught sight of each other."

It's possible that the affair happened later, because there is no evidence of any prolonged connection before 1937. And besides, all through the early and mid-thirties, Dietrich was busy becoming a huge star in Hollywood, having liaisons with costars and leading men: John Gilbert, Richard Barthelmess, Ronald Colman, Brian Aherne, Maurice Chevalier, Viennese matinee idol Hans Jaray, Douglas Fairbanks, Jr.; and women: Mercedes de Acosta and Elizabeth Allan; and, of course, her mentor, the director Josef von Sternberg—or, as director Joseph Mankiewicz referred to him, "Joe Stern from Newark, New Jersey."

From 1930 to 1932, Remarque was living in Berlin, at 5 Wittelsbacherstrasse, working on *The Road Back*, when he was not traveling or "visiting." Ruth and Jutta, unaware of each other's existence, continued to work on the new villa. They both had a great deal to say about it. Jutta took the tone of a very good, very helpful child: "My dearest Daddy, today Mr. Benrath sent three samples, two of them I ordered, the third would be for your couch. I had him make exact notes for you, so you are well informed. If you like the fabric for the couch, you need only to tell me the name of the firm and the measurements; it will be sent to you directly and all will be taken care of. I think the three fabrics fit well together, but of course this is just my suggestion. I hope you like the second fabric, which I picked for the sofa and the two chairs."

Ruth was amazed at the way Remarque was living. Though she came from a comfortable background, her family had nowhere near the kind of money that Remarque was spending daily. "He let me choose whatever I wanted in furnishing the house. I got most of the things together in a reasonable amount of time. I loved two very expensive but extremely good stores in Berlin and Vienna, so I went to them. I got the linens there—sheets, towels, luxury bathroom items. . . . I had great fun. And the same with picking the garden furniture, and the kitchen things. The whole thing was up to me. I could spend what I wanted. He never checked up. I know this because the buyer at the store asked me if I was Mrs. Remarque. . . . Funny, Boni couldn't decide between people and he couldn't decide between things. So, he needed me."

Remarque managed to cope with the rather fraught situation of the two intensely competitive women decorating his home simultaneously but independently: Jutta from the sanatorium in Davos and Ruth from Berlin and Vienna. Somehow Remarque was able to finish *The Road Back*, after informing the twenty-one countries holding the foreign rights contracts that he had decided to change the ending. He even volunteered to return all the advances; however, none of them accepted his offer. Who wanted to jeopardize the potential results of a literary wunderkind? They patiently awaited the result. The book was critically and commercially well received, but seemed lackluster in contrast to *All Quiet*. The novel, dealing with the return of the defeated soldiers after the armistice had been signed, had run in serial form just like its predecessor. In Germany, it was carried by *Vossische Zeitung*, in Paris, it was in *Le Matin*, and in America, in *Collier's* magazine. Otto Klement, wishing to repeat the experience of the last movie, went with Universal again. Although it acquired the screen rights, and the picture that was eventually made was successful, there was a six-year hiatus in between. In 1931, the studio considered it too soon to make a picture so similar in theme to *All Quiet*. Remarque would be competing against himself.

Remarque preferred *The Road Back* to *All Quiet*, for he felt it accomplished just what he had set out to do. He had wanted to elaborate on the horror of war's aftermath, showing how it destroyed even those who survived.

The book had its supporters and detractors, but did not create the same maelstrom of controversy as *All Quiet*. The respected German writer Ludwig Renn, author of *War* and an obvious competitor, told his socialist colleagues that *The Road Back* was "a disappointment for Ullstein." Richard Katz, a Berlin journalist crony of Remarque's, recalls how they got back at Renn when he was visiting Remarque at his villa. Renn was anxious to gain support from German exiles for the leftist movement against the Nazis:

We let [Renn] talk and stared at one another over a bottle of cognac that was on the table. Lake Maggiore shimmered through the open window.

"And you?" asked Renn. "What do you think of Stalin?"

I was discourteous enough to point then to a work of Negro sculpture, standing on the fireplace mantel.

"A fetish?" I asked Remarque.

"Yes, a fetish," he noted. Renn had his answer.

Heinrich Mann, despite his brother's antipathy toward Remarque, gave the book a good review in the *Vossische Zeitung*. The *London Times*, however, called it a type of "degenerate realism," and William Faulkner, in reviewing it for the *New Republic*, sneered, saying that the book was "created primarily for the Western trade, to sell among the heathen like colored glass." Published in Germany during the Depression, *The Road Back* had advance sales of 100,000 copies.

Remarque's drinking and divorce, as well as the political climate, were depressing him. Less than a year earlier he had stated, "No desire for war really exists in the German people," and "I have no opinion of Hitler. I know nothing about him. I never occupy myself with political questions."

For a brief time, this was true. When he thought he was in love with Ruth Albu, he was able to be the passionate humanist he wished to be. Before the Reichstag election, when the Nazis, with their 196 deputies, were on the ascent, and before President Hindenburg appointed Adolf Hitler chancellor of Germany, before the suspension of civil liberties and a free press, before the Enabling Act, which gave Hitler full constitutional control, before Germany became a dictatorship, in the waning days of the Weimar Republic, Remarque was still detached and naive about what could happen in Germany.

At the moment he believed he was getting free of Jutta, he began work on *Three Comrades*, his love paean to her; his working title was *Pat*—based on the heroine, Pat Hollman. Ruth shared Remarque's work-in-progress struggles during the writing of this book, which, ironically, featured Jutta, who once again seemed very much a part of their lives.

"Sweet Little Monkey," he wrote in a letter to Ruth in late 1931, "I was not able to finish my work. I could not do it here. I wasn't able to sleep and too nervous from smoking and being alone—and sitting at home. I will try to finish in Berlin and be done with it by the end of the month. It's too long; half of it isn't good and needs to be edited out," and then cryptically he writes, "How are you doing? I hope everything goes well without complications.

Don't get up too early. Write to me if you can, just a note. . . . Buy what you need and pamper yourself."

The relationship with Ruth was more complicated than it seemed. She was his true cultural comrade, and he felt he could discuss anything with her, from the writing of his books to his dealing with rug merchants. But she wasn't always around. She began to spend more time in the pursuit of her acting career. Remarque wanted to continue their comfortable relationship, in which she served in a nurturing and advisory capacity.

She recognized this and tried to soothe him in this poignant letter: "Dearest, dear! I am with you and kiss you! And the joy and pain is equally great! I only know I'm staying with you, I'll hold your hand, two aging children. . . . But despite it all, you must know I am faithful to you and myself. I am devoted, devoted, devoted! . . . I am always with you. You'll never be alone. A coaxing kitten, a raving body, a soft smooth blanket, how often I hold you in my arms—even if you don't like it when I call myself a 'Mother,' but I was one and I am one. You shall always feel good with me! Beloved soul, beloved body—what can I promise you to make you happy?"

Ruth began to get work and recognition in Berlin and Vienna. She also had an ailing father to take care of. So, she was busy and sometimes didn't write to Remarque, which provoked him into temporary ardor and concern: "You really ought to write to me how you are doing, my little one! Just a note—just three words—I am fine!" He writes from the Hotel Majestic in Berlin, where he is incarcerated, forcing himself to write without interruption. He is lonely. He misses her and his dogs. He had six in Ronco at the time. His favorites seem to have been Billy, the Irish terrier, and Tommy, a mutt. "I should have brought Tommy. I didn't, because I thought it would be too boring. Now I am missing him. I will return soon. Please write to me, tell me you are up and about—that you are well again—that you are better—that I will be content."

It was not the time, however, for him to see theirs as the core relationship. He cared for her deeply, needed her, but his muse was devoted to Jutta, aka Pat Hollman, and he had to follow it.

Remarque anguished over *Pat*, straining to finish the entire book within a fixed time frame, as he had the others. This was the book that drove him to change locale and lead a monastic life (which he could never quite manage) in order to work on it. Eventually, the manuscript of what became *Three Comrades* was finished during his exile from Germany; it would be 5,500 pages long (all drafts) and would rest in the repository at New York University. But in Holland, in Berlin, in Arosa, in St. Moritz—he didn't believe it would ever evolve.

"Autumn storms" was how Remarque referred to the encroaching Nazi takeover of Germany. In 1932–33, the Brown Shirts belonged to what was called the SA, a private militant arm of the early Nazi party. The movement, though young, was insidious. For Remarque, the warnings were increasingly louder and clearer. He knew he was being watched by the government and tried to arrange his finances so it couldn't seize any of his holdings. He was highly suspect because of having a second residence in Switzerland, where he could bank and stash his royalties. He had to act quickly. Part of him knew it; the other part couldn't actually believe it.

His main financial adviser was his agent, Otto Klement. But it was Ruth Albu who proved indispensable on several levels. Not only was she his business liaison between Germany and Switzerland, making sure his money got out safely, but also she was keeping his books for him. And she knew enough about his finances so that if the government asked, she could provide answers to protect him.

In the spring of 1932, the German government seized Remarque's account at the Darmstadt and National Bank in Berlin. Although there wasn't a great deal of money in it—20,000 marks, which was the equivalent of $5,000—the action served to warn him of future intentions toward him. The government accused him of having a residence in Holland, which was false, and of banking outside Germany, which was true. But still he stayed on, traveling back and forth from Switzerland, until the galvanizing moment.

In the wee hours of January 29, 1933, Remarque was drinking in a bar in Berlin. His dog Billy was with him. A friend of his, and an informer against the Nazis, joined him at his table, patted the dog, ordered a drink, and very casually passed Remarque a note under the table that said, "Get out of town fast." Remarque had one more drink, took his dog, got into his Lancia, and drove straight through the night and next day until he reached Switzerland, arriving with nothing but the clothes he was wearing.

Hitler officially became Germany's chancellor just after Remarque crossed the border into Switzerland. And Remarque did not return to Germany until 1952, when he was accompanied, along with some fanfare, by Paulette Goddard.

From Switzerland, Remarque made it clear why he had departed: "In the year 1933 I had to leave Germany because my life was threatened. I was

Remarque with his favorite dog, the Irish terrier Billy.

The beloved Lancia, named Puma,
was a gift from Ullstein Verlag, Remarque's publisher.

neither a Jew nor oriented toward the left politically. . . . I was a militant pacifist. . . . It's more by luck than good judgment that I am on the side I now stand on. But I know that it happens to be the right one."

Joseph Goebbels, who launched the initial campaign against Remarque, sneered that without the National Socialists his antiwar book would have lain in the dirt of low sales, to which Remarque countered, "It is apolitical. And at first the impression it made was entirely nonpolitical. Only through its success was it drawn into the political debating arena. I think it was more the number of copies sold than the book itself which was the object of attack."

Later, after Remarque had exiled himself, although Goebbels still alleged that Remarque understood and had catered to public taste, he relented by saying that they were losing a "valuable citizen." He requested that Remarque return to Germany. Remarque spoke freely from Switzerland: "What? Sixty-five million people would like to get away and I'm to go back of my own free will? Not on your life!"

Remarque on Lake Maggiore, ca. 1931.

A view of the waterfront at Ascona, the nearest big town to Porto Ronco, where Remarque frequented the cafés.

CHAPTER FOUR

THE HONEY POT

1936–1939

IT WAS CHARLIE CHAPLIN and *Modern Times* that transformed Paulette Goddard from celebrity to star. After the release of the picture in 1936, everybody wanted her professionally and otherwise, but only Chaplin could work with her. She was his contracted player, and though their relationship was profoundly professional, he was also, according to many sources, her great love. There is the story that in 1974, when he was honored by the American Film Society, she went in full, bejeweled regalia, sporting her best pieces: the jumbo star sapphire ring, and the big ruby collar with star rubies hanging from a huge carved star-ruby pendant. Squatting down beside him, she crooned, "Hello, baby." Whereupon he turned, eyes filled with tears, and said, "Oh, oh! My little baby." And she said, "Yes. Your only little baby."

But when she was once asked what she felt about the fact that she and Chaplin, married to different people, both ended up in Switzerland at the same time, she said, "He has his mountain; I have mine. Separate mountains is the only way this country could remain neutral," after pointing out that she lived in the Italian part and Chaplin in the French part.

There were hints of Paulette's dissatisfaction with Chaplin as far back as 1935. Before they were married and before *Modern Times* had premiered, she had begun to go out on dates when he was working late or if he had gone to bed early, and then she would sneak back in and put her purse and shoes in

LEFT AND ABOVE: *H. G. Wells with Paulette, who is flanked by Charlie Chaplin, Jr., left, and Sydney Chaplin, right, at La Mirador in Palm Springs. Jinx Falkenburg and Paulette on the court at the Chaplin house, ca. 1935.*

A view, from the garden, of the Chaplin house on Summit Drive in Bel Air.

the refrigerator, retrieving them in the morning. She was restless at some of their stuffier dinners, and by 1936 had begun a heavy flirtation with Tim Durant, Chaplin's best friend.

Chaplin and Goddard, however, were a favorite couple with the Hollywood columnists. Rumors of an impending marriage circulated endlessly. Her salary reportedly rose from five hundred to a thousand a week on his payroll. From 1932 on, they were allegedly married. Paulette was satisfied while waiting for Chaplin to come up with another project for her. He was trying. He began to adapt a novel called *The Regency*, by D. L. Murphy, and then became intrigued with an original screenplay called *White Russian*, which would costar Paulette with, perhaps, Gary Cooper. (Three decades later, Chaplin finally made the film, retitled *The Countess from Hong Kong*, with Sophia Loren.) He then debated a remake of his own *Woman of Paris*, with Paulette recast in Edna Purviance's original role. Nothing came of it.

Also circulating were rumors about Paulette's restlessness, her shopping sprees, her devotion to Chaplin's boys, her determination to be a better actress, and her interest in other men. Another of her interests was the diminutive, witty Anita Loos, whom Paulette referred to as "the working Dorothy Parker." Because she was one of the few top women writers in Hollywood, she ran with the "in" crowd and found herself at the Chaplin-Goddard parties: "Now Charlie, as the author of his own movie scripts, was given to reading them aloud to guests after dinner. Excellent as those scenarios were, they failed to hold attention after several readings. So Paulette used to sit on the floor behind Charlie's big armchair, under which she stashed a bottle of Dom Pérignon champagne to help keep her alert. Even so, those recitals were frequently interrupted by the snores of Mrs. Chaplin."

Also present in Chaplin's group was "a companion from his days of poverty in London. By now Constance Collier was a famous Shakespearean star but when she was a showgirl in London, she'd been the inspiration for Max Beerbohm's heroine 'Zuleika Dobson,' a siren who caused the entire student body of Oxford to commit mass suicide out of love for her—after which Zuleika moved to Cambridge."

Loos compared this with Paulette's effect on men. The three women were made for each other. Loos wrote, "Both Paulette and I, closing the generation gap that separated us from Constance Collier, latched onto her for being as bored as we were with the petty gossip and never-ending business talk about films. Mrs. Chaplin, in particular, was getting restless."

To stanch the boredom, Paulette took acting lessons with Constance Collier, who, like a wise courtesan aunt, taught her the etiquette of being a coquette. In 1964 they acted together, and triumphed in Mitchell Leisen's *Kitty*.

There was, however, a good deal of frivolity in Paulette's life just after *Modern Times* made her a star. She might have seemed almost a parody of indulgence. All her life Paulette paid scrupulous attention to the latest in fashion, and as a result, she was fashionable but had never quite arrived at her own style. Jinx Falkenburg, one of Paulette's treasured chums in the late thirties and through the forties, thought Paulette was the epitome of style:

> She was the first person to take jeweled charms off a bracelet and set them in a gold compact, an idea that became a fact. One night when we were going out she tied a velvet band around her head, took a dozen pairs of earrings, and clipped them on in a jeweled fringe. She has a black jersey formal that's bare on one shoulder and ties on the other shoulder in a large, soft knot. Some women would have perched a clip stiffly on top of the knot. Paulette took a wide gold and emerald bracelet and encircled it. She can put the same individuality into a $3.95 playsuit. She'll tie a sash around the waist pirate-fashion, put a clip on the shoulder, and you'll never know it's the same outfit. She's always willing to share her ideas. She'll say: "Why don't you pin your hair back this way, or wear your flowers that way?" And bang! You've got a brand-new effect. She never wears stockings or uses perfume.

Jinx Falkenburg was seventeen years old and on the tennis circuit when she first met Paulette. She had been asked to the Chaplin house to play doubles, and, although an accomplished tennis player, she was also a tongue-tied, awestruck teenager. Tall and leggy, with all-American good looks, she felt insignificant if not invisible in contrast to Paulette, who, she recalls, was dazzling in her designer tennis outfit with a tailored ermine polo coat thrown over her shoulders. The first image of Paulette never changed for Falkenburg: "I had never seen anybody so at ease, so graceful and so gracious. She could talk to anybody." Falkenburg felt twice blessed when Paulette not only talked to her but made her a friend.

Suddenly, Falkenburg was part of the Chaplin coterie and invited to the various parties, which, mostly took place around the tennis court. "The pool house," recalls Falkenburg, "was like an estate in miniature." She would sometimes stay there in one of the guest rooms when she had a match early the next morning. Those times were charmed. She got to be a champion at her own game as well as to worship an idol. "I wanted to be like Paulette and look like Paulette. I thought she was absolutely perfect."

Paulette and Chaplin at the premiere of Modern Times, *1936.*

Because Paulette was so beautiful for so long and a petite five feet four inches, she got away with wearing clothes that were basically too young for her; it was only when she hit her mid-sixties that she began to look like she was stuck in another era, with her eternal auburn pageboy hairdo, her dresses with capped or puffed sleeves, her matching bags and shoes, and her violently pink lipstick. She was always quite fierce about obtaining just the right thing that would enhance her style. Relentlessly, she would track down what she felt she just had to possess, as in a letter she wrote to a shopping service at *Vogue* magazine: "Gentlemen, I have been reading in *Vogue*: 'Wear large-lens sunglasses,' but it does not say where they may be obtained, and there is no place in California that I know of where they can be purchased. Does your service send such things on approval? If so, I should like six pairs with various colored rims. If you cannot arrange this, would you be kind enough to advise me where I can obtain some."

She was meticulous about the luxuries she owned. She kept scrupulous records of her furs. Storing them, and then withdrawing them when she went to New York, London, or Paris, she kept a list of them and their various stages of upkeep: "Long ermine wrap (faint yellow streaks starting around the collar), black lamb coat (repair pocket linings), ermine coat, brown-and-white fur coat, beaver jacket (add hood?), black jacket with white ermine trim, white velvet coat with fox trim (clean yearly—lining?), gray fur coat, brown seal coat (secure hooks), strip of eight white ermine skins."

In February of 1936 Chaplin took Paulette and her mother on a grand tour of the Orient. The Japanese adored Chaplin and were bound to embrace *Modern Times* with even more fervor if its distribution in Japan coincided with a personal visit.

Photographs show the trio riding atop elephants, tanned and bursting with health as they stood on the deck of a cruise ship taking them through the China Seas, and arriving as guests of honor to a flurry of flashbulbs, and it seems this was a happy and successful trip. Chaplin and Alta looked like the proud parents of the glowing Paulette, who had—according to Chaplin himself—gotten married to him shortly into the trip: "We stayed away from Hollywood for five months. During this trip Paulette and I were married. Afterwards we returned to the States, boarding a Japanese boat in Singapore."

His terse statement seems to lay to rest the rumors that persisted long after they had been divorced about when, and whether, they had been married. At that time one's career might not recover from an actor being called a tramp

Chaplin, Paulette, and Alta sailing the China Seas during the supposed honeymoon, 1936.

RIGHT: *Chaplin's golfing friend, Tim Durant, with Paulette and Chaplin at the Brown Derby, ca. 1937.*

Paulette, Alta, and Chaplin in Burma, 1936.

or a drunk or a Communist. The studios dictated conduct: if an unmarried couple were living together (it was called shacking up) and they were stars, their opportunities were definitely limited and their careers tarnished. When Vivien Leigh won the role of Scarlett O'Hara, one of the most fiercely sought-after parts in the history of movies, she and Laurence Olivier were deeply in love, but not living together. It was that unspoken code that kept the almost perversely independent Paulette Goddard herself from running across the lawn of Tara in a silk gown and morocco slippers. In fact, Paulette had been given the role of Scarlett, and it had been taken away from her.

The Selznicks lived across the street from the Chaplins. Other neighbors included Harold Lloyd, Ronald Colman, Kay Francis, cowboy star Tom Mix, and Douglas Fairbanks and Mary Pickford. It was a built-in coterie. Tennis was the rage, and since everyone had courts, they would make the rounds in their whites, becoming familiar with one another's household customs. In the beginning, Chaplin goaded Paulette into becoming an avid natural player: "The way I learned to play tennis was when I was married to Charlie and he said, 'The day you beat me I'll give you a thousand shares of AT&T.' He didn't know that I had drive—I didn't either. I just thought, 'I'm going to beat him! I'm going to beat him!' So I got Bill Tilden and all the great tennis players and never stopped taking lessons for six months. I got in high-training condition, went in, knocked him off at tennis, and never played that well again. And I still have the stock, thank God!"

The other sport that they embraced was golf, which Paulette took up with a vengeance. Paulette and David O. Selznick had always been friendly but reserved with each other because of their potential professional relationship. One day they got to talking about golf out at the Lakeside Country Club. It seemed that everybody but Selznick knew that Paulette wielded a mean club, but from the way she talked to Selznick, she sounded like an amateur. Soon, they had arranged a match for rather high stakes, and Paulette was getting a whopper of a handicap. She didn't ask for it, but humbly accepted Selznick's gallant offer. She then proceeded to cream him. It was on the eighteenth hole, after she had holed in, and in one under par, she squinted up at him, green eyes glinting: "Not so bad after all, am I?" And he, grinning ruefully: "No, not bad at all, you little devil." Right then, he glimpsed his Scarlett, filed it, and went on to a game of tennis doubles with her, Chaplin, and his wife, Irene.

While Paulette was waiting for Chaplin to create another vehicle for her, she aligned herself with opportunity. She was truly gifted at turning situations to her advantage. One Hollywood veteran put it this way:

> How else could she have withstood, no, triumphed over what Hollywood had come to know as "the Chaplin situation"? Here she was, an unknown member of the Goldwyn Follies chorus who did a bit in *The Kid from Spain*. Chaplin spotted her. The eventual outcome was that four years later he put her into *Modern Times*, where she was good, but nothing cataclysmic. Meanwhile she became—or did not become Mrs. Charlie Chaplin, even though Randolph Churchill announced their marriage to the world. [Chaplin very much admired Sir Winston Churchill, whom he had initially met at Marion Davies's beach house in Santa Monica. When they saw each other again, he was Churchill's dinner guest in his hotel suite, where he met Randolph, Churchill's son.] For five years she was subjected to the most trying, the most heartbreaking situation in which a woman could find herself. But it did not get her down. Instead she seemed to have turned the mystery of her relationship with Chaplin to her own advantage. For more than four years after she did *The Kid from Spain*, she never faced a camera. But she got more publicity than half the stars in Hollywood. . . . There was no one like her.

Socially fearless, because she had access to everyone, she skillfully piloted her hostess role—with an eye out for the press, as is evidenced in a 1936 cable from New York to Chaplin's secretary, Catherine Hunter: "I'm giving a theatre party tomorrow night for ten for Margaret Sullavan's opening play, *Stage Door*. Guests include Mr. and Mrs. J. O'Brian, Mrs. Newbold Ryan, Mr. William Rhinelander Stewart, etc. Thought this might be a local news item for you. Arriving back TWA 9:50, Saturday, October 24. Okay for pictures at airport."

A highlight of that evening must have been seeing the man who gave her her first diamond, William Rhinelander Stewart. Paulette believed in recycling people. She never held a grudge; there was always room for rekindling. As she said to Anita Loos, "I never lose track of a jewel or its donor." Ironically, this philosophy was shared by Marlene Dietrich, who became her arch-enemy once Paulette was being seen with Remarque; it is evident in a story that Remarque related in his diary of 1949. He was never truly "over" Dietrich, but he had gone on, as she did. He wrote, "Saw Puma Saturday night; pretty, lively. Told stories of Gabin, also of her new boyfriend Michael Wilding (was 38, looked 24). How she had met Gabin, with his wife in an antiques store in Paris. When she left she neither turned right nor left, but crossed the street in the middle so he could see her walking, see her legs from the shop window. Same thing with her: you never give up a man, you only add one.'"

Paulette was also intrigued by intellectual men, and during the late thirties she was often in the company of such first-rate minds and family friends as Aldous Huxley, whom she seriously charmed, and H. G. Wells. Wells became a house guest, not unlike Sheridan Whiteside in *The Man Who Came to Dinner*, by George S. Kaufman and Moss Hart, since he arrived for the night and ended up staying over two months. During this time, Paulette took Wells away to Palm Springs to be her partner in a tennis tournament. The bespectacled, pigeon-breasted Wells dashing toward the net for a save seems a situation that only Paulette could have brought about.

Paulette recalled H. G. Wells's rather eccentric expression of affection for her: "He stayed at my house and when he'd burned enough midnight oil talking, he said to Charlie, 'I have nothing more to say.' So, he went to Palm Springs and spent a few days there, and he came back and said, 'I have something you're going to love. I have a sackful of stones for you. I found them outside in the desert while I was walking.' And I said, 'Well, what am I going to do with it?' And he said, 'You can use it as a doorstop, but if you love stones, here they are.' Wasn't that sweet?"

"Every day I start my education" was her motto, and during this time, in between tennis, golf, parties packed with every illustrious star, director, and producer in Hollywood and imported from Europe, swimming, shopping, flirting with Jock Whitney and Tim Durant, among others, she ordered serious books: "Dear Miss Goddard," wrote a book tracer. "We find that *Werther* by Goethe is out of print."

"Paulette's secret," says her friend Celestine Wallis, "was that she narrowed in on what interested her at the moment. She made her need so clear, so pulsing, that everybody wanted to be heroic and fill it."

There was one person who fervently did not wish to cater to Paulette. Kono Torachi was more than the traditional Japanese houseboy, and in fact Chaplin described him as his "secretary." Since Chaplin's early days in Hollywood, Kono had established himself as indispensable to the star and his household. He was a true gentleman's gentleman, and although he got along with the other women and wives in Chaplin's life, he did not take to Paulette. He had been used to reigning supreme over the two-story mansion on Summit Drive in Bel Air. He oversaw every inch of it: the large circular driveway filled with black and white gravel, the enormous living room with an almost constantly lit fireplace, the well-tuned piano, the dining room modeled after William Randolph Hearst's in San Simeon, the three over-sized bedrooms and baths on the second floor, and the great hall of a kitchen and servants' quarters on the ground floor. He liked the house before Paulette appeared on the scene and took as much pride in its dour grandeur as Chaplin: "I built my house in Beverly Hills . . . perched on a hilltop, fronted by a lawn that came to a point like the bow of a boat, a house with forty windows and a large music room with a tall ceiling . . . the organ room, which was long and narrow like the nave of a church."

After 1932, as Paulette became an increasingly frequent presence at the house, gradually moving in, Kono became increasingly dissatisfied, to the point of churlishness. The final straw was when Paulette became Mrs. Charlie Chaplin and began to redo the house as well as their way of living in it. She installed her own Scandinavian maid and brought two bulldog pup-pies. She took over the middle upstairs bedroom and bath, making it her bower, filled with her clothes, jewels, and such prized possessions as a small Cocteau drawing of her profile. She placed fresh flowers everywhere, high-handedly gave orders to the staff, and extravagantly redecorated the house, bringing to it colors and life it had never known. Kono took his leave.

Paulette used to knit, and Diana Vreeland first met Paulette about 1936, when Paulette was on Long Island visiting relatives. They were both attend-ing a garden party, and Diana Vreeland went over and by way of introduc-tion said, "What's a nice girl like you doing sitting and knitting?" Whereupon Paulette smiled most winningly and said, "Well, your whole day is wasted. I've at least made a sweater."

In reminiscing, Paulette contradicted this: "It wasn't a whole sweater. It was a midriff. I used to make two sleeves and tie them together." She went on to give an exacting picture of life among the rich and famous where she was just "one of the boys."

"That was when I was out at Jock's. Whitney. That was *la dolce vita*. They used to serve a silver tray for breakfast holding double martinis. . . . And I'd stare at it. Because I was always more or less on a health kick. And I'd think, 'Will I beat him today?' So I'd push it aside—this is about ten o'clock in the morning—go out and play golf, get a stroke a hole from everybody, and come home with my sweater and a little pack of money. It was fun. Women didn't play golf very much then, but I used to love to play for money.

"Until I won the Pebble Beach Championship. And *everybody* was furious because I played at least ten strokes below my handicap. . . . I was pressured

Paulette with Bob Hope, taking a break from her usually serious game, ca. 1939.

The famous fight scene in The Women, *directed by George Cukor:
from left, Norma Shearer, Joan Fontaine, Rosalind Russell, Paulette Goddard,
and Mary Boland, 1939.*

playing for the prize. So I took the prize and never played again. Because I knew that for the rest of my life I'd be trying to make that score. And I knew I couldn't do it. . . . So I gave up entirely and started playing tennis. . . . I used to play [golf] with all the boys—Howard Hughes, Pat DeCico, Bruce Cabot, Bob Ritchie from El Morocco. They used to have a club: The Cad's Club, and I was the only woman who played with them. It was a riot. Pat used to get so mad at me if I beat him that he'd break his clubs. Oh, I had more fun!"

As a new star, Paulette was eager to assist any public attention that was brought to her. Fan clubs were not only an enormous morale booster, but valuable publicity as well. Paulette fueled her fan club's already avid interest. In a report to her fan club at this time, she gives an amazingly detailed description of a whirlwind of social activities:

> Returned from Palm Springs about a week ago and it's been a round of parties ever since. It has completely upset my routine, inasmuch as neither Mr. Chaplin or I ever go out much. However, we had a very good excuse, for Igor Stravinsky, the famous composer-conductor, was in town. He conducted the Los Angeles Symphony Orchestra not only in a repertoire of Russian music, but several of his own compositions, together with the ballet *Petrouchka*, which my dancing teacher, Theodore Kosloff—with whom I've been studying for the past four years—conceived and directed. . . . Incidentally, I was originally to have been in it, necessitating eight weeks of rehearsal with Kosloff, but my ski accident ended that. [She took the boys skiing in Sun Valley and had a relatively minor but painful accident, breaking several small bones in her foot.] . . . Last Saturday I was hostess to Stravinsky at a tennis tea party. That, with a dinner party given by the Harold Lloyds for a cousin of the Rockefellers, will give you an idea of the whirl I've been in.

Paulette was meeting everyone—whether it was George Gershwin or Igor Stravinsky. Paulette and Chaplin were at the center of a small world and apt to be asked to every event that counted.

One night, Stravinsky was to be the guest of honor at a dinner party hosted by the Edward G. Robinsons, who were known for their art collection, their liberal views, and their ability to cull vital and distinguished guests. Chaplin had been reluctant to attend that particular dinner party because he found himself at odds with Stravinsky, who was sure that he had heard one of his compositions used in *Modern Times*. His lawyers were on the case, but Chaplin was determined to ignore the whole matter. However,

Paulette had already accepted the invitation, and Chaplin, in a show of good sportsmanship, felt that if he'd ignored Stravinsky thus far, he could ignore him over dinner. There would be plenty of stimulating company to keep him occupied. Douglas Fairbanks and Sylvia, his new wife, would be there, as well as the Frank Capras and Ernest Hemingway's favorite "Kraut," Marlene Dietrich, whom Chaplin found interesting, although, apparently, this was not mutual. According to Maria Riva, "Dietrich did not like Chaplin. She considered most comedians of the silent era 'low-class circus performers.'"

It was not Chaplin's evening to be intrigued. Gershwin had that market cornered. Paulette was his dinner partner. He wrote about it to a friend, Mabel Schirmer: "Dined at E. Robinson's the other night at a party mainly for Stravinsky. Many celebs were there. Sat next to Paulette Goddard. Mmmmmmm. She's nice. Me Likee." He was never to recover from his infatuation—although, according to Oscar Levant, he understood her baser nature, calling her "a little gold-digger."

At thirty-eight, on any given night Gershwin was putting on his top hat and white tie more often than not. He was at the pinnacle of his fame, having composed the scores for such Broadway hits as *Lady Be Good*, *Funny Face*, *Strike Up the Band*, *Girl Crazy*, and *Of Thee I Sing*, and the innovative opera *Porgy and Bess*. He and his brother had "gone Hollywood," writing the score for Fred Astaire and Ginger Rogers's *Shall We Dance?* and working on their new picture, *A Damsel in Distress*.

George lived in a big house with an Olympic-size pool, drove around town in a Cord sports car, and squired various beauties. His interests included Ginger Rogers, Simone Simon (*The Cat People*), and Elizabeth Allan, who was also seeing Marlene Dietrich. When he met Paulette, everyone else fell by the wayside. Even his work suffered until she told him that she would be "a damsel in distress" if he didn't get back to work on that picture. Gershwin, in fact, was partly responsible for Paulette's dancing opposite Astaire in the 1941 movie *Second Chorus*. She had met Astaire on one of the Sundays around Gershwin's pool and she had discussed her dancing lessons. The pay-off arrived three years later.

Gershwin was also responsible for Paulette's introduction to Mexico. While visiting Mexico, he had met with the muralist Diego Rivera, and had been deeply taken with both the country and the artist. He passed along his enthusiasm to Paulette, who later embraced Mexico like a long-lost relative and became Rivera's muse and savior.

Anita Loos felt that Gershwin, however, "fell hopelessly in love. He used

Chaplin and Paulette with her favorite wit and friend, Anita Loos.

Paulette and her ardent admirer George Gershwin, in Los Angeles.

to follow Paulette everywhere, came to life in her presence as nobody had
ever seen him before." Oscar Levant: "He fell madly in love with Paulette.
He was more in love than I'd ever seen him." Harold Arlen: "You know, he
wanted to marry Paulette Goddard. We sat by his pool talking about it. She
was a great girl, but George's life-style was very free-wheeling. I knew that
marriage would tie him down, so I told him that he would have to give up
some of the freedom he had. He didn't say anything because I knew—all of
us knew—that he wanted to get married."

Though she referred to herself as Mrs. Chaplin, and others addressed her
as such, Paulette would not publicly admit that she was married, nor, at the
time, would Chaplin. In fact, he announced their marriage at the premiere
of *The Great Dictator* in 1940, when their relationship was considered to have
already unraveled. It is difficult to understand just why they were so evasive
about it. It was almost as though they had gotten caught up in their own
game. Paulette, when she looked back, referred to herself as having been
married—certainly about 1937, at the time of the Gershwin flirt. There
were, of course, different versions. This was Paulette's:

I was married to Charlie and that's why George fell in love with me.
Because I was unattainable. If you know his pattern or his story in any
way—absolutely unattainable was what excited him. I would go down on
Sundays and have lunch at his house. He lived with his family, his mother
was alive then, and we'd go Sunday, we'd sit by the pool, and we'd play
records. Always his own. And he'd always have these terrible, terrible
headaches. And this last Sunday that I was with him, he was absolutely
screaming in pain with a headache. And the family was calling the psychi-
atrist in New York saying how he was frustrated in love and this and that.
And I just finally gave up. I didn't say anything to them. I just said to the
chauffeur, "George is very, very ill. Pack a bag and take him to Cedars of
Lebanon." And George had come out of the sun and was holding his head,
screaming on the stairs, "Paulette, *help* me, *help* me, I'm in terrible . . ." It
was really something frightful to see.

So the chauffeur took him. And the doctor called me from the hospital
and said, "He's in a coma and will never again regain consciousness. My
diagnosis is that he has a tumor of the brain." And other doctors came and
operated and he had a tumor the size of an orange. And Charlie and I
mourned George. And that was it. . . . I had only known him for about six
months. We'd go to parties sometimes because Charlie was working at

home. And he'd let me go with George because I've always been a one-man
woman. Believe it or not. . . . When I was married to Charlie, that was it.
And he knew it. . . . But George wrote a couple of songs for me: "The way
you wear your hat/The way you sip your tea/They can't take that away from
me."

Warmth, sentiment, nostalgia were not part of Paulette's makeup. The
time with Gershwin was a sweet, romantic scene between a married woman
and a dying genius. As she said, "Charlie and I mourned George. And that
was it." For Gershwin, there were those who thought it meant a great deal
more. "Adulation to her is as normal as breathing," Constance Collier commented about Paulette.

David O. Selznick had perhaps not called Paulette a "little devil" for nothing. As soon as he was committed to making the movie of *Gone With the
Wind* and began his search for Scarlett, Paulette got herself a top agent (she
hadn't needed one for years, with Chaplin acting in her best interests), who
just happened to be David O. Selznick's brother, Myron. Following the loss
of Gershwin, who had made a lot of contacts for her, Paulette was newly
determined not to let her career take a dive. Chaplin wasn't coming through
for her, didn't have a picture written, and didn't know when he would
deliver a "talkie." It was time and he was nervous, so instead of working, he
would retreat to Pebble Beach with his friend Tim Durant. Ostensibly they
went to play golf, but as events began to unfold, it looked as if the retreat was
more of a separation between Paulette and Chaplin.
 "If I had gotten to play Scarlett, my life would have been a much deeper
red," said Paulette in wistful reflection. At that point, the role meant more to
her than anything else—her relationship with Chaplin and the boys included. There were rumors that Myron Selznick thought of her as more than
a client and that they were often seen entering the jewelry salon of Saks Fifth
Avenue in Beverly Hills. It was unlikely that the biggest agent in Hollywood
bought Mrs. Charlie Chaplin jewelry, and at Saks. A more likely explanation
would be that Paulette could not pass a jewelry store without going in. Her
favorite lark was to try on thousands of dollars' worth of jewelry—much like
a child playing dress-up—whether she bought anything or not. And it
didn't matter who was with her. Man, woman, old, young, business or social,
she would drag them in to witness her ritual. Undoubtedly, Myron Selznick
thought her very beautiful in the Cartier diamond choker or the pavé dia-

mond and ruby earrings, but his gifts to her were two choice roles under a David O. Selznick contract, along with the understanding that she was being groomed for Scarlett, the role of a lifetime.

Chaplin balked at the contract. He became rigidly territorial: Paulette was his creation, star of his pictures, his wife, and besides, his company was paying her $2,500 a week whether she worked or not. He was also unsure of her ability without him at the directorial helm. She had appeared to be a natural in *Modern Times*; her performance was so free, winning, vital, and true. Chaplin had worked indefatigably for two years to capture that performance from Paulette. He doubted, as did Irene Selznick (who was a moderate friend of Paulette's), whether she could come within yards of approaching the role. In fact, the only one who was really enthusiastic about Paulette as Scarlett—that is, a year prior to the screen tests—aside from her agent, Myron, was her mother, Alta.

Chaplin relented and consented. Paulette could sign a five-year contract with Selznick, which would state that Chaplin could reclaim Paulette's services by giving Selznick sixty days' notice. Chaplin was doing his best to stall for some time. While Paulette was cast in her first talking role as the third lead under Janet Gaynor and Douglas Fairbanks, Jr., in Selznick's *The Young in Heart*, Chaplin was trying to persuade H. G. Wells to write an original story for his long-awaited talking debut. He had written a screenplay in collaboration with Tim Durant, but the project had been abandoned as being "not suitable for the times." The reason behind the statement was that he had heard about Paulette's flirtation not only with Tim Durant (who had just divorced his wife, the daughter of E. F. Hutton) but with the dashing twenty-five-year-old Earl of Warwick, who was working as an actor in Hollywood under the name of Michael Brooke. When asked about a romance with Paulette, Brooke said without chivalry, "I am backing the field. There is always safety in numbers."

Daniel Selznick took Paulette's side against Chaplin: "Of course Chaplin was a genius, which made up for a lot, but he was so gruff and not terribly charming. . . . I believe that he moved on first—that there were other women while he was with Paulette. And my impression was that she was very proud, and she wouldn't have stood for a second to allow herself to be either replaced by or in competition with some other woman. She just would have walked."

In his autobiography, director Jean Renoir wrote about the breakup of the marriage:

I asked her how Chaplin could have been so mad as to break up their marriage, and she answered that it was not he who had left her but she who had left him. The reason was that he reserved all his comedy for his films. In real life, according to her, he was not at all funny. Then there was the huge house they lived in, a solemn, English-style house, like a tomb, she said, without a single picture in it, the only objets d'art being a collection of figurines in English porcelain enclosed in a glass-fronted showcase. But above all there was the fact that genius is hard to live with. It is very exhausting to stay on the high mental level of an exceptional person. One needs to sink back into good, solid mediocrity in order to get one's breath. . . . [Paulette says she] keeps company only with remarkable men, but she changes them often. [Almost the exact opposite of Remarque's comment about Marlene Dietrich's propensity.]

Psychologically, she probably did walk, but she stayed firmly in Chaplin's house with her mother while she made two of Selznick's movies.

According to David Thomson in his biography of David O. Selznick, *Showman*, Paulette stayed in the house on Summit Drive when, in fact, "by 1937–38, Chaplin had lost interest in Paulette except as a property." And clearly, she went into training for the role of Scarlett, first by charmingly inserting herself into the Selznicks' lives—especially Irene's, who called her sugar and was marginally fond of her, but Daniel Selznick felt that his mother was not taken in: "If she wanted to be somebody's friend, she had the capacity to ingratiate herself so tremendously that I think she could have won almost anybody over. I think that women basically disliked her, but if there was somebody whose friend she wanted to be, she would make a real effort. And whether because of Mother's social position or whatever—you know Paulette obviously wanted to be Irene Selznick's friend, cultivated her, which I think my mother suspected. My mother would get upset over matters of principle, morality, integrity." Selznick makes it clear how his mother might have felt about "the flirty, wicked-eyed neighbor, so full of mischief," as David Thomson describes Paulette.

The Young in Heart, a United Artists film, produced in 1938 by David O. Selznick, with a screenplay by Paul Osborne and Charles Bennett, was considered a first-class comedy. It starred Janet Gaynor, who had recently wrung hearts in the original version of *A Star Is Born*, Douglas Fairbanks, Jr., Paulette Goddard, Roland Young, Billie Burke, Richard Carlson, and

Minnie Dupree, who had played, as a young ingenue, on the stage with Douglas Fairbanks, Sr., at the beginning of the century. Years and years later, she was playing a very old lady, with Douglas Jr. as leading man.

An aside to all this is that during the filming of *The Young in Heart,* Douglas Fairbanks, Jr., was having a major affair with Marlene Dietrich. He also was to be supplanted by Remarque—new to Hollywood—who had just left Europe with the help of Dietrich. And during the years of Remarque's affair with Dietrich, she strayed frequently, which compelled him to do the same, although not quite as wholeheartedly as she did. He found enormous comfort in the arms of Garbo, who was a great friend of Charlie Chaplin's during the time he was married to Paulette. Bringing it full circle, in Remarque's last novel, *Shadows in Paradise,* published posthumously in 1971, the protagonist, Robert Ross, a German exile in New York and Hollywood, decides to see a Paulette Goddard film and asks his friends Greta Garbo and Dolores Del Rio along.

The plot of *The Young in Heart* concerns a larcenous family of actors who learn to go straight through a heartwarming experience. Paulette plays Leslie Saunders, the first in a long line of bland names. She is the new boss of former wastrel Fairbanks. The part is definitely that of a second banana, although her reviews said "amazingly effective" (*New York Times*) and "Paulette Goddard hasn't much acting to do as a clear-eyed girl in love with Fairbanks, but she is an eye-filler and possesses an exciting screen personality" (*Variety*). Actually, she looks a bit frowsy and frayed. It's mainly her hair, which is unbecomingly flat on top and then curls in bunches around her ears. Her figure is chunkier than in later films, and she seems on the ordinary side. However, her voice sounds softer and her demeanor is less brittle than in later work. She doesn't get a chance to shine much in this one. Douglas Fairbanks, Jr., called her "very fine looking. Beautiful may be an exaggeration. . . . She wasn't a great star at all. . . . She was a very accomplished, attractive leading lady. . . . Chemistry? No. It was professional. Very good-natured. Vital. Energetic. Conscientious about work. That's about all."

Daniel Selznick remembered her later, in the forties, as a giant star:

In the period of the forties—when she made *Kitty*—she was a big star. The trailers said it all. They said, WAIT UNTIL YOU SEE PAULETTE GODDARD! They let you know what the audience's relationship was to the movie that was going to be coming out. That was her Paramount period and she was a big star. Absolutely. I mean a tremendously big star. She had the kind of spirit and gumption and vitality that I don't think anybody else had. What these qualities really conveyed was a real intelligence. All that animation and energy really had to do with how bright her mind was, how quickly she observed things, how quickly her mind turned over. Goddard and Lombard were two of a kind, I think. Absolutely bright and absolutely desirable.

By 1937, Selznick was casting *Gone With the Wind* in conjunction with the filming of Paulette's first two pictures for him, the second being *Dramatic School*, in which she was on loan to MGM, and which was also released in 1938. She was making an effort to keep her private and professional demeanor in check and be less like Cleopatra and Lola Montez (to whom she had been compared by Jock Whitney). Luise Rainer, a back-to-back Academy Award winner for best actress in *The Good Earth* and *The Great Ziegfeld*, was the star of *Dramatic School*. She was a slim young Austrian actress with enormous dark eyes and delicate, rather haughty features. She was not as glamorous as Paulette, but she looked high-born, sheltered, and high-strung. Paulette, though on the small side and slender, seemed rough in comparison. Although the two women were deliberately indifferent toward each other, animosity lurked.

Rainer, the star, wore a long camel's-hair coat to the set. Paulette, in the supporting role, arrived each day in sable. Finally Rainer commented on their different styles. "Yes," said Paulette, "I like a short coat and you like a long one."

"I always thought she was very beautiful," says Rainer, "and she didn't particularly interest me. She seemed very secure, and she had a terrific zest for learning. She tried to make up for something—her background, maybe. But it was as though she had a fever to grasp what was not given to her in her early home life."

Two other beauties were in the cast of *Dramatic School*—sixteen-year-old Lana Turner, who called Paulette "Butch" and whom Paulette called "Schwabby," in reference to the legendary discovery of her while she was sitting on a stool at Schwab's Drugstore. And there was Virginia Grey, who had a very different memory of the usually assured Paulette: "I watched her do a scene with a group of girls. She seemed the most confident of the lot. But afterwards, when she picked up a comb, her fingers were trembling."

About 1941, while in Hollywood, Erich Maria Remarque discovered his attraction to his fellow émigré, and they proceeded to have a brief but intense affair. "The person I knew very well was Remarque"; Rainer speaks softly, as many women do when recalling Remarque. "He had a little bit of a crush on me after Dietrich, and we saw each other quite a bit, and he was disturbed when I married my husband. He called me at five in the morning and said, 'What do you want to do with that bookseller?' [Her husband was the publisher Robert Knittel.] I liked him immensely. I thought that Erich, except for the drinking he did at the time, was a gift to women. He was intelligent, he was well educated, he had a marvelous sense of humor, and he was not arrogant in spite of the many qualities that could have made him arrogant. He was quite simple."

Her voice hardens when she talks about Paulette, whom she became reacquainted with after she and Remarque had married. "Paulette once told me that when she married Remarque she thought she was going to get a terrifically exciting man. But actually, she discovered that he was too simple—not simple-minded—but not that kind of exciting man that she had pictured when she first met him."

Who would play Scarlett O'Hara was the big question in Hollywood in 1938. It was the most sought-after role in film up to that point. The tension surrounding it was dramatically increased by the fact that every other aspect of the production had already been decided upon. George Cukor, known as the Women's Director, was set to direct the Greatest Woman's Role Ever. Sidney Howard would write the screenplay, adapted from Margaret Mitchell's novel. Metro-Goldwyn-Mayer would distribute, after waging a neck-and-neck competition with Warner Brothers. If Warner's had won, the whole topography might have changed, with two of their contract players in the leads. Errol Flynn would have been a much less expensive Rhett at $50,000 than Clark Gable at $150,000, and Bette Davis would have been a darker and perhaps funnier Scarlett. Olivia de Havilland, who was with Warner's and was loaned out, was the first choice for Melanie either way. But Gable wasn't called the King for nothing, and Jock (John Hay) Whitney, Selznick's emotional and financial consort, made the official announcement that his king had crowned another king: "It has been obvious from the day Mr. Selznick bought *Gone With the Wind* that the public has felt an enormous concern in the bringing of this great book to the screen. As a company, we have been through a trying and difficult time involving unusual delay in order to satisfy this genuine interest. Mr. Selznick has felt all along that Clark Gable was the one and only 'people's choice' to play the role of Rhett Butler, and only through an arrangement with Metro-Goldwyn-Mayer, to whom he is exclusively under contract, would he have been able to make *Gone With the Wind* as the world wants to see it."

Paulette didn't mind the competition for the role of Scarlett; in fact, she relished it. She had competed for *The Young in Heart* against actresses Margaret Lindsay, Pat Patterson, Dorothy Hyson, and ravishing young Vivien Leigh. She knew that Selznick had wanted Leigh for that film but didn't feel she was quite right for the rather ordinary love interest, and wanted to save her for something more captivating. So Paulette had won the first round, and was confident going into the second one. Besides, being a Jewish Scarlett could add a certain dimension to the role. Paulette didn't talk about the fact that she was half-Jewish, but she didn't deny it either. She would rather not have discussed it, but if pressed, she would admit to it. Chaplin had instilled in her the spirit of the liberal free-thinker and speaker, fighting against demagoguery. Although Selznick, Cukor, the Warner brothers, Goldwyn, and Mayer were the monarchs of the movies, the political and social climate in 1938 did not embrace Jewish movie stars.

"I mean, God knows, there were many, many beautiful Jewish women, but she didn't seem Jewish, in any way, shape, or form," Daniel Selznick contemplates. "And yet, when you think back on it, you realize maybe there was something about the energy, the drive, and the charm that was Jewish."

Two years later, during the time Chaplin was being accused of Communist sympathies, she was to appear as Hannah, "the Jewish ghetto washerwoman," in Chaplin's *The Great Dictator*, his talking parable of Hitler's Reich. Her role was described as "a symbol of downtrodden humanity in the chaos of war." In 1938, however, a Jewish Scarlett was not to be.

Katharine Hepburn postponed her opening of *The Philadelphia Story* because she wanted to play Scarlett so much. Bette Davis, flushed with her successes—and Oscar—for playing the southern schemer in *Jezebel*, felt that she was the only possible Scarlett. Jean Arthur, Loretta Young, Ann Sheridan, Joan Bennett, Priscilla Lane, Frances Dee, Tallulah Bankhead, Lana Turner, Doris Jordan (later Doris Davenport, opposite Gary Cooper in *The Westerner*, 1940), Jane Bryan, Margaret Tallichet, and Edythe Marrener (later to become Susan Hayward) were other contenders. In his frustrated and blunt confidential memo of October 21, 1938, to George Cukor and Daniel T. O'Shea and Henry Ginsberg, David O. Selznick rails against casting a well-known actress and throws Paulette an extremely left-handed compliment:

> I am still hoping against hope for that new girl. . . . If we finally wind up with any of the stars that we are testing we must regard ourselves as absolute failures at digging up talent; as going against the most violently expressed wish for a new personality in an important role in the history of the

Paulette with Sylvia Ashley Fairbanks (who would later be a girlfriend of Remarque's) and Douglas Fairbanks, Sr.

Paulette and Chaplin in The Great Dictator, *their second and last movie together, 1940.*

American stage or screen; as wasting the opportunity to create a new star; as actually hurting the drawing power of the picture by having a star instead of a new girl, in whom there would be infinitely more interest in this particular picture; and as actually, in my opinion, hurting the quality of the picture itself by having a girl who has an audience's dislike to beat down, as in the case of Hepburn, or identification with other roles to overcome, as in the case of Jean Arthur. (Paulette Goddard also has plenty against her in the way of the public's attitude, but I think that when it comes time for the final decision she at least has in her favor that she is not stale. For this reason, I think George ought to devote particular attention to the dramatic sections of the Goddard test.)

After saying for years that she really had nothing to tell the press until she had done something, or had something to show for herself, after *Modern Times* Paulette made up for lost time. Her revelations and contradictions were distasteful to the public, which was what Selznick pointed out. An example of the way she was doing herself wrong was the magazine headline SHE REFUSES TO BE MRS. CHAPLIN for an article that quoted her as saying, "The contract I had with Selznick called for me to remain single. I thought the clause was a good idea. All leading ladies should be single, shouldn't they?" She was ahead of her time in her irreverence. But the article pointed out, "Whether or not she thinks failing to admit her legal marriage is good publicity, Paulette should know a bit about opinion in that great part of the United States which is not Hollywood. There marriage is something to cherish, not to hide nor use for sweet publicity's sake."

Ultimately, Paulette's detractors and supporters were equally confused. No one knew what to think of her. "On the other hand," says the same article, "there is something admirable in the fact that she has not depended as an actress on the influence of Chaplin. . . . Thus her refusal to acknowledge herself as Mrs. Chaplin is silly and stupid, and at the same time, highly laudable."

It was said that Selznick needed to see a marriage certificate before he could grant Paulette the role, or that the real problem was whether Chaplin would release Paulette from a contract—if in fact they had a written contract—or that Chaplin would begin his next film and be able to legally recall her no matter where she was in the filming of *Gone With the Wind*.

Selznick scheduled three screen tests for Paulette, playing opposite Jeffrey Lynn as Ashley; they were coached by Constance Collier and directed by George Cukor. She had requested that one test be with a Rhett, suggested

Alan Marshall, who had been her co-star in *Dramatic School*, and was turned down—even though Marshall was Selznick's second choice for Rhett.

"Dear Mama," she wrote to Alta, again in New York for a visit with the relatives. "No Rhett, no sizzle. Hope the screen test doesn't fizzle."

Selznick's memos show that he was increasingly partial toward Paulette, impressed with her screen tests, and attempting to keep a negative publicist, Russell Birdwell, at bay. If Paulette had a concrete and powerful enemy at this time, it was Birdwell, who gave Selznick regular predictions of doom if she were to be cast: "It will throw us under the shadow of such a resentful press that all of our good public relations work of the past will be completely dissipated. I have never known a woman, intent on a career dependent upon her popularity with [the] masses, to hold and live such an insane and absurd attitude toward the press and her fellow man as does Paulette Goddard."

Selznick seemed able to withstand the fear of impropriety surrounding Paulette and Chaplin. Chaplin's contractual rights to Paulette were more on his mind, as he indicated in a particular memo of October 21, 1938, to George Cukor and Dan O'Shea:

> I have looked at the new Goddard test—the one she made with Jeffrey Lynn—practically daily since it arrived, to see whether my first impression of the great improvement in her remained; and I must say that each time I see it I am more and more impressed. As much work as possible should be done with her. Incidentally, the point in her contract about which I have written you, concerning Chaplin's rights, should be straightened out immediately if it needs straightening out. It might be wise for you to make clear to Goddard that unless this point is straightened out . . . and unless we get a further extension of the contract to a full seven years, she is not going to play Scarlett.

During the testing and the waiting, Paulette, who as Chaplin described her, was "a creature of whims," decided that she wanted to return to the stage—real acting instead of posing and dancing. She had gotten fired up by Paul Osborne, the playwright who had written the screenplay for *The Young in Heart* and had encouraged her to try summer stock and to get in shape with a wonderful coach named Paul Stevenson. Since Chaplin and she were emotionally estranged, activity with publicity was the key. It was announced that she would star in *Accent on Youth* at the Cape Playhouse in Dennis, Massachusetts, in the summer of 1938. She had ignored or forgotten about

Paulette and Chaplin making a glamorous public appearence.

publicity commitments for her new releases under her Selznick contract. This could have been the reason why Selznick paid $1,000 to buy her out of the stock contract, or it could have been that he wanted all of his possible Scarletts to stay in a row.

Paulette reported the incident to Alta: "Fiddle-de-sticks," she wrote. Michael Hall, a former actor, was very close to Paulette and remembers her reaction. He had met her while she was filming *Sins of Jezebel*, where she played a bargain-basement version of Scarlett, Egyptian style. Hall had once asked his friend George Cukor about it, and Cukor had said, "As far as I'm concerned, I think Paulette has the part." Hall felt Paulette was not so sure.

"You know what those bastards did to me?" she railed. "They called my agent and told him to tell me that I had the part, and that if I wanted to sign the contract, I had to bring Charlie's and my marriage license to Selznick's office to prove that I was married to Charlie. Can you imagine playing with me like that? That was the way they got—those goddamned bastards! They were trying to fool me into thinking that that's why I didn't get the part, because I wasn't married to Charlie. Well, I showed them! Charlie and I got on a boat for China with Alta—practically the next day we took a boat. We went to China and I married Charlie on the boat. The captain of the ship married us." (In fact, the three of them took the trip to China in 1936, two years earlier.)

In 1937, Hall had met the costume designer of *Gone With the Wind*, William Menzies, in London. Menzies said he was desperate. The production was set to begin in a couple of weeks. He had to make at least four or five major dresses for Scarlett. He went to Selznick's office to plead his case. He had to know who was playing the part before he could start delivering costumes that were due. It made him look bad. Henry Ginsberg and Jock Whitney were in the office with Selznick. Menzies asked, "Well, is it Paulette?" And they decided right there. They all agreed. Yes, it was Paulette. Scarlett would be played by Paulette Goddard. All right, fine. The designer left the office and told his staff to begin making dresses for Goddard's measurements and to book her for a series of fittings. A week or so later, he heard that Scarlett would be played by Vivien Leigh.

Hall lamented: "I never told Paulette that she had the part, because it would have been too devastating for her to know that. Because she was so headstrong and she often made these decisions all on her own—with an often misguided sense of spirit—and I knew that would just kill her, that she had lost, because of her own ego and will—lost probably the greatest female part in movies of all time."

No one actually testified to seeing a memo describing the near-spiritual experience of finding Vivien Leigh, but there is an excerpt from a 1941 article written by Selznick titled "Discovering the New Ones": "Before my brother, Myron, Hollywood's leading agent, brought Laurence Olivier and Miss Leigh over to the set to see the shooting of the Burning of Atlanta, I had never seen her. When he introduced me to her, the flames were lighting up her face and Myron said: 'I want you to meet Scarlett O'Hara.' I took one look and knew that she was right—at least as far as appearance went. Later on, her tests, made under George Cukor's brilliant direction, showed that she could act the part right down to the ground, but I'll never recover from that first look."

Judging from this, Myron seems to have had a conflict of interest. However, the agent was in a difficult position since Olivier was also his client, and a bigger one than Paulette. Olivier had asked Myron to do something for the then-unknown Vivien Leigh—to at least get her an introduction to Selznick. Whatever feelings of hurt or betrayal Paulette had were camouflaged under bravado mixed with umbrage, and her story about how it happened is quite different: "Charlie wouldn't release me from his contract to do the part. And I'd been tested and my costumes were made and Vivien Leigh came to my house for tennis with Olivier on Sunday and the Selznicks were there from across the street, and David saw her and that was it. And the night before, Charlie and I had met with David, and I was crying, sitting on the floor and sobbing because Charlie said, 'It'll take you a year longer if you use Paulette. She wants to go to parties, she wants to go out, she wants to have a good time, and she's not serious, so I won't release her.'"

If Paulette's version is to be taken seriously, it is a wonder that she was able to work "under" Chaplin on *The Great Dictator*.

When *Gone With the Wind* was completed, Paulette requested that the movie be screened for her, as she would be out of town and would miss the premiere. Her request was refused, even though there were screenings for various VIPs.

In 1940 Paulette starred in an antiwar plea filmed for United Artists at Goldwyn Studios. *Bundles for Britain*, as it was called, also starred Douglas Fairbanks, Jr., Merle Oberon, Laurence Olivier, and Vivien Leigh. Making the picture was very much the right thing to do. She got along perfectly well with Leigh, against whom she competed a bit later, to win the role of the half-breed Louvette Corbeau in the Cecil B. DeMille extravaganza *Northwest Mounted Police* (1940). Much later, in the sixties, when Paulette met

Leigh in London at a party for Constance Collier, she wrote to her mother that Leigh's face looked like that of a "disappointed pansy."

Oddly, in 1944, after Paulette's marriage to Chaplin was long over, and Carole Lombard had been killed in a plane crash, Clark Gable turned romantic attention toward Paulette—enough to propose to her. Paulette politely refused. She always hinted that she was sorry, but felt that the timing was off. It was too soon for either of them to marry again. "We have one tomorrow: Ourselves" was one of Paulette's most frequent expressions.

In 1939, Selznick again loaned Paulette out to another studio, this time MGM. The picture was *The Women*, to be directed by George Cukor, who had been out of a job since Clark Gable had had him fired as a "faggot" from *Gone With the Wind*. In *The Women*—based on Clare Boothe Luce's Broadway hit and adapted for film by Paulette's buddy Anita Loos—catty rivalry reigned; sisterhood was anathema, off camera and on. No man ever entered the picture, which was full of divas such as Norma Shearer, Rosalind Russell, and Joan Crawford. Paulette played Miriam Aarons, a fierce character with an undeniably Jewish name but no other ethnic references. Paulette's memorable Miriam was a "predatory chorus girl and home-wrecker."

The secret of the success of *The Women* was that the actresses enjoyed their feline nastiness to the hilt. Paulette remarked that Russell was so good because, in fact, she was "just a nasty bitch." She had never been particularly interested in Norma Shearer as an actress, but thought she was credible in *The Women* because "she had all of her close-ups redone ten times. Her husband owned the studio—Thalberg, you know. And they'd cut everyone else out of the scene." She and Joan Crawford—who some of the others felt was the most venomous of all—became friends while making the picture. The two were not dissimilar in their unmasked aggressive intelligence and deep-seated need to climb.

In *The Women* it was the truly realistic fight scene with Russell that catapulted Paulette into a star position, leaving others in the cast, such as Mary Boland, Virginia Weidler, and Aileen Pringle, behind. The only other two-fisted women's brawl to rival Roz and Paulette's was what Steven Bach has termed "the champion catfight of all film history," and is between Marlene Dietrich and Una Merkel in Joseph Pasternak's *Destry Rides Again*. A nod to the ironies: Paulette's social position and increasing box-office popularity made her more desirable at that moment than Dietrich, whose Svengali-Trilby pairing with director Josef von Sternberg was beginning to pall on Hollywood; they had not had a hit since *Shanghai Express* (1932)—both *The*

Scarlet Empress (1934) and *The Devil Is a Woman* (1935) did not go over well at all. As a result, when Pasternak thought of who could play the very American role of Frenchy (formerly called Angel), the saloon manager and "chantootsie," Paulette Goddard was at the top of his wish list. She was sent the script to consider, and was inclined to do it, when Chaplin finally came up with a shooting schedule for his long-awaited talkie, *The Great Dictator*, starring himself as half-Hitler, half-barber, and Paulette as Hannah the washerwoman. Still indentured to her husband for this one picture, she had no choice but to turn down Angel in *Destry Rides Again*. Her future nemesis Dietrich took it. Dietrich's career was reinvented through this role. But she almost didn't take it, and needed some serious convincing and cajoling. This was done by her lover at the time, Erich Maria Remarque, who, because he had known the screenwriter, Felix Jackson, back in Berlin when he had been Felix Joachimssohn, was sent the script to read after it had been turned down by Paulette. Remarque was to be the conduit for Dietrich. But in 1941, Paulette got to play Frenchy in the radio version.

Dietrich's comeback outdistanced the mark Paulette made in *The Great Dictator*, which balanced things out, placing them neck and neck in their careers and a lot more. Not only did they both play baseball for charity, but they were captains of opposing teams. Dietrich led the Leading Men while Paulette was at the helm of the Comedians. They also took some of the same lovers—although their techniques and appeals differed sharply. While Paulette had what William Saroyan coined as "more fun appeal than sex appeal," Dietrich was dry ice, simultaneously steamy and frosty. Paulette admired men and listened to them. Dietrich basked in their desire for her while often scorning them at the same time. Paulette, although younger than Dietrich, seemed to get her elder's discards when it came to men. Dietrich found Bruce Cabot "stupid" and John Wayne grossly undereducated, where-as Paulette seemed to think they were just fine. Paulette inherited Remarque much later, but was certainly aware at the time of Dietrich's throwing him over for the French actor Jean Gabin. Remarque never got over the humiliation, mentioning it in his diaries throughout his life.

Whereas Paulette had a lusty appetite for sex, Dietrich was certainly reserved, if not dubious, about the act. Maria Riva tells the story of her mother's conversation with Remarque following their first real moment of excitement. It was in June of 1937 at the Lido in Venice. She was having lunch with Josef von Sternberg when Remarque came up to their table and introduced himself. Von Sternberg was soon forgotten and he quietly left. They talked into the night. Remarque finally looked at her and said, "I must tell you—I am impotent." Her response was "Oh, how wonderful!" and then to Riva in recounting the moment: "You know how I hate to do 'it'—I was so happy! It meant we could just talk and sleep, love each other, all nice and cozy!"

It was common knowledge that Dietrich was bisexual; in fact, Ruth Albu felt that it was only women from whom she got genuine sexual satisfaction. One of the many women she was supposed to have desired was Claudette Colbert, whom Paulette disliked intensely. While Dietrich did not bother to hide her erotic feelings toward women, there was little mention of anything bisexual about Paulette. But in 1940, when at the urging of Aldous Huxley as well as through the influence of the late George Gershwin, Paulette took her first trip to Mexico, she fell completely under the spell of the celebrated couple Diego Rivera and Frida Kahlo, and with Kahlo, it is thought, fell under a sexual spell as well. The *Hollywood Reporter*, in discussing a contemporary film project about Kahlo, suggests the same: "Kahlo's volatile 24-year marriage with Rivera is also ripe with dramatic possibilities, each having several affairs, with Kahlo's involving Russian revolutionary Leon Trotsky, Japanese sculptor Noguchi and several women, reportedly actress Paulette Goddard among them."

In her biography of Kahlo, Hayden Herrera has presented what she thinks the Rivera-Kahlo-Goddard triangle was:

> When the divorce proceedings were initiated, there was a rumor that Rivera was planning to marry the pretty Hungarian painter Irene Bohus; but though she became one of his assistants after the decree was final, and though Frida was certainly jealous of her, eventually the two women became . . . close friends. . . . Perhaps there was a triangle: a photograph (published in October 1939) showed Bohus and Diego in Rivera's San Angel studio; both artists are painting the famous American movie star Paulette Goddard. Rivera is widely believed to have been romantically involved with Paulette Goddard, who had taken up residence at the luxurious San Angel Inn, just across the street from Rivera's studio. The press made much of this affair, and so did Diego. But though Frida was displeased by Rivera's infatuation, she and Paulette, too, became friends, and in 1941 Frida painted *The Flower Basket*, a charming still life tondo for her ex-rival.

According to one source, Paulette delicately referred to lesbians as being "double-gaited." According to another, her reference was somewhat rougher. "That old dyke" was the way she spoke of Dietrich. The two women closest to her were Anita Loos and Constance Collier, both lesbians. Though involvements have been suggested between Paulette and Frida Kahlo as well as Mrs. Jack (Ann) Warner, who was reputed to have been one of Dietrich's lovers, it could have been just Hollywood talk.

If put to the test of what would be necessary for survival on a desert island, Paulette probably would have opted for a man and jewelry, whereas Dietrich's choice might have been more domestic and magnanimous: a stove, a man, and a woman. Dietrich loved to cook, but Paulette loathed it; and while Paulette revered jewels, Dietrich took only mild pleasure in them. Dietrich was, however, extremely preoccupied with beautifully cut clothes in the most luxurious fabrics. Remarque's diary entries are full of shopping with Dietrich, attending Dietrich's fittings, or shopping for Dietrich. Although she did have a substantial amount of jewelry, Remarque felt it didn't add up to more than bits and pieces, that there was nothing outstanding in the whole lot. He had a suggestion: she should round up a good deal of it and have the mass turned into one fabulous bracelet. She demurred.

"Marlene," he coaxed. "What if I paid for the transformation?"

"You mean, it's a gift?" she asked.

"Yes. In a manner of speaking."

"Then why not just buy me a marvelous new piece of jewelry?"

Perhaps she took Paulette's lesson to heart. It didn't work, however. Remarque stuck to his original offer, and she accepted, compiling her odds and ends into a celebrated and startling piece that became a topic of much gossip.

By 1939, Paulette had been exposed to an elitist insiders' world for long enough to be considered a part of it. She had been assimilated into Chaplin's household, his family, and his work. His friends had become her friends: John and Elaine Steinbeck, Robinson Jeffers and his wife, and the Arthur Rubinsteins. Jean Cocteau found her scintillating and suggested that she play Madame Du Barry in a film. "I can smell her French blood," he said, even though she had none. Howard Hughes wanted to do all kinds of business with her. H. G. Wells, at eighty, felt rejuvenated by her, and was about to insinuate himself into her personal life more than was wanted. Having been a house guest of Paulette and Chaplin's, he acted as an authority on their marital status and wrote about it in his memoirs:

I had an amusing time at Santa Monica with Paulette Goddard, with whom I discussed and negotiated a divorce from Charlie Chaplin. They had never been married before his film of *The Great Dictator* was released in New York. But they had discovered that living out of wedlock is extremely inconvenient in America, because, since divorce is so easy there, there is no excuse for unsanctioned cohabitation. Divorced people however are perfectly respectable. Accordingly, having arrived at a practical equality of income, so that there was no monetary squabble possible, and having long since discovered each other's intolerable side, they decided to divorce. In order to do so, they had to marry. They came before the screen at the first night of their last film together (*The Great Dictator*) and Charlie made a brief speech thanking all that vast audience for honoring "me and my wife Paulette Goddard" by attending his modest show. By the laws of the State of New York, that was a common-law marriage, and all that remained was to induce Paulette not to see interviewers about their subsequent divorce.

A low blow from an old friend, Paulette felt over forty years later, when in 1984 Little, Brown finally sought to publish the memoirs after there had been a long staying order dictated by Wells's will. Paulette's position, according to her lawyer and executor, Richard Kay, was "that the statements made in the paragraph do not accurately reflect the facts and, on her behalf, I wish to request that the paragraph be eliminated in its entirety." Subsequently, Richard Kay assured Paulette that he had been told that the offending statement had been removed.

The idea for *The Great Dictator* came during a particularly difficult period—personally and professionally—for Chaplin. Not only had his relationship with Paulette come apart and he had no film he wanted to make, but he was troubled by the rise of Hitler. "How could I throw myself into feminine whimsy or think of romance or the problems of love when madness was being stirred up by a hideous, grotesque Adolf Hitler?" Chaplin wrote in his autobiography. Chaplin's good friend the director Alexander Korda suggested that he film a story about Hitler and a double—direct opposites with the same face and mustache—Adolf at the height of his twisted powers and the tramp as a downtrodden Jewish barber. "I could play both characters," Chaplin recalled of Korda's inspiration. "It suddenly struck me. Of course! As Hitler I could harangue the crowds in jargon and talk all I wanted to. And as the tramp I could remain more or less silent. A Hitler story was an opportunity for burlesque and pantomime."

Though a good idea at its inception, it didn't really work by the time the picture was in production. Chaplin had thought it would be an important

tonic that people laugh at Hitler, the clown dictator, who was too prepos-
terous to be taken seriously; he felt that the real danger was in giving him
credibility.

"Had I known of the actual horrors of the German concentration camps,
I could not have made *The Great Dictator*; I could not have made fun of the
homicidal insanity of the Nazis," Chaplin lamented.

After Paulette and Chaplin's estrangement, and Chaplin's endless golf
games with Tim Durant in Pebble Beach, and weekends at John and Elaine
Steinbeck's in Monterey, he moved back into the house with Paulette and
Alta during the filming of *The Great Dictator*. He moved back to a Paulette
who was bored, restless, and angry with him, but who had become a success
in Hollywood. It had become clear to Paulette that Selznick was never going
to make her a star, and Selznick was tired of her demands when Paramount
gladly picked her up and signed her to a seven-year contract with options
that would bring her a salary of $5,000 a week. It was serious money for the
time; however, Paramount was producing rather fluffy fare—college-
campus musicals and arch comedies striving to be worldly. The leading
ladies were attractive but fell short of the necessary star wattage. About the
time Paulette was signed to "boost the ratings," actresses like Ann Sheridan
and Ida Lupino had already departed, and Mary Carlisle, Frances Farmer,
Marsha Hunt, Gail Patrick, and Shirley Ross were waiting for their moment.
After a modest first assignment for Lux Radio Theatre of *Front Page Woman*,
co-starring Fred MacMurray, and directed by Cecil B. DeMille, Paulette was
put by Paramount at the helm of their first-class pictures. *The Cat and the
Canary* was a comedy–ghost story that co-starred Bob Hope. They were a
droller, sexier, and older Mickey and Judy team; their interplay was charismatic and funny, translating into a box-office bonanza. They were the *It* couple at Paramount.

There were many father figures in Paulette's life. She had not heard from
her own father, Joseph Levy, since childhood. However, he got in touch
again when she married Chaplin, the good father who made her a star. She
developed a theory: "Nobody in Hollywood ever had a father." She cited
Ginger Rogers, Rosalind Russell, and Garbo, though she thought that
Marilyn Monroe and Dietrich had fathers "in the background." "Even the
men worshiped their mothers. They never had a father. Well, Clark Gable
had a father and it showed. But that's it."

Joseph Levy resurfaced in the late thirties in an attempt to claim a portion
of Paulette's fame. "I never saw my father until after I married Charlie. . . .

He'd stand up when we'd go into a premiere and say, 'My baby, my baby!' That was my father. And then he sued me."

The trouble began in September of 1938, when an interview with Paulette, written by Kyle Crichton and titled "The Perils of Paulette," ran in *Collier's* magazine. The article was full of deliberate evasion and misinformation on the part of Paulette. With Paulette's tendency to re-create herself, she said that Levy was her stepfather and that she was the daughter of J. R. Goddard. In a psychologically interesting way, she had combined her father's first initials with Uncle Charlie's last name. Levy—spelled Levee in some instances—had been working out of Syracuse as a salesman for Warner Brothers. After reading the article he retained a lawyer named Charles Schwartz, claiming that his mental and physical condition as a result of the article had lost him his job. His initial price for restitution was $150,000, steep for a job that paid $150 a week. Shocked and dismayed, but in an effort to placate him into settling out of court, Paulette decided to pay him $75 a week. This amount did not sit well with Levy, who then increased his suit to include $600 a month for personal support. His statement was that he should not "be required to lower his previous standard of living merely because Miss Goddard was unwilling to provide him with the means."

At first Paulette refused to go to court and tried to dodge the publicity attached to the case, but then, in a turnaround, she filed her defense with Louella Parsons, whose column in the *Los Angeles Examiner* was read as gospel by many: "I've never known my father. He left my mother when I was a very small child and never contributed to my support. Mother took care of me until I was fourteen, when I went out and started earning a living for both of us. I pay him $75 a week, which should be adequate."

"Paulette has the sympathy of Hollywood," decreed Parsons.

Eventually, Paulette won the case and ceased any payments to her father. In a pathetic attempt at retaliation, upon his death in 1954 Joseph R. Levy left one dollar to his daughter in his will.

Paulette recalled how, during the filming of *The Great Dictator*—as with *Modern Times*—Chaplin was both paternal and perfectionist. "He always made sure that I was not only in the light, but the right light—the best light. He didn't use close-ups. They weren't loving. . . . Charlie would shoot like we were on a proscenium. And just throw the light. And I'll tell you, the greatest comedy lighting in the world is the bright light. Just get out there in the bright light. It cleans everybody out. They don't look fat, they don't look dirty. They look clean and lovely and that's comedy lighting."

Although their working relationship was as passionate and as intimate as any affair, Paulette and Chaplin were no longer lovers. "It was inevitable that Paulette and I should separate," Chaplin wrote in his autobiography. "We both knew long before *The Dictator* was started." But as in many long-term relationships, they were loath to admit it. Paulette, recovering from the ordeal with her father, seemed to stall, certainly until she was sure that Chaplin was involved elsewhere—which she was soon to find out. In June 1943, there was a paternity suit filed by the starlet Joan Barry, and at the same time Chaplin was falling in love with Eugene O'Neill's seventeen-year-old daughter Oona. Paulette deliberately ignored these situations.

During the final few years of her marriage, she was extremely busy living out her fantasy of becoming a top star. She was reteamed with Bob Hope in Paramount's sequel to *The Cat and the Canary*. This one was called *The Ghost Breakers* (1940). Paulette plays Mary Carter, a singer who inherits a spooky castle on Black Island off the coast of Cuba. Hope, who gets top billing, plays a radio commentator who is wanted for a murder he didn't commit.

The whole production shows more expertise than the first film. Again, it was produced by Arthur Hornblow, Jr., but this time the clothes were by the great costume designer Edith Head, the director was George Marshall, whom Paulette's frequent co-star Macdonald Carey remembers as being "a great director for staging business," and the screenplay was written by Walter DeLeon, based on a play by Paul Dickey and Charles W. Goddard— not Paulette's uncle Charlie!

Paulette doesn't look quite as radiant as she did in *The Cat and the Canary*. Strangely, her face resembles the young Bette Davis's in *Of Human Bondage*—it's a little sharp at certain angles. Paulette was now thirty and her figure was at its sleekest, and in fact 1940 was the year that the illustrator Jefferson Machamer and a jury of artist colleagues voted Paulette as having the world's most beautiful body. That might have been one reason Paulette was always doing bathtub scenes: "Every film I ever made had a bathtub scene. And you always wore the little bikini underneath the water, even in the DeMille pictures, and the hair piled up, and the arms out and free, and it made it look very suggestive."

Paulette and Hope were never more appealing than in *The Ghost Breakers*. They do a mean rumba that started a fad. Hope is actually romantic; Paulette is funny, sparky, and natural. The trick photography and animation for the ghost sequences is superb. A baby-thug-faced Anthony Quinn appears as Ramon Maderis, with a twin, and both attempt simultaneously to romance

Paulette, who has eyes only for Hope. Of all her screen lovers, Hope was the one with whom she had the most chemistry.

"Part airplane" was the way Paulette described Howard Hughes, with whom, during the waning days of life with Chaplin, she played a lot of golf. There were always two or three of what she called his "henchmen" around, whom she liked better than Hughes. She would talk to them during the game and then go off for a beer with them afterward. It would seem that Hughes had more use for Paulette than she did for him. "Howard proved disappointing. But his ego was great. . . . He wouldn't talk to anybody but beautiful women. He had a couple of aides who would procure for him."

Paulette knew about many of the women who either had slept, were sleeping, or wanted to sleep with Hughes in the hope that he would propose, which he had a habit of doing. Even though Paulette was sleeping with him, she wasn't impressed, had no designs on a future with him, and pitied the actresses who did. "He absolutely proposed to everyone. He knocked them all off. Hedy Lamarr, Jean Peters, Katharine Hepburn, Norma Shearer. . . . Norma said to me, 'I'm going to marry Howard. You mustn't tell him.' She wanted me to know right away because I was going with him—but it wasn't anything romantic, yet. . . . Howard always fell in love with the same girl. Jean Peters was a composite of all of them put together. He even went with Hepburn for three years and gave her a set of golf balls at the end of it. She was really happy with them. She ruined it for everybody. And then there was Olivia de Havilland. I mean, big, heavy romances. And they never knew where he lived."

When he wanted to have a private conversation, he would have it only in his car. He never had a phone, and could not be found unless he chose to appear. Paulette was one of the few women he could depend upon to respect and protect his eccentricities—after all, she did it with Chaplin. She was there for him in her own irreverent way.

He was always the same. More than Lindbergh, he actually *was* an airplane. He lived for that, dressed for that. . . . Then, the only people who knew what he was like were the ones that were associated with him. If he wanted to talk to you, you'd have to drive around in some lousy little car that nobody would recognize. An absolutely unique character. . . . He wished to live and have sex. . . . He had so much. That's what knocked him out. He was really mad. He'd have five or six girls a day. But it was kind of chaste because he only did it one way. That's one person who never kissed anybody on the lips. . . . I know because he went through the whole town and they'd come crying to me. I don't think he ever had it straight.

Once, inadvertently, they were almost partners in crime. The story that Paulette tells captures the skewed essence of having something as simple as a dinner with Hughes:

I had a very bad thing with him. He was deaf, I mean extremely, and we were sitting in Palm Springs and he wanted to tell me something, so he wrote it down. You could hardly believe this with such a smart fellow. He wrote it down on a piece of paper and I read it and tore it up. So then I wrote my answer and he tore it up, and then he wrote me something else. We were having a lovely dinner. Chicken with hot biscuits, his favorite. And when I'd torn the notes, I threw them in the ashtray. I didn't feel like a spy or anything.

I was married to Charlie at the time, and the District Attorney called my house and asked for him. Then Charlie came in to me and said, "The District Attorney wants to see you on a very private matter at the Ambassador Hotel." . . . So, I went to the hotel and they produced a man. A young man, looking very European. And they said, "Have you ever seen this man before?" I said, "No, I never have." I was scared to death. I mean, the District Attorney was my friend. I couldn't imagine! . . . He said, "Well, this man is trying to blackmail Howard Hughes for $100,000 and says you're in on it." . . . I said, "He does? Well, what is the evidence?" So they brought this piece of paper, the note that I had written to Howard, and he'd pasted it together. . . . And I said, "Well, of course I wrote that note and I tore it up and put it in the ashtray." So they said, "We just have to run this guy out of town. We'll have to ask Howard Hughes for $100 to run him out of town." Turned out it was the waiter in the restaurant.

I'd never played the spy game. Before or since. But it's such a stupid thing, because we weren't having a romance. I was sitting there having supper. Chicken and biscuits. In Palm Springs. And we were talking through those damn notes. Well, then Howard and I became very close . . .

Women were madly in love with him because of all that money. Of course. What else? . . . And he was very attractive. Because he was so peculiar. But I must say that what he got out of his money was to have it all his own way and he overdid it and he kind of wore out early.

The Great Dictator began filming on September 9, 1939. By the time it wrapped, in March 1940, it had cost over $2 million. Chaplin wrote in his autobiography about the picture's whopping cost: "*The Great Dictator* was difficult to make; it involved miniature models and props, which took a year's preparation. Without these devices it would have cost five times as much. However, I had spent $500,000 before I began turning the camera." It opened October 15 of that year at the Astor and Capitol theaters in New York, and met with near jeers. The public didn't want a serious Chaplin film. They found it too long, redundant, and pious. They resented being force-fed propaganda at the end when Chaplin as Hitler makes a humanist speech for brotherhood. A good portion of the reviews mirrored the audience: "She [Paulette], and the star, too, could do with a professional director and makeup man. Miss Goddard adds nothing but a pretty face to the film," said one critic (E. Creelman, *New York Sun*). What was imperceptible to the public at large was the double message that Chaplin sent in his closing speech. He was talking to his fellow man, and also to his wife, Paulette, who shortly after the picture opened would leave him: "Hannah, can you hear me? Wherever you are, look up! Look up, Hannah! The clouds are lifting! The sun is breaking through! We are coming out of the darkness into the light! We are coming into a new world—a kindlier world, where men will rise above their greed, their hate, and their brutality. Look, up, Hannah! The soul of man has been given wings and at last he is beginning to fly. He is flying into the rainbow—into the light of hope. Look up, Hannah! Look up!"

Before she left Chaplin, Paulette went with him to the White House in 1941, where they were guests of President Roosevelt. She found herself looking up into higher than Hollywood circles, specifically at Harry Hopkins, adviser to the president, with whom she would become involved. Simultaneously, she was about to stare down the face of scandal.

TRAVELER WITHOUT A COUNTRY

1 9 3 3 – 1 9 4 8

EMIL LUDWIG, A writer in exile, spent an interesting evening in Ascona with Remarque on May 10, 1933. "The night of the public burning of the books . . . I invited my friend, Erich Maria Remarque, to drink with me. We opened our oldest Rhine wine, turned on the radio, heard the flames crackling, heard the speeches of the Hitler spokesman—and drank to the future."

The picture of the two of them toasting while their words were being burned is dramatic; they were celebrating their survival. It was Dr. Joseph Goebbels again—of the white-mice scourge—who had organized the public burning of books in the square in front of the Berlin Opera House. From the Nazi point of view, the act was a cleansing of degenerate art written or painted by subversives. The creators might have fled, but their country would see to it that their works burned eternally in hell. Some twenty thousand books were thrown on the funeral pyre that night, accompanied by a ghoulish ceremonial speech before each author's work was demolished. Remarque's "speaker" was typical of them all: "Against literary betrayal of the soldiers in the world war, and in the name of national education in the spirit of self-defense, I consign to the flames the work of Erich Maria Remarque."

Otto Klement, Remarque's agent, who, according to one of the many versions of the story, had sounded the warning note in Remarque's ear to flee, remained behind, sitting in his office near the Opera House on the afternoon of May 10, 1933.

Two Storm Troopers presented themselves at Mr. Clement's [*sic*] office and announced that they had been assigned to see that no harm came to him during the sacred ceremony. Presently, they had become bored and asked if they could borrow something to read from the library. He invited them to help themselves. One selected *All Quiet on the Western Front*; the other took Remarque's *The Road Back*.

"They sat reading them," said Mr. Clement, "blissfully unaware that the government was burning those books only a stone's throw away."

This report was written from a 1939 interview with Remarque. Kyle Crichton—who misspells Klement's name—is none other than the journalist who, a year earlier, had written the damaging article on Paulette that had provoked her father to sue.

The book burning was reported to have a positive side effect: "At the reception in Manhattan by the American Jewish Congress Dr. Ludwig boasted that the Nazi burning of his books and those of many a Jew and Pacifist, including Erich Maria Remarque, is helping to boost their world sales, quickening the flow of royalty checks to Switzerland where friends Ludwig and Remarque bank their money in gold francs."

Remarque was becoming used to adversity. The Irish Free State had banned *The Road Back*; his novels were also banned by Russia and the Eastern Bloc; his divorced wife was determined to come and live with him in Switzerland; *Pat*, the novel he was working on, was giving him a hard time.

Felicitas von Reznicek had done some freelance work for Remarque back when he was an editor at *Sport im Bild* and had socialized with him and Jutta. The last time she saw them, Jutta was undergoing a health cure at Davos and Remarque was at her side, ever solicitous. When their divorce was being processed, von Reznicek took Jutta's side, stating that she "was not in agreement with the way he put his divorce through, but was in no doubt as to its necessity." She recalled that Remarque later praised her for supporting his wife when the majority sided with him.

The bottom line was that after their divorce, Jutta remained financially dependent upon Remarque; however, this basic need was disguised by a kind of moral and political subterfuge. Jutta claimed to feel threatened by the

National Socialists in Berlin. The premise of this is puzzling for two reasons. The first was that although the wife of Remarque, Jutta had never aligned herself with his beliefs or what *All Quiet* espoused. The second was that even if she did have dissident feelings, she was well connected and would have been protected. Her sister, Edith, was married to Heinrich Göring, brother of Hermann. Heinrich, the good brother, was known to have assisted many people who were opposed to Hitler's Reich, so it would seem that Jutta would have been safe within her own country. That she chose to live as an exile with her ex-husband was often a burden, and yet, curiously, sometimes a convenience in an alien environment. Speaking Italian, she paved the way with the local people, helped to get him settled in his house—renamed Casa Remarque, occasionally decorated his arm with her exceptional beauty, and provided a familiar presence to a man who increasingly sought to be grounded.

For the next two years, from 1933 to 1935, Remarque lived the life of a relentless playboy. His German work ethic was constantly pitted against his heavy drinking and serious sybaritic tendencies. Torn by this dichotomy in his character, most of the time following his move to Porto Ronco he gave in to his less appealing side. He would take his Lancia (Puma I) and make the rounds of his favorite places, such as Davos, St. Moritz, Venice, Rome, Paris, and the French Riviera. He was a well-known figure at expensive restaurants, nightclubs, and after-hours bars. Sometimes, when he was accompanied by Jutta, he would drink very heavily and Jutta would leave him and return to the hotel, either calling a cab or getting a ride home with some accommodating gentleman. Remarque would either make his way back by dawn, wake up in a hotel room with a warm-hearted but unfulfilled prostitute, or drink until after the sun came up, have a big breakfast, and then go for a shave and a massage. "Nobody said anything because he really only behaved outrageously toward himself," recalled Victoria Wolff, a friend during his early new life. She, too, was an exile from Germany who found artistic and political refuge in Ascona, but unlike many of the other women in his life, she was not in love with him. "I understood him. I, too, am a writer," she has explained. "He acted like a mentor, sometimes. He pushed me. He told me what to do and what not to do. It made him feel stronger about his own work when he told me what to do. For instance, he would say, 'What are you going to write now?' And I told him the idea and he'd say, 'Much too early. Wait two, three, four years. Then you can do it. It's too early now. You haven't lived through enough.'"

Wolff witnessed the beginnings of his Ascona persona. It was a time when the town had its own distinct identity and was considered a sort of Continental Bloomsbury. Although it was a sanctuary for émigrés who had fled Hitler's Germany, it served as a wellspring of creativity for well-known, free-spirited artists and writers. The colony included the biographer Emil Ludwig and the writers Thomas Mann, Franz Werfel, and Stefan Zweig, among others. They would frequent the Café Verbano or the Café Schiff, sitting and talking until the wee hours.

"Ascona is a very little place," says Wolff, "and everybody knows everybody. Everyone goes to the Al Porto or the Café Al Pontile. Everybody meets around six o'clock without an appointment. . . . Boni would often sit in his car with a glass of wine and talk to people for a long time. He had the most beautiful car imaginable. The Lancia. Gray, with gray interior. Convertible. And just elegant. He drove it like a champion. He was a perfectionist in his driving. The car is now in the Lancia Museum in Torino. Boni and his car; they were famous."

Ruth Albu, an authority on Boni's heart and responsible for his Swiss well-being, was still very much in the picture—certainly enough to know that "Victoria Wolff was not Boni's type." It was she who had known Wolff in Berlin and had arranged for the two writers to meet, confident that their muse would dominate the relationship.

Albu understood better than anyone what was happening to Remarque during those years of adjustment. She knew of his wandering soul, his proclivities toward drink and wasting his talent. She knew of his inextricable attachment to Jutta, and how Jutta tormented him, which even he could not fully grasp. Albu realized there was no real future for her with Remarque, because "He always knew exactly what was right to do but couldn't do it." Both she and Remarque were on the road a lot, she in plays, he, playing. Through letters, they talked of sorely missing each other and of possible meeting places, but it was mostly an exercise in frustration. However, if anybody could, she kept him honest, using a form of "tough love," admonishing, warning, even badgering him to keep on track. In her letters, there is a combination of scolding and yearning:

My Sweetheart, I would really like to know if you are still at home, or where I should try to place you. Sadly enough, the idea of your diary-letters was never realized. I worry very much about you, that you don't write and suddenly will be overwhelmed by deadlines for a novel, and you have to force yourself to meet them. But maybe I just worry too much and you will surprise me, as you have done before, with written chapters. Nevertheless you do have the possibility to affect the world and future generations and therefore it would be a shame if you don't pull yourself together. I have the feeling that I have to scold you, it can't harm you, even if for once I'm in the wrong, and then I will apologize. If I imagine you in your paradise of a home, sleeping, reading, talking without any goal, I am appalled.

Did you get fat? I am kissing your fat—if you're fat—your fox-eyes, your good eyes—teacher's eyes, and love you.

Jutta lived on and off with Remarque in Porto Ronco. She had a very close woman friend named Bettina, who often accompanied her when she went off on a sojourn, staying at a posh resort or grand hotel. The nature of the relationship with Bettina is curious. She is revealed through Jutta's letters and in Remarque's diaries as being half nanny, half soul sister. It is clear that Jutta needed someone to take care of her. In this letter, written to Remarque on November 7, 1933, from the Hotel Claridge in Paris, one can see the vast contrast between Ruth Albu's concerns and Jutta's:

Dearest Babusch, I hope you received my letters. I wrote two, following the Renoir catalogue. I'm always very happy when I hear from you, and I am always writing to you. I'm sitting downstairs in the writing room. My room is terribly cold. Today I will get another room on the second floor. The heating is better there. The whole heating system seems to be a problem here. . . . I feel a cold coming, headache, fever. Bettina will come soon and prescribe something. She always has advice, which is especially wonderful when one feels as forlorn as I do. . . . I think I have the sleep disease, can sleep for twelve hours in a row, without moving. I hope you are well, Babuschka, don't you want to come? Or should I come to you, in case you get too lonely? All my best, as always, your Peter.

Remarque had been working steadily, and he did finish a draft of *Pat* in January of 1933. He had a habit of asking for friends' opinions about new work, and then not respecting what they had to say. He sent *Pat* to a friend in Berlin named Lotte Preuss (thought to be the same person as Lolott, Remarque's love of 1921).

"Dear, dear Erich," wrote Lotte Preuss. "I wept while I was reading it, I wept while I'm writing this. It overwhelmed me. . . . A wonderful piece of poetry, the most beautiful love story I can think of. You should get the Nobel for it. I would have loved it if somebody had come yesterday and had said something stupid about you, so that I could have yelled at them and told them that they're a bunch of stupid lice."

Remarque thought of *Pat* as the completion of a trilogy. Its theme was infiltration and readjustment following World War I, just as it had been for *All Quiet* and *The Road Back*. What made *Pat*, aka *Three Comrades*, singular was that it could not be published in Germany and that it featured a passionate love story. Remarque's ongoing faith in comrades is explored to the full. The three of the eventual title are as passionate in their way as the lovers. It was a tough book for Remarque to structure and went through many rewrites. Although the book was not published until 1937, it was completed in 1936 and heralded by Remarque's English publisher, Hutchinson: "I have just read your new novel about the very sympathetic young people who so valiantly try to battle through the postwar years, running a garage. Each page of the book was a true joy, and I would like to congratulate you heartily for the major effect of human warmth which emanates from your characters and tell you that you have been masterful in achieving your goals."

After finishing *Pat*, Remarque's choice of title for the English publication was *A Bit of Life*. Hutchinson suggested *We Were Young, We Were Gay*—gay in the old-fashioned sense. Remarque dismissed this less than gripping suggestion, and finally came up with the title that stuck: *Three Comrades*.

But in 1935, he was still struggling with fulfilling his contractual obligations. Little, Brown, his American publisher, was waiting. Klement, his agent, was goading—eager for the book's completion so that a movie sale could get under way. A. W. Wheen, Remarque's English translator, was arduously translating each rewrite. "I have had to revise my own work as radically as Remarque has done his," he said. Remarque, caught between exhilaration at having escaped Hitler and depression at being without a country, found work difficult. The reverberations of being charged with literary treason were immense. It was cold comfort that he was in the distinguished company of Sigmund Freud, Emil Ludwig, Tucholsky, Heinrich Mann, and Karl Marx. Their branding had also been severe. Marx was called an instigator of social and class conflicts: Mann, an exponent of decadent and perverted fiction; Ludwig, a falsifier of German culture. Goebbels's victory cry that ended the book-burning ceremony chilled Remarque again and again: "What a century. What knowledge! It is a joy to be alive!"

Remarque managed, however, to get great pleasure from life itself. "A clear, wintry day in spring," he begins his diary on April 4, 1935, in Porto Ronco. It is the first entry since 1918. "The wisterias in bloom on the house as well. Went walking in the garden with Peter and the dogs in the morning. Again and again it's the simplest things that give the purest pleasure—the bright, waving green of the meadows, the cadmium yellow of a primrose, the odd red flowers among the host of white ones on the huge camellia—the young dogs with their flapping ears, as they tear away at a reed they've found—the pure, fresh air over the lake, Peter's lovely narrow head against the blue of the sky . . . the purest joy: but is it enough? Wouldn't objectives be better? Better than joys even?"

Although there are many passages like this one in the diaries that seem to suggest a happy personality, Remarque was deeply complex and prone to dark mood swings. He never knew how to have a simple relationship. Victoria Wolff remembered how mercurial he could be: "He could be dangerous," she has said, referring to their time in Ascona. "He could be intelligent, witty, friendly, and then cut you off the next moment. For instance, he is nice to you now, and he meets you tomorrow and says, 'What's your name? Oh, yes, I've heard of you.' Why? It was his nature, double-faced."

Remarque, who considered Wolff a friend to her face and had her believing she was a writer of substance, notes in his diary: "Spent the evening with Christa Winsloe and Victoria Wolff. Artistic and bourgeois temperament side-by-side. Both writers. With and without atmosphere."

As with his most important relationships, his with Ruth Albu would be complicated. In the days when letters were the form of exchange, their outpourings of love, hesitancy about love, recriminations about love, and general torments and musings were still unusual. The letters are highly intelligent, expressive documents of a floundering affair. They perfectly reveal the "Remarque malaise." Here was a good woman, good for him and to him, whom he could not appreciate or accept.

Albu wrote him in 1932:

It's over a year now that you were very much in love with me. . . . It was beautiful then; even you have to admit that. Then there was no Johannes in sight. Whenever you mentioned her it was with an almost negative tone and the interest you showed for her was merely that of one human being for another—especially when one has shared so many important years together. . . . I encouraged you to establish a friendly relationship with her. . . . I loved you and believed in our relationship and left you to go to Vienna. Two weeks later I returned, you were working—I sat in your hotel room. At night you passed by me with Johannes. When you came to the room you complained about your work. After another two weeks you had to leave, you needed to be alone, you went to Holland. . . . Two weeks later suddenly a phone call promising a trip together, tomorrow, or the day after tomorrow. I didn't hear from you for another week, when you finally called again to ask me to meet you tomorrow! During that time, I called around, you weren't staying at the Majestic. I knew where you stayed! You wanted to spare me so you lied! The next time we met it was in Locarno. My nerves weren't in the best shape. As long as I've known you, you've always been miserable, always hoping to sort things out once you knew where you belonged. . . . You, or we, then bought your house. I don't want to point out all the details which should still be fresh in your memory. . . . Today, you still relate to Johannes as "your wife," which, of course, she still is even if you are divorced. Whenever you mentioned her to me you made it sound as if it never would be the same between you and her, and yet now I know, she is the one and only for you. When you claim you still love me, it's a mistake on your part. . . .

You know that I admire your work and that I believe in your future. I have given you more leeway than any other man in my life, but the right to own two people I won't give you. It wouldn't be just—I haven't even got half a man. I am again and again dumbfounded by your matter-of-fact attitude. You take me for granted, but not any longer.

Please write to me honestly that you can't fulfill my expectations in our relationship, so that I can finally be cured and give up all last hope that I still foster in my heart. I can't go on like that any longer and despise the way we lead our lives.

It is only sad that most likely you will read this letter as an attempt on my side to win you over. I swear I have no such intentions. I wish I could miss you. Ruth.

Remarque answered her from Ronco, from the house she had found for him:

It is hard to respond. What can I say? Words always spoil everything. . . . I can say: Yes, I am weak and tired and haven't even started, and I can say: Yes, maybe I am not capable of love, but who could wish more than I to be able to, and I can say: Yes, go away from me, free yourself, I'm not worth another human being who voluntarily and vehemently enters a relationship without regrets, I am only half—never fully there, I am not enough—I only take, I never give. . . . However, not all is just weak, flat, lazy, and wrong. No, somehow I know that I couldn't suffer so much if there weren't something else there which I can't explain or even understand, from which I shy away, yet call it by its name: fate.

. . . I always wanted to play and I always loved the buoyant, the carefree, the risk—I tuned into it—I fed into it—I lost myself in it. How long is it that I could be on my own? Didn't I always strive for happiness? And didn't I always know: to start means to destroy?

. . . I can't say anything about me. I am so used to lying, and now, when I could push aside all the well-known phrases, I feel so ashamed because I am so caught up in them that it drives me to despair.

No, I can't love the way you want it and need it, but one shouldn't condemn someone's desperate efforts in a sudden and mad hope to jump once more into a life, to take it on once again, to be taken in by life again.

I avoided, circumvented it as best I could; I didn't want to fall into this strange failure, into this twilight; I wanted clarity and happiness—I wanted to live. But now sometimes I see this unavoidable slipping as a preparation for the bare, hopeless heights of my work. I hate my work: She [Jutta] ruined everything, she took my warmth, she takes the little I love, she forces herself into my living and being without me being able to believe in her or in me. I observe her, cold and with spite, and I know I will never love her, and I also know I can never go back again.

. . . Love is for me what remains indestructible: the relation to another human being, not to a woman. My relationship to you is indestructible. You will leave and always think that another was the reason for it. You won't be able to understand that it is not so. . . . I never saw anything else in your relationship with me but an unexpected beauty, a greatness, which I wanted to hold, but was not made for. Give me time; I will try again. . . .

I just got back yesterday. After Florence I had a car accident. I thought of you during all my days on the road. Now, I'm not saying it right again. But try not to read the false in this letter. Read what I wasn't able to say.

In 1993, Ruth Albu Morgenroth was eighty-five years old. She received her last letter from Remarque shortly before he died, in 1970. In it he says he feels older than his years and is sick. In the letter he affirms a vintage statement. He says theirs is an indestructible relationship, that they've always belonged to each other, and that he wishes that he had known what she knew then. How happy their lives could have been.

Remarque's stepmother, Maria, committed suicide around 1943, causing his aging father to move in with his daughter Erna and her husband, Walter

Rudolf, in the German town of Bad Rothenfelde. Remarque would visit there only once, nearly twenty years later, when he attended his father's funeral. By 1935, he had already moved his money from Germany, and by all available reports did not attempt to get any in to his family. After Erna Remark Rudolf had sold the bulk of Remarque's war diaries and letters, relations had been strained. For several years, Remarque had attempted to track his material down, but to no avail. His sister's betrayal and avarice would cause Remarque to always use various signatures, and result in his complete lack of interest in the family. Later, when he was idyllically happy in one of his most passionate relationships, with a beauty named Natasha Paley Wilson, he treated his father to a vacation in Rome and Venice, where he spoiled and patronized the old man, who announced that he was having the time of his life. But in the years when Remarque was adjusting to his fame, his millions, and his feelings of permanent dislocation, he could not deal with his family in any sustained way.

He was far closer to his family of animals. Billy, Gitta, Tommy, Pat, Carrie, and Roelly were the dogs, and there were assorted cats and kittens at all times. It was the only way he could be a good parent, for he had no intention of having children. According to Virginia Wolff, he was adamant about the subject early on: "When I first came to Ascona and he didn't know me and I didn't know him, something came up and I said, 'I have to go home now with my children.' and he said, 'Oh, you're the one with the children. Immigrants have no children. They have no time for children. And life is too hard for children.' And Jeanne, of course, wouldn't have spoiled her figure for anything."

Physically, Ascona looks like the ballet set of a happy village. From its long quay with cafés overlooking Lake Maggiore to its pretty town square and narrow, winding streets filled with small, elegant shops, it is totally charming. The character of Ascona—cosmopolitan, friendly, informal—played a large part in Remarque's successful repatriation. Richard Arthur Firda wrote about how many of the Germans in Ascona considered Nazi Germany "as a menace of certain but short duration." And Firda also notes that Remarque, once in Ascona, refused to take a position against Nazi Germany:

> If he was a generous host, he still remained a solitary figure in the midst of his conviviality. . . . Remarque never took an open political stand against Nazi Germany in any of the emigrant journals and newspapers then starting publication in those countries where such activity was still possible. He seems to have sought the way of genuine non-political alignment. As

Thomas Kamla has noted, Remarque's "name rarely emerges in conjunction with the liberal humanists, leftist intellectuals, Social Democrats, and Marxists who attempted to form a political front against Nazism after 1935." . . . Kurt Tucholsky's earlier prophecy that "we cannot count on Remarque" had come to pass. Even now he was unwilling to join hands with the majority of his fellow exiles, however solicitous, who were in fact preparing to leave Swiss territory for other areas of Europe.

Remarque saved his opinions and his philosophy for his work. If he was asked about his deepest convictions, he would refer to his novels, saying that he didn't like to talk about such personal matters. However depressed, restless, or inebriated he was at this time, he still managed to write a novel that completed a cycle and began a fresh literary reputation. Although *The Road Back* received some favorable reviews, it did not get the kind of attention given to *All Quiet*, but Remarque always thought the book was one of his best.

The writing of *Three Comrades*, dedicated to J. Z. R. (Jutta Zambona Remarque), was as emotionally wrought as the relationship depicted in the book and the real-life one with Jutta. In 1936, as Firda reports, "Remarque announced to Alfred McIntyre of Little, Brown that he would never again sign a contract with a specific date of termination, noting that the book had cost him blood and nerves, and that as a writer he would lose time and money if he missed his deadline. McIntyre's response was sympathetic but to the point. He assured Remarque that he would never make a contract, or take one over that would involve an advance as large as this one had required."

Remarque's agent, Otto Klement, who had moved to London shortly after Goebbels's book burning, traveled to Hollywood in 1936, after stopping in New York to make a deal to serialize the novel with *Good Housekeeping* magazine. In Hollywood, he had meetings with Sam Goldwyn and Louis B. Mayer, who were going to buy the novel for MGM. He met with Joseph L. Mankiewicz, who was to produce it, and F. Scott Fitzgerald, who was to write the screenplay. For Remarque, Klement was his Seeing Eye dog in a world he was yet to know. He had no English and little desire to pull up stakes again. He loved and understood Europe, and as long as he had loyal and adventurous scouts, all was well. For Klement, *Three Comrades* would be his most creative and illustrious project yet. He had steered it admirably for his most prestigious client. Through subsidiary rights and the film sale, he was trying to restore the financial leverage that had plummeted with the loss of the Third Reich market.

As late as October 1936, Remarque was still searching for the proper title. Although he liked *Three Comrades*, *Good Housekeeping* didn't. In his diary he writes, "Kept thinking of *Dust in the Winds?—Small Lives?—Twilight?—Dream of the Night?—Our Little Life?* Keep looking, brother!"

He held out for *Three Comrades*, which was published in America by Little, Brown on April 26, 1937. The Dutch publisher, Querido Verlag, which supported many writers in exile, published the book in its original German, as *Drei Kameraden*, in 1938, but was forced in 1940 to cease its distribution when the German army invaded the Netherlands. Remarque was indebted to Querido for its bravery, and many years later, in his letters to Paulette, he would often sign them "Your Querido."

In a sense, the three comrades themselves each represented one of the three most dominant characteristics of Remarque: the romantic, the practical, and the elusive. He is Lenz, one of the hero's comrades, who scoffs at love: "The whole thing is a swindle. A wonderful swindle by Mama Nature. Look at the plum tree, for instance, making herself more beautiful than she will be afterwards. It would be terrible if love had any truck with truth."

He is Robby, not unlike Hemingway's heroes of a "lost generation," as Firda points out: "I had known women, but they had only been fleeting affairs, adventure, a gay hour occasionally, a lonely evening, escape from oneself, from despair, from vacancy. And I had never even wanted anything else. For I had learned that there was nothing else one can trust but oneself, and one's comrades, perhaps. Now I suddenly say that I could be something to someone, simply because I was there, and that that person was happy because I was with her. Said like that, it sounds very simple, but when you think about it, it is a tremendous thing, a thing that knows no end."

And he is Pat Hollman, elusive because of her fate: "The girl sat silent beside me; brightness and shadow through the window glided across her face. I glanced at her occasionally; she reminded me again of the evening when I had first seen her. Her expression had become grave, she appeared stranger than before, but very beautiful; it was the same expression that had moved me then and had not let me go. It seemed to me as if there were in it something of the secret of quietness that things have that are near to nature—trees, clouds, animals—and occasionally a woman."

The real Pat Hollman was not as tragic nor as graceful. Jutta was increasingly becoming a thorn in Remarque's side. Although he allowed her to live with him, she rightly perceived that she was not entirely welcome. Periodically she would clear out—usually in a sulk—and take up residence at the Hotel Lancaster, on rue de Berri in Paris, or at the Grand Hotel

Kurhaus in Davos. She would send the bills to him, along with letters of recrimination. She could not tolerate his seeing other women, which he was doing to excess, with a particular concentration on a mysterious "E." He never mentions her name in his diary, but apparently her beauty and appeal were legendery. Everybody wanted her, and Jutta found it hard to bear the gossip about Remarque's squiring her and others around. It drove her to the limit when Remarque would downplay his amorous activities.

"Boni—How unjust you are to be so unreliable," she wrote from Paris on November 3, 1937:

> What other excuse will you come up with now for not calling—for not giving me a sign? Why don't you say that you don't want to see me, that you have other things in your head? I would find it understandable, but don't pretend. . . . Why hide your head in the sand? Be a little good to me, Boni. It's so insulting when you lie to me.

More for himself than for her, Remarque answered Jutta's letter in a diary entry: "Marriage always means being on the defensive. Possession means loss. You can't possess any person. In the imagination at the most. And then it's an illusion. Wanting to possess somebody is a sacrilege."

The year 1936 was one of escapades, dabbling, lumbago, and leisure. "I'm living like a retired colonel" was the way Remarque put it. He had a bad back condition, and he didn't know what to write next, but it seemed that his physical and mental torments had lifted for the moment. From his diary, one can see the writer hungry for a project and in the process of experimenting. He works at capturing a character's condition through a single image: "His face was wrinkled, like the seat of an old pair of trousers" or "He was such a bore that the clock stood still when he entered the room." He is increasingly fascinated with the macabre printed in the tabloids.

In fact, Remarque was drawn more and more to the exotic and to the erotic, neurotic, and sordid sides of human nature. Dr. Ralph Gerard, an artist and friend of the late actress Lilli Palmer, and an Ascona dweller, uses the word *Machiavellian* in association with Remarque. He felt that Remarque did have a taste for the sordid, and a need to experience the whole spectrum since "the sordid provides for the sublime."

In May, Remarque went to Budapest with "E.," his main lady friend. His descriptions range from the sublime to the base, yet because he enjoyed himself to the extreme, he expressed an unusual exuberance. He took steam baths in the morning, went to the tailor, breakfasted with E. on the terrace, made midmorning love, fell into a deep sleep, lunched with E.'s aunt, who was a countess named Edelsheim, had tea, visited a painter for cocktails: "The painter, tall, brown, makeup, red carnation, suede shoes, homosexual, led us to a painting titled *Poison Mixer*, and declared to have painted it with blood from his heart. The expression was enough." In the evening, he would cut loose and visit first what he called "our restaurant with the gypsies."

> With Countess Edelsheim and E. to the Holub restaurant. Had stuffed cabbage and beer on wooden tables. . . . Finally E. and I to the Tabian Bar; rendezvous with Bornenusza. Bar is orange, red, green, blue. Terrible. Wonderful black drummer. I borrowed money from Deppo, the concertina player. Knew him from Berlin. Then to Plantage, a homosexual bar. Pretty mulatto. Bornenusza said she was from Berlin. Then to the Parrot, a dusty, big place. Later to the Arizona Bar. On the other end of our table, the real homosexuals. . . . Met Ria. Charming. Wanting to be more than just a bar girl. Back to the Moulin Rouge, where Bornenusza had made a sentimental attack on E. . . . then a rendezvous with a young Danish girl, together. E. superior. By 5 A.M. at the hotel. . . . God's good old air, fresh and moist from the rain . . . small laughter, chatting about the day, the great security in being together with the magic glimmer above it all.

After E. departed, there were others whom he took up with casually and reported on perceptively, as always:

> Monique Nègre. Beautiful eyes, with which she looks at you quietly, astonished and sincere for a long time. . . . Later, met two girls from the Parisienne Grill. Remembered to have made some kind of date. Both very beautiful. Brown swimsuits. Laid in the sun. Then up to my room. A little earlier met Ria from the Arizona Bar. Was told she was crying and waiting at night in the bar for me. Why wait for me? Some old empty straw? Maybe that's just the reason. Love is looking for empty cases to fill them. Later Lise came to my room. Straight, broad shoulders, tanned, with blue blouse. . . . In the afternoon . . . Monique was there. . . . Sweetly confused, happily listening to my silliness. In the hallway, she did not want to leave. I promised to call. I forgot.

He took the train from Budapest to Vienna, where he reunited with Ruth Albu, whom he hadn't seen since early 1933. Now, she was married to a man named Ulrich ("met Ruth's husband. Nice"), and the three of them went to a suburb of Vienna called Grinzing for the year's new wine. The next day, he saw her alone: "Tender memories. All remain. Just a light shadow of the years passed, which only makes it sweeter, more secretive and beautiful. Went to the bar in the Grand Hotel, had a few martinis, she was light, swinging, happy, and as she assured me, uninhibited. 'That must be the end,' I said. 'That you are here,' she said, 'that you are alive will always make me happy.' That's the end, I thought. She left."

His 1936 diary reveals a personal dichotomy: an observant and penetrating writer living alongside a confused and wounded spirit. Many of his novelistic themes are woven into this one year of diary keeping: his enforced wanderlust, his endless search for home, the available women he doesn't want, the constant pursuit of a great love, political limbo, the power of memory versus the experience of the present, the romantic versus the cynic. His entry upon leaving for home—meaning Switzerland—is touching. He seems very vulnerable.

Departed. Dining car. The waiter sat a girl at my table; red hair, very pale, with green eyes. Strangely transparent and full of charm, deeply colored lower lip, wide mouth. An artist, Rimgard Kell. Was on her way to Lugano for two weeks. Shared some wine. Whitsuntide Sunday. 10 A.M. customs. Swiss breakfast with the young artist. Later lunch at 1 in Zurich. . . . A little homesick, a small wanderlust. Thought of E. Thought: I would like to be able to cry once, but in such a manner that all the old crust and the rust dissolve and youth, and the great longing, the big desires, can emerge from beneath. Sentimental. Made up letters in my head, often promised, never written . . . everything is passing. That existence is an illusion . . . Bellinzona. Mr. King's taxi. Home. The dogs. The kittens. . . . Prepared my desk for writing. But will I work? . . . Will I finish my book?

[June 2] Wanted to work. No energy. . . . Where to? Into the slow, slow dying. . . . Went to Zurich for the afternoon to see a Chaplin movie: *Modern Times*.

There is no mention of Paulette's performance. He was more interested in getting very drunk afterward and ending up at a hotel that he did not recall checking into: "In the morning I was given a toothbrush, soap, had a bath and breakfast before I went back."

His bitterness toward his countrymen was surfacing alongside his increasing desolation:

Two fat, tipsy Germans with glasses. Recognizable from afar: "Where do you have the German flag? It's a pigsty here! Hey, band, play the Adolf Hitler march. The champagne tastes like the cork!" One asked a woman to dance, he stood at attention. His hands were on the sideseams of his pants and his heels were clicking. I think that's the way they fuck too.

[June 4] . . . Took my beloved llama blanket and a hot blanket to bed and sweated. Lumbago . . . 38 years old. My God. . . . Tired not only in my bones. I wrote a few letters. I don't like to write, either letters nor books. . . . I'm much too tired for my age. I don't know what I want. Any goals? Oh, God, what kind of goals are these one believes in? If I don't know from where, or from what, or where to—what are these goals other than self-deception?

Remarque's writing was always fresh and palpable when he stuck to description rather than ruminative turmoil. He studied émigrés and wrote knowingly about their adjustment-without-assimilation in a new city or country. He also could capture a locale simply and vividly.

He took E. to Venice and the neighboring towns of the Veneto in the summer of 1936. E. lived in Frankfurt, which made it increasingly difficult for her to get out, to travel freely, and to meet Remarque: "Called E. Missed her. Seemed so far away. Strange that politics can do that: not allow people to see each other whenever they like to." But Remarque was no stranger to the idea of thwarted love, a recurring theme in his life as well as his work. In the novel *Flotsam* (1941), a relationship is threatened because of political conditions; in *Three Comrades*, the relationship between Robby and Pat is doomed by her terminal illness. Obstacles against freedom pained and preoccupied him.

It was about this time that he began to be more vigilant and even slightly suspicious about his business affairs. In July, Otto Klement sold *Three Comrades* to MGM, and Remarque says in his diary, "Can't quite believe it yet. Maybe I will be able to buy a Cézanne!" And then two days later, his mood was more cautious: "Telegram from Klement. Asked for power of attorney. Debated it. This way he could collect the money from me. Difficult decision when dealing with a rather large sum. I finally sent him the document with a few changes. Curious what will come of it."

Jutta was back in the house that summer of 1936. She came and went at will. While there, she was mostly part of his social schedule, accompanying him to restaurants and dinner parties. Jutta's friend and nanny-companion, Bettina, often joined them. Jutta was still referred to as his wife, and in a sense he still thought of her as that and would always feel responsible for her welfare, but he complained about her being spoiled, egocentric, sensitive, and moody in his diary: "One should never marry a woman. . . . A husband is and always will be ridiculous, women have a feel for that. They betray them hopelessly."

No matter how much she irked him, his outward behavior toward her didn't change much. He was unfailingly courtly. The following excerpt from his diary gives an idea of the lengths he went to in order to please her, while he drank himself into near oblivion. It also gives a sense of the extravagant life of the émigrés, who were enjoying the good life while, as Remarque put it, "Europe was dying."

> Asked barman to congratulate Peter with flowers from me for her birthday. . . . Had Tavern host congratulate Peter. . . . Music. Drank a lot. . . . Home, I felt sick. But a birthday is a birthday. In the morning presented Peter with one hundred twenty-dollar coins. . . . Decided to have a party at night: Hallgarten, Reymont, Olly, Zei, Dispekers, little Holzer, Honigs, and us. Had caviar and sandwiches. Olly grilled wonderful sausages outside. Zei made fireworks. Very funny improvised cabaret. Holzer played Napoleon in the show; Zei demonstrated grotesque dances; Honig danced a belly dance, and a wonderful, almost too real performance of a chimpanzee. Peter presented a fashion show with evening gowns. Reymont appeared as a nun in a bath cloth. Grete D. almost naked. Nothing to it in this neighborhood. Had cognac, beer, and wine. Later, Alfredo came, bringing four Italo-Egyptians with him. . . . Peter was happy.

During the summer of 1936, Remarque's art dealer, Walter Feilchenfeldt, visited him, bringing some great art—a landscape by Renoir, two drawings by Degas, a watercolor by Cézanne. Remarque decided to buy the Renoir and the Degas drawings, but the franc was going down and so he delayed payment, which Feilchenfeldt allowed since he was such a good customer.

This was the same summer that Remarque told Peter about E. and smoked too much, got a new pipe to cut down on the cigarettes, and found he smoked even more. He ate shrimp and crab at nearly every meal. He had a major exhibit of his Persian and Turkish rugs in Zurich. Three litters of kittens were born. He began to drink whole bottles of kirsch or wine in a sitting—good wine to be sure, such as Lafitte 1911—and listened to the abdication of Edward VIII on the radio.

It was the summer that his hypochondriacal tendencies escalated; if it wasn't his heart, it was lumbago; if not that, it was his lungs. Remarque made a deal with Peter that every time he had too much to drink in town, she could summon the horse carriage belonging to the local carpenter to come and pick them up, thereby calling attention to his condition in front of the town.

For the first time, early in the fall, Remarque's sister Erna and her husband, Walter, came to pay a visit. It was a prime example of how he was manipulated because of his fame, wealth, and courtly spirit. Erna had sent him a letter hinting that something was terribly wrong and insisting upon a visit. Remarque, alarmed, called her in Germany. She acted secretive and didn't want to talk on the phone. He told her to come right away. He records the reason for the visit: "Picked up Erna and Walter in Lugano at night. She came with her husband. All worries unnecessary: she just wanted my German savings account so they can build a house. Nice company! All this excitement for that!"

He was also making anti-Semitic remarks in his diary: "Nice Jewish gymnast has left. . . . The less likable Jew with thick glasses stayed on. . . . Rode over to the Dispekers', he was complaining about the climate, the rise of expenses, and Switzerland in general. Jews don't fit in the countryside. . . . Called Feilchen [Remarque's nickname for his art dealer] in the morning. Asked me to send the paintings back! No word about our agreement. Once a Jew, always a Jew. . . . With Zei to the Nelly Bar. Family Tuchman. A very fat mother, two pretty daughters. Boringly stupid Jews. Rare! Stupidity is rare; boring rather often."

That fall, the German consulate began to harass Jutta by giving her trouble about her passport—all because of Remarque. She applied to renew it, and was told she had to wait nine months. Remarque was concerned about the political climate in Germany and what this snafu might mean, as well as about being stuck with her for a lengthy amount of time.

At least he was writing well again and was finally able to finish the last revised draft of *Three Comrades* for publication—even though it had already been sold in an earlier version to MGM. It gave him the first feeling of contentment in a long time. He was able to enjoy the privileged life in Ascona, although he was also uneasy about the trouble to come: "How much uncertainty in all this peace."

His peace was about to be shattered. Hitler was firmly established as chancellor, and Dietrich was about to reenter his life.

Prior to Remarque and Dietrich's fateful meeting in the summer of 1937, Remarque had spent a mostly indolent year, traveling between St. Moritz,

Paris, and the French Riviera. His coterie of friends included Louis and Mary Bromfield, Henry Bernstein, "with his huge Jewish profile, pains in his heart when he dances, and the manner of an old roué—a good manner," Kay Francis, Eleanor Boardman, Rose Warwick ("beautiful and quiet, only sometimes she flings glasses across the bar"), Georges Simenon, "who nowadays writes only six novels a year," William Wyler, the producer, Leni Riefenstahl, and many others. He felt the need to get out of Porto Ronco when an irritating wind called the *Föhn* blew in, because it seemed to bring on certain ailments. He complained of lung inflammation and severe eczema. He had been forced to give away Roelly, one of his favorite dogs, because of the same eczema caused by the climate. He entrusted the five remaining dogs and various cats to Jutta when he took off on a trip.

Financially he could afford to take time off from working. The American sales were strong for *Three Comrades*, Universal Pictures was finally going into production on *The Road Back*, after having optioned the rights in 1931, and *Three Comrades* was also to begin filming. Otto Klement, again in the States, was beginning to annoy Remarque: "*The Road Back* is being filmed, too. Didn't know about it until I read the newspapers. Klement has been in America for nine months for me and has arranged it, but he didn't even tell me. Crazy way of behaving!"

The Road Back starred Andy Devine and John King, and was directed by James Whale, with a screenplay by R. C. Sherriff and Charles Kenyon and a musical score by Dimitri Tiomkin. The movie itself has some uneven acting, but the handling of the material is interesting. The film self-consciously compliments itself for its political bravery, and the omniscient narrator at the beginning of the film makes a statement in stentorian tones. He tells the audience that at first, because the subject matter was censored, Universal halted filming. The real reason behind this dramatic announcement was that the studio felt that the material was too close to *All Quiet*. When it finally went into production in 1936, the film version veered sharply away from the novel.

There are, however, some startling sensibilities. For instance: "War brings out the best in men . . . it's a privilege to die for the fatherland," says one German soldier. The themes are familiar but more pronounced in this picture than in the earlier, more emotional *All Quiet*.

The picture endorses the idea of showing the Germans as sympathetic. These Germans who were spurned upon returning from the trenches still had to make the difficult readjustment once home. This is Remarque's point about the universality of the psychological experience of war.

Although the scenes are stiffly played, the content of the material, the way the labored process of reentry is depicted, is searingly informative. Remarque's humanist platform reached maturity in this work.

The climactic event is when a veteran shoots a man who has taken his girl while he's been away. He goes on trial for murder. The prosecutor makes the point that, once having fought in war, one is trained as a cool killer. The best defense is given by the character played by Andy Devine, who points up the irony of the situation and refutes the argument that the court is trying to establish: "If a man's been forced to shoot men who've never hurt him, why can't he shoot a man who's ruined his life?"

Ernst speaks bitterly: "You can't wash four years of killing off the brain with the one word *peace*. You never helped us find the road back to life. You were too busy scouting heroism, unveiling memorials, and hoarding food."

The production of *Three Comrades* had its own problems. Joseph Mankiewicz was to produce and Frank Borzage to direct; F. Scott Fitzgerald was writing the screenplay, and Robert Taylor and Margaret Sullavan had the starring roles.

In his screenplay, Fitzgerald, who had intended to honor the story of the hardships of three veterans being assimilated back into civilian life of the Weimar Republic, instead drafted a screenplay depicting the rise and ongoing horrors of the Third Reich. Mayer, behaving like a mogul, was nervous about the backlash from the German government if he exposed Nazism as an evil force in his picture. He brought in a co-writer, Edward E. Paramore, in an attempt to dilute the message. There are several versions about this. Ilan Avisar, in his book *Screening the Holocaust*, suggests that "Fitzgerald's efforts . . . were frustrated by the revisions of producer Joseph L. Mankiewicz, who sought to blunt the political denunciations, and director Frank Borzage, who shifted the emphasis to the story's romantic content."

In his *City of Nets*, Otto Friedrich gives another version, with Mankiewicz the unlikely hero of the film—even though he softened the original script:

> The script, written by Fitzgerald (and rewritten, to Fitzgerald's dismay, by the producer, Joseph Mankiewicz), blurred the identity of the various factions fighting in the streets, but it was clear enough that the Nazis were Nazis. Mayer invited an official from the German consulate in Los Angeles to a private screening. The German official came, saw, and disapproved.
>
> Mayer apparently was quite willing to make changes. Mankiewicz, however, refused. Joseph I. Breen, the head of Hollywood's self-censoring Production Code Administration . . . offered what he considered a solution:

Let the rioters be clearly identified as Communists. Mayer ordered that the changes be made. Mankiewicz threatened to resign, and to explain his reasons to *The New York Times*. Mayer shrugged and decided to leave the movie alone.

Ultimately, the watered-down version was popular with the public. Remarque's comment in his diary was terse: "October 20, 1938—Saw the film of *Three Comrades* on Monday evening. No good. Sullavan was good."

In the spring of 1937, Remarque had his last sexual encounter without love for a while. It happened in Zurich:

Arrived around one in the afternoon. . . . Ate at the Reblaube in the evening, then went on to the Terrace Bar. . . . Drank vodka. A lot of it. Made a lot of acquaintances right away. Afterwards went to the apartment of S., a kind of high-class bar call girl. Modern-style apartment. Very clean, big, new, with lace covers to protect the furniture, lovely woodwork, just like an older girlfriend of hers: S. woke her up. S.'s motto: whoever eats my bread must be at my disposal, even if he has to clean the flat when he gets up in the morning. Hard as nails. Of course she had to build up the apartment herself, bit by bit. Chattered. In the end the others left. Then she phoned a girl upstairs to come down—a half secretary to Thomas Mann and Wolfe, Langhoff, Elsie Lindt. Quite pretty. Came down in her dressing gown. Well-educated. Amusing to see how S. overplayed her relationship to her. Conversation about writers. I acted stupid. Used the name Breslauer. Packed up about six A.M. Streets of Zurich wet with morning rain.

Ruth Albu's theory about Remarque and women was that "Boni was drawn toward women who would hit him on the head. There definitely was a touch of sadomasochism." This dynamic was part of his relationship with Dietrich.

The story of Remarque and Marlene Dietrich has been largely underestimated. Their affair lasted from 1937 to about 1941—for Marlene it was after Douglas Fairbanks, Jr., and before Jean Gabin. For Remarque it has been set as shortly prior to his emigration to Hollywood, and shortly after. In fact, the relationship—the attraction and caring for each other—lasted for over thirty years, until Remarque's death in 1970. It might be an exaggeration to say that it was the most profound relationship for each of them, but for Remarque—with his diary as proof—it was the most tumultuous and obsessive one of his vast experience.

Dietrich was one of Remarque's greatest passions and remained a lifelong friend.

They had been slowly moving toward each other for a long time. They had originally caught sight of each other at the Hotel Eden in Berlin in 1931. They had frequented the same cafés, restaurants, salons, and events in Berlin; they shared friendships with Max Colpet, Leni Riefenstahl, the actor Willi Forst, Billy Wilder, Tilly Losch, Elisabeth Bergner, among others; they both stayed at the Hôtel Lancaster when in Paris and at the Hôtel des Bains on the Lido in Venice. They both loved good food and romantic love. Sexually, neither was overzealous.

According to "The Child," as both Dietrich and Remarque referred to Dietrich's daughter, Maria Sieber Riva, her mother met Remarque at a restaurant on the Lido. Dietrich was having lunch with Josef von Sternberg when Remarque approached their table:

> "Herr von Sternberg? Madame?"
>
> Although my mother resented strangers approaching her, his deep voice, with its cultured tone, intrigued her. She looked up into the finely chiseled face, the sensitive mouth; his falcon eyes softened as he bent toward her.
>
> "May I introduce myself? I am Erich Maria Remarque."
>
> My mother held out her hand, he raised it to his lips in homage. Von Sternberg motioned to the waiter for another chair, saying, "Won't you join us?"
>
> "Thank you. May I, Madame?"
>
> My mother, enchanted by his impeccable manners, smiled faintly, inclined her head, giving him permission to sit.
>
> "You look much too young to have written one of the greatest books of our time." Her eyes had not left his face.
>
> "I may have written it solely to hear your enchanting voice tell me so." He flicked his gold lighter, extending it to light her cigarette, she cupped her pale hands around his bronzed ones, inhaled, the tip of her tongue dislodged a speck of tobacco from her lower lip. Von Sternberg, the consummate cameraman, left quietly. He knew a great two-shot when he saw one.

In his biography of Dietrich, Steven Bach sets the meeting in the restaurant at the Hôtel des Bains on the Lido in Venice and adds that Dietrich's husband, Rudi Sieber, was also there.

What is certain is that they met in August of 1937, and Remarque stops writing in his diary, so there is no known record of his early days with Dietrich. His diary entries stop exactly on July 31, when he took Jutta to dinner at their favorite Monte Verità in Porto Ronco, and begin again in

The fragile beauty of Jutta Remarque, ca. 1937.

The romance continues: Remarque and Marlene Dietrich in Cannes, ca. 1939.

December, in Paris, at the Hôtel Prince de Galles, where he went with Jutta but had dinner, presumably without her, with Dietrich's husband, Rudi Sieber, and his mistress, Tami. In the meantime, life was filled with "sun and booze." And art. His dealer Feilchenfeldt was bringing him treasures: a Polish carpet, a bronze, a Greek vase, a Han vase, four tiger china vases, a Korean vase, a red dragon carpet, a small Holbein carpet. He had become a member of the Aquarian Club in Zurich; an interest in the zodiac had developed when he started consulting a local Porto Ronco astrologer called Lamby. He had become increasingly dependent upon Lamby's readings since moving to Porto Ronco. It was Lamby who had predicted the emergence of a "blonde Venus" in Remarque's life. But by the summer of 1937, Lamby's life had become sad. His wife had taken steps to commit him, and he was leaving Ascona. He would go to Basel and then to an asylum in Germany. Remarque mourned Lamby's decline: "A man for whom the stars hold no more secrets—apart from that little bit of life on the darkest of them."

Not only was Jutta being given trouble about her passport, but Remarque's was being held in abeyance. He needed approval from the Swiss authorities to travel. Clearly the German government was trying to tell him something. He was becoming fixated on movement, dreamed of home, and felt somewhat trapped in his Porto Ronco refuge. "I just can't go on without a passport," he writes in his diary. "I must do something. Otherwise this place will turn into a prison."

But Remarque was a privileged prisoner, taking delivery of 170 bottles of 1934 Moselle wine or a new Chinese Chou bronze, sending his Daumier to an exhibition at the Zurich Kunsthaus, rowing out on Lake Maggiore, reading voraciously, and making judgments in his diary: "John Dos Passos *42nd Parellel*. Interesting composition, but it doesn't work all the same. *Pao*, a Negro novel by a Hungarian. Good. *The Ball*, by Irene Nemirowsky. Very perceptive, Jewish, quite unmerciful to herself. Klabund's Chinese translation. Great stuff. Brilliant and dense. Read Al Capone's biography. The forerunner of modern dictators. Only more humane."

At the end of June, he was able to get Panamanian passports from Athens, Greece, for Jutta and himself, which would free him to travel to France and then Venice in August, because, as he noted about his inner state as well as the political one, "It's getting quieter. Quieter and more restless."

The day after Remarque and Dietrich met at the Hôtel des Bains, they met again—by chance or design—on the Lido beach. Dietrich was holding a book of poetry by Rainer Maria Rilke. Impressed, Remarque commented on her good taste, whereupon Dietrich began reciting poem after poem from memory.

By December of 1937, they had become an item. Douglas Fairbanks, Jr., who had spent approximately half a decade as Dietrich's lover, was out, but, in retrospect, not entirely down about it. They had been together in California and then had a flat in London for several years: "She was the one who persuaded me to go back to Hollywood to do *Prisoner of Zenda*, which I was hesitant to do. She talked me into doing it, which was a very wise thing. I was dragging my feet, but she could be very persuasive. . . . And then Remarque came on the list . . . but even later on, after we'd separated and I'd married, she would always call. She was very friendly with my wife. She'd call up every birthday and Christmas, say 'hello' and 'how are you?' and wanted to know all about the children and so forth. She was like an old friend. And so we kept on in the relationship as friends for years afterwards."

In December of 1937, both Remarque and Dietrich stayed at the Hôtel Prince de Galles in Paris. Remarque was with Jutta but longed for Dietrich, who was there with her husband, Rudi, her daughter, Maria—called The Child—and Rudi's mistress, Tami. Remarque saw a lot of movies: *Stage Door*, which he called "very well acted. Good milieu. Material: Edna Ferber; Marx Brothers: quite good as a variety turn, otherwise pathetic; *Saratoga*, Jean Harlow's last film. Strange, a dead woman's film. It was all in the walk, face, hair. A few scenes were played by a double."

Because of Dietrich, Remarque became increasingly aware of the movies, even though he'd already been involved with them through his books. To be with a star as self-centered as Dietrich required constant attention. During the time that they were lovers, he became her closest adviser. Although their affair was just putting down roots by December, he did not sound elated, which was quite in keeping with his character: "Not happy, not sad. Memories and the present keep crossing. I could work, if I were on my own."

An extraordinary confluence of events began in the new year. Jutta had left Remarque in Paris a few days after they'd arrived and had gone to Vienna to be with her sister Edith and brother-in-law, Heinrich. They were holding a family conference in a safer place than Germany in order to make some sort of a plan. Jutta was being required by the German government to reside in her own country. She was not Jewish and therefore had nothing to fear. Unless she was married to a Swiss taxpayer, she could no longer remain as a resident in that country. Germany would not extend a visa to permit the ex-wife of a traitor also to betray her country. Although her brother-in-law, Heinrich, was Hermann Göring's brother, there were not too many new strings he could pull at that time.

Jutta, her sister Edith, and Heinrich had a semblance of an idea, and summoned Remarque, who extricated himself from his new love to go to Jutta's aid. Whatever transpired in Vienna wreaked some emotional havoc. A guess would be that Remarque initially balked at having to be the rescue net. It would seem from his movements that he was in a spin. He left Vienna, touched down in Paris again—perhaps for some consolation from Dietrich, then on to Porto Ronco for Christmas, and then to St. Moritz to meet Dietrich on January 5. Whatever his reaction, it was certainly enough to trigger this abject letter from Jutta that greeted him on arrival. She had gone from Vienna to her retreat in Davos.

The first letter in the New Year. For a whole year I didn't exist for you; it didn't hurt me so much as it insulted me. Once, it would have been unthinkable for us. That we are now so separate, because I still love you with all my heart, is clear. The meeting in Vienna was not only disappointing for you. I know I was miserable, and behaved like a silent louse, but you weren't the Boni I know either. What I hear from people about you, I don't like very much, but you have written a good book, and I am loyal to you. What I want to know is if we will still live with each other. It's a success if I know that someone accepts the feelings I am able to give. It's upsetting that all this should have been in vain. I'm fine. I'm learning—with difficulty—to live alone. I'm probably separated from my husband for good. Even so, it's difficult to accept this ending, and I may do many unnecessary things—but I feel alive again. Please send me a sign. I'm staying here for another ten days. Farewell—with all that truly belongs to you.

Jutta joined Remarque in St. Moritz, and on January 22, he remarried her. His reasons were straightforward: it was the only decent thing to do. Her reasons—however much in real peril she felt—were more complex, but she came out of it with her financial, political, and psychological problems eased. Emotionally, it still was not good, but at least, now, she had some room to maneuver. She was legally back in the picture.

For Remarque, it was purely a marriage of convenience. He was determined not to let it be a millstone. "A talk with Marlene," he writes in his diary of February 1938. One can only imagine how it went.

For the moment, the big problem was not Jutta but the darkening political situation in Europe and his suspicions regarding Otto Klement. Remarque noted in his diary on February 20, 1938, that a call from Knopf confirmed that there was $5,000 missing, which he blamed on Klement.

He continues with further disturbances: "Eden, the English Secretary of State, has resigned. Piece of luck for Italy. Now they'll probably get the loan from England that they need to continue their opposition against England. English policies: the bane of Europe for the last twenty years. . . . Heard the Hitler speeches. We're in the mire, and there are darkest expectations for the future. . . . The night sky with all the stars—shining down on martyrs, idiots, madmen, fanatics, the dead and wounded; on Spain, concentration camps, meadows of rotting narcissus, criminals and their crimes, and the 20th century."

Remarque was an autobiographical novelist whose life—as much as he railed against it—dictated and served his art. His passport troubles, which began as tiresome, ended in March of 1938 as destructive on a grand scale. He was deemed null and void by the German government, which stripped him of his citizenship. The document signed and sent by the Gestapo agent Dr. Lange to "The Reich Leader of the SS and Head of the German Police in the Ministry of the Interior" is as chilling as it is thorough. It is a prime example of twisting information in order to justify obliteration:

> The German-blooded writer Erich Paul Remark has German nationality status. He left the territory of the Reich even before the assumption of power and resides in Porto Ronco near Locarno in Switzerland. On the basis of a reference in a Paris newspaper he is said to be living at the present time in St. Moritz. . . .
>
> Erich Re-mark [*sic*], with support from the Jewish Ullstein Press, has for years, in the most sordid and base manner, insulted the memory of the dead soldiers of the World War and already, as a result of that, excluded himself from the German community.
>
> With the money acquired in this manner he bought himself a villa in Switzerland. In Porto Ronco, near Locarno, he maintained, until recently, an active social life which was exclusively limited to emigrants, Jews, and Communists. . . . [Remark's] associations also unequivocally show that he clings just as much as he did earlier to the Jewish-Marxist seditious ideas. . . .
>
> I am therefore proposing to deprive Remark of German citizenship.

In the event that domestic inquiries should prove to be successful, I shall recommend the retroactive confiscation and seizure of his assets.

According to an account in the Paris newspaper of January 27, 1938, Remark is supposed to have remarried his former wife Ilsa (née) Zambona, born August 28, 1901, in Hildesheim. After the conclusion of the inquiry I shall, if appropriate, recommend the extension of the deprivation of civil rights to the wife and any children.

There were several more go-arounds before the smear campaign was complete. The final approval came from the Reich Ministry of the Interior on June 8, 1938: "In reference to the deprivation of citizenship proposal made by the Reichsführer SS and the head of the German Police . . . I concur in the deprivation of citizenship of the German-blooded Erich Paul Remark and the proposed extension of it to include his wife Ilse (née) Zambona. (signed) Schumburg."

Remarque would preserve and heighten the sense of alienation due to his new status as a citizen of nowhere in his next two novels: *Flotsam* and *Arch of Triumph*.

Even though his relationship with Dietrich was somewhat nurturing, he felt severely shaken. The first time he was irrevocably changed was through Fritz Hörstemeier; the second time was through fame; the third was through his loss of citizenship. He began to concentrate on minutiae while waiting for bigger ideas to form: "Looked at the newly laid out rugs. There's nothing from which one can't learn how to write. One only has to look for it long enough. . . . Idea for a small book: travels in a room. Story of a rug, reflecting a painting, a sculpture, watching an ant who has lost her way, a cat."

He concentrated on the blows being dealt Europe and humanity:

On the 11th in the evening the start of the conquest of Austria. A clear war—bloodless—the clearest there ever was. . . . In Vienna they already have named a place after Hitler. The world consists of servants. . . . Everybody expects war. I don't expect it yet. European depression. Caused by one man and one country. . . . Letter from Marlene. Depressed . . . world situation is helpless, dumb, murderous. More than just political. More than just economical. Socialism, which mobilizes the masses, is destroyed by the masses. The same right to vote fought hard for, has extinguished the fighter. If the masses count, then demogoguery also counts. Human being is closer to cannibalism than he believes. A hundred years ago the last witch was burned. Tortures were only suspended in Germany under Frederick II.

And how long ago were the Inquisition, the witch hunts, the slavery? It's not yet time to look back on them.

Finally, toward spring, an idea arrived: "Thought about a novel of a man without a passport. . . . Cleared my desk. Normally a sign that I will start writing. . . . Started a little work. The theme is still too unclear. What doesn't help: to have to put pressure against the pressure from the outside. One world against the other. But isn't it too late already? Missed out on so much. Too many tensions in the middle of a circle of laziness, passiveness, and standing on the sidelines. It's never too late. Never too late even to learn English. But I need some wind. This year is paralyzing me slowly. I'm too little alone. Much too little."

He was alone even less for the next several years. He seemed to be caught up in the vortex of the rich and famous and was unable to let go. "A deeply private person needing considerable affirmation" was the way Luise Rainer regarded him. He wanted to be alone—but in good company.

Curt Riess, his colleague from *Sport im Bild* days, met up with him again in Paris in the late spring of 1938, when he was with Dietrich: "He was spending a few weeks with Marlene. I had seen from the immigrants' newspaper that the Germans had lifted his citizenship, and so I mentioned it to him. I had already been expatriated three years earlier. It seemed to upset him. 'Now,' he said, 'now I am really an emigrant,' although he had been one for years. . . . He lived surrounded by other people and their intrigues. He despaired and thrived on them. He was particularly involved with other immigrants, and whether he knew it or not, he studied them. Many of them appeared much later in the novels he wrote, the most successful of which was called *Arch of Triumph* and was another worldwide success."

Remarque was also drinking heavily. His consumption was becoming legendary. The major women in his life all had been concerned for his safety and health first, but then, there was his sexual appetite, or lack of it.

Even during the beginning of his time with Dietrich, in Paris and the south of France in late 1938 and 1939, he was so out of control that she—as world-weary and blasé as she seemed—panicked. At all hours of the morning she would recruit friends to search for him in the various haunts, find him, and bring him back to the hotel.

Like all drinkers, Remarque could get quite determined and wily over what was his necessary intake; Curt Riess recalled one dinner in Ascona:

My wife and I were invited to his house. We stayed at a hotel in Ascona, but came to him for dinner, which started with six or eight people at the table. A tin of caviar was placed in front of each of them, together with each having his own bottle of vodka. During dinner there were various wines and later whiskey and then champagne. And finally, when we were all really in various stages of drunkenness, Remarque insisted on driving us back to the hotel in his Bugatti. We declined, but he insisted, and we wound up not in our hotel but in a nightclub in Ascona, where we waited—since we couldn't drink anymore—while he continued until the place closed down. Then, and only then, he took us to our hotel, and I asked him to promise that he would drive directly home.

The next day at noon or one o'clock he came to fetch us at the hotel. . . . He had not gone home, but he'd gone to his baker, and then he told us one of his typical stories. He was irritated that the nightclubs in Ascona close at three o'clock in the morning, a time when he frequently would find himself still in need of an alcoholic beverage. He had found that a small bakery on his way was open all night baking bread for the next day. So he arranged for the baker to take the stock for him of various bottles of whiskey, gin, and some wine, and he would appear at all hours of the night and would buy— yes, buy back—his own whiskey by the glass!

By late spring of 1938, Remarque's attachment to Dietrich had become quite intense, although she was already sprinting ahead, leading him on in a not-so-merry chase. She was inconstant. She would cook for him, often spend the night with him, worry about his drinking and that his "genius would wither," but she would not be faithful to him. She was rapidly becoming his favorite form of torment. In his diary, the recorded scenes between them often read like highly charged drama: "Cocktails at the George V. Got back to the hotel late. Marlene was offended. Went out alone. Along the Champs-Elysées. I followed her. Went alone to the Tout Paris afterward. Met the Opels. Marlene called. We left to change bars and meet her. We'd been told the Monocle. A few minutes later Marlene turned up at Tout Paris. She looked for me later without my knowing it. Got home about six in the morning. Marlene, up and dressed, was waiting for me."

There was a charming contrast between Dietrich the bewitcher and Dietrich the hausfrau. When she wasn't running him ragged with her other affairs, she was giving him a gemütlich family evening. She would spend hours—often half a day—preparing a delicious dinner for Remarque and her husband, Rudi, and sometimes a few guests. But these occasions were never lavish, very social, or "Hollywood." They tended to be relaxed and easy: "Spent yesterday evening with Rudi S. Marlene had been cooking since 4 for it. Clear soup, beef and veal goulash, potatoes with parsley, and Berlin pancakes with apricot filling. The best I've ever tasted. Marlene had burned her hand in the fat. She appeared in a white smock." Or she would prepare something more casual: "Champignon soup, boulettes, scrambled eggs, and Serbian risotto."

Remarque found himself spending a good deal of time with Rudi Sieber. He tolerated him—but just: "Spent the evening with Rudi S. The gentle paralysis of a totally unimaginative yet unimpeachable existence. Bourgeois attitudes are fatal. Lack of imagination is disarming. . . . Rudi is a priceless study of a glutton who always takes offense if everything is not right. Gluttony without intellect is sometimes rather hard to put up with. Tami and I try to convince him that he must get to work: get out of this dependence on the Puma. Don't think he really wants to, despite his fine words. Too lazy, too comfortable."

At that moment, women rather than men were preoccupying Dietrich, a situation that simultaneously amused and repelled Remarque. He thought he was sophisticated enough to handle her liaisons with her last lover, the writer Mercedes de Acosta, and her latest passion, the Canadian whiskey heiress Jo Carstairs. However, he seriously balked when she left his company for that of another woman. The comings and goings, pushes and pulls of both of them were dizzying. He, with Jutta, Porto Ronco, his drinking, the pressure to write, and she, with her strange brood of husband, his mistress, and child, her need to revive a flagging career, her need to be desired by many, her overwhelming self-absorption. Their lives during this period, as recorded by Remarque, come across as misdirected farce. It is sometimes difficult to comprehend how they actually had time for any of the usual rituals of a day. Remarque records in his diary:

[*June 25*] Reached Paris after 7 in the morning. The Puma came running to the station. To the hotel. She's taken care of everything. Right away played me some of her records and a Stravinsky *Rite of Spring*. Coffee. As was to have been expected: too much anticipation on both sides, misunderstandings. It was very much my fault, according to her. I'm a dirty player. . . . It carried on next day. Each did their little bit toward it. . . . Ate at Fouquet's in the evening . . . then Le Tout Paris. . . . Ended up at Caprice. Phoned right away. Asked if the Puma would collect me. Yes. Then I'll come home.

Arrived. To and fro. Puma's version: I'd arrived, woken her up, and announced that I wanted to leave again right away. Later told her she ought to get some sleep. Puma gave me a right hook in the face. Disappeared. Came back. The Puma. I said, "Oh, there you are again." In her room. I stayed. Storms rumbling. Lightning, and the long, soft night breeze, the joy of intoxication, and the return home of the will-o'-the-wisps, the long road along the adventures of the heart.

[*27th June*] . . . Sense of animal well-being. Went out to eat with the Puma. . . . Then Hermès to try on a white bathing costume; Agnès, hats. Tired. Went home. Had a sleep. . . . The sleeping Puma. Walked about softly. A bit like in *Three Comrades*. Puma with the astrologist in the evening. I'm sitting waiting. . . .

[*28th June*] . . . The stargazer told Puma that she could only love somebody who had been born between June 21 and July 15, or in August. That made the Puma happy.

[*30th June*] . . . Sent flowers to Puma, Peter . . . and Mercedes. Orchids and lilies for the Puma.

[*2nd July*] . . . Puma's been to the lady-doctors with her daughter. Had her examined, glands malfunctioning. 2,000 white blood corpuscles too few. Far too much calcium. . . . Then began on Marlene: abscess of the liver. Half-functioning thyroid. Growths. Then the Puma had had enough. Terrible, if it's right. Abscess of the liver—the life-line in her palm, that's cut short . . . it doesn't do to think about it. M. was depressed. I comforted her. If the diagnosis is right, then it can be treated. If it's a con, then don't get steamed up about the diagnosis. . . .

[*6th July*] . . . Family, too much of the family. . . . Evening at the Tout Paris. Marvelous armagnac. All in a very good mood. In the end Rudi S. on the trumpet, Marlene on violin, and me on the piano . . . Got home about 5. . . .

[*8th July*] . . . Le Tout Paris . . . Scheherazade. Cognac . . . Caprice . . . Then some house or other which had flagellation and a fat Madame. Very well-built Negress from Martinique. Gin. Got back in the morning.

[*9th July*] It's cold in Paris. . . . I'm increasingly toying with the idea of leaving for Porto Ronco. For the silence, for the inescapable, solitary evenings, when I'll curse myself for having left. Everything is wearing thin, getting too touchy and rather bourgeois. Marlene reproaches me for having married. Rightly and wrongly. Peter reproaches me with Marlene—wild and pathetic. Wrongly. I explain to Marlene that marriage means less than having someone who is mostly in America and seeing them from time to time. She says she waited for me, but you can't stay alone, especially in the situation she was in. Right and wrong on both sides. Quite a complicated mess. Then there's the family: friendly, understanding, kind—but there all the time, even when they aren't there. And The Child, too. A crowd of hangers-on that I would never get so close to if it weren't for M. It kills the freedom in me, it makes me dusty and gray, even when there are no problems. It changes M., too. Even when we're alone. Everything had a different ring about it, there's a lot of emptiness where there should be fullness . . . I do things that are childish and silly; I realize it as I do them in spite of it. I should live in a different hotel. I ought not to know the family. Too much comfort blunts you. And sharpens and tires you altogether.

Eleven days later, he changed his mind. Instead of fleeing to Porto Ronco, he dutifully chauffeured some of "the family" from Paris to Lyons en route to a holiday in Antibes. Remarque took The Child and the Puma in the Lancia; Rudi and Tami went in their Packard. They all spent the night in Lyons, where, as Remarque noted, "Everything was bright and cheerful. Puma happy." The next day, Rudi took off for Antibes, but Remarque, Puma, and The Child were stuck. The heroic Lancia had stalled out. One of the coil windings had broken. They had to stay another day until an expert repairman was located. Nerves were frayed. They called Rudi in Antibes and arranged for him to meet them outside Cannes. As Remarque comments drily, "Reloaded cars because of The Child. Then I went on alone."

Maria Riva, in her biography of her mother, describes that summer of privilege, and the Hôtel du Cap in Cap d'Antibes, one of the most luxurious hotels on the Riviera, where the celebrated "gathered . . . to observe each other and exchange their privileged gossip." It was a place where one dressed up and showed off designer clothes and jewels from the vault. Dietrich, Remarque, and Riva's father had connecting suites, while Tami and Riva were down the hall. Riva describes in sumptuous detail three-hour luncheons followed by naps in cluttered rooms before the round of parties in Cannes or Juan-les-Pins.

Remarque was a semi-willing victim of this sybaritic lifestyle. He berated himself in varying degrees of severity for being unable to resist it. And even though their affair continued until 1940, Remarque and his Puma were at the height of it that summer. When they were domestic and sweet together, he often referred to her as Marlene; otherwise it's Puma. Curiously, for all their worldliness and sophistication, their carryings-on were clumsy and immature. The diary tracks the escapades of their relationship:

[*1.8*] . . . Had a letter from Puma's mother yesterday. Warning and begging me to break off the affair with her, otherwise consequences for her in Germany. Still no real idea who is behind it. Possibly Herr Vollmoll, who often wanted to take Puma to Germany, and perhaps blamed me for the snub she gave him . . . or perhaps the boss-Nazi himself, who has gone head over heels for Puma's latest film. . . .

[*4.8*] . . . The family—the surroundings—at the moment all very nice and charming—are suffocating me. There can be no love where the family comes as part of the deal. . . . The Puma squatting down, beautiful and pure seduction. This strange touch of iciness in her. . . .

[*15.8*] . . . Saw Kennedy, the American ambassador in London. Morgenthau, the Treasury Secretary of America, a big, quiet Jew, very pale. . . . Got a new cabana, to one side. Better for thinking in. The situation with the Puma is better. Was about time. Mostly my fault.

[*22.8*] . . . Had a row with Puma. Not my fault this time.

[*23.8*] The row with Puma went on. . . . In the evening had another row with Puma and got back my car keys, which she had annexed a week earlier. . . . Whatever happens is okay. Even loss.

[*31. 6 a.m. Wednesday*] The situation: for several days Puma has been completely under the spell of another woman. Began around Friday. At the next cabana to the Puma's was a fat homosexual man—round, spongy face and tattooed arms—with a very masculine-looking woman—gray-black hair, tattooed arms—and a pretty blond girl and a younger man. Not quite sure that it's a crisscross relationship, man-man, woman-woman. Puma was rather interested. Then around Friday she was sitting over there, introduced by an English actor, and aroused by things she was told about the woman with the tattoos: apparently fabulously wealthy, the owner of her own island with 150 people living on it an hour from Miami, built hospitals, lived quite independently, etc. . . . Puma very impressed with the whole situation. . . . On Friday evening Puma was at a party nearby. . . . The lesbian was there. Saturday afternoon Puma was sitting outside the cabana with her ears pricked up. . . . Margo Lion was at our cabana so Puma was already rather nervous and aroused. . . . [Margo Lion, an actress, appeared with Dietrich in a musical called *It's in the Air*, where they sang a song to each other called "My Best Girlfriend." Lion and Dietrich were very close.]

. . . Puma disappeared at about 6, as there was a party at Elsa Maxwell's in the evening. . . . Fetched Lion out around 8, and saw Puma sitting there all dressed and ready to go, white paillettes, white fox-fur coat, an hour too early, sitting with the homosexuals. . . . I went up to my room and waited for Puma to come before she left, as she always does: she came—for one minute, fleeting cool: "Adieu, mein Herz"—without a word whether we were going to meet up later. Only asked me, "I hear you're going out for a stroll?" I said I was going out, as I couldn't work in the light of the room, and the hotel was dead. I heard later that she had quite forgotten to come and say good-bye—it was Rudi who had reminded her. A quarter of an hour later I went to dinner with Tami. In the hall were the partygoers. . . . Puma sitting with the homosexuals, with her face turned toward the door. Rudi came up to us, wanting us to go with him, we talked, then went on, past the Puma, who didn't look up but glanced at us from behind as we walked past. I spent the evening alone with Tami. I heard later that Puma, at the Maxwell party, talked Rudi into looking in at the Bastide, an attractive bar in Cannes. She only told him as they went in that they might meet the fat homo there (otherwise he wouldn't have gone), but really meant the lesbian with the tattoos, who was simply called Jo. . . . Next morning, as I came back from a swim around twelve, Puma was sitting over at the homo's cabana: looked up, saw me, looked away, and didn't speak. I was furious, and in the afternoon I drove to Monte Carlo to see Peter, who had just arrived to celebrate her birthday. . . . Drove back later. Found a rather lie-ridden letter from Puma, who acted innocent and wanted to know where on earth I'd gotten to. Then on Monday morning she appeared in my cabana. She'd come from Jo, told me she had waited for me in the evening—because she knew I wasn't there—and later admitted she had been with Jo. I was very calm and friendly. The main reason for Puma's arrival was to complain about Rudi and Tami, who had been very reserved earlier in the evening—Rudi was furious about the Bastide and the lesbian because once upon a time he had lost the Puma to the lesbian Waldorff. . . . I told the Puma that I found it childish of her not to have spoken to me. She lied, tried to get out of it, cried, said nobody understood her, etc. Big scene, well played. Finally she said the woman interested her, and as I remained friendly, I got a naively proud account of all sorts of things: such and such a look, things she'd said, the way she held her hand, etc. . . . Puma spent the afternoon with the homos. I was introduced, pushed off, then Puma came round to us occasionally, rather ill at ease, overfriendly because of Rudi. Tennis at six. Puma turned up with Jo. Wanted to show herself off. Played doubles—Puma badly, me worse, stopped after a short while and then Puma played singles with her daughter. Puma left with Jo afterward. The rest went to the bar expecting to find Puma and Jo to arrange the evening; nobody there. Waited until 9:30. Rudi and I had two vodkas. Then I went upstairs, having decided to eat alone at the Eden Roc. I went over to Rudi: heard that Puma had just walked in, furious. I went over. Puma was incredibly nervous, kept powdering herself. I explained to her that we had waited for her and even sent Tami up to ask her what was being planned for the evening. She claimed I had arranged it all in the morning, invited all the people. Not true. She was afraid of Rudi. Finally we came to an agreement. She rushed down the stairs ahead of us to get to Jo and brief her. . . . We all had dinner at the Eden Roc. I talked a lot of nonsense, but drew Jo away from the Puma in conversation. Then we went on to Maxim's. Puma sat next to Jo. . . . Rudi, Tami, and I sat at the corners. I didn't talk much. Puma chattered away. A few women with bare breasts. One naked. A Hawaiian atmosphere, à la Juan-les-Pins. Puma wanted me to dance with her. I didn't want to. . . . Later Puma went to Jo's for the night.

[*1st Sept. 7 A.M.*] . . . Puma's escapades liven things up no end. The report continues: Tuesday morning nothing to be seen of the Puma till midday. . . . She was nervous. Bought a record: "The legionnaire with nobody tattooed on his heart." Puma was really shaken as the record played, showing me she had goose pimples listening to the song, and I laughed as my life may be falling apart. Went home afterward. I was very nervous, a bit afraid of driving the car. Puma in my room. . . . Tried to get some sleep alone in the afternoon, managed an hour. Heart was pounding. Sweating. Really in a state . . .

[*2nd Sept. Friday*] Yesterday sent some flowers and a note to Puma in the morning. Went round to Rudi later. Puma was already up. Looked strange: no makeup, her eyes wide apart, her skin rather sallow and dull, very like a Puma. . . . Not beautiful, interesting. The rather pale, rather vague blue eyes. Saw her again later, after tennis. Even that was overdoing it a bit. Feilchen and Marianne around midday. Puma went to eat with us. Talked about nothing but Jo: her island, her boats, the Bahamas, freedom, the radio station, foreign countries, and her own sense of oppression; about how she never even got to Italy, and then about Sternberg and all he had seen: the West Indies, Bali, etc. . . . All in some naive way against me, especially when I said that under some circumstances you could see more of life sitting at a table than on a trip around the world. . . . I have to become more romantic and interesting for the Puma. At the moment Jo represents romanticism, freedom, the exotic, adventure. I am the familiar, the secure, the bourgeois (by my very association with The Family—though it was she who created the association), and at the moment she remembers only the bad times we have spent together—as a contrast to the ideas she contracts from the other woman.

I should become more interesting through a) work; b) work that has got something to do with her; c) not necessarily living in the same hotel; d) what is known as romantic panache, pushing myself a bit, doing the things that a woman likes, dressing very well, always being a cut above the rest, etc.

. . . Had dinner at the Pavillon Bleu. At once there was an unpleasant atmosphere between Rudi and Puma. Caused by Puma, who was as nervous as hell and ordered for us all, while Rudi wanted to study the menu in peace. Rudi drank a lot of vodka, Puma kept signaling to me what a sacrifice it was, in short it was unpleasant. I bridged the situation. Later, the others drove home, and Puma and I stood on the street without a car, Puma having wanted it that way earlier when I wanted to bring my car along; so I stood there, interested to see what would come next. What came was good. First of all the Puma convinced me that it was only for my sake that she wanted to go to the Bastide, the homos' bar, as I had said at lunchtime that I definitely wanted to go back with her. Only that was no reason not to be in my car. Then she explained how Rudi had been so offended, otherwise he could have taken Tami to see the place. Finally, she came out with this: Jo and her entourage were eating at Sartori's in Antibes, and she had said that after dinner she was going to the Bastide with me or with us, but it was very doubtful whether Jo would come, as she had no car and was so far away. I had to laugh when I imagined Rudi and Tami at the Bastide, and I said, too, it would have been better for us to have gone on our own, whereupon the Puma looked at me wide-eyed and announced that it made no difference to her. . . . A moment later, Jo and her troupe arrived in a taxi. They made a good entrance. We went home about three in Jo's taxi, which had waited. I'm not quite sure what it was all supposed to mean; whether my car had to be left at home to hide something—or that she wouldn't have to drive back home alone with me—or, rather unlikely, because she was scared that I would drive too fast: probably the second. Unmistakable progress in relationship. Back at the hotel Puma phoned me again to ask whether I would like to say good night once more. I went over. Assumed that she was doing it to be sure that I wouldn't come later, when she was away with Jo. Puma acted tired, melancholy, had a bath, and went to bed before my eyes. I left, knowing that five minutes later she would be trotting happily downstairs. Considered it quite a passable performance.

Just as Remarque was pretending everything was all right with Dietrich, Jutta was pretending things were fine with Remarque. Occasionally, in an effort to steer clear of the Dietrich entourage, Remarque would meet with Jutta—in Monte Carlo, for instance, which she loved, and where, eventually, she would reside until her death. He would dine, dance, and talk into the night with her, and she would allow herself to think that they might have another chance. At the same time, she was determined to be detached, yet always failed, as is clear in this letter sent from Littlehampton, Sussex, Great Britain, in 1939:

Beloved Son, Father, united in death—Crucified One!

What a wonderful sign to have so many words coming from you to me. I kiss you!

How good that we don't live together—the sweet longing remains—and once—even if it's a long time away—to sleep together, sleep, sleep!

Originally I intended to go to the French Alps in the middle of February—maybe our trains will pass each other—maybe I will be closer to your heart, once you have succeeded with your other difficulties, and we can meet again.

Farewell. I kiss you. I hold you close in my arms. You know I am strong. I hold you tight! A stream of life goes out from me to you! Inexhaustibly!

Remarque would never again allow her the emotional position that she wanted. She would never stop wanting it. And he would never stop wanting Dietrich, until he married Paulette and his health began to falter.

His passion for his Puma seemed most feverish during the time of the triangle with Jo Carstairs, her tattooed lady. His diary entries are unique in their ability to capture an intelligent mind caught in the throes of an obsession.

[*4th Sept. Morning*] Got up at six yesterday. A strange situation: I sang, and deliberately and spontaneously began to cry. Very slowly, and not much, in front of the mirror, half ironically and half for real, half serious and half something else; not play-acting, more out of curiosity: even willing myself to, willing myself to shed tears . . . and then, a certain tranquillity and control.

Played tennis. Afterward Rudi came and told me Puma had already gone to Jo, had had her cases packed. I went to the beach around twelve. Half an hour later the Puma arrived, ready to go, obviously in some discomfort about how to put the trip to me. I hardly listened to her, was very lively and merely told her about my work, my marvelous mood, and how everything had suddenly come alive . . . and how youth had suddenly returned with its storms and wide horizons. . . . For I had seen that I was on the wrong track with the Puma; and I would certainly have lost her had it not been for this incident, which had stirred me into action and benefitted me in every possible respect. I have been awakened, and am alive.

I took the Puma back to the hotel. Jo's two shadows were waiting in the bar. Both rather embarrassed when they saw me. I was totally at ease and cheerful. Jo came, and was equally embarrassed. I reminded them to take some blocks of ice with them on the boat, to keep the drinks cool, and was quite in control of the situation and pleasant. Then I left. Puma called after me that she would phone. . . .

[*6th Sept.* 6 A.M. *Tuesday*] Puma phoned at lunchtime the day before yesterday. Said she would get back around 8 o'clock, but we weren't to wait. In the evening I drove to Monte Carlo to see Peter. It ended in a scene. . . . Came back. Found a note saying that Puma wasn't back.

. . . Yesterday morning . . . still no sign of Puma. We were really worried. At the hotel. Packed. At last I saw the fat queer outside talking to Tami. So they'd arrived. The boat was moored down in front of the cabanas. Puma sent word that she was here. I went to my cabana a little while later. Pretended I didn't see the boat. Did some work. Puma waved and shouted, I waved back. . . . We were all rather furious that the Puma didn't come down from the boat and had indicated via Kater (The Child) that she wanted to stay longer. Puma called to Rudi to tell him to come aboard: he said that he couldn't swim after a meal. Then after a short while Puma announced that we should send a car to the Port d'Antibes around 4, as they wanted to go for a drive around then. Presumably at first she had wanted to stay longer on the yacht. Hence the stay in the harbor. I had no urge to take part and help her out. Rudi went to the hotel to find out what was happening, whether Puma was staying or not. At 5 he told me to get the cases ready that were to go by train, and that we were leaving in the morning. I went up. Puma was in her room, very nervous. I advised her to stay. She made out that Rudi was spoiling her life with his room reservations, tickets, etc. What she was saying was crooked. In fact the dirty bitch had long since arranged with Jo that the queers would also be in Paris on Wednesday at the Hôtel Prince de Galles, where she then booked rooms for us, too, on the pretext of better service. . . . Later Puma came in and told another brilliant pack of lies: On the phone to Rudi she had meant 8 o'clock in the morning, not evening.

She forgot to explain why she had added that we weren't to wait for her at dinner. She lied and lied, ruthlessly and naively. Remarkable, the total absence of the thought of whether she was hurting the other person with her unnecessary explanations, disclosures, etc. Extraordinarily selfish. In everything she does she sees only what she wants to see, and holds that to be right. She takes offense if she causes offense. If she hurts another, then she's the one who's hurt. . . .

. . . She wanted to eat alone with me. I suggested taking the others along. She declined, heroically. I said, then let's take it as a kind of anniversary celebration. It was just a year ago that she had come to Venice. Okay. We arranged to meet at ten in the bar. She wanted to have a drink with Jo beforehand. At ten she arrived in the bar with Jo and the other two: one of them suggested eating in the Pavillon Bleu. I agreed. Made a couple of light-hearted comments to the Puma about our dinner à deux. She did the usual trick: declared she wasn't going, she was staying with me, and had to be persuaded to go. Was glad to go. Pavillon Bleu and then on to the Bastide. Without fatty. The three of them were terribly childish. Laughed and giggled about nothing. Not that I don't understand. It's the best thing possible. But I took a good look at it all and told myself: There's nothing left over of you and for you. . . .

. . . We leave in two hours. I know I need have no illusions. It's over and done with. I'll come to terms with it. It was a lesson. It was my fault in many respects. I'll have to become more disciplined. Work. Not let things drift. Keep an eye on myself. Learn languages. Work. Make something of myself. I've already become livelier in the last few days. The world is open to me.

[*7th Sept. 10 P.M. Paris*] . . . Slept in Lyons on the way. Only two rooms, one for Rudi and Tami, the other for Puma and me. Puma was even rather tender. This morning, too. Left for Paris at 9. Sang, laughed. Good spirits until evening. Had the hood down all day. Drove fast. Somehow thought I had made up for it all. Puma open and friendly. I'm sitting waiting now. Jo and the queers arrived this morning.

[*9th Sept. Friday. Lunchtime*] Went for dinner at the Tout Paris with Puma and her entourage. They didn't fit in. Good. I did fit. Puma was surprised: blue suit, white shirt. Her favorites. Little touches are the best ones. I was slim, full of life, and well dressed—quite enough to get the Puma interested. Mercedes de Acosta, Puma's last homosexual lover, was present, a tragic muse. Of the two sugar daddies, Mercedes was the better. Then the walk home: Puma and Mercedes in front, her arm around Puma's shoulder, the present sugar daddy suffering along behind. That common bitch of a

Puma! It has to be seen! Took Mercedes home. . . . Later went to a homo place in Montmartre: the Isis. Fantastic place. There was a show. Two queer can-can dancers. It was eerie. A singer in an evening gown, a man just the same. A Torero, like a girl, with castanets. A tap dancer lit up with blue spotlights. The audience was genuine, devoid of any pose. Men with makeup in women's costumes. The few normal folk who were there seemed unreal. Went on from there to Scheherazade. Puma had the urge to sing her songs. She sang. Wasn't too happy. She only wanted to do it for Jo. She was disturbed by my presence, which, without my saying a word, forced her to occupy herself with me. Talked to me all the time, drinking at the same time. She was drunk afterward in the car, without anyone noticing it. Told me not to leave her on her own. Said good-bye on the sixth floor. Puma shook hands with Jo, turned on her heels, and I followed behind her. A good scene. Took Puma to bed. Phoned Jo. Puma went to sleep very quickly. I left. Heard a record player. Six in the morning. Jo's room. Playing the Legionnaire song. I felt sorry. Must have thought I was sleeping with Puma. I phoned her again. Then went to bed.

Got up early yesterday morning. . . . Arranged to take language lessons. Sent the Puma some white orchids and a note to remind her of when we started, and the love that there had been this time a year ago. Went home. To Rudi's to fetch my watch. When I came out, there was Puma. Went down to my room with her. She was sweet. She remembered. Wanted to wear a wedding ring again. I felt that the affair with Jo was already on the wane. I also felt that my new manner was the right one. . . . Ate dinner at Fouquet's. . . . When I left, Puma came in with her entourage. Sat with them afterward over coffee. Jo disappeared. I saw that Puma wanted to be alone. Went to the hotel. As I was getting the key, saw Puma walk by to the lift. Got in too. Puma was rather embarrassed that I had noticed that Jo had gone upstairs and she was following after. I laughed, asked for the fifth floor. The lift boy had already pressed the sixth. I laughed. Puma laughed, rather embarrassed, ran out to Jo's side; the lift boy called after her that Miss Carstairs's room was in the other direction. I laughed after her.

Went to bed. Relaxed, untensed, slept right through till 9 this morning. Could sense that it was all over.

But now I've got to create some tension for myself, so that I don't lose the good condition I'm in.

From the end of 1939 until late in 1941, when his next serious love, Natasha Paley Wilson, was to appear, Remarque is an increasingly diminished mere mortal, battling, thrashing about, wooing and attempting to tame the wild Puma. His defenses were a sense of humor, his sharp writer's eye, his good instincts for survival, and his appreciation of aesthetics. As much pain as Dietrich caused him, he was thrilled by her, which he used as justification for enduring her shenanigans. The waning year would bring him constant new resolves, which he constantly would misplace.

[*9th Sept. Cont.*] . . . Learned some French. . . . Went to the Bibliothèque Nationale. A Persian exhibition. The little animal carpet by Peytel. The large counterpart to the Ardubil carpet. Some nice ceramics. But the high point was the miniatures. A 13th-century collection, absolutely spellbinding. The sweetness of the colors, a harmony of reds and blues—impossible to grasp. Wonderful naive and sophisticated art. . . .

Sent the Puma some cakes, the kind that get stuck around your teeth.

[*10th Sept.*] . . . Read Rilke, *Book of Hours*. Thought for a while. Puma phoned at two. Wanted to go out with me. . . . Went to the Persian exhibition, then to the Deux Magots Café. Talked about me, my work, the new impetus, films. Puma went to the church once, in between, alone. . . . Took the quiet, gentle Puma to the Ritz, where the others were waiting, and went home. . . . Phoned Peter. She cried. Felt lonely. Terrible. Advised her either to come to Paris, or to drive to Paris via Porto Ronco. What can I do to help her, without going back to her? I can't go back. That would be the end of my life.

[*13th Sept.*] . . . Puma came round about two yesterday afternoon. I was in bed. She joined me. It was a Puma on the attack. Didn't know whether to be glad or not. . . .

. . . Puma called me at 2:30 A.M. Wanted to tell me she loved me. Later she was in my room, in the sitting room. I heard something and got up, could smell perfume, but there was nobody there anymore. . . .

. . . Sent the Puma some chrysanthemums. Bought some fruit: damsons, nuts, grapes, and peaches. Sent them up to the Puma, who came down a short while later wanting to go for a walk with me. Champs-Elysées . . . Had orange juice and champagne at Fouquet's. Then on to Knize's. . . . Puma tried on some dresses. Suddenly Jo and her friend came in. Puma and I soon left for Schiaparelli's. Puma was beside herself. Lay down on the floor and said it was the first time she had felt nothing at the sight of Jo. Had coffee at the Ritz, then went to the Ostertag's [a well-known jewelry store], where Jo and her friend were waiting. I said good-bye, after I had looked at a bracelet and had asked about American rings. Had an hour's sleep in the hotel: Puma sent me some flowers. Telephoned her: Tami told me that she had come home, changed into a black dress, and disappeared like a flash with a new dress under her arm. The flash-in-the-pan at Knize's doesn't seem to have had a very lasting effect. We'll have to wait and see.

Spoke to Peter on the phone. Talked about an ultimatum from the Sudeten Germans. Six hours, expiring tonight. Must keep my ears open. Summoned Peter to Paris. Damned close to war. Perhaps even tomorrow. . . .

Half past nine in the evening. Puma's great orange and pink autumn flowers are glowing in the lamplight: I'm sitting by the radio . . . to see if there's going to be a war. To see whether I'll make it to Porto Ronco, to fetch everything away.

[*14th Sept.*] . . . Heard today that people born in the last war have been called up. . . . Puma heard that stateless persons in France were being sent to the military. Was very upset because I've been in France for 4 months now and should long ago have got myself a Carte d'Identité. Sat by the radio till midnight. Ultimatum expired. Eleven dead. Czech government was demanding first order, then negotiations. . . . Puma was hatching plans the whole evening. Wanted to travel to Porto Ronco for me, wanted to get us all on board the ship and travel to the American Embassy. Got to the hotel about two A.M. . . . an incident in the lift. The boy asked: "Fourth?" I said sixth. And at the same instant Puma said fifth. . . . She explained that she wanted to see if Jo was okay. . . . I went away. Was cleaning my teeth when Puma came in. Told her to go and get some sleep. She said she had plenty of time: Jo was asleep in her clothes and couldn't be woken. This was a bit much for me: this consideration and at the same time the deceit. Rightly or wrongly I felt that I was relegated to second place . . . when she acted in the afternoon as if the other affair was all over and ours was the coming thing, then for Christ's sake she ought to make up her mind and not vacillate! I began with the American consulate: I said she was not to waste her time, I would go myself. She was offended: back and forth. I was angry about her nervousness, which came from the fact that Jo had gone to sleep and that upset her. Put things more or less to rights. We lay on the sofa in the salon for a while, then on the bed: Puma was careful not to let any artificial situation develop. I saw that she wanted to go. She even tried to get out of staying by saying that she had to give Rudi and the others the latest news. I said we could phone them. She said no, if they were already asleep we would wake them unnecessarily. She would go and see.

Got a phone call this morning. We are to go to the American Embassy at a quarter to three. The political situation is critical: a plebiscite that comes to the same as secession, or war. Relations between the Sudeten Germans and the Czechs broken off. 18 dead already.

I've got to make a decision! Get out of this nonsensical backing and forthing! Be decisive! Get a grip on myself! Let go of what doesn't belong. Enough of chicanery, women, and amours! . . .

[*18th Sept.*] . . . In the afternoon of the 14th went to the American Embassy. Got a visa for 12 months, which took only ten minutes, thanks to Marlene. Together with the Puma afterward. Good. Said she loved me. . . .

. . . Mercedes de Acosta was telling me tales about the Puma, the practical joker. How one morning she had called the doctor, because in the afternoon she planned to fall off her horse in order to win back Sternberg, who was angry with her. Sent herself flowers, so as to be able to say they were from Mercedes. . . . Indisputable exhibitionist. . . .

. . . Met Puma and Tim [part of Jo Carstairs's ménage] in the cinema: *Pepe le Moko*, and American version with Boyer and Hedy Lamarr, who was Hedi Kiesler from Salzburg. . . . Told Puma that I was meeting Ruth Albu later. She stiffened rather. Left. When I went into the bedroom, she was standing behind the door. Later I saw that she had hidden all my shoes, so that I couldn't go out. But I managed to find a pair. . . .

. . . Puma made some wild comments, because she was angry I had found a pair of shoes. . . . Also, very cold, thinking I had started something with the chambermaid. According to her, I had cold hands and a smear of lipstick around my mouth. Ran away. Came back, very excited, wanting to kill me. In the end I managed to half convince her. Went to Korniloff's with Jo and Tim and Mercedes. Puma let her hair down, played the child—said it was because of the shock she'd had. Prince de Galles. Puma was ill. On to the Boeuf afterward. I just sat around quietly. Said a calm good-bye in the lift. Puma didn't phone me again. Had a bad night. I'm still not over it yet.

[*19th Sept.*] . . . Slept with the Puma. She was half asleep when I came. Wearing Jo's bracelet and ring. And a nightdress. I didn't touch her. . . . She was tender in the morning. . . .

[*20th Sept. Early afternoon*] Ate lunch yesterday at Fouquet's with Mercedes and Puma. Mercedes told Puma that I was the best man she's ever had. Made little impression on her. Mercedes said Puma ought to marry me. Puma said I had promised to. Not exactly spoken from the heart—more with a certain satisfaction that she had wrung that from me. . . .

Went to a French film with Mercedes at ten. . . . Then back home. The phone was ringing in Puma's room. I went, saying that she should call me when she'd finished. She lay in my arms, told me some story about having pains, which was totally unnecessary. I made some jokes, and she went straight to sleep. . . .

. . . Why do I go along with it all? I'll wait until Jo comes back or Puma goes to London. [Jo had gone to London, which is why the Puma had spent her nights sleeping with Remarque.] Everything's gone downhill since Jo's been away. Naturally: I am here, and that is uninteresting; the one who is away in this situation draws all the attention to himself. I think I can now only save something of it all by leaving. Before it would have probably been the wrong thing to do. But not now. Maybe, too, I ought not to sleep with her without sleeping with her. . . .

[*23rd Sept. Friday*] . . . 21st. Had breakfast with Puma at midday, in my room: fried sole and coffee. Drove into the Bois around three. Splendid September day. Two hours of continual skirmish. Puma told me how she loved men. Fast, misty-eyed, uninhibited, when it comes over her, etc. Then she said that she didn't need men. She'd never felt the lack of one in bed. Only women—Jo. That was just the problem. That was what got her excited. Long conversation. In the end we had a bite at Fouquet's, then I took her to Schiaparelli's. At the door she said, "Why not talk about what we really think now?" Went to get a monocle and a pair of glasses. . . . Went to the Louvre with Puma in the evening: medieval, Roman, and Greek rooms lit up. Afterward ate at the bar of the Tout Paris. Went home. Puma suddenly discovered that I'm in better training. Fell in love. After all that talk, suddenly. I couldn't manage it. Heaven knows why not. We slept close together, however, with Puma clutching me tight. Puma in love again in the morning. . . . Both of us rather infected by desire and lack of it. Went to Knize's, for Puma to try on some outfits. Then Van Cleef, the jewelers. Chose a wedding ring, which Puma wanted to have from me. . . . Went to bed with Puma that night. Afterward she slept clutching me right through till morning. Had taken off Jo's ring and bracelet.

[*25th Sept.*] . . . Chamberlain-Hitler conference broken off, the Czechs mobilized, some of the French, too, impossible demands from Germany, etc. Took the news along to Fouquet's. Said I would probably have to go to Porto Ronco tomorrow after all. Puma was upset. . . . It's all a bit like in the war again: uncertainty, expectation, tension. . . . Awaiting news of the English cabinet decision.

[*27th Sept.*] Disturbing days: war—peace—war. Report on latest developments: sort of obstinacy, thought I'd been running about after the Puma too much. . . . So, now, Puma had been looking for me, came down, we talked, packed later. Went to Fouquet's for dinner with Jo and Tim. . . . I gave Jo a copy of *All Quiet* with a dedication, which amazed the Puma. Had a good conversation: Puma claimed I had sparkled, but I hadn't. Talked about how Puma built up all her lovers, then left them behind, broken. Puma denied it. Sternberg. He had, according to her, been hysterical in the old days—and still was for that matter. . . . Back to the hotel. Went up to the 5th floor. An hour later Puma rang and said she loved me and had no desire to go to Jo. Good ploy, mixed with the truth. I said, then she should come down. She twisted out of it, skillfully: last evening, etc. I said it was also the last for me, but I wasn't sentimental. . . .

. . . On the morning of the 26th, sent over a letter to the Swiss consulate to get a visa. Meanwhile, the Puma arrived with the newspapers, telling me I wasn't to travel, as there would be war by evening. The situation was very bad, it's true. . . . She ran out, saying she'd be right back. I waited, then went to the bank to get another $5,000, then came back to carry on packing. Puma walked in about 10:15. I was angry. I had heard earlier from Rudi that she was at Knize's trying on outfits. She claimed she had told me. I was really furious! Took her out of anger and love. She ran upstairs afterward. . . . Went to get gas for the car: it was already hard to come by, but got some by giving a tip at the garage . . . had a test drive in the rain, the gray Puma's cover had always let water in; I left it at the garage. Later went up to the blond Puma, who was doing her packing in her blouse and panties, with a huge ruby bracelet from Ostertag's on her arm, in a good mood. We ate together in her room, then went downstairs, as it was time for her to meet Jo. . . . Later all the rest came up to hear Hitler's speech. Drank cocktails, then Rudi fetched his car, we drove out to the Avenue Foch . . . and listened to the speech of the man who decides the peace of the world. Certain cause for hope. . . . Marlene was enthralled by the manner in which he spoke— clever, etc.; a great big baby-brain. . . . Later, after dinner, drove to Rudi's flat with Marlene. An eerie picture: everything packed up, the mirror smeared over, departure, the end of the world. . . . I thought of my house and every- thing in it in Porto Ronco, standing there waiting for the Italians. . . . Puma was impersonal. We left. Rudi stayed. I took the Puma up to the hotel. I told her that our morning's agreement did not stand. Told her to go to Jo, I had given her permission. . . . She seemed happy. I went with her and said good- bye outside Jo's door. Was very tired, in any case. I went downstairs to my room. As so many times before.

From 1938 on, Remarque realized that it was very dangerous to travel even as far as Switzerland, even with a visa, which Dietrich had secured for him. Dietrich was still a German citizen and protected by a passport. Remarque felt increasingly trapped in France, and she was packing up in preparation to go back to work in Hollywood.

The diary does not specifically address the fact that Remarque was really working very well at this point. He was finishing up *Flotsam*, the first of his "exile novels," and beginning a rough draft of his next novel, *Arch of Triumph*, which dealt, among other things, with his semi-imprisonment in France and his tempestuous relationship with Dietrich. Also, because he rarely boasted, he does not mention that it is mainly due to him that, ironically, Dietrich is leaving to resume her career. He had read the script of *Destry Rides Again* and had strongly advised her to seize the day and accept the transforming role. The last entries until 1939 reveal the attempt to maintain equilibrium within an abnormal relationship being carried on in an environment of hysteria.

[*28th Sept.*] . . . Puma came at about 2. Wanted to go with me to the British consulate. We went and were told to wait. Puma went into action and fetched the American consul in from a radio shop to help, and we got our visas! . . . I took Puma to Schiaparelli's and went home. The news getting worse all afternoon. I wanted to set off to Porto Ronco by train that evening. Phoned Feilchen, who assured me he would move out the most important things. . . . Went upstairs and saw Rudi, who was still wanting to rescue the most unlikely things: bottles $^{1}/_{4}$ full of vodka, vermouth, etc. I promised him I'd get rid of everything. He started packing. . . .

[*29th Sept.*] Spent the evening with the Puma two days ago. Went to bed. She was tired, but hesitant, too. The uncertainty of everything. Early next morning she came to me, in my arms. Something wasn't quite right. Some gray shadow over it. Probably all manner of things, the war, her departure, Jo, etc. . . . Did some more packing in the morning, took some things to Rudi's flat. . . . Rudi wanted to leave around 9, but his tires had been slashed, so he got away only at 11. Lunch in Puma's room, ready to leave for the Hague at 6. Report on the conference between Daladier, Chamberlain, Mussolini, and Hitler. Puma didn't want to leave. Preferred to stay. . . . Later went up to the Puma, who was sitting there in bra and pants, sorting out letters from my rivals, Fairbanks and Warwick. Had a good laugh. She read them out loud, of course. Told me that mine were too literary. True. Ought to write more simply. [Remarque was always terrified that Dietrich would sell his letters and make a nice profit exposing every fiber of him to the world. She never did.] . . .

[*4th October*] . . . Had breakfast yesterday morning with the Puma. . . . Later on to Ostertag's, Van Cleef's, where I saw some wonderful bracelets, then on to Chanel's. . . . Puma tried on some pajamas and later chose an outfit at Rochas. . . . Puma was happy, because it was all fun for her. . . . Later took her to Ogilvie Sisters' to have her hair washed. I wandered around, got a powder case for the Puma, and then went back to collect her. . . . Puma's hair was like golden silk after being washed. . . . Before bed she worked on herself for a half hour, while I lay in bed and watched. . . .

This morning I wanted to get up early, in secret, but Puma kicked up a row. . . . Puma went off to Knize's and an interview, I went to Opelka's to try on a suit, which didn't fit. Ordered a coat. Came back. The Puma was sitting looking lost in her room, in her brown outfit and brown cap. Was sad and quiet. I wasn't really sure what she wanted. I wanted to leave her alone, but then I realized that she didn't want to be alone, that she was sad because she ought to be happy that The Child was coming back in the evening and the others in the morning, the fact that she loved them and yet wished they were not coming—the fact that the holiday was over. [Rudi, Tami, and The Child had taken a short vacation to the south.] . . . At the moment I'm sitting waiting for her. I'm full of love. I can't help it. . . . Wanting to hold on, not being able to. . . . I'm aware of it all. I'm not under any illusions. Just let me have this one evening. . . .

[*6th Oct.*] . . . Met Brigg in the Café de la Paix. He told me about the trip with the gold [Brigg, Remarque's business manager, had taken gold out of a numbered bank account in Luxembourg and deposited it in Remarque's Swiss account.] He told me about Peter with her plans and her attitude to me. Not very nice. Looks as if she wants money, money, money. She's embittered to the extreme. Firmly convinced of the injustice I've done her. No attempt to understand. Settle the accounts. It'll not be easy. . . .

. . . Phone call from Puma. Fouquet's with Puma and Mercedes. Talked about Garbo. Puma was rather anti. Said Jo didn't like Garbo. Backbiting. Mercedes against Jo. Puma against Garbo. . . . Later, on to the Café des Deux Magots in the church square, with the brightly lit terrace and the falling twilight. Puma was sweet and affectionate. Across the bridges through the velvet-black Paris, autumn in the air, the light breathing in the great gray distance of the sky, and Puma with her head on my shoulder.

Dietrich was still vacillating about when to sail for America, still a bit unsure about a final commitment to star in *Destry Rides Again*. Remarque, feeling exhausted, wanted her to leave.

[*13th Oct.*] . . . Puma looked very beautiful in a blue velvet outfit, almost black, and her hair falling down onto the white fur. Rang the astrologist Sturgis, who advised her to sign contracts by Saturday. Went home, chatted, rubbed our faces with Ettinger cream, and slept like babies. Puma had a headache in the morning. . . . I phoned Peter, who is arriving tomorrow to stay at the Hôtel Jubilee. I'd already been warned by Brigg. . . . Tami was rather bitchy, asking me if Peter was coming because I was having trouble with the Puma—not entirely wrong. . . . Puma, meanwhile, has suddenly decided to leave on Oct. 28th. I advised her to go to London on Sunday and do the American trip with Jo. After all, she would have Fairbanks waiting in Hollywood. She said she would have to refuse that. I asked her why. She said because he would never stay with her unless she slept with him. I replied, well, of course she would sleep with him, what else? She stared at me. I said, after all it was like that in the old days. She said now things were different. She was in love with me. I said, so she wasn't before? No, she said, not like this, differently. . . . Then she explained to me how it wasn't easy to live alone for a woman. . . . She told me how Dolores Del Rio hadn't wanted to leave her husband behind when she was going to England to make a film. She'd been quite beside herself on the voyage over. Later, the Puma met a friend in England, who had had a friend with him who was very unhappy. He said that Dolores had left and he was still shattered by it; it had been such a great affair. But in spite of it, Dolores would already be looking forward to getting back to her husband in Los Angeles, as soon as she was on the boat. I asked the Puma how long these shattered feelings lasted in her. Answer: one week. . . .

[*16th Oct.*] . . . Puma. Thrilling night. Deep sleep, close together. . . .

[*21st Oct.*] . . . Puma has seen Jo, who had lost her tan, and, according to Puma, was no longer so sure of herself. Before, she had been a woman who could summon a sailing yacht from one moment to the next, self-assured, radiant, with the romantic appeal of all the money, the island, the boats, the tropics—even the room, the balcony, the breakfast, the carelessness had played a part. Today it was just someone who had begged Puma as they parted: "I'll see you again, won't I?" and our Puma is already miles away, talking pretty nonsense about guilt and innocence . . . and already looking for some means to get rid of the so-called responsibility. I tried to talk her out of it, said that nobody ever gets anything that they don't take away from somebody else: Jo had taken something from me, and now probably she was going to lose it again, maybe even to me, but that was no reason for anyone to talk of guilt. She said, of course it was. She had told Jo then that she was unattached. . . . I was a little bit hurt at the amoral Puma, who was being very moral, and thereby revealing herself to be ten times more amoral than before. Soldier, there's only one thing to do: forget it, don't get attached, stay free!

[*23rd October*] . . . A silver October. Went for a little walk. To Van Cleef's. I bought a bracelet that the Puma rather liked. . . .

[*October 25*] . . . Jo left around noon on Sunday. . . . Slept with Puma in my arms that night. . . . The matter of the bracelet: I had seen golden bracelets with Puma. One which she had liked, I had brought and given to her. At first she was happy. Then Rudi told her he had seen a nice bracelet with white stones in a shop on the Avenue Victor Hugo. Later Rudi called me, under instructions from Puma, to find out what the bracelet from Van Cleef had cost. . . . The end of the story was they wanted to buy the other one rather than have the one I'd bought for Puma. So I told him the price. He responded that the other one was more expensive. . . . Later, annoyed, went down to Puma about the matter. A flood of words back and forth— she had only thought . . . etc. Now she wouldn't think about it anymore because the difference in price was too extreme. She'd only been interested in the first place because the bracelet had unusual stones. I told her that we could also buy the other one. She: Forget it. The doorbell rang, announcing a salesperson from the other store with the bracelet with the stones, like a deus ex machina. She said she only wanted to show it to Rudi once more. Rudi came, said it wasn't the right one, the salesperson left. Big talk. The Child was asked. It turned out that it was the right one after all but had been moved to a different place in the window. But Puma didn't like it anymore. So we went to Van Cleef in the afternoon to exchange the bracelet I had given her, which had also lost favor. Puma couldn't find anything else she liked. Finally, she admired one with sapphires and small round diamonds. But Puma didn't like sapphires. Thought it would be nicer with just the baguettes. The owner advised her to take the one with sapphires, but agreed that the diamonds did sparkle more. Puma wanted the one with baguettes. Baguettes were bigger and more valuable. I couldn't take much more. Finally, things were settled and the baguettes were put in place of the sapphires to see how the baguettes would look. I had to laugh. It was almost funny to see how my Puma had become this little greedy person. It wasn't a big thing. Just a brilliant, twenty-one carats, for six hundred and fifty thousand francs. They showed us two others for three million. . . . In a neighboring room, Chevalier was just buying something for his wife. . . . Puma overheard the word "ruby," was jealous of the present for the other woman, wanted to know what it looked like, went into the room and introduced herself in a most overwhelming way. I have to remember it for a character in a novel. . . .

[*October 27*] . . . Had dinner with Puma in the room. . . . We slept, awoke, and then the old spiel started all over again. I wasn't taking care of her hot Vichy water, her warmed-up robe, etc. Seems she needs a better kind of servant. . . .

. . . You lived a life with Peter [who was] not caring and indecisive, don't do that again [now]. . . . You have had enough of your role as a film assistant. . . .

[*October 28, Friday*] Yesterday at noon Puma came up to my room in a black fur hat, black suit with a fur collar, very pretty. Was nice and sweet. . . . In the evening, Puma wanted to show me a watch with a gold wristband she had bought me. She showed me the bracelet from Van Cleef's with the exchanged baguettes and another one she had seen at the Ritz that matched one of her rings and she told me it cost as much as the baguettes. I really didn't care. I noticed that the watch was exchanged for the more expensive bracelet that Rudi had bought her. I usually don't take gifts, but this was too calculated to pass up. I told her I would have to get used to the idea of wearing golden wristbands. . . .

[*November 1, All Saints' Day*] Fouquet's with Puma, who overate. . . . Got sick very nicely: Threw up the caviar, the dessert, the main dish. . . . Then I massaged her feet while laughing and talking, she turned around and fell asleep. . . . In the morning Puma was tender, sweet and intimate. No sex. Told me that she loved me and would be very unhappy in America. I told her that she would find someone to massage her, to brush her hair, to chat with, and to sleep next to. Maybe it's true that women need more tenderness than sex. True with Puma for sure. Maybe it's on the edge of homosexuality—maybe also possible that tenderness is more than sex—more a finding together and belonging together. I noticed that it's almost more pleasurable to see her running around without any shyness, naked in my arms, playing around in the morning—it's more than just sex. Although! I'm not quite sure. I told her it had been different before. . . . We will see. The separation will show us. I'm not unhappy about it.

[*November 3*] Puma went with Warners, Cary Grant to Maxim's, for dinner. I went to Feilchen's hotel room to look at Cézannes. Watercolors, two landscapes, a head covered by a straw hat from the back. Bought it. Back to the hotel. . . .

. . . In the morning . . . to Cartier's, where we found the bracelet Puma truly liked best.

[*Monday, November 7, and Tuesday, November 8*] . . . Puma in the bar dressed in a velvet suit and top hat. . . . Talked about Rudi marrying. Rudi was like a child, she said, could never leave him. . . . Had too many martinis. Puma took me upstairs. Wanted to put me to bed, long discussion, said good night forever in the hallway. Finally we both had to laugh and went to bed.

. . . Puma said there was no unhappy love before two people had had sex. Only afterward. She said for her the decisive moment was the excitement coming through a man. The most attractive man for a woman is the one who cares least . . . the staring, straying glance in company, which will stray again and stare once more. She found it irresistible when jealousy and desire come together. Sometimes she had had this feeling with Sternberg. The strongest memory she had of him was one night when he had taken her, out of jealousy, because she had called him from Ronald Colman's after she had been with him and Colman had left for the studio. Sternberg had come immediately. . . .

[*November 12*] . . . Had dinner with Jack and Ann Warner. Did it for Puma. Simple man. Somewhat crazy wife. To Monaco. Drank Pernod. Puma danced with Jack, also later with Ann. Went to the Sphinx. In one room two girls were making love. Ann Warner was very interested in it. I almost fell asleep. Puma and I had a misunderstanding about the evening and when we returned to the hotel, I went to my room, slept alone.

The next morning slept, walked around, Puma came, we laughed. Later went to Feilchen, who had a huge Daumier: *Don Quixote*, a wonderful picture, it is in my room now. . . . Gave Puma a massage with oil. . . . Had pears and oranges during the night. . . . Puma took a radium bath with lots of foam in the morning. Laughed a lot. Bath was pretty good. I could not work my magic.

[*November 17*] Yesterday in the afternoon we saw two of Puma's movies at the custom's office: *Dishonored* and *Shanghai Express*. . . .

In the morning, to the custom's office again. Two movies: *Morocco* and *The Devil Is a Woman*. *Morocco* was good, the second, terrible, no bones, soft and no optical teasers. The role Puma played was badly arranged and also badly acted. . . .

Excitement in the world about Germany. . . . Destruction of all houses and business, thousands of Jews arrested—all this because a seventeen-year-old Polish Jew had shot the third secretary of the German embassy in Paris, a certain van Rath—the truth behind it was a homosexual affair. The feeling of living on top of a volcano.

[*November 22*] Departure. In the morning strange feeling in my back and in my legs. Measured thirty-eight-point-five-degree fever. Headache. Departure chaos, Rudi, Tami, The Child—it made no sense to drive them to Le Havre. Accompanied Puma to the hotel lobby. They left. The summer has ended.

In 1938, Remarque finally did go home to Porto Ronco and managed to work intensely, finishing the first draft of his novel *Flotsam*. The combination of the house, the beauty of the area, his attentive and sympathetic housekeeper, Rosa, and his pets—especially Billy—brought him profound relief. On the other hand, because of his nature, it couldn't last too long. It was interspersed with longing for and fretting about his Puma in Hollywood. When he did not hear from her for a while, it was Rudi who was the intermediary, bearing news of her well-being. Indeed, the dynamic was of a family, though a very peculiar one.

After Dietrich was somewhat settled, she began a loving correspondence with Remarque, which buoyed him tremendously—so much so that he developed a theory that a warm and receptive Puma allowed him to do his best work. He made her his muse during this time. When he was in favor with her, his world smiled; when she frowned at him, he felt emotionally, psychologically, and creatively destitute.

Maria Riva saw Remarque through a child's eyes as "a debonair fox, like an illustration out of *The Fables* of La Fontaine, even the tops of his ears pointed slightly. He had an innate theatricality—an actor in a heroic production standing perpetually in the wings, waiting for the right cue." In retrospect, she calls him "a tragic hero," because of his exile, which created a deep and visible sadness in him.

From December 1938 until March 1939, Dietrich allowed him to believe he was her only love and true anchor. She was in Hollywood; he was in Porto Ronco. There were daily cables sent back and forth between them. She took the time between promoting her stardom to search out the perfect living quarters for him. In his diary entries he constantly refers to her as "sweet." He felt wonderful about her—with an absence of suffering for the first time in ages. Clearly distance was necessary for the relationship to be successful.

Although it had been reported that Remarque was writing *Arch of Triumph* in the summer of 1939, with the main female character, Joan Madou, mirroring Dietrich, in fact, he was much too involved with Dietrich to be able to write objectively about her.

In fits and starts he was working on *Flotsam*, his novel about the plight of exiles in Europe. The title in German, *Liebe deinen Nächsten*, or *Love Thy Neighbor*, carries a cynical message regarding the refugees and the countries that temporarily harbored them. Remarque used the third-person narrative for the first time, yet his protagonist, Ludwig Kern, is similar to his other leading male characters in that they are all versions of himself, his beliefs, and his experiences. Kern is a twenty-one-year-old refugee, half Jewish, forced to flee Germany when he is barred from continuing his university studies. He is a Candide-like figure in that his soul remains pure as cruel obstacles present themselves. There is a deviation from Remarque's former work in a strong alternative protagonist—an older man named Josef Steiner, who teaches Kern the tricks of the refugee's trade. Symbolically, when they stand together, there is a chance for them to outwit each unfolding terror. Psychologically, Remarque has created the father-son team of his dreams. Although they are separated several times, Steiner always appears just in time to help Kern out. And as Remarque continued to build his oeuvre, his female characters became less idealized or stereotypical and more rounded, interesting, quixotic, or downright odd—as is Joan Madou in *Arch of Triumph*.

In *Flotsam* there is Ruth Holland—Jewish, spirited, and compassionate, who has been unlucky until she meets up with Kern. She allows him to love her and help her; in return, she becomes a loyal friend, partner, and lover. Their relationship in the novel has a picaresque quality in that they are constantly enduring and surviving hair-raising episodes. Ruth Holland resembles Ruth Albu, who was the first to help Remarque adjust to his role as an exile, and it is this theme of the exile, of not having valid papers—a passport, visa, bank acount, and so on—that is the subject of *Flotsam*, hence the title.

In the forties, Remarque wrote endlessly in his diary about not knowing where to go or what to do. His conscience fought being overtaken by the trap of "the good life": fame, fortune, beautiful women; in a sense, his battle was to remain an outsider, *Ausländer*. Continuing to feel a permanent loss of identity after leaving Germany was a way to salvage his history. As a writer, his difficulty with assimilation was a primary theme.

In his book *Understanding Erich Maria Remarque*, published in 1991, Hans Wagener writes about the background for *Flotsam*, with its startling statistics and conditions:

Shortly after the National Socialists' rise to power on January 30, 1933, the floodgates opened for thousands of refugees to flee Nazi Germany. . . . Most of the refugees first went to neighboring countries . . . but after Austria was united with the German Reich in March 1938, and after Czechoslovakia had been taken in March 1939, more and more refugees went on to Switzerland and France. . . . Laws were originally designed to prevent the influx of foreign workers so as to protect the home economy. They now worked against the refugees, who were denied residence and working permits and consequently sent across the border to other neighboring countries.

Remarque was luckier than most. He was protected by his fame and contacts. However, the Swiss authorities were not particularly neutral or benign toward Remarque and Jutta. The country's relationship to Nazi Germany was a delicate one, causing the Swiss to uphold the Germans' rigid immigration and work-permit strictures regarding exiles. In his examination of *Flotsam*, Hans Wagener charts Remarque's travail as a refugee, and one can see where the impetus came for him to expand on that theme:

Remarque himself did not suffer physically from being in exile. But he did encounter annoying bureaucratic difficulties with the Swiss, and also later with the American authorities when his wife Jeanne wanted to emigrate to the United States. Furthermore, when he was in the United States he was affected by the curfew laws that prevented him from leaving his home at night, just like all other "enemy aliens." He had lost his German market and did not have the support of his German readers. He could not travel anymore to or in Europe and thus lost the emotional support and integration into the society of his homeland. And so he shared his heroes' suffering in emotional respects, their experience of emotional isolation, of being cut off from their accustomed environment.

Compared with his other works, *Flotsam* did not do well for Remarque. The timing of the subject matter was off. The story was too sensitive for both European and American markets. All the same, it was serialized in *Collier's* magazine from the translation by Denver Lindley, published in America by Little, Brown, and it was sold to Metro-Goldwyn-Mayer. In 1941 the movie was released by United Artists as *So Ends Our Night*, starring Fredric March, Margaret Sullavan, Frances Dee, Glenn Ford, Anna Sten, and Erich von Stroheim. The cast was considered first rate, although the reviews of the picture were tepid; it was the general consensus that the performances could not rise above the material. The Austrian actor Erich von Stroheim added to his portrait gallery of villains by playing the Nazi Steinbrenner—shortened to Brenner in the film. The creation of this character and his fate was significant in Remarque's psychological expansion. He came to grips with his fury against the Nazis by having his older protagonist, Steiner, murder the malevolent Steinbrenner.

Remarque spent most of 1939 in a state of outrage, caused more by Marlene Dietrich than by what Germany was doing to Europe. He was deeply troubled by the political situation, which was escalating into the Holocaust, but his affair with Dietrich was paramount in his mind. After being led into the pipe dream of finishing his work and then falling into the welcoming arms of his goddess in Hollywood, he was in for a real pratfall.

Before he faced the romantic fireworks in Hollywood, there was the matter of his business management. Remarque allowed Klement to continue handling his affairs in the States even when he seemed convinced he was being cheated. He did try to protect his interests somewhat by hiring a European representative, referred to only as Bing. He didn't seem pleased with him, either, as he notes in his diary: "Bing wanted to get a higher percentage; greedy Hungarian and Jew." Remarque's mistrust of those he supposedly trusted was a trait that would become increasingly entrenched. Even when he found meticulous care and business acumen somewhat later on in the lawyer Harriet Pilpel, and in the agents Robert Lantz and Felix Guggenheim, he still was skeptical and grumbled about being taken advantage of.

The biggest blow during this time was the death of his beloved dog Billy, whom he took almost everywhere. He noted that Billy was getting old and had begun to sleep on his back, as aging dogs do. Remarque records his passing: "Billy is dead. He died at 3:30 today. I had gone with the three dogs in the afternoon to Ronco and back; about 100 meters from the house I saw that Billy was walking rather stiffly; I thought he was tired. We went into the house. Soon afterward, Rosa came to tell me that Billy had collapsed. He lay there in cramps. Tried to get up, could not any longer. I called the doctor and went upstairs. . . . I wasn't by his side when he died. By accident, the doctor dropped by. He suspected strychnine. Many people here put it out in front of their houses. "

Remarque began to feel very anxious as the time approached for him to set sail for America. He was sure something would go wrong and he wouldn't

LEFT AND ABOVE:
Remarque in Paris, 1940.
Harriet Pilpel, Remarque's
brilliant lawyer and
confidante.

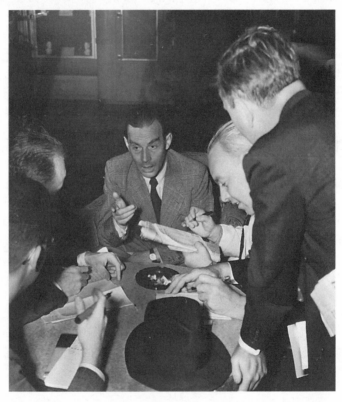

Remarque, in exile, gives a press conference on the Queen Mary *upon arrival in*
New York, September 1939.

get to see his Puma again. His fears were legitimate. War could be declared, or bueaucratic steps could be taken to prevent his leaving Europe or entering the United States. He also anticipated that Jutta would act up, get sick, create some ruse to detain him. Ironically, just as Dietrich arranged for him to sail on March 18 on the *Queen Mary*, she informed him of her desire to return to Europe and, in fact, had booked return passage for all of them in early June. They would again all go to Paris and then on to Antibes. It would be their last vacation in Europe for quite a spell.

When he finally sailed from Cherbourg, he must have had a sense of solidarity—even if he wasn't sure it pleased him. He was surrounded on the ship by Rudi, Tami, The Child, The Child's new governess, and Klement, who had obtained a visa at the last moment.

Five days later, he saw the skyline of New York for the first time:

In the morning very early, around 5:00, the skyline of New York, gray against a light sky, surprising and not surprising, seen often in pictures but more impressive, of course, seeing it physically. . . .

Hotel Waldorf-Astoria. Beautiful, and despite its skyscraper size, somehow intimate. . . . Went to the Empire State Building. Wonderful view. . . . The cars like toys below. But most beautiful was the sound of the city—dark thunder held back like the motor noise of a racing car. . . . Lunch with Littauer from *Collier's* at the Chambord Restaurant. . . . Later to the Savoy Ballroom, Harlem, a huge black establishment with thousands of blacks. A little like the jungle. All colors from white to black. The smell of thousands. The pushing. The glances, the walk. . . . Up the stairs beautiful figures with wonderful legs.

As Remarque and Dietrich drew closer to their meeting, the tension that could so easily turn acrimonious began again. The day he arrived in New York he wrote: "Called Puma at noon. Was insulted because I hadn't called right away, was cool because I hadn't done what she wanted me to do." On March 24, he began heading toward her:

Left at noon on the Twentieth Century Express. Black men in the hallways. The huge station. Read Rilke and studied English.

Arrived at 9:00 in the morning in Chicago. . . . Hotel Blackstone with view of the lake. . . . Noticed on the train that Americans take good care of their suits. . . . Called Puma. She was again strange, somehow demanding and slightly hurt. Discussion if she would come to the train or not. I said no because she was talking about reporters. We'll see what will happen. Don't anticipate anything good.

The Super Chief leaves in 5 minutes. Where to? And will I ever come back? Don't be afraid, soldier!

Dietrich sent a chauffeur to call for him in Pasadena, and after a ride through the "long and flat city," he saw "Puma in front of her house in a yellow suit. Beautiful and shy. Showed me the house. Nice yet ugly; seems to be very comfortable and has been prepared for me with enormous care."

They were soon fighting—about his work. She was very disappointed that he had been writing about emigrants in his new book instead of working on *Ravic*, the early title of what would become *Arch of Triumph*. Ravic was the name of the alter-ego character who gets involved with Joan Madou, modeled on Dietrich, and it is the story of their relationship set against the backdrop of Paris. She was looking forward to seeing her influence on Remarque's talent, and was also disappointed that he hadn't brought with him any material that could have shaped itself into a movie for her. Aside from sporadic love-making, according to the diary entries, the feeling between them had eroded into almost constant bitterness, with only short respites.

To Warner's studio to see *Dark Victory*, a film with Bette Davis. Good. . . . Puma told me yesterday that after we made love, she had dreamed she had been together with Bette Davis. Not very pleasant to hear. . . . The evening seemed to go well, we went to the Beachcomber, then the discussion about marriage, and the whole thing turned into something nasty, and now I'm sitting here; I will sleep alone for the third night and if this continues I will soon leave. Even with this kind of treatment, Puma had the nerve to ask me why I wasn't coming over into her bed. I responded I didn't want to sleep with such a bitch. She just laughed and now I'm back in this damn room, and feel like a prisoner because I live here and can't leave and she knows it.

And then, a few days later: "Everything okay again. The fight of the 8th was a first-rate fight. . . . Afterward, days of complete happiness. . . . In the morning in the sun by the pool. Puma cooks and bakes."

Although Remarque was considered very much a celebrity and his name was linked with Dietrich's in all the columns, he did not fit in—mostly by his own design. Within a year, when the war was raging in Europe and he was forced to emigrate, as much as he had antipathy for Hollywood, that was where he settled. The impressions that he formed during his initial visit never changed. He was guilty of a double standard, however, since though he had complete disdain for the colony of celebrities, he enjoyed observing them:

> One evening to the film guild, exhibition of film stars. Sat at a table with Gary Cooper, Lili Damita, Dolores Del Rio, Errol Flynn. Lots of reporters. Everyone is posing all the time.
>
> An evening party—the birthday of Gregory Ratoff—together with Constance Bennett, Norma Shearer, Mayer, Goldwyn, Zanuck—one worse than the other. . . . Douglas Fairbanks, Puma's earlier lover, with a very rich but terrible-looking woman. . . .
>
> Last night party by the Charlie Feldmans . . . Myron Selznick, Sternberg, Puma, and I, the young Laemmle, Milestone, etc. Puma a little proud of me, because other people thought I looked like a movie star . . . film stars are impersonal and distant. . . .
>
> . . . Saw *Wuthering Heights*, a ballet [Remarque's sense of humor] by Wyler. Party afterward. . . .
>
> . . . A big party for the Duchess of Westminster . . . in one corner sat the former lovers of Puma: Colman and Fairbanks, hand in hand with his new wife, which made Puma depressed.

For all its frivolity, Hollywood has always been politically alert. During that time, with so many exiles attempting to settle, yet having roots and often family left in occupied countries in Europe, the imminent war overshadowed the gaiety: "Roses, flowers, lots of sun, swimming. Always some feeling of departure; always the political thunderstorm warnings."

However uncomfortable he was in Hollywood, Remarque gained advantage there. He had entered American life at the very top. His English began to improve; the Hollywood beauties became aware of him, which he didn't mind in the least; and he made some kind of home and life with Dietrich.

Shortly after Remarque had arrived, he had bought her an Afghan dog, which became highly agitated when they started to make preparations to leave (they took him with them on the boat). Remarque was disquieted:

> I'm trying to write an outline for a story for Puma. It's difficult, she makes so many demands. I'm tired sometimes. It's better not to be together from morning to night. But then I miss her.

The pool, the flower in front of the window, the big soft dog, who slowly got used to us, the cool nights, the Beachcomber, the endless city—not so easy to leave right now.

In the middle of June, "the family" en masse, including Josef von Sternberg, Jo Carstairs, and The Child, "pale and fat," arrived at the Sherry Netherland Hotel in New York, where they stayed before sailing to France. An incident at the customs house just as they were about to leave concerning clearance papers, taxes, and citizenship turned into high drama, but it all ended well.

To the customs house. Everything seemed to be all right. I needed an explanation from Little, Brown that tax would be paid by them. . . . At noon lunch with Littauer from *Collier's* and Lindley at Chambord. Discussed Klement's case and arranged for him to get no money. Initialed the contract so he couldn't do it. He would have sacked the money again. . . . Call for Rudi from the customs house; he was asked to bring receipts of the tax returns of the last 3 years. Didn't have any. Much excitement. . . .

Next morning, packed, signed contracts, suddenly bad news: Puma had been visited by two tax officials from New York, first asking for $120,000 and later for a $240,000 deposit. They explained that the luggage would be confiscated, etc. What chaos. A lawyer was called; Jo, Sternberg, and Rudi hid out; I sat in my room. Puma tried to call the secretary of the treasury, Morgenthau. In the meantime, they found among Puma's papers a certificate that she had become an American citizen. They had to let her go. They wanted to get hold of Rudi. In the meantime, someone gave me a registered letter, someone I didn't know. I refused to take it, because it could have been a summons. Around 12:00 we made the decision to go on board and fight it out there. Brought our luggage there. Jo picked me up. The others had already gone with the tax official. I went to Jo's cabin, locked it. Shortly before 3 A.M., the time of departure, Jo came and said everything was all right. Told me that Puma had given her jewels to the captain and that they were safe. We learned that Rudi was held for an hour and a half at the pier. Everybody was overjoyed, we ordered champagne and caviar and celebrated that Puma had saved her jewels. Suddenly twelve boys appeared with an official, again to pick up Rudi. Puma was storming, the lawyer was storming, the customs officials were storming. As Puma fought, she was applauded and photographed. She was excellent. The boat was held for another hour and a half. Finally, the customs officials left with Puma's jewels anyway. We departed.

Remarque was miserable in Paris. Dietrich was cold to him, wouldn't sleep with him, and forgot his birthday. As was typical behavior with them, when she gave him a present of a cigarette case a few days late, he returned it to her. Even The Child was getting to him, although he felt sorry for her: "The Child—too much and too little is unbearable. Actually, she is really to be pitied with this big clan."

And then, shortly before they were to leave for Antibes, his misery was alleviated for a brief moment by Dietrich's candor about her inner workings:

As long as Jo Carstairs had taken what she wanted without asking, everything was fine. The moment she fell in love and did only what Puma liked, it was over. . . . Puma explained that she had been much bolder years ago. She had charmed Sternberg by being mother, whore, lady, and first-class cook all at the same time. She had been obscene one minute and the next would be sitting on the bed of her child. She had to have a man every night, was not able to sleep alone. If she had a fight during the day, at night the restlessness would set in and also the certainty that everything would be all right. That all had changed after John Gilbert's death. That was the first time she had realized that one could not get back another human being. Not through begging, wanting, asking. One evening he had gone and not come back. That had changed her. Until then she could have had everybody she liked. . . . I made the mistake of talking to her about Dolores Del Rio. She darkened and became furious. She was right; one could not react this way about another woman with her.

Remarque understood that Dietrich needed scenes and tension and in between was gentle. He understood that as much as he swore to extricate himself from her and "the family," they all served a purpose for one another. It would be easy to say that he was the accommodating masochist to Dietrich's demanding and demeaning sadist, but it was deeper than that. Dietrich and the family represented the last vestiges of the Old World: caring, sybaritic, royal, intricate, familiar.

In between Paris and Antibes, Remarque had gone to Porto Ronco with the sole purpose of packing up his prize possessions—his art, rugs, Tang horses (all but one, which he gave to Dietrich), Chinese bronzes—and having them shipped through Holland to the United States. It was the only instance when he went to Casa Remarque not to write. It was just as well, or he might have been tempted to stay. He packed and left quickly, saying his farewells to Rosa and Joseph, who would keep the home fires burning. No one could know it would be nine years before Remarque would return to his beloved Swiss sanctuary. He set off to Antibes.

In Antibes, the family had grown to include Josef von Sternberg and his new lady love, Dolly Mollinger, Charles Banbury, Joseph Kennedy and his brood, and, of course, Jo Carstairs and the ubiquitous Tim. Although everyone was a bit more muted because of the political atmosphere, there were still games in the moonlight. Dietrich had a small reprise of her liaison with Jo Carstairs and wore her gifts of the bracelet and ring once again; Tami was suddenly vociferous about wanting to marry Rudi; The Child, with the new nickname of "little Kater," was busy diving for octopus with the Kennedy kids and hoping that her secret crush, Jack, would join them.

The days grew fewer before war. Remarque made futile attempts to work on a second draft of *Flotsam*. Dietrich was about to leave for America to begin filming *Destry Rides Again*. Jo Carstairs was dressing like a woman to try to interest Dietrich in a new way. Much restlessness. They all passed around the latest literary discovery: Henry Miller's *Tropic of Capricorn*.

On August 16, 1939, everything happened at once: "Yesterday morning chaotic packing. Sternberg came and announced warning for the beginning of the war on Sunday. Had heard it at the Spanish embassy in Berlin. Puma was very nervous. . . . Good-bye from all the others—the Banburys, the Charles Boyers, Norma Shearer, then back to the room. . . . We departed. . . . The small, light, bare station of Antibes. The blue train. Puma went on. Rudi insulted her at the last moment when he said in the future she ought to respect him more. . . . Waving—the summer came to an end."

Life as they knew it also came to an end. What continued was Dietrich's imperious behavior. After consulting Ambassador Kennedy, and being assured that he personally would act to protect her family when the time came, she sailed off to America to keep her rehearsal schedule, leaving The Child specifically in Remarque's care. Maria Riva remembers her mother's very words: "My only love—I give you my child. Protect her, keep her safe— for me!"

Within days Kennedy left the south of France. Dietrich was still in transit on the *Queen Mary*. As Riva recalls, "The message ran through the hotel like a flash fire: 'Go, get out. Leave France—fast!'" Remarque, the guardian, was panicked. He tried to get through to Dietrich on the *Queen Mary* and could not. He did not know quite what to do without her counsel: "I want to leave and yet don't want to leave: Switzerland is hopeless, once the war starts; but I want to leave from here, too."

Finally, when he reached her in New York, she wanted to know what was wrong, if he was sick, what was going on politically. She had been cut off from late-breaking news during the last leg of her crossing. As soon as she docked in New York, she used her influence to book passage for the family on the *Queen Mary*, which would sail from Cherbourg on September 2. In the face of difficult conditions, Remarque exerted himself to get them there.

He left on the twenty-sixth with Kater in the car, which was not running well. He noted in his diary that they had trouble getting over the mountains near Cannes. They supposedly were the trailblazers, being followed by Rudi, Tami, and the dog—Teddy—in the Packard. They couldn't find hotel rooms because there was mobilization everywhere. Finally, Rudi found them two rooms. They drove all the next day because the car kept stalling, and reached Paris late at night, where he spoke to a high-spirited Puma, who had arranged for them to take the next boat.

By the next morning the occupation had escalated considerably: the phones in the hotel were blocked and no telegrams could be sent. Remarque stored his beloved Lancia in a garage while Rudi secured their tickets on the *Queen Mary*.

Remarque felt guilty and obligated: "A terrible feeling to leave now. Everything in me is against it. Many thoughts, contempt for myself combined with a certain commitment. . . . The contempt for myself because I am leaving Peter behind, the thought and the knowledge not to be able to do otherwise, because I don't want to lose Puma. The idea to end a lot with this one move. . . . I still don't want to leave. I don't want to run away. But Puma will be scared to death and she also needs me. I love this town and I want to stay, knowing I would not, that the ship would leave with me."

Being emotionally torn was not new to Remarque; what was new was a betrayal with danger attached. Although he had called Jutta and told her to get herself to Biarritz and wait there until he could secure her passage, in her eyes he had deserted her. She would never let him forget it.

Remarque had no choice but to get out when he could. The passage was highly charged for him, as he notes in his diary:

On the 30th left Paris for Cherbourg. With a heavy heart. *Queen Mary* huge and safe. Days with little radio. No newspapers. The number of passengers was tripled. The library, etc., had been turned into sleeping areas. Suddenly the news like a bomb of the invasion of Poland. Of the declaration of war by England. Slow creeping start of the war. The silence in the lounge on board while the news was given. The slow speech of the king of England. This morning arrival in New York. Since yesterday a zigzag route due to the U-boats and the accompaniment of war boats. The news that the ship *Athenia* had been torpedoed. Friends of Jo Carstairs on the pier to help with the luggage. Phone call from Puma. Typically, after all the excitement, she tells me all her little worries. . . . Called again: wanted only to talk about me. I was astonished. Of course she talked about herself. At night I slowly got more and more enraged about this reception. When Puma called me later I yelled at her. . . . Hardly slept. The shaking city with its towers.

. . . Sternberg was suddenly on the phone, saying something about the war being wonderful, reuniting everything, and now he had to say good-bye because he wanted to go out to dinner with Puma. I nearly vomited. Puma said she would call me back later. I told her not to bother.

After days of train travel, Remarque was back in Hollywood again—this time for several years. Dietrich met him at the station: "White suit, very thin, strange, looking miserable." She had rented him a spacious bungalow at the Beverly Hills Hotel; she had a smaller one just behind his. It was probably the first and only gesture of subservience on her part.

He immediately entered the colorful, western world of *Destry Rides Again*. He was on the set a good deal. Billy Wilder remembers, "Erich made a bit of a nuisance of himself. He watched Marlene. He watched Stewart. He wanted to rewrite but no one had asked him."

Remarque began tentative work on *Ravic*, Jutta was sailing for New York, and Dietrich was falling in love again—this time with her co-star, Jimmy Stewart. Dietrich later confessed to Remarque that she had slept with Stewart from the very beginning—when they were being outfitted by the wardrobe department. She did her best to hide what she could from Remarque, who, while having to make a major adjustment, was also in the sickening position of perceiving something he did not want to know.

Jutta, meanwhile, had arrived in New York and been detained on Ellis Island. The combination of her German origin and her Panamanian citizenship caused immigration authorities to stamp her documents with "Doubtful Visitor, No Immigration Visa." Her hearing was scheduled three days after her arrival. It did not go well, and the Board of Special Inquiry refused her admission into the United States. Remarque, whose attitude was one of mild

Lupe Velez, "the Mexican Spitfire,"
who briefly enchanted Remarque, at
Ciro's, in Hollywood, 1941.

LEFT: *Marlene as Frenchy in* Destry
Rides Again, *1939.*

Directer Josef von Sternberg, Marlene Dietrich, and Remarque at a premiere
in Hollywood, 1938.

concern because he was still so embroiled with Dietrich, nonetheless went into action against the Immigration and Naturalization Service by retaining Isaac H. Levy, an influential lawyer. Levy was able to arrange with the Mexican consulate Jutta's entry into Mexico, where she would be safely housed until the time that the application for United States citizenship could be properly processed. The twist to the story and to Jutta's ordeal is this: it seems that Dietrich had pulled some strings at Immigration to complicate Jutta's admission into the States. Remarque's diary entry for October 31 attests to this: "At noon Klement called. He told me that the lawyer from New York, Levy, who was working for us to get Peter out of Ellis Island, had undergone many complications to do so, because Puma had interfered against it with the help of someone in a Washington immigration department. I thought it was impossible, but I haven't seen Puma yet." The issue of Dietrich's running interference is never mentioned again in the diary. In fact, there are only two more rather passionless mentions of the whole episode.

The case of Jutta Remarque eventually concluded more happily than many others. Since she was associated with a VIP, a good deal of bureaucratic treachery was circumvented. However, the ordeal remained vivid for her, as did the resentment against Remarque for inadvertently having caused it by not bringing her over with him in the first place. Twenty-five years later, still in touch with each other, Remarque asked her to recall for him her stay on Ellis Island. He asked her, not as an exorcism—provided they'd never properly talked about it—but as a means of research so that he could write affectingly about the experience in what was to be his last novel, *Shadows in Paradise*.

As early as 1940 Remarque was having heart problems, which were exacerbated by Dietrich's passion for James Stewart, who, meanwhile, was said to be going out with Loretta Young but was actually more serious about Olivia de Havilland. Remarque noticed that although Dietrich's apartment was "a kind of shrine for Stewart, his picture next to Sternberg's on her desk, his flowers next to her bed," she still came running to him with every little thing. He had contempt for his role as an often-spurned lover, but seemed to accept—with a sort of rueful resignation—his role as adviser to the queen. However much she enraged and humiliated him, he felt inextricably bound to her and loyal in his "duties." It was a bit excessive, however, that she was jealous of his having to go to Mexico to comfort Jutta.

There had been a New Year's Eve party at the Jack Warners'. Dietrich began to throw herself at Stewart, doing everything she could to be noticed by him, to his increasing discomfort. Stewart kept a reserve, and finally left.

The very next day, at Chasen's, Remarque was having dinner with the German writer Carl Zuckmayer when in walked Stewart with Olivia de Havilland, and then some time later, Dietrich with Orson Welles. An unhappy configuration. No one acknowledged anyone. The next day, Dietrich, in tears—a rarity for her—called Remarque, asking him to come to her bungalow. He responded, of course, and recounted the following story, true or not, in his diary:

> She was totally disheveled and desperate about Stewart, who had told her it was better to forget the whole thing. She'd seen him with another girl, whom he had been seeing in New York. Slowly she came forward with the truth. She'd slept with him from day one. It was a dream: it had been magical. For him, too. Suddenly, she was able to speak about it. It had all been poetic and romantic, hour by hour. That had held her bound to him, making her happy and unhappy. She never knew from one week to the next. He had never talked about love, but told her he was not in love, couldn't afford it. She had broken down because he didn't want to be loved. It had bothered him to be responsible for anybody. She had become pregnant by him the first time they'd slept together. Didn't want to abort the child, in order to continue sleeping with him. But she gave in to his wishes; when he had left for New York, she had gone to the doctor—alone, at night, with Nelly, her hairdresser. The doctor had not remembered their date. She had sat on the stairs, waiting. The next day the doctor came. He prepared the instruments, sterilized them. Puma was alone with him. While he was sterilizing the instruments, the doctor was eating. Puma was so alone, just waiting, looking at the boiling water. She held her hands to her ears while the doctor was working. He asked her whether she was doing that because of the pain. She said she didn't want to hear her own screams. While he was working he asked her if she knew an actor X, whose Christmas celebrations were well known. Later, he proudly showed her what he had cut out. Puma got into the car with Nelly. There was Christmas traffic in the street—lots of pushing and shoving. . . . Stewart hadn't called for twelve days while he was in New York, even though he knew that she would have an abortion. She was not even angry with him. She blamed herself for getting pregnant. She blamed herself for having been too aggressive at this party. What a way to start a New Year. . . .

Dietrich's obsession with Stewart continued well into 1940. She even hired two detectives—one to watch Stewart's house, the other to watch Olivia de

Havilland's. Remarque's obsession with Dietrich continued apace, manifested by the fact that he recorded her every move. He was attempting to work steadily on *Arch of Triumph*, the novel that Dietrich had fueled, but it seemed to pale in comparison to daily life around her. His tracking of her machinations is a truly fascinating document of an over-the-edge relationship, intertwined with the rest of the extended family and their doings.

The war encroached: German troops on the Dutch border; Germans were in Holland, Belgium, and Luxembourg; cannon fire in Belgium; windows shot out in England; the Germans were at the Channel at Laon, in St. Quentin; Hitler was in Paris; battles in France and Belgium; Calais was taken. "Politically it's dark," Remarque records. "Churchill instead of Chamberlain. The Germans for the next century will be the most hated people in the world."

As his involvement with Dietrich continued, there were new figures in the landscape. Charlie Chaplin's favorite golf partner as well as Paulette Goddard's ardent admirer, Tim Durant, appeared on the Ciro's–Casa Mañana circuit to woo Dietrich as well as de Havilland. There was Countess Dorothy di Frasso, whose house Dietrich had rented on Benedict Canyon during an earlier Hollywood stay, and who was extremely colorful in her own right. Born Dorothy Taylor in Watertown, New York, she had inherited $12 million from her father's leather goods business, and as Jean Howard (once married to the agent Charles Feldman) commented, "She had put her mark on many men, but never more rewardingly than with Gary Cooper. Dorothy and Gary were a modern-day Pygmalion and Galatea in reverse. I don't know whether it's true, but once when Dorothy and Gary didn't show up at a party hosted by Tallulah Bankhead, she was heard to drawl in her best Alabama accent, 'He must be worn to a Frasso.'"

Also part of the Remarque-Dietrich coterie were Dolores Del Rio and Orson Welles, Spencer Tracy, Hedy Lamarr, Loretta Young, Noël Coward, Max Reinhardt, the Edward G. Robinsons, Hedda Hopper, Greta Garbo, Gaylord Hauser, Vera Zorina, Elisabeth Bergner and her husband, Paul Czinner, Charlie Chaplin, and Paulette Goddard. At this time, Remarque gave her only a mere mention: "At night party at the Beachcomber, Dolores Del Rio, Orson Welles, Chaplin, Paulette Goddard, Diego Rivera, who had to flee Mexico, threatened by arrest, suspect in Trotsky's assassination." Remarque was clearly more interested in Rivera, Goddard's new romantic involvement, than in her.

Remarque's conscience about writing was keener than his application during this time, although he was slowly drafting what he still called *Ravic*. The setting was based on the Hôtel Ansonia in Paris, which had served as a shelter for many exiles and colleagues of Remarque's—among them Billy Wilder, Franz Waxman né Wachsmann, Max Colpet, and Friederich Hollander. Ravic, his hero, a refugee who had been head surgeon at a hospital in Germany, was closer psychologically to himself than any of his previous protagonists. Ravic's real name was Ludwig Fresenburg, and he had been living in Paris for two years at a refugee hotel called—instead of the Ansonia—the Hôtel International. He found work as a "ghost" surgeon for a much less estimable French doctor, performing, among other unfortunate surgeries, incomplete or inadequate abortions. As described by a nurse in the French clinic who didn't like him, "Mr. Ravic is a lost man. He will never build a home for himself. . . . There is no longer anything sacred to Mr. Ravic."

There was a more significant reason that the book was dedicated to M. D. than his relationship with Dietrich. In Joan Madou, his main female character, he had scooped the essence of Dietrich's effect on him and put it on the page. Joan Madou is the darkest, most difficult, and most destructive of his fictional women. There is a fusion of Joan's quixotic, often chaotic ways and those of Dietrich. In the first paragraph, his description of Joan's looks is that of Dietrich's: "He [Ravic] saw a pale face, high cheekbones, and wide-set eyes. The face was rigid and masklike; it looked hollowed out, and her eyes in the light from the street lamps had an expression of such glassy emptiness that they caught his attention."

Dietrich had championed the writing of this book she always referred to as *Ravic* even after the title had been changed to *Arch of Triumph*. Although he never read his work in progress to her as he did with Jutta, she knew he was basing Joan Madou on her and expected to be offered the role, if not to play it, when the movie rights had been sold. She never thought that he would take forever to finish it, or that the character's relationship with Ravic would be so unsparingly drawn. She finally recognized the angst that she created within Remarque, but it took *Ravic* to point it out. Not only did Remarque expose Dietrich's traits and his obsession with her, but he disguised a female character, Jill Carstairs (after Jo), as a man and created a lover who is a successor to Ravic—an actor in the Jean Gabin image—who, in an act of agonized passion, kills Joan Madou. This act would seem like a wish fulfillment of Remarque's at various times, safely expressed between endpapers.

When *Arch of Triumph* was first serialized in *Collier's* magazine in 1945, the affair between Remarque and Dietrich had been over for quite some time. It was Dietrich, in fact, who seemed to cling to the memory of their past intimacy, as is clear from the following letter and notes she wrote him through the forties:

Paris, December 1, 1945—Elysées Park Hotel, Rond Point
I don't know how to address you any longer—Ravic is in general pretty good. I am writing to you because I had a sudden longing, not the one I had so often. Maybe I need a liverwurst sandwich—the remedy for the depressed. Paris is in gray fog. I can hardly see the Champs-Elysées. I'm confused and empty and without any goal. No running around after food and pilots any longer . . . I just don't know where I ought to be. Last night I found behind a picture three letters from you in which you give me good advice. The letters are without dates, but I know the time when you wrote them. They bring up memories of a time when you were furious with me because I had become too bourgeois. . . . You have ended up in a row full of hand-crafted cross stitches, and remain a measuring stick for me. . . . I am no longer in a row of hand-crafted cross stitches! I have revolted against it, torn the stitches away from me with not always the fairest of weapons, to free myself, and now I'm alone in my freedom and lost in a foreign city and find your letters! And write to you for no reason. Don't be angry with me. I long for Alfred [a fictitious little boy Remarque concocted whenever Dietrich withdrew from him], who writes: I thought love was a miracle in which two people together are much lighter than one is alone.

The letter is signed "Your doubting Puma."
Dietrich's notes are more those of a concerned wife than a pining ex-lover. They were written from the Plaza Hotel about 1944, when Remarque had not only moved to New York but into his own apartment from the Ambassador Hotel, where he had been staying.

[Note 1] Put the leftover rice in it and warm it up. Kisses.
[Note 2] No salt! Just steamed. Thought you would come home and want something to eat. Kisses. I'll call you later.
[Note 3] My pressure cooker broke, therefore so late. Turn the lid to the right to open. Kisses.
[Note 4] This is beef without any fat in its own juice. You can eat the meat or throw it away. The juice is the main thing. Easter kisses and thanks for my bells. I am washing baby clothes and will go to the children. [This one

jumps to 1948; with the birth of John Michael Riva, she became a grand-mother.]

[Note 5] Beloved, tried to reach you but in vain—only hope that the fact that you didn't answer means that you are out—therefore well again. [Remarque was beginning to suffer from a variety of ailments, such as lumbago, heart and arterial problems, Ménière's disease, and an extremely painful neuralgia condition known as tic douloureux, or trigeminal neuralgia.] The girl said you always accept your calls—you are probably not so ill that you can't call at all. I am leaving for Washington and come back next Friday. Ten thousand kisses—Your Puma.

For Remarque and Dietrich there was one element that bound them, more than any other, that went beyond their day-to-day dissonance, and that was being a refugee. They had escaped together, yet shared the love of the place that had forced them into exile. She had been his means of getting out. When he felt tortured by her, he didn't understand it, because suddenly she would then love him. He never quite grasped what she was doing, but he trusted that the love would endure long after the torment receded. The evidence is the last note on public record that Dietrich sent to him, dated February 8, 1962: "Beloved—I'm asking you for a translation of a text I spoke for a film about Hitler. The film is good—otherwise I wouldn't ask you. I'm longing for you every second in all eternity. Your Puma. Yes, I will of course speak your words; to the film, I mean. I speak your words in life anyway."

In May of 1940, Remarque moved into a rented house at 1050 Hilts Avenue, Westwood, Los Angeles. He felt, falsely, that he had finally extricated himself from her: "Her power is broken. . . . And I have learned that I can live without her." But they continued to see each other and he continued to buy her bracelets, meet her at Ciro's, have her cook for him, listen to her litany of lovers, and massage her breasts with a special cream to keep them firm, as well as massaging her feet.

For his forty-second birthday, Remarque received from Jutta a key ring, a cigarette box, and an ashtray with a light attached—"good for drunks" was Remarque's comment. Josef von Sternberg presented him with a picture of Venice, and Dietrich's gifts were a watch, a map holder, a white canary, and two yellow nightingales in "a beautiful cage." On this day he presented Dietrich with the best gift of all: a large aquarium fully stocked with battle and zebra fish and various other exotic species. They witnessed the installation together, absorbed the instructions, and fiddled around with it all afternoon. "Puma excited about the fish," Remarque reported. Owning and maintaining an aquarium seemed a point of mutual pride. For a few weeks they settled into a gentler pattern.

A year later he wrote across the entries of this temporary happiness: "At this point, you idiot, you should have given this beast a thrashing, and have gotten yourself out of the picture."

After James Stewart, Remarque had to endure watching Dietrich dance the rhumba (*the* dance that year) with her next two flings: John Wayne and George Raft. But at a benefit at the home of Gladys and Edward G. Robinson, he watched someone else do the rhumba, and perhaps saw a hint of things to come: "Paulette Goddard, nicely tanned, was dancing the rhumba. Full moon."

If he had had some kind of premonition, or even an attraction, it would wait a good decade to evolve. In the meantime, on New Year's Eve of 1941 in New York, he met two women with whom he would become involved—one who would replace Dietrich as his obsession.

Although he was receiving telegrams from ladies with no last names—"SALUTATIONS TO THE MISSIONARY OF THE DRUNK NIGHTS—LONGINGLY AND LOVINGLY—LISL"—his real affairs were of a deeply serious nature. Remarque, who was now staying in New York at the Sherry Netherland Hotel and preferred it to Hollywood, wrote of his preference to his friends the writer Franz Werfel and his captivating wife, Alma Mahler Werfel, who had been the mistress of the illustrious painters Oskar Kokoschka and Gustav Klimt, and was the widow of Gustav Mahler, the composer:

> You beloved ones! Pack your suitcases, leave our sweet home; leave the avocados on the strong avocado trees and come. At "21," they serve partridge, one cries thankfully into the Chateaubriand, and neurosis flies away like a hangover in a Turkish bath. . . . It is beautiful here! Adventure hangs like a liverwurst in the butcher shops downtown, in the large caravans around Central Park. The air tastes good. . . . Rembrandts and Vermeers are here, and I drank the Renoirs. The art dealer Thannhauser in addition to Bilka-Kümmel (iced Kümmel, Franz) has dozens of Degas works—it is a heavenly night ballet all around us—then there are some Picassos, Cézannes, Manets, Pissarros, van Goghs—all in a tiny Amsterdam house in the middle of New York . . . and at four o'clock in the morning we made it to the Champagne Room (that's our name for it) of El Morocco and on to the Dream Room of the Monte Carlo. . . . We went through Harlem,

Chinatown, Brooklyn, overate in Czech, Jewish, Greek, and French restaurants, and carefully examined the drinking supply of the city.

The year 1941 began with new romantic possibilities. The theatrical producer Gilbert Miller, "Divan the Terrible" (a nickname earned by amorous skills on the casting couch), had given a party where Remarque brought Jutta, whom he had gotten out of Mexico on a temporary visa while securing one for himself. His Panamanian passport had expired, making him, as he called it, "a white nigger" in America. Both he and Jutta would have to return to Mexico in May of that year to renew their refugee passports. But in January in New York, at a grand apartment with a great art collection that belonged to Kitty, Gilbert's wife, Remarque felt freer than he had in a while.

Greta Garbo caught his attention first with her "beautiful dark voice." Unfortunately for Remarque, she was with her steady companion, the seer of nutrition, Gaylord Hauser. They left early, but Garbo noticed him.

Next at the party he was introduced to the exquisitely fragile-looking Natasha Paley, a socialite with a Russian pedigree who was much photographed by Horst, among others. Remarque was entranced: "Met Natasha Paley, the new Mrs. Brown. Pretty and fragrant. Talked with her for a long time." (Natasha Paley was a model and actress of Russian descent who was born in France. She went to New York in 1935 to appear in the French version of Roy del Ruth's Folies Bergère; she also had a part in George Cukor's film *Sylvia Scarlett*. She returned to France in 1936, but maintained a second residence in New York.) Three days later they met in the afternoon: "Tender beginning, warmth, words, light playing, soft skin of the face and of the hips, suddenly, more. . . . My feeling: to fall in love with her."

Oddly, a painting by Cézanne got in the way of his two new romances.

When Remarque had gone back to Los Angeles and moved in 1940 into the 1050 Hilts Avenue house in Westwood, his Swiss art dealer, Feilchenfeldt, arranged to ship, by way of Holland, the bulk of his art collection to him on the West Coast. Kept company by van Gogh's *Yellow Bridge*, Daumier's tall, linear *Don Quixote*, his paintings by Degas, Utrillo, Delacroix, Renoir, Picasso, Toulouse-Lautrec, and Cézanne, he felt a new surge of comfort and confidence. Though still crated, more of his collection had also been sent: four Chinese bronze pieces from the Han and Chou dynasties, a Han dynasty vase, two Egyptian female mummy portraits found in Fayum dating from the first century, nine pieces of ancient Chinese pottery, and eight figures from the Tang dynasty, which included musicians, dancers, a buffalo cart drawn by a buffalo, and a lovely little horse. The most comprehensive portion of his collection was the Cézannes; he owned three oil paintings and nineteen watercolors. When he moved to New York in 1942, the collection was loaned indefinitely to the Los Angeles County Museum of Art and put on public exhibit there for over a year.

Dietrich, who had seen the collection, became fond of one of the Cézannes and very much wanted it for her birthday. He resisted. It was during his stay in New York at the beginning of 1941 that he realized, despite Garbo and the fragrant Natasha, that the old Puma still had a claw in him: "Went to a party given by Rudi S. Told me that Puma had called. Was insulted because I had not sent her the right gift, even though I knew how much she loved the Cézanne. To think, she had paid $2,500 for a desert house—I could buy two Cézannes for that! Of course, she didn't mention the Tang horse [he had already bestowed the horse on her]. What a child . . . today I was considering sending her the weaker of the two Cézannes she favored, but thought later that it was not necessary."

He was cautious with Natasha Paley, not so much because she was the new Mrs. Charles Brown, but because she seemed delicate and refined. There was something about her that could break. He was the one who was used to feeling breakable. "She is so defenseless, it prevents me from taking her," he wrote shortly after they had started to see each other. This was not the case with Garbo, whom he had simultaneously begun to see. He found her accessible, caring, and candid. She would call him if she wanted to see him, and then they would go off and explore New York—the galleries, the Empire State Building—and she would advise him to cut down on alcohol, to stay away from nightclubs, and out of Harlem. He promised her he would try.

At this point, Remarque was trying to take it all in: to Harlem for a jitterbug contest, to the fight between Joe Louis and Red Burman, to Elmer Rice's play *Flight to the West*, to the Museum of Modern Art, the Metropolitan Museum of Art, where some of his paintings had been shipped and were on display, to the dog show at Madison Square Garden, to the musical *Pal Joey*, to hear Father Divine preach to his congregation, and then on to "Mother Holmes" to observe a black religious ceremony.

He finished the first draft of the Ravic novel and gave it to Denver Lindley to translate. He began to ready himself for his return to Los Angeles in March.

Jutta Remarque remained in New York, taking a room at the Pierre Hotel, for which Remarque paid $400 a week. Ruth Marton recalls his response: "'Four hundred dollars for one room at the Pierre! But I mean if that's what she wants, so okay.' She was with him when he had nothing, and I think he never forgot that. And she was an expatriate because she was Mrs. Remarque."

Two weeks after the Millers' party, Greta Garbo entered Remarque's life. It is strange to think of Garbo as being an interlude for Remarque. He was puzzled why she pursued him, but willingly allowed himself to become "slightly infatuated." In the beginning, it was almost as though he was so detached that he was on the outside observing them together, rather than being gripped emotionally. They went for long walks along the beach at Santa Monica with his two Kerry blue dogs he had bought when he moved to Westwood. They laughed, talked, hugged, kissed, and to top off the walk, Garbo would show him a handstand in the middle of the road. "Every dog on the road knows her," Remarque wrote affectionately. They went to the movies—*That Hamilton Woman*—and Garbo sobbed when Lord Nelson died. They visited the Botanical Gardens, went for a long walk afterward, and then back to Remarque's house, where they cooked hamburgers, ate ice cream, and sat in front of the fireplace listening to records. In one afternoon walk with her, "She rolled up her sweater. The smooth brown skin. Brought her back to the house. Leaned over the gate. She slowly moved backward toward the house. The beautiful face under the hat. The silk ash-gray blond hair. She wants to go to India." The romance heightened.

Another time Garbo came to fetch him for a walk. When they returned to Remarque's house, she seemed different—livelier, a bit nervous. They shared a candlelight dinner with Gypsy music and then: "Went upstairs. She entered the bedroom, the light of the dressing room behind her, softly flowing over her shoulders, enchanting her outline, the face, the hands, the trembling, something imperceptible shook her, then the voice, the dark . . . the absence of any form of sentimentality or melodrama—and yet full of warmth. . . . Spent afternoon with Garbo, strolled around, watched the sunset."

Garbo was worried about gossip concerning them that was printed in the *Examiner*. She called for him at his house and they took a stroll "through bushes and over fields. Garbo lifts off her blouse. The most beautiful tanned back and the most beautiful straight shoulders, more beautiful than Puma's, whose shoulders are a bit too high. Farewell in the car. Garbo seems soft and opens up. And, idiot that I am, called her a little fool. She froze. I had frightened her. She called later. Thank God."

More gossip is spread by word of mouth in Hollywood than in the columns. Unless Hedda, Louella, or Sheila had managed a real scoop, an item was already lukewarm to cool by the time it hit print. Dietrich had been so busy with Gabin that the impact of Remarque and Garbo hit her late. They were at his house sharing one of their enchanted evenings when she called, angry, wanting him to come over. He refused. She kept pushing him until he told her why: "Puma began to blackmail Garbo. Says she has syphilis and breast cancer, can be arrogant and ugly, etc. A bombardment of jealousy, and then, confirms her love for me. Finally, I go to her. Puma warm and caring. I stay until 5 A.M. No commitments."

Remarque remained interested in Garbo. It was spring of 1942, but no matter how many peonies he sent to Garbo, she was undecided and didn't know to whom to belong. He reports: "I'm slowly getting impatient with her. I tell her that to Puma, men are like hotels; some are better, some are worse, but it makes no difference in which one she lives."

Garbo remained confused, but continued to see Remarque: "Garbo picked me up. Drive to the ocean. Walk the beach. Gentle wind, tender words, soft ocean. Garbo, the barefoot, big-foot beauty."

Although Garbo sent him a bucketful of red roses on occasion, their relationship petered out gently. He thought of her, but it was more like a refrain: "Garbo, all the nights with her, sitting in the dark. Never liked to switch on the lights. A strong solitude. Take her as an example, soldier!"

Although Remarque was fed up with Hollywood as early as spring 1941, he did not "scratch the Hollywood scab off his bones," as he put it, until October 1942. Many factors interfered. Chief among them was his shaky immigration status. He was required to go to Mexico so often that he figured it was cheaper to remain near the border until his business looked to be more settled.

While Remarque remained in Hollywood, there were many new women in his life. He was not seriously intrigued, and found fault with most of them.

Sylvia Ashley Fairbanks, widow of Douglas Sr.: "Glassy eyes, long, dangling arms like a monkey. Brought her home. As usual she forgot her key and we had to use the back entrance. A lightness; easygoing extravagance."

Dolores Del Rio: "Every part of her was beautiful—even her toes."

Greer Garson: "A red-haired amazon in a black tuxedo."

Frances Cain, a young actress: "Took Frances Cain to the Scheherazade. She was happy. She danced with a lightness and most charming ease, which seems to compensate for her lack of intelligence."

Frances Robinson (later to marry Edgar Bergen): "Pretty, boyish, simple, sensible. For the time being."

Greta Garbo: "With curls and red fingernails, came from the studio. Tired, older, a little sad."

Natasha Paley Brown: "Call from Natasha. Devoted, full of love. Stars in her absent eyes."

Clare Luce: "Author, blond, fragile, not that young, intelligent, witty, and charming, a beautiful profile.... Took Clare home. The dark room. The soft emotions. The devoted face. The whispering in the dark."

And then there was Lupe Velez, known as "the Mexican Spitfire." She stood out in a dispirited year when he said, "To fuck a woman is only a small thing—to fall asleep and to awake with her is a sign of deep trust." He seemed to enjoy both with Lupe, who appears in his descriptions to be relatively unneurotic, volatile, sensual, and funny—in other words, a tonic.

> White teeth, trembling, sparkling, crunching, shivers—talked till morning. ... Lupe is happy. A wild time. She bubbled "Yes, yes, yes, you got me." Unpretentious reverence.... Lupe's until six in the morning ... untamed, wild, trembling, feeling, childlike behavior ... nonstop laughter at Lupe's stories.... A beautiful, wild, smart child. Jumped around imitating people, even Puma.... More Lupe stories: How Puma had tried to start something with Lupe about ten years ago, and therefore had gotten in trouble with Cooper [Gary]. Lupe was hiding in the closet watching Puma, who was naked under a fur, trying to seduce Cooper, without any success, because Cooper was truly in love with Lupe. Lupe made wild remarks about Puma's breasts. Brought her home later; she [Lupe] hadn't slept with a man for years, was afraid—yet she looks like sex incarnate.... Strange and charming mixture of slang and teenage lingo, a very young feeling. Complete devotion, shameful like a child and yet knowing it all—harmless and dangerous. In her white robe in her white room with the little wooden Madonna, made in Germany, red with lipstick, kissed over and over. Following me like a shadow down the stairs to the door.

Lupe Velez provided just the irreverent and fun time that he needed. She was sophisticated, had had at least one female lover, and was buoyant, resilient, a good sport. Clearly, she adored Remarque, and her letters to him are effusive: "My Darling, Even though I won't be with you tonight I'll be thinking of you constantly and I hope you don't flirt because I hate to do to you what the dame did to the little rooster, bang, bang, bang. I love you, I love you, I do. More and more every day." And "My Darling, Just to tell you how sorry I am I laughed at your little man but I am more sorry about my garlic stink. I promise never to do it again so please forgive me. I love you more than anything in the world and I ain't kidding."

Ironically, for Remarque, the beginning of the end with Lupe Velez had something to do with Dietrich. Remarque had spent Christmas Eve with Lupe. He had presented her with a beaver coat, which she had then decided to exchange for a bracelet. Who should walk into the jeweler's while Lupe was there but Dietrich, who felt it necessary to advise Lupe on a present for Remarque: a ring, which she knew he would never wear. Lupe, the innocent, bought him a fat gold ring. Witnesses who happened to be in the store at the same time: Oskar Homolka, Olivia de Havilland, George Raft, and Fritz Lang. None of them were friends of Dietrich's, but for Remarque the town was getting too small.

When it was over, Lupe sent him a telegram that was without rancor; it was as sweet as their affair had been: "Is it true that a new love should die so very soon? Why? Hope all is well. My best to you—Me."

Remarque was bitter, but not about Lupe. It was Dietrich who still got to him: "Puma wanted a double magnum to take me down. Bitching about Lupe, she called me without any scruples. Wants part in Gabin film. As expected, good old career whore!"

During the time just before he left for New York, he went to the Charles Boyers', where he listened carefully to Chaplin tell him about his future wife: "Chaplin talked about Paulette Goddard and the attempts to change an inferiority complex and powerlessness into a superior philosophy. Said he didn't mind if she came home with jewelry given to her by other men. He'd never given her the jewelry she wanted."

One day Remarque would remember and change all that.

On December 11, 1941, there was a blackout in Los Angeles, America declared war on Germany and Italy, and many things changed for Remarque. He decided to pack up his house on Hilts Avenue and move to the Beverly Wilshire Hotel. Marlene Dietrich and Jean Gabin broke up—for the first time; there were many partings before it was finally over and he went on to Ginger Rogers. Orson Welles split up with Dolores Del Rio, leaving her free for the attentions of Remarque. His finances were worrying him—his 1939 Swiss tax situation was in such disarray that the Swiss government had frozen some of his assets, and the IRS was bearing down heavily on taxable income earned from book profits in the United States. He worked hard to make progress on *Arch of Triumph* and to find a German title for his novel *Flotsam*; he finally came up with *Liebe deinen Nächsten*, in English meaning

Natasha Paley Wilson, the actress and model who was one of Remarque's great loves, ca. 1945.

LEFT: *Marlene with her Afghan dog, a gift from Remarque, in Westwood, 1940.*

Remarque with Jack Warner and Mervyn LeRoy at the Santa Anita racetrack in Los Angeles, 1939.

"Love Thy Neighbor." His tendency to use an apolitical title proved unpopular with the German and Austrian exiles, who urged him to get more political and less understanding, to get involved. However, he had a major insight about his work and what he thought was the big mistake in *Flotsam*: "The use of autobiographical happenings—always weaker than imaginary happenings." During this time, his usual nocturnal activities of drinking and womanizing were greatly impeded by a decree from Lieutenant General DeWitt that Japanese, Italian, and German aliens be put under curfew from eight P.M. to six A.M., starting the last Friday in March. During the daytime, they had to stay within a five-mile radius of their houses.

Remarque not only suffered under the curfew but was frightened by its implications. "This curfew makes everything seem unrealistic, it's like waiting in a glass house: I read, move, don't work any longer, sleep, I'm without excitement or rebellion, just accepting the fact that we don't live any longer in Germany because we think democratic—and live in a democracy halfway incarcerated because we are Germans."

Those last months in Hollywood were inglorious ones for Remarque. He was very much involved with "Dietrich-bashing"; he made disparaging comments about her looks: "She didn't look well—kind of empty and wasted, no facial expression . . . so plain . . . like a ghost's face."

Although he was concerned about how long he could remain in California, seeing that all enemy aliens were going to be asked to leave, he regularly abused his curfew. He describes a wild night with Vera Zorina, the beautiful ballerina wife of George Balanchine, who was in Hollywood working on a film, accompanied by her mother and her agent. Remarque took up with her briefly but intensely: "With Zorina to Oskar Homolka, birthday party. Brecht, Feuchtwanger left on time for the curfew. I stayed with Franz Werfel and his wife, a wild blond woman, drinking, violent. Had brought Mahler into the grave, other lovers like Gropius and Kokoschka must have escaped her. Werfel won't. We boozed. I couldn't care less about curfew. Sometime much later I drove home, very insecure, crossed the white line several times."

Remarque finally decided to leave Los Angeles. He made up his mind to finalize his business with the Los Angeles County Museum of Art, where his collection would be exhibited on loan, and then depart for New York by October 1942. He had been living with a sense of helplessness and indolence for too long a time, and was hoping to reclaim his sense of purpose on another coast.

Even though the plan was set in motion, there were diversions and obsta-

cles. There were more women to squire about and become entangled with—
among them the actress Luise Rainer, with whom he found great comfort
speaking German. Rainer had recently come out of an upsetting marriage to
the playwright Clifford Odets, and although Remarque felt that she was
pretty and somewhat kindred, he also reports that she was lost: "I can't give
her what she wants."

Before he left, Remarque received news that made him distraught:
Osnabrück had been bombed, and was severely burned and gutted. He
mourned his past and berated himself for his luck at leaving it behind: "Erna
and Elfriede there, nothing I could possibly do. Thought of what I could and
should have done before, as well as for my father, the city, the Dome, the
green Katherine church, the walls, the mills, the schools. Go on, heart. Go
on, soldier. In spite of everything."

Astonishingly, the draft approached him, and he made the wry note
that aliens could never be officers, so he was to actually comtemplate being
a soldier again. He appealed to the draft board to allow him to leave for
New York. They gave their nod—for the time being. He left within the
week.

For the next six years, Remarque exchanged Ciro's, the Beachcomber,
Mocambo, and the Little Troc for El Morocco, Le Pavillon, the 21 Club, and
the Casino Russe. "Headquarters," he called them. He entered the same kind
of life in New York that had run him aground in Hollywood, with the
exceptions of access to the theater, more varied cuisines, and an introduction
to an exciting art market. He stayed at the Sherry Netherland Hotel, had a
major reunion with Natasha, who, after only a brief marriage to Charles
Brown, was being seen around with Jack Wilson, who, although homosexual, was to be her next husband. No matter how deeply felt her affair with
Remarque would be—and it would indeed last for over seven years, outdis-
tancing any of his others—he would remain a married man.

He would tryst with Natasha through her marriages and in between them
all over the world; as Victoria Wolff put it, "Their love was right but their
timing was off." They seemed to believe that forces were endlessly thwart-
ing and separating them, that they were a modern Romeo and Juliet—their
meetings took place in Rome, Venice, and Verona.

Dr. Thomas Schneider of the Remarque archive in Osnabrück felt that
Natasha was the great, pure love of Remarque's life, and if we judge from
what must have been one of Remarque's last letters to her during their affair,
he could be right:

Love of my life for so many years: let me tell you on this emotional night again and once more: that I have loved you with a love that has been rising and forever mounting and that it was the glory and the substance of being alive. Every butcher can be in love for a few weeks and months, but you by being you and with your love have made me (and I do mean in the highest, not the obvious-seeming sense of the word!) love you in a golden spiral of seven years, seven mythical years, seven years of renewal. They were seven most important years of my life, years that could easily have been the years of my worst misery. Thank you, thank you, thank you. You made me hope again, you made me positive again, you made me want to be creative again. In your beloved eyes, my life began to collect itself again. Thank you, thank you, thank you.

My last written word, which might reach you in Europe, again is: thank you for it all, Natasha.

As exciting as the love may have been, by 1943 Remarque was expressing doubt and displeasure in the diary. The recordings of his emotional barometer in regard to Natasha are indicative of all his major relationships. A pattern can be seen of his idealism shattered and then his attempts to sully the love and then his remorse. These entries cover a small span of time in 1943:

[*June 18*] Slept the whole day yesterday. Natasha came when I was just getting up. Thought it unbelievable. Explanation, discussion, fight continued throughout dinner until 2 A.M. . . . . She left. I went to El Morocco, and escaped with Pat, the cigarette girl, to Reuben's [famous sandwich restaurant and hangout of the forties and fifties]. . . . Natasha's picking on me all the time. I won't change my life—even though it's not ideal—to live as she wants me to. One needs contrasts and therefore looks for them. Can't help it. Forward, soldier!

[*June 29*] . . . Drank everything there was, in the end crème de menthe. To Bee's [a favorite brothel in Harlem]. A beautiful young Creole girl, Dolores. Home. In the afternoon with Natasha, who looked tired; she insists on separation; just to remain friends. Can't see a future with me for herself. . . .

[*July 6*] . . . A late call from Natasha, accusing me again of burnout, laziness, etc. I responded that I simply tried to survive the war and tried to spare myself for the years to come after the war. I also suggested that we shouldn't stay in touch any longer—something I had learned from my time with Lupe: better an end with terror, than a terror without an end.

[*July 8*] . . . Had a talk with Natasha without any results. Around three her phone rang. She pretended it was another lover. I didn't believe her. She screamed at me: Finished. It's finished. I left.

Sent her flowers today with a collection of Greek, Etruscan, and Egyptian jewelry. Sent it to her via a taxi. I pray she got it.

[*July 13*] . . . Yesterday at Salz's; we sold another Renoir and a Degas. [Sam Salz was his New York art dealer, who bought for him but also sold pieces of Remarque's collection that would bring him in the cash to continue to buy art.] At night to Natasha. We went together to a 1,000-people dinner at the Waldorf. . . . Natasha and I left early to be alone. No such luck; we went to El Morocco and right away [acquaintances] appeared, who literally clung to our table. We disappeared to Reuben's, where Natasha admitted during our talk to having had an affair recently. I took her home. Deep in thought. Phone call from Natasha late at night. I told her off; I had finally realized I had overcome the suffering inflicted on me by Puma in the only possible way: by falling in love with Natasha. Now I had to overcome Natasha!

[*July 15*] . . . [Natasha] is weak. On one hand she wants her independence, on the other a stormy and never-ending love affair. She speaks of a future together, and when I offer her one, she retreats.

[*August 15*] . . . Have the shakes every night. . . . Because of Natasha, I now understand Puma much better. Natasha's "if I could only trust you"—and when she finally can she gets bored and leaves. Get away from it all, soldier. Even Puma is on my mind again.

Aside from Natasha, there were other—seemingly incidental—women with whom he was involved. His pattern consisted of having one major female "tormentor" in his life, with several dalliances on the side. Tallulah Bankhead, Sylvia Ashley Fairbanks, the starlet Frances Cain, a singer named Reva Reyes, Gloria Swanson, Greer Garson, Luise Rainer—all entered and exited for cameo roles.

While Remarque had been in Los Angeles, something unspeakable was happening to his beautiful younger sister, Elfriede, back in Germany—and because of him. He did not hear about it until afterward.

Remarque had not been in touch with Elfriede since the mid-thirties, when she had written him a sorrowful letter with a request for money: "I have swollen legs again and the doctor fears it is water. . . . I have to rest a lot. Unfortunately I have very little money and therefore I want to ask you to pay another month of my health insurance. I don't know how to raise the money as much as I try and sweat over it. Otherwise I will get along somehow. I should drink a lot of red wine, but I can do without, too."

Later, she weaned herself away from Osnabrück when her sister, Erna, her brother-in-law, Walter Rudolf, and her father moved to the German resort town Bad Rothenfelde. In 1941, she met and married Heinz Scholz, a soldier in the army since 1940, moving to live with him in Dresden. She entered professional life by becoming a *Damenschneidermeisterin*, an accomplished ladies' dressmaker. By 1943, she was running her own dress shop for the well-to-do women of Dresden. In December of that year, Elfriede Remark Scholz was beheaded. The following is excerpted from the published document tracing her misdeeds, which led to her execution:

The Death Sentence Against Elfriede Scholz

In the name of the German People in the Case Against the Ladies' Dressmaker Elfriede Scholz, born Remark, from Dresden . . . who is currently in detention, accused of demoralization of the Armed Forces, the People's Court of the First Senate, based on the testimony of October '43, has recognized the following as law: Mrs. Elfriede Scholz, born Remark, over many months of unfettered, hateful, defeatist rumor-mongering, in conversation with a soldier's wife, has made the following declarations: She, herself, would like to send a bullet through the Führer's head. Our soldiers are nothing but cannon fodder, and the Führer must have them on his conscience. She would like it if the soldiers at the front would learn that their wives back home have died in aerial bombings. She would like it that women still convinced of impending victory lose their husbands at the front. As a dishonorable fanatic propaganda disseminator on behalf of our enemies, she is without redemption. She is therefore sentenced to die.

Her landlady, Mrs. Toni Wengel, during many conversations had concluded that Elfriede Scholz was someone who did not believe in our ultimate victory. That she never misses an opportunity to pose disdainful questions such as whether she, Mrs. Wengel, still believed in victory. Mrs. Wengel says that she, with quiet conviction, always answered this in the affirmative. In addition to Mrs. Wengel, Mrs. Scholz also tried to bring her defeatist conversions to the attention of Mrs. Ingeborg Reitzel. She knew Mrs. Reitzel as one of her customers . . . they had become friendly acquaintances. . . . Several of the particularly characteristic and demoralizing, defeatist remarks of Mrs. Scholz are stuck in the memory of Mrs. Reitzel. She, for instance, said that once Mrs. Scholz had said to her: "What kind of luck and happiness has he brought us? All the people who are going to the front are nothing but cattle and cannon fodder. He'll have all of them on his conscience. If I had the opportunity I would be delighted to send a bullet through his head myself, and I would be happy to take the consequences. . . . If I could do that, at least the German people would be free of this terrible man. I would be delighted to sacrifice myself. . . . Is this idiot going to wait before he . . . considers a peace? Is he going to wait until all of our cities and towns have been destroyed? . . . I have traveled a lot, and I've made the acquaintance of people all over. When those enemies come into our country, it's not going to be anywhere near as bad as they tell us. They are all much better than we have been told, and we Germans are really responsible for the fact that we are the most hated people of the world."

Mrs. Elfriede Scholz agreed that as a pessimistic person she may have expressed herself as doubtful about the potential ending of the war. But she's only done that to induce her neighbors and friends to strengthen her beliefs. For instance, she knew exactly what Mrs. Reitzel, a convinced National Socialist, is and was. She also knew that Mrs. Reitzel's husband was an officer in the army on active duty and was a dedicated believer in National Socialism. Mrs. Scholz thought and hoped that she might . . . possibly be converted by those two people. In addition she says that she has not expressed herself exactly as Mrs. Reitzel has testified.

In truth, however, she had no intention of being converted to a National Socialist belief by Mrs. Reitzel. On the contrary, she wanted to induce Mrs. Reitzel into following her line of thinking, of defeatism and degradation. When Mrs. Reitzel testified and quoted the remarks that so clearly stayed in her memory, and described the ironic and disdainful approach of Mrs. Scholz, she was so convincing in the eyes of this tribunal that there can be no question that [she] is a trustworthy witness and that as such she is cognizant of her responsibility. . . . All of this leads us to feel that there can be no doubt that things happened exactly the way Mrs. Reitzel says they happened. . . .

When Mrs. Scholz tries to base a part of her pessimism on the influence of her brother, the author of the ill-reputed masterwork *All Quiet on the Western Front*, that really is not an acceptable excuse . . . particularly since she testified that she has not seen her brother in the last 13 years. No. She herself is a shameless traitor. . . . She is a propaganda agent of our sworn enemies. For someone as debased and honorless as this woman, there can be only one form of punishment, a death sentence—an execution.

At the trial and sentencing on October 29, there was an attempted appeal for clemency given by a woman lawyer, whose name is not mentioned in the document. As the plea was presented gingerly and without true conviction, there was no question that Elfriede was doomed.

In addition to the question whether clemency and a backing away from the death sentence would prove helpful and beneficial, I would like you to consider the following personal moments. The condemned Mrs. Scholz is naturally pessimistic largely as a consequence of her severe illness. She has been suffering for years from a form of osteoporosis and only through the constant taking of various medications is she able to continue to perform any work at all. In addition to that she suffers from pernicious anemia, which makes it necessary that she be kept alive through a series of liver injections. The fact that she doubts anything and everything is partly based and excused by these serious illnesses. In addition to that, obviously one should consider the fact that she is the sister of the ill-reputed Remarque, whose train of thought, she, in her youth, must have listened to and absorbed. . . . She has not had any contact with her brother in 13 years, so that a direct influence can no longer really be considered. In pleading with you for clemency I would like to have you also consider that the detrimental remarks of the condemned regarding the outcome of the war were made after her sister had been completely bombed out and that the big bombing attack on Hamburg, of which she had just recently learned, had affected the entire family of her husband. . . . As to whether the only proper punishment for her acts is the death sentence, we should consider not only what we see objectively, but also what we know subjectively. We should not lose sight of the fact that we are dealing with a person who is suffering from several illnesses and, as a consequence, has become a pessimistic and questioning human being.

Lastly, I would like you to consider . . . the circumstances that her husband has been at the front, as a soldier, for three years, and that he has every intention of staying in the service. These are the summations under which I hope you will consider clemency.

Elfriede Scholz was beheaded in the Plötzensee prison on December 16, 1943, at 12:57 p.m. Her sister Erna received a letter from Elfriede that was written hours before the execution:

Dear Erna!

I am now in Plötzensee for the second time. And today, at one o'clock in the afternoon I won't exist anymore. Everything I own I leave to you. It all belongs to you. Even my life insurance. I don't think Heinz really deserves that I still think of him lovingly and kindly. [There is no recorded explanation for the implication against her husband. It's possible he didn't stand up for her.] But I forgive him everything and I forgive everybody else everything. To you and Ludwig and the parents, a last, loving salutation. Yours, Elfriede

Shortly afterward, Erna received a bill from the German authorities for the costs of Elfriede's execution:

Fee for the Rendering of Death Sentence . . . . . . 300 marks
Cost of Execution . . . . . . 122 marks and 18 pennies
Cost of Detention in Prison from Oct. 29, '43, to Dec. 16, '43 . . . . . . 73 marks and 50 pennies
Postage for the Sending of This Statement . . . . . . 12 pennies
Total Costs . . . . . . 495 marks and 80 pennies

This amounted to about $120. The bill then states that the obligation to pay lies in the hands of Erna Rudolf, as the sole heir of the effects of the ladies' dressmaker Elfriede Scholz, born Remark.

What is curious is that Remarque makes no mention of Elfriede's murder in his diary of that year. That he might not have known anything about it seems impossible. However, this diary entry appears in June of 1946: "Letter from Feilchen. The first news from Germany. A few days ago a letter from my sister Erna. Lives near Leipzig, alone. Husband is prisoner of war. My father seems to still be alive. She saw him last in 1944. His wife, mentally deranged, had just then committed suicide. My sister Elfriede in 1943, due to subversive remarks, was jailed, convicted by the people's court, and executed in Dec. 1943."

A month later, he mentions it again, having found out the name of Roland Freisler, the presiding judge who had delivered the sentence. Those are the mentions, without any elaboration or emotion.

That the news reached Remarque so very late is contradicted by his old journalist colleague Curt Riess, who writes:

Toward the end of 1943 I had once again gone to Washington and had taken a few days' vacation in New York. I had to bring Boni a very sad bulletin. His sister Elfriede had been executed by the Nazis. I heard about it a few days before the news appeared in the media, although it really had very little attention. . . . Boni was shattered. He said: "If she had not been my sister, probably nothing or very little would have happened to her." He had not been on particularly good terms with Elfriede; he found her end senseless and frightening. After the war he went back to live in Switzerland. He apparently expected and waited to be reinvited to come to Germany, but nothing like that happened. None of his former friends or acquaintances who had remained in Germany contacted him. Later on he once said to me that they were probably ashamed.

It was not until 1948 that a letter written by a stranger filled Remarque in on the details of the tragedy:

Dear Mr. Remarque, My name means nothing to you. We are simple, country people. Since my marriage in 1937, I have lived in Berlin. Every time I read your name, I am impelled to report to you about the sad event and the details of which are probably unknown to you, and of which I am particularly aware since I was an eyewitness. . . . I was in the visitors' gallery; I was supposed to learn how the law was being administered. . . .

I want to tell you of my admiration for your sister's demeanor during the trial. She answered all questions in a calm and composed way. But she really never had an opportunity to explain her political viewpoint, since the president of the trial—of the court—whose name was Roland Freisler, interrupted her twice by saying: "I am not going to give you the opportunity here in my court to continue to wallow in your defeatist propaganda." He compared her several times to Charlotte Corday, but it was never clear whether he admired her or thought her one of the instigators of the great revolution. . . . Every time the court entered the room, and when the judgment was read, all of us visitors had to stand and raise our hand in the Nazi salute, which your sister declined at all times. Calm and resigned, she accepted the reading of the death sentence, and she never budged when the handcuffs were put on her and she was led away. The court assembled in the great hall of a former girls' high school. One of the leaded windows showed the black, red, and golden German eagle with the inscription "United in Law and Freedom." The witnesses for the prosecution were never sworn in, since it was assumed that Germans would tell the truth, even if not under oath. During your sister's case, the president, in his most cynical and sarcastic way, said to her, "Your brother, unfortunately, got away. But you are not going to get away."

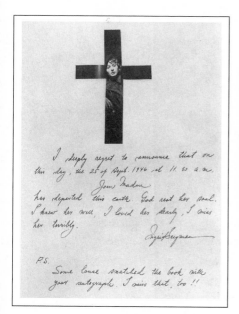

LEFT AND ABOVE: *A letter from Ingrid Bergman to Remarque after she finished filming* Arch of Triumph.

Charles Boyer and Ingrid Bergman in the film of Remarque's book Arch of Triumph, *1948.*

Elfriede Remark Scholz, shortly before her beheading by the Nazis in 1943.

I would like, dear Mr. Remarque, to congratulate you on having gotten away. . . . I can only get an approximate idea of the fight for existence that was faced by all emigrants. . . . I hope that my letter has been able to give you a little more detail regarding the final hours of your sister, and with best regards, Claire Lehmkuhl.

There are two postscripts. The first is that on December 16, 1968— twenty-five years after Elfriede's execution—the town council of the city of Osnabrück chose to honor her by naming a street after her. The affixed plaque reads: ELFRIEDE SCHOLZSTRASSE. The second is that in 1964, Robert Kempner, a lawyer and longtime friend of Remarque's, tried to find documented material related to the court hearings and thereby get the case reopened. He was unsuccessful. On the day of Remarque's death, he received information from the high court in Berlin refusing to reopen the case of Elfriede Scholz, born Remark.

The next several years were not productive for Remarque. His guilt about his sister's death might have contributed to his overwhelming lassitude and wastrel ways. He constantly reinvented loss and sorrow for himself, and yet recorded his busy evening schedule: "One evening with Natasha; one with Carol Bruce, one with Peter; one with Mona Williams. Day before yesterday, Millicent Hearst. A gentle night with many women, for so many years now everything seems to be for the last time. Sylvia Fairbanks beautiful, yet a bit harder; Mona Williams gray; Christina Patino with shadows under her eyes. Maybe the last time, the last years, maybe the last life. Later to El Morocco."

His fascination with Bee's brothel in Harlem grew to the extent that he was there a few times a week. The way he talks about Bee and her "girls" conjures up more eroticism and sympathy than lust: "A cab driver wanted to see my I.D. before he drove me to Madame Bee's. I sat with two of them, listening to their dream of having an establishment of class, while the morning sun shone through the torn curtains." "Ended the night at Madame Bee's place, where something slim came into bed with me." "Again to Bee, who had talked about a bronze she has. The sacred home of a chatty, simple Madame, who wore the medals of a navy officer on her bathrobe so she wouldn't forget to pray for him."

As the war continued, Remarque became increasingly unsure about himself as a writer. Projects had dwindled or fallen through, such as a screenplay he had been planning for Dietrich titled *Beyond* that was scrapped and then later, in 1947, produced as *The Other Love*, starring Barbara Stanwyck and David Niven. His work on *Arch of Triumph* was slow and unsure: "Worked despite awareness that I'm not good at it at all. . . . Today I worked a lot; still suspicious about it. . . . Got stuck with my book. Started a new chapter."

Moving to his own apartment in the Ambassador Hotel (between Fifty-first and Fifty-second streets on Park Avenue), hanging his van Gogh, and arranging through Sam Salz for his paintings to be shown in the prestigious Knoedler Gallery helped somewhat to reassure him: "Paintings. A Cézanne from Salz. Rugs, Chinese, Sung porcelain. The peace, [the balance] one can still find only in art. A Corot with a silver sky means more than ever before."

There was progress on the book. His affair with Natasha settled into somewhat less of a struggle, but he still accused her of nagging and of speaking French whenever she found someone who could understand, thereby totally excluding him. (Remarque refused to learn any languages other than English.) She also accused him of being a true German in his heart because he had predicted that the war would not end until the fall of 1946, and so she deduced that he believed the Germans would still put up a great fight.

This last struck a chord of fury within him: "Tasteless! To blame me for the umpteenth time for being German. A waste of time to explain to this she-goat that I've had my hands full getting rid of my complexes, without having them served up again and again by her!"

Remarque continued to take care of Jutta, upon whom he bestowed records, china, silver, cigarettes, stockings, and flowers; she happily accepted the gifts and tremendously looked forward to her bimonthly dinners with Remarque at the 21 Club, where she always ordered smoked salmon, lobster, and champagne.

As for the other women in his life, Dietrich had moved into her husband's apartment upon the breakup of her relationship with Jean Gabin. (Remarque records: "Looked well and relaxed. The gentle tap on the heart. The confusion of memory and fantasy.") Lupe Velez had committed suicide at the age of thirty-four. Remarque was shaken: "Lupe killed herself last night. Supposedly because of an unhappy love affair and because of a child she carried by a French actor. Pictures in the paper. They described her bedroom— the bed—the blue pajamas. One of the police officers said that she looked so small in the outsized bed that at first they had thought she was a redheaded doll. Little left to say. She was so full of life. Sorrow."

Arch of Triumph appeared in 1945, published by Remarque's new publisher, D. Appleton-Century Company. (He had followed his translator and editor, Denver Lindley, from Little, Brown. He would loyally follow him to a few more houses.) Orville Prescott, of the *New York Times*, wrote: "Erich Maria Remarque's new novel, *Arch of Triumph*, is the best he has written since *All Quiet on the Western Front*, which means that it is very good indeed." *Collier's* magazine purchased it to run in installments. Remarque asked for $50,000 in toto, they agreed, and he celebrated over a dinner at Brussels—one of the poshest restaurants in New York at that time. Two days later, he bought one of Degas's dancers in oil and a seventeenth-century Indo-Isphahan rug for $1,100. "Good for protecting the animal rug," he noted.

That same year, Remarque became a client of Harriet Pilpel, a partner at the prestigious law firm of Greenbaum, Wolff & Ernst. A long and trusting relationship was to follow. Their meetings tended to take place over luxurious lunches at the Chambord Restaurant, where Harriet Pilpel would fight being swept away by Remarque's charm while she worked on setting his affairs in order. For Remarque, their relationship—entrenched as it became—was strictly business-oriented. Harriet Pilpel, with her dark hair, alabaster skin, and keen, merry brown eyes, was most attractive, but she flaunted her cerebral side, which Remarque did not find particularly romantic.

Pilpel not only worked to have him pay less taxes in any given year but explored the possibility of assigning one-half interest in *Arch of Triumph* to Jutta; she even suggested divorce as a means of decreasing Remarque's tax burden. Harriet Pilpel's advice regarding Jutta Remarque was sound, but too late. On January 1 of that year, Remarque had already made a commitment to Jutta by promising her in writing 15 percent of the net receipts of *Arch of Triumph*. Nobody could quite understand why, nor could he be dissuaded. After his death in 1970, Paulette was left with his legacy of $50,000 to Jutta, and did not appreciate paying it.

The title for Remarque's next book, *Spark of Life* (*Der Funke Leben*), had come to him years before he actually started writing it. The book takes place in a concentration camp, and it would be his personal apologia for what his country had done. Starting in 1945, it took him five years to write it, and he started from scratch several times. This book became a journey into a darkness he had never known, a severe departure in style and content. It would be an exploration of and an exorcism from monstrosity. Hans Wagener has pointed out that with *Spark of Life* Remarque has made a departure from his other novels since he is not writing about what he himself had experienced. He therefore had both to interview concentration-camp survivors and to take into account written documents of what life had been like "under the conditions he wanted to describe." He knew it would be a very controversial book for his fellow Germans, who wanted to forget "the atrocities of their countrymen." As a result, Remarque had great difficulty finding a German publisher. In the dedication, found in the Library of Congress manuscript copy only, he states:

> The biggest Swiss publishing house which had made a contract for *Spark of Life* refused to print the book after it was delivered and gave as a reason that the book and all other books of the publisher would be boycotted in Germany if it appeared. Other publishers wanted changes. When the book finally came out in Germany the reaction was to a large part hostile, guarded, and resentful—to a smaller part the book was received without objections.

The first American edition of the book is dedicated, "To the memory of my sister Elfriede."

Juxtaposed to his diary entries about the progress of the war at this time was a typically decadent scene Remarque describes after a dinner with the head of *Collier's* magazine, at the Brussels Restaurant and a nightcap at El Morocco. Later Remarque found himself with two girls in an apartment: "Late night surprise: The two beautiful girls posed. The blonde squatting in an armchair, wrapped in an ermine cape, the brunette in a mink on the couch, both naked, both very beautiful. Suddenly time stopped. The driver outside patiently waiting. Back at 7:30 in the morning."

As Germany fell, he reports in his diary:

[*April 12*] Hannover, Osnabrück, Duderstadt, and other cities taken. Still somewhere real resistance. The gold treasure of the "Reich," paintings, Goethe archive, were found in a salt mine near Weimar. Prisoner camps were dissolved. Sanatorium of mercy killings discovered, 8,000 dead people. Russians in Vienna. . . .

[*April 18*] Roosevelt died on the afternoon of the 12th. Echoes from around the world. Friday, the 13th, a one-minute pause of commemoration in N.Y. Thunderstorm in N.Y., and at the same time in Washington.

Vienna capitulated. Yesterday Magdeburg. 300,000 prisoners in the Ruhr-Pocket. Papen was caught. Most likely had himself caught. . . .

[*April 28*] Berlin is surrounded. Battles below the earth (underground tunnels), Stettin fell. Regensburg fell. Prisoner-concentration camps for forced foreign laborers liberated. Gruesome photographs. Many thousands starved to death. Buchenwald, Belsen, Erla. Human beings incarcerated and burned alive, or forgotten. The folk of the poets and thinkers that it once was; the folk of murderers and hangmen now. The commander in chief of the Belsen concentration camp, Krämer: "clear conscience, only 1,000 died per month."

[*May 2*] Mussolini was shot. Supposedly Hitler died yesterday, fell or suicide. Germans and Italians signed unconditional surrender. Berlin fell. Hamburg fell. Munich fell. Rundstedt captured. The end is near.

[*May 7*] Germany surrendered. Papers rained from office buildings. Noon: not official yet. Russia hasn't agreed yet. Emotions strangely subdued; more a release of tension than exuberance.

[*May 9*] In between Hitler's death, Goebbels's death, not confirmed yet. Göring was taken prisoner. Not Himmler yet. Pictures of Berlin in ruins. . . .

[*May 28*] Himmler was captured; suicide, potassium cyanide. . . . Tokyo was bombed; for the most part burned.

The German Nazis are all complaining that they are not treated according to their rank and interrogated by higher officers. Göring and Himmler expected to chat with Eisenhower. Complete ignorance of their reputation abroad. . . .

[*Sept. 12*] Since July: Atom bomb. Japan abandoned the war. Americans landed in Japan. Peace. The Day of Armistice: honking horns. The noise of children's trumpets. Reminds me of an idiotic carnival. But supposedly also: people kneeling on the sidewalks, in Times Square, in churches. . . .

From Europe there was good news and bad news for Remarque after the war. The good news was that Rosa and Joseph were still in the house in Porto Ronco, and that it was intact, with a garden that was wildly overgrown. From Paris came the amazing news that the Lancia he had left in a garage six years earlier had not been seized by the Nazis and was still there. The fee for the storage couldn't take away from the joyful thought of racing his first Puma once again.

The bad news came from the tax man. He hadn't paid most of his European taxes for years. He had tried to sell stocks in Zurich, but it was impossible since the money was being blocked by the Germans. He had paid $60,000 in taxes in 1945, but that was only an installment, and because of his dual residency and his complicated financial status, he would be in a tax snarl for most of the rest of his life. There were other problems, such as Enterprise

Pictures, which produced the film of *Arch of Triumph* and which Remarque was convinced had siphoned off profits. But he could be peculiar about money, particularly small amounts.

"Remarque was a stickler for every little penny," recalls Robert Lantz, "and so when a $20,000 contract for *Heaven Has No Favorites* arrived by messenger, he couldn't get over the fact that he had to pay the messenger's fee of $1.98."

Remarque was increasingly concerned about his father, although true affection remained suspended, as it always had been. It seemed that "the old man," as Remarque referred to him, got in touch only when he needed money. After the war, Remarque made a special effort for his father because of what he had suffered. The murder of his daughter, the suicide of his second wife, and his own fall, which resulted in a broken thigh bone, rendered him a pathetic figure to Remarque, and one who needed to be pampered. His concern is recorded: "Letters from my father. Tried to transfer money to him from Osnabrück. Sent packages. Take a long time to arrive. A British censor had, on top of everything, wrongly rewritten the address. The 81-year-old man doesn't know where I am and why he doesn't get an answer! Am worried about my father. Packages take 5 to 6 weeks; heard to my dismay that the first three sent may take up to 4 months!"

Remarque worked to get his father a visa, and out of Germany into Switzerland, as well as sending money and CARE packages regularly. His father wanted "refreshments," as he called them: cigars, chocolate, a pipe, tobacco, and information on his favorite movie star, Ingrid Bergman, who would shortly be signed to play Joan Madou in the movie of *Arch of Triumph*, a part that was thought to be destined for Dietrich, but one that Remarque— had he had his way—would have seen go to Garbo.

The women of his past were beginning to age. He still ran into them in the small and elite world they shared. Garbo, on the arm of George Schlee, husband of the designer Valentina, looked "uncombed," as he put it, and Natasha was often puffy around the eyes. Dietrich was back—although not entirely successfully. She appeared at the beginning of 1947:

> Puma called, came over, wanted to start anew. Had had an unsatisfying affair with an American actor; Gabin and boredom lay ahead, and she therefore decided I was the right one to stay with. Stayed here the first night. I didn't want to; steered clear. At first nothing. Then it started to rise.

I felt nearly nothing. Just slight resistance. I took her home in the morning, was pretty drunk. Tried. I don't know why. Yes, I wanted her again. It was okay because I didn't feel anything any longer. It's strange how one's body reacts. She's changed. She appeared heavy, the face broader, older, flabbier. No, that's not so. She does look good. A columnist had written about us again. Had a fight with Peter about it. Stupid. She can't expect me to be alone or not to appear in the papers. With Marlene: nothing left, really.

A few days later, Dietrich took her cue and said good-bye again. "Touching, despite everything," he records. "These farewells are harder than before, each time more intense, because with it is the farewell to beauty and youth."

At the end of July 1947, Remarque had a new hearing in New York regarding the matter of his citizenship. He was grilled about Nazism, Communist affiliations, breaking his curfew, his separation from Jutta, and his relationship with Dietrich. "I am now 49 years old and have to respond to this!" he notes. "Longing for Europe."

On August 7, 1947, both he and Jutta were made naturalized citizens by the United States of America Southern District Court of New York. Remarque celebrated with Natasha by having Wiener schnitzel at the Blue Ribbon Restaurant. Shortly afterward, he made several patriotic statements regarding his new prize: "I am not German anymore, for I do not think in German nor feel German, nor talk German. Even when I dream it is about America, and when I swear, it is in American."

Though he loved being in New York and becoming an American, it was not easy to belong after having been a traveler for so many years. Remarque read Kafka and longed for Europe again. He began receiving cards and letters from Porto Ronco from friends who were already back, and it made him feel it was time to go there again. Remarque was also worried about taxes due and the fact that he was spending too much. He felt that it might be cheaper to be in Europe.

It was Robert Lantz who, inadvertently, helped him with his money problems. Remarque needed an honorable agent to make him a bonanza of a deal. Lantz was his man, although at the time neither felt that the offer being made by Universal for a reissue of the film of *All Quiet* would cause much excitement. Lantz recalls:

Bob Goldstein of Universal International was a close friend of mine. One day he called me and said, "Erich Maria Remarque needs some agency advice on a deal with Universal. And I don't want to give it to him. You certainly know who he is and speak his language. Would you like to call him?" And I said, "Of course, I'd be delighted, honored."

I called Erich at the Ambassador Hotel and he said, "I have a very tiny problem and I would appreciate it if you would like to take care of it for me. Come and see me."

And I went to see him and we liked each other a lot. I mean, he was such a charmer.

And he said, "I have a deal with Universal for *All Quiet on the Western Front*. Now, of course many years have gone by. The war interfered with the proper release of the picture. And these crazy people think they would like to re-release the old movie in some countries probably for the first time. And, oddly enough, under my contract made a hundred years ago in Germany, they can show the movie at this point only if I consent. They think that with my consent, it will publicize the old novel and I will make money that way. They are crazy and will lose their shirts. Who wants to see this old movie? But what do you think?"

And I said, "Well, if you have a right, however farfetched it is, they should pay something. They have more money than you. We'll ask for something."

And he said, "I'll tell you what. If you can get me five thousand dollars, I'll be a very happy man. Because I tell you, there will never be another penny!"

So, I called my friend, Mr. Goldstein, and I said, "He will give you the right to release the picture for fifty thousand dollars and twenty-five percent of your gross receipts."

So Bob said to me, "Fifty thousand dollars is not unreasonable, and at least you will make five thousand dollars commission. I will also give you twenty-five percent of the gross, because between you and me, it's not worth five bucks. Nobody will ever see another penny! This is the craziest enterprise! But if Mr. Remarque agrees, I agree. It's crazy!"

I was brought together with Harriet Pilpel and a deal was drawn. Remarque was thrilled to get an outright payment of fifty thousand dollars. It was money then. And he said, "Not only will I pay you the five-thousand-dollar commission, but I'll take you to lunch at Chambord."

End of story it seemed. Then, one morning, I got a letter in the mail from

Universal, and it contained one piece of paper. It said: This is a statement for the last six months, and a check was enclosed to Robert Lantz as the agent for Erich Maria Remarque. It was for six hundred thousand dollars. Some such figure. I mean unbelievable!

Now remember Bob Goldstein was a close friend; I called him and said, "Listen. We have to do something quickly, because I don't want to involve Remarque in this, but somebody has made a terrible mistake, and that check was ..."

He said, "No, they didn't make a mistake. That is what is due. Twenty-five percent of the gross receipts of the picture. So, let us all learn for the rest of our lives, one never knows."

When Remarque wrote in his diary, "Longing for Ponto Ronco. Longing for security. Somewhere to belong," he could not have anticipated the shock of actually being there after nine years. He put all of his faith into having a personal revival in Europe of everything that mattered to him.

He was booked to sail on May 12 on the *America*, docking in Le Havre. He would go to Paris, Zurich, and then on to Porto Ronco. In the weeks that preceded the trip, he grappled with demons and disabilities. His drinking was out of control; he could not seem to rein it in, and as he ruefully noted, with age, hangovers take longer to subside; there were also increasing instances of sudden impotence, which he first mentions in his diary of 1948. He fretted about the collapsing economy and his difficult relationship with Natasha, and suffered from the trigeminal neuralgia—so much in fact that a dinner party was arranged just so he could meet another sufferer.

Harriet Pilpel invited him along with, among others, the novelist and playwright Edna Ferber, who had the same agonizing facial pain. Also at the dinner was Luise Rainer, with her new husband, the publisher Robert Knittel. Remarque only mentions that he had many cognacs and went later to El Morocco. Edna Ferber, in her diary, makes a passing mention of the evening: "To Pilpels'. Met Erich Maria Remarque, author of *All Quiet on the Western Front*." Neither mentions their common bond.

"Tax troubles; lawyer troubles; publisher troubles; work troubles; will not finish the book on time. Once to be free of pressure," he writes in April. But apparently pressure was following him right to the boat. The film of *Arch of Triumph* had just been released to poor reviews. The newly formed independent film company Enterprise Pictures had offered a purchase price of $100,000 for what was to be their first property on any terms that Remarque wished. He would get $133,000 out of the first million dollars of net profits as dividend and 20 percent thereafter. What became complicated was the fact that although Harriet Pilpel was negotiating the full deal, Otto Klement had already made a prior deal with one of Enterprise's partners, David Loew, whereby he would receive 4 percent of the net profits after Remarque's share had been deducted. As Harriet Pilpel wrote in a memo to Morris Ernst, "This was not disclosed to Remarque at the time and it makes Klement an interested party whose advice is not entirely objective since he is personally involved."

Lewis Milestone, who had made a classic film of *All Quiet*, was set to direct, Ingrid Bergman and Charles Boyer were signed to star as Joan and Ravic, and the American novelist Irwin Shaw was to write the screen adaptation. He withdrew, however, when he and Milestone disagreed about the treatment of the material. Milestone and his producers wanted Bergman and Boyer to smolder in a love story: Shaw followed the storyline of the novel more closely, depicting the German exile's ordeal in Paris, and his strange obsession with the small-time actress-singer Joan Madou. Lewis Milestone, along with the screenwriter Harry Brown, replaced Shaw and wrote a screenplay that was in keeping with the producer's vision. Boyer's Ravic was turned into an Austrian, and the emphasis was indeed on the love story. The heads of Enterprise, Einhorn and Loew, along with the producer of the film, David Lewis, had their eyes on censorship from the very beginning— especially because they were a new company and could not afford any tangles.

Remarque allowed the changes perhaps because of the substantial profits to be made from a commercially geared picture, but the film was not to be a success. As *Newsweek* put it, "the arch not triumphant." And Remarque was soon to engage in his only lawsuit, against Enterprise Pictures for withholding profits.

But on the day Bosley Crowther's review in the *New York Times* came out, Remarque, Bergman, and Boyer went to the circus. Boyer held the bad review in one hand, and ate a hot dog with the other.

Remarque wrote an enormously flattering letter to Ingrid Bergman. Even though he had wanted Garbo, he did not let on any disappointment about the film's reception:

> Strange, I know that having seen Joan on the screen, I will not be able to recall her face back from my imagination. It will be from now on always your face. Already, looking at the crucified photo in your letter, I believe she

looked like you. [Bergman's next film was *Joan of Arc*.] This is not an accusation of mental murder; it is a story of death and resurrection.

From now on nobody will ever think of her [Joan Madou] in other forms than in the storms, lightnings, and landscapes of your face, and I, wanting it or not, will be included in the magical exchange. So hail and farewell. She died a beautiful death in your arms.

The Sunday before he left for Europe, he took Dietrich, his muse for Joan, to the Metropolitan Museum of Art to see the unicorn tapestries. Afterward they went to Mrs. Herbst's, a Hungarian pastry shop, for strudel and coffee. He writes, "It was everything I had expected, hoped for years ago. She wants to go back most likely. And since it was expected and not received years ago, now, one doesn't want it anymore."

Up until practically the day of departure, Remarque had passport problems. Not only did he want to go "home" again to Porto Ronco, he wanted to do research for *Spark of Life* and visit occupied territories. He appealed to the passport office, explaining he was writing a book set in Germany in 1945, and, since he had not been there since 1933, he needed to do some research. He asked to stay about a month in the American and British zones, and to visit Munich, Stuttgart, Frankfurt, Hannover, Berlin, and Osnabrück, as well as some schools, camps for displaced persons, camps for prisoners of war, and former concentration camps.

Letters were written for him, but despite everyone's efforts he was denied entry into Germany. On the day before he sailed, Remarque was issued passport no. 200106 and a visa.

Natasha was waiting for Remarque at the George V in Paris. They fought almost immediately. "N. wanted to go to Biarritz on the 15th. I wanted to go to Zurich on the 29th. I suggested we combine both trips, making them at the same time, otherwise the earliest I could be back in Paris would be on the 7th or 8th and then we would only have a week together before she would have to leave for Italy. She: wanted to swim in Biarritz, and expected to be indisposed the week before, so therefore wanted to go later. I: just because of this stupid swimming I have to race back and forth between Ascona and Paris."

They finished a bottle of cognac and agreed to go their separate ways. For the few nights before he left for Porto Ronco, he would go out drinking and find her asleep when he got back to the hotel. He writes: "Nothing stirred. After all I had lived here in earlier days with Marlene."

In Zurich he was greeted by his old art dealer Walter Feilchenfeldt, his wife, Marianne, and a nine-year-old godson, whom he met for the first time. Feilchenfeldt had treasures to show: a van Gogh, drawings from the Lichtenstein estate, two Rembrandt drawings, and two Brueghel prints. Remarque began to feel at home. He walked along Bahnhof Street—the main shopping street in Zurich—he had coffee in the garden of the Baur au Lac—one of Zurich's grandest hotels; he celebrated the day. At night, he had a lot to drink, "light wine, but a lot."

It was raining when he reached Porto Ronco. He could see the lights through the windows, and everything looked cozy and welcoming. Inside, his father was waiting for him—physically fragile, but chipper, with Spatz, the one dog left. Rosa and Joseph came out to help with the luggage. The sensation of being there, finally, was overwhelming emotionally.

Everything as I had left it. Toothpaste, letters, pencils, paper, all in the same spots. A Rip van Winkle. Sleeping Beauty dreams. One awakes—and it's ten years later. Strange effect. Touching and mysterious. That it can pass like that, completely gone, that among the stormy existence a piece of life can disappear like that as if it never happened. The force of matters: to put two ends together, ignoring the in-between. Walked around. Books, things, suits: awakening memories. Painful, touching. Ghostlike. . . . Next to my bed, my note pad was still on the table on which I had written the night before. . . . I started to look around on the desk, to look for my original Goethe manuscript, and I found it and the faded handwriting said: "Whosoever comes into the world, builds a new house; he departs and leaves it to another, and that person will change it. But no one finishes it." I felt as if I had stepped through a wall of glass and that the nine years had not existed, these nine years that had been filled to the brim with excitement.

RINGS ON HER FINGERS

1 9 3 9 – 1 9 5 1

BY THE TIME *The Great Dictator* had been released, Paulette's marriage to Chaplin was over, but through him she had undergone a firm indoctrination in liberal politics. She had also been around his politically aware friends and could, on occasion, be convincingly outspoken. In early 1940, Paulette and Chaplin were guests of Roosevelt in the White House. Harry Hopkins, Roosevelt's special adviser, was quite taken with her, and after that initial visit, became her official escort at various White House functions. "He was the Kissinger of the day," she recalled. And it was he, not Chaplin, who paved her way to becoming a favorite with the Roosevelts: "Harry picked me up at the St. Regis and said, 'What would you like to do today? Would you like to go to the races or would you like to visit the old boy up at Hyde Park?' I said, 'I think I'd like to go to the country and see the President.'"

She and Harry Hopkins had set out for lunch with FDR, but she had insisted they stop along the way to peruse a flea market (Paulette could never resist anything remotely connected to shopping), which delayed them considerably. With anybody else, it might have endangered the relationship, but not with Paulette: "The first thing that FDR said to me was 'Goddard, you're late!' And I nearly fainted. I was so shy with him. There we were at lunch and that was his greeting. It absolutely stunned me. And then he said,

'Why aren't you talking to me? I invited you so we'd have some fun and talk.' And I said, 'I'm shy with you because you're so—eligible.' He said, 'I'm not! I'm married among other things.' And I said, 'Well, you're handsome and I'm speechless.' And we became great friends."

She also made sure that she was friends with Eleanor. When she visited at the White House, Roosevelt would say, "Paulette is staying to play backgammon with me after dinner," and Eleanor would counter with "She is not! She is going to the the-a-ter with Harry, and me and the boys."

Not only did the Roosevelts vie for Paulette's company, but also John Ringling North, Lord Mountbatten, Anthony Eden, and Winston Churchill. Paulette had met and, by her own admission flirted with, Eden at a dinner that she had attended with Lord Mountbatten during the elections for prime minister. She recalled,

> We were in one of those great houses of England owned by Lord So-and-so. I was staying at the house and he was staying at the house so I flirted with him a little bit. But I didn't know we were going to be house guests for a week. At that time John Ringling North was trying to court me, but I was in England and he was in New York. So, he said, "What can I do to keep you on the string?" I said, "You can send me steaks and caviar!" This was when they had rationing. So, he sent me—twice a day it would come by Air Post—first the big steaks from 21 and then the caviar!
>
> And Eden was such a beautiful man. So charming. But he was running for election then and he had to go to all these meetings with constituents, and they were hiding me from the constituents because there wasn't supposed to be a film star visiting alongside a politician. And I felt like Lady Chatterley's lover because I'd want to go outdoors all the time and I'd have to go through the back gate because the constituents and their wives were coming through the front.

Paulette's liberal mix of politics and pleasure put her in the middle of a Mexican fracas involving the artist Diego Rivera and the Russian exile Leon Trotsky. It had all started as an article for *Look* magazine in 1940, titled "Paulette Goddard Discovers Mexico." She and Chaplin were separated, she had just finished co-starring with the young comic-comer Bob Hope in Paramount's *The Ghost Breakers*, and she had decided, for a little rest, to accept an all-expenses-paid trip. She took her mother, who had generally felt much more deprived by the end of her marriage than had Paulette.

The trip was timely for another reason; it was used as an escape from yet another scandal—this one more dangerous than the one in Britain.

It happened one night at Ciro's, a favorite haunt of Remarque's and Dietrich's, as well as of almost every other celebrity. There are several versions of the story. Paulette was dining with the Hungarian-born director Anatole "Tola" Litvak, who had been married to Miriam Hopkins and had directed as well as romanced Bette Davis in *The Sisters* and *All This and Heaven Too*. At that time, on that night, he was supposedly mad for Paulette. They were seated at a banquette. Paulette's shoulder strap popped, her bodice slipped down, Litvak held up the tablecloth to shield her, she slipped prankishly under the table, he followed, and they carried on under the table. According to other versions, Paulette dropped an earring under the table, Litvak went to retrieve it, and Paulette soon followed him under the table, and so on.

Paulette's comment regarding the much-publicized episode was "Isn't that silly?" However, Litvak took the brunt of the rumor and, according to some, he never quite recovered his former stature. The indignity of the event was made worse, according to the late director Jean Negulesco, by the fact that "'Tola' got a mouth infection at the height of the scandal."

Paulette was captivated by Mexico, and Mexico was crazy about her. *Look* took many pictures of her as a celebrated tourist playing with burros, petting livestock, roaming the open markets and filling her bag, her arms, and her mother's arms with flowers and pottery. Of the Churubusco Monastery garden, she said reverentially, "It makes a girl think." She posed at the Palace of Cortez, walked over the cobblestones of Cuernavaca, visited an old grandee, who kissed her hand and told her to beware of slick gentlemen who pretended to be grandees, and then, when she was in the courtyard outside his stables, he roped her and announced, "To the real grandee, three things in life are important—his horse, his gun, and the ladies." "In that order?" asked Paulette. At a bullfight, "Paulette was cheered by the crowd. The matador dispatched a bull in her honor. Some low fellow said the matador was an amateur. "Perhaps," said Paulette, "but the bull was a professional."

Paulette later recalled the excitement of the bullfight and of being involved with a ritualized sport that was so primal: "The impresario of the bull ring in Mexico City liked me. He made me the 'Madrena'—the Godmother. And I was so involved in it—it was like a whole life for me. And I'd run into the chapel because there was no ladies' room in the bull ring. I'd have to go somewhere, so I'd go in the back of the chapel, or in a pew or a confessional or something. I learned not to have any champagne before I went to the bull-

*In Mexico in 1940: Paulette keeping company with the Mexican film star
Cantinflas,top, and, above, photographed by* Look *magazine.*

fight. Because it was right after lunch when I went into the chapel, they'd be on their knees praying and crying out for help before they'd go into the bull ring. It was fabulous. I was as close to that as I was ever close to anything."

George Gershwin had originally told her about Diego Rivera, who was not only a great muralist but a Mexican veteran of revolutionary barricades. He was also a notorious ladies' man, forever ready to paint and woo whoever thrilled him. He was immediately entranced by Paulette, and appointments were made for her portrait to be done. Conveniently, Paulette was staying at the posh San Angel Inn, which was right across the street from Rivera's studio. And so, "amid Aztec and Mayan relics in the studio of Rivera's modernistic pink and blue house on the outskirts of Mexico City, Paulette posed in what the artist called a classical boudoir scene—'Milady of 2,000 years ago.'"

In 1936, Rivera had been a member of the Mexican contingent of the Trotskyite International Communist League, and had been instrumental in getting the Mexican government to grant Trotsky and his wife, Natalia, political asylum. Trotsky's entry into Mexico signaled the beginning of a full-blown affair with Rivera's wife, Frida Kahlo. Whether Rivera knew is difficult to pinpoint, but he and Trotsky had a bitter fight—presumably over politics—that left them polarized. "The real problem," according to Hayden Herrera in her biography of Frida Kahlo, "was that Rivera's Trotskyism was neither consistent nor profound. He would say things like: 'You know, I'm a bit of an anarchist,' and behind Trotsky's back he would accuse him of being a Stalinist. With his anarchic attitude toward any dogmas or systems other than his own, Rivera was incapable of staying obediently under Trotsky's ideological wing or serving as a reliable party functionary."

When an assassination attempt by a group of Stalinists was made on Trotsky's life in May 1940, Rivera was suspected of being the impetus behind it. Paulette had been posing for Rivera, and luckily her portraits were well under way when Rivera was forced into hiding. Paulette, in fact, had been the one to warn him of his impending danger and help him escape. Supposedly, Rivera and Paulette drove to Dallas together and flew from there to safety in Los Angeles, where he then departed immediately for San Francisco to fulfill a contract he had with the Golden Gate Exposition to paint some frescoes. In an interview he gave upon arrival, he attributed the highest honor to Paulette for helping him "escape from Mexico with my life."

He honored her again—more libidinously this time—in one of the murals he painted for the exhibition. As Herrera describes it: "Rivera and Paulette Goddard hold each other's hands while also embracing the tree of love and life. Her blue eyes and his brown ones are amorously interlocked, and her virginal white dress is pulled up to show her lovely legs. She represents 'American girlhood,' Rivera explained in his autobiography, 'shown in friendly contact with a Mexican man.'"

Years later, Paulette recalled her time in Mexico and making the dramatic escape:

> Mexico is part of my life. Every time I'd get off the plane, Diego would be there with flowers and the mariachi band. It was so long ago when I first started sitting for Diego. And we had a date with Trotsky the afternoon he was stabbed with the ice pick. We were on his daily date book for 4 P.M. tea. And I was sitting for the portrait around noontime. I'd always be sure to get there for the great Mexican lunch and I'd only sit for about an hour. But I was sitting that day and waiting until it was time to go over to see Trotsky, and two cars came up filled with men in black suits and all the rest of it. And I was sitting looking out the window and I said, "Look, Diego! I don't know what's going on, but I've seen enough in movies to know we're in trouble." So he lay in the back of my station wagon on the floor and I drove him out.

Rivera, who ended up in Los Angeles for a bit, stayed with Paulette and Chaplin, but Paulette claimed that Chaplin did not like him—or any of her friends—and that he was forced to go stay with Dolores Del Rio.

Back in Hollywood, Paulette was determined to save her career. *The Great Dictator* did not provide her with the momentum that she had hoped for, and although *The Ghost Breakers* was received in the ebullient and larkish manner that it was made, she needed a smash, a part that would elicit surprise and elevate her.

Paulette's social success with movie moguls—such as Selznick and, of course, Chaplin—preceded her working relationships with them. Before they started working together, she and DeMille got along famously. She recalled:

> He used to invite me to his ranch in the country. Some ranch! He would say, "Bring your most glamorous clothes." And there'd only be four or five for dinner, and he'd have everything in flames and you'd have to protect your hair from flying around because everything was flaming behind you. Not only was everything flambéed during the dinner, but at the end there

Paulette with the Mexican artist Diego Rivera,
whom she always saw on her trips to Mexico.

Rivera painted this 1940 portrait of Paulette.

was cherries jubilee to top it off. DeMille would hand me a gun as I went down to my cabin, and he'd say, "In case of wild animals." And I said, "The only wild animal I'm leaving up here!" He thought I was quite amusing. He was terribly flattered at that. . . . But it was marvelous to be there. Everything was organized, completely disciplined, dinner at eight, eight oh-five would come the caviar for me—nobody else would get any, just me. And the men all had to put on their Russian silk jackets for dinner—he had one in each dressing room. . . . It was as though we were living in Roman times. Before the fall. It was fabulous at his place. I thought I was in a movie while I was living!

DeMille was about to make a picture for Paramount called *Northwest Mounted Police*. It was to be his first full-length feature in Technicolor, out-DeMilleing any of his previous pictures. Gary Cooper, Robert Preston, Madeleine Carroll, and Preston Foster were already set to star. The part yet to be cast was that of one Louvette Corbeau, a fiery half-breed. Marlene Dietrich had expressed interest, and after playing Frenchy in *Destry Rides Again* was available to play almost anything. Simone Simon, an exotic French actress who had made a hit in Jacques Tournier's *The Cat People*, wanted the role, but young Rita Hayworth, with her Latin background and lush looks, was the best contender. Paulette was also interested. She had once written to DeMille in 1936 from China, saying, "I look forward to working with you someday."

Her agent, Myron Selznick, met with resistance at getting her a screen test for Louvette. She wrote to DeMille asking for the role, but her letters were getting her nowhere. He was not at all convinced that this advanced ingenue could meet such overtly steamy requirements. According to Morella and Epstein, Paulette went into an orbit of preparation to change his mind:

She conspired with Wally Westmore, head of makeup at Paramount, with Natalie Visart, DeMille's costume designer, and with associate Bill Pine to transform her appearance into that of the character's.

One day DeMille's personal secretary, Florence Cole, knocked on the door of her boss's office and announced, "Louvette is here to see you." . . . In DeMille's words: "Florence stepped back from the door, and a dark girl, with eyes that could smolder or melt, came in, made up as a half-breed and costumed as such a girl would dress on the wild Canadian frontier in the eighteen-eighties. . . . She gave me one insolent look and said, 'You teenk you wan beeg director, hah? Me, Louvette, show you!'

"That was enough; Paulette Goddard had the part."

Suddenly it seemed Paulette's career was flourishing. After the release of *The Ghost Breakers*, the public was clamoring for more of Goddard and Hope. Paramount immediately signed them for a rematch in *Nothing But the Truth*, which was set to open in 1941. What with *The Great Dictator* about to premiere, the two Hope picture hits, Louvette about to smolder, and being considered to dance opposite Fred Astaire in his new picture, Paulette was hot. Chaplin finally gave sanction to their marriage at the premiere of *The Great Dictator* by announcing to the thrilled first-nighters, "My wife, Paulette Goddard, and I hope you enjoyed the picture."

Just as it seemed her work was going well, Paulette was also being targeted as someone associated with Communists by the baiters who were becoming increasingly active in and around the FBI. Her involvement in the Rivera-Trotsky incident, as well as her attachment to Chaplin, put her on the well-known lists that were the scourge of every liberal, creative person making a living in the arts. A letter from within the FBI to the director of the agency confirmed that Paulette was among those being watched closely for Communist activities:

Dear Sir:

Enclosed herewith is a Paramount Studio contract list as of September 30, 1941 which was turned over to the New York City Field division [Note: the continued sentence has been blacked out] with a notation that Frances Farmer and Paulette Goddard, actresses, and Dalton Trumbo, a writer, were contributors to Communist Party causes.

These three were not alone. A pervasive list was submitted, including among the actors Walter Abel, Mary Anderson (Mrs. Jack Benny), Jack Benny, William Boyd (Hopalong Cassidy), Madeleine Carroll, Claudette Colbert, Bing Crosby, Eva Gabor, Sterling Hayden, William Holden, Bob Hope, Veronica Lake, Dorothy Lamour, Fred MacMurray, Mary Martin, Joel McCrea, Ray Milland, Robert Preston, Alan Ladd, and many others. The actors with "Special Contracts" included: Fred Astaire, Charles Boyer, Melvyn Douglas, Betty Hutton, Raymond Massey, Basil Rathbone, Rosalind Russell, Barbara Stanwyck, and Vera Zorina. The producers included Cecil B. DeMille; the directors, Mitchell Leisen, Elliot Nugent, Mark Sandrich, and Preston Sturges; and the writers, Charles Brackett and Billy Wilder.

Although under surveillance well into the fifties, Paulette managed to have ten prosperous years. After that she was of an age where there were fewer and fewer roles. However, at the height of her career, nothing could stop her—not even Chaplin. She left him after *The Great Dictator* opened. Chaplin, in his autobiography, makes it clear that knowing it was going to happen did not make it any easier: "It was inevitable that Paulette and I should separate. We both knew it long before *The Dictator* was started, and now that it was completed we were confronted with making a decision. Paulette left word that she was going back to California to work in another picture for Paramount, so I stayed on for a while and played around New York. Frank, my butler, telephoned that when she returned to the Beverly Hills house she did not stay but packed up her things and left. When I returned home to Beverly Hills she had gone to Mexico to get a divorce. It was a very sad house. The wrench naturally hurt, for it was hard cleaving eight years' association from one's life."

The break was actually more wrenching and painful than Chaplin implied. One of the reasons Paulette moved out so quickly was because her mother, Alta, who had married Earl K. Fleming, a Los Angeles mining man, on April 2, 1940, had left him by October of the following year. The single reference on record about him is in a 1962 letter to her mother in which Paulette is giving her some real estate advice and snidely suggests that they call up "that land expert, Earl K. Fleming." In the divorce suit, Alta charged him with extreme cruelty and nonsupport. Paulette, having marital troubles of her own—although in a highly civilized manner— and feeling responsible for her mother, decided that it was the right time to break from the past. It was a time when she could well afford it: she was a top box-office earner, and she could already anticipate the settlement she would receive from Chaplin.

She began her new life and bought a Normandy-style house off Coldwater Canyon in Beverly Hills. The house was decorated by Harold Grieve, an art director on some of Ernst Lubitsch's silent movies of the twenties. When she bought it she commented on her nomadic nature: "I don't like to collect anything I can't pack . . . I've never had a permanent home . . . I have no roots anywhere. I love being wherever I happen to be . . . I'm a Gypsy who likes to go first class."

Jinx Falkenburg, who became Paulette's housemate for a while in 1943, described the house in an interview: "Her home is a medium-sized, secluded house perched up in Coldwater Canyon, and there's no tennis court or swimming pool. . . . The furnishings are gay and casual. . . . The rooms are in gray and white with touches of sunny yellow and always a vase of red roses or camellias. Her particular joy is a slot machine in the playroom, which she keeps filled with money, and then plays feverishly, trying to cash

LEFT AND BELOW:
Paulette shared this house in Coldwater Canyon for a while with Jinx Falkenburg.

Paulette made a rare appearance in drag in the 1941 film Pot O' Gold, *with James Stewart.*

Director George Marshall talks to Paulette, with Veronica Lake and Dorothy Lamour in the background, on the set of Star Spangled Rhythm.

in on herself. I think the simplicity of her living is best illustrated by the time we were both weekend guests at a Texas oilman's mansion. When we walked in and were practically bowled over by its luxury, Paulette nudged me. 'Gee,' she whispered, 'this looks like a movie star's home.'"

The effect of the house was much like the writer William Saroyan's description of Paulette: "What she has is an inner twinkle and it goes around in a strictly nonsorrowing frame; all of it is attractively tough, challenging, mischievous, coquettish, wicked, and absolutely innocent."

A peculiar contract was drawn up in May 1942. It came on the brink of their breakup and was an agreement between Charlie Chaplin, "Producer," and Paulette Goddard, "Artist." It would seem from the content that Chaplin had definite plans for another feature picture starring himself and Paulette, or perhaps he only hoped to make a picture and wanted to guarantee her presence, sufficently blocking any other opportunities. Although the contract gave her only two weeks to disengage herself from any other project should Chaplin go into production, it provided her with the kind of advance she couldn't refuse: $100,000.

There were twenty-eight clauses in the contract—twenty-eight ways that Chaplin tried to exercise control. His is the only signature on it. Paulette seems never to have signed it. However, when she was chosen to play opposite Fred Astaire in his next picture, *Second Chorus*, and was ecstatic over the coup, Chaplin attempted to stop her—at least until *The Great Dictator* was released. He also could have been stalling for time, hoping that she would sign her next contract with him, but Paramount outbid him. Myron Selznick, still her agent, was able to renegotiate her contract with the more than eager Paramount. She would receive $85,000 per picture. She had the right to make one outside picture a year. And the contract guaranteed her at least one picture a year for ten years. Plus they had given her sixty days' notice prior to sending her the script. It was one of the better deals in Hollywood.

Although her acquisitions were famous, her eventual settlement from Chaplin was kept secret. All that was known was that it was staggering, hovering around the one-million mark, which was a vast amount in those days of war, Depression, and inflation, worth about $17 million today. Charles Chaplin, Jr., remembers his ex-stepmother as saying, "I think your father lost a lot when he married me. I even got the yacht."

Despite Paramount's heralding "Fred's Best Yet . . . Cause He's Got Paulette," her reputation even after starring in *Second Chorus* did not include

Paulette danced with Astaire in
Second Chorus, *1941.*

*Ray Milland, Susan Hayward, and John Wayne starred with Paulette
in the 1942 film* Reap the Wild Wind, *small compensation
for losing the role of Scarlett in* Gone With the Wind.

dancing. "I had a wonderful time with her. She has a great sense of humor," said Fred Astaire, gallant off as well as on screen. "But the movie we made wasn't one of the best," he had to admit. Everyone was a good sport about it, however, and Paulette voiced awe at having even gotten through it: "I'll never try dancing on the screen again. I was determined that the dance would be good. Imagine me dancing with Astaire. And I guess it was all right. We did it just once, one Saturday morning for the cameras. Just one take. I'm glad it was all right, because I couldn't have done it again."

The supporting cast was an interesting one: Artie Shaw (on clarinet), who later escorted her about, Charles Butterworth (on guitar), and Burgess Meredith (on trombone/trumpet) all played musicians in a band headed by Astaire. Meredith was really the odd man out. He was a serious, often classical actor, whose forte was the stage, where he had recently scored a substantial hit in Maxwell Anderson's *Winterset* (as well as such plays as *High Tor, The Star Wagon, The Playboy of the Western World*, and *Liliom*). He was a bantam red-haired intellectual, a divorced charmer. Paulette was drawn to him one day as he sat over to the side of the stage, slouched across a canvas chair, lost in a book. She had noticed him often before. He was known as the cast wit. "That Burgess Meredith," she had said, "is a deep one. I'm not sure that I get his message. How can so intellectual a guy be so witty?" She began to find out.

She did not recall, nor did he, what he was reading that day. Paulette chatted him up by saying that she had read the book a month before and thoroughly enjoyed it. Meredith smelled falsehood and proceeded to ply her with questions about the text, all of which she answered promptly. Afterward he commented, somewht chauvinistically, "How do you suppose that a beautiful chassis like that ever got attached to a 24-karat brain?"

Like practically everybody else, Meredith felt a strong attraction to her, but he saw something the camera didn't: "She was very attractive physically. Probably three times more in person than on film. She was not an actress that the camera found to be lovelier than she was. I think it didn't do her justice. She was a very dynamic presence, and she was a very skilled conversationalist, a very joyous one."

Meredith also has an opinion, without frills, of her abilities as an actress: "I think that she was always inhibited somewhat in her acting. She overstudied, and although she had a good deal of concentration, she didn't have much freedom. She never got 'the Method' going in herself."

According to Meredith, they met on the set and then, "We just went out. It was at the end of her session with Chaplin. She was kind of out on her own. . . . None of us were doing what we could well in that picture. She certainly wasn't a dancer. I certainly wasn't a musician. But we met there. And then kind of went on and on, and for some reason got married."

Chaplin, Meredith, and Remarque were not tall men. All tended toward melancholy, all tended to be loners; all were exceptionally bright and talented. Two were also rich. Meredith, while well off, was not in the same financial league. All were vulnerable to Paulette's most prized asset: vitality.

After the filming was over for *Second Chorus*, Paulette and Meredith kept low-key company. They enjoyed their autonomy and they felt free to go their separate ways. In fact, between 1941 and late 1943, when they finally married, the main thrust of their relationship was business via real estate.

Paulette often visited a farm that Meredith owned as a respite from her Hollywood filming schedule, which was becoming somewhat frantic. Four of her pictures were released in 1941 alone. Following work on *Second Chorus*, she was loaned out to United Artists and went right into *Pot o' Gold*, directed by George Marshall, co-starring James Stewart and featuring the veteran character actor Charles Winninger (Cap'n Andy in the 1928 movie of Edna Ferber's *Show Boat*) and the band leader Horace Heidt. Next, working simultaneously, she filmed Paramount's *Nothing But the Truth*, directed by Elliot Nugent and co-starring Bob Hope, and *Hold Back the Dawn*, again for Paramount, produced by Arthur Hornblow, Jr., directed by Mitchell Leisen, screenplay by Charles Brackett and Billy Wilder, co-starring Charles Boyer and Olivia de Havilland and featuring a top-flight supporting cast of Victor France, Walter Abel, and Rosemary DeCamp—later known as Margaret on Bob Cummings's early sitcom, *Love That Bob*.

There was no chemistry on screen or off between Stewart and Paulette during the filming of *Pot o' Gold*. Stewart must have been more than preoccupied with his affair with Dietrich. In fact, Paulette was singularly unimpressed by Stewart: "Anyone can gulp," she said.

The most arresting part of the picture is Paulette in drag, and reminiscent of Dietrich, doing a musical number called "The Gay Caballero," where she's dressed as a seductive rake escorting two señoritas—strutting and serenading them, as she wields a large cigar.

Thus far, Paulette had made popular pictures, and with Chaplin—because he was who he was—landmark ones, but she had yet to give a "quality" performance in a "quality" picture all on her own. *Hold Back the Dawn* was that picture. Based on a story by Ketti Frings (1958 Pulitzer prizewinner for her play *Look Homeward, Angel*), it concerned the plight of émigrés seeking entry into the United States and being detained in a Mexican border town. Paulette played the "bad girl" of the story, an ex-dancer named Anita who used to partner refugee George Iscovezcu, played by Charles Boyer. She appears genuinely flirtatious around him. It also carried some associations for Paulette, who was becoming increasingly allied with Mexico and the powers that were there politically and artistically, even though her time with Diego Rivera was over.

Edith Head did not have fond memories of Paulette on the set: "She would carry around a cigar box filled with jewels. And then open the box and pass it around for the girls to see. I only remember her taunting my staff with that damn cigar box full of jewels."

For every Paulette-basher, there were ten who championed her. She did a lot of radio during this time: Lux Radio Theatre, Cavalcade of America, Silver Theatre, Hollywood Hotel, Screen Guild Theatre. On the last, she did five gratis appearances for the Motion Pictures Relief Fund, and was celebrated with a party. One of the favors was an autograph book; in it were some lively sentiments:

"To Minnie, the first, the Minniest of all Minnies . . . I also loved Minnie the second . . . to Paulette, my darling, with so much of everything, Andre Tola." (This was from Anatole Litvak, her Ciro's pal.)

"To grateful PG for all you have received, don't even try to thank me. Mea culpa. Burgess Meredith."

"J'aime les fleurs, l'intime sauvage et aussi la douceur de votre bouche rouge et aussi votre physique aggressive. Et aussi Paulette et aussi ça maison. Jean Renoir."

"Remember, dear, that it is better to travel hopefully than to arrive. But it's just as well to travel with beautiful luggage. Your servant, dear. Michael Arlen."

"Oh, that the fair should be so cruel. George Jessel."

"Hell, why don't I ever get to stay for breakfast? James Bessie."

"Can you beat it? Can you picture PG asking me for breakfast? Hell, I love her just the same. Hedda Hopper."

"I never knew that stepmothers were no nice, Charlie, Jr." (In parentheses, he puts "Chaplin," as if she wouldn't know.)

Paulette celebrated her thirty-first birthday at Remarque's favorite haunt —El Morocco in New York. She sat with the owner, John Perona, Wooley Donahue, and Winston Guest. Several reporters tried to join her table for an interview, hoping for official confirmation of her reported divorce in Juarez, Mexico, over the weekend. "I have nothing to say," she said.

The Federal Bureau of Investigation filed a document that coincided with her Mexican trip to file for divorce in June of 1942. The document was far more devastating than anything Paulette could ever do to Chaplin, who was leading his own life—as she was—but was about to be excoriated for it. Freedom as he knew it began and ended with a young woman named Mary Louise Gribble aka Joan Barry aka Joan Berry aka Mary Louise Berry aka Joan Barratt aka Mary L. Barratt aka Joanne Berry aka JoAnne Berry. In the FBI file she is listed as "VICTIM." Charles Spencer Chaplin is the "CHARGED." The "character" of the case is titled "WHITE SLAVE TRAFFIC ACT":

Investigation of CHARLES CHAPLIN, well known movie personality, initiated on information that he caused victim to travel from Los Angeles to New York in October, 1942, in order that she engage in sexual intercourse with him and his friends. Facts developed reflect he paid her way to and from Los Angeles to New York; that on or about October 19, 1942, she stayed with him at the Waldorf Astoria, New York City and did so engage with subject. Further, that CHAPLIN put BERRY under contract to his studios about June, 1941, shortly after meeting her; that he coached her for a contemplated screen career; that he became intimate with her three weeks after their first meeting; that she stayed all night with him in his home some fifty times; that through CHAPLIN's intimate friend and pimp, one TIM DURANT, two abortions were committed on BERRY; that she broke her contract with CHAPLIN Studios in May, 1942, but thereafter CHAPLIN continued to be intimate with her and supported her. BERRY claims that CHAPLIN is the father of her child born October 2, 1943, as a result of their intimacy about December 23, 1942. Civil suit to determine paternity presently pending Los Angeles Courts. . . . CHAPLIN denied allegation, however agreed to pay some $20,000 to BERRY pending determination by blood tests four months after birth of child.

Paulette was apoplectic about "how they broke Charlie." Many years later, she reflected upon it:

I've always said that any greatness is resented by contemporaries. I've never seen it fail. I have a whole list of them that I could make, of people who have been ostracized by their peers. And Charlie's peers were, for God's sake, Darryl Zanuck, Jack Warner! I mean, *really*! They resented him and the minute he did one little thing—I mean, I don't even call it a "thing."

To have an affair with a girl! What's wrong with that? So this girl ran down to Hedda Hopper and cried her eyes out. "He promised to make me a star!" Well, for God's sake, Howard Hughes promised to marry them all. Who *didn't*? Everyone promised me, too. But I said, "Let's see the contract!" That's when I was in my teens!

So anyway, she cried to Hedda, and they were happy to have something on Charlie. Louella was happy too. She worked for Hearst. You see, Marion Davies was *madly* in love with Charlie at one time. This is strange. This is the "Citizen Kane" bit. Just so much that he was the great love of her life. And she had every reason to be because he was *enchanting, captivating, fascinating*. And sweet. I mean, you couldn't know anyone who was so perfectly charming in every sense of the word. Difficult, but charming. But Hearst found them together and took a shot and I think somebody was killed—I forget who it was, a director—in the melee, and it seems Hearst thought it was Charlie. When he found out it wasn't, they got after him and the whole press turned against him. Finally, with the Berry girl they could hang something on him so they took him to court and threw him out of the United States of America. All because he had an affair with the most *ghastly* girl. I mean, I was quite surprised at his taste.

It was a difficult time. I had left him and he was sitting in this empty house. It's such a normal thing to have some girl there for dinner. And what they do afterwards, after dinner, is certainly private business. I think that's all under the heading of "Sport." But to ostracize a man the way they did!

They absolutely hated his talent. He was just too good for them. Whenever there was a list of the most loved people in the world, there was Jesus Christ, Buddha, and there were two or three more, and then Charlie. He was the best loved in the whole world. Everyone adored him. He was enchantment itself.

Paulette very much approved of Chaplin's marriage to eighteen-year-old Oona O'Neill, daughter of the playwright Eugene. She felt that Oona profoundly understood him and made a whole new life for him.

Interestingly—after all the concern regarding first the Goddard-Chaplin marriage and then the divorce on June 4, 1942, in Juarez, Mexico—when attorneys for the FBI searched the records at Cuernavaca and Cuautla in Mexico, they found no record of a divorce between the two.

Four Paulette Goddard movies were released in 1942. DeMille asked for her again in *Reap the Wild Wind*, and the concept of that picture seemed to compensate for her loss of Scarlett O'Hara in the epic that DeMille didn't get to make. This one starred John Wayne, Susan Hayward, and Ray Milland. "She was in her prime," Ray Milland said, "but there were some ripples of discord between Paulette and DeMille. . . . Both ladies had to back-seat it a bit because of the giant squid."

"DeMille actually used to invite people to come and watch him direct Paulette Goddard," she recalled. "Then he'd give me a loud Belasco treatment. He thought the way to get the best work from me was to break my spirit. I never realized that I had any.

"After my first picture with him, *Northwest Mounted Police*, he swore he'd never have me in a picture again. Then he asked for me in *Reap the Wild Wind* and we went through the same thing again."

It was an adventure picture, a real swashbuckler with John Wayne as Captain Jack Stuart battling with lawyer Steve Tolliver (Ray Milland) for the attentions of Paulette Goddard, whose character has the most unfortunate name of her career: she is called Loxi and is a sassy southern ship owner. The climax of the picture is an underwater sea battle with a giant mechanical squid.

As expected, the picture was a huge hit. Susan Hayward, who had found Paulette to be her career nemesis, not only loses John Wayne to her in this one, but she comes to a watery end by drowning in a sunken steamship. By 1947, when *Reap the Wild Wind* was re-released by Paramount following the success of DeMille's *Unconquered*, starring a definitely older Paulette opposite Gary Cooper, Susan Hayward's career was on the ascent and the marquee billed her second and Paulette fourth.

Ray Milland's year with Paulette was 1942. They were immediately cast together again in *The Lady Has Plans*, a cloak-and-dagger comedy of mistaken identity that was originally meant to star Madeleine Carroll. It featured Roland Young, Albert Dekker, Margaret Hayes, and Cecil Kellaway, with costumes by Edith Head, and was directed by Sidney Lanfield.

Another of Paulette's successful comedy pairings was with Fred MacMurray; they were deft, breezy, and sexy together, creating droll romantic friction. *The Forest Rangers* was their first movie together, although they had co-starred in *Front Page Woman*, a program that was part of DeMille's Lux Radio Theatre.

Hollywood was joining the war effort in a big way by making quickie big films brimming with big stars performing tiny bits. The roster of talent was eye-popping. In *Variety Girl* of 1947 there was Bing Crosby, Bob Hope, William Bendix, Barbara Stanwyck, Gary Cooper, Dorothy Lamour, Sonny

Tufts, William Holden, Lizabeth Scott, Burt Lancaster, Sterling Hayden, Robert Preston, Macdonald Carey, Cecil B. DeMille, Mitchell Leisen, and Pearl Bailey singing "Too Tired," the song that made her famous.

The premise was slim, padded, of course, by the special appearances. The stars had trademark bits such as Ray Milland answering a phone by reaching up above the ceiling light fixture in a satire of his alcoholic machinations in *The Lost Weekend*. Paulette appears briefly in a bubble bath, which was becoming her proverbial prop. "When in doubt they float me" was her comment about the recurring piece of business.

Paulette also appeared in *Star Spangled Rhythm*, a 1942 "defense film," another quickie packed with big stars performing tiny parts. The cast included Bing Crosby, Bob Hope, Mary Martin, Dick Powell, Franchot Tone, Ray Milland, Dorothy Lamour, Vera Zorina (Remarque was having an affair with Zorina at this point), Veronica Lake, Alan Ladd, Susan Hayward, Fred MacMurray, Robert Preston, Cecil B. DeMille, and Preston Sturges. There were sketches by George S. Kaufman and dances choreographed by George Balanchine. George Marshall directed the all-singing, all-dancing extravaganza.

There was a formula to these pictures: the "little" people would gape at the stars, often doing lavish impersonations of Hollywood power in order to "con" those stars into performing in a variety-show benefit. Then the "little" people would work to put on the show before they got caught. Everything always turned out "swell."

Paulette's mother moved back to New York for a while in early 1943, leaving Paulette to her own devices. At this point, work came first. Carroll Righter, astrologer to the stars, had predicted that she would be on a roll for about a decade, and Paulette, sensible as she was, seemed eager to fulfill the prediction. Ironically, a tragedy proved to be one of fate's lucky strokes.

After one of the bloodiest battles of the war, the island of Corregidor, in the Pacific, fell in May of 1942. Ten nurses were able to escape and make it home. The director and producer Mark Sandrich, who was on the FBI's closely watched list along with Paulette, managed to make the story of these nurses into a film called *So Proudly We Hail*. He got permission from the government to make a completely authentic picture, with an intelligent screenplay by Allan Scott; he hired one of the nurses, Lieutenant Eunice Hatchitt, as his technical adviser, and he got his first choice of stars: Claudette Colbert, Veronica Lake, and Paulette Goddard. Little did he know that he was in for another kind of bloody battle: Colbert and Goddard fought through the entire filming. They took an instant dislike to each other and escalated it daily.

Paulette with Charles Boyer in Hold Back the Dawn, *her real first dramatic role (1941).*

War nurses Paulette, Veronica Lake, and Claudette Colbert taking a break on the set of So Proudly We Hail, *for which Paulette received an Academy Award nomination, 1942.*

A good deal of attention was paid to Colbert's valiant head nurse and to Paramount's newest hot property, Veronica Lake, as the grieving (her soldier-fiancé has been shot by the Japanese), temporarily psychotic young nurse who, in order to enable her comrades to escape the Japanese, puts a grenade in her blouse as a diversionary tactic and blows herself up. It was Paulette, however, who got noticed. The film critic Alton Cook wrote in his review for the *New York World-Telegram*, "The surprise of the group is Miss Goddard, until now not much more than a fluttery pretty-pretty but this time an actress of vigor and zest for life."

In between filming, Paulette went off to Mexico as if it were just around the corner. While there, she seemed to be quite busy. It was said that she was having an affair with Avila Camacho, the president of Mexico, and when she came home with a jade and emerald Aztec necklace from the national museum and wouldn't name the donor, fuel was added to the rumor. She took a gigantic gold watch off the wrist of a high-ranking Mexican general and kept it for herself after she convinced him that it looked too feminine on him; she was honored with a fiesta and a bullfight in which the president's brother, Máximo Camacho, was the star matador; another matador, named Manuelo Capitio, was also sweet on her. If she was in Mexico when he had a fight, he always put her in the honored guest box, so that she could receive the ears of the bull in a silk bag, as well as the matador's hat.

She made the rounds in more than the bullring. Jinx Falkenburg, who accompanied Paulette on a trip there, got caught up in the fiesta life. Paulette knew everybody: government officials, dignitaries, matadors, artists, movie stars. In Mexico City, Taxco, and Cuernavaca, they would go to the races, to bullfights, to parties. Falkenburg felt a bit like a tag-along until Paulette made her co-hostess of a bash for the Mexican cognoscenti, an endeavor that elevated Falkenburg.

Along with her mother and Anita Loos, Jinx Falkenburg was the closest woman friend Paulette had. And being her friend was always an adventure. When Falkenburg was in Mexico with Paulette, Maximo Camacho wanted to buy Paulette a ring but didn't know her size. Paulette, trying to facilitate the giving of the gift, asked Falkenburg to take him her emerald band so that he could size her new gift. He was to take the measurement and Falkenburg was to bring Paulette's ring back. Camacho mistook the enterprise to mean that Paulette wanted to give him a personal token of hers and that she had no desire for any gift. He kept her emerald ring. Falkenburg finally told Paulette about the strange and awkward mixup, and Paulette found it more humorous than anything else. A short time later, she invited Falkenburg to be her housemate on Coldwater Canyon.

For Christmas of 1943, Paulette sent six dozen pairs of nylon stockings to Burgess Meredith, who had been made lieutenant by the U.S. Air Force and been sent to England to make training films. She attached this note: "To insure your popularity with the 'birds.'" At that point, there was quite a bit of emotional insurance that the two of them would get married, but in the meantime, Paulette kept more than busy. Because of her fine work in *So Proudly We Hail*, she was being seriously considered for the coveted role of Maria in the film verson of Hemingway's *For Whom the Bell Tolls*. She lost out to Remarque's current but brief flame, Vera Zorina, who was later replaced by Ingrid Bergman.

And it was Paulette who, at Oscar time in 1944, was nominated as Best Supporting Actress, against Gladys Cooper and Anne Revere for *The Song of Bernadette*, Lucile Watson for *Watch on the Rhine*, and Katina Paxinou for *For Whom the Bell Tolls*. Paxinou was the winner, but Paulette felt like one. It hadn't been her favorite role, but it had taken her to her favorite destination: recognition.

Paulette repeated her role in *So Proudly We Hail* for the Lux Radio Theatre. A more glorifying role was the one she gave to the war effort: "Rita Hayworth and Greer Garson collapsed on grueling bond-selling tours, but Paulette Goddard, who is smart as well as oomphy, doesn't intend to have that happen to her. Paulette's getting into condition to do the country for the Treasury Department" was just one of the many items carried by the columns. She also received some adverse publicity for cutting her war-bond tours short because of her filming schedule for her next picture, *Standing Room Only*.

"Paulette was a trouper, an amusing woman, who not so amusingly stole top billing from me," said her co-star, Fred MacMurray. Paulette created a fad with one of her hair styles in this picture. She wears it in two bouncy, bowed bunches on either side of her head. Louella commented, "That hair style that Paulette Goddard started seems to be catching on. Two pugs behind the ears with flowers. Caution: not everyone can look ten-years-old."

The political jam that Paulette was skirting during this time because of Chaplin is reminiscent of Remarque's attempts to sidestep the political heat that he had inadvertently created. Neither of these two people were political activists, yet neither dodged controversy; both said what they had to say, and both ended up with sizable FBI files. The activities of both were documented as subversive within approximately the same time period. In a memorandum of 1943, Chaplin was cited as "receiving advice from his friend Paulette Goddard. She said that Chaplin wasn't getting the proper publicity and that it would be a good idea for him to first of all buy a $1,000,000 war bond, strictly for publicity. . . . Paulette Goddard also suggested that inasmuch as Chaplin had learned that the FBI was making inquiries concerning him, he should go directly to the Director and find out what those 'bastards' are doing investigating him."

Remarque was blasted in a chilling letter, accompanied by candid photographs of Remarque, Dietrich, Gabin, and von Sternberg, written by an anonymous "Deep Throat." It is addressed to J. Edgar Hoover and starts, "Dear Edgar, seems we are friends. You have done so much for this country," and continues along in a sanctimonious fashion until," Now these German men, what are they doing here in our country? Picture making and writing is a small excuse. Why so close to the girl [Dietrich] as constant company? Why? Looks more like watch dogs. This girl is supposed to be an American citizen. Does she display our flag in her car? . . . Yes, she goes to camps which should not be allowed, for it gives a chance over the air and a code could be quite the thing for the Germans. . . . I wouldn't trust a German born if they said I am an American in a hundred years. . . . I think this gang should be gone over with a fine tooth comb." Nothing came of this, but it described a climate of highly strung political paranoia.

Paulette was never afraid to add her name to a good cause, and when messages of support were sent from Hollywood to the International Convention of Solidarity with the Spanish Republican Refugees, the names included Paulette Goddard, John Garfield, Orson Wells, Groucho Marx, Ring Lardner, Dalton Trumbo, Lion Feuchtwanger, Heinrich Mann, and Franz Werfel. Remarque's name did not appear. Nor would it appear in Paulette's life for several more years, for in the meantime, she loved someone else.

Just before Lieutenant Burgess Meredith returned to the United States as Captain Burgess Meredith, Paulette made another movie, called, appropriately, *I Love a Soldier*, produced and directed by Mark Sandrich, co-starring Sonny Tufts, and featuring Beulah Bondi, Ann Doran, and Barry Fitzgerald. Paulette plays a welder in a defense plant who meets a soldier at a USO dance, falls in love, but hesitates becoming a wartime bride. Love conquered all by the end of the movie, which was not a hit.

An interesting footnote to the film was that when the National Safety Council heard that Paulette was going to portray a welder, they began to worry. Colonel John Stilwell, president of the council, requested that the studio cover her up safely because "the problem of getting women to wear proper protective clothing has been a very real one." The studio retorted with "She'll set a fine, shapeless, all-inclosed example." The colonel responded diplomatically, saying that safe clothing "need not detract from feminine charm." Paulette wore an authentic, all-covering welder's uniform.

Just as Meredith landed on U.S. soil, Paulette was off on an overseas tour of fourteen U.S. Air Force bases in China, Burma, and India. She had told her friend Falkenburg that for two years she had been longing to do a tour but filming had always gotten in the way. She had caused a sensation when appearing at the Hollywood canteens, and now she would wow the actively fighting soldiers. It was such a thrill for the pilots Lieutenants Duane C. McDonald and Francis M. Stefanak to fly her over that they turned down offers of a hundred dollars and more to trade places with envious comrades.

It was called "flying the Hump" (meaning, over the Himalayas). Paulette was accompanied on the tour by the actor Keenan Wynn, who organized the show—scripting and directing it, the actor William Gargan, and Andy Accari, an accordionist. They covered over 38,000 miles in two and a half months. Hedda Hopper commented that "it was the toughest air travel possible for a girl who wanted to appear always at her best: fresh, feminine, and as if she had stepped out of a beauty parlor." Paulette was not only the first woman to fly into this territory, but she and her companions flew farther into China than any of the other entertainers. They listened to the boys beg to keep their illusion that America was a Shangri-la. They refused to hear from any civilian that life in the States wasn't exactly the same as they had left it. Paulette's motto was to give son, brother, sweetheart, or husband the impression that everything was plentiful, that pretty legs still wore silk stockings, and that you could still eat steak every night of the week. That was what they wanted to believe; that's what they were fighting for; that's what they were coming back to find. The experience that Paulette provided them came back to her twofold.

She recorded some of her impressions in a journal: "These men were wonderful," she said about the crew. "They did everything possible to make me comfortable, and treated me as though I were a guest in their own living room at home. They were so hungry to have a girl around that one of them—I won't tell his name, for he took an awful lot of kidding—offered to brush my hair. He'd do it for hours. After we'd reached our destination in China, some of the boys at the field found out about it. They made his life miserable, so he told them they were jealous."

I brought back thousands of messages from soldiers to their loved ones. They more or less fell into five categories: Tell Mom I'm okay; tell Mary I sure do still love her; tell Pop to take care of my dog or horse and car; tell Chip not to date Mary or I'll knock his block off when I get home; tell them all that I'm doing okay, that my morale's good but that I sure would like a home-cooked meal. Most of them haven't seen a civilian white woman in so long they act shy and afraid on first meeting. They didn't whistle at me or wisecrack. They waited to be spoken to before they spoke. I made a point to kiss one GI—just one—at every place we stopped. I never asked his name. I just walked up to the first GI I saw, kissed him on the cheek, and said: "This is for all of you swell guys." And I'll be darned if most of them didn't blush. Once a boy came up and asked if he could smell my hair. He took a long whiff of it and said: "Gosh, that will have to last for a long time." Everyone sent me expensive perfume before I left. I took it all along with me. I'd heard that GIs love perfume and I was going to give them the best smell they'd had in the South Pacific. We went to a zone in China where dead Japs still littered the ground; there were bodies all over. They needed to smell something sweet.

Most of the time our arrival at a camp wasn't announced in advance, and the look on those boys' faces was something I'll never forget. In their honor I wore pin-up dresses for every show, whether it was for ten men in a hospital tent or seven thousand in an outdoor hillside theatre. I often heard the officers say, "If you're going to wear that dress out here tonight, be careful of malarial mosquitoes." Before I left I'd been inoculated against everything, and I mean everything. I was worn out. When it came time for my vaccination, the MD asked where to put it, and I told him, "Any place where the Screen Actors Guild can't find it." He did what I'd told him and from then on, I couldn't find it.

When we were in General Stilwell's territory, some Chinese troops under a Chinese sergeant put up a special tent for me. When I thanked him, he said, "We'll put up another tent for you in Tokyo. Then you can thank us." I think that the American soldiers will return with a tremendous respect for their fellow man, regardless of race or color. . . . Barriers of race and creed are battered and broken down. It really should be a better world when it's all over.

The boys called me Madame Cheesecake because I always tried to look my best. I wore shorts and a halter with a lot of flowers in my hair, or those bare-midriff dresses with sequins on them that the boys like. In many places I slept on sleeping bags on the ground or in a specially erected tent, which was true glamour. I washed my face in leftover tea, creamed it with castor oil, and scrubbed my teeth with grapefruit juice.

They all had names for me. With our boys it was Miss Cheesecake, with the British it was a more formal PG, and the Chinese called me American Girl of Electric Form or Miss Precious Cargo. I was with the GIs all the time I was in Asia. I had three squares with them, ate their rations, underwent the same living conditions. It was a tremendous emotional experience. The three most popular questions they asked were, "How's the morale of the people back home?" "What's on the Hit Parade?" And "How is Lana Turner?"

Keenan Wynn kept a journal that he later published. It was called *A Trouper's War Diary: Over the Hump to China*, in which he gives a vivid account of how rough their trip was, as well as an entirely sympathetic picture of Paulette:

On the way to the airport a GI driver nearly killed us trying to impress Paulette. It seems impossible that by this afternoon, just six days from Wednesday to Monday, we will have covered over 15,000 miles.

. . . Last stop is India before flying over the Hump. The Hump is the nightmare of the Air Transport Command. . . . Must fly anywhere from 19,000 to 30,000 feet to get over the Himalaya peaks. They've had planes shot down in daytime, so we wait for night.

February 27: The Hump. Yesterday they lost a C-46 with twenty-one aboard. We go in a C-87 or a converted B-24. We get chutes and oxygen masks. There is only one seat, for Paulette. The rest sit on baggage. We take off in 20 minutes, have our masks on at 22,000 feet. . . . Doors blow open, cold as hell. . . .

February 28: China. Played first hospital and first show today. Hospital up worst road yet. Hospital show terrific. Visited wards afterwards. Burned P-40 pilots. Ouch.

February 29: Chungking, China. . . . Facilities unbelievable. Lived in hospital and had broken beds with dirty sheets. First shower in five days.

March 17: . . . A short time overseas makes you realize many things. This was our first day with sheets and pillowcases for some time. . . . If this seemed a luxury to us it is easily imaginable what it must have meant to Paulette. She gave performances daily under conditions which seemed difficult to us men. Yet she was able to walk out on that truck or platform or bamboo stage, looking like she had just stepped out of a bandbox. We men went quite often without a shave or clean clothes, but Paulette made it a point always to look her best, and thus able to take the men out of their jungle surroundings for an hour and a half and return them to thoughts of the States and the girls they want to see.

April 5: Had crazy pilot, awful takeoff. Cut engine and at last minute dropped wing, coming in ballooned 75 feet. Heat is terrific. Took off and flew into worst storm yet. Really sweated this one out. Was lost with no radio contact. . . . By following only visible road we finally found landing strip. I got off and kissed the ground.

April 6: Paulette on verge of hysterics from fatigue.

They had to cancel their shows in Delhi and Calcutta. The army doctors ordered Paulette to the hospital for rest before they would allow her to fly home. Andy Accari, the accordionist, had already been shipped out, having barely missed suffering a cerebral hemorrhage. Wynn and Gargan gave one show by themselves, which didn't go over, because Paulette was the one the boys wanted to see. "She did a fantastic job," Wynn said. "She's a true American star."

When she returned to civilian life, Burgess was waiting for her. Neither seemed swept away. Meredith has said, "She was a good girl and a valiant one." Paulette has said everything from "We got married for tax purposes" to "I feel this is right. We are congenial—we have so much in common. We like to laugh, to study together, and Burgess takes great pride in my career" to "I never doubted that he was the one. He has something of the gamin about him, too. He loves to laugh and play and cares little for the things money can buy. We both have our work, and we are going to try our best to make a go of our marriage."

Anita Loos questioned whether Paulette could do without diamonds as her best friend, whether she was sated with jewelry and palatial homes. "Are you the appointed captain of industry?" she once asked Paulette. "Because as a real captain, Burgess's salary isn't overwhelming." Paulette defended her intended: "He is such a fine actor, and when the war is over he'll do big things."

Probably the most likely version of how they ended up married had to do with a farm. Shortly before Meredith went to war, he had acquired a seventy-acre farm in Spring Valley, near Suffern, New York. With his future uncertain, he turned to Paulette: "It's never amounted to anything but a deficit, this farm of mine, but maybe you could do me a favor and keep an eye on it whenever you're in the East." Paulette agreed to do better, by buy-

Paulette's mother, Alta, was at her side for all important events such as getting the marriage license with Burgess Meredith in 1944.

LEFT: *Irene Selznick looks across at Paulette, right, next to Daniel and Jeffrey Selznick, after her wedding at the home of the David O. Selznicks, 1944 .*

Ready to leave for the overseas tour into China, Burma, and India with William Gargan, Andy Accari, and Keenan Wynn, 1944.

ing it. She then rented the big house, retained the guest house, and set up a long-distance arrangement with her friend Constance Collier, who became somewhat of a partner by residing on the farm, looking after the sizable vegetable garden (the seventy acres had been planted by a produce company) and the one thousand chickens, keeping records of their eggs, and getting a cut of the proceeds as they began to sell to local merchants and then to furnish restaurants such as the 21 Club. They were in a sort of business, but kept it friendly and rural. Letters were dispatched regularly from Hollywood to England, keeping Meredith abreast of the enterprise. At first he teased her about horticulture and animal husbandry, but when the balance sheets began to arrive, he paid all due respect. Soon, their business and pen-pal-ship gave way to a deeper understanding and appreciation.

One day Paulette came home from the studio to find two dozen long-stemmed roses from Meredith. The card read just "Burgess." He continued to send her the same amount for weeks on end until he came down with a harsh case of pneumonia. The next time she heard from him, the letter was postmarked New York, where he had been sent on "detached duty." Paulette was just about to go overseas on her tour and was leaving from the East Coast, so they met for a date. They talked about books and music and art, whereupon Meredith told her that he'd picked something up for her that he hoped she'd like, but it was so big that he would have to pack it up and ship it to Hollywood. It was a canvas by Covarrubias, one of Mexico's leading artists. The choice of gift was a good way into the cultural side of Paulette's heart.

Before she departed overseas, he clucked over her, giving her copious advice on how to combat whatever might befall her. She told him he was fussing over her, to which he responded that when a man had asked a woman to marry him as often as he had, he began to feel a bit proprietary.

According to Anita Loos, Paulette told her that upon returning, "I staggered off the plane in California and found Burgess waiting there. The first thing he said was, 'Gee, you look awful!'" His candor seemed to erase all the "double entendre which had nauseated her for weeks," perceived Anita Loos. Paulette had had her intense share of being ogled by soldiers, hence Meredith's remark was a relief. "And when Burgess added, 'Let's get married,' I let him lead me straight off to the license bureau."

They were married at the home of Irene and David O. Selznick in Beverly Hills, across the street from the Chaplin house. Paulette was thirty-three, Meredith was thirty-six. His two previous marriages had been to Helen Berrian Derby (who had divorced him in 1935 after three years of marriage and who committed suicide five years later) and Margaret Perry, daughter of the theater producer and guardian angel Antoinette Perry, whom he'd married in 1936 and was not yet divorced from when he met Paulette. Only seven other people were present when they took their vows, and that included the chaplain Stanley Brown, who had pronounced the standard "to love, honor and obey." "Obey is in all my ceremonies," Paulette told an interviewer. "It's a classic." She went on with gusto about the wedding: "A private drove some of our guests to the Selznick house and guess what his name was? It was Love, so we invited him to attend our marriage. After it was all over, little Jeffrey, the David Selznicks' elder son, said, 'Paulette, this is the nicest Sunday I ever spent.'"

Almost as if to make up for the expediency of her first wedding and the secrecy of her second, Paulette was very excited about her third, even though it was private and the press was grateful for such details as that the bride wore a natural-colored, Empire-style linen dress and had a gold chain bound around her hair and carried no flowers; that her mother was one of the guests; and that Irene Selznick was matron of honor. "It's the first religious service either of us ever had in any marriage—and I think it's important to have such a ceremony," Paulette told Louella Parsons, who went on to write an assessing postscript about the seemingly blissful bride: "Paulette has always been an enigma to me. She has, I think, as fine instincts as any actress in Hollywood, but there is something of the gamin in her. . . . She is like a gypsy with her love for pretty things, a desire and flair for jewelry and gay colors. Nearly everyone in Hollywood felt she would marry a rich man so she could have all the material things in life—the houses, the clothes, the furs and the jewels."

After the wedding, it was business as usual. Paulette and Meredith moved into her house on Coldwater Canyon, and visited the farm, and Alta began a small real estate venture for Paulette by moving into a house her daughter had bought in Santa Monica, overseeing its renovation, selling it, and repeating the process again and again. Paulette's business tentacles were stretching, perhaps because of the success of the farm. She built a $35,000 chicken coop on the farm, she and Meredith bought a bicycle shop together, and she bought and sold a lot in Mexico City to Arthur Murray for one of his dance studios.

Paulette's defense of their absence of a honeymoon set the tone for their laid-back, un-Hollywood style: "Why, we would rather be here in our home than anywhere else. Burgess has been away for so long and so have I, and where could we be happier?"

Happiness was intense, if short-lived. Paramount had come through for Paulette in a big way by casting her in the title role of *Kitty*, which was based on a bodice-ripping novel by Rosamund Marshall. It was to be the answer to Kathleen Winsor's blockbuster *Forever Amber*, which Paramount had just lost to 20th Century–Fox. By choosing Paulette, they demonstrated their faith in her box-office sales and her acting abilities.

During the filming of *Kitty*, a lot of effort went into the conversion of Paulette from Kitty as eighteenth-century Cockney street urchin to a duchess. Phyllis Laughton was Paulette's dialogue coach, working with her several times a week for many weeks. Paulette frustrated her because she showed more exuberance off screen than on. She attributed this to the fact that Paulette had been weaned on Chaplin's martinet style as a director; they had had their own symbiotic way of working, whereby he could tap just the right place to get what he needed. After Chaplin, Paulette waited to be tapped in the same way, and when she wasn't, would become stiff and unyielding. Leisen was a good director for her, patient as well as inventive, but even he had trouble with her on *Kitty*. For all the coaching, she couldn't get the Cockney accent. Then he had a brainstorm.

Actress Ida Lupino's mother, Connie Emerald, was a Cockney. Leisen requested that she move in with Paulette and that the two speak only in Cockney dialect from breakfast to bedtime. Also, any direction that he gave to Paulette on the set was in Cockney dialect; any time the actors talked to Paulette off screen it was in dialect.

On the set of *Kitty*, Paulette was overheard saying to her friend, coach, and farm partner, Constance Collier, who had a plum role in the movie, "You know, I'm going to have a baby." The set was supposed to be closed to reporters, gossip columnists, and the like—in fact, it was Paulette's first closed set—but somehow the news leaked into Louella Parsons' ear. In an unusually kind act for a gossip columnist, she called Paulette to check the story. "For heaven's sake, Louella, that's not true—it's a line in the picture—don't you dare print it!" She had hoped to keep her pregnancy a secret for three months. She was just finishing *Kitty* and would be between pictures. Plans were being made to do a picture called *My Favorite Brunette*, reteaming with Bob Hope, but in the meantime, she would have been able to collect a weekly salary of $5,000. If she was pregnant, she would be on automatic suspension from Paramount, which is what happened, and she was out about $60,000, as well as having the Hope project scuttled.

Paulette miscarried in January of 1945. She had been pregnant five months. It was the only time that anyone had seen her really down. She had

TOP AND ABOVE: *Paulette in one of her many bath scenes, here with Gary Cooper in* Unconquered, *1947. Paulette with her great friend and acting coach Constance Collier in Paramount's* Kitty, *1946.*

suffered an ectopic pregnancy and had been rushed to St. John's Hospital in Santa Monica, where abdominal surgery was performed. She received several blood transfusions and slipped in and out of consciousness during the night. The way Paulette remembered the event much later reinforces the trauma: "My blood count went down to thirty and I died for two hours. Nearly died. But I'm awfully glad I didn't. Because afterwards there was a sense of urgency. . . . Some women, if they don't have a child, suffer all their lives, but I just never thought of it . . . until that very bad thing."

Friends attempted consolation. Flowers and notes came in from those who felt close: Joan Crawford, for instance, sent Paulette an elaborately glamorous bed jacket and Clark Gable sent flowers with a note simply saying, "Clark."

Kitty, the picture that was generally considered to represent the peak of Paulette's popularity, was completed in mid-1945, but its release was delayed until spring of 1946. Real security—as real as it gets in Hollywood—would come with the reception of that picture, although Paulette had already been voted one of the top actresses of 1944–45 in a popularity poll. She won for *Standing Room Only* and *I Love a Soldier*, ranking with Margaret O'Brien (*Meet Me in St. Louis*), Ann Sheridan (*Dough Girls*), Barbara Stanwyck (*Double Indemnity*), Maureen O'Hara (*Buffalo Bill*), Myrna Loy (*The Thin Man Goes Home*), Jean Arthur (*The Impatient Years*), and Carmen Miranda (*Something for the Boys*).

Kitty opened at the Rivoli Theatre on March 31, 1946. Paulette's reviews were better than her Cockney accent: "Paulette Goddard has worked up blazing temperament to go with her ravishing beauty in the title role. If she is less fetching as a late eighteenth century duchess, it is because the script turns thin on humor and drama. In any case, she gives the work the correct touch of wry romanticism." The picture was a big hit, earning $3.5 million in domestic gross rentals, and Paulette renegotiated her contract at Paramount: two pictures a year for six years at $100,000 a picture. (Prior to *Kitty* she had made $132,737 a year, which was lower than the salaries of Bette Davis, Gary Cooper, Claudette Colbert, Fredric March, and Charles Boyer. With one picture, she sped ahead of them.)

Paulette was becoming a real estate wizard. She bought a house, sight unseen, from her old tennis partner, Errol Flynn. He had sold the house to the painter John Decker and was about to foreclose a $10,000 mortgage held by Decker's widow. Decker's claim to fame, which seemed to duly impress Paulette, was copying El Grecos, Modiglianis, and other paintings by celebrated artists. Paulette received a call from Decker's widow asking Paulette to buy the house, which she would sell to her for $16,000, whereupon she could pay off Flynn and still have money to put down on a house she wanted in the San Fernando Valley. So Paulette bought the house and immediately rented it to the director John Huston for $500 a month. Years later, in the early seventies, she sold the property for $125,000 to Hugh Hefner for a Playboy Club.

She and Meredith moved out of the Coldwater Canyon house, rented it, bought a house on the beach in Santa Monica, sold it, and moved into a Hollywood apartment complex that was owned, as well as being decorated, by none other than one of her favorite directors, Mitchell Leisen—who also designed costumes. For special stars like Paulette, he would even make party dresses: "I would go to parties and Mitch would make my dress, sewing it right on me—like a gold lamé that really fit. He just loved to make clothes." Another director also had a penchant for designing for Paulette: "DeMille used to get a sensuous delight out of designing my shoes. Those little moccasins I'd wear in *Northwest Mounted Police*—he'd take a close-up of the shoes." And then, she admits to her most serious weakness: "You really become like a family, you know, working on a film. And everybody gets emotionally involved with each other—I used to get involved with the directors."

While recovering from the miscarriage, Paulette hired an economics professor at the University of Southern California to give her a course at home. As one of the richest women in Hollywood, she wanted to know more about every angle of investment—because 92 percent of her income was taken in taxes. Meredith would point proudly to her and say to friends, "See what I worked up from a two-dollar license."

She learned about operating a small business, and soon she and Meredith owned an antiques shop in Pomona, New York, not far from their farm, where, as Paulette liked to put it, "Antiques could be purchased for a mere life's savings." Her business prowess, managerial skills, and sales pitch were becoming impressive. As the columnist Earl Wilson said, "Lana Turner acquired more men than anybody, and Paulette Goddard latched on to bales of that green stuff with the pictures of dead presidents on it." Paulette might have taken a lot of ribbing regarding her monetary chin-ups, but everybody knew how serious and capable she was of accumulating whatever she set her sights on.

Jinx Falkenburg had since married the show business personality Tex McCrary, with whom she had a popular radio show called "Tex and Jinx." Meredith, always quick-witted, was one of their guests; he was on primarily to discuss Paulette and their new antiques business, about which he said that the antiques were "very expensive and probably fake." He jokingly implied that the antiques might be younger than had been advertised by Paulette. Meredith then recounted that he and Paulette had recently invited the playwright Charles MacArthur to dinner and had offered to give him a good price if he bought their Chrysler. "I don't need it. I already have two cars," he told them; however, by the end of dinner he had almost relented. Once home, his wife, the actress Helen Hayes, built back his resistance—until Paulette called, saying that she didn't want to hurry him, but that Bing Crosby was determined to buy the Chrysler, thought it was a steal. She said, with great conviction, that she told Bing that MacArthur would be given the first right of refusal, that it was entirely his decision. MacArthur bought the car then and there over the phone. Later, Helen Hayes saw Crosby at a function and apologized for buying the car from under his nose. "Why, I never talked to Paulette about a car!" Crosby said. Meredith's tag for the story was that MacArthur had since visited their antiques store and, upon leaving, temporarily couldn't find his coat. "Oh, I should have known," he said. "Paulette's sold it."

While Paulette was waiting for *Kitty* to open, a new project was afoot. She and Meredith went to New York; the trip was partly to take in some theater—sorely missed by Meredith—but mostly to meet with the great French film director Jean Renoir. Renoir was an old friend of Meredith's, as well as an old friend of Chaplin's, as well as an old friend of Jean Gabin and Marlene Dietrich's. Paulette and Renoir were to discuss the collaborative launching of the film *The Diary of a Chambermaid*, which was based on the novel *Celestine's Diary* by Octave Mirbeau. Paulette, along with Meredith, who would write the screenplay as well as appear in the film, was soon to become co-producer, star, and principal stockholder of the project.

Renoir describes Paulette as "still the waif of *Modern Times*, except that the rags had given place to clothes of the utmost elegance. . . . She is a beautiful woman with a lively mind; one can never be bored in her company. . . . She keeps company only with remarkable men, but she changes them often."

Renoir also relates an anecdote about Paulette and his wife, Dido, during that time in New York: "Paulette promptly took Dido under her wing, acting somewhat as her sponsor in the American way of life. 'Have you any jewels?' she asked. Dido confessed that she did not own a single one of any value. Paulette gently rebuked her. Every woman ought to possess a store of jewelry in case she should fall out with a man whom she regards as the keystone of her life. Jewels are small, easy to carry, and easy to hide. You put them in your handbag, and off you go. Dido listened gravely but did not seem convinced."

Before she began *The Diary of a Chambermaid*, she and Meredith went to London and Paris. The trip was mostly for Paulette to relax and do one of the things she loved most—shopping. Her passion of the moment was the clothes of the great Russian designer Valentina (whose husband, George Schlee, kept company with Garbo). Paulette was five feet four inches, and proud of maintaining a weight of 128 pounds, which today, for her height, might be considered a trifle chunky, but because she dressed herself shrewdly and expensively with clothes that pushed her in and up, her figure was always admired.

Paulette started working on *Diary of a Chambermaid* in early 1945.

About *The Diary of a Chambermaid*, Jean Renoir said, "I shot it at the beginning of a period when I was seeing things in a more concentrated way, more theatrical, with fewer reverse-angles. . . . I saw the scenes rather as small groupings, added to one another—scenes which would almost be sketches, that is to say, outlines. . . . My first project had been in silent days, and at that time I saw it very romantically, in the style of *Nana*. . . . I revived the project because I very much wanted to make a film with Paulette Goddard.

The controversial novel unmasking the decadence of the French bourgeoisie had been a stage play, and then was adapted into a screenplay by Burgess Meredith, who had worked with Renoir before. Together they had made the war documentary *A Salute to France*, starring Claude Dauphin. Meredith, and Paulette; a third party, named Benedict Bogeaus, formed Camden Productions in order to make the feature as an independent film and Paulette went out and did the fundraising. Renoir describes the free-spirited Bogeaus as "the proprietor of an independent studio which functions like the studios in France, that is to say, which leases its facilities to individual producers, and doesn't even include sound," but he went on to allow that he shot "in complete liberty with much improvisation."

"Moonbeam" was the name of the dye color used on Paulette's hair for her role as Celestine, the serving girl and the mercurial gold-digger in *The Dairy of a Chambermaid*. She had been moving toward blonde as Kitty, and in fact, the two roles were not dissimilar. Kitty is a more obvious, romanticized version of a woman who champions the heights but understands the depths, whereas Celestine is darker, more victimized, and feral.

The cast—Francis Lederer, Judith Anderson, and Hurd Hatfield—all had

The Merediths at the Stork Club, ca. 1946.

Paulette, Burgess, and friends in St. Moritz, ca. 1948.

William Paley, center, gazes across the table at Paulette, Mrs. William Paley, and Jinx Falkenburg during a benefit lunch, ca. 1950.

a touch of the sinister in their screen presences. Irene Ryan, who later became famous as Grandma on *The Beverly Hillbillies*, is the plain, old scullery maid. Burgess Meredith plays a most peculiar character named Mauger, a retired army captain who eats rose leaves and beetles, sleeps with his elderly maid, and intentionally kills his pet squirrel. The British actor Reginald Owen is the half-senile husband of the dominatrix, played by Judith Anderson.

Paulette's future did not depend on *The Diary of a Chambermaid*. Later, a successful remake was directed by Luis Buñuel, with Jeanne Moreau playing Celestine. The Renoir version got a cool reception. The chambermaid's romantic choices seemed unsympathetic and unappetizing to the public, who were used to the comedic Paulette, making her way into the right rugged arms. The cineasts, such as Raymond Durgnat, criticized her lack of a substantial grasp on the role: "Paulette Goddard alludes to both an American brashness and a French knowingness, but fulfills neither, still less exploring the interactions between them."

The themes of the picture also thwarted it commercially. Avarice and equality were a tough sell for a studio like RKO, which was going to be the distributor (this was Paulette's one outside project a year) but bowed out. It simply served to fuel Paulette's determination: "They said it violated all the accepted standards of picture-making. I framed their letter and took it as a challenge. I recognized their business sense. My reaction is not a criticism of the studio. It just is not my conception of what picture-making ought to be." United Artists picked up the film for distribution, earning them a nasty position on the FBI's "confidential" list of Communist Infiltration of the Motion Picture Industry, alongside *Scarlet Street*, produced by Walter Wanger, directed by Fritz Lang, and starring Joan Bennett and Edward G. Robinson; and *Three Strangers*, directed by Jean Negulesco, with a screenplay by Howard Koch and John Huston and starring Sydney Greenstreet and Peter Lorre.

It was general knowledge that Paulette, through Meredith, was politically involved and active. She, along with Meredith and John Garfield, were leading members of the Hollywood Democratic Committee: Hollywood Independent Citizens Committee of the Arts, Sciences, and Professions. She was on the National Win the Peace Committee, some of whose goals were bringing the GIs home from Asia, unification of China, self-determination for Korea, independence for the Philippines and Puerto Rico, and relief for "victims of aggression" in Germany and Japan. To the Democratic way of thinking, these were hardly subversive activities, but they were to the left of the right, and once Paulette's name was on a few lists, it seemed to be included everywhere in the FBI files.

Paulette was also part of Mobilized for Democracy, along with Dorothy Parker; Helen Gahagan Douglas, the congresswoman and wife of the actor Melvyn Douglas; and the writers Robert Rossen, E. Y. Harburg, and Donald Ogden Stewart. She was on the Committee for the Use and Development of Atomic Energy. She served on the American Committee for Yugoslav Relief, which supported the Yugoslav guerrillas who put up a fierce battle against the Nazi occupation of their country.

Paulette got more and more involved, taking sides against fellow members of the movie industry when testimonies began in front of the House Committee on Un-American Activities. Samuel A. Tower's article in the *New York Times* was a harbinger of what was to come:

Three Hollywood stars, leaders in the Screen Actors Guild, stated today that their profession contained a "militant, well-organized, well-disciplined minority" of Communist leanings. They declared that the group was tiny and had made no headway.

The three actors, Robert Montgomery, George Murphy, and Ronald Reagan, . . . joined Gary Cooper, in giving their views on communism in Hollywood before the House Committee on Un-American Activities, conducting an inquiry into the degree of Communist infiltration on the film industry.

Another group of Broadway and Hollywood artists, professing their belief "in constitutional and democratic government," disclosed after the hearing that its members had banded together to form the Committee for the First Amendment of the Constitution, to oppose the inquiry on the grounds that it "stifled" the "free spirit of creativeness" and violated the constitutional right of free expression by investigating individu beliefs.

In an informal news conference in the hearing chamber, [actor] John Garfield and [dancer] Paul Draper, acting as spokesmen, listed among the Hollywood members of the new committee Paulette Goddard, Henry Fonda, Gregory Peck, Van Heflin, Myrna Loy, and Burgess Meredith; and among the members from Broadway George S. Kaufman, Moss Hart, Olin Downs, music critic of *The New York Times*, Minerva Pious, the Mrs. Nussbaum of Fred Allen's radio show, and Louis Calhern, actor.

In 1946 Paulette helped the war effort again, entertaining American troops in Frankfurt, Wiesbaden, and Heidelberg, Germany. This trip was fairly easy, as it was only six days, but she worked hard, making many appearances at army installations before soldiers, for WACs, for Civilian Actress Technicians, for Army Hostesses, for Army Librarians, and for all American and Allied personnel and the wounded in the army hospitals.

Paulette received a letter from an American serviceman, which she kept, and it was found among her personal effects after her death. Its tone of brash, brave, unabashed romance could represent the Everyman American soldier's salute to a beautiful woman. He writes:

> When you visited China in the Spring of 1944 at the Kweilin air base, I plucked a small nosegay of violets and left them for you in a .50 caliber bullet case full of water, with a note reading: "These are the first violets of the year to lift their faces above the antique square of old Cathay, quite undaunted by warring man. I plucked them forth for the loveliest fate a violet could wish—to bask in the light of your bright eyes.
>
> You did me the honor to wear them in your hair. . . .
>
> Incidentally, now that it's no longer a military secret, your code name in army radio was "goddess."

Shortly before Paulette left for Germany, her mother married for the third time. The man was Don Jacobson, who had worked for the railroad, was semiretired, and was extremely handy at helping Alta in renovating, renting, and managing the houses that Paulette had bought. There were two in Beverly Hills and two at the beach—one in Santa Monica, and one in Trancas Beach, north of Malibu. Don Jacobson was the answer to both women's worries: Paulette's, that her mother would become old before her time, therefore making Paulette seem older, and Alta's, that she would become a burden to Paulette. Occasionally, one could wonder who was burdening whom. Paulette was planning to accompany Alta and Jacobson on their honeymoon to Mexico, but plans for her six-day tour and then meetings in London about a picture interfered.

Meredith genuinely enjoyed Alta's company—as did Chaplin and Remarque. "Maw, I used to call her mother Maw," Meredith recalls. "She was a good friend of mine. She was very, very personable with a big laugh. She never lived with us. We'd go to see her or we'd meet. But she kept her own. On the surface, their relationship was perfect—a shining example of a mother and daughter. Their private memories, or hells, or whatever never came out. Her mother and she were very close and very, very dear to each other, I think. I remember hearing that they got even closer toward the end. Finally, they were all each other had."

Despite an acrimonious split later on, Paulette and "Buzz" Meredith's marriage was an intelligent collaboration. He reported that a major factor in their separating was that they were apart so much; she was filming in Hollywood, and he was working on the stage in New York or filming in Europe. The facts do not totally bear this out. In 1946, it was true, he was in New York a good deal of the time, while she was in Hollywood making a Paramount picture with Mitchell Leisen called *Suddenly It's Spring*, a situation comedy with Fred MacMurray. This was her modest comedy following her baroque epic. She and Meredith had decided that it was smart for her to alternate the kinds of pictures she made so that she wasn't always type-cast.

Paulette had just renegotiated with Paramount yet again. This time it was $1,000 a week, forty weeks a year, with a lifetime guarantee. It enabled her to buy whatever she wanted and do whatever she wanted. That deal may have been her professional undoing.

In 1947 DeMille approached Paulette to star with Gary Cooper in *Unconquered*. The cast included Howard Da Silva, Boris Karloff, Cecil Kellaway, Ward Bond, Katherine DeMille, Henry Wilcoxon, Sir C. Aubrey Smith, and Virginia Grey. The screenplay was by Charles Bennett, Frederic M. Frank, and Jesse Lasky, Jr.

Paulette, who was now thirty-six, had worked with Gary Cooper, who was forty-six, in DeMille's *Northwest Mounted Police*, but had not played opposite him. He was a DeMille favorite, and Paulette had been trained by the director to always watch Cooper. "He said, watch Coop if you want to learn how to use props. He said it is not to be believed how Coop times his movements. He said, now watch him. You're going to make an entrance here and he isn't going to say anything. So, I'm coming into the tent and Coop's frying bacon. And every time I'd come in and take a look at him he'd have the bacon in the air at the same time."

Abigail Martha Hale is played by Paulette in a mobcap. She is an English convict who has been sentenced to deportation to the American colonies.

Unconquered was the waterloo of the relationship between DeMille and Paulette. DeMille was always willing to put his actors in a certain amount of jeopardy for a shot. When Paulette had made *Northwest Mounted Police* for him, and even *The Forest Rangers*, she did not have the box-office clout that she had at this time. As a full-fledged star, she was not about to stand in the middle of a scene involving firebombs being thrown every which way onto the set. She refused point-blank to do the scene. DeMille became apoplectic, yelling at her in front of everyone. Although reduced to tears, she would not be moved, demanding that her stand-in be called to do the scene. Reputedly, DeMille bellowed, "Get her out of here—before I kill her!"

DeMille did use a double, who wore a wig, which caught fire in the picture. Paulette, with no wig, could have been disfigured. DeMille never used her again. Her statement concerning him and the debacle was probably more demure than she felt: "Mr. DeMille wouldn't speak to me for years and years."

The $2.5 million film did not get good reviews. After *Unconquered*, Paramount had nothing to offer Paulette, and so she threw herself into working on the antiques shop, High Tor Associates, on Route 202 between Haverstraw and Suffern, which she shared with Meredith. At considerable expense they had remodeled the chicken house as the shop. Meredith recounted its history at an opening celebration for the new shop: "This was a chicken house which I started some time ago before Paulette and I were married. I would have had to raise chickens for five or ten years to earn back what it cost. Furthermore I'm allergic to chickens.

"The chickens came before the chicken house was finished. The gardener telegraphed Paulette asking what to do with the chickens and she replied, 'Put them in the guest house.' They remained there for several months. Subsequently, I started the antiques business in the chicken house because I thought as long as we're going to lose money, let's lose it on old things."

Paulette and Meredith presented a dashing appearance at the opening of the shop. Meredith arrived in a Jeep full of greens from the garden. He wore a plaid mackinaw open over a blue shirt and orange tie. Paulette made an entrance and seated herself under her portrait by Rivera. She was wearing a dinner gown, by Valentina, of brocaded ivory satin, covered up at the top, parted at the midriff, and short at the bottom. Her legs, tan and bare, gleamed below the white satin. Her hair was pulled tightly back from the left side and left flowing on the right. She carried a woven, solid gold Van Cleef & Arpels purse worth $6,500.

The guests and visitors wore a mix of country boots, wool socks and mufflers, and mink coats. Helen Hayes and Charles MacArthur were there, as were the playwright Maxwell Anderson (author of the play *High Tor*), Arthur L. Mayer, owner of the Rialto Theatre, the columnist Earl Wilson, and Jinx and Tex McCrary, who were going to do a recorded broadcast of their radio show, "Hi, Jinx," from the shop.

The show was in tune with the character of the shop—informal and a little zany. Helen Hayes talked about how she had once been in the strawberry and egg businesses; "False Jinxenburg," as Jinx was joshingly called, told a tale about a green wool blouse in Orbach's department store. Meredith admitted that one of the big problems with their enterprise was keeping Paulette from buying everything in the shop for herself. She would suddenly decide she wanted an item and then stick a SOLD sign on it. Every morning when Meredith entered the shop, there were a lot more SOLD signs than when he'd gone to bed.

The High Tor enterprise seemed to reveal the irreverent heart of the Goddard-Meredith merger, indeed beginning to be more merger than marriage. Although she called him "Sugar" and he called her "Miss Busymitts," it seemed that business came before most other things.

Without much warning, Paulette's career, along with her marriage, was slipping. Paramount had yet to come up with anything for her. It was hard to understand, since only two years earlier, with her rival Claudette Colbert having left Paramount, Paulette, along with Dorothy Lamour and Betty Hutton, were its top female stars. Although Paulette was never directly accused of being a Communist, she appeared on almost every FBI list, and was outspoken against HUAC when the chance arose—as it did in 1947 on the radio program "Hollywood Fights Back." There didn't seem to be a tie-in between her speech and Paramount's lack of a suitable property, and it was never documented in any direct studio blacklist. Joined by other well-known speakers, such as Lucille Ball, Judy Garland, Frank Sinatra, and Robert Young, Paulette spoke eloquently in defense of the Freedom of Information Act, as well as objecting to political persecution of the Hollywood Ten.

And in the fall of 1947, Meredith went to New York to star in a revival of J. M. Synge's *The Playboy of the Western World* on Broadway. Off Broadway, their friend John Huston was directing Jean-Paul Sartre's *No Exit*. Meredith was looking for a vehicle for both of them. Paulette had expressed interest in returning to the stage but was ambivalent. A play about the founding of the State of Israel called *A Flag Is Born* was on Broadway that season, starring Paul Muni and young Marlon Brando. John Garfield, Meredith, and Paulette liked the play and planned to open it at the Studebaker Theatre in Chicago. That plan fell through, but Meredith persisted. He settled on Maxwell Anderson's *Winterset*, which would run at the Gaiety Theatre in Dublin in August. He would reprise the role of Mio that had won him plaudits in New York, and Paulette would play the smaller role of Miriamne. It turned out to be a perfect plan, since they were both going to be filming for Korda in London—he with *Mine Own Executioner* and she with *An Ideal Husband*. After their films had wrapped they went on to Dublin.

Just as at fifteen a blond Paulette had threatened to strike against Florenz Ziegfeld and his production unless he retracted a statement about preferring brunettes, in 1947 Paulette and her hair would cause trouble, shutting down *An Ideal Husband*'s $2 million production.

Paulette had brought over her own hairdresser, a Swedish woman named Hedvig Mijordu, whose hands, she swore, knew just how to turn her into the blackmailing, upper-class, British Mrs. Cheveley from *An Ideal Husband*. It almost became an international incident; Paulette suggested that there wasn't one English hairdresser competent enough to do her hair. Twelve British hairdressers took arms against foreign labor by walking out of the London Film Studios upon finding out who had done Paulette's hair. Their striking put nearly a thousand actors, actresses, and technicians temporarily out of work. Korda was losing more than $12,000 a day because of it. The executive committee of the National Association of Theatrical and Cinema Employees Union recommended that the strike be abandoned, but the studio's makeup artists and hairdressers refused. Meanwhile Korda, through the Labor ministry, was able to get a work permit for Hedvig Mijordu, and eventually the atmosphere on the set returned to normal.

Despite having Michael Wilding as a co-star, a strong cast that included Glynis Johns and Constance Collier, among others, glorious rented jewelry, and gowns designed by Cecil Beaton, Paulette was not a success in this film, which did not do well at the box office.

From London, Meredith and Paulette went to Dublin to do *Winterset*. The Dubliners didn't quite know what to make of Paulette on stage or off. She was too old for the very young girl in *Winterset* and didn't really have enough skill on stage to get away with it anyhow. She did have enough self-awareness to know that regardless of how big a movie star she was, on the stage she was a novice. "I'll never forget that first performance," she recounted. "On a movie set you are surrounded by people and cameras, and there is a feeling of proximity and warm companionship. When a scene begins, the lights flash on, and as the cameras roll there is utter silence.

"My entrance in *Winterset* was made in complete darkness, and I had to cross the full width of the stage; and as soon as the curtain went up the audience began talking. They had come to see the 'fil-um' stars, and immediately began to discuss us in whispers. You know—'Gee, where's the di'monds?'

"That was the longest walk I've ever taken, and I've never felt so alone in my life.

"But the feeling soon wore off, and everything was fine, until they began throwing pennies at us—large, oversize British pennies. That, we found, was because there was a line which the audience regarded as sacrilegious. We took out the line and, after that, no more pennies."

The play broke house records, despite mediocre reviews. The public clamored to see the stars.

Paulette was out of the country a lot in 1948. She went to Paris and bought clothes from Balenciaga, Schiaparelli, and Grès and to London to buy antiques for the business. In order to contradict rumors that their marriage was in trouble, Paulette would make statements such as this one: "In one big way, I'm more independent since my marriage. I simply mean that I'm less dependent on others for happiness and comradeship than I used to be. I now have all the understanding and comfort I need right in my own home with Burgess." Their marriage, however, was not to last another year.

Complicating matters was her next project. It was to be called *A Mask for Lucretia*, with Paulette playing Lucretia Borgia and Mitchell Leisen directing. He was one of Paulette's favorite directors, because he knew how to make her limitations look like assets. Leisen's last project had been directing Marlene Dietrich in *The Golden Earrings*, which had been a hit. He was confident about his Renaissance tale of the dastardly doings of the Borgias, which later came to be called *Bride of Vengeance*.

The film journalist James Robert Parish had this to say: "It was such a turkey that the studio held up its release for well over a year, not knowing how to slip the lemon quietly onto the market . . . from the start the project went badly. Ray Milland later said the picture portended so badly that it was the first picture he rejected in all his years at Paramount."

It was around the time of *Bride of Vengeance* that Paulette became reacquainted with Clark Gable. One night, so the story goes, Paulette was at a party in Brentwood with the director John Huston, who was separated from his wife and Paulette's good friend Evelyn Keyes. Prior to her official estrangement from Meredith, Paulette had romantic escorts, which she always believed in having for the in-between times. She was concurrently seeing the writer John Steinbeck and the actor Hurd Hatfield, who had been one of her co-stars in *The Diary of a Chambermaid*. Paulette often culled her dates from the friendships she had had during her marriages. For example, out of her marriage to Chaplin she extracted Aldous Huxley, George Gershwin, Tim Durant, Harry Hopkins, and Howard Hughes. During her time with Meredith—known as her "intellectual marriage"—Huston and Steinbeck, along with their wives, Evelyn and Elaine, provided a good deal of their stimulating social life.

The party that night was held inside because of the dense fog. Clark Gable, not one of the guests, was driving home from somewhere else when a car came careening toward him on the wrong side of the road. He swerved, hit a ditch, and skidded across several well-manicured lawns until he rammed to a halt into the porch of a large house. The guests, including Paulette, streamed out to see what had happened. Gable, whose car was in worse shape than he was, got out, was given a drink, and joined the party.

That was the beginning of his reuniting with Paulette in a different way. According to Paulette, they never would have had a chance had he not been driving alone: "Clark never went out without his publicity man. And his publicity man chaperoned us through our romance. He'd have a fit when somebody else would give me a present and it would get in the papers. He really resented it. He was that protective of Clark. Once Clark gave me a medallion. It was some kind of Saint Christopher, I think, and my skin turned black. And somebody said, 'Look, it can't be gold!' And it got in the papers. His publicity man gave me hell, and he said to Clark, 'How could you not give the girl a real gold medal? For God's sake, it's in the papers!' He warned Clark, 'That girl's dynamite! Watch out for her!'" Eventually Gable heeded the warning, and literally kissed her off at the airport on her way to Mexico in 1949, but for a good time, he was smitten.

The incriminating headline of an article by Charles Pool read, IF SHE WANTS HIM, SHE'LL GET HIM. IF PAULETTE GODDARD MAKES UP HER MIND TO BECOME MRS. CLARK GABLE, THE MOST ELIGIBLE MAN IN HOLLYWOOD MIGHT JUST AS WELL STOP STRUGGLING. GODDARD NEVER MISSES.

Gable was seeing a lot of Paulette before her divorce from Meredith was final. One particular source says that they saw each other daily, took meals together, swam together, watched home movies together, and laughed uproariously at almost everything. Gable did not think it was funny, however, when Paulette made an arrangement to meet him at Rosarita Beach, a resort in southern California, and John Huston just happened to be staying there at the same time. "Johnny" Huston, as Paulette called him, seemed to be a factor in her romance with Gable—so much so, that he was present when Gable proposed. Paulette recalled, "Clark proposed to me in front of Johnny Huston and all my friends. And that was the time in Hollywood when everybody drank so much. I was carrying someone's drink to them by the pool. Fully dressed. And Clark said, 'Now I'm going to ask you something in front of all these people.' And you know how I hate a direct question. I always have too quick an answer and I don't really mean it. And he said, 'I want you to marry me.' And I said, 'You what? You don't need a wife, you need a nurse!' So he pushed me into the pool. I mean, to see the faces of all these sodden, drinking people. And Huston's face. You can imagine."

Paulette's one outside picture, made for Columbia in 1948, was the end of her star tenure with Paramount; in fact, she would never make another picture for them. *Anna Lucasta* began as a prestigious project. Myron Selznick, still her dutiful agent—although rather beleaguered after three of her flops—carved out the deal for her. She would star as the battered belle Anna Lucasta, the title character of a play by Philip Yordan that had been a hit on Broadway in the mid-forties. Yordan, partnered with Arthur Laurents, had adapted it for the screen, and Irving Rapper was signed to direct. Susan Hayward had been Columbia's original choice but was unavailable, so Paulette stepped into a salary of $175,000 and a percentage of the profits. She was supported by a decent deal and a cast that included Broderick Crawford, John Ireland, Mary Wickes, Will Geer, Whit Bissell, William Bishop, and, playing her abusive, incestuous father, Oscar Homolka, who happened concurrently to be the hard-drinking best pal of Erich Maria Remarque. At night he would be on a bender with Remarque, and during the day he would knock Paulette around on the set—in character, of course.

The story dealt with a dysfunctional farming family of Polish background, living and sparring in Pennsylvania. In the play, because of her perverse father, Anna runs away to the big city and turns to prostitution. In the movie, she's merely a waitress with a wilted reputation. She is lured home again in order to land a rich, college-boy farmer with substantial property, and in doing so, to provide financial and social restitution to her family.

As much as Paulette threw herself into the role, it seemed hard for her. She did research on prostitutes—went to red-light districts to see where they lived, how they worked, how they walked, how they laughed. She had a masseuse come on the set because the role made her so tense. Mary Wickes, the salty, venerable character actress of stage and screen, recalls the uncomfortable atmosphere on the set: "Paulette didn't even know our names. She was extremely professional—came in, got into makeup, knew her lines, and went home. She was totally noncommittal—a bit of a bitch, really. She did have a good figure, though."

The film received bad reviews, and *Cue* magazine wrote of Paulette: "Most of the time, she slouches through her role like a party of the second part in a nightclub Apache dance—all sin, scintillation and sex."

Anna Lucasta was withdrawn after playing in theaters for only a week. In 1958, it reappeared as a moderately successful remake with an all-black cast, starring Eartha Kitt and Sammy Davis, Jr.

Paulette's career had reversed itself extremely quickly. Before *Anna Lucasta* was released, she increased the speed of her downward spiral by making a quick movie in Mexico called *The Torch* during the time she was also obtaining a divorce from Meredith there. Meredith had said, "It costs more to marry a woman with a large income," and Paulette replied, "Actors are for Dr. Menninger. The ideal man is one who has $8 million and no complexes. To such a man could I give security." She bought into *The Torch* by becoming an associate producer. This gesture of belief in a clearly designated less-than-B picture could have been a reaction to having had a Paramount project canceled.

She had been slated to co-star with William Holden in *Beyond the Sunset*, but it got postponed indefinitely, and again Paramount had nothing for her. She somehow got another contract from the studio that didn't want her. Her deal was for one picture a year for ten years, with script approval, sixty days' notice prior to the start of production, and all the outside work she could get. For a divorcée about to be forty in Hollywood, it was not too bad.

Leo Rosten wrote a seminal article called "Hollywood: The Movie Colony, the Movie Makers," and fifteen years later followed it up with "Hollywood Revisited," in which he examines the Hollywood "still absorbed in its own world and its own values, but making movies with new care and incomparable know-how to meet television's challenge." In this article he looks at the elusive reality of stardom:

> A star may have less talent, less character, less beauty, less ambition than a dozen competitors who remain unknown; but the star possesses some internal flair, some catalytic capacity to evoke excitement or response. It is extraordinary how rarely a star takes hold of the public affection and how great is the fascination which the old stars still exert. . . .
>
> . . . Insecurity has always characterized people in show business. . . . "You're only as good as your last picture." In few industries does success come so rapidly or on so spectacular a scale; and in few do careers collapse with such bewildering speed. Luise Rainer won two Academy Awards in a row, then could not get a job. Greer Garson, Veronica Lake, Jon Hall, Sylvia Sidney, Dennis Morgan, Paulette Goddard, Paul Muni, Deanna Durbin, Simone Simon, Lisabeth Scott—each a box-office magnet for a while—suffered a sudden debacle.

If Paulette was dismayed by her life, she didn't let on. If the role of the star was not suitable for her anymore, she would play the role of the gorgeous, bejeweled, bewitching vagabond. She justified her dismissal from the elite colony in an airy, slightly superior way: "I just did what came naturally. I was a natural, as they say. I was supposed to be unconventional. The others played the game seriously. I was only in it for the fun. And I gave it up because it ceased to be fun. It became so grim. Everybody on the set. And they all thought they were doing something new and they were doing the most old-fashioned kinds of things. . . . I'd leave Hollywood with my full makeup on the night I finished my picture and go straight to New York and then to Paris. They'd have to call me at Maxim's or somewhere like that. I had a romantic feeling about the world."

A great friend of Paulette's at this time was the outrageous Surrealist painter Salvador Dalí. They shared an interest in the ridiculous and the grotesque. She and Dalí reminisced about the time when he and Gala, his wife, were at Thanksgiving dinner at the Merediths'. It was just before the breakup of the marriage and, in fact, she felt that what occurred at the dinner was the *coup de mort*: "Gala and Dalí, it was when you were at my house in the country with Burgess. You came for Thanksgiving Day and I thought, What could be provocative for you to eat? We had a little pig running around, and I had the cook kill it; she put an apple in its mouth, which is classic for Thanksgiving. Burgess came to the table and fell straight on his head. It was his pet. I didn't know it. He said, 'Leonora, Leonora!!!' Remember? He couldn't eat, couldn't come to dinner. But it was so delicious!"

Meredith's mourning of Leonora quickly turned to outrage. They had been so estranged that Paulette had not even known which pig was his pet. It seemed the final blow: Paulette arranged to have the art collection crated and shipped out, as well as all the Early American furniture and antiques. She was especially concerned about keeping the Rivera portrait of herself that had been hanging over their mantel for many years.

Paulette had made arrangements for packing up and fleeing to Mexico. She was to report for work on *The Torch*, and equally important, would be able to get a fast divorce in Cuernavaca. She wrote Meredith from there about the removal of the Rivera, informing him that a representative of a packing and shipping company would call within the next few days to arrange for the crating and shipping of the painting. Meredith replied that he would be glad to give her one half of the painting: "The other half under our community property law is mine."

Although Meredith was said to be fed up not only with their geographical differences but their material ones, he reminisced with little bitterness:

> She took all of our collection of valuable paintings. And I was glad to have her have it. I didn't want to fight—so it ended. . . . I was not able to give her the kind of comfort she was looking for, and so we separated. It wasn't anything severe, but it was a drift apart, and God knows that I wished her well. We had a separation that was without any rancor, and a good deal of relief. . . . I had a pulling down of the curtain on her, I know that I had to do that. It's funny how thoroughly the curtain came down between us. I'm an adjustor at heart, and when it didn't work, it didn't work. My career went on, so to speak, though in those days being a star with one of the major studios was the whole thing, and I was never that. . . . Her stardom ceased rather suddenly. For no particular reason. In those days stardom seemed a little less on the basis of talent. It had to do with who was a favorite in some places, and I think she must have fallen out of favor in ways I don't know. Because it wasn't long after we separated that she was dropped from Paramount. . . . But she always seemed to have her own money. She was a highly paid actress, and she was always well off—better off after we split up. . . . But I had a great admiration of her spirit—without half knowing or trying to know what the hell lit the fuse. . . . I have no idea what she did afterwards. I got involved in my own life, and the last thing I wanted to think about was her.

In 1951, Meredith married for the fourth time. She was a twenty-year-old "exotic" and Broadway chorus dancer named Kaja Sundsten. A little over a year later, he filed suit against Paulette for $400,000 of communal property. Paulette rose to the occasion by waging a countersuit, which questioned the credibility of their quickie Mexican divorce and thereby cast doubt on the validity of Meredith's new marriage. A settlement was made out of court, in Paulette's favor.

Meredith had one more encounter with Paulette. He was going through some drawers and came across an old savings-account book of hers that had eighteen thousand dollars in it. "This could only happen to Paulette" was his comment. He also found a whole group of small drawings that George Gershwin had done of her. He contacted her and arranged to get a package to her. "So the little pig turned into a savings-account book. The End," Paulette said drily. She seemed to have the last word, until Meredith outlived her.

Newly divorced, Paulette danced at Mocambo with Clark Gable. The columns reported she was wearing a form-fitting, split-to-the-knee Parisian gown that Meredith had brought back from France for her just before they'd separated. The columnist Dorothy Kilgallen wrote, "The movie colony still hasn't latched on to the fact that its most torrid current romance stars Paulette Goddard and Clark Gable. But only because P & C have been doing such a good job of keeping their atomic secret."

Nothing much came of it. Gable, known for being tight with money, never indulged Paulette in the manner to which she had become accustomed. The end of Paulette's romance with Gable reputedly took place at the Los Angeles airport, where, after chauffeuring her there in his Rolls-Royce, he sent her off to Mexico with only a casual kiss on the cheek, witnessed by a herd of reporters and photographers.

At the end of the year, Gable surprised Paulette, and everybody else, by marrying Sylvia Ashley Fairbanks, who had spun her own web around all of them. She was the widow of Douglas Fairbanks, Sr., who had been the best friend of Chaplin. As Mrs. Fairbanks, she had known Paulette well and, once widowed, had taken up briefly with Paulette's husband-to-be Erich Maria Remarque.

Paulette started looking around again.

Her good friend Celestine Wallis had a theory about her relentless energy regarding men: "She appreciated being desired. When you have been abandoned by your father, it is a very great thing to have men desire you, to prove to yourself that it wasn't your fault."

By 1950, Paulette was over forty but had plenty of admirers. The writer John Steinbeck not only squired her about but gave her a gift of a trailer and formed a production company with her called Monterey Pictures. They had a three-picture deal, and the first one was for *Cup of Gold*, based on an early Steinbeck novel. "We've got the money, and we've got the release," said Paulette. Their film ventures never got off the ground.

Stanton Griffis, a former ambassador to Spain and Argentina and chairman of the board of Madison Square Garden, was also around Paulette. A blueblood from Boston and a "magnate," Griffis owned a yacht where he entertained in the lavish manner that Paulette found truly nurturing. As a balding, sixty-three-year-old bachelor whose circle included Richard and Dorothy Rodgers, Danny Kaye, Edna Ferber (for a time, until she read him the riot act over a Bund meeting that was to be scheduled at Madison Square Garden), Max Gordon, Moss Hart, Theresa Helburn, and Lillian Hellman, he made an extra splash with diamond-decked Paulette on his arm.

Perhaps because she felt somewhat impoverished by her change of status, Paulette took comfort in flaunting her jewelry during this time. Wearing her diamonds like a coat of arms, she would sail into the 21 Club ablaze, causing Mack Kriendler, one of the owners, to exlaim, "Paulette! What happened? Did you find a diamond tree?"

Her reputation preceded her and served her astonishingly well. Paulette herself recalled how she would push a situation as far as it would go to come around her way: "One night I was at the Jules Steins'—whom every-body knows—for dinner, and there was this man there by the name of Dodero, who was the Onassis of his time—only he was from Buenos Aires—an Argentinean ship owner. He was there with a charming young girl, very, very young, very sweet, and I wanted to leave early as usual. So Dodero said, 'Oh, *please*, let me take you and Anita home.' And I said, 'Oh, great, I'd love to go.' But then he said, 'Oh, *please* stop at El Morocco with me!'

"So I said, 'Oh, all right'—because they were so nice—and coming into the club they had a vitrine with an exposition of Dalí's jewelry . . . and there in the vitrine were the famous ruby lips!

"And I just stood there and *stared* and *stared* at it for a long, long time. It fascinated me. And he finally said, 'Do you like that?' And I said, 'I think it's absolutely *fascinating* and I've never seen anything like it and I suppose I never will. So I'm having a very good look.'

"Well, the next day his secretary rang my doorbell and he had a big bunch of red roses, and he said, 'Here's a little remembrance from Señor Dodero—he left early this morning for Buenos Aires.' And I opened it and it was the ruby lips! . . . And I was so happy! And I said, 'Oh, please tell him . . .' And she said, 'I don't have to tell him anything. He knows you'll be happy. He knows you'll love it and you'll never forget him.' And then he died—quite soon afterwards. . . . But we had that marvelous evening, sitting there at that corner table, talking, and everyone was staring at us as if we were the rising sun!"

For most of 1950 Paulette was not working. Her regimen remained ex-actly the same as it had for two decades. She ate no sugar; breakfast was black coffee and fruit juice, lunch was usually meat and iced tea, and dinner was hearty. She was a great walker—even in Los Angeles, never carried a hand-bag, would frequently get thirsty, and would stop in at various familiar restaurants and ask to "borrow" a drink. Her dress size was 12, her shoe size $4\frac{1}{2}$B, her weight between 118 and 128. She was still giving interviews with good quotes, but she began to recycle her stories, adding even more hyperbole. Her friend Jinx Falkenburg encouraged the press to write about her, and often fed items to the columnists to keep Paulette's name and ego active. Sometimes she would even be there during an interview, acting as fan and coach. One night, for instance, they were having dinner with John Ringling North following an interview, and Paulette was trying to recollect for him her own favorite quotes: "I told Jinx that I'm not temperamental—I just know what I want, and if I don't have it, I try to get it."

Ringling listened, wrote it out on a napkin, and then suggested a revision: "This sounds more like you, Paulette: 'I never know what I want, but I always get it.'"

Paulette was thrilled. "I love it like that! Perfect! Jinx—have them change it! Promise they'll print it John's way!"

At this point, Paulette began revising her Hollywood beginnings to the press.

With little to do, Paulette left for Paris shortly before the summer of 1950. Perhaps she needed to give herself a fling, reminding her of the good old days before a swan song of sorts: summer stock. Paulette had agreed to play Cleopatra in George Bernard Shaw's *Caesar and Cleopatra* for four weeks, touring Massachusetts.

From Paris, she was keeping in touch with her various beaux. Along with Clark Gable, John Huston, John Steinbeck, Stanton Griffis, the television producer Cy Howard, and the actor Hurd Hatfield, she was also seeing the playwright William Saroyan. The story goes that she cabled Saroyan from Paris, stating that she would arrive in New York for the opening of his latest play and that she expected him to escort her. He didn't want to offend her, but there was the problem of his current companion, a charming young actress. Contracted to write a movie, he phoned the head of the studio and arranged for his actress friend to be flown out to test for a role on the day of his Broadway opening. The expenses would be deducted from his film salary. At first, the young actress balked at missing the opening, but was convinced that her own career should not be sacrificed. She went to Hollywood, and Paulette was escorted to the opening as she wanted. The play was a hit; the young actress's screen test was a failure; however, her relationship wasn't. She flew back the next day to reclaim it.

Soon after, there occurred another humiliating episode. The circus was in town, playing at Madison Square Garden. Paulette proudly claimed that she had attended the opening with Cecil B. DeMille, who was planning to make a blockbuster movie about aerialists under the big top. It was to be called *The Greatest Show on Earth*, based on John Ringling North's story, for which DeMille had acquired the rights. One of the leading roles, that of a "girl" aerialist, was coveted by many of Hollywood's leading ladies, most of whom had long left girlhood behind. Hedy Lamarr, who had starred for DeMille in his last hit picture, *Samson and Delilah*, was the top contender for the role. Lamarr was the love of the magnate Herbert Klotz, who was also seeing Paulette, who lusted after the role of the aerialist. Marlene Dietrich, close to fifty, was also not disinterested.

Paulette wasn't DeMille's date for the opening of the circus. She happened to be there, spotted him in his box, and was invited to join him. Once there, she made it known to him how much she wanted the role. She vowed to be on her best behavior. Soon after, she sent him a note to that effect: "Dear C. B.: I'm sorry I missed saying goodbye to you after my thrilling evening with you at the circus. I do hope and pray that I get 'The Part' in your coming film. I will be a good, good girl. In the meantime I shall be working hard in summer stock. Yours, Paulette. P.S. You can get me from Paramount. I have pretty feet, too. Love, P. G."

DeMille's response in a note: "Yes, your feet are beautiful. What bothers me is that those same lovely feet might be tempted to walk off the set a second time."

Paulette's response in a telegram from New York: "Hope all those rumors about my going into *The Greatest Show on Earth* are true. I'm returning Monday to sign the contract."

The postscript to this bit of aggression was that she had already lost the part of the aerialist that she wanted. It had gone to Betty Hutton, and what was left was the part of the elephant girl—a physically demanding and less glamorous role. Her competition was Dorothy Lamour, Gloria Grahame, and Lucille Ball. Gloria Grahame was chosen. Paulette had been bypassed for two roles in the same film.

In the summer of 1950, Paulette returned to the stage. Although she had said just three years earlier, following her experience doing *Winterset* in Dublin, that playing the same role day in and day out was boring after the first week, and that she had no interest in a further career in the theater, she soon changed her opinion. She talked about her new venture with the relish of a young initiate: "I've wanted to do this—to act on the stage, to be in this play—for a long time."

Bob Ulman was the press agent for the tour that played Olney, Dennis, Falmouth, and Beverly, Massachusetts. Ulman recalled, "The audiences were thrilled! She really had no stage technique. But she did have a certain flair on stage, and she did have her looks. . . ."

Paulette defended her decision to do summer stock: "Certainly I didn't do this for money, or for self-aggrandizement. I am on vacation now between pictures. I have a ten-year contract with Paramount Pictures—that sounds like a life sentence, doesn't it?—but the contract says I can do what I like between pictures. If I wanted, of course, I could have made an outside picture. Or I could have loafed."

Paulette did need the money—at least to continue living as she had been. The big pictures and big husbands weren't in front of her anymore. She was on her own again, with a mother and mother's husband to support. She claimed to be rapturously enjoying her freedom, embracing the gypsy life. Curiously, a year before they were to transform each other, she was espousing the very life that Remarque rejected—that of a wanderer. From an Ohio newspaper in 1950:

PAULETTE GODDARD CONFESSES TO WANDERING GYPSY LIFE. Gorgeous Paulette Goddard, one of the world's most flamboyant and shrewd stars, threw up her long-fingernailed hands today and confessed that she was a mere wandering gypsy. . . . "Sure, I'm a restless nomad. In fact, I've sold all my possessions, at profit of course, and just strictly live out of three suitcases. My home is where I hang my diamonds. . . . Actors originally were vagabonds, and that's the way they should be. . . . Possessions are a false security. They bog you down. And nothing is going to bog me down."

The footloose glamour queen . . . does have one possession left. An eight-acre beach promontory along the California coast, which supports nothing but 900 trees and a teeny trailer, gift of author John Steinbeck. "It's a dream spot," Paulette sighed. "Good real estate property, incidentally. But I don't think I'll ever build on it or subdivide it. I live a beachcomber's life there. I only keep one bathing suit and two towels in the trailer."

Early in the new year of 1951, Paulette was taking jobs she might not have agreed to fifteen years before. She posed for an ad for Ayds, a new reducing chocolate. "It works!" says Paulette Goddard. She is pictured on the Ayds candy box looking slim in a housedress. She also posed for an ad for Sylvania Radio-Television Service, in an evening dress.

The stage was set for the entrance of Erich Maria Remarque.

CHAPTER SEVEN

NEW MOON

1 9 4 8 – 1 9 5 8

REMARQUE TURNED FIFTY in June of 1948 at his villa in Porto Ronco. "Never thought I would make it," he writes in his diary. He spent it quietly and with some irritation, trying to work on his new novel, *Spark of Life*, in his bedroom while his father wandered about the house looking for something to do. He notes in his diary that he received telegrams from friends including Puma and Natasha and that he got a call from Peter. He also records that he contracted lice: "God knows how I got them. Didn't sleep with anybody in Paris."

He was finding it awkward, sometimes anticlimactic, to get used to being home. Life was too quiet. He wasn't working well. He had grown too accustomed to New York and to his relationships, especially with Natasha. He had not heard from her since his arrival and it was making him anxious, even though he recognized the "Puma syndrome." "My damned addiction for scenes," he acknowledges.

Spark of Life (the working title was *The Image of God*) was as painful to write as it would be to read. Hans Wagener, in his *Understanding Erich Maria Remarque*, notes the immersion in the grim conditions of the small camp within the first few pages of the novel, where "Remarque uses grotesque contrasts when describing the cruelties committed by the SS: 'Buchsbaum, as a matter of fact, [had been] not quite complete: three fingers, seventeen teeth,

ABOVE: *Remarque at his desk in the living room in Porto Ronco, ca. 1951.*

LEFT: *The main square of Ascona.*

"Drinking freed, relaxed, minimized, enlarged what was projected, what was hidden in the chambers of my psychosis." From Remarque's diary, 1954, Porto Ronco.

the toenails, and a part of his genitals had been missing. He had lost them while being educated to become a useful human being. The subject of his genitals had provoked much laughter at the cultural evenings in the SS quarters.'"

Arch of Triumph and *Spark of Life* were both published in America by Appleton-Century-Crofts; *Spark of Life* appeared in 1952. Even before the first draft was completed, *Spark of Life* was looking problematic. As Hans Wagener notes:

> The subject was considered likely to become too melodramatic and was tackled by comparatively few writers—among them the most well known were Alexander Solzhenitsyn, André Malraux, and Arthur Koestler. Remarque recognized this problem. But in addressing this topic he did not wish to write a documentary type of work, as did later authors such as Rolf Hochhuth (*The Deputy*, 1963) and Peter Weiss (*The Investigation*, 1965). Instead he felt that as a novelist he should write a work of fiction. In his dedication, Remarque justifies this choice:
> "To write a documentary about concentration camps was not intended— although every detail of the story is documented. This was necessary and— alas—material for it existed in overwhelming masses—there were photographs, films, books, diaries and thousands of witnesses to interview."

With *Spark of Life*, more than any other book, he makes his position against Nazi and Communist totalitarianism clear. He is a pacifist without any affiliation. For Remarque, writing the book was a necessary exorcism. By graphically depicting Nazi horrors, he could come to some sort of terms with the death of his sister Elfriede. Until he began writing, he had remained relatively quiet about her murder—according to all available records. Even in the book, he does not directly re-create the atrocity. However, as Hans Wagener notes, "at one point Remarque sarcastically states that 'one of the first cultural achievements of the Nazis had been to abolish the guillotine and reintroduce the hatchet instead,' an obvious reference to his sister. There is one scene in which Remarque alludes to the persecution of anyone who makes the slightest defeatist remark. . . . Remarque was well aware of the fact that by killing his sister Elfriede, the Nazis demonstrated that they actually intended to murder him."

Remarque isolated himself in the house in order to work on this book, which he found slow going. He wrote to Harriet Pilpel that the solitude, the "flowers, mountains, stars and the lake" and his cat for company were a good

Hitler's bunker and Eva Braun were part of Remarque's collection of photographs gathered while researching Spark of Life, *published in 1952.*

Remarque's film debut as Professor Pohlmann in A Time to Love and a Time to Die *with John Gavin, 1957–1958.*

way to begin his fiftieth year, but Remarque was clearly lonely. So that close to a month after he arrived in Porto Ronco, he left for Rome, hoping for a rendezvous with Natasha. Natasha was at first "indisposed," and then took off for Palermo for a ten-day stay. She was determined to travel and avoided him. This led him to drink heavily and carry on with whomever he could find. Natasha heard what he was doing, which only drove her further away. He recorded this particularly empty time:

> Had a lot to drink during the past few days. Met: Dorothy di Frasso, Michael Washinsky, Merle Oberon, Orson Welles, Ludwig Bemelman, and others; on the last day also Natasha's Italian prince, Raimondo di Lanza. Too much to drink. Annoyed and ashamed of myself. I'm afraid of what people are going to tell Natasha and how she is going to react to it. Last night dinner with Feilchen [his European art dealer]. Distracted—didn't recognize people from the night before. Today in the sun. For the first time since my trip to Rome, I worked again. Worried how Natasha will digest the Roman gossip.

Back in Porto Ronco, he took up with Ellen Janssen, his neighbor's daughter, but thought only of Natasha. Through his diary entries, the patterns of his blatant obsession can be observed. The intensity of his desire, the revulsion with that desire, and then the expiation of the revulsion are similar to his Dietrich dilemmas, but because he is older, his besottedness seems heightened: "At noon to Ellen Janssen. . . . Ellen under the shower. . . . Suddenly for the first time homesick for America. Has something to do with Natasha. . . . Called Natasha in the morning in Paris. Fear was justified. She had heard. . . . She felt insulted. Good-bye, see you in New York. Hung up. Wrote her a letter today. Explained it wasn't pleasant to know that she had wanted to go to Palermo for ten days. Also other things from before. The guy in Paris; the other one from Palermo, who had called at three in the morning. . . . There is something that tells me: maybe it's better to say good-bye. Am I incapable of it? . . . Have to hold on to her."

His bad behavior and guilt continued. He went to the Tavern, a little restaurant in Ascona with a terrace, regularly for the remainder of the summer. He notes that several factors drove him there and were responsible for his obstreperous behavior. The rains were heavy and unrelenting at that time of year in the Ticino; his father was demanding and was distracting him; Natasha's husband, Jack Wilson, was sending her gossip-column clippings linking her with Remarque, which she would forward to Remarque. It was all too much, so he would go to the Tavern to drink and forget—as he did on one particular night that he happened to remember. Later that night, he went with his crowd to a beautiful house owned by a woman named Gypsy Pamealdi. There, he ate Vienna sausages and drank copious amounts of wine and cognac. In his cups, he found himself making love to two women, one after the other, on a wet stone garden table: "It was really nice, the wet garden with the wet stone table, for a while. Later the bar girl Tildi from the Tavern, blond, quietly steadfast, and suddenly giving in. . . . That has to stop! Have to work! I am not master any longer when I drink. Can't stop it."

That he managed to work at all, and on such a book, was a feat. His drinking escalated, along with his sexual exploits. He was engaging in ménages, but there was a blend of the prurient and the compassionate: "Yesterday Anita, Renée, and Giselle. . . . Into the early morning. Drank Mosel. Bought 'Holbein' rug from Anita. Needs money."

While Natasha continued to torture him—discussing her ex-lovers, such as Saint Exupéry, flaunting her current dalliances, and then dutifully ministering to her husband—young Ellen Janssen was available, adoring, yet observant. She had grown up watching Remarque. Every summer from the age of fourteen, she had gone to visit her mother, and had been dazzled by her mother's famous neighbor:

Oh, I thought he was terrific. I loved his house so much. It was so absolutely devastatingly beautiful. . . . He had the most beautiful Impressionist pictures you can imagine on the wall. He had bookshelves all around. He had an enormous desk. [The desk is at New York University, set in a facsimile of his working space.] It was absolutely crowded with stuff. He would say, "It will take care of itself by staying there." If you came into this room you were just enfolded by beauty. . . . He loved to collect. But he was a little tight with his money. He always said, "I am a Cancer, and Cancers always hold on to their money." He bought the most expensive suits for himself, and if you touched his sleeve it was always cashmere. He really knew what to do with money, which is very rare.

By the summer of 1948, Ellen Janssen, then in her twenties, had fallen in love with Remarque. Soon, she would work for him as a secretary, typing up his manuscripts, but that summer, with her youth, blond hair, and tanned shoulders, she became an important diversion. In looking back, she says she must have been in love with him, because she remembers telling him that she would always be there. She was well aware of his reputation as a womanizer and bon vivant—the side of him that caused David Niven to comment, regarding Remarque's Hollywood days, "When Erich Maria Remarque was not wrapped around Marlene Dietrich or other local beauties, he acted as a sort of liaison officer between the German-speaking foreigners, the Garden of Allah set, and Musso and Frank's Restaurant on Hollywood Boulevard."

Ellen Janssen (now Dunham) understood how complex he was: "He was not in love with every woman that he was with. He was very romantic. He might have had one-night stands, but I don't think he had affairs unless he was emotionally involved and romantically involved. He was very sexy, and when he drank, he went out at night and couldn't seem to curb himself. But he wanted to have every relationship be a romantic one."

In the next couple of years, Ellen Janssen was an integral part of *Spark of Life* and the working world of Remarque. Their relationship grew in intensity, even though he writes in his diary, "She knows that it isn't really love, I know it too, don't need to try." Not only did she type for him, she became an extension of his words—the next step in the precious process. She recalls being part of his "grail," and she was especially gratified to work on *Spark of Life*:

> He wrote very distinctly—only in German. You could read every word. And he would never scratch something out and rewrite it. It was there—every sentence was there in his mind, and that's the way he wrote it. . . . Just draft after draft, but perfectly whole. Because I typed it up for him, he was scared that I would talk about it. . . . He was very, very sensitive about this particular book. When I met him as an adult, I was married to a German. He was half Jewish and there was a very tough time, when I went back to Switzerland, and my husband ended up in a camp. . . .
>
> I lived in Germany during part of the Nazi regime and during the beginning of the war, and so I knew something about it.
>
> Well, Remarque wrote something like "And the bells would ring," and I would say, shyly, "You know, there were no bells to ring, because all the bells were being melted into cannons at the time."
>
> And then he said, "Well, maybe at that time, in this particular place there were bells."
>
> He didn't like it at all if I criticized anything, but of course I knew the atmosphere under the Nazis so much better than he, because I had lived there. And there was another thing I criticized. And there, too, he would argue with me about it, but he always changed it afterwards. But I just hated to tell him anything, because he didn't like to be told. For instance,

there was a big issue over the Nazi wives, the ones who had a lot to say. He would describe the wives. He would have them sit in their pink chiffon gowns on overstuffed French furniture and not do anything, just be plump and passive. And I said, "The description of your milieu is wrong. That's not the way they were. They used to have sort of hand-loomed dresses, and they believed in being natural and not wearing silk and satin. Their style was different. They would have modern, hand-crafted furniture."

Then he said, "The next thing you're going to tell me is that they were wonderful people."

I said, "No, I'm talking only about the backdrop. The milieu should be right when you write something." At that moment, he would sacrifice being right for his pride, but later he would always change it.

Both *Spark of Life* and his next novel, *A Time to Love and a Time to Die*, depicting life after the Third Reich, were novels of conscience rather than of firsthand experience. America responded positively to these looks into existence in a concentration camp and the aftermath of war in a German city. But the Germans criticized Remarque for his lack of verity. He just couldn't win with Germany. Hans Wagener writes:

> Probably neither one of the novels will be considered great literature by literary historians. Whereas the vital theme of the will to survive against all odds in *Spark of Life* is a bit dated and clearly places its author in the first half of the twentieth century . . . the development of the heroes in both novels from passive acceptance of their fate as dictated by the political system, through an individual, critical analysis, and finally to active resistance is testimony to Remarque's change into a political writer with a message. They demonstrate once more that, in spite of his own opulent life-style, Remarque was taking the side of those who were victims of twentieth-century history and that he was now posing questions that would increase his readers' political awareness.

Writing *Spark of Life* may have been an important step in his professional maturity, but it was grueling. He would refer to it as "this stupid book" in a letter to Alma Mahler Werfel. He could not wait to be done with it. In his diary he writes, "Important: when I'm done with this book I would love to write a humorous story, or a play."

Though Remarque wanted badly to settle down, he also felt compelled to be constantly on the move after a while. He seemed to need to wander, and he kept up a steady round of trips between Paris, St. Moritz, Porto Ronco, and Venice. After some particularly severe drinking bouts, when he dented his Lancia twice, he recorded, "Feeling that I have to leave soon." He thought about a title for his next book: *The Big Restlessness*.

Ellen Janssen recalled some insightful and amusing times before he began traveling: "He was a fabulous raconteur. He would tell jokes—mostly Jewish jokes—and he was very good at it—at doing the accent and everything else. He was very, very entertaining, full of stories, and he had this beautiful, soothing voice. He was very sensitive to voices himself, and as soon as I got a little excited and my volume would go up, he'd say: 'Keep it down.' We spoke mostly in German, and his German was beautiful and very well chosen. A very pure German was spoken where he came from—in Osnabrück."

Remarque, who had never been close to his father, found himself making up for lost time during these days. Remarque wrote to Harriet Pilpel that his father was "well, quite charming and looks like seventy [Peter Remark was eighty-five]. He is somewhat disappointed—expected much more entertainment, does not say it, understands that I must work, but I feel it. He is an old man of action and still not one of contemplation. But it will somehow work out, I hope."

Ellen Janssen recalls that Peter Remark was "a little ga-ga" when he came to stay with his son. "We lived next door and sometimes he would come by. I would invite him down for a drink—our house, just like Boni's—had steps that led down to the entrance. He said, 'Well, I would like to, but I don't have any money with me.' He had the idea he would have to pay for it."

Peter Remark may well have been a little vague, but he was also mischievous. Ellen and Remarque used to sunbathe without any clothes on, because there was nobody around. The old man would be out fishing on the lake near the house. Boats would come by, passing him while he fished, and Remarque would be lying there without any clothes on—lying flat so he couldn't be readily seen. The passersby in the boats would call out to the father, "Is this the house of the famous writer Erich Maria Remarque?" whereupon the father would say, "Yes, I happen to be his father, and my son is lying right there." They would come in close for a look at the startled and furious famous writer.

That fall Remarque bade farewell to his circle of friends and particularly notes in his diary two women friends (Herman Hesse's widow, Hellen, and Karen Horney's daughter, Brigitte). He packed his father off to Bad Rothenfelde, Germany, to resume living with his daughter Erna and her husband, Walter Rudolf. He settled with Joseph and Rosa nine years' worth of their salary. He visited the widow of his old comrade, the German writer Emil Ludwig, who had emigrated to Switzerland at about the same time. Ludwig had died in Porto Ronco a short time earlier, and in his frequent mood of self-deprecation Remarque reports, "I, bastard that I am, hadn't done a thing." He is beginning to feel his mortality as he records his visit: "Went the last day. Lunch. Clearest day. The marble terrace. The wide lake. Numerous bees in the aster flowers. Sad. Laughed when she talked about Ludwig's extravagances. Gave her a check made out in francs; has no money, just the house and garden. But has style. The big porch, bees buzzing. Full October sun. That's over too. Emden, Schleber, Ludwig [all comrades and early émigrés]—all gone. And I am the only one left."

His nostalgia continued when he stopped in Paris en route to New York. He stayed at the Hôtel Lancaster:

I'm living in the same room as before when I was here with Marlene! Saw the rose in the window of the bathroom, the light from there. It was once like that, at dusk, when she came in like a butterfly, beautiful, and the bed welcomed us. There was never a man who was able to look fearless at his memories. Can one love again after the first time? No. Yes. One grows. One changes. The strange thread of memory. . . . Start of a book: I stood at the window. It was gray outside. October dusk. Behind me, you were sleeping. And suddenly, the thought that one of us had to die first. I turned around. You were breathing—then the painful adventure of love. . . . You are gone. I'm standing at the same window, in the same hotel room. It is October and I remember the time I thought you were gone for good. It was worse than dying.

He arrived back to "the fast life of New York" and to Natasha, who he was afraid was about to embark upon another affair. He was surprised at Harry Truman's victory as president; he retrieved his paintings from the Knoedler Gallery and the Metropolitan Museum, and sent his van Gogh to be shown at the Cleveland museum; he complained about his chronic headache of unsettled taxes and gift taxes which was easier to dismiss when he was in Europe. He swore about a bill from Harriet Pilpel's firm, Greenbaum, Wolff & Ernst: "Bill from Ernst: ten thousand dollars! Thief!" He followed his favorite routine: had dinner at 21 with Peter; met with art dealer Sam Salz, who showed him a Matisse, a Bonnard, a Vuillard, and other treasures; bought two Chinese bronzes at an auction; ate oysters and pot au feu at Chambord, still his favorite restaurant for lunch; in the afternoon saw

"Puma, looking very pretty," and in the evening, Natasha—they dined on smoked sturgeon, smoked ham, and cheese and drank wine.

That night he got violently sick. He was dizzy, he vomited repeatedly, and Natasha went home. She had an aversion to being around sick people. The next day he was diagnosed as having Ménière's disease. No one knew how it occurred, this sudden distortion of balance. He was given injections and sent to bed for three weeks. The disease seemed to reflect his emotions about Natasha, for as soon as he felt stronger, he was gnashing over her again: "With N. the traditional December trouble. Doesn't want to make love to me . . . refused when I tried to take her in my arms, tried to fend me off like a dog. Usual debate. Had I nothing else in my head but sex? Sickening. I do only if two people have slept together for years and one suddenly doesn't want it any longer—then, yes, I have sex on my mind."

He ended the year accepting that he was caught in static and familiar territory: "When Jack has his arthritis, N. takes care of him and mothers him— with me she hardly showed up. Sadly, the real care does not go to me. Same thing earlier with Puma. Strange: it is in my horoscope. . . . Last night to Torbergs. Puma was there. Home with N., who wanted it. I found that I couldn't. Rain outside. New Year's Day. Cyclamen from Puma. Red azaleas from Garbo. Also from Puma a dressing gown and a blue scarf. . . . Didn't work yet."

Remarque began the New Year, 1949, by not working, not smoking, and with a tirade against the election of Harry S. Truman, which, in a sense, shows how truly American he considered himself: "Thought about the New Year's words of one of the most important people of the next four years: Truman said 'I would rather have peace in the world than be President.' Incredible naiveté. Overestimation of simple ego; enormous danger of ambitious stupidity. One can vary that: I would rather . . . than possess a Gauguin, or get a Nobel Prize, or . . . what a terrible comparison! For four years as a president, a man from Missouri who hasn't accomplished much yet, has overlooked many things and yet talks of peace for the whole world. One can only hope that he wasn't thinking that through well enough. I want to believe that this was a deeply sacrificial quote, and not impudent idiocy, which seems to be making the rounds."

Remarque's disenchantment was becoming all-encompassing. He was also on the verge of being frightened. Whether as a result of the Ménière's disease or not, he was suddenly impotent and definitely unable to work. And one exacerbated the other. He called it his "sterile limitation." Natasha seemed to be part of the cause. She had trouble differentiating between the eloquent writer Remarque and Remarque the person and lover. It was paralyzing him: "I have to work, if I don't get to it, it will end badly for me. Deadline for *Collier's* is April 1. Can't get my act together. Not to smoke is a big obstacle, and then this constant nagging. Natasha asked: Why wasn't I talking the way I was speaking in my letters to her? I: After being speechless for a moment, stumbled but . . . I . . . She: 'So, this isn't literature?' I: No, but when writing one concentrates differently, one has more time. She: Then it is literature. Your letters are literature. I: My goodness, yes, I suppose so, sometimes."

If he was not working, it was impossible to keep the deadline. He made a lunch date with Kenneth Littauer, his editor at *Collier's*, and Denver Lindley, his translator, to acknowledge his problem. He drank too much and ended up pronouncing, "A writer does not finish a book, he abandons it!" which became his catchphrase.

The sexual obstacle with Natasha was reaching a point of obsessed hysteria. He railed against her, yet longed for her; he blamed her for a sterility that reached beyond the physical. His tone in the diary is of someone close to his wit's end:

I think I've had enough of it. Even so, my horoscope advises me not to make final decisions and rush into things. I think I've had more than enough. I think I haven't fucked her once in '49, or if once, just the act, without passion. Then she'd have her period or a cold. Even a mule would become neurotic if she sits twice a week for four hours in front of you on the couch. Add to it the frustrations of not smoking and the dizziness in the head, and worried if I am capable of ever working normally again. And then this stupid goat who says, "You can't talk about anything but your Ménière's!" . . .

This morning a whiff of reason. One becomes what one endures. This bird whose life I don't dare criticize has without any caution dared to criticize mine. . . . N. might be a border case—some of her affairs show that, Cocteau, for instance. . . . Nothing is more difficult than to break loose from a zero. She has no understanding, blind egotism, she is always on the side of illogic, she is petty and there is a cosmic idiocy to her. . . . Besides her beauty, God knows she doesn't give me any inspiration, enthusiasm, or a constructive moment in the last years—just the opposite. And to think of all the letters I wrote to her that I had squeezed out of myself—much too many! They overwhelmed her. She couldn't take it. Some women obviously can't bear my written expression. Marlene couldn't either.

The next entry in his diary is charged with anger and contempt about Natasha. He had had Garbo and George Schlee, Garbo's frequent escort and the designer Valentina's husband, over for dinner.

Garbo walked lifting her skirt high over my Polish rug. Her beautiful, smooth legs. Natasha appeared. During dinner she offered one of her disapproving remarks, like "That's old news. Everybody knows about it. Why are you going on about it? I haven't heard anything interesting out of you for months." Later, she tried to patch it up. I told her to forget about it, but she went on and on. She declared suddenly that I could sleep with her if I liked to. I said, "But I thought you were indisposed." By that time I had drunk two thirds of the bottle of Armagnac. I said that it was a damn cheap shot just at the last moment before leaving on a trip—to have a quickie just to make sure she still had me, etc. Which is exactly the case.

That finally gave her the chance she needed. Major scene: "How I despise you! How I have always despised you! You with your cheap mind! You may have talent, but your mind is cheap!"

Dramatic attempt at departure. I: "Now, here's your chance! Take it!" After weeks of frustration I said, "Go ahead!" She: "It's finished! It's finished!" I handed her her things, and then held her at the door. It just was not the right farewell after such a long time together. I should have let her go. But who would? I told her that she should think what this crazy business was all about, and could she be really honest for once. If she was despising me so much, why had she stayed with me for so long? Couldn't she understand that her sudden mood swing—wanting to sleep with me—could be interpreted as charity? . . . The heart of the nonsense was what I most resented: to sleep together before she left, so that all could be erased and she could leave happily, feeling assured.

At some point I said something about her not sleeping with me for months. She: "It's your fault." She said it briskly, turning away, and then whirling back on me: "You have forced me before when you wanted me. Why not now? If you wanted me, why didn't you insist and force me to?" I said because her resistance had been going on too long. Because I had been sick. Because I didn't want to. When I mentioned pride, she said, full of contempt, "You have no pride, with your cheap thoughts!" It seemed to me as if Marlene was coming back at me. I should have let it go. I would never get any peace with this jealous, ungenerous, malicious being who is constantly on the lookout to snag, hit, or stab. I told her at the door, "After this time with you it will be a pleasure to meet any other human being. It will be a relief."

He began to write again—marginally. He recorded in his diary: "Rewrote four lines of the start of the first chapter today. What an achievement!" By spring, he was in a real work crisis. He was grievously behind on the novel, and although he had two drafts, they were not satisfactory enough for him to feel that he could meet his deadline at *Collier's*. Ironically, the matter was taken care of by a series of events. Kenneth Littauer, his editor at *Collier's*, had resigned, causing *Collier's* to decide not to extend Remarque's contract and giving them the right to terminate. Denver Lindley, who usually translated Remarque, had not as yet translated anything substantial, so anybody else who would get a manuscript would get it in German. Harriet Pilpel attempted to save the day by contacting *Cosmopolitan* magazine and offering them—hot off the press—the new Remarque novel. They were polite but cautious. Under their new editor, Herbert Mayes, they accepted no material that they had not previously read. Luckily, Mr. Mayes was fluent in German.

Remarque sent the last draft, representing about 300 out of a probable total of 500 pages, of the novel to Alice Sheridan, associate editor at *Cosmopolitan*, and received the kind of letter he had never known: "Here is the manuscript of your first novel [last draft, in fact], which Mr. Mayes has read . . . as Mr. Mayes will tell you in a personal letter, he considers this a very fine book. He thinks it is extremely well written and has fine prestige values. Unfortunately he does not see it adaptable to *Cosmopolitan*'s serial program."

Remarque noted the rejection brusquely in his diary: "*Cosmopolitan* sent first book back—unusable. Expected it. One failed. Probably all others, too. Not made for it."

Perhaps it didn't sting as much as it might have, because Natasha was agreeing to sleep with him again. Like someone in love for the first time, he was thrilled, kicked up his heels, and "Sent N. daily flowers throughout the week, which touched her more than I had expected." He was able to stave off the dark for a while longer.

Eventually, *Spark of Life* took off, but not without a degree of humiliation. After Remarque had explored serial possibilities with *Cosmopolitan*, *Saturday Evening Post*, and the *Ladies' Home Journal*, and had been turned down by all of them, *Collier's*, which had initially rejected the book, purchased it. Knox Burger, *Collier's* fiction editor in the early fifties, recalls that it had been an "unlikely subject" for them and that the manuscript had been "a bit windy." After a "big chunk" was cut out of it, it ran about 15,000 to 20,000 words, and was billed as a "novella." Burger had done the cutting with Remarque's and Harriet Pilpel's approval. He remembers Remarque as charming, and wishing, because the author was so gracious, that he had had the benefit of seeing the whole novel in print.

Upon signing his contract for the whole novel with Appleton-Century-Crofts, Remarque received the check for his advance: $7,500 for what the publisher referred to as "the concentration camp book." Appleton promoted the $3.75 hardcover book with the customary publisher's fervor, never directly mentioning its subject matter in the promotion release:

JUST KEEP IN MIND THAT THIS IS THE BEST NOVEL EVER WRITTEN BY A MAN WHOSE NAME MEANS MAGIC TO MILLIONS: WHOSE *ARCH OF TRIUMPH* WAS BOUGHT AND READ BY OVER 750,000! . . .

Once back in Porto Ronco, Remarque was still obsessed by one woman (Natasha), who sent him telegrams signing her dog's, not her own, name. He was often drinking through the night, becoming foolish and reckless more often than not. He was reluctant to be alone, yet restless and intolerant with friends. Jutta was still coming for extended stays at Porto Ronco; she was chronically sick and needed money. "It's idiotic to be here still together. Damned weakness, always giving in to someone else," he wrote in his diary. His father was increasingly fragile and needed to be supported. Remarque's own physical maladies were not abating; the trigeminal neuralgia could be excruciating. He had back problems; his second vertebra was not aligned, and he had an occasional return of Ménière's disease. He felt his sex life waning and wrote, "When I was six I thought my penis was there only to urinate with, when I was sixty I knew it"; this was something he had read, and then he wrote, "It's over, man, don't fool yourself." His blood pressure was up, and he was tired too much of the time, and frequently bored. This was a man who had wealth, fame, and a courageous new book coming out, but who dreamed of shit:

Slept and dreamed. Pictures in my semisleep. The enchantment of life: Children playing in a southern street, jumping rope; thought that such a summer afternoon must be a memory for a dying person. The same as a drink of fresh water must be to a person dying of thirst. . . . Then a dream that I had a child. It was shown to me dressed in a green shirt. I did not understand why. I remember that the mother seemed to be a strong, fairly good-looking girl. I remember that I liked the thought of having a child in my dream, even later on, while normally I dislike children. . . . In between dreamed of shit again. Jammed up the john, which didn't work, and flooded over. I had taken a shit during a meeting, wanted to clean it up before the others came back. Helpless. Hopeless. Years that first give and then take. Whoever hasn't developed his own life by a certain point will find it getting darker year after year.

When his personal self-esteem was at its lowest, his work always distracted him and kept him going. He had an idea for a new novel that he records in his diary: "I would like to write a story about a man (immigrant) who tries to rescue his wife; love, camp, death, Lisbon, Foreign Legion." These were the seeds for a novel he would write over a decade later. It would be called *The Night in Lisbon*.

Remarque spent New Year's Eve, 1950, in New York at the home of the theatrical producer Gilbert Miller and his very social wife, Kitty. Among the guests were Natasha ("very beautiful; with the Empire laurel leaf in her hair I had given her three years ago"), Cole Porter, Millicent Hearst, the Brian Ahernes, Rex Harrison, Lilli Palmer, and Paulette Goddard. Remarque listed Paulette but doesn't mention anything about her. He was still in painful pursuit of Natasha.

He was fifty-two years old and things were about to change drastically. His astrological chart, drawn up by Carroll Righter, astrologer to the stars, said so. He would soon be done with his obsession with Natasha, but it would get worse before it got better.

In the afternoon I called for N. for the second time at Mainbocher. [Natasha worked as an executive assistant to the designer; she also modeled for him, as well as for Avedon. She certainly did not have to work, but chose to.] They did not know whether she would be coming in the afternoon. I called her at home. She is not there. Don't know whether she's pretending not to be home. I am shaking inside, part excitement, part after-effects of alcohol. Damn! I am still dependent. A hundred times I have hung myself. I let myself down again and again.

[The next day] I had sent blue and white lilacs to her office with a note asking her to call. She received it at three. Shortly after three, I called. She was not there. Called again at four. She was there. Told me that she had been busy. Nonsense. Went to lunch before one, could easily have called. She came over in the evening. I always felt during the few hugs and kisses that nothing was going to happen. After dinner, she read magazines. She said that the dog should get infra-red treatment. I said that this would be easier in the bedroom, since the fixture is in there. She said that we could not leave him alone, and that she wanted to finish her coffee. She slowly drank the coffee and continued to read. Finally disgusted, I prepared the things for the dog. Undressing in the bedroom, she got into bed wearing her white slip. I asked her whether she didn't want to take it off. "No." In protest, I wore my underpants into bed. She was sucking and cracking a peppermint candy, which she put into her mouth just as I climbed in. She was noncommittal; I didn't react. We lay there for a time. Finally, I: "This is the first time that I've been to bed with a woman who is eating a candy." She: "Why don't you relax?" I: "How can I be relaxed? You have a slip on, and out of protest, I am now in bed with my underpants on." She: "They're hideous. They should be white." I defended my underpants and tried to relax. We talked over the dog. Finally, she turned around and pretended to sleep. I thought that she was asleep. Finally, after about half an hour I turned off the lamp; she woke up, was very cold. I put on my dressing gown, took the dog outside, and gave him a massage. She got dressed. We made small talk, and then, good-bye. Should she call? Certainly, why not Tuesday? . . . Urgent desire to have the strength to simply finish it once and for all. It's no use. Everything is like before. I am becoming an impotent neurasthenic with ulcer and heart troubles, that's all, and life passes by.

In the summer of 1950, a catharsis came in the form of a famous New York psychoanalyst named Karen Horney, whose daughter, Brigitte, had a house in Porto Ronco and was within Remarque's circle of friends and acquaintances. Brigitte had told him that "God is in the details," when he had "sunk so low that it is shameful; I drink so much and I can't stop myself." She had produced one of those "details" by introducing him to her mother, who immediately took stock of him, but didn't start to work with him until they had formed a social alliance. They began by enjoying food together—Brigitte and Karen Horney would bring Remarque a jar of caviar from Zurich, along with wine, cheese, and raspberries. Remarque would abstain from the caviar, which he didn't particularly like.

His first breakthrough with Karen Horney came as he was evaluating her appearance: "Karen delighted over her steak. . . . Delighted over everything. She is secure with her gray-white hair, her coat, the hat sitting at an angle, which she thinks is elegant, the earrings from Brigitte, and two watches. Compared to her, I feel phony, with my preference for elegant women, society, have to think about that. There is something in it! Take Natasha, the princess. What would have happened if she'd been simply N. Smith? Much less."

It was fitting that following a long, turbulent, but also vapid winter in New York, Remarque began his search for renewal in his haven of Porto Ronco. Karen Horney quickly perceived the nature of Natasha, whom she evaluated as a type, as Remarque records in his diary: "Once they notice that they have the other in their power, they lose interest. If the other escapes, then they claw for him. And they clamp down on the relationship until it doesn't function anymore. They are destroyers. It is typical that they want revenge for something that happened in the past. Only their feelings count. They attempt to push aside others' feelings by domineering and getting the upper hand."

Horney asked Remarque for his definition of love. She asked him what he wanted. "After thinking about it: To be outside myself, not in myself. The other person has what reason and understanding cannot give."

Through his work with Karen, he began to question his entire inner structure and outer behavior. Natasha was the symptom to trigger his own deep feelings of malaise—playing itself out in always positioning himself as the victim. He calls it "victim cancer." In mid-August, he underwent a genuine catharsis, where all that was buried began to unearth itself. His analysis, rewarded in budding self-awareness, is dramatically documented in his diary:

[August 15] . . . I always wanted to be more than I am, or wanted to appear more than that which I am. Always. . . . Perhaps I have found the source of my neurosis. . . . The two things in my life: to appear to be more than I am, and the almost morbid dependency on love. Also, I am too sensitive; I am always acting the worldly man, the cavalier, the ladies' man—yet at the same time, I feel that I am a swindler and I'm no good as a writer, which will one day become apparent. The cause: my childhood. For the first three years, until my brother Theo died, I am haunted by the words of my mother: that I was a very tender child, but had to be neglected, because it took three years for my brother to die. [This is the first time it is revealed that his brother suffered a prolonged illness.] Thus: insecurity, loneliness, denial, feeling like I came in second and therefore was not lovable. I am also beginning to connect the not being loved with loneliness, world anxiety, chaos, sense of hopelessness, the enormous exaggeration of love—whose loss results in: world anxiety, chaos, senselessness. That's why I hang on to love and make renewed attempts to save what is lost. It looks like I have a bad case of masochism when I constantly make excuses for my loved one, when I give up more and more, only to finally lose.

I also have uncovered these memories: that I was ugly, because my sisters, who were pretty, were treated better. I still remember my aunt's saying: "Perhaps he'll outgrow it." And I remember reading a story by Christof von Schmidt, and going in to my parents and asking them for a different name. I wanted the name of Harras, who, in the story, was the faithful vassal of a knight, who was in trouble. Harras, with two pistols in his hands and a knife in his mouth, jumped into the room to save his master.

I had dreams that my parents were ruined and that I, returning rich from abroad, would save them, obtaining cool satisfaction.

Not that I was not loved, it's just that I had less than others. Many of my problems could be a result of all this. Maybe I try too hard to make up for everything now. Such as passing a beggar without giving, and then returning and giving him something and feeling embarrassed. The opulent "throwing" of Christmas and birthday presents, rather than giving with friendly words. I am able to write about tenderness more than to talk about it. My need to criticize is part of my neurosis. The dislike of people, the sarcasm, the denial. There is a similarity in every one of my love relationships, which are loaded (I load) with difficulties, and continue to exist on a one-sided basis.

I have to find out the cause of my resistance to actual work. Maybe I don't entirely believe in it, thus try to avoid it. Daydreaming, building dream castles is my great problem—typical for the alienation of self. . . .

Have to find out why I'm oversexed, why everything is based on sex. Automatically, with every woman; the closeness of every relationship before it actually starts. The overexcitement, which then is externalized and leads to nothing else.

My name-dropping; during a conversation, everywhere, knowing that it is unwise and yet I do it anyway. Always the same. Always to demonstrate that one is lovable.

Always my feeling that my love would grow and grow and never die; it's the others who would not continue. But what did you, great lover, with all your devotion, give to your family? Your sister is dead; she could have been saved. You did not want to support all of them from Switzerland. You were ashamed of your family. You made your father a captain; you raised their social standing. You bothered very little with them. You wanted to hide them. Your father was grateful for the little you gave. You never wanted to really give. Think of all your talk about generosity. What have you ever given? [Out of diary sequence. This paragraph was written five days later.]

All the realizations: the drinking, the lies about car races, the lies about war things, the totally slanted and wrong structure about everything, everything! And for this reason: an important, important day!

As part of his treatment, Karen Horney advised Remarque to write about Natasha, which he did—penetratingly—in his last book, *Shadows in Paradise*, which was published posthumously.

In April of 1951 Remarque met up with Paulette Goddard, and for the first time—because they had been in proximity before—acknowledged the romantic possibilities. He was seeing an entertainer named Gypsy Markoff, whom he admired: she had been in a Pan Am plane crash while touring for the USO and undergone nineteen operations. Since the USO was not an official part of the government, she could only be compensated by the airline and not by the government, and was $40,000 in debt. Her hard-luck story drew him in.

Remarque was seeing Gypsy Markoff in the evening of the day he ran into Paulette. In conjunction with Carroll Righter's astrological predictions, he had decided to move out of the Ambassador Hotel and had just rented an apartment at 320 East 57th Street: "2H rooms, fireplace, view over Manhattan." "Did not believe it. Decided day before yesterday—just like that." It was as though something were guiding him.

Four years before, he had wandered into Hahn's, one of the poshest florists in Beverly Hills, to send hyacinths to Natasha. As he ordered the flowers, Paulette walked in. According to Anita Loos, "He sent the flowers, but he asked Paulette to dine." On April 30, 1951, he only mentions in his diary that he ran into her on Fifth Avenue. He expected and had hoped to run into Natasha. Paulette asserted, "He asked me to dinner the next Friday night. I had to break a date to go, but after that we always had dinner together."

Things progressed rather quickly, although Remarque is reticent in his diary. At first, he reports the events without comments: "On the evening of the 4th Paulette Goddard dinner at Pavillon. She only got one necklace from safe. A 'choker.' To Copacabana after Pavillon. Two Jewish comedians, very good. I don't have the right appreciation for comedians. Then to El Morocco. I don't remember how Paulette got home." (He later reports that he sent a note of apology.)

"On the 8th with Paulette to Pavillon. It became a heavy evening. Drank a lot. With Bruce Cabot, the Cassinis. Club. Lost Paulette."

His diary entry for the next day notes: "At noon, went for a walk with her. Pretty gray dress, through the green park, she looked young, ate at the Stanhope, then back."

Later, he went on his rounds without her to the Knoedler Gallery, then to a dinner party with David O. Selznick and his new bride, Jennifer Jones, Joan Bennett, and Anita Colby. He "drank too much again," and went on to El Morocco, where he drank more. He got home to a photograph of Paulette, which she had had delivered.

The rest of 1951 was spent struggling with the last chapter of *Spark of Life* while beginning to be energized by Paulette. Although he did not care for one of her best friends, Anita Loos, referring to her in his diary as an "idiotic monkey," he was starting to be smitten by Paulette. She disarmed and beguiled the depressed Remarque, just as she had done so many years before with the depressed Chaplin. Her tonic was as potent as ever. Remarque's escalating ardor, combined with the struggle to be level-headed, is affecting. The diary entries, tracing the growth of their relationship, move from New York to London to Porto Ronco to Paris to Madrid:

[May 19]: . . . Paulette in black sweater, gigantic white skirt; $100,000 of diamonds around her neck. Very pretty, radiating life. . . .

[May 24]: Ate at Paulette's yesterday evening. Her brand of economy: whatever is not finished is stored in the refrigerator. . . . At night, she is resting next to me. Strange. Familiar apathy. . . . Paulette suddenly decided to fly to Paris on Monday. Did I object? Quietly, she is putting a loop around my neck. I would prefer to be alone. . . . Finished book! Now, only translation needs to be read. . . .

[May 28]: . . . In the evening Paulette. Bread, lobster, blueberries, butter. Paulette brought sprats. Stayed. Until yesterday at noon. Breakfast, took her home. In the evening, we ate here. She left by herself. She is: clear, understanding, childish, shrewd, dangerous, simply there. Good conversations. Quick and to the point. She is pretty in her many dresses. Radiates in the morning, with untied pajamas. Marlene complains about her.

[May 30]: . . . Depressed yesterday. Much pain in back of head, eyes. No reason. In the evening Paulette; Balenciaga dress—black, dramatic with pink. . . . Next day to Pavillon for lunch with Marlene. The usual hen party. N. was there. She avoided me, got up and left. Afterward, I felt weak and sweated (although this has happened to me with Paulette, too). Marlene about Paulette: her theory, Paulette has troubles with money. . . . In the evening, Paulette—buzzing, lively, laughing around. I'm sorry for the person who falls into her hands! He'll have half a leopard around him. . . .

[June 19, Paris, Hôtel Lancaster]: . . . Last night telephone conversation with Paulette. That devil had spent the weekend in Fairfield, because she is in a play for Jack Wilson this summer! [Jack Wilson was Natasha's husband.] She was there to study N., I bet. Certainly.

[June 26, Porto Ronco]: . . . Still thinking of Natasha; Paulette . . . Nothing from Natasha on my birthday [his fifty-third]. Anticipated the worst with Paulette's visit. Could be those newspaper articles about Paulette and me. Found out only today that Paulette had sent flowers for my birthday. . . .

[July 5]: . . . Letters from Paulette. As before: not full, but clear. Undecided, distant, evasive reaction. She wanted to come; I wanted to avoid it. I will lose her; then I'll have regret.

[July 23]: . . . Had been drunk for more than two days. One evening I ended up flat on the Piazza (with van de Velde, my Dutch publisher). Paulette is on the *Ile de France*, left on the 18th. Letters and cables. . . .

[August 4]: . . . Paulette in London. Telephoned. Letters. Paris. Telephoned. Letters. Arrives Wednesday. . . .

[August 2]: Paulette arrived during a storm, rain, floods on the 8th or 9th. Bellinzona, no train, bridge near Biasca destroyed, highway under water. I waited, then finally went back home. Street to Locarno was flooded; stayed at Bruno Canavese's; connection with Paulette, who was alone on the road. She finally got back across the flooded Tessine bridge. Got a call that Paulette had gotten through. She arrived at eight in the evening. She had been the only one who managed with the post bus to get through with a suitcase full of jewels (and that diamond necklace), a makeup case, and a basket with a magnum of champagne. She waded through water up to her stomach, street construction, and across miles and miles of broken railways. She drank vodka and ate caviar. She was radiant. Not cold at all. . . .

Paulette wanders through the house, goes swimming, laughs, relaxes, happy, clear, goal-oriented, and apparently without any complexes. She feels good to me. She moves things into the right light. She's beautiful, and walks around like a clever seventeen-year-old. . . . Good, slightly guilty (because of little work done) days with Paulette.

[September 15]: Paulette, beginning of Sept. to Paris for a week—to see Anita Loos, etc. Back on the 9th. Swimming, sun, eating, drinking, laughing—I can hear her, from the upper rooms, laughing alone. . . .

In the evenings with Paulette, all the candles are lit. . . . She is delightful, refreshing, and lively. . . .

[October 1]: Paulette left for Paris yesterday. Before that: Bally and Bodo

Brunner here . . . disturbed over Paulette's presence; Bodo, like most men, practically fell over Paulette; had typical reaction when he saw that she was polite and uninterested. . . .

Paulette got drunk one evening. Had too many grappas. Fell down, walked around in her nylon panties to her own surprise. Finally, the scampi and grappa came up and then there was peace. A lot of warmth from a real person.

Evenings. The cat, sleeping on the chair; Paulette is in front of her on the floor, watching her, falls asleep herself. Morning, noon, evening, this warmth: arms that reach high above her neck, the total ability to let go. That which has always been impossible for me. Head above water, while swimming, natural, proud. Everything that I do not have.

[October 20]: Gray days. . . . Telephoned with Paulette in Madrid. Will return today. . . . Found a yogi, influence of Paulette, tried to exercise with him. . . . Drank too much again . . . sent flowers to N. and a few lines. Had dreamed that she stood somewhere in the street here in Ronco. Depressed afterward. . . . Strange, I have the feeling that it's over, over in me. As if now that Paulette is here the other thing is in the shadows. . . .

[November 7]: . . . Don Antonio, priest from Ronco, falling all over Paulette. Paulette, since she had promised, went to church with me on Sunday. . . . I assume that my trip to Germany will be very brief. [He was planning to go to Germany for the first time in twenty years to do research on his next novel, *A Time to Love and a Time to Die*, concerning a soldier returning home from World War II. Remarque felt, for authenticity, he needed to see Osnabrück in order to conjure up the appropriate sensations.] Paulette was refused visa for Germany. . . . It's good to have someone here. Does one work less?

[November 16]: . . . Will not go to Germany before December, visa expires end of November, too short. Paulette's visa declined by German consulate in Zurich (they never change).

[November 18]: . . . In the evening to Tavern, drank. Finished several bottles. At some point Paulette was angry. The reason was because I had told the barmaid to get her a taxi, that she should go and I would stay. She screamed and hit me. It was upsetting. There was nothing I could do. She was insulted, on the stairs, in the car. I had no desire to hit her. Outside it was impossible to calm her down—there were too many people and it was raining. And then at home I didn't want to do anything with her. The whole thing was stupid and should not have happened. . . . Gradually, I desire to go to New York.

[December 9]: Paulette left on the 7th. To Barcelona to make a film [*Babes in Bagdad*, United Artists, released in 1952]. She called today. Those were good, happy weeks we spent together. Warm, lively, close. How little one needs to write down, if one is happy.

[December 14]: . . . Worked on my new book. . . . Europe has become too stifling for me. Things like *Der Spiegel*, a magazine that is looking for old materials about me with which to blackmail me; they bother me more than they should. Letters from Paulette, poetic and with feeling. Telephone calls from her. The scale: knowing that if I were to make a decision between her and N., it would go to her, without regret, but with reason. Otherwise I would be like someone who has hidden himself and pretended to be dead. . . . I have no desire to go to Germany. Not only because of the *Der Spiegel* matter, but other things. The only reason to go is to see my father and to pick up the money from Dresch [a leading German banker] before he goes bankrupt or whatever.

[December 19]: Call from Paulette in Barcelona. Cheer. Still occupied with the *Der Spiegel* matter. Decided not to go to Germany before summer. First, finish draft, the new one. Then I'll start the new book and so forth. I tried to think about when my complexes became stronger. It started after *All Quiet on the Western Front*, the fear. I had the fear of a swindler. At the same time, the past, which reemerges. Just like now. Always. As always, the fear of what might happen. And how I can do it. How I can earn enough for Peter, for me, the house. Just like the movies, books are in a crisis because of TV.

[January 1, 1952, Porto Ronco]: . . . Read into the New Year in the bathtub. Later a call from Paulette. She was with Spaniards. She wanted to go to sleep yet was excited. Had drunk some champagne. Delightful—that slight confusion of love and not understanding why we are apart.

Shortly into the new year, Remarque understood a bit more about the ways of Paulette. She always seemed to know just how to do things, but occasionally her plans backfired. Since she had been denied a visa into Germany, she decided to try a connection. She gave her passport to Stanton Griffis, former United States ambassador to Spain and Argentina and a spurned beau. He had wanted to marry Paulette; she had put him off. Even if he hadn't shown it, his pride had been wounded, so giving him her passport was unwise. He confiscated it because Paulette—vanity in full cry—had altered her birth date. Remarque, amused and annoyed, writes in his diary, "Now she is without a passport. . . . Griffis, seventy years old, took revenge like an old woman.

He fits a certain type of American who, behind his smiling façade, suddenly shows his real face. That's why he was ambassador to Argentina and Spain. Polly had been careless. Now she had to get a new passport from Washington, which can take a long time. Exactly what the old guy wanted."

With Paulette more and more in his life, work took on a new resonance, as did time. "Twenty-three years ago I published *All Quiet on the Western Front*. In another twenty-three years, I will be seventy-six years old. My life is practically at the end. How quickly twenty-three years pass! How much faster will the second twenty-three years be? And should I get as angry over things?"

The intent of his work certainly had changed since the publication of his most famous novel. It has been said that *Spark of Life* was the turning point into a new way of thinking, a new expression, a new form of protest. Striking out against political oppression had seen him through *All Quiet on the Western Front*, *The Road Back*, *Flotsam*, and *Arch of Triumph*. Simultaneously he had been in combat against oppression in his serious romantic relationships. Now, there was new growth on both fronts. He addresses himself to a different kind of future, seriously, and then humorously in regard to a different kind of woman: "Something is stirring in me as if my life of fifteen years ago (before I went into passion) is coming back. I probably don't even realize yet how much I have lost and destroyed; but if one really comes back again, and starts again, then nothing was lost."

Richard Arthur Firda captures some of the reasons why *Spark of Life* was such a watershed:

> In the 1930s and '40s . . . Communism and Fascism became for Remarque the harbingers of tyranny symbolized in the mass state. Tyranny, Remarque believed, was a resolute part of political conflict, especially in Germany itself. Yet in each one of his novels, the author confirmed his stand against group resolution of political conflict under the banner of either Socialism or Communism. It was always a chief interest of Remarque to portray the way of individual enlightenment in the nightmare of political and historical change. *Spark* places the reader for the first time, as no previous novel by the author had done, into the extreme center of that change itself. Hope emerges there as a sustaining quality of human life and without a strain on the probabilities. *Spark* is a fine imaginative work on one of the darkest passages of human history.

This is not to say that Remarque forgot what Germans had done in Germany and elsewhere. If anything, he devoted the major body of his work to exploring, exhuming, and exposing the German consciousness, and examining the aftershocks of the atrocities. One of the biggest testaments to Remarque's courage and success in writing *Spark of Life* was that in 1952, in conjunction with the American publication, it was published in Germany by Kiepenheuer and Witsch.

In 1952 José Ferrer, the man the *New York Times* called "the man of the month, last month, and probably next month," became interested in a possible dramatization of *Spark of Life*. He got in touch with Remarque, who was interested and began putting down ideas. A month later a contract arrived, but Remarque was beginning to have second thoughts. A letter to Harriet Pilpel reveals how exacting he could be in business matters:

> I tried to wade through the Ferrer contract. To do it . . . and to concentrate on a new book is too much. It is to do the work of an agent, a lawyer, and to repeat it all in letters and phone calls and to be an author besides.
>
> I am very interested in the deal; but either one has to have somebody who knows all these things exactly or one has to do it oneself. That I give you instructions and you go to Reiskind [Edwin M. Reiskind of Friend and Reiskind, the lawyer for Ferrer] and Reiskind to Ferrer and back is a waste of everybody's time and money.
>
> The problem is: a) Ferrer is an actor & a director & a producer—as far as I know not a playwright. He will contribute valuable advice and ideas, but can he write? Or have I to do all the writing? b) The side-rights. Film, television, etc. He wants 25% as co-author, 40% as producer. That gives him 65%. He forgets that the contract format is for plays, not for plays after books. The nature of the book has to be considered.
>
> The best will be to wait till I am back. . . . It will only cost a lot of money to negotiate in this difficult way.
>
> What about your 10%? And what about your fee?
>
> I propose: to try to close one contract for the rights for the play—and separately to negotiate the other. Which means: if Ferrer wants the book for a play (without me, but maybe another author) that is one thing, my cooperation another. The first should be possible without the other.
>
> It is difficult to explain. I have nobody to type English. I just can't write reams of difficult English. I must work on my book. . . . Love, Eric.

After many discussions and a lunch meeting, Ferrer decided the material was too grim for the stage.

There were many requests for foreign rights for *Spark of Life*. Small outfits as well as large approached Appleton-Century-Crofts. The Mada Publishing Company in Tel Aviv, Israel, offered Appleton $25,000 to publish in Hebrew, saying, "It is unlikely that our Government will authorize a larger sum for publishing rights." And owing to a serious paper shortage in Israel, Mada planned a limited edition of 1,500 copies.

Remarque was always very pleased to be published by a small house because he thought them to be more meticulous; the advance was secondary. When a request came for the right to publish *Spark of Life* in Icelandic, Remarque said, "Yes, please do. Advance is not too important—ask them for an offer."

In New York, Appleton-Century-Crofts went into a second big printing of *Spark of Life* two weeks prior to publication, and promised the most sustained ad campaign ever for one of their books. It was immediately fourth on the best-seller list; Daphne du Maurier's *My Cousin Rachel* was first, and Herman Wouk's *The Caine Mutiny* was second. Appleton-Century-Crofts put $20,000 into their initial advertising campaign: they took out five consecutive full-page ads in the *New York Times*, as well as full-page ads in the *Chicago Tribune* and the *Herald Tribune* and released posters and imprinted postcards. They were rewarded by brisk sales; Orville Prescott in his *New York Times* book review made it clear that he thought it a worthy if not tough subject: "To read *Spark of Life* is a heartrending experience. . . . *Spark of Life* is not just pitiful and horrible. It possesses great narrative power and authentic suspense hinging on the question: Which among the tormented will be alive to witness the certain defeat of the tormentors, the defeat of which is heralded by the sound of the approaching American artillery?"

Despite the success of the book and the efforts by the publisher, Remarque decided to leave Appleton-Century-Crofts, get out of his contract, and go to Harcourt Brace with his next novel, *A Time to Live and a Time to Die*. His editor and translator, Denver Lindley, had already signed a contract with Harcourt Brace, and Remarque was interested in following him. His advance for the next novel was $30,000, with another $10,000 upon delivery. Remarque was quite pleased: "Did not get everything, but enough," he records.

Paulette was still in Barcelona, finishing *Babes in Bagdad*, but she kept up a steady dialogue with him. Lively postcards, chatty, witty letters, and sexually charged phone calls would become her hallmark through twenty years of being with, yet often away from, Remarque. As Anita Loos put it in assessing Paulette's fabulous appeal to men, "She was hard to get." It was her elusive yet emotionally vibrant quality that so appealed to Remarque. "Good to have her more and more," he records. "It is something one looks forward to. . . . One should not stay with people who are going down; this sounds heartless, but most of the time one cannot help. . . . One should not let them hang around, otherwise they take you down with them. Everybody needs positiveness."

In contrast to Paulette, Jutta, his father, his sister Erna, and her husband all made demands on him. For him, Paulette represented the most positive and independent energy force he had ever experienced.

The plan was for Paulette to return to Porto Ronco, and then they would go to Paris, back to New York, and then, in the summer of 1952, to Germany. The day before Paulette was to arrive, Remarque came to a major realization: he was moderately happy—if a little stir-crazy. For months he had been very much alone, missing Paulette, but diligently working to complete a first draft of the new novel. For the first time in his diary, almost daily he writes, "Continue to work." On March 3, 1952, he looks back, and forward: "For 13 years, I have not spent this many evenings at home. The last time was in Westwood. That time in Hollywood! The last year with Natasha! That time with Marlene! Was I crazy? Probably. For sure. Paulette: the frontal experience—be open."

The knowledge that Paulette was for him was confirmed in Paris. They left Porto Ronco under a full moon; everything seemed perfect.

"Ate in train with Paulette. Everything is always the first time for her. [One of the big secrets of her triumphs.] In the morning Paris, Easter morning. Noon to Place de la Concorde. Ate at Maxim's. To Musée du Jeu de Paume, pictures. Paulette loves Degas. . . . Then a walk. Paulette, who is always hungry when looking at delicatessen stores, becomes crazy and buys everything. In the evening to Tour d'Argent. Paulette drunk, magical. . . . Yesterday on ship. Two large luxury cabins. Warmth. Trust. Feeling. Lively. Love. So many things are simpler. Everything is normal. No neurosis. No more guilt. Paulette is good for me."

In March, Remarque and Paulette made a trip to New York so he could move into his new apartment at the Ritz Towers, which was finally ready. This was to be a more permanent winter base—he had bought this apartment rather than renting, as in the past. Jutta, who had decorated much of the house in Porto Ronco, had once again been busy measuring, buying curtains at Altman's, finding just the right Windsor chairs, as he wrote to Harriet Pilpel: "I will just have a bed in my apartment—no sofa, no chair (will borrow one and a card table to write on) and a few lamps. It will be

Paulette and Erich on the terrace of Casa Remarque, ca. 1952.

Paulette snapped by Remarque on the stairs leading to the dock, ca. 1951.

rather bohemian—a few rugs, books, but no place to sit or to put things. I am looking forward to it."

It didn't seem as though he needed anything else in the apartment but Paulette. She made him feel as he never had in his life: "Every evening with P. Time flies. Still, wonderful feeling. No more anxieties. The wonderful view outside the window and her influence. I get up early in the morning. Read Yogi—Hatha Yoga. Occult. Bought Bible. . . . At home a lot in the evening. Eat lobster, beef tartare, salads (Old Denmark), drink Moscow Mules and here and there a Chambertin '37, mild and strong, the way one should be oneself. My glasses, bought at Baccarat, are extremely thin. P., who is warm, radiant, and complete, wanders through the apartment, the streets, and the meadows of Central Park. We spend the evening without light, because so many lights are outside the window, creating a sense of the un-real, and then P., with her beautiful carriage, shoulders, and back, comes to me. Rain, thunder, blue clouds in front of the window. How could I live so long without a view? In every respect I have a relationship: it's in the eyes, intellect, spirit, and soul."

One night while he was still in New York, Remarque finished Graham Greene's novel *The End of the Affair*. That very evening, he ran into Natasha in the street. She asked him up to her apartment and he went—for a short visit. He found her "lovely, fragile, nervous, and wilted." He told her he would call her before he left for Europe. He didn't.

In late June, Remarque sailed on the *Nieuw Amsterdam* with Paulette at his side. They docked in Amsterdam, spent a couple of days going to the Rijksmuseum to see the Rembrandts, Halses, Vermeers, and Ter Hooches, then they went on to Germany—first stop, Berlin, and finally, Osnabrück. Remarque records his first sensations after twenty years away:

German officials in green uniforms. Checked passport: "We did not expect you," the one who checked said. He wanted my passport one more time to show a colleague who didn't believe that it was me. We went on. Gray skies, people on bicycles. The Dutch student who was driving us: "What do you feel after coming here for the first time after twenty years?" "That it's raining," I said.

We went through Osnabrück. There was the church tower without any enclosure—everything in ruins. Hakenstrasse No. 3, my old home, was not there. Most of the streets were new. Johannes church was not totally destroyed. Suesterstrasse destroyed. Vogt house as well [the home of Karl Vogt of the Vogt Brothers, who had employed Remarque in an early job as a tombstone salesman]. Hoberg house and garden to a lesser extent. [Karla Hoberg's house was where he took respite after the overwhelming success of *All Quiet* and was able to write some of *The Road Back*. Although the intent of the return to Germany/Osnabrück was specifically to do research on his new novel, *A Time to Love and a Time to Die*, the trip would also serve as background for his later novel *Der schwarze Obelisk* (*The Black Obelisk*), to be published in 1956 in Germany and in 1957 in America.] We saw everything only by driving by.

We got to Bad Rothenfelde and saw my father on the balcony of a pretty house. He was standing with my sister Erna, her husband, Walter, and their fourteen-year-old son, Klaus. My father was in good spirits; my sister looked pretty—although wilting a bit—I have to remember that she's 52. I like the 14-year-old. In the evening to bars. Fat, sharp-eyed owners with their typical comments. Much wine, home late.

With Walter Rudolf to Hannover, and then into Berlin, where there were mostly empty places, rows of empty blocks where houses had once stood. In the evening, we went through the town. We ate at Maison de France, where there were no German wines. Paulette and I sat outside. Like being under water. The people seemed totally strange. I had no connection. It was something foreign. . . . It was like a dream. Everywhere we went seemed unreal—the sounds, the people . . . seemed as if they would all disappear. No feeling of humanity, warmth, or reality. Everything felt separate . . . as if on a stage—in a bad play. Neon lights, the street shadows, the ruins, the German look; this unreality, this artificiality was impossible to penetrate. It was a city of masks: the people were empty, empty, like zombies. Raped souls. Souls that have been commanded down to the last breath, whispering, silence. There was so little noise. The politeness was mechanical. Inappropriate faces were made at me, however. There were looks. Suddenly, I realized what I had always known: that one could command them to do many things. Instead of souls, they have mirrors that reflect what has been ordered to be done. There is hardly any humor anywhere, in anything. Berlin is a city without illusions; life is naked; it functions. There is still the pressure of danger. One looks up as soon as an airplane flies overhead. Will it bring bombs again?

. . . The Berlin zoo had been bombed out. All the elephants except for one had been burned. The last one stood there, waving his head back and forth. Crocodiles were burned. The apes, lions, and tigers ran away. After a hunt, they found the apes in an antiques store, throwing old china around. The birds survived the Grünewald fires, and lived in the ruins, singing in the ruins above death. Life started to beep again, flowers started to bloom among the ruins.

... In the afternoon to visit Lotte Preuss [a former lady friend who had written him an impassioned letter about *Three Comrades*—not a sentence of which he believed]. Lives on a wide street, many flowers, balconies. The room was somewhat stuffy. Lotte is too fat, smelled bad, bad odor from mouth. Kissed me, had to hold my breath. No hot water in the house. We sat on the balcony. Through all the years she had kept her excitement for me alive. My miserable attempt to explain to her that there is nothing between us anymore, that it had been a youthful episode, that she is making more of it than she should. It was terrible, this conversation with this aging woman. She told me about a book she had written about me, and that I had to provide her with the ending. She wanted to publish my poems and my letters to her. Her frightening conviction that she is the right one for me. I had to get away. I called a taxi. She went with me to the train station. Her shabby coat of green-blue velvet, gathered in the back, the hat with the veil, the fat face, the hopelessness, the tragicomic silliness; it was all wrong, and touching, but nauseating.

In the evening, a visit with Dr. Johann Stumm, Berlin chief of police. Terrible boredom. New house, garden, guarded by police. A burgher family: a wife with a behind the size of six horses' asses; a daughter with a hamster back, and the host, jovial, mayoral, very much Berlin. Regarding the horrors: the cases are all exaggerated in the press ... finally, I left.

During his visit, various people—whom obviously he hadn't seen in years—came to him asking for money, which he gave. He found these experiences disturbing and evocative. For example, there was the widow of an estimable physician, who had "disappeared." She went to visit Remarque at the Hotel Steinplatz, where he was staying. They reminisced. Athough she knew all of the fashionable restaurants and clubs, most of her teeth were missing. She explained to Remarque that no matter how she tried, she could not get fat because of such long periods of hunger during the war. Then there was the waiter, who had been an actor, and while serving Remarque reminded him of his illustrious bygone career. Remarque, ever polite in situations that saddened him, smiled and nodded, privately recalling only one film role the waiter had played—that of a waiter.

On July 22, Remarque and Paulette left Berlin: he flew to Munich and she to Paris, and their separate lives began again. He says, "It was good to have seen it all. A cycle finished."

A new cycle had begun with Paulette. They would be nomads together. They would winter in New York, summer in Porto Ronco, and spend time in between in Paris, Venice, Rome, and Milan. They played quite hard, and spent lavishly, so they had to manage to fit in enough work to maintain their mutual standard of living. Paulette, who adored Paris—mainly for the shopping—spent a lot of her time there at the couture houses. She was always proud of having an "off-the-rack" figure, which made it so much easier to walk out with a few creations. Sometimes Remarque would accompany her, sitting with his leg crossed, smoking and smiling indulgently and saying, "Yes, Mummy, I like that." (He liked to call her Mummy, and she often signed her letters to him "Mom" or "Ma.") When she was not buying dresses, she was in some jewelry store, spotting things that she would longingly tell Remarque about later. As much as Paris pleased her, Rome became their city. Paris held too many memories of Marlene for Remarque to ever be entirely comfortable there with another woman. He and Paulette often went to Rome and lived in splendor at the Hotel Danieli for as much as a month at a time. After they were married, they rented a palazzo there for several seasons.

Paulette began to fit in with some of Remarque's friends, but others disliked her intensely. Most could only observe their relationship without really understanding it. Long before they married, they were a seemingly devoted couple—just as Paulette had been with Chaplin years before. From the beginning, although they had separate residences (which they always maintained; eventually it was individual apartments in the same building), they were perceived as a serious couple.

Paulette seemed all the more American in Porto Ronco. She had a grasp of Italian, with which she could make herself understood, and was admired for her efforts. Most feel, often inexplicably, that she did make Remarque happy. Licci Habe, the wife of the German journalist and novelist Hans Habe, and a longtime dweller in Ascona, was around Paulette through the friendship of their men. She was never close to Paulette, but over the years the four were together often enough for Licci Habe to form definite opinions and theories: "I think they had quite a lot of things in common. They both adored money, and they both had money, so they couldn't say, 'You love me for my money.' Both had a name, so they weren't vying for those things in their relationship. Both were very good-looking, both were successful, and both liked beautiful things—especially Paulette. I never saw anybody who was so adoring of gifts—any gifts at all. Once she explained to me why she received so many presents in her life. We were all together at a restaurant on New Year's Eve, and the owner was giving ashtrays away. They were the most horrible-looking things, but Paulette just raved about them. It was puzzling. When we got outside, she told me her philosophy. She said, 'Listen, Licci. If you get something, you have to make a lot out of it, because otherwise, you won't get anything. You have to be happy to get presents.' She explained to me something peculiar that always made me a little sad. She said that for her, presents were her salary. And so she got from Erich the most beautiful things. Never small stuff. Big diamonds. Big rubies, and sets. She had sets of jewelry that she called her 'pullovers.' Meaning that she could 'put' a matching diamond or ruby necklace, earrings, and bracelet over anything and look wonderful. Erich gave her a ruby heart brooch from Bulgari's in Rome that could have belonged to a queen. It wasn't for people just walking around. But that was her standard."

Robert Lantz concurs. It was a hot summer night in New York, and he and his wife, Sherlee, had just moved into a new apartment, which was bare and yet to be decorated. They had a few guests over, including Remarque, Paulette, the painter Rolf Gerard, and his wife, Kira. Paulette's beauty was certainly decorative, as was Kira Gerard's jewelry. She wore a large yokelike necklace that looked incredibly impressive. Later, Lantz asked Paulette how she had liked Kira's jewelry, to which she replied, "Splinters, my dear, splinters." Lantz recalls that Paulette had one ruby necklace that Remarque had given her that dropped clear over her shoulders, but that basically she bought for investment, not pleasure.

In addition to jewels, Remarque indulged Paulette's passion for caviar, which he did not like at all. Licci Habe remembers one particular event that was indicative of Remarque's passion and deference toward Paulette. It was the evening before his birthday:

Six of us were invited to dinner, and Erich had decorated his huge terrace overlooking the lake. He had put carpets down, hung Renoirs on the stone walls, and had even managed to hang a chandelier. It was an early, warm evening of June 21—the longest day of the year. The famous Rosa was in the kitchen making something. I don't remember what kind of dinner we had. I only know that Erich brought out a jeroboam of champagne, and caviar. Caviar! The kind of jar you see in stores that takes up the whole window. Well, he bought the whole round thing, and he didn't even eat caviar! He didn't like it. But Paulette adored it. So, on his birthday he brought enormous amounts of caviar for her. And with a big spoon—like a ladle—he dished it out.

So I said, "Erich, you are serving caviar like goulash!" Poom! He put it on the plate. . . . But he didn't touch it. He just enjoyed the ceremony. You don't do that if you don't love somebody.

According to some, generosity was not one of Paulette's attributes. As it had been with Dietrich, Remarque once said to his friend and fellow Ascona dweller Victoria Wolff, "If I were sick all the time, Marlene would be wonderful. Unfortunately, I'm not always sick. Marlene just gives and gives. And Jeanne [Jutta] just takes and takes." Wolff does not remember his talking much about Paulette. However, she has her own memory of Paulette's lack of largesse: "We were in Zurich in the garden of the Hotel Baur au Lac, and she told me that she had a beautiful present for me—just beautiful. I said, 'What is it?' She said, 'You'll love it. I'll go up to my room and get it for you.' And when she came down, she brought the fashion magazine L'Official, a French fashion magazine that weighs about six pounds. She said, 'Oh, you'll love it! It has marvelous things. I just clipped a few pages out, because I want to have those dresses copied.' So that was her present for me."

The actress Evelyn Keyes, who at one time had been married to John Huston and had remarked that Paulette actually swam in her diamond necklace—keeping her head way above water—candidly recalled Paulette's nature: "Perhaps what I should have copied was her acquisitive talent. Not only did she have plenty of diamonds and emeralds picked up from some man or other, she also had gathered a fine collection of paintings, of the Modigliani and Renoir genre. Generosity for her did not always operate the other way around. One Christmas I gave her some perfume; she responded by sending over a half-eaten turkey."

Ellen Dunham, formerly Janssen, remembered her being generous on several occasions. "She was very, very nice to me when she lived here for periods of time after Erich died. She was very thin and we had the same figure, and when I was invited out to a dinner party and had to be dressed to the nines, she would lend me one of her evening gowns. I would go over, we would have a bottle of champagne together, and she would give me a dress to wear."

Dunham also remembered a rather nasty tale, about how after Remarque had died, Paulette would always go to Olly Vautier's (Ellen's mother's) house for Christmas luncheon. She loved venison, and so Ellen would always make a venison roast for her and would serve the meal on plates that happened to be the same service as one that Remarque owned. And Paulette would say, "Oh, they're the same plates as Erich's and I hate them because you can't really see what you're eating because they're so busy. I like white plates. If you want the rest of my service, you can have it."

"I said, 'Yes, I would love it because you can't buy it anymore.'

"So, a few days later, her chauffeur came over with a big box; inside was only part of the service—everything was imcomplete, and some of the pieces were in disrepair." Ellen Dunham is of the opinion that "all of Remarque's friends absolutely hated her. Absolutely detested her. She was so hard, and she would take off when he was sick, and she was bored stiff with Ascona."

In late November of 1952, Karen Horney was diagnosed with lung cancer and died a hideous death by choking two weeks later. This was a major loss for Remarque, which was somewhat softened by his perception of what he now had: "Life that goes on: Yesterday evening call from Paulette. The warmth, intensity, precious with the melancholy of time, the never-owning, the possessing—well, it's like possessing a rainbow."

Life indeed went on to completely alter Remarque's perspective of what Dietrich had meant to him, now that he had what he considered to be a lasting love. While Paulette was away filming, he had dinner at Dietrich's. She, too, had moved into a new apartment. Remarque was disdainful: "One evening at Puma's. Gave me something to eat. She ate potatoes with butter. Glued to her TV set, half-furnished apartment, not enough light in the living room, awful blond and beige of the floor. Hollywood elegance. . . . Gone, this beautiful legend, Marlene Dietrich. All over. Old. Lost. What a terrible word."

Perhaps he protested too much. He was feeling safe for the first time, and perhaps was exercising the luxury of being smug and a bit brutal. Paulette soon returned to set the tone for his next several years: "P. rearranged things in the bedroom—the rugs, the furniture. She lay in her underpanties on the floor, like a picture in *Esquire*. Then later in the kitchen washing dishes, half naked. I took a nap with her and then we went for a walk. Park Avenue with the Christmas trees, the department stores on 5th Avenue decorated with many lights. How colorful! How wonderful!"

All through 1953, as Remarque struggled to finish *A Time to Love and a Time to Die*, he was tinkering with what he called "the Vogt novel," which would become his tenth novel, his most autobiographical, and, some say, his finest, most mature work. Its title would be *The Black Obelisk*.

He felt like a hack writing *A Time to Love*, because Harcourt Brace was impatient to receive a best-seller and Denver Lindley was eager to get the work completed to coincide with his contract deadline. He wanted a final draft, to prevent Remarque from continually changing the text on him. The more impatient he was, the slower Remarque worked. He was earning a reputation for being not only pokey but difficult to reach, unavailable when it was urgent, and almost impossible to correspond with when he was in Switzerland. Business associates always tried to tag him before they would receive his disappearing-act letter on the day of his departure.

It was Harriet Pilpel who now appeared to help with these sorts of situations. Pilpel was a master at dealing with Remarque. Discreet, warm, amusing, and with a mind like a steel trap, she acted as the go-between. She was reverent and practical with him. She devoted enormous amounts of time to his and Jutta's complex tax matters, as well as structuring his contracts, answering copious numbers of inquiries regarding rights and permissions, taking personal meetings with publishers, editors, and potential clients, as well as handling his occasional lawsuits/legal tangles. She also acted as a sensitive, optimistic adviser, laying out what would be the best plan of action for him.

Though she was completely devoted to Remarque, she often irritated him—certainly her huge bills, which seemed to arrive all too frequently, made him very grouchy. But he never considered leaving her for another firm. He appreciated her unswerving concern for him; he valued her incredible prowess, and he always knew he could unburden his less desirable traits upon her: his crabbiness, his doubts, his fears, his need to go over every detail of his business matters.

Remarque reveals in his diary that he had outlined *A Time to Love* ten years earlier, which checks out with the Remarque archivists Dr. Thomas Schneider and Angelika Howind, who think that there had been a proposal and an outline for a novel circulating that was originally called *Der Funke Leben (Spark of Life)*. It was retracted and later evolved into *Zeit zu leben und Zeit zu sterben—A Time to Live and a Time to Die*. The English version substituted the word *love* for *live* because it was more commercially viable. The novel deals largely with the subject of concentration camps in the East and a German soldier's attempts to come to grips with his conscience. It appears that the book, and its possibly negative reflection upon the German "image," caused a major flap and resulted in a voluminous correspondence between the German publishers, Kiepenheuer & Witsch, Remarque, his agent Felix Guggenheim, and his secretary Olga Ammann. The outcome of which was an effective publisher's censorship (with Remarque's concurrence) and the printing of what amounted to two versions of the story. The censored one appeared in Germany and Warsaw Pact countries. It wasn't until thirty-five years later that Kiepenheuer came out with an edition that represented the original text. In the archives lies documentation of the censored text and its many versions, but what is also documented is Remarque's obsessive involvement in each stage of the manuscript. Those close to Remarque felt it came from a deep-seated insecurity and the inability ever to top the success of *All Quiet*. Denver Lindley, who was in a sense his faithful Seeing Eye dog, wrote to him in Porto Ronco in a letter dated February 26, 1954, commenting on the process: "Your changes for the first four chapters are now in hand. I have made almost all of them and I must say I think the net result is very good. . . . In a few cases I have made the changes in different words from yours to accommodate the eccentricities of English usage. There are some things one cannot do in English ('it were the rats' is impossible: 'it' always takes a singular verb) but it's really amazing what one can do, if you begin by taking a deep breath."

Ernst Graeber is Remarque's protagonist in *A Time to Love and a Time to Die*. It is interesting that Remarque felt such antipathy toward this work as he was doing it—both he and Ernst were undergoing somewhat the same spiritual, moral, psychological, political, and emotional crisis. No wonder the work was arduous; he was constantly exposing his own nerves, twofold. In order for Ernst to return to his native city during a three-week furlough, Remarque had to return to the ruin that was Osnabrück.

Remarque, of course, heightens Ernst's experience, turning it into an odyssey: his home is destroyed. He can't find his parents. During his search for them he meets again the daughter of a family friend; the daughter is being guarded by a Nazi informer who sent the girl's father to a camp. A clandestine romance develops between Ernst and the girl, Elisabeth. Marrying her would signify the maintenance of old values, yet Ernst is influenced by childhood friends, now high up in the Gestapo, who represent the new Germany. He is torn between being smart politically or saving his soul. At first he is dazzled by what connections can do, but his salvation begins when he meets a particularly odious SS man through those connections.

The weights are lifted from Ernst's eyes as he realizes that if he listens to and digests these atrocities, he will become like those committing them. He seeks the counsel of his former professor, Pohlmann, a German Aryan who is himself in hiding because he had hidden a Jew.

"Pohlmann's answer is that . . . the burden of responsibility lies with the old and not the young."

Eventually Pohlmann is arrested and charged with collaboration. He disappoints Ernst, who is evolving into a die-hard anti-Fascist. Pohlmann doesn't belong in the old Germany, won't function in the new one, and thus, his spirit must be buried. Although his role in the novel is a featured one, Pohlmann is conceived and executed as a natural tragic hero. In a sense, it must have been a schizophrenic endeavor to write about young Ernst and aging Pohlmann, for Remarque was looking at two sides of himself, had he remained in Germany.

In *A Time to Love*, Remarque also continues the exorcism of his sister's murder, as Hans Wagener points out: "There are several indirect references to Remarque's sister Elfriede Scholz. . . . The most obvious reminder of Elfriede is . . . when Graeber sees a newspaper photograph of the head of the German People's Court, Freisler, the man who sentenced Remarque's sister to death. The newspaper reports that four people had been beheaded because they did not believe in the German victory anymore."

The fate of Ernst Graeber is chillingly ironic, and very much in keeping with Remarque's own cynical view of life. The Russians break through the German lines, and a bloody battle ensues, from which Ernst emerges unharmed—except psychically. He feels the waste of war in a ragingly profound way, and so when ordered by a brutal Gestapo officer to shoot four Russian prisoners, he kills the officer instead. He turns to the Russian soldiers, indicating that he is freeing them: "The Russians looked at him. They did not believe him. He threw down his rifle. 'Go, go,' he said impatiently, showing his empty hands." As Ernst walks away from them, one of the soldiers picks up the rifle and shoots him in the back.

This is the first book dedicated to Paulette—"To P. G."

The next few years were relatively benign and productive ones for Remarque. He still had the Ménière attacks, for which he received nicotine-acid injections, and he slept a lot, because Paulette adored sleeping, but psychologically and physically he had rallied. He had stopped drinking, made all the more difficult by the fact that Paulette had no intention of doing without her vodka and pink champagne.

They had been together for two years. He wanted to play the piano again, and so Paulette ordered him a spinet. This was cause for great excitement and celebration. He rearranged the room for it, bought a special lamp, and when the piano arrived at noon he sat down and played until dusk. His thoughts went back to the time in 1919 when he'd had to sell his piano in order to get his first novel published. That evening, in gratitude, he gave

Paulette one of his Chinese Tang horses and took her to dine at Pavillon.

Enormously happy with Paulette, Remarque found he was playing the piano and painting again, as he hadn't in years. He was seriously questioning his future as a novelist. And he would soon write his first play, which would have its premiere in one of his least favorite cities: Berlin.

Paulette maintained her independence with her own busy schedule, which he very much approved of. He seemed to worship her. Occasionally, he accompanied her to a television studio, for her appearance on *The Milton Berle Show*, *The Sam Levinson Show*, and *The Martha Raye Show*. He would sit in the control room and be amazed by how it was all done, and by Paulette. "They shoot with many cameras. They sit in glass cages likes a bomber crew, with many gadgets. The blue lights from the ozone lamps; the romance of technology. How quick Paulette was with her responses."

In the late spring of 1953, Paulette was off to Hollywood to film her third movie of that year, *Sins of Jezebel*. She would be gone about a month, during which time he continued to wrestle with *A Time to Love*, somewhat encouraged that he'd written seven chapters without revisions—only to become undone by Hemingway's winning the Pulitzer Prize. He records with rancor: "After 30 years of work for his weak last work, *Kiss of Death*. He should get the Nobel Prize for his complete works: Deadly Kisses!" In fact, Remarque was making a joke about the Nobel Prize and the Hemingway oeuvre, not realizing Hemingway would indeed get the Nobel Prize the next year. But Hemingway's tribute seemed to annoy him so much that he decided to plan out the rest of his own literary life—having been told by an astrologer that he had twenty more years. He called it Program for Future: "1953: one novel; 2 plays or 3 sketches. Then: plays for 15 years. A few novels here and there, songs, music, chamber music, opera, musicals (the novels in part will be satires. I want humor). Beginning at 70: large novels; lyrics. Two books: Letters to My Son, and Essence of Life (a short book). Will see what becomes of it."

Remarque returned to Germany that summer on his way to Ascona. He had one funeral to attend—that of Joseph, his devoted houseman, who had died at forty-three after working for Remarque for twenty-two years. He went on to Bad Rothenfelde for a day to see his father, who was now eighty-seven and with whom he now had a moderately good relationship. Remarque found himself studying his face, feeling it might be for the last time.

At the beginning of 1954, Remarque spent some time in London with Paulette, who, at forty-four, was making her forty-fourth movie, *The Unholy*

Four. He then left her and continued on to Porto Ronco, where he read Malraux, bought the Swiss artist Paul Klee's *Pink Witch* for Paulette's room, and thought about success and happiness:

Desire to get on with other things. Enough of these dark times. Thought about my complexes. Thought that one is strongly connected to the success of *All Quiet on the Western Front*. That I don't want to belong to it, and yet do belong to it more than any other. With the success of that first book, I immediately became an outsider. . . . I always think that I don't concentrate enough to get more done. But I notice this emotional concentration even when I'm reading newspapers. I physically feel things—an increase of breath, heartbeat, rushing of blood—even during the simplest show or movie. Maybe I'm not as unfeeling as I thought. I always try to suppress feelings—forbidding myself to feel happiness, to open up and allow it to penetrate. I think of it as if it were a criminal act. Giving in, is weakness. My reason for drinking so long: I'm unable to face people sober, even myself. Drinking freed, relaxed, minimized, enlarged, projected what was hidden in the chambers of my psychosis. . . . The deepest feelings I remember ever having: the few times I went with Fritz Hörstemeier to paint . . . probably because I was totally relaxed. I have to start from there again—to find that feeling, enlarge it, transfer it to the present. Otherwise, I will not live.

Remarque was an omnivorous reader, and like most writers, extremely discriminating, giving the nod to few. But when his reading took him places he could not hope to go in his own writing, his admiration turned to envy and seemed to result in a loss of creative ego. Malraux and Baudelaire caused him to flounder again: "Read *Voices of Silence*, André Malraux. Brilliant. Sometimes even too brilliant. Very interesting theories, results, and views. Embarrasses the art historians; he makes more associations and has more understanding. Same as Baudelaire, who knew more about art than ten professors who wrote about it . . . everywhere one can find excellent formulation and very often depth. . . . I'm stuck on second chapter, time to stop, in despair."

Although he and Paulette were not officially living together, he worked to make Porto Ronco feel like home for her. He was always trying to think of what she might like, such as the shipment of white hyacinths that he had planted in her honor. Her long-distance calls to him did everything, he said, short of magic. So when, after she was finished filming, she wanted to meet him somewhere "fun" in Europe, he was happy to leave Porto Ronco, something he wouldn't ordinarily have done. "Strange," he comments, after a "call from P., sparkling and questioning whether I would come. Strange, my entire life is spent defending and excusing myself for working."

He took the Lancia, called for Paulette in Malpensa, Italy, and drove to St. Moritz, where they shared a gigantic suite (separate bedrooms). They stayed for a month, relaxed, she skied while he watched her from the terrace. Even though relaxed and reasonably happy, he was upset about the new novel, how the German publisher was receiving it, and the compromises that he had made that had to do with the current German mentality. He would forever speak out against the Germans, in his diary as well as publicly:

Kiepenheuer & Witsch are afraid of the book. The Germans are afraid of everything. And since the Germans are so sensitive, publishers want to justify their every action. . . . They want to change Communist to Social Democrat; they want to take out the last three chapters, and they tell me, "You were not here. You couldn't know everything. It was different than what you think." . . . With silent disgust, finished German edition for Kiepenheuer, sent it off. Read in *Times* . . . that Judge Fritz Eickhoff found 20 Nazi policemen not guilty. The accusation was that while driving through the Warsaw ghetto, they had shot 20 Jews, because their captain had told them that Jews were not worth the gas if they didn't shoot at least one of them. The judge said that the 6 jurors declared that the accused did not realize "that they had committed a misdeed." Nauseating!

At the end of March, he and Paulette returned to Porto Ronco, and within a few days she left again, to do some looping (voice-over) in London. Remarque drove her to the airport in Milan in a Jaguar she had recently bought herself, and as he was driving back to Ascona, something strange occurred: "Without any reason, I ran into a wall by the lake. There was not much traffic, it was a straight road, I was driving in 3rd, I don't understand it. Because of the contact with the wall, the front wheel blocked; if I had been driving faster, the car would have rolled over. . . . The car was badly damaged on the right side and had to be towed away. . . . Later, P. called, and I didn't tell her anything, but the next day it was in the papers that we had been in an accident, she heard it on the set, called again, and I explained what had happened. The eerie thing is that Righter had forecast that accident practically the day before, so that I drove extra carefully with the car in 3rd gear, but despite that, if I had been going 20 kilometers faster, the car and wall (because it was so thin) would have gone over the embankment."

*In the living room at Porto Ronco,
1954, four years before Paulette and
Remarque married.*

RIGHT: *Skiing in St. Moritz, ca. 1953.*

The funeral of Remarque's father, Peter Franz Remark, in Bad Rothenfelde, 1954.

Carroll Righter was Remarque's Hollywood astrologer, whom he had started using in 1940 after he had been recommended by Dietrich. Righter, who valued Remarque as a "long-time client," gave him a special rate of a hundred dollars for a yearly chart, and drew up monthly lists consisting of good and adverse dates.

A few months later, in June, he had taken Paulette to Malpensa and was coming back in a driving rainstorm, and had just come to a stop light when the gear shift broke—it just fell apart in pieces. All he could think about was if it had happened a half hour earlier, when he was racing along the road with Paulette.

The next morning he got a call from his brother-in-law, Walter Rudolf, telling him that his father had died. In three days, Peter Remark would have been eighty-eight years old. Remarque felt guilt and sadness that he had not been in touch more often:

> I had wanted to visit him on the 12th for his 88th birthday. Now he will be buried on the 12th. I am mourning. Why didn't I go sooner; if I had only written him that I was coming, then he would at least have had something to look forward to. Strange: as if a piece of me has passed. Sad thought, mourning, regrets.
>
> I arrived on the 11th at noon in Osnabrück. Walter met me at the station. To Rothenfelde in the afternoon, to the cemetery. Looked at deceased in the basement of the church. The coffin was open, the waxen face of my father with hands as young as those of a young man, a distant look. He had died in the morning of the 9th at 8 A.M. He had gone the Sunday before to church without a coat. The church was cold, he had caught a cold, and by afternoon he had a high fever. They gave him penicillin, and by the next day his temperature had dropped, but he wouldn't eat. He got up in the afternoon, walked through the living room, and looked out the window. He 'had to see whether everybody was still there.' Wednesday morning, he drank some fruit juice, and a little bit later my sister wanted to give him cognac with an egg; she placed the napkin around his neck, turned around to beat the egg in the cognac glass, turned to give it to him, saw that his eyes looked strange and far away; she called out, "Father!" shook him, he sighed twice, and then it was finished. . . . The nurses came to wash and dress him; the barber shaved him and cut his hair.

After an eight o'clock Mass and nine o'clock funeral, there was a traditional breakfast, followed by a lunch in a local hotel for all the relatives whom Remarque had not seen in thirty years. Remarque then went back to look at his father's room.

Looked at his things, which were clean and orderly. He never wanted to give anybody any trouble. His room was empty, cleared, nothing left of him. I looked at pictures, his belongings. He did not have a single book of mine. I never thought of giving him any. I wanted to bring him my last one as a birthday gift. Many things too late. Why didn't I come sooner? I could have done it. Why haven't I done many things?

In the afternoon, the relatives left, except for Aloys. The next day I got up early and went to the grave. In the evening, I went back to his room, but by evening there was a trace, as if something had returned.

Just as we wanted to drive to Osnabrück, a thunderstorm came up. As we sat in the car, it started to pour. I felt that it came from him, that he did not want me to leave.

I had the same feeling in Osnabrück. I walked through the streets, through Hakenstrasse, Suesterstrasse, with the moon following. Something had ended, totally.

The lonely station, me waving, Walter and Erna staying behind.

Next morning I decided to have a Mass read for him. Something had to happen. He had to have help. I chose from the Tibetan *Book of the Dead*. Sent telegram to Walter to have a Mass read. Since this was his belief, then he should have what he believes in.

Felt better. But something has changed forever.

Everything that Remarque wrote addressed issues that seemed timely and important. Many people felt he had more talent for being provocative than for being a great writer. In 1954 his Austrian friends Marietta and Friedrich Torberg recommended him to the director G. W. Pabst, who hired him to write a film script about Hitler's last ten days in the bunker.

The film script was based on the book *Ten Days to Die*, by Michael A. Musmanno, who was an American judge at the international tribunal of the Nuremberg Trials. Hans Wagener summarizes the film's essence and Remarque's intent: "The film followed the actual historical action very closely, except for the introduction of the fictional character Wurst (played by Oskar Werner), 'a young captain who is finally shot in a confrontation with Hitler himself. Wurst's idealism is sensitively contrasted with Hitler's decision to flood the Berlin subway system as a last stand of insanity against the Allied invasion of Berlin.' During an interview in Vienna, Remarque stated that he had taken on the project as a result of his lifelong concern with fascism in postwar Germany."

This was the beginning of Remarque's promise to himself that he would take a rest from writing novels and turn to plays and, more and more, film. Even though Remarque had done several drafts of the screenplay, Pabst overlooked his efforts in the final credits, which read, "According to a film story by Erich Maria Remarque. Scenario by Fritz Habeck." In fact, Remarque was not really able to move easily into a second career as a screenwriter or as a playwright. Four years later, when he adapted his own *A Time to Love and a Time to Die* for film, the final credit was given to Orin Jannings.

His work on the script for Pabst had gotten into the papers, and his brother-in-law, Walter, who felt close to Remarque after the death of his father, wrote a proud and generous letter to him:

> We learned through the papers that you are hard at work. They told of the script for the movie *Hitler*, which is to be filmed in Vienna. We wish you all the best in this hot and controversial affair. . . .
>
> Your money was plenty and what is left will be used for the stone. Music, nurses, and priest are already paid.
>
> Dear Erich! Can't we give you anything you might like? After all you will be in Europe until the end of the year, maybe the piano would give you some respite from your work? Just send a postcard saying you want it, and we can take care of its transport to you right away.

With Paulette near his side, not much seemed to bother him. Inching toward divorcing Jutta, he was still hesitant—as he noted in his diary, even more so after spending a rather drunken (twelve bottles of beer) evening in Munich with Ingrid Bergman and Robert Rossellini. Bergman and Rossellini both confessed that their relationship wasn't ideal, but with three children and so much publicity, divorce looked impossible. Remarque knew how much his own divorce would cost him and was stalling, despite the fact that he "would not keep the house [Casa Tabor] without P."

In August 1955, *The Last Act*—for which Remarque had done the screenplay—opened the annual film festival at Edinburgh, Scotland. Remarque's only published political essay, the title of which—"Be Vigilant!"—was the last, cautionary line of the film, was handed out. The article, a warning against what had happened in Germany, ended dramatically:

The great part of the German people want peace and democracy and have had enough of Hitler and his associates; nonetheless, the forces of reaction are not dead.

They are agitating and working and awaiting their chance, and they do not consist solely of former Nazis; they also include those circles which helped the Nazis to power, which did nothing to check them when they could still have been stopped, which put false patriotism above the concept of personality and responsibility, and which worked hand in hand with the Nazis for their own ends.

Let us hope that God will never allow them to come back to power.

But simply hoping is not enough. Education in active democracy is more important. Twelve years of education in intolerance and a couple of hundred years of training in blind obedience cannot be so easily eradicated.

That is why this film was made.

That is why its last words are: Be Vigilant.

At the age of fifty-seven, Remarque had finally begun to try to please himself. He was simultaneously working on a play, *The Last Station* (*Die letzte Station*), and on a novel, *The Black Obelisk* (*Der schwarze Obelisk*). As it turned out, the play, newly titled *Berlin, 1945*, premiered at the West Berlin Renaissance Theater as part of a cultural festival. This version of the play was performed only in Berlin and never published—in German or in English. Hans Wagener feels the play reiterated the themes of the novels:

> The combination of a life-threatening situation and a love story is obviously vintage Remarque. The theme of denunciation typifying the Third Reich had already been treated in *A Time to Love and a Time to Die*. The idea that the Nazis would retreat underground and then resurface has already been expressed . . . in the epilogue of *Spark of Life*. Furthermore, the theme of the final revolt of the individual against the dehumanizing dictatorship of the Third Reich. . . . Finally, Remarque's anticommunism—his belief that communism, like fascism, is a dictatorship—has already been illustrated in *Spark of Life*.

Perhaps Remarque's first play would have had a better chance of exposure and endurance had the estimable playwright and adapter, Peter Stone, been allowed to remain on the scene. At that time anything that Remarque wrote was an event. News of the first draft of a Remarque play came to Stone in the

form of a phone call from the producer Warner LeRoy, who had taken an
option on it, even though it was written in German.

Stone already had a certain entrée to Remarque, through his mother and
stepfather, who were friends of Remarque's and had a house near his on
Lake Maggiore. That association made it all the more comfortable for the
young playwright to be working with Remarque. As Stone recalls,

> The play had never been performed anywhere, and Warner wanted to
> put it on Broadway, so he asked me if I wanted to, in effect, write it with
> Remarque. It wasn't to be an adaptation of the play. I was to redo the thing.
> And we met many times up at his place on Fifty-seventh Street and in
> Warner's office a few times, but mostly in his apartment. We did a lot of
> work on the play; we actually arrived on a draft together. I enjoyed the
> process very much. He was obviously an interesting man.
>
> When we finished the play, there was a sort of hiatus, and then Erich,
> for reasons that were never made clear, decided he didn't want to do it. He
> didn't want it done. I never discussed with him why, but it was decided,
> and therefore shelved.

It was 1955 and Remarque had been with Paulette for over four years, so
their relationship was not new. Stone felt Remarque was very happy with
Paulette as well as amused by her:

> I went on seeing Remarque and Paulette whenever I was in Switzerland
> visiting my parents. I saw them before and after they were married.
> Remarque would sometimes come over to my stepfather's house alone. He
> would sit and drink a great deal of cognac and talk. He was an extremely
> handsome man. Not in the Hollywood sense, but he was a very, very attrac-
> tive man. It was clear why he was appealing to women. And he used to tell
> sort of naughty—not bawdy—stories about Paulette. It was a fantasy of his
> that she couldn't wait to collect his money. It was a running joke with him.
> How, for instance, when there was a storm on the lake, he would wake up
> in the middle of the night and hear her putting all the metal furniture by his
> window . . . or take the rugs: his passion was collecting Oriental rugs, which
> are quite large, and the only way to collect them is to pile them one on top
> of another, so that he would have them five, six, seven deep in a room, and
> he would love peeling back the corner of one to show another. And he was

always convinced—he'd joke—that Paulette would slip one of these out from underneath the others—which would be quite a chore—and send it off to her mother to keep as an investment. Paulette was always terribly worried about security, and jewelry, furs, and objets d'art were very important to her. . . . And so furs, jewelry, and art took on a much deeper meaning. She had great insecurity about the future. And he would joke about this when he was sitting drinking brandy. But it was clearly joking. They clearly got along extremely well.

The first production of Remarque's play *Berlin, 1945* was in Berlin—directed by Paul Verhoeven, with Kurt Meisel and Heide Marie Hatheyer, one of Germany's best actresses, in the principal roles. Remarque had stayed at his favorite Hotel Steinplatz during the entire rehearsal period because he got an enormous charge out of working with the director and cast and reshaping scenes for an exciting deadline and immediate payoff. He wrote immodestly of the results to Harriet Pilpel on October 10, 1956: "The play in Berlin was an extraordinary success! It had more than 30 curtain calls and the reviews were good. They say that it was the most spontaneous applause since the war; in fact, they hadn't had a success like it for many, many years, and that now Berlin had some of its old theatre glamour back!"

As Remarque was getting on with the new, he was shedding the old. Happier and more secure, he was also more ruthless, refusing to play the victim anymore. He was especially harsh toward those whom he had long perceived as manipulating him—Dietrich being one, as he makes clear in a letter to Alma Mahler Werfel: "As to your question: I have seen Marlene. . . . Do you know the sensation of feeling embarrassed with oneself to have taken someone so seriously once, who is nothing but a beautiful flirt? One cannot bring oneself to tell that to the person, and therefore one is always just a little bit too nice, even though one is disgusted. The stench of publicity of middle-class exhibitionism and false feelings, the pains which are lies, this stuff gets into my nose and smells like an old grocery store. Air, please! Small egotism is the worst, especially if it pretends to be altruism."

Jutta Remarque had long been her husband's albatross—psychologically, financially, and medically. According to him, she was mostly an imaginary invalid, with no known debilitating illness. One thing was clear. Jutta had suffered in some way and received a great deal of medical attention. By the end of 1955, Remarque was close to hitting his limit of tolerance. He had begun the year just barely avoiding being a passenger on the last voyage of the *Andrea Doria*, and he would end the year by trying to avoid being sunk by Jutta Remarque. In a memo sent by Jutta's lawyer, Maurice Greenbaum, to Harriet Pilpel, Greenbaum presented Jutta's litany of complaints: that Remarque had ignored her when she was in the hospital, had not helped her out with medical expenses and had been in the Hôtel Bisson in Paris with Natasha during some of this time. In addition, she had told Greenbaum that Remarque's tax return only reflected his U.S. income and that he had other income abroad.

Erich did not want to return. Increasingly, he would travel, not leaving word where he could be reached, or simply not responding to the correspondence at home in Ronco. When in New York and faced with some unpleasantness, he would let it be known that he was en route to Switzerland. This time, however, he was far from elusive in a letter he wrote to Harriet Pilpel from Berlin, tackling the Jutta syndrome: "I will have to do something about Mrs. Remarque, who seems to now have 3 doctors and a lawyer. I will pay part of her expenses but not all, since she has quite a bit of money in stocks but pretends (and believes, she has a strong insecurity complex) she is starving—and since she has a martyr complex, too, she will have 6 doctors when she knows I'll pay for it all. Understand me, please, she is really sick, I believe, but the reason (ulcers) is psychological. I would like to have your opinion on that, too. I am rather depressed tonight and the only reason I can find is that I have to wait longer to see you. . . . Keep well and don't betray me too much."

This signing off is curious. Occasionally, through their many years of intense correspondence, it might be deduced that he and Harriet Pilpel, for perhaps a brief spell, meant more to each other than merely friendly associates. From 1955 to about 1957, his letters seem quite flirtatious. He addresses her as "Darling," flatters her liberally—almost courting her at times: "I will be very happy finally to come back and to go with you right away to the Chambord. All my love, Eric"; he advises her, comforts her, and never mentions Paulette. It is all inference, subject to conjecture, and perhaps he was just being playful. Or perhaps, because he was more productive, and felt freer and more creative during this period, he was more generous in his expression toward those who he knew were loyal to him. In his diaries he treats her rather brusquely, saying that she "depresses" him, and is always making sour comments about her bills, so it might be a certain shrewdness in wooing her once in a while into making the best deals for him.

Harriet Pilpel, however, was not overly impressed by Paulette Goddard. A good amount of animus existed between the two women, although certainly Harriet Pilpel was perfectly professional—even after Remarque's death, when Paulette fired her. Harriet Pilpel had several recollections regarding Remarque and Paulette:

> First of all, Erich was more French than German. In looks and in manner, he was very much a romantic. He really was a divine man. I remember he told me when he was serious about Paulette that what he needed was a very bright Jewish girl so he would know what he was doing. . . .
>
> Then there was a pleasant day trip that I took with Paulette. It was a day climb somewhere near Ascona. Paulette, who must have been in her late forties, early fifties, came out of her room wearing a hot pink jumpsuit and received wolf whistles all day long.

Jutta Remarque had spent practically a lifetime attached to her celebrated husband. She claimed that Paulette had sexually trapped Remarque, and that by the time his health began to fail in the sixties, she owned his body and bank book. Until Remarque's dying day, Jutta was sure that they would get back together. Ironically, Jutta during the early days of her marriage to Remarque was reported to have been notoriously philandering. The filmmaker Leni Riefenstahl, best known for *Triumph of the Will* and *Olympia*, her 1936 account of the Berlin Olympics, recounted a striking example, in 1927, of Jutta's callous infidelity and Remarque's pitiful desolation:

> Remarque wanted to meet a good friend of mine, Walter Ruttman, a film director, so I promised to arrange a pleasant evening at my home. . . . I was surprised when I greeted Frau Remarque, for she was wearing an elegant evening gown, as if she were going to a gala. She looked wonderful with her red curls, held in place by jeweled combs, and an almost pure white complexion. She appealed not only to me and to her husband, but also, and most of all, to Walter Ruttman—as soon became apparent.
>
> At first it was a lively and cheerful evening. We drank wine and champagne, and, perhaps as a result, Frau Remarque behaved so seductively that she completely turned Ruttman's head. At first I thought it was only harmless flirting, but as the mood grew more animated, Ruttman and Frau Remarque got up, leaving me alone with her husband. They retreated to a dimly lit corner while I remained with Remarque, who tried to drown his jealousy in liquor. . . . Remarque sat on the couch with downcast eyes, his head drooping sadly, and I felt so very sorry for him. All at once Frau Remarque and Ruttman were standing in front of us. "You've been drink-

ing too much," she said accusingly. "Herr Ruttman is taking me home. I'll see you later."

I squeezed poor Remarque's hands, then followed by the other two, I went to the lift and saw them down to the front door. As we said good night, I pleaded: "Don't make your husband suffer so much," but she merely smiled and blew me a kiss. . . . When I went back upstairs I found a sobbing man whom I tried in vain to comfort. "I love my wife, I love her madly. I can't lose her, I can't live without her." He kept repeating these words, his whole body shaking, and when I offered to call a taxi, he refused; so I stayed up with him until dawn. . . .

Two days later Remarque called me. His voice sounded hoarse and agitated: "Leni, is my wife there? Have you seen her, has she called you?" Barely waiting for me to say no, he shouted into the telephone: "She hasn't come home, I can't find her anywhere." Then he hung up.

That evening he came to my flat and wept without restraint, drinking one cognac after another. He kept answering me that his marriage had been unruffled, indeed very happy, until this meeting with Ruttman, and he was at a loss to understand his wife's conduct. He blamed it on some spell, but was certain she'd come back; and of course, he would forgive her completely, so long as she came back. However, she didn't come back. Nor did she get in touch with me. I tried for some time to call Ruttman, but no one answered the telephone.

For almost two weeks, a desperate Remarque came to my place almost every day. Then, unexpectedly, he told me he couldn't stand being in Berlin anymore and was going to a spa; he simply had to get away. He never got in touch with me again.

Perhaps working on his new novel, *The Black Obelisk*, which in Germany was subtitled *The Story of a Belated Youth*, acted as the catalyst for Remarque to proceed with a divorce action against Jutta. Remarque's fictional alias, Ludwig Bodmer, works as a tombstone salesman in the small industrial town of Werdenbrück in 1923, during the peak of inflation in Germany. He moonlights as an organist playing for the Catholic services in the local insane asylum, where he meets and becomes romantically involved with a schizophrenic patient named Genevieve Terhoven, whose other personalities are Jenny, a "distrustful, unattractive person, discontented with everything," and the fair, unintentional siren Isabelle, who "lives in a dream world divorced from reality and seems light and weightless." Isabelle is the version of Genevieve that captures Bodmer, who, as Firda notes, "seems to be worshipping an idea rather than flesh, the idea of love rather than love itself." Bodmer speaks through Remarque's memory of an early Jutta: "During the first weeks this was all very confusing, but now I am accustomed to it. . . . At first I could hardly believe that she was sick at all, so playful seemed her alterations of name and personality. . . . Finally I realized, however, that in the silence, behind these fragile structures, was a quivering chaos. It did not quite penetrate, but it was close at hand, and this, combined with the fact that Isabelle was just twenty and, because of her illness, sometimes of an almost tragic beauty, gave her a strange fascination."

Even though this book—as future ones would be—was dedicated "To P. G.," it was the look of Jutta and Dietrich, who were similar, that inspired his heroines. The delicate Natasha of his last novel, *Shadows in Paradise*, was indeed the delicate Natasha, his former tormentor. The vital American Jewess, Paulette, did not become a part of his fictional canon. His heroines, for the most part, bedevil and confuse him.

Just as Jutta Remarque appeared in many guises in his books, so Osnabrück would continue to reappear though he describes it quite thoroughly in this novel. It was the first time he had tackled his past in such an imaginative and vital way, devoid of any agony during the writing of it. "I had been thinking about writing *The Black Obelisk*, about treating that early part of my life, for years. . . . But there were so many difficulties. I wanted to write about Genevieve. . . . I thought I might do a novel just about her, but it seemed to me it would have been too static with not enough interest. Then I gradually came to feel that I wanted to write about all the other things at the same time—the tombstone business and—that Genevieve could be part of the whole. Scenes with her could be worked in among others, and the whole thing might be moving."

The Black Obelisk provided Remarque with strength that he had not felt since the writing of *All Quiet*. In the first few sentences of the last chapter, he walks away from it all for the second time—fictionally, for the first: "I never saw any of them again. Occasionally I planned to take a trip back, but something always interfered and I thought I had plenty of time. Suddenly there was no more time. Night broke over Germany, I left it, and when I came back it lay in ruins."

Remarque and Jutta were technically married for twenty-four years with a nine-year period in between when they were divorced for the first time. However, even when married for the second time, they were estranged for nineteen years. Remarque's decision to divorce Jutta for the second and final time came in 1956. In June, he wrote her from Porto Ronco of his decision to divorce her. Her response of July 1956 provides insight into their marriage from her point of view; her side of the story, more mysterious, made slightly less so by this letter:

Dear Boni,

    . . . A divorce can only clear our relationship, not that it will help me any, it's too late for that, the damage is done. To describe this condition, lasting for years, as a misunderstanding is bitter for me, especially after you refused a divorce in 1952 and I had to pay for this condition in the meantime with my health.

    All of this waiting was unnecesary, and it's rather cruel to find out after such a long time that you thought it was all just a misunderstanding. You will understand that I see it that way. . . . The decision is yours. . . .

    The most important thing is to get it over with in a quiet and peaceful way. Any kind of excitement, tension, or pressure is hardest on me. After the last fourteen months I cannot risk my health again like that. . . .

    . . . The summer here isn't easy for me. The high humidity is hard to bear. I have great pain. I always have to stay in bed, which weakened me. . . . We tried to get a new medication; two scientists in Copenhagen developed it, and treated patients with Crater disease successfully, but the American Drug Administration hasn't allowed it here yet. We are trying to get it via Canada. . . . I have been treated for a long time with something similar— injections— which try to heal through the bloodstream. The new medication works directly—locally. . . .

    I hope you are well and wish you a wonderful summer.

Best greetings,
Peter

For the better part of the following year, Remarque was elusive and admitted to being so; in a long-overdue letter to Harriet Pilpel, he cites arduous involvement with the production of *Berlin, 1945*, a recently diagnosed heart infarct, and a moderately puerile desire to have somebody else take care of unpleasant matters: "I beg you to pay the bills now if they are normal, otherwise send me a cable. I guess the hospital bills have to be paid right away— Mrs. R. is not able to attend to this as her new attorney cables—she was of course able to get an attorney. If you have any funds paid to me in your holdings anymore, please pay the necessary and tell me how much it was, and I will send you a cable."

Nothing more would happen with his play for a long while (until 1973, when Peter Stone finally got to adapt it as *Full Circle*, directed by Otto Preminger), but his divorce and return to the States were encroaching. Again and again, he turned to Pilpel for professional and personal counsel about everything, but at this time, especially to rant about Jutta and the hovering financial obligations that would be attached to the severance: "I would like to suggest at the moment that she should leave the Pierre—she doesn't want that at all! but I think it not absolutely necessary that I should pay for it. All that can be seen to later. What I would like to know is in what way there could be a legal claim. When we married in Switzerland we married not under a community property agreement. . . . I have not answered the lawyer of Mrs. R. and will not do so. I will write her, as I did before, console her (since neurotic sicknesses are exactly as real ones), and tell her—very friendly—that if she wants a lawyer to negotiate, it would be best that the lawyer contact you."

Although the terms of the divorce agreement were not indecent, they were binding. Remarque was to pay Jutta the sum of $25,000 by June 1958. However, he was to pay her during her lifetime—as long as she did not remarry, which she scrupulously never did—the sum of $9,200 at the start of every year beginning in 1957. In the event of Remarque's death after January 1, 1967, Jutta would receive $50,000.

Then there was the codicil to the agreement: as long as Remarque was alive and Jutta was alive and had not remarried, he would make a payment held in escrow of $2,300 in addition to $9,200 yearly.

Harriet Pilpel took good care of Remarque, finding legal loopholes that let him hold on to as much income as possible. He would not be the one to file for the divorce; that would have to be left for Jutta, for if he did, she could hit him for staggering alimony, which would lead to a complex tax situation. Remarque was determined not to be taken for so much that it would gouge into his lifestyle and his future with Paulette, whom, at this point, he was contemplating making his wife. So Pilpel and he began to work out the components of a game plan.

In order to get a quick settlement, Remarque agreed to pay $50,000 as security, although he was unclear how he could lay hands immediately on that sum. As a compromise, Pilpel suggested that Remarque leave Jutta all his literary properties and contracts affecting them and, in addition, a "chattel mortgage" on his van Gogh painting (worth about $25,000 in 1957), with a right to withdraw the mortgage and substitute cash, securities, or art equivalent in value. Remarque felt that if a settlement could not be struck, he would not contest the separation. He was afraid that there might be charges against Paulette, and so would litigate only the question of support.

Remarque's not being able to find an extra $50,000 might seem exaggerated, if not improbable, but Remarque lived beyond his income, making no concessions where luxury was concerned, or his international tax situation—dating back to 1930. And finally he spent more on Paulette, for whom he bought more grand jewels and good art than he had for any of his other women. He had also been supporting Jutta Remarque in style—as much as he complained about it and she denied it. He also sent his family in Bad Rothenfelde steady money, although not great sums. His tax situation was expensive; he had to pay Swiss taxes from 1940 on, American taxes, and in addition, from 1929, the Germans pursued him for taxes on back royalties.

The paranoia of a self-made rich man is that he will lose it all, which is why Remarque pushed so hard all the time, chastising himself when he let up.

In a Greenbaum, Wolff & Ernst memo concerning Remarque's divorce, alimony is ruled out on a technicality, and a lump sum is favored. If Remarque were to pay Jutta her $25,000 as alimony, he would have to give her additional alimony with which to pay the taxes on the agreed-upon amount. Harriet Pilpel convinced him that legal language would make a real difference.

In order to protect himself in the long run, he had to pay, and did, grumbling all the way. One could almost think he was stalling by the way he would stop things from going forth—such as his agreeing to leave Jutta the first $50,000 in his estate but then violently opposing any long-term security arrangement. He stopped the procedure so many times that Jutta boasted to him of having eight attorneys so far. "I warned him," recalled Pilpel, "that we should settle this before Louis Nizer becomes the ninth."

Remarque was certainly not stalling in a will that he had drafted in December of 1957, in which he refers to Paulette as his wife, having already decided they would be married:

> FIRST: I give and bequeath all clothing, jewelry, books, pictures, paintings, silverware, china, glassware, works of art, automobiles, household furniture and furnishings and other personal and household effects owned by me at the time of my death, to my wife, PAULETTE GODDARD REMARQUE, if she survives me. . . .

THIRD: All the residue and remainder of my property and estate, real and personal, of every kind, and wherever situated, I give, devise and bequeath to my wife, PAULETTE.

On May 20, 1957, Jutta was granted a divorce from Remarque, who was then free to marry Paulette Goddard, which he did nine months later.

Shortly thereafter, Jutta departed from the expensive Pierre Hotel, which had been her home for over fifteen years. She relocated for a while in Munich, then went on to Italy, then the French Riviera, and finally Monte Carlo, where she died in 1975. Her infrequent letters to Remarque over the years show that she did not change much—although she mellowed a bit. The letters are mostly concerned with payments and taxes, or her ill health.

Remarque was ready to return to the States. He would travel on the heels of a strongly positive reception to *The Black Obelisk*. The critics—particularly those in the *New York Times* (Sunday book review and the daily paper)—celebrated this high point in Remarque's oeuvre. In his review, Charles Poore writes:

> The less things change in the novels of Erich Maria Remarque the less they are the same. When we open one of his books we know just about what we will find there: antic figures in chaos, modern men and women fighting and making love in some dark backwash or some looming apocalypse of war. Yet he always makes them new because he has a dazzling facility as a storyteller. They are as contemporary as a weather report, and, in the light of events, often as surprising.
>
> . . . All values are questioned smartly and discussed mercurially; the boobery and the bourgeoisie are recurrent targets of opportunity. . . . The climax of comedy always blends into the beginning of terror, to be succeeded by new, albeit stark, comedy.
>
> "Is your world collapsing?" Bodmer's friend asks.
>
> "Daily," the new Candide replies. "How else could one live?"

The fact that the word *Live* was changed to *Love* in Denver Lindley's English translation of the original German publication of *A Time to Love and a Time to Die* made a sizable commercial difference. In 1954 Universal Studios bought the rights to Remarque's novel for $50,000 up front. Remarque never liked the new English title. He felt that it altered the meaning of the work, but understood that some of what Universal had bought was the title of a best-seller. At the same time, Universal was also paying him $115,930.96 as an installment for the rerelease of *All Quiet*.

This helped to soothe his pride for being turned down by every major magazine for the serial sale of *The Black Obelisk*, as well as being unable to obtain a film sale. Yet, when Joseph Mankiewicz expressed interest in producing it, Remarque turned him down, saying in a letter to Harriet Pilpel that he was a "dilettante who would never get anything done." So, the movie was never made—at least not for an American audience. (Thirty years later, it was made for German television.)

In the summer of 1957, Remarque's mood and countenance belied the little song that he wrote for Paulette:

> When you start very low there is much ahead of you.
> Don't walk too fast on the top.
> There is only room left for you to go down.
> Walk slow, start low.

Remarque was at the Bel-Air Hotel in Beverly Hills—at the behest of Douglas Sirk, the director set to film *A Time to Love and a Time to Die*—to adapt the novel. He was breaking new ground everywhere. Paulette had given an interview saying that they would soon be married in St. Moritz, and in an interview he gave to the *Los Angeles Times* in 1958 he said, "Usually I'm so tired after I finish a book that I don't want to have anything to do with it for a few years. But *A Time to Love* dates back to 1954. I met [the film director] in New York and found him an extraordinarily understanding and capable man. He knew what he wanted to do with my book and persuaded me to write the screenplay.... A writer has to know—and trust—a director. There's an old rule for writers, 'When they make your book don't go near the studio or you'll end up with a fine pair of ulcers!'"

His enthusiasm continued in an interview he gave to the *New York Times*: "It is very interesting writing for the movies. The difference between writing a novel and a movie is like driving a truck and a sports car. In the movie the story must move fast. Keep it going and it will come out all right. You have a good term in English—storyteller. That's what you have to be in the movies."

Remarque's attitude toward Hollywood eased, and he agreed to act in his own film. He would take the small but choice role of Professor Pohlmann, since he liked and trusted Douglas Sirk so much. Sirk understood that movie audiences were not ready for a reindoctrination to Hitler's Holocaust in all of its permutations, or as he put it, "Hitler's empire of a thousand years of history. Furthermore, I thought 'die' balanced 'love' very well. And going back to my idea of a title being a kind of prologue, it announced the theme of the picture. The terrible incongruity of killing and young love."

Ernst and Elisabeth, the young lovers, were played by the newcomer John Gavin and the Swiss-born actress Lilo Pulver, about both of whom Sirk said, "It should be the vehicle of a star, and this was the reason for picking Lilo Pulver . . . for the other part. She, too, was unknown in the States, though she had a small and good reputation in Europe." Remarque had casting approval of both leads, although he was particularly interested in the choice of Gavin for Ernst Graeber, for whom he felt, as he did with all of his protagonists, an inexorable affinity.

Twenty-eight years after he turned down the opportunity to make his film debut in the leading role of Paul Bäumer in *All Quiet*, Remarque found himself on location in West Berlin, about to go before the cameras. Sirk began shooting his exteriors in the ruins of the Tiergarten area, where embassies lay in rubble. Remarque, never more restored and sounding like a young and tremulous actor—which, in a sense, he was—wrote a love letter to Paulette from his favorite Hotel Steinplatz on the night before the first day of filming:

> My beloved little baby, it's Sunday and I'm sitting here not knowing what to do. I've worked. I've studied my part (tomorrow we start shooting). I've walked and now it is 6 o'clock in the afternoon and the most beautiful behind in history walks just out of the Carlton Hotel to charge into a steak of tremendous proportions. I spent two days to combat the flu—one alone with a partridge and a bottle of Bordeaux and two hours of blissful adoration of you. . . . The cold is gone and I am in love with you like you with Mr. Bollinger [the champagne]. This here is so provincial the eye cannot rest anywhere—there is not even a beautiful old face. There is a transportable mirror in my room . . . it makes me slightly melancholical to see only my mournful face in it.

The next day he sent her another letter—one of the few he dated, October 7, 1957—reporting on his supposed debut:

> Dreamboat of Cleveland, I was supposed to start today, we had a hearse, a coffin, and lots of tombstones on the set, I was trembling with stage-fright, and then it got too dark and all the excitement was in vain—tomorrow I

have to be ready at 8 in the morning. Ah, what respect I suddenly have for acting. Lindley [Denver Lindley, his translator, and his wife had recently been introduced to Paulette] and wife are just squares. They admired you to the sky, but they can't talk, they just stare. So do I when I see you. The miracle of you slays me now for seven years relentlessly and more and the longer I know you. Bless your little black heart . . . I just worship you!

He signs it "Anton." Almost always, he uses some kind of swaggering alias in his letters to Paulette, as well as to her mother.

John Gavin was essentially in the same position that Lew Ayres had been in decades before. He was young and green, and this was his big break. The enchantment was somewhat greater for Gavin than Ayres, however, for he not only got to be in something by Paramount but got to act in a key scene with Remarque himself. "Every moment with Remarque was golden," Gavin recalls.

I met Mr. Remarque in Berlin for the scenes that were to be shot there. To my knowledge, he had never performed in a film before or after. I certainly didn't have any judgment at that stage of my life, but I had the feeling that he did it very well, and that he was very strong and impressive in what he did. I so enjoyed meeting him on several levels. Personally, he was worldly and urbane and extremely kind and generous in his time and in his comments to me. Professionally, it was interesting and pertinent that he was playing Professor Pohlmann, who was the conscience and the chorus of the drama that he put together. The character blended into what Remarque was. To me, they fused, not only in their persons and personas, but what they felt and what they stood for. The professor was a character who was aghast at the inhumanity that was taking place before his eyes. I think that Erich Maria Remarque was still aghast; it wasn't outrage, but I think he was profoundly saddened that these atrocities could have taken place. That I was able to do that role—I was young and green and really awful in the several roles that followed it—but I was able to do that role as well as I did was because it was a rich role and I could do it by instinct. And it was because of him. The real come-to-life feeling and empathy of dealing with a character in that picture was in my work with him. He was so solid, so centered that I felt an enormous communication with him—not only as a person but as a character! Pohlmann meant so much, and when he looked at me with those eyes, he just pulled me in and kept me there.

Gavin was so affected by Remarque, who was quite taken with Gavin, that they got together after the filming was finished. It was a memorable visit for Gavin, who, obviously, was aware of Paulette's presence in Remarque's life:

> My wife and I called on him at his apartment, which was identical in layout—and separated by one floor and a ceiling—to Miss Goddard's apartment. We'd gotten to meet her by then as well, and she couldn't have been more lively, kind, or generous. At any rate, his apartment was a very interesting man's apartment. His walls were replete with fine paintings, including a very generous sampling of the Impressionists. He had beautiful antique furniture, but it was frequently threadbare; he hadn't bothered to get it recovered in places. He had splendid Oriental carpets. There were also manuscripts piled all over the place. He served us a Piesporter Goldtröpfchen which was a plot point—that wine—in *A Time to Love*. He served it in Baccarat glasses that I have never seen before or since in my life. They were very simple wine goblets that were so fine, so beautiful, so delicate that, as he showed us, you could take the crystal goblet at the rim and you could press on it and it would go out of round without breaking—almost as if it were made of a rubber material. Remarque didn't show us to be pompous; he genuinely enjoyed his crystal and informing us about it.

Gavin remembered their divergent style in identical apartments: "Miss Goddard's apartment, in contrast to Remarque's mishmash of beautiful things, looked as if it were ready to be photographed for *Architectural Digest*."

And that was very much Paulette. Presentation was foremost. Remarque, however, deeply understood and indulged her. Like a good father, he understood Paulette's Jewish roots that made her detest the Germans, her tendency to learn only what was necessary to get by, and finally her voracious appetite for clothes, jewels, gifts, and compliments, which was one that would never be satisfied. This was the sum of all the parts that he accepted in his love for the new Mrs. Erich Maria Remarque.

CHAPTER EIGHT

FOURTH CHORUS

1951–1958

PAULETTE UNDERSTOOD REMARQUE from the moment they met. Contrary to the popular myth that she was a rich and free spirit, roaming the continents, feeling no need for a permanent home or relationship, she wanted both, and saw the same desire in Remarque. Although it seemed that she had had it all before, at age forty-one, she felt this was different. No doubt there were other factors than Remarque's intelligence, charm, and good looks. His fame, wealth, and villa in Switzerland all helped secure Paulette's attachment to him. She loved being on the estimable writer's arm; she relished the places they went and the gifts she received, and she prized Casa Remarque in Porto Ronco. She found it most enchanting in the early years they were together, while it was still a haven, a love nest, an enormous pied-à-terre. The first time she visited it, in July 1951, she claimed it, writing to him, "I will adore my new house with you. If you have plans to go off to other places I will make the house on the lake my headquarters until you return."

When she first arrived on the train from Bellinzona to Ascona, she found a quaint little Swiss village with lots of pretty shops in back of the large town square that faced Lake Maggiore, with palm trees lining the lakefront and snow-capped mountains in the distance. For many years she would promenade across that square, giving the people sitting in the cafés something special to watch as she went by in her rather out-of-place, and occasionally out-of-season, clothes.

It took about five minutes to get from the village of Ascona to Casa Remarque in Porto Ronco. Ronco was the highest point in the area, and the car would have to proceed up a steep incline where, at the crest of the hill, an oversize door that opened directly on the road could just be made out through the lush foliage. Once inside, there was an enormous living room that ran from the road on one side to the lake on the other. Bright with the golden light of Switzerland's Ticino, its floor covered with rare Oriental carpets, its walls hung with van Goghs, Cézannes, Renoirs, and Degas, precious objets d'art on tables and pedestals, it was a grand but welcoming room. Remarque's huge wooden desk, strewn with correspondence and manuscripts and journals, sat in one corner, a looming presence, and a large, often blazing fireplace kept the room cozy at all times. Clearly, it was a room well lived in and much loved.

The rest of the house was relatively simple. The "servants'" quarters and kitchen were on the basement floor below the living room, and there were two bedrooms and two baths on the second floor. Running the width of the living room was a terrace that overlooked the vast lake and gave the unearthly sensation of being suspended over the water. It led to smaller terraces on lower levels, lined with pots of bright flowers in bloom, which in turn led to paths through the lush cliff-hugging garden that dropped all the way down to the lake. The spectacular and panoramic view of Switzerland into Italy was mysterious and beautiful: the climate in this particular part of Italian Switzerland can change dramatically many times during the course of one day, and bright sun can suddenly become obscured by many strange cloud formations, fogs, and mists.

The lush, multilevel gardens that tumbled down the side of the hill from the main terrace were filled with every kind of flower, bush, and plant. The terraces were intersected by paths, where daily Paulette would take long walks alone or accompanied by one of the dogs, returning with a basket overflowing with the brightest flowers, which had been planted by Joseph, the gardener. They were all heavenly bursts of color and fragrance: yellow, pink, and coral roses, acres of mimosa, hot-pink azaleas, and sweet peas in pale pastels. After jewelry, Paulette loved flowers, and every place she lived was always full of flowers. In the early years at Casa Remarque, Paulette either believed, or convinced everyone else, that she had found nirvana.

Paulette would dress casually, in resort style—with a bit of Swiss Miss thrown in. A full skirt, low-cut blouse, espadrilles, and a bandanna tied over her hair, accentuated by large hoop earrings, was a favorite morning outfit. Paulette and Erich were late risers. If it was a beautiful day, Rosa served them breakfast on the terrace. They both like muesli, fresh fruit, rolls and muffins, and coffee. Occasionally, Remarque would have a *palatschinke* (a large, crêpe-thin apricot pancake) and a piece of grilled meat.

In the beginning, Paulette unintentionally diverted Remarque from his work. She was so pretty, so full of life, and so available while there in Porto Ronco, that he was in an almost constant state of happiness. When Paulette was in residence, he attempted to work but often ended up having a massage and reading while she walked, picked flowers, or swam. There were steep stone steps that led down to a dock on the lake. Paulette took a daily swim here, sometimes in the nude, with Remarque watching proprietorially, occasionally taking photographs.

They lunched either on the terrace, with such guests as Hans and Licci Habe or their neighbors Budy and Robert Keibel, or in Ascona on the main square, at the Café Al Porto or Café Al Pontile or Café Schiff, after which Paulette made her tour of the boutiques with Remarque. Paulette always shopped with Remarque's encouragement and indulgence. From the very beginning of their relationship, he bought her whatever she wanted, and she always wanted something. She could not go into a store without making a purchase, whether it was a pair of cabochon ruby and diamond ear clips from Bulgari or a grosgrain hair band from Elizabeth Arden. Jean Tailer, who had met Paulette at the Palace Hotel in St. Moritz during her marriage to Burgess Meredith, felt that Paulette's still being in her prime was a major asset: "I think she was really happy with Erich. She had everything she wanted, and she still had her looks."

Dinner was the main event of the day. Paulette would dress up, and they usually went out. They might return to Al Porto or Al Pontile, where what they ate was guided by Paulette, who always requested plenty of fresh fish and vegetables. They often ordered a bottle of Soave to start—before Remarque began to drink seriously. Occasionally this ended with a scene, but it was usually smoothed over by the next day. Despite the occasional feud, the life, the villa, and Remarque were a dream that Paulette felt was long over-due. She had had several low points before she met him.

In fact, Michael Hall remembers his first meeting with her, in 1948, while she was filming *Bride of Vengeance*, when she was nervous and angry from the frustration of lost stardom. He was still a relatively young actor, studying with Constance Collier, who was always talking about how amusing and interesting Paulette Goddard was. At this time, Hall happened to be work-ing on another movie, which was next door to the soundstage where Paulette was filming; his trailer–dressing room was outside the entrance to her soundstage: "One afternoon, this enormous door suddenly rolled open and this steaming tigress burst out, wearing a sort of Babylonian Cecil B. DeMille seductress's outfit with a veil going to the ground. She was really fierce-looking and was furiously smoking a cigarette. She was in a rage about something. She was pacing back and forth. I saw her do it hundreds of times—she always did that when she was agitated and angry. I thought: This is a woman in distress. I went up to her and said, 'Miss Goddard, my name is Michael Hall and I'm making a movie next door, and I'm a friend of Constance Collier's and Phyllis Willburn's.' [The latter was Constance Collier's companion, and then later became Katharine Hepburn's companion.] And she said, 'Oh? So what?' It was so rude, I just wilted, and then said, 'Oh, well, I'm sorry. I didn't mean to bother you,' and went back into my dressing room and slammed the door. I could see her looking after me from where she was, and then she resumed pacing until they called her to the set. She went back in, closed the door, and I didn't see her again for about a year or so."

The time after her marriage to Meredith and before her relationship with Remarque began marked the period—1949–1951—when Paulette's career and position were slipping. When Hall met up with her again, he found her more defensive than fierce. She had just ended her affair with Clark Gable, in late 1949, and was trying to learn to work in television. She had a job in Armstrong Circle Theatre, co-starring Lon Chaney in a movie for television. Paulette was badly in need of coaching. Hall understood the demands of the medium and was moonlighting as a coach when Phyllis Willburn called and asked him to help Paulette.

Hall rather reluctantly admitted he wasn't doing anything and could coach her:

So, I called her, and I went over, and she was very gracious and kind—at first. She was staying in her studio house off of Sunset Boulevard, which was all sort of strange and vacant. Her mother had been living there and Paulette was just visiting. I remember this one huge studio room with an L-shaped seating arrangement and an enormous coffee table in the center. On it, there were two bowls, one filled with chewing gum and the other with packages of cigarettes—all sorts of brands and matches from everywhere she'd ever been. But these were huge bowls—fourteen, fifteen inches across. I'd never seen anybody have that many packages of chewing gum!

So we began to work together, and I went every day to teach her this part. We worked on the lines all the way through, because you don't learn the whole thing; you learn it piecemeal. She was extremely difficult to work with. Her memory was actually pretty good, but she would get sort of sulky. She was still very, very beautiful. Perky and pert, but had a very aloof quality. Very seductive, however. We got along pretty well, but she resented any kind of suggestion that I would make. She wasn't learning her lines quickly enough, and every day she said, "It didn't go well today. We had to do these takes over and over."

Finally, I said, "You know, you've got to change your pace. You really have to speed it up and get with it." And she said, "What do you mean?" I explained to her that in TV, they can't take the time. It wasn't like the old days in movies when you broke for a gracious lunch. Anyway, she took umbrage, got very angry with me, and said, "Who do you think you are, telling me?!?"

I said, "Well, I'm the voice of experience, and you either listen to me or you won't make this movie very well. And if you don't make it well and quickly, they won't give you any more jobs."

Well, she looked at me as if she could kill me.

Then I said, "All right, let's go. Come on, hurry up. Let's go, get with it!"

She really was very offended. I said, "No, don't be offended. Let's just do it. Now, get it over with and do it!"

She said, "Who do you think you are? Charlie Chaplin or something?"

I said, "Yeah! Okay. Think of me as Charlie Chaplin, but do it. Now, learn your lines and stop fussing around!"

That's what she needed. She needed somebody who would stand up to her foolishness and nonsense. And from that moment on, we were pals. She blossomed, and learned her lines. And I directed her in those scenes, because in TV they basically told you where to stand and didn't give you direction. You directed yourself, which Paulette had no idea how to do. She wasn't like Dietrich or Garbo, who knew their way around a set and looked out for themselves. Paulette looked to the director to transform her; she trusted him to do that.

Paulette and Michael Hall had a brief encounter when they were more than just friends. It was one of the rare instances when Paulette became physically involved with a younger man, but she could not be forthright about it. She introduced Hall as her nephew. They remained intermittently romantic for a while, and then continued a friendship up until the final stage of her life. Hall felt that he was as close to Paulette as anyone could be to her. "Even with Erich," he notes, "she was often a little removed. With Erich, she frequently removed herself physically, if not emotionally, from his presence. Paulette always kept herself at a remove. I thought that perhaps it was because her father slipped away from the family, and she always felt a kind of insecurity with relationships. She probably felt as if nothing was permanent, so she didn't want to make any firm relationships with anyone, in case they might go away or die. I think she was terrified of that."

She was close enough to Hall to confide some secrets and truths. As she got older, her skin, always thin and delicate, deteriorated to a desperate condition—eventually diagnosed as melanoma. It looked patchy and flaky. She wouldn't shake hands, and she avoided being kissed on the cheek—by women at all times. She could never consider a face-lift. She confided to Hall that, as a child, she had such terrible acne that she would bake in the sun for days on end, trying to burn it off. It worked on the surface for years, but then caught up with her. One of the many dermatologists who treated her will never forget her very real anguish and hopelessness. She called the condition of her skin "a small, but significant tragedy." She railed against his inability to do anything for her, called him some small and significant names, and finally didn't return.

Hall feels he did have insights into her character that others missed. He saw her as a courtesan; "like a reformed whore, she doesn't like dirty jokes or anything like that . . . she didn't like anything that was smutty or naughty." Regarding her intellectual interests, he insisted, "Paulette was no intellectual. She pretended to be. She faked it. Before someone would finish a sentence she would say, 'That's right!' So they thought she got it, but she didn't get it. She'd look at me and say, 'I don't understand. What are you trying to say? Well, say something!' She would get angry because she didn't understand. Yet she wouldn't really educate herself. Even though a lot was missing, she got by perfectly well by pretending."

The seven years with Remarque before they married were a long trial period, a test of how resilient she was. She had finally found where she wanted to be, and yet she wasn't sure of any of it. The wealth, which was high on her list of desirable factors, was not the key factor in this relationship, although, when Remarque finally asked her to marry him, she confided to Michael Hall:

"It's the most wonderful thing! And Michael, it happened just in time."

"What do you mean?" he asked.

And she said, "Baby, I was broke! I was broke! It happened just in time." Through her "courtship" letters to Remarque, one can see her concern about money. Practically pelting him with funny, chatty, caring, and seductive "long notes" from wherever she was, she reveals an undertone of insecurity and need. There is also no doubt of her sincerity. She had the most wonderful of all men, and she knew it: "Hooray! I've found the Holy Grail! It is in a chair, by a large desk, with a lite shining upon it, in a shrine by a lake—overlooking the universe." This was one of the early notes in her substantial correspondence with Remarque. He was in Porto Ronco; she was in Spain filming the low-budget *Babes in Bagdad*, co-starring Gypsy Rose Lee.

Eventually, Paulette couldn't bear to be trapped in provincial Ascona with a husband in deteriorating health, but in the first throes of their romance, after they had been in Paris together in June of 1951, the earth moved:

I'm so in love that I've become completely idiotic. I swoon at your voice (like the kids with Frank Sinatra). How did this happen and why did you leave me? I hated your being on the boat alone. Never let this happen again! I also hate everyone in Paris, because I am not there with you. Remember my instinct told me to take off in advance, but I would have missed the "most important part." The part that made me want to belong to you. This love business is an extraordinary, biological thing. My body changes and is so alive. I'm never tired and always well.

Absolutely nothing happened at the Wilson weekend. [Paulette was invited, much to Remarque's chagrin, by Natasha's husband, the producer Jack Wilson, to discuss theatrical prospects.] Jack told me you were mad about Nat, but I don't mind. She seems scrawny & unhappy. . . .

May this excitement and idiocy and hope never die. I hate everyone, they all seem like sleepwalkers. You are everything that is aware & alive. . . . It just occurred to me that Natasha will be in Europe before me. Could it be that—horrors, now I will not sleep.

Paulette made sure to let him know that what he loved, she loved. And previously not the maternal type, she put a soothing hand to his brow: "Am désolée about the neuralgia. How cruel to have to carry your own hell with you into the remotest and most tranquil of places. This must be fixed! Will work all forces constantly. Your Mom."

From the start, Paulette's correspondence with Remarque is lively and self-effacing. Because they were both so independent, and not young, they had quite a bit to work out. As Paulette's career was winding down, she was forced to actively seek employment and took pretty much what came along.

During this time, between jobs the Hampshire House was her base in New York. It was widely reported that she was renting a house in Switzerland because Remarque did not want Jutta to hear that another woman was occupying the house a good part of the year. They attempted to play down their relationship for as long as they could so that Jutta would not charge years of infidelity to the cost of their eventual divorce.

"The great spell is still working, Señor. I trembled when I received your letter, before reading it! This is not fear, but that magnetic spell that was put in force before you left me! Your shrine at the Hampshire has grown to enormous proportions—dead flowers, scraps of cables, envelopes, French francs, etc. I will never tell you all. Your Swiss friend, P.G."

After her first trip to Porto Ronco, in July of 1951, Paulette immediately gave it as one of her mailing addresses to her mother, who was living none too happily with her third husband, Don, in one of Paulette's houses, on Alta Loma Road in Hollywood. Alta would soon get to know and "worship" Remarque, as her daughter did. He was the ultimate surrogate father and husband that both had been seeking. In a sense, he rescued them and gave them respectability.

In the summer of 1951, Paulette was off with Anita Loos to London and Paris on an assignment for *Look* magazine. Just as she had done for Mexico several years earlier, it would be "Goddard's Guide to Paris" and "Goddard's Guide to London." She was on an upswing, having appeared as the queen of the fashionable New York Art Students League Diamond Jubilee Ball, wearing a borrowed diamond tiara from Van Cleef & Arpels and a filmy costume that exposed her still-alluring midriff; she had also just done a *Milton Berle Show* guest spot. Eager to please and show her worth, she wrote to Remarque:

Darlink amour love, Now that my coffers are replenished I am ready to take off with a clear conscious [a Freudian misspelling]. I put the TV money in my sock instead of burdening myself with a car. Also *Look* is giving me $2,000 expense money for a week in Eng. & one week in Paris—of photos— which seems an honest way to make a living. Anita will do the articles & then I dump her. I swear never to mention such mundane things again. But this is my way of explaining my plans. I waited in vain to receive your itinerary, so went ahead without consulting your plans. Was this a bad thing to do? Have I done a wrong thing? Tell me. Aren't you sick and tired of receiving mail from me? All that too is ended, because here I come! Absolutement le vôtre aussi. Old Faithful.

Paulette played no games with Remarque in terms of her objectives. With admirable brazen charm, she moved right in on him, never faltering in her belief that she was a big part of his life. Her letters to Remarque during most of the fifties offer the best of Paulette. These letters mark her summer in England and Paris and into the fall and winter on location in Spain, and set the tone that she took toward him for the duration of their relationship. As Lois Granato puts it, "Erich was the only one Paulette never had a bad word about."

Dearest darlink, What is my address in Porto Ronco. Let me know where my maid [Anita Visconti] is to stay & I will send my mail to her hotel. Do get her a minimum rate room, but nearby as she can take complete care of me and my room & bring my breakfast & do my clothes etc. etc.

Off to Blenheim for the weekend with Anita to visit your rival [Lord] Marlboro. His complaint is that he can never manoeuvre me because I never stay long enuff. (elusive, that's me) We will get sun and photos of croquet and the gentleness of stupidity. His name should be Bland M.—Princess M. will be there also visiting his son. Am wearing one of my cheap cotton dresses, because you said no silk in the country. Hell, I venture Margaret will have an osprey hat.

... We stayed at Kitty Miller's [Lord Marlboro had at one time been smitten with Paulette. He and Kitty Miller had been part of the Chaplin set and she had retained them as social contacts ever since] last night on the way back from Brighton. Their house is fine. A real home. I see them now in a different light. The place was really perfect. (for England).

Arriving Paris Wed. Will phone because I will be happy & excited to be there and want to share it with you. Perhaps you will return with me for a few days. . . . A few days with thee in Paris. That would be the thing.

Planning to leave nite of Aug. 7 for Porto Ronco. Mission accomplished. So much to see & do with thee. My my whatta LIFE.

In Barcelona to film *Babes in Bagdad*, she took one look at co-star ex-stripper Gypsy Rose Lee's figure and went into a flurry of ballet classes and rigorous massage. The two women became friends through healthy competition. Feeling sleeker than when she had arrived, Paulette turned up for lunch at the studio commissary in pedal pushers, an off-the-shoulder gingham blouse, and freshly pedicured bare feet.

"Where's the plow?" asked Gypsy.

Paulette stars with Gypsy Rose Lee in the Danziger brothers'
Babes in Bagdad, *1952.*

Paulette and Erich just after their low-key marriage,
in Branford, Connecticut, 1958.

"I feel in a back-to-nature mood this morning," Paulette said, "and surely you would know about that!"

Another example of their good-natured rivalry came about when Gypsy Rose Lee received a splendid Christmas gift from her husband, Billy Rose. It was an oversize brooch of emeralds and rubies, set in gold—a handmade piece from Mallorca. Paulette, knowing her jewels, gasped: "There isn't any name for it—it's bigger than a brooch. Why, it's so big, Gypsy could wear it as a complete costume!" Paulette continued to write Remarque from Barcelona:

[Hotel Ritz, Barcelona]: Dearest Warmth, My heart may be broken but my body will be perfect when we meet again. I do the ballet every morning at 11, then the massage. Taking only one cocktail before the late dinner then early to bed (2 A.M.). The dining room opens at 10 P.M. Will be in the groove for Paris!

While reading your letters I have a habit of holding my breath. Your latest arrived before I had breakfast (2 P.M.) and I nearly fainted dead away before coming to the end. The mail is delivered here at 1 P.M. & 9 P.M. No one begins work until noon, then home for lunch until 4:30. Have never been so conscious of time altho I don't know what day it is.

Bought & sent a divine grilled (½-inch thin—like lace) fire screen that holds two bottles of wine. Have Joseph bill me for the Swiss customs. The screen is not for me. It is for The House for Xmas.

Evelyn Keyes is going to marry Cantinflas (the C. Chaplin of Mexico).

Once in Spain, Paulette found that it wasn't so easy to get back to Remarque. The producers of her movie were the sweet-natured Danziger brothers, Harry and Eddie, who had Paulette dressed by Balenciaga but found their picture shooting way over schedule. Paulette knew that it wasn't ideal for her new relationship, but since there wasn't much she could do about it, she wrote him endless letters:

Dearest One, 2, 3, 4, 5, & 6: I adore your photo with the DOG. One day I hope you will look at me like that with complete surrender & real affection (but never let me see it!) What a loving soul you are—with a golden hatchet in your pocket. The letters do not flow & overflow from me now, because I have no more complexes or fears. No more passionate outpourings. I simply sit complacently waiting for the rug to be pulled from under me. Am prurient with well-being. I love you—completely—unreserv-

edly—absolutement. My future work is cut out for me. It is a most constructive job. My work is to please you, tease you, love you, hate you, feed
you, eat you—Be cat & mouse. And pick up a few bucks along the road for
Our Old Age Security. I'll save mine—You can spend yours! Then when
you are 80 you will be completely dependent upon me and I will have you
docile & tamed at long last. If this arrangement does not interest you I can
change to suit your requirements. But I will always be your own. P.

P.S. 11:30 P.M. Jesus Christ—Another fiesta (holiday) tomorrow, so no
work. Will spend a frantic weekend writing you many times. Desperate
again. Thought I was closer to being on my way home, so I got quite flip.
Your own Pete.

Paulette's homesickness accelerated to the point where she almost poked
fun at it, but it is so plaintive that two thoughts occur: either Remarque had
uncovered Paulette's deepest fears of abandonment and feeling unmoored,
or she was milking a powerful theme—in him—for all it was worth.

Dearest Warmth, I wanted to phone today, but did not, because I knew I
would cry. Am so homesick. Let's face it! Being homesick is a vicious circle.
I simply cannot eat here away from you, hence my blood pressure is way
down to 100, which would make anyone feel like crying. If anyone asks me
where can I eat, where do I have appetite I say "in my casa" and big croco-
dile tears pour. Am feeling sorry for myself. But remember what fine
appetites we have, everywhere together. If this picture does not end soon I
will go into a decline like Camille, only I will have pernicious anaemia. Am
starving for you and all for love.

Enclosed is tea to try for the stomach!

I will be 1,000% strong when I pack away some mounds of Rosa's noo-
dles—with you in the house near—always near—never again. Mom.

It took years for Remarque to agree to marry her, but she declared herself
in the first round. One can't help but think that the confidence and eager
projection came from a certain amount of desperation: "I hope you do spend
this time training for a long run. Can you imagine how beautiful and fantastic the House will be in 24 years? Let me garner the loot. Let you sit at the
desk and watch it come in and let's play games together in every hotel in the
world. I love you, Erich. Never again without thee. Never, never, never!"

For the first time, both of them seemed to have a relationship beyond all
value. This was no one-sided desire. Paulette was still very much a beauty,

and as Anita Loos put it, "I always thought gentlemen preferred blondes until I traveled with Paulette."

As much as she swore fidelity of heart, soul, and mind, Paulette was always on the move. She worked a lot during the fifties, although not on any good films. She also invested in her movies, although not very lucratively. In 1952–53, she made three movies—each less distinctive than the last.

Though her films weren't any good, her image in the press improved. Her behavior during *Vice Squad*—released by United Artists in 1953— was a case in point. Although technically she was still under contract to Paramount, nobody even mentioned the term *loan out* anymore. This was welcome work. Paulette's co-star was Edward G. Robinson, who was also suffering a career comedown, but his was for solely political reasons. The Korean War meant that the House Un-American Activities Committee was Red-baiting once again. Robinson had been put on a "gray list," which had the same ominous repercussions as the blacklist but was supposedly unofficial. Paranoia was back, as the studios and unions were demanding testimonies of fidelity and purity from everyone. Paulette, too, would soon come up against this, but for the moment was grateful to be co-starring with someone of Robinson's stature.

Paulette's financial deal couldn't have hurt her attitude. Robinson had agreed to a $50,000 salary for the entire picture, which was budgeted at a mere $200,000—$15,000 of which went to Paulette for only three days' work, which was all that was required of her. She slinked her way through it as "the head of an escort service," winning friends and admirers. "It's just as if a new star had been born," said the wardrobe mistress. "Why Paulette, who has always acted as if she were a queen, goes out of her way to be nice and complimentary to the people who work beneath her. Only the other day she was so grateful at having a dress altered in the middle of the day's shooting, instead of the schedule being changed, that she came all the way back to wardrobe to thank us personally."

Edward G. Robinson also admired the "new" Paulette: "Paulette Goddard will always be a big star, a name to contend with. If in the past she has not always been totally cooperative, we have seen no signs of that during this production. She has been a joy to work with."

Hollywood journalists such as Vincent Rodgers chewed on Paulette's "reformation": "Could the fact that Miss Goddard is now investing much of her own money in the movies she is making have anything to do with the new personality? Does she want to avoid the costly setbacks to a movie production with which, at first hand, she is so expertly familiar? . . . Always one of the most uncooperative actresses with the press, Paulette Goddard has been the subject of as much myth and literary speculation as Garbo herself. So much so in fact, that she has remained very much a woman of mystery. Now she even receives the press with open arms."

There was nothing new in Paulette's attempts to be clandestine about her personal life. She was overwhelmingly happy with Remarque, and although it was the reason for her behavior, she was guarding it as carefully as jewels in a vault. She still threw reporters off the scent by going out with, and accepting gifts such as a star sapphire from her old flame Cy Howard, whom she seemed to be able to keep on a string indefinitely, as she mentions in a letter to Alta some time later: "Saw Cy Howard in Paris. His wife is going to have a baby next week and he says it is not his! He says he still loves and adores me, but why shouldn't he?"

The next picture Paulette made, *Paris Model*, was negligible, but during its filming she made an amazing statement to the press: "Actors and actresses who say they never go to see their own pictures are talking through their hats. You don't have to be a Freud to know that the most fascinating person in the world—actors or anybody—is yourself. Nobody on the screen fascinates me as much as Paulette Goddard. I'm probably her greatest fan, bar none. I see my own pictures six or seven times. I take them in to see what I do wrong and what I do right. There's always room for improvement. And anyhow, I enjoy it."

She rather liked being back in Hollywood, and if she felt obsolete, she covered it with a bitchy sort of panache in a letter to Remarque. Perhaps she was in training for the television remake of the 1939 movie *The Women*, in which she would play the extremely catty role of Sylvia originated by Rosalind Russell. Her friend Jinx Falkenburg had written a book, launching a whole new career for herself, which she writes about in a letter to Erich:

Dear love, I thought Jinx's book a far better character drawing of an idiotic glamor girl than the one Anita Loos worked too hard at making idiotic [Lorelei Lee in *Gentlemen Prefer Blondes*]. Bet you Jinx sells more copies, too. The public seem to like their idiots sincere, not manufactured. Sincere like Mickey Rooney, Clark Gable, & June Allison (she is no. 1 box office now). Did you ever hear of her?

Wait 'til Marlene's book comes out: "The Beds I've Slept In"—Oh brother. I do love you. I like you very much, too. I liked your ads on *Spark*, I love your photos, your letters, your hands, your cats, your breakfasts, your

mouth, your hair pills, your deep & devious ways, your sensitivity, your stub-
bornness, your plans, your dreams, your hair (the way it's long), your body
warmth, your super-philosophy, your humor, your wildness, your chain-
breaking, your physical strength, your soul's energy, and the millions of
facets unknown.

Paulette also consistently wrote him openly provocative letters. It seemed
she was able to excite him as nobody had:

Why do you want more photos and what are you doing with them? If it is
for the old hex bit, everything you've got is working. My heart, soul, and
body reacts with you always inside me. How can I walk about with you
inside me? . . . I did not finish writing the hex because of fear of mail censorship. Here it is: "that he will explode like Oscar Wilde in a deathbed of
satisfaction." . . .

Lover, Lover, Lover: Thank you for the letter and bath of love. Received
two letters & your photo (in one day!) which sends me! You are a very physical looking guy. Will play with the photo like a cat with a mouse. Some
days I will hide it, then take it out slowly and watch it for a few days, then
hide it again. . . . [She puts a star by the words "physical" and "lover," and
then has a key at the end of the letters.]

*physical = F——Y
*Lover = Querido

As Paulette was trying to finish up *Babes in Bagdad*, she wrote a letter to
Remarque that is very honest about the industry itself and also shows that
she had a sense not to take it too seriously:

Whatever I am doing here is certainly the wrong way to live. Picture
making is for another kind of "mensch." It's nice to be a movie star & collect
the dough, but the actual making of the film is a horrible experience. It
could be fun, but everyone takes it all so dead serious. My makeup woman
is in hysterics because I have one eyebrow higher than the other. I let her
pull out my one nice brow, to please her, and paint one on—discovering too
late she pulled the wrong brow, and so it goes. Everyone connected with this
epic is an outcast—either blacklisted in England or have-beens in America,
so everyone is completely off-center—like the people in Ascona. . . . I love
you madly, Sierra Sue.

Her crack about Remarque's cherished Ascona would become one of the few points of contention between them. Paulette grew bored and irritable in Ascona. She found the people and shopping too provincial. The Italian that she spoke didn't make her any more comfortable there, because although it was technically in the Italian part of Switzerland, the language most spoken was German, due to the many émigrés who had settled just before Hitler took power. Paulette made herself a stranger and therefore was never accepted. She would end up there, however, totally dependent upon its people to care for her during her final years. Casa Remarque, the sanctuary that she praised during her early years with Remarque, was eventually to become half prison, half hospital.

Just as Remarque had hired the sharp-shooting lawyer Martin Gang to handle his suit against Enterprise Pictures for payments owed him on *Arch of Triumph*, Paulette now hired him after finishing *Babes in Bagdad* to defend her against her own studio—Paramount Pictures. Her complaint was not negligence, although it might well have been, for Paramount no longer offered her even a scrap of work. However, Paulette was defending herself against having to prove she wasn't a Communist. Paramount had requested a letter of American allegiance from everyone under contract. Paulette had complied and written her letter, which then was judged as not meeting the requirements: "I am not now, nor have I ever been, a Communist. My allegiance is to the United States." Paulette refused to be dictated to, to allow her freedom of speech to be reconstituted in such a way. The right-wingers were also bearing down upon Chaplin again, and Paulette felt particularly incensed about it. He had come to the States for a Hollywood screening of his latest picture, *Limelight*, after which he would sail back to Europe on the *Queen Elizabeth*. While at sea, he received word that the U.S. attorney general was suspending his readmission to the United States until a new examination of his qualifications had been weighed. Although never a U.S. citizen, he was in exile again. And once again, Paulette was a rebel by proxy. But Martin Gang was finally able to persuade Paramount to cease and desist.

There were two more upsetting episodes during this time. The remarried Burgess Meredith waged a $400,000 suit against her for his half of their community property. Although it was settled out of court, the action caused her a good deal of bitterness and legal expense. The next year, in 1954, Joseph Levy died, his will dictating a bequest of one dollar to his daughter. "We won't think about it," she wrote with simplicity and dignity to her mother, but offered her help if needed: "If you feel we should pay funeral expenses, then I think you should make the offer and payment in your name. . . . You let me know what you feel is best in the matter. Of course I would reimburse you for everything, but not enter it in any way."

The nadir of Paulette's movie career was a toss-up, the critics agreed, among *Sins of Jezebel* (Lippert, 1953), *Charge of the Lancers* (Columbia, 1954), and *The Unholy Four* (Lippert, 1954).

Outwardly, she showed her usual enthusiasm toward her new projects. No matter how dreary they might be, she preserved her movie-star sensibilities. In an interview about *Sins of Jezebel*, she was brief but positive, segueing—a bit defensively—into what was happening to her career: "*Jezebel* is a Biblical story, and I loved doing it. Another picture I completed is *The Charge of the Lancers*, in which I play a gypsy. That was fun, too. And I have a tiny part in a film called *Paris Model*. I don't have any ego about the size of my roles. Some of the best pictures I've made had small roles for me. *The Women* and *Hold Back the Dawn*, for example. I think it's very difficult for an actress to be colorful for one hour and 45 minutes. I used to say I'd rather have a short part with long eyelashes than a long part with short eyelashes."

Paulette was excited about playing Jezebel, the gorgeous siren, and was vigorously preparing, as she writes in a letter to Remarque from London, where the picture was being filmed: "Life is good. Life is beautiful. . . . Am off for the day, preparing my body for Jezebel and you (hair, nails—toes & fingers—massage, exercise & steam). Three weeks of preparation, to give you the 'peak' of me."

Paulette and Remarque's romance was now a conversation piece in New York, London, Paris, St. Moritz, Rome, and Hollywood. Elsa Maxwell wrote glowingly of them in her column in the *Hollywood Reporter*: "But this much is true, they have spent more time together this past year than any other unmarried couple I know—and they seem more important to each other than ever. . . . It's easy to see Erich's charm for women. I said as much to him not long ago, adding 'But in Paulette, Erich, you have met your match. With good reason I call her my bronze butterfly.' 'Her wings may be bronze,' he said, 'but she can fly higher than any kite I've ever seen.' These two people, I think, give each other something both have been seeking—companionship."

Cole Porter agreed. Occasionally he traveled in the same social set as the two of them, and one time happened to be at the Palace Hotel in St. Moritz at the same time that they were there. Having dinner with the glamorous pair became a delightful habit, as he says in a letter to Paulette: "We missed

TOP AND ABOVE: *Paulette wore her famous "engagement ring" diamond necklace to a New Year's Eve party in St. Moritz, ca. 1954.*

you and Eric in the grill tonight. Your table was occupied by a dull-looking gentleman & a lady who looked like quite a good horse."

"They had so much to say to each other," Porter recalled of Paulette and Remarque. "And they were so full of laughter."

Paulette had to be cagey during these years. She arranged to be away or making a film if Remarque needed to be alone to work, and then would make herself available when he sought her company. Occasionally, she'd make him wait a little too long, so that desire would give way to anxiety and real need. He, on the other hand, never let her know that there was a possibility of marriage until around 1956.

In 1955, he was going to meet her in Paris, where she was staying at the Ritz Hotel for a protracted amount of time. Her sojourn was ostensibly for a purpose. She had been asked—although not signed—by producer Bill Marshall (married to the French movie star Michelle Morgan) to make a French movie whose working title was *Angel Puss*. "It will be called *Angel Face* when it's released in this country," Paulette explained. "I play an adventuress."

Instead of speaking "Hollywood French," Paulette decided to tackle the language, enrolling in courses at the Sorbonne. Never a halfway person, Paulette threw herself into this project: "I go to the Sorbonne all day long studying French. I'm in a small class, and fortunately it's all of young men. But I wear one of my old wedding rings so none of the young men will ask to carry my books home from school."

Paulette moved from the Ritz into an apartment on the Left Bank. She spoke only French. She dressed in black and wore comparatively little makeup. "Big eyes are the rage," she said, "and I never had any problem with those." She took it all very seriously. For a little diversion she did go out with King Umberto of Italy once or twice, collecting a diamond and emerald pin. Perhaps feeling guilty, she wrote to Remarque, "This is not the greatest time for us to be in Paris together. No walks or leisurely lunches in the sun. I too am all purposeful, but simply to make you love me. Here's to high hopes for the future. That will be sumpin'. This place makes me feel romantic. I'm nuts about you, and being alive. Please order the champagne rose per la casa.

"I forgot to tell you that I am happy to be 'with' you. Also that I think we have a marvelous life full of the present & even greater future!"

Paulette never made the picture *Angel Puss*, but that year she decided that she wanted to work on a project with Remarque. Her first thought was that she would star in a screenplay that he had written, to be financed, perhaps, by the Danziger brothers. Where business was concerned, she believed in bygones, and the Danziger brothers were very rich, having inherited Luna Park (Coney Island), which had burned down, allowing them to collect insurance of $8 million in cash. They wanted to make another film with Paulette, as she exuberantly explained in a letter to Remarque:

> They are anxious to know if you would do the screenplay and how much. Naturally they want an original from you, but did not dream you would take the time and effort. Now this is a group that works on "if money." "If money" means a percentage after cost, but a fair down payment date that production starts (I will arrange for your money to be put into escrow).
>
> They suggest your doing a property like Strindberg's *Dream Play* but I think they are wacky. I would suggest a mystery melodrama (a thriller) set in any locale that has flavor—Venice, etc. What a wild stab for an idea. But, my God, I would like to see an emotional thriller. I think we would hit the jackpot.

Paulette never did act in anything Remarque wrote: however, a screenplay collaboration was attempted. It was titled *L'Americana*, and at first the credit read, screenplay by Melchior Sirr, a chosen alias that happened to be a fictional protagonist in an early Remarque short story. Next, the credit read, by Paulette Goddard and Melchior Sirr, and finally, by Paulette Goddard. The reason for all this name shuffling was that although Paulette had wanted to collaborate, she had no interest in writing. Remarque ended up writing it—perhaps with some of her suggestions—and gallantly put her name on it. Today, this slim (eighteen pages) unproduced screenplay is copy-righted in her name.

Through the mid-fifties, Paulette worked a lot in television. Highly paid, grateful for the work and exposure, she attempted to respect the medium, but it was not like the old days. "I love doing TV," she announced in an inter-view, and then, "It's such a breakneck pace, you know. It's kiss and go with your leading men. You meet them in the morning and go right into a clinch. The filming is over before you get to know their last names. As for 'live' TV, it's like a premiere on Broadway that closes after the opening night."

While in London, Paulette filmed six episodes of *Errol Flynn Theatre*, an anthology series that was never shown in the States. Back home she did a *Ford Theatre* (she described her role as "a fallen woman"), a *Bob Hope Special*, a series called *On Trial*, and the *Martha Raye Show*. There was a lot of advance talk about Anita Loos's writing a TV series for Paulette called *White*

Collar Girl, but it never came to anything. What is interesting about it is that Paulette wanted it to materialize. Lonely and concerned for her mother, who was separating from Don Jacobson, her third husband, and missing the old ways of Hollywood, she wrote to Alta about her hopes for a long run: "My T.V. series will be made in N.Y. or Hollywood. I hope Hollywood, it would be lovely to come for a good long stay."

Remarque, busy finishing *The Black Obelisk* and planning for the premiere of his play *The Last Station*, retitled *Berlin, 1945* (September 20, 1956), in Berlin, might not have minded Paulette's absence. He clearly adored Alta, and partly because of problems with his own mother, he encouraged Paulette to lavish attention upon her. His wishes must have created complex emotions for Paulette, who had always taken good care of her mother anyway. But Remarque spoiled Alta shamelessly—in word and deed—which made Paulette quite jealous. Remarque's affection for Alta was reminiscent of another time. Michael Hall recalls Paulette's telling him that Chaplin found her mother so attractive that he said he wanted to take her to bed. Remarque, in his letters to Alta, is very attentive and just short of seductive. An example of a letter written in the late forties (Remarque rarely dated his letters) addresses Alta's severe gynecological problems: "My poor little baby, I hear from Paulette that you are still suffering terribly. You don't know how sad that makes me. I wish I could fly over, borrow from some Saint his power of working miracles and put my hands on your head and say: Alta, irresistible Darling of the Gods, get up and let's go to Chambord or the Pavillon and have a Champagne Dinner. . . . Believe me that I am thinking all the time of you. . . . Love as always from your son-in-law."

In 1956, Paulette's potential TV series written by Anita Loos fell through and she returned to Remarque's side. Paulette persuaded him to take a bit of a holiday, and so they were off in her new Jaguar to Cannes, Monte Carlo, and Nice for a few weeks, and then on to witness his play in Berlin, where the press referred to her as "Frau Paulette," leading to the rumor, seized upon by the American press, that she and Remarque were married. Immediately following the rumor, she took off for Hollywood to star in a *Climax Theatre* for CBS. More than ever, she was on the defensive—forty-seven years old—and a frau but no Mrs.; she hammered her free-spirit theme in an exclusive interview with the Hollywood columnist Sheila Graham:

Erich and I will marry eventually. I believe in doing everything eventually. . . . You see I'm not ready to settle down. I have no roots anywhere. I love being wherever I happen to be. Right now I'm crazy about Hollywood.

I can't think of a nicer place to be. When I'm in Hollywood, I think the same. And also in France, England, Germany, where I am.

"If I have a home at all, perhaps it is in Switzerland. . . . and I have some of my paintings there. But most of them are with my mother, here in Hollywood. I don't care for possessions, only for things I can pack. . . ."

She was wearing a double diamond ring and other diamonds scattered on her yellow summer dress. "Every jewel I'm wearing is new," she told me.

"Are they real?" I asked, forgetting myself for a minute.

"What a foolish question," reprimanded Paulette. Then I asked a sillier question. "Did you buy them?"

"I never have and I don't propose to start now! . . .

"I keep getting offers for my life story, but I'm too busy living it. I'll wait until I'm eighty. My mother is a little worried about my philosophy of life. 'What will you do when you're lonely at seventy?' she asks me. That's when I'll get the education she couldn't afford to give me." . . .

Paulette, full of energy and good health, laughing easily, a loaded bank account, a girlish figure, taking her fun and romances in stride, no regrets, free as the wind. She'll always have a good time. And I can see her still drinking the champagne she adores, when she's eighty. She has everything—almost.

In 1957, the producer Robert Whitehead asked her to return to the stage in a national touring company of *Waltz of the Toreadors*, co-starring Melvyn Douglas. Her initial instinct was to back off when told what part she was being offered. Her retort to Whitehead: "In this play I have to identify myself with a character that doesn't suit me—a spinster. If, however, you want me to do Moll Flanders . . ." But she accepted the role—mainly for the chance to work with Douglas: "He is such a fine actor and teacher. For the first time I came to know what timing meant—how to wait for the laughs and how to speak the lines to get more." When she showed up for rehearsal in January in chilly Pittsburgh, she wore a floor-length sable coat with a hood. "I like this coat. It picks up my spirits," she said.

Paulette and Remarque's marriage seemed to be looming for everyone but them. She had the gifts of a soon-to-be bride: the new sable, and a knockout engagement ring, described in a Sotheby's catalogue as "'monture Van Cleef & Arpels.' Estimate: $40,000–$50,000." She had announced that they would be married in St. Moritz in December of 1957 and, in fact, they already had reservations at their favorite Palace Hotel and a justice of the peace lined up.

When the ceremony was abruptly canceled, the press could get little from them except terseness.

Paulette: "I believe in five-year engagements."

Remarque: "There's nothing to be canceled."

Paulette was an old hand at manipulating the press into jumping to some sort of conclusion—usually erroneous. She took a certain amount of pleasure in throwing them off the scent. Remarque, who never really understood the American press and its lust for gossip, did not. Unlike the weaving, dodging Paulette, he would just shut the door. Two different styles, but their sensibility was the same: none of anybody's business when or if they took their vows.

Two months later they did get married, and the delay had nothing to do with cold feet or disaffection. It was a pesky, contractual reason having to do with a play that Paulette had resisted from the start. She was committed to being in a *Waltz* that neither she, nor, she felt, the audience enjoyed: "Opening nite again, and they don't seem to like this play a'tall! Who does—not us!"

She was to open in Chicago, then to St. Louis, on to Pittsburgh, then Detroit, and then Philadelphia. She had hoped to suspend production for a month in order to wed Remarque in "their place," St. Moritz, but she could not figure out a way, and in fact, until the producer, Robert Whitehead, found a suitable replacement, Paulette was stuck with the entire tour. Michael Hall recalls:

> She was not pleased from the start. She had assumed that I would play the part opposite her, and it would be just perfect. Well, she got involved with the production and realized that the boy who played it originally was going to play it again. So, she didn't have her pal with her, and then she got a little frightened.
>
> She opened in Chicago. . . . But she didn't like the play, and didn't like the way she was being treated by the boy who was playing opposite her. During rehearsals he would refer to Paulette as "her." "Tell her to move over there when I'm over here." She wouldn't tolerate that kind of insolence. She said, "You know what I did? I stopped the production in a dress rehearsal after he had been rude to me backstage and I said to the director, 'Would you please tell this young man that my name is Miss Goddard, and I want to be referred to as Miss Goddard when he is talking about me or to me. Is that understood?'" She left the stage and when she came back the boy called her "Miss Goddard" from that point on.
>
> One night after the show, she telephoned me and told me that she was

leaving to marry Erich Maria Remarque. I had not been kept posted about their comings and goings because I'd been involved with her and it was awkward, I suppose. At any rate, she thought he was fabulous and she was thrilled.

On New Year's Day, 1958, Paulette saw the rest of her life fall into place. She heralds her news in a letter to Remarque:

Darling Bunnykopf! This is much too good news for me to phone. Must put it in writing so that it is impressive. I am clear of *Waltz* irrevocably and amicably. . . . Leueen McGrath, the scared ghost that you said would be perfect casting, is starting rehearsals Monday, Jan. 6, to replace me. That was the earliest date she could start, so after 3 weeks rehearsal she will open in Philadelphia. That leaves me Pittsburgh & two ghastly weeks in Detroit. But they honestly did their best to relieve me, so everyone is happy except me. I am hilarious! with joy.

She gets $500 per week, so that pleases Douglas and Whitehead. But they will miss my little magic. Douglas said so.

. . . Now we can start all plans rolling. Let's do everything! Let me have your congratulations. I did my 100th performance last Saturday. Quite adequate. More than most. I adore you. Mom.

And so finally "Mom" and her "Bunnykopf" married on February 25, 1958, in Branford, Connecticut. She wore to the ceremony the baguette-diamond wedding ring that Remarque had bought for her, blocking questions about why they hadn't gotten married before by saying blithely that they had just not gotten around to getting their license for a while. They chose Branford as the site because, as a headline trumpeted, it was "Nearly All Quiet." They wanted to escape publicity, but were greeted upon arriving at the law offices of Town Court Judge Cornelius Driscoll by thirty-five reporters and photographers. Remarque said nothing, but for Paulette, it was reflexive; she waved her ringed finger and said, "The press had us engaged five years ago. I guess that made it official. Anyway, I feel I've known Erich all my life."

The ceremony took ten minutes. Paulette gave her age as forty-two. Remarque gave his correct age of fifty-nine. They were attended only by Paulette's attorneys, Robert Morris and Halsey Crown, and their wives. A newspaper article by Josephine DiLorenzo reporting the event had almost nothing to enhance: "For the ceremony in the second floor office above Main St., Paulette wore a burgundy wool dress, a short matching jacket with a very wide mink collar, brown suede pumps and a brown ribbon hat on her pageboy-style auburn hair. She carried a full-length mink coat. Remarque wore a double-breasted blue suit of European cut."

Their honeymoon plan was unusual but true to form, somehow. They would spend it in New York, where Paulette planned to move into her newly rented and still unfurnished apartment at the Ritz Towers, having taken an apartment on the fifteenth floor—one floor above her new husband's. "We're planning to keep both apartments," she explained. "When people work as hard as we do and keep different hours it is better to have separate apartments."

Anita Loos, who was not well liked by Remarque, sang his praises and rejoiced in their union:

> But at long last came a marriage that made up for the perils of the two previous ones. Erich Maria Remarque fulfilled every one of Paulette's tough requirements. More than handsome, he was elegant; more than elegant, he was a wit; more than witty, he was a famous writer; his anti-war novel, *All Quiet on the Western Front*, had won him worldwide renown. He had become a connoisseur of every amenity: art, women, jewels, food, and wine. His appreciation of Dom Perignon champagne and Persian caviar matched that of Paulette herself.
>
> Erich had a gallantry toward women that has now gone out of fashion. As a European and German-born at that, he was not quite as bewildered as most men are by the enigmas his bride presented; he merely put them down as "shenanigans" and they amused him. But Erich also considered Paulette seriously as the greatest specimen in all his collections, more fascinating than his Egyptian bronzes or his Monet water lilies.

"Not the Goddard!" Marlene Dietrich had cried upon hearing of Remarque's plans to marry Paulette. There were others who were alarmed. There were people who thought that Paulette was "not quite right." Max Colpet, Remarque's old friend, felt that even at that late date, had Dietrich capitulated and agreed to marry him, Remarque would have disentangled himself from Paulette. Maria Riva recalls how "appalled" her mother was at the news, and how she expressed it:

> "What insanity! He is not really going to marry that Goddard woman, is he? Doesn't he know she only wants him for his paintings? I am going to talk to him," and she did. Boni asked my mother to marry him; if she refused, he

was marrying Paulette, which he finally did. My mother's only comment:
"Now, just watch. Now—she'll try to kill him. He was a great writer, but
about women—always so stupid!"

Remarque had once warned Clifford Odets to "never fall in love with an
actress." (Too late, for Odets was about to marry the actress Luise Rainer—
unhappily, as it turned out.) Remarque continued his "Ides of actresses":
"These actresses [are] so typical. . . . They hit you hard on the head and you
fall, you are stunned—you don't know where you are."

After the wedding, from that moment forward and much for the better,
Remarque knew exactly where he was with Paulette. He got her, he continued to want her, and he knew that to keep her was to give to her, and to let
her go:

[January 1959]: Thank you, most adorable Sputnik (circling now the orbit
of New York) for your cables. . . . In the meantime, I bought a very small
Renoir . . . and now I must work to get the money and to pay for the Renoir
(a little girl's head) with it. Simple, isn't it? The Renoir, of course, will land
in your bedroom. . . .

The first evening here was rather tough alone. I always heard you bark-
ing and calling, all through the night, and I was twice up to look out. . . .

The house is listening, especially around six, even in the afternoon for
your quick steps—alas, they are stepping around Fifth Avenue now. Enjoy
it, Baby! In the stars is a contract for you. In my heart is another one, lifelong, no options, no possibilities to break out. . . . Bless you, Ondine! Your
Père Noël.

As for Paulette, she was aware that Remarque's health was beginning to
slip. She knew he had headaches. She knew he had heart problems. She
treated him seriously, but with a light touch, as if to ensure—always—that
he wouldn't get any heartaches from her. It was part of an unspoken deal.
She understood his pride in her, valued his faith in her. And although she
would continue to drop her sometimes silly and disdainful quips about all
sorts of things, she understood that she could never, ever treat Remarque
with anything less than devotion. Whether she truly adored him or not, she
knew the rules and played her cards. Her lip service was so smooth, her presence so fulfilling, that he never stopped delighting in her. It might have been
her last and greatest performance of a lifetime. Her true nature was that she
could never be totally there for anyone. She wrote him, "So close & enrap-
turing I feel with you. An ocean is not a barrier, or is it?"

MR. AND MRS. ERICH
MARIA REMARQUE

1 9 5 8 – 1 9 7 0

PAULETTE STARTED OUT her new married life with a misspelling on stationery, "Mrs. Eric Maria Remarque," and a quick trip back to Los Angeles for a guest appearance on a television series. A thrilled Alta sang her daughter's praises to her new husband: "Paulette was like an angel from heaven. . . . The first week she was on location—up at 5 a.m.—studio car picked her up at 5:30—home about 7 p.m.—on with her cooking outfit—chop vegetables—cook a delicious dinner— then out with the lights at 9. How she does all that in a day I can't understand." Paulette was also negotiating for the sale of her Trancas house property: she had an offer of $75,000, but wanted the offer paid with one half down and the rest in monthly installments over a five-year period ("but in case they renege on payments, I want to be sure the property reverts back to me"). She made time to write regular letters to Remarque, who was mostly in Porto Ronco. Battling a weakening heart and struggling with his next novel, *Heaven Has No Favorites*, he was grateful for her funny, bitchy, and informative letters. This one was from New York:

> It makes me sad to be writing to you. I don't realize my achy missing you until I try to touch your heart by letter. So much I want to know & to tell you, too.
> Anyway to facts. Humidifiers here cost $6.94, so I bought three—recklessly. . . .

The Remarques in Ascona, ca. 1958

In the garden at Casa Remarque, ca. 1961.

Have cooked two absolutely great suppers. Easier & better than ever. Just give me one hour & any request & it's yours to dine. Am practicing for the nites when we don't have steak or lobsters or caviar.

Have seen *Touch of the Poet*. It is vile, dull & pretentious. A 3-word description of Mr. Clurman [the director Harold Clurman]. You can see his heavy thick knuckles in every obvious cliché! . . .

When I go to your apt. to sleep, after undressing in 14D, I always stop and listen for your bark. I still expect you to be in that great wolf-bed. I love the place. The landscape is superb. Right down to Wall Street. One must keep an eye on the stock exchange, you know. . . .

Please give me a complete résumé of your visit to the Dr. But every detail, please.

I have the address of the No. 1 heart specialist in Europe. . . . He is mad about artists & appreciates their worth. Especially yours! . . . You are my life, love & happiness—P.

Paulette took to her new role with pride and her own special brand of brash flair. After all, she was The Actress, and most everything related back to her. She told everybody that her hair smelled like pencil shavings (Remarque used only pencils, and they had to be Eberhard Faber #1), and she was tickled at his success in playing the role of Professor Pohlmann on the silver screen—her territory.

Whenever Paulette returned to Europe, they continued to travel to their favorite cities. When they were in Milan—a fashion capital that had seen it all—Paulette made heads turn, particularly when she wore her red-dyed ermine coat with the hood. "I guess they saw my movie," Remarque would say sarcastically, as though they might be looking at him. Actually, Remarque himself had gotten some good reviews, but the *New York Times* film critic Bosley Crowther was hard on his performance: "Stumbling around in a small role of an aging schoolteacher is Mr. Remarque, who might better have saved himself embarrassment by staying as far away from this pastiche as he could."

At home, Remarque was writing his play *Berlin, 1945*, aka *The Last Station*, which was completed in the spring of 1956. He had begun working on it right after he finished his screenplay *The Last Act* (based on Michael Musmenno's book *Ten Days to Die*) and it was considered somewhat of a spin-off. He was determined, as was Paulette, that *Berlin, 1945* should have a Broadway production. Remarque felt a certain urgency to establish himself as a playwright. Perhaps brought on by the fact that he was having heart problems, his concerns for the play loomed large. Remarque was rather rigidly overseeing Denver Lindley's English translation and worried about proper representation for the play in the States. His European agent, who had an office in Paris, was George Marton, whose sister, Elizabeth Marton—also an agent—had an office in New York. Paulette suggested that he give the play to a large, prestigious agency in New York, but Remarque, loyal as always, decided to honor George Marton by entrusting the play to his sister Elizabeth. Paulette then got into the act of helping to seek a production and advising Elizabeth Marton on how to package it. Marton was busy negotiating with the producer Warner LeRoy, who was offering a $5,000 advance. Paulette's choice was her old friend the director-producer King Vidor, but he would pay only $4,000. She decided to go with LeRoy but to bring in Robert Whitehead as executive producer. (Whitehead had recently, and indeed amicably, released Paulette from *Waltz of the Toreadors*. This is a perfect example of Paulette's realistic approach to the business.) "The play is very hot!" Paulette wrote to Remarque in encouragement. "Other producers are interested too . . . *Berlin, 1945* is more timely now than when it opened."

The production didn't come to pass at that time. Warner LeRoy did indeed renew the option for another year, and the dramatist Peter Stone prepared an adaptation of the play, which Remarque was not satisfied with, according to an in-house memo written by Harriet Pilpel. It was an awkward situation, seeing that Stone was related to Elizabeth Marton. (Stone's stepfather was George Marton.) Remarque felt that someone else would have to be called in, but by that time the option and a good deal of enthusiasm for the project had run out. LeRoy did not renew and the matter was dropped.

Although he was not considered a success as a playwright, Remarque felt his technique in fiction was allied to that of a dramatist, and attributed this factor to his success as a novelist: "Perhaps because I'm a playwright manqué. . . . All my books are written like plays. One scene follows upon another . . . I write by ear. I hear everything that I write. I choose words for their sound. Because I am musical, because I was once quite a good organist, because I really wanted to be a musician, my novels all sound good when they're read aloud. I find easy what other authors find most difficult: writing dialogue."

Aside from *Berlin, 1945*, which would eventually be titled *Full Circle*, produced in the States in 1973, Remarque wrote two other plays and one set of scrawled notes for a play. *The Homecomimg of Enoch J. Jones*, which he did in the late fifties, had only one amateur production, in Remarque's hometown of Osnabrück in 1988, and *Brunnenstrasse* (*Fountain Street*), about the division between East and West Germany and the children of Hitler's followers, was never put on.

Remarque was also keeping notes for *La Barcarolle—A Study in Brown*. The notes are written in longhand in a German-English patois. A guess at when he attempted to write this play would be shortly after a minor stroke in 1964, because what can be deciphered of the English feels struggling and disjointed.

Paulette never stayed with Remarque for very long. "We get on very well, I must say. I'm gregarious and he's sedentary; it works out fine," Paulette said about her marriage to Remarque as she prepared to take off to Hollywood for a role in a new television series, *Adventures in Paradise*. Before leaving New York for Los Angeles, she dashed off some news and loving reassurance to Remarque—as was her custom before and after almost everything she did:

My only love, crush, passion, and sweetheart: Now that the first shock of separation is over, I can gird my loins and tell you that your pigeons miss you frantically. I have not been in your apartment so far, but see them batting around by my window.

Am having lunch with Pam Churchill at Pavillon today. She is here with Leland Hayward. A real husband-snatcher strictly. It's okay when she tampers with a European husband. To them it is a sideline. But Leland being a typical American will get a divorce & do "The Rite Thing." Funny if she turns him down. Marriage would cut off her other sources of income: Agnelli, Baron Rothschild. You can see I am back in the Haute Monde. But not much, mein lieber, not much.

Am taking a real sure massage diet & have lost your favorite 3 lbs. How in God's name is your poor leg [Remarque hurt his leg when he took a bad fall after drinking at home and almost fell in the lake] and your headaches? I hope they never, never come back! Be sure to do some mild neck & body exercises in that clean, clear virgin air. Maybe a swim? I am nuts about you too. Mom.

From Los Angeles Paulette wrote,

Dearest love of my life or anybody else's life: No one knows but thee or better than thee why I'm writing with red pencil. It is My Day.

What a barren arid place this is. One forgets that the vacuum here is indigenous to the place, the only thing that makes it unique.

Dinner with Anita Loos, who was a loyal friend and admirer, ca. 1959.

Paulette guest-stars in Gardner McKay's television series
Adventures in Paradise, *1959–1960.*

But the trip was worth it just to see my Ma's joy. She is all well & looking great again. I think it is your attention and kindness that makes her feel normal again after Don and then the medical business. She thinks you really care for her. She is going to have a face-lift job as soon as I leave. The same Doc that did Loretta Young, Roz Russell, Hedda, Louella, Jack Benny, Gypsy Rose Lee, etc. I know that it is her crush on you that gives her the courage! Love, love, ain't it amazing?

I have the handsomest leading man in the world, so says *Life* mag. this week. He's on the cover. But he's an amateur and has to rehearse 8 to 10 days for each show. So far the only snag.

I know my letters are no compensation for the vast distance between us, but will pelt you daily with all my longing & love.

Gardner McKay, the recipient of the "handsomest man in the world" title and the star of *Adventures in Paradise*, has his own startling and unkind memories of working with Paulette:

They were the early years for me and the late years for her; I'd sailed a lot and studied acting a bit, and really wanted to be a writer when this *Paradise* thing came along and obliterated all reality in life. Paulette was part of that.

It was one of the first episodes of *Adventures in Paradise* and she was playing Suzanne Pleshette's mother in an episode that was trying to be as grand as Somerset Maugham's *Rain*. I thought of myself as a complete womanizer until I worked with her. Until Paulette Goddard, I thought the only woman I could not handle was the tipsy older woman at a party. No man can deal with her. There's no defense. Insult them and they go berserk.

Anyway, for some reason, on the set Paulette wouldn't leave me alone. She was quite beautiful, but older than my mother. She seemed to be about seventy, and I wasn't wise enough at that time to understand the beauty of much older women.

Paulette would start first thing in the morning. She said whatever came into her mind, usually something to do with fucking, and moved her hands freely whenever I stood close to her. It wasn't Tourette's syndrome, was it? Unbelievably, the A.D. had to stand by during rehearsals to keep her straight. First and last time for that.

Through Paulette, though, I learned what the word *harassment* means. It's amazing, isn't it, but it really does take a firsthand experience to give a man the impact of the idea. I can see now what women are complaining about and I can sympathize with them. Also, it widens the range of the he-she exploitation, the way women want it to be widened, and that is: if there can be dirty old men, there can be dirty old women, too. Paulette was indeed ahead of her time.

Paulette reported to Remarque McKay's weaknesses and problems:

Only one day's shooting and my "leading man" cracked. He's 6 feet 5 inches, 27 yrs. old, but the weekly T.V. grind got him. They handed us 40 new pages of dialogue on the set yesterday & he said "goodbye, I'm going to have to learn it" and took off. . . .

[Five days later]: . . . Well, the secret is out about delay in schedule. We rehearsed all day Fri. and The Boy is a creamy, divine actor but—he stammers! when tired or confronted with the smallest conflict (me, for one) he suffers terribly from embarrassment. Rather tragic. He's ready to give up the business. Says he hates to be an actor. Who wouldn't, in that condition. It was painful to watch him suffer, so I told the producer to send for a specialist in curing stammers, simply with breathing exercises, no analysis. . . . He arrives on Monday. That's life in the tropics.

There had been a time, shortly before Remarque and Paulette were married, when he considered selling the house in Porto Ronco. Weary of his complicated tax situation plus the psychological history that the house represented, he felt that perhaps he would be better off if he moved to New York, with protracted stays in Rome, Paris, and St. Moritz. The impulse did not last long. Paulette was horrified at the notion—ostensibly because he would be forfeiting his treasured sanctuary, his peace of mind, his peace in writing. Perhaps, however, there was something ulterior: Remarque's being in the house for a good portion of the year was her freedom, and the house would be her legacy. So, she was adamantly against its sale.

Soon after she and Remarque were married, a major remodeling of the house was started, but this time it was Remarque who initiated and executed it. Realizing that Paulette had to roam, he was canny enough to know that she had to come home eventually, and would do so more readily if a more opulent house greeted her each time. Paulette was relatively passive during the process—pleased, but occupied with her own doings and, if anything, a bit inconvenienced when she was in Ronco. As far as Remarque was concerned, she always managed to be a good sport. Paulette wrote Alta about what it was like: "We are both camping out in the living room. Am using my bathroom for a clothes closet. The old walls had to be stripped down to the foundation because the plaster caved in all over the house. Naturally a repaint job has to be done thru-out. . . . There have been 8 workmen on the place two weeks now & the upstairs is only one-half finished. Probably three more weeks to go. They start at 7 A.M. so the whole place is jumping very early! . . . Nothing new, just enjoying life in Switzerland!"

Paulette returned to New York, leaving Remarque in his redecorated house working on his novel *Heaven Has No Favorites*. Alta was visiting New York and staying in Remarque's apartment, which she would do periodically into the sixties, using it as a second home. Mother and daughter would do the town, each reporting faithfully to Remarque of their adventures. Remarque, always generous toward his two ladies, began to take on, in his letters to Paulette, a wistful tone of martyrdom coupled with increasingly hyperbolic adoration. Occasionally, his knowledge of her minx side would come through, but mostly until the end of his life her pedestal grew, as in these examples of his devotion, most likely written in the fall of 1960:

Bicky, the whole house was very happy when your cable arrived. As you know, I was flying next to the plane in a little space capsule made out of love and intensely good wishes—and, of course, I woke up exactly at the time you must have arrived in New York, sent a thousand loving thoughts over, and had the feeling that all was well with you and New York. . . .

Life in the village has, as by magic, with your departure become wintry. . . . Our house is different. It blazes into the night with all its lights and tells again and again the oldest story of the universe. It is still full of you, and your rooms are too. Last night I heard you tapping around as it is fitting and expected you to come in with apples or cheese rinds. Then I remembered. . . . Have all the joy you can, my love! That's why you went, don't forget! And all the love to you and your Mama.

I just have had a silent walk through the garden, brought with me a few last roses and put them in the blue vase in your room. . . . I am truly happy that you are in New York, my golden one, you certainly have deserved it to go to the big city again and I hope only that you have all the joy you can find. Missing you already terribly, the two feelings are holding themselves in a strange balance, and one is necessary for the other, which means one is only bearable through the other. If you enjoy yourself immensely, the missing is easier to bear (or let's say much easier), it would only be terrible if you wouldn't enjoy yourself at all. So, you see, that's the mystic balance.

. . . I am quite well, I know you want to hear about that, and it is true (so far!). So, my love, just have all the fun you can have, and have the feeling at the same time, that it is quite good for your husband to stew in his own juice for a few weeks. Give your Mama all my best wishes—it is a rather wonderful feeling to know you are both together.

My Little Baby, it's raining outside, so you really are not missing any golden autumn here. . . . I am rather pressed and harassed by a slew of things: the dreaded last corrections of the book, tax things to look for . . . and people here who want me, or think I could help them with their pressing troubles.

It is enough if you bring some dancers. [This is in regard to their "art and antiques trafficking." To create tax loopholes, they would often move their acquisitions from continent to continent or, in Alta's case, from Hollywood to New York, and sometimes to Europe. Here, Remarque is talking about part of his Degas collection.] Maybe the musicians and the dancers, but if it bothers you, forget about it. If you want, send 6–8 or ten bronzes, rather 6 than 10. (The blue ones.) I will write later about these problems. Let's first get our own things a bit straightened out.

Once and most of all: You are the most divine and gorgeous creature . . . and I am happy that you are alive although it be in America (for a short time). Fix your coat [her sable coat was giving her trouble; she felt it didn't fit right and embarked on a series of complex alterations], Baby, take your time for it, and don't mind if you need a few more days or a week for it. Arrange everything, work too, so that you can leave with an easy heart.

In 1960, Paulette got a part opposite Reginald Gardiner in the play *Laura*, written by Vera Caspary and George Skylar, playing the title role, which Gene Tierney had originated in the 1944 film. Said one appreciative critic, "Paulette lends her own vivaciousness to the part of the not too moral Laura and still delineates the character perfectly. Her rich, warm voice projects and she lights up the stage with every move."

Paulette was pleased with the project and wanted Remarque, who was not in good health, to come to the States to see her. He did not feel well, and according to a member of the medical profession, was pre-aphasic long before he suffered a mild stroke in 1964 and, in fact, might have had a series of tiny stroke during this time. This is where Paulette's affections fell short. She was good at prescribing any number of resourceful-sounding antidotes for whatever ailed him, but when she wanted something from him—some sort of activity, such as coming to America to see her in *Laura*—it was difficult for her to understand his medical shortcomings. He plied her with telegrams:

FLOWERS IMPOSSIBLE TO SEND BUT OUR HEARTS AND LOVE AND CLAP-
PING HANDS. YOUR HUSBAND AND ROSA.

MISS YOUR BLISS BABY. ALL LOVE, ABSTRACT UNFORTUNATELY.

She wanted him in person, putting such pressure on him that he actually considered flying on Friday the thirteenth, a more abhorrent idea for him than for most. He was abjectly apologetic because he could not get a flight out. The following excerpts from his letters reveal their relationship from 1960 on: his vulnerability, his willingness to please, his dogged endeavors to get his work done, the reassurance of his love, and his state of disrepair:

My adored and most fascinating daughter of your Mom—this is the second letter following the first which told you I would try to get tickets for Friday the 13th. Alas, all the beds are sold out and the plane goes only once a week, Fridays. There are no other planes . . . but I made a lot of hubbub and they managed that in the next tourist plane (without beds) they got a place and, as a special favor, one bed installed for me. The doctor has strictly forbidden that I fly the whole trip sitting up. So, happily that is solved and I am leaving here 4 days later. . . . I am very sorry about it, beloved creature, but there are no other planes, it seems. . . . Could you forgive and wait till the 18th before you get a divorce? I promise you to manage that my next books only play in places in which you like to stay! And never anything with a time limit! . . . I'm working against time, will not get through, but will bring it all with me to finish over there. Since New Year I have constantly trigeminal neuralgia. Am on the drugs morning, midday, and night, otherwise rather chipper and extremely happy now to be in ten days off and right into your arms. . . . I am dreaming three nights in a row about you and boy, what dreams! It's time to come back! I adore, worship, and love you. . . . You are the most gorgeous thing alive. Sometimes I have a stroke of reflection and then I realize what an all-around love athlete you are, how full of love and ready to spill it all at once and have more. . . .

Last night I dreamed of you, very intimate and very much in love, not just sexy, but holding you and feeling your skin and being unbelievably in love. Even awakening, finding myself alone, it was such a warm and marvelous feeling that I thought, closing my eyes: All right, once more! . . . It is such a fantastic joy to have you, even if you are not around.

Today it looks like rain, which will stop when you are arriving—and, if not, we will celebrate with caviar and champagne. We even have a dozen bottles of Soave, now. This might be the last letter before you are leaving. So, it's time to tell you that I adore and worship you and that I had a lovely time here because you had an exciting time over there, that I love you more than yesterday and yesterday more than before yesterday, that for the first time my life is full since I am with you. . . .

Would you like a few weeks in Paris? I, rather! But I want first and all— about fifty more years with you. Bless you that you don't quite know how marvelous you are!

I am working through all my stuff like mad to go to Malpensa—and fly to you, who are the center of my heart, whom I love, adore, worship, and embrace with every thought in the most pitiful way.

Bellissima . . . We must never part for such a long time again, it is cruel, unhealthy, idiotic, and inhuman. I had slowly the feeling that I would stay incarcerated in this flowering paradise here forever. . . . I wanted to make some money here to entertain you royally this year, but it is not worth the absence. I've written about 120 pages now of a good book [*Heaven Has No Favorites*] and an absolutely perfect film for you, and I will finish it over there. . . . I have writer's cramps, hearts cramps, and head cramps. . . . We have a new camellia . . . which is called: General Paulette—Mexican red with a bit of white and in the form of a carnation. It got the best place in the garden. . . . The heart of my heart, the life of my life is seeing plays in N.Y. without me. Enough of that! I'm starting to pack. God bless you, my love-liness and light of my eyes. Kiss your mother for me. With you I intend quite a lot of other things too.

Absolutely Unique-one, I am writing to you on this day because tomorrow I will be a year older, and so, as a comparative youngster, I want to tell you that my life with you has been a parade of superlatives so far and that I have the most wonderful expectations for the time to come. It all has been noth-ing but joy and love and great feelings, and you have been Cleopatra, Huckleberry Finn, Theodora, and my pal, Venus, and my head-scratcher, the mythical Prince of Thebes, and the best cook between Sardi's and the Pavillon—all rolled in one and still quite a lot to spare. So, my wish for the next forty years is very simple: you, and that means: everything! . . . Just come, light of the West, with laughter and beauty and the unfathomable magic which is always around you like a coat of gold. . . . I will go to the year 7500 (and higher). God bless you, beloved jewel and handiest cook! Other people make such a fuss about their cooking, you just buy a book in a cig- arette store and do it left-handed! Your sprite-man of 61 years old.

Mummy, the weather here is so terrible that I earnestly think you should stay a week longer in N.Y. if you like it. Here . . . it rains cats and dogs. . . . Even when my poor heart breaks I have to offer you the choice! This is the worst summer I can remember here as far as weather is concerned, and the best one, as far as you are concerned—I am so nuts about you that I some- times look like an idiot. . . .

I am best with work. Slowly, I am going through the chapters for the last time. . . . I want you desperately, darling, but I fear you will get bored in this terrible climate. Of course, we will go to Milano etc. before we go to Paris, but I must finish this book here and it might take a week or so longer than the first of November, before we rush off. . . .

Tonight I have a party for Isaac Stern, the violinist. . . . The party is over. There is no party without thee. . . . Everybody was happy—except me who is enslaved by you—and who cannot enjoy anything when your gorgeous face is not shining at the top of the table, not to speak of your other limbs. When I think of your behind a Niagara rushes at once over, through, and in my brains and I have the feeling to faint. Do you think I will ever see it again?

The weather is today again beautiful—but, my love, don't rush back—do what you want to do and enjoy yourself to the hilt (with men over 70).

My knee is quite good already (without ever looking at the doctor again after he bored into it to get some water out of it for the laboratory). I cured it with compresses and long underwear. I love you so much that there is no room in me left for any misery. . . . I miss you terribly though but I am very happy to miss you so terribly because that means I am terribly in love and heaven thanks you don't just hate me! Absolutely the great combinations of being pitiful and enviable at the same time.

Japan [Paulette very much wanted to take a trip there with Remarque], my beloved sweetheart, is out because I can't interrupt two books, a play, etc., and I shouldn't risk the strain. I have been more sick than it looked and why play around for Buddha? For you, it's different—you are my love and my life and we'll go to the East leisurely next year. . . . Believe me, never shall we be separated again, even if it bores you to death.

In tone, sentiment, humor, and topic, there is a symbiosis in their correspondence. What can also be seen in some of Paulette's letters is her uncanny ability to keep him reeled in, swearing intimacy and yet remaining distant. They both preserved the technique of long-distance cherishing until the day Remarque died. It is evident that he begins to fade from about 1964 on. There is a sameness to most of their letters: they discuss missing each other; they discuss the glorious plans of when they will be together and how they will fulfill all of each other's expectations when they are finally together, physically, emotionally, and spiritually; they discuss acquisitions; Remarque gives Paulette monetary chores to take care of and dictates what art should be moved where; Paulette reports on accomplishing her various tasks, as well as the state of her mother, her career, her diet, her social life, and her businesss acumen; she gives him advice and remedies; he gives her money and gifts; she thanks him lavishly for his generosity; they both itemize the cost of everything; they both discuss money and material things a great deal; he worries; she reassures:

Dearest only one, most extra-sensory one: Am doing a small radio show Sunday for which they will send you a victrola with 50 long-playing records of your choice. I also get a year's card for theatre meals at Sardi's. . . .

PLEASE wait for me to go to Zurich with you. It will be such fun to try the Impala on the Gottardo [the Gotthard Pass, which runs through the Swiss Alps]. I'm game for anything as you well know.

Staying home tonite to move all the "objets" to a safe place for tomorrow when the furniture goes into storage. [During this period, while she was nomadic and he was mainly in Ronco, they were using her apartment to store most of their valuables, while renting his apartment to Alta. For the next several years, they would mostly be in Switzerland during the summer, and Rome, Milan, and Venice during the winter—with Paulette darting to and fro as usual. When she went to New York, she and Alta would share his apartment; when he went to New York alone, Alta was sent somewhere for a posh vacation.] . . . It is sad to give up the tiny apt.—I loved every minute right up to the last. But since I have had to run the stairs 8 to 10 X's a day, as you did, I am fed up with the dual arrangement. Isn't that a blessing?

Saw Chas Jr. [Charlie Chaplin, Jr., whom she had taken care of as a boy and who would later commit suicide]. He wanted to give his 18-month-old baby girl to me—Imagine! He is an alcoholic and not able to care for it. . . . She was killing. So cute. Not pretty—But a blonde with Indian features & skin— My! Something for the 1970s. Very strange & sober little tyke.

Dear Cookie, you will be happy to know that Serge Obolensky will be married next month to Harry Hawkes's last young wife. She is tall & thin—like him—and has a head like a pin—like him!

Saltz tried to wiggle out of sending some Chinese figures and bronzes. But I pinned him down. Taking him tomorrow to . . . an exhibit of 16 Chinese bronzes— Big deal—16! you have 60, but I want to price them! Just for edification, not to sell! Please don't worry. . . .

Huxley [Aldous] was in town for one day—tea at Anita's on his way for a six-week seminar of lectures at Cambridge. Needs the dough. He asked me to go with him to a Zen lecture with a Zen dinner. He bought me the $3 book on Zen Diet and I've been on brown rice ever since! 3 days now— nothing on it but that sea salt— Have lost 4 lbs. and feel simply hilarious. I take no liquid but tea—and very little of that. Dining out I can have caviar and sole or lobster or baked oysters. Are you interested? Your own devoted, adoring wife.

Ritter of Ritter Furs is thrilled I will wear his sable coat on my T.V. show. The chubby one. Going down to the dress district to get 6 free gowns from a new house. . . . It is true the real Mrs. Remarque is in Ascona? Your perennial girlfriend, Mom.

Dearest Dream-Boat Best in the Entire World (& I should know)— Unequalled Man Power— Your evening with Isaac Stern is an Ascona classic—Mine too— Leonard Bernstein phoned invited me to dine with Stern when he plays here in Oct. Like a boob, I accepted with delite. Next day two tickets came in the mail at $50 each! At least you heard him play and saw him eat! Me—nothing!

Saw Kennedy-Nixon debate. They are both schoolboys. It was like a Junior debate on Civic Rules at a N.Y. High School.

Dearest Summer Kinder—Went to Loo today. Mr. Caro, in charge, said he would be glad to ship all your Tang ladies and bronzes via air-freight. He says the cost will be about $300 or $350. He said the alternative and safest way would be to take them with me by boat the next time. The charge is zero % except very small cost of packing. Also 100% safe & sure. You decide which you prefer next time I come by boat—in winter and bring many things. He had some marvelous things in his shop, but nothing as great as yours. I like him. He is not a grifter like all the other poisonous creatures. . . . I certainly am preparing myself for a Dealer's career for the Golden Years! . . .

Will be so happy to get home and simply stare at you, wunderkinder. What's going on chez vous?

Paulette's instincts and intuitions were so sharply honed that Gypsy Rose Lee called her "the real stripper; [she] knew what was underneath everything." She also gauged what people needed. If it was an item, she would not seek it out or shop for it, but if it fell into her hands, she would cheerfully send it to the person for whom it was right. She was forever sending Remarque uplifting printed matter, including Baudelaire's "L'Invitation au Voyage," which Paulette retitled "L'Invitation à la Casa Remarque."

During the writing of his next two novels, *Heaven Has No Favorites* (Harcourt, Brace and World, 1961) and *The Night in Lisbon* (Harcourt, Brace and World, 1964), Remarque found that Osnabrück was frequently on his mind. He had renewed his friendship and correspondence with his dear old friend Hanns-Gerd Rabe, who was a committed Osnabrücker throughout his life. With his health eroding, Remarque found nostalgia comforting, but not so much that he wished to go back and spend time in his home town. In fact, he resisted every opportunity. He attempts an explanation in a letter to Rabe: "I just received your letter and do not want to wait until I come to Osnabrück . . . before I reply. Strange that you should think that I have a love-hate relationship to Osnabrück and look negatively upon answering from there. Nothing could be farther from the truth. I have been wanting to go there for many years now, but whenever I get to Europe, I travel mostly via Paris or Milano to my house in Switzerland and time flies by so fast that I must rush back here without stopping by in Osnabrück. I love that city as much as you do. We both were born there and grew up there. To you over there, I am considered a child of the world, here my friends call me an Osnabrücker. One should never deny something and as you know, almost all my books feature O. in the background."

Heaven Has No Favorites was an exception, taking place instead in Paris,

Rome, the French Riviera, and Ascona. It was Remarque's "jet set" novel, with racing-car drivers and their glamorous lives as its subject. Inspired by his early days working as an editor for *Echo-Continental* when he was allowed to test-drive the rubber company's cars, and by his more than thirty-year friendship with the German star racer Rudolf Caracciola, Remarque, who was a would-be racer himself, had done more than enough research.

Considered one of his most minor novels, it had a rich history. In 1924, it had been written as the sketch "Vendervelde's Race"; then it was a short story called "Beyond," which was sold to United Artists, who made it the movie *The Other Love* in 1947. In 1927, while working as the editor of the Berlin sports and society magazine, *Sport im Bild*, he wrote the novel *Station on the Horizon*, which was never published in book form but ran as a serial in *Sport im Bild*. In 1977, it became the movie *Bobby Deerfield*, starring Al Pacino and Marthe Keller.

Clearly, the story held an attraction for Remarque, as it did for others who fostered its incarnations. It contained the commercial elements of romance, glamour, and heartbreak, but, as Hans Wagener summarizes the plot, it had a surplus of hairpin twists.

The aging race car driver Clerfayt visits his former co-driver, Hollmann, at the tuberculosis sanatorium Bella Vista located high in the Swiss Alps. There he meets an attractive and sensitive woman, Lillian Dunkerque, also a patient, who, after learning that her condition has worsened in spite of her diligently following all the hospital's rules, decides to leave the sanatorium and her lover, the Russian émigré Boris Volkov, to live life to the fullest before she dies. She goes to Paris with Clerfayt, and during the trip the two become lovers. In Paris she settles in a small hotel, and to the dismay of her uncle Gaston, a spendthrift who administers her small inheritance, she orders a number of expensive dresses from the fashion house Balenciaga. In the meantime Clerfayt, in Rome on business, meets his old lover, the sophisticated Lydia Morelli, intending to forget his affair with Lillian Dunkerque. Back in Paris, however, he falls in love with Lillian, and later tells her that he wants to marry her, retire from car racing, and take over his company's car franchise, which will soon become available in Toulouse. Eventually he takes her to a neglected house on the Riviera which he bought a long time ago, and makes plans for them to live there. But an average bourgeois life is not what Lillian wants. She decides to leave Clerfayt, but ironically Clerfayt is killed in an unimportant race through the streets of Monte Carlo. At the railway station, she meets her former lover, Boris Volkov, who has been

looking for her. Lillian goes back with him to the sanatorium, where she
dies six weeks later.

There were several versions of Lillian Dunkerque, depending from which
emotional vantage point Remarque was writing, and she grows in stature
until she becomes the main character in the novel, whereas in past editions it
was Clerfayt. Early on, Lillian clearly evoked Jutta: her illness, her beauty,
and her shunning of anything bourgeois. Next, Lillian was Dietrich—for
whom the part in the movie was intended—mainly because of Remarque's
idolization of her, not to mention her tendency to be an inconstant lover.
There was a pinch of Garbo to Lillian in the combination of her self-
containment and her hoydenish zest for life. He dedicated both the German
version of the novel and Richard and Clara Winston's English translation to
Paulette. "To Paulette Goddard Remarque" reads the inscription. Though
he had her in mind for the film, Remarque never mentioned for which role,
and in truth, she would have been perfect, if not more suitable, for the role
of Clerfayt's sophisticated ex-lover, Lydia Morelli, who was based on
Remarque's ex-lover Natasha Paley Wilson. It cannot be known what he
really had in mind for Paulette, because although the property was purchased by Columbia Pictures in the mid-sixties, it was not made until 1977,
and by then it was too late for Paulette to play either role.

Zen had entered both of their lives—in the beginning through Paulette's
enthusiasm—though perhaps it had a deeper, more mystical meaning for
Remarque. Paulette embraced some aspects of the Zen diet and some exercises—veering into yoga—while Remarque pondered the spiritual and
philosophical ideas connected to life, death, time, and destiny. He used these
ideas in *Heaven Has No Favorites*, threading them through the character of
Lillian, who, as Richard Arthur Firda points out, "is thus kin to Remarque's
early visionaries, those of *The Dream Room* Circle and Bodmer's lover,
Isabelle, in *Obelisk*. Like Fritz Hörstemeier and Isabelle, Lillian Dunkerque
is an intermediary between spiritual and earthly values."

She undergoes an ecstatic, somewhat psychedelic experience when visiting
Sainte-Chapelle in Paris: "She felt she was breathing light; it was as though
the blues and reds and yellows were coming through her lungs and blood.
. . . She was not isolated and solitary. Rather the light received her and sheltered her, and she had the mystic feeling that she could never die."

As Firda puts it in discussing Lillian's entrance onto a loftier plane, "The
vehicle for this experience is art and through this device, Remarque reaffirms
his commitment that art justifies the search for a perfect life."

Then there was Lillian's other side, inspired by Paulette, but more mystical:

> When the first things arrived from Balenciaga, Lillian did not hang them in the wardrobe. She hung them around her in the room. The velvet dress hung above the bed, with the silver one close beside it, so that she could touch them when she started up out of sleep, out of primordial terror dreams, the dreams of falling, plummeting alone, with a smothered cry from endless darkness into endless darkness. At such times she would stretch out her arm and grasp the dresses, and they were like silver and velvet ropes which she could use to draw herself back out of the shapeless greyness, back to walls, time, relationships, space, and life. She ran her hands over them, felt the cloth, and stood up and walked about her room, often naked, and felt that her dresses surrounded her like friends. . . . Only a woman could know, she thought, how much comfort there could be in a tiny hat. She wandered about at night among her acquisitions, held the brocade up to the moonlight, pulled a small cap over her hair, tried on a pair of shoes, and sometimes a dress. In the pale light, she stood studying herself in the mirror, looking into the muted phosphorescence, into her face, at her shoulders to see whether they were already gaunt, at her breasts, to see whether they were already drooping, and at her legs to look for those concave curves of emaciation in the thighs. Not yet, she thought, not yet. . . . And the image in the mirror smiled and questioned and looked back at her as though it knew more than she herself.

Heaven Has No Favorites and his next novel, *The Night in Lisbon*, were not well received by the German critics, who tended to dismiss the novels as fluff, romantic diversion, and superior pulp fiction, and the author as lightweight. Marcel Reich-Ranicki made the unkindest cut of all to any serious writer by judging the works as "facile." And, of course, Remarque's "defection" from Germany and its literary establishment still carried deep enough resentment to infect the criticism of his work. The general complaint was that he had not come even close to writing another *Magic Mountain*.

The American critic Maxwell Geismar hailed him as a major voice for *The Night in Lisbon*, and compared him to one of America's greatest writers, "for precisely like Hemingway, Remarque has an extraordinary sense of surface texture in his prose."

Germany was increasingly on Remarque's mind again and overtures, holding mixed messages, were being extended from the homeland. The interest in him personally had never really flagged, but although he was sought after for an interview by the prestigious paper *Die Welt*, he was still reviled enough for West German officials to quite consciously neglect any moves toward restoring his citizenship.

With his feelings of hostility in check against the German machine of right-wing politics and big business, Remarque went to Germany in 1962, agreeing to give the interview to *Die Welt*, and perhaps to meet with Hanns-Gerd Rabe, who was attempting to reunite Remarque with Osnabrück. Although he had had another small heart incident, he prized his mobility and was determined not to be always left to work in Porto Ronco while Paulette visited the emporiums of Europe and New York.

Actually, Paulette was at loose ends. She wanted to do a film in Europe, supposedly so as not to leave Remarque for an extended amount of time. The fact was that the Hollywood studios were not beckoning for her to play a lead for the kind of money she required. But she was willing to consider any money-making prospects that were not downright demeaning—for example, there had been talk of her writing a column or newsletter from the viewpoint of a "non-innocent abroad." Although technically she was represented by the William Morris Agency, Remarque's people—Robert Lantz and Harriet Pilpel—were all for offering their assistance. Harriet Pilpel, ever helpful, understood the delicate situation of roles for Paulette and wrote to the producer Paul Lazarus, diplomatically stating, "I am sure she [Paulette] would be absolutely delighted at the prospect of playing in a motion picture. . . . I do not think that at the moment she is contemplating a lead: rather some kind of character part which I know she would do very well."

In his interview for *Die Welt*, Remarque spoke boldly; he denounced the Nazi government for his depatriation; he proclaimed himself a free citizen of the world and a man with three viewpoints: German, Swiss, and American. He spoke as a conscientious objector and a pacifist. He condemned Berlin and the Wall. He condemned his sister's murder. He was puzzled by his German colleagues and comrades who had remained to suffer stoically, in silence. He was in Berlin, he was in Munich speaking out, but he did not go back to Osnabrück, where people waited, led by Hanns-Gerd Rabe, to bestow honor upon him. Perhaps he could not finally accept that.

Paulette wrote him during this time:

Dearest Love and Cooky—Here's the scandal sheet: Sinatra has been getting "girls" for Kennedy. Sinatra called off his marriage to that dancer because she liked J.F.K. better! Burn this letter.

Charles (Chaplin) has had a baby starlet girlfriend for 3 yrs. and spends every weekend with her in a Suisse village smaller than Vevey. She is a young (23) Jayne Mansfield [type] & he can't stand all those kids at home. Ironic. Now don't get any ideas because you still have to "make" me. . . . Absence does not make the heart fonder, but more lecherous. But only for you. . . . But I love the theatres, shops, dinners with a backdrop of 12,000,000 people rushing to grab it all. Your Zen fren', P.

Remarque would pine for her and she would pine back. Almost every letter displays this ritual, although both keep up the amusing, entertaining banter—Paulette being more successful at this. As their marriage endures, he is increasingly the abandoned yet indulgent parent and she is the frolicking teenager. Excerpts from letters written in the mid-sixties contain a unique quality of new lovers, forever planning their rendezvous:

REMARQUE: I'll find somebody, expectation of my life, my liver and my longing, to pick you up in the early morning at Malpensa, but you must, as I have asked yesterday, tell me if you are arriving on the 1st or 2nd of May. . . . Would you like to bring something? Perhaps a few of the Degas drawings? Or one of your little Renoirs? . . . I can't think much of anything except that stronger and stronger, and glowing more and more is the expecting of you; it is blinding my eyes, and the trumpets of welcome are already starting to rehearse all over the mountains, and the winds are full of calling your name.

PAULETTE: Dearest Love, Am so ready to get home to you. Read your beautiful letters over & over, missing you to the ultimate degree! When Ma read your letter to me—we both cried—blubbered.

I went to Valentina's annual cocktail party . . . and when George [Schlee] and she began to extol your virtues to me over a vodka, I burst into tears, so you see your emotional Mommie is boiling over. Only one more Sat. nite to howl without you.

. . . I don't know why I feel so guilty this time about bringing pictures, etc. back. I even think & feel that the tax people are digging into every detail. Just a feeling.

. . . Are you positively expecting me? I am positively madly in love with you. Your Leopardo.

REMARQUE: About ten times a day the ritual is a visit of the lonely bachelor at the shrine upstairs with a face in the pink room there like a moonstruck hippo! . . . The trembling is starting which will continue till the 2nd or 3rd of May, getting stronger and stronger, the breathless vibrations of a heart in love, waiting, hoping, expecting, impatient, and, in the most exciting way, sure.

Enjoy yourself the last weeks in New York. Take it all with great gaiety and without regrets, because you will go back in the Fall, together with me, and this will be only a reconnoiter trip, a soupçon of recognition, a fast reunion with your Mama and your hometown and there is more to follow! Laugh and be happy. Here in the alps is sitting your husband, tending flowers, chairs, trees, the terrace, and the fabulous garden of emotions which are jumping all around him like the fountains on Sunday night at the Place de la Concorde. Remember the tulips and narcissus and the light and the dancing waters? So it is with thee and me and so it shall and will be more and more.

PAULETTE: Dearest, my cable was too excited to be explicit. . . . I leave May 1st . . . arriving May 2nd. . . . Should be home by 9 A.M. That will be 3 A.M. by my clock. I don't mind if you don't meet me. It's the only non-stop $7\frac{1}{2}$ hour flite, and very easy for me.

Callas will be singing Medea at La Scala sometime in May. Will you find out when—so we can surely be there?

Am home to early bed tonite to dream and think of you. This weekend am attending another Alan Watts Zen Seminar—3 sessions a day! All more interesting than the vile plays I've seen. The worst play yet was *The Connection*. So dull it was nauseating! . . . All my love and wishes and plans and bones for you.

After the visit, Paulette is back in New York. Remarque, who has returned to his Swiss perch, is more reassuring, counseling, complimentary, and yearning than ever.

REMARQUE: I had the feeling last night, you were opening the door to come in—and it was the cat, coming from your room, meowing softly, wanting to get out to catch the moon, which was full red and gorgeous.

. . . You and your Ma must decide what you feel is right about the sale of the house [this being the house that Paulette owned and where Alta lived, on Alta Loma Road in Los Angeles]. Only one thought still: Money for real estate should be invested (in real estate, possibly) right away—or it shrinks. Same with paintings. Tell me how the Parke-Bernet sales went! At

Sotheby's a cat went for 100,000 Swiss francs. Next to Parke-Bernet is the shop Klejkamp. Friends of ours. Give them my regards and ask them if they still have a blackish, smallish cat with gold earrings which they had when I was last there for $600. If yes, tell me. I might get it for you.

REMARQUE: Mama . . . I, myself, think that the best thing to keep in the world at this time is real estate property. It will go up and up, and all one can do later is regret to have sold it so cheaply. It even happens with pictures. I could regret that I've sold the Degas . . . today it is not so expensive anymore compared with a year ago. (I don't regret it! I bought the Monet!) But think it over carefully. I know that you and your Mama consider that you'd make a nice profit (in numbers only!). But think of the old paintings!

Otherwise I was revived, and, of course, mortally struck at the same time by a call from you which brought you into this big icy room—so clearly came your voice and your fantastic presence. . . .

It is a great surprise to Rosa and me that the most gorgeous thing in the whole garden are the tulips you brought last fall from Locarno. I think you bought them at the hairdresser and all the professionals [green thumbs] here smiled indulgently and we put them in the spot of earth in front of the kitchen window (Well, P.G.'s tulips, you know, God knows what she's got there). Well, they are, each flower, as large as giant cabbages, a flaming, indescribably beautiful silken red, so enormous that we can see them on the other side of the lake. People try to steal them! Rosa is flabbergasted! So am I! Well, Mama did it once more! Everybody is craving for their name! Well, P. bought them either at the hairdresser or in a tabac shop. Not in a flower shop? God forbid! So, we don't know the names of these monsters of screaming beauty. They just fell from heaven—as you did, Queen of the brightest nights. . . . I love, worship, adore, and cuddle you. . . .

Enjoy yourself to the hilt, my love. . . . I am tossing and turning on the storm of love, and at the same time, also safely in this haven.

PAULETTE: Oh Dad, Poor Dad—Your last letter was so sad. Why don't you lunch on the Piazza these warm golden spring days? I know there's no place like home, but a good walk in the sun can make you love it even more.

Why do you wish I were twins? When you know that I am? So are you! Your presence is here—on T.V. *All Quiet* this week. On the newsstands—your paperback novel [*Heaven Has No Favorites*]. Edward's Drugstore has stocked fifty copies. Says they're selling like hotcakes.

Don't worry about my T.V. crisis. The shows were to be taped at 10 A.M.

—which meant up at six for hair & makeup. Also, the five programs were "Games"!—called *Password*. I backed out after I saw Van Johnson & Jane Fonda perform it. Really idiotic. Am still doing my dramatic spot. Am inarticulate this A.M. because it's Sunday and I want you and crave your presence. Wish you were twins!

Am Seeing Huxley tonight after his lecture. . . . Supper at the Plaza.

Mon.—Shopping with Jinx.

Tues. Alan Watts lecture in the Village.

Weds. Opening of the circus. John Ringling North & 80 friends.

Thurs. Ball of the Year—I make a presentation for something or other.

Fri. Photos of my Antique Exhibit at the 18th century Carnival—I call it A Room at the Ritz.

Sat. & Sun. Alan Watts' Zen Seminar and lectures

Great variety here. One can dip into any way of life. I'm doing it all in one month!

Your flowers were gorgeous again. Red Glads in the black Chinese vase. Shrieking "Hello Mommie" when I come into the room.

Why do you stay in the house all the time? Are you feeling okay? Please tell me in your next note. I worship your letters & you.

REMARQUE: Today, Kleopatra, came your second letter, yesterday the panicky one. . . . It's all over, you are right, jobs like the ones you refused you can get all the time, it's much better to do dramatic ones. (Of course, oh twin! you can do them if you change your gorgeous mind—that we know) but do just what you really like to do. We are not so desperate for money or work! Look at even the greatest actresses getting old—Duse dying in Pittsburgh, the ridicules of Mistinguette on tour as an ever-young grandma and so on. The best and last star part of an actress is marriage at the right time. Basta. Anything else should be just velvet and only if you like it.

Time of Indifference, shot at Cinecittà in Rome, put Paulette back in the movies. After a long retirement, this return to the screen would be her first and last. She filmed in the summer of 1963 in one of her favorite cities, playing opposite Rod Steiger. In the initial stages, she thought she had returned to some kind of glory. The producer, Franco Cristaldi, had dangled prestige and histrionic opportunity before Paulette—as well as a weekly salary of $3,375, of which she was extremely proud. She crowed in a letter to

Remarque about being a substantial wage earner again: "Am taking the $1,860,000 lira check to the bank tomorrow to see how it can be transferred to your account. I want you to have the 1st dough, so you will feel why I'm here. It's very nice to have."

The movie, referred to in Italian as *Gli indifferenti*, was based on a novel by Alberto Moravia, and featured two other powerful actresses. Paulette could deal with playing Claudia Cardinale's mother, an aging yet still beautiful countess on her uppers; however, it was in Shelley Winters that she met her rival. Paulette did not agree with Winters about the role Winters was playing. By Winters's account, she was "playing a remittance woman, sort of Paulette's personal saleslady and cosmetologist." By Paulette's account, Winters was playing her maid. They approached their roles completely differently. Winters held a cynical view from the beginning, noting that Cardinale was the producer Cristaldi's girlfriend and hence the reason for making of the picture, which, as she puts it, "started in chaos and ended up in shambles. It seemed that the producer, Cristaldi, was making a film about a romance between Claudia Cardinale and Tomas Milian—and the director, Maselli, was making a political picture about the rise of Fascism. . . . Everyone in the film spoke a different language. Rod Steiger, Paulette Goddard, and I sort of spoke English. Tomas Milian, who was Cuban, spoke Spanish, and Claudia Cardinale just made sounds. She had been born and raised in Tunisia, had spent a few years in Spain, and had arrived in Italy at eighteen. . . . The film director, Francesco Maselli, barely spoke English."

Although Winters felt the picture was a shambles, she concedes that there were some good things in it—namely, Rod Steiger's performance and, interestingly enough, her work with Paulette, whom she recalls with fond amusement:

I think my scenes with Paulette Goddard were very funny. I remember one in which I was giving her a facial. I had worked with her in *The Women* and she had worn different sets of jewelry every day and she did the same in this film. It was rather difficult to get around her diamond necklaces while I was giving her neck and face a facial, but we had very amusing scenes together. She was indeed fun to work with in this film, rather zany, and she would tell me long, rambling stories about how stingy Charlie Chaplin was, ignoring the fact that she was the only woman in his history who got a lot of money and jewels from him. I told her about the open house on Sundays at Charlie and Oona's that I had gone to. She was amazed.

"I can't believe he spent money on food for strangers, talented or not," she said.

Rod Steiger, who enjoyed being in Rome, recalls the turmoil on the set, and between the two women:

> *Time of Indifference* was a very good piece of material, but didn't come off because of miscasting, besides which there was a lot of dissension on the set and Maselli, the director, was driven crazy. Eventually, he had a nervous collapse and was taken away. Paulette was always very professional with me, and she was very funny. She was a very good comic actress. She was just wonderful working with Chaplin; the only other actress who could keep up with him was Marie Dressler. But on our picture there was this rivalry between Paulette and Shelley Winters. It was the craziest thing. They couldn't even enter through the same door without deliberately bumping into each other, trying to push each other out of focus. The culmination of their competition came when they both complained about the color of their hats that they had to wear in one particular scene. The irony was that we were shooting in black and white, but they both just frothed away anyhow.

Paulette was not pleased with the way she looked in this picture, but she had also not been in a film for ten years, since she was forty-four. Her new diamond and ruby necklace, a gift from Remarque worth a quarter of a million dollars and so heavy that she could wear it only for short spells, was some consolation. Paulette was not one to anguish over anything for too long, but her looks had been a major contribution to her fortune, and now, she would either have to take on the mantle of a character actress, like Constance Collier, or stop making movies.

The American audience could not have cared less about the movie, which puzzled Shelley Winters, who thought it was worthy of a late-night television showing at least. However, the review in *Variety* came forth with the plaudits that Paulette had rarely gotten at the height of her beauty. "Paulette Goddard probably walks off with honors as the aging mother still obsessed by her man and the maintenance of a status quo—at all costs. Her near-finale scene in which she suddenly and finally realizes the truth is shattering in its power."

The Italian press heralded Paulette, making it clear that she could have had a new career in Italy had she wanted it. But their reviews were too graphic for her, pointing up things that she did not want to see:

PAULETTE GODDARD, whom we have never considered a great actress and whose roles were usually quite obvious, here is greater than Gloria Swanson in *Sunset Boulevard*. At 53 years of age she has exploded with a part greater than herself. Although she has selected to act in the "old-fashioned manner" with the grimaces of that epoch, only in this way could she rightly represent a middle-aged woman still greedy for the fruits that her teeth do not allow her to bite anymore. It is a pathetic character in her iron consistency, in her intrepid imbecility.

In late 1963 the quality of Remarque and Paulette's relationship altered considerably when Remarque suffered a stroke that left him partially paralyzed on his right side and temporarily affected his speech center. The stroke, although considered a severe warning, was not in the major aphasia category. Still, it caused him a setback from which he never fully recovered; in her, it provoked a complicated set of reactions. She was at turns frightened, annoyed, revulsed, bullying, maternal, overly alluring, and then finally, much the same toward him as she had always been. The real difference was that she avoided spending long periods of time with him, which made him pine for her all the more, feeling deprived and often desperately lonely. He had had the stroke in Porto Ronco. Soon after, Paulette returned to New York "to do the season" with plays, shopping, lunches, dinners, and galas. She carefully researched how to help him, finding the very best doctor in Zurich to visit him in Porto Ronco, but she did not rush back to his side. They planned for her to come when he was rehabilitating—around the middle of February; both seemed to think that best. His letters to her and to Alta convey a sorrowful yet valiant figure who would be extremely grateful for the company of his wife, yet who comprehends her need not to see him that way. He writes in January of 1964 to Alta:

> This is my first letter since two months and I am writing it to you to tell you that we love you. Paulette is coming on the 11 or 12 of February and will stay quite a while—two months I guess.
> As you see I am making lots of mistakes. But the doctor says it takes time and it will get better in time.

It was a slow process, perhaps made slower by Paulette's postponed arrival. In the meantime, his overall condition had been diagnosed as arteriosclerosis, manifesting itself in a stroke. In a mid-February letter, Paulette was authoritative and compassionate:

Walter Alvarez is the genius doctor in the U.S. for your problem. . . . When I see Ibanez [another expert] Tues. he will submit several suggestions for our next move. Altho so far they all say—rest, rest, rest.

I love you so much, that I have trouble breathing when I think of you. Otherwise I am feeling so very well, that something MUST be wrong!

Remarque's almost daily letters to her struggle toward normalcy (these are some of the few that he dated):

Feb. 15th: Little princess of rubies, I am sitting quietly here writing you somewhat slowly my first letter. It is raining outside—naturally. . . . I hope you had a nice trip and the fleurs arrived in time. Snow and furs, wonderful. . . .

It is very difficult to be tender, mama, if one is writing so slowly and has to watch it all time and makes mistakes.

But my heart is full of you, little chimpanzee! Love to your mama, too. Eric, your pupil from ground school, 8th grade.

Feb. 18th: . . . I am not good today in writing. I am sorry about it but there it is. I better stop. Must be patient. Don't worry. I guess it changes. A pity that I can't tell you better how I love you. Please have a lot of fun and pleasure! . . . I write like an ape. But I love you more every day.

Feb. 19th: . . . I will try to write to you often. Exercise and a wonderful habit to learn the language again. . . . My letters will be only short. I am getting too impatient to spell so slowly—because I am very patient in holding you in my hands but very impatient in my love to show you my progress. That was a word, wasn't it?

The first camellia on the terrace is out. Pink and incredibly beautiful. Close the windows—it's too beautiful. No, open them wide. Love, my life. E.

Feb. 24th: . . . I was at Pedrazzi [his doctor in Ascona] to take blood, etc. He told me he thinks I don't need special exercise, it will come by itself because nothing is damaged. . . . Contrary he thinks too much electric shocks, etc. would be not so good, and that natural movements were enough. [At this point in the letter, his writing begins to buckle.] I am sorry, Mama, I will stop. [He tries to write a sentence containing the word *depression*, can't get the spelling right, and after several attempts, gives up.] I feel well. I walk every day. It is only English I can't write. It will come. But it makes me a bit sad not to be able to write you gorgeous love letters. It will come again. First I must learn German back. Not all at once. One after the other. Don't worry! It will come back. I don't worry myself. Always was stupid and need time. Pedrazzi thinks I am better. . . . The address on the envelope I wrote already very well, n'est pas?

Miraculously, Remarque managed to pull himself out of his "prison" in record time. He wrote to his old friend Victoria Wolff that the thought of his "young" wife made him "race." In a little under a year, he was writing, conversing, traveling, keeping his diary again, and his latest novel, *The Night in Lisbon*, was being published in America. In October of 1964, he and Paulette went on a small holiday to Venice, Florence, and Milan. In his diary, Remarque writes with a new economy and gratitude—upon hearing of the fatal heart attack of his old friend George Schlee: "The sudden flash, no one can escape. . . . Thank God, that I can get excited again. During my depression in the beginning of '64, everything was dead. For what, had been the question. For the short time? The first big brush with death, my own."

After the trip, they went their separate ways—he back to Porto Ronco and she to New York. The pattern would resume and they would start missing each other anew. She would not be there to see what Remarque referred to as "the invasion of Osnabrück."

Since he would not, and now pleading health problems, could not go to Osnabrück, a troop led by Hanns-Gerd Rabe would come to him in Porto Ronco to bestow upon him their highest honor: the Möser Medal of the City of Osnabrück. If we judge by Remarque's diary, it seems it was more of a momentous occasion for them than for him:

[Nov. 1, '64]: Yesterday morning, the delegation from Osnabrück. The Lord Mayor Kelch, the directors Voss, Kuehler, five senators, a photographer, a reporter, a radio man, Hanns-Rabe as journalist, all together eleven people. Small speeches, the presentation of the Möser Medal, a certificate, and an old map of Osnabrück. Touching and boring. What should one do with eleven people with whom one has nothing to discuss? Served them foie gras, lox and champagne. They left at 1 o'clock. Had traveled for 15 hrs. through dense fog, had seen nothing. I was very tired in the afternoon. I dreaded the evening. Had invited all to dinner at Feldpausch. They arranged everything. Candles, silver, and at the end a special cake with the names of all my books and a marzipan representation of the crest of

Remarque on the terrace at Casa Remarque with its sweeping views of Lake Maggiore, ca. 1964.

In a local Ascona ceremony, Paulette looks on while Remarque is presented with the Distinguished Service Cross of the Order of Merit of the Federal Republic of Germany, 1967.

Osnabrück. That did it. The menus had ribbons in black and white, the colors of Osnabrück. The manager of the restaurant was from Osnabrück and knew this. I would not have known it. The Lord Mayor took the marzipan crest with him. I was happy when it was over—tired and bored, but touched that the eleven had traveled so far and had not even had beautiful weather here in Ticino.

Osnabrück would continue to be very much on Remarque's mind. In the mid-sixties his correspondence with Hanns-Gerd Rabe resumed, continuing until his death, and he wrote with increased passion and nostalgia for his hometown: "Please send my greetings to all my old schoolfriends again, and tell them that I very often think of the happy old days of our youth—that's probably always the case when one gets older. Youth then often seems strangely close, as if it were only a few years past instead of more than half a lifetime away."

Through these years, Rabe never gave up on the idea of Remarque's return. And each year Remarque would dicker as to whether he should go and then back away: "Nothing will come of my trip to Osnabrück this year; it is too far and too exhausting, also emotionally, strange as that may sound."

The Night in Lisbon, translated into English by Ralph Manheim and published in 1964 by Harcourt, Brace and World, was dedicated "To Paulette Remarque." It was the last of his émigré novels and a feat of construction. It is virtually a long monologue told by a German refugee named Schwartz (this being an assumed name, after he had taken the identification papers off a dead man whose name was not really Schwartz) during the course of a night spent in limbo in Lisbon. He tells his ballad-like tale to another, younger refugee, to whom he has given his passport with which to flee to freedom in America. His story is strange, compelling, and, ultimately, at least for one influential book critic, Maxwell Geismar of the *New York Times*, "It is almost a manual of underground refugee existence, depicting the life and 'culture' of the hunted and dispossessed during these years. . . . In some respects Erich Maria Remarque has had a curious career, but it is a great tribute to this aging literary veteran of World War I that now, at the age of 66, he has produced what may be his best novel. A famous European counterpoint to Hemingway, Remarque has, through the years, almost converted a handsome minor talent into a major one; whereas Hemingway almost reduced his own large talent into a more limited one. . . . In this novel Remarque reveals his extraordinary talent for entertainment and narrative suspense. He is a very gifted artist on the human level who can be playful, witty, nostalgic and tender in turn; like Charlie Chaplin he is both hilariously funny and a great tearjerker."

The Night in Lisbon was the first novel in which he used the real name of his hometown, Osnabrück, as well as the names of some real streets. He was ready to embrace certain aspects of his roots, whereas others he still found troublesome. He chose to withdraw instead of reaching out when his sister Erna phoned him with the news that her husband, Walter Rudolf, had died of emphysema. He writes in his diary, "Thought about whether I should go to Rothenfelde, decided not. . . . Her [Erna's] stepson Klaus arrived with his fiancée. She will not be alone now. Trip would have been too long and difficult for me. It's cold already and cumbersome, also I risk having another attack, and I cannot give more than warmth. Hate myself for that."

The next day, he comforted himself by buying a Degas drawing from his art dealer Walter Feilchenfeldt's widow, Marianne. Two days later, Paulette arrived "happy and beautiful." He presented her with a pair of bronze earrings in the shape of cats' heads, they went to the village, ate at one of their favorite restaurants, Al Porto, and afterward "made many purchases."

When Paulette was back, the whole town of Ascona was primed for observation and gossip. In Ascona, they cast more aspersions than accolades, but there was one thing that everybody agreed upon: Paulette was fascinating.

The small town watched and seemed to take on the role of a disapproving headmistress. It tsked in unison at Paulette's always overdressing and wearing bright colors, spike heels, and unnaturally colored furs, such as her red nutria. With her penetrating voice and autocratic manner, she snubbed those who held no interest for her and she did not tip well. She refused to speak German, and she would leave a party when bored—which was often immediately after she had been fed. She lived by her own rules in a town that was circumspect, provincial, and extremely proud. Unlike Hollywood, it had no reason to understand or accept her.

Remarque's good friends tended to be creative, intellectual, and well-to-do; for the main, they accepted and were amused by Paulette—the men being more impressed. Through the sixties, the writer Hans Habe was probably Remarque's closest male friend. Similar to Remarque in style, flair, and interests—including roving eyes—Habe was a good foil for Remarque and vice versa. "They exchanged brains" was the way his widow, Licci Habe, put it. Licci, who was his sixth wife, recalls her husband's view of Paulette: "Hans felt as I did, that she was clever. Absolutely. You don't have such success with such clever men if you are an idiot, and not only because you want jewels. She was a clever, intelligent human being—in an abstract way. Hans always said, 'Paulette is the only person in the world who talks abstract. One sentence is good, and the next one is strange. It finishes nowhere.'"

The foursome would often get together in the evening, with raucous, if not downright acrimonious results. Everything would start out smoothly enough; Paulette usually wore black, to accentuate her famous cabochon earrings or the ruby-lipped brooch designed by Dalí or the collar of rubies and diamonds or the all-ruby heart brooch. There was another reason for Paulette's wearing black—her least favorite hue—to the Habe house. Several times she had tried to coerce Licci Habe into visiting the safe where she kept her famous jewels, "but I saw to it that I never had time," Licci Habe says. "So Paulette wore black in order to display her jewels to me." Remarque would be gracious but removed until he began to drink, when he would become increasingly charming, playful, even rambunctious. This was after his stroke, and Licci Habe recalls that "Paulette was very, very anxious that Erich shouldn't drink. It was always the same thing when they were invited to our place. She would say, 'Erich, you're not drinking.' And he drank. And she would say, 'If you drink one more, I'm going.' And she always left. Always!! She got up and left him alone, because he had no driver's license. At that point, it had been taken away from him. But he was happy, because when she was gone he could speak German."

Licci Habe feels that theirs was a "very large love," but that there were large quirks as well. One was that there was a feeling of artifice about their relating: "You had the feeling they were playing a game. You know, like a Noël Coward play. They played something. They fought constantly in company," she says. "Actually, she was the one. He didn't fight. He would laugh and laugh, which made her all the more furious. And he would do a funny little thing, which drove her nuts. When he drank, he wouldn't let anyone take away his empty glass. He mixed drinks, you know, and he would yell out, 'Don't take away the glass!' And he would be lining up all his glasses like little soldiers. Just out of fun. Fun for him; not for her.

"Another thing which made her furious was when he spoke German. If he had somebody around him who spoke German, he started to speak German. It made Paulette very angry. At the dinner table, Erich would speak German with me, and Hans would be a good host and speak only in English with Paulette. She hated the Germans passionately." Others—such as the painter Rolf Gerard and the defense lawyer, Dr. Ralph Rosenbaum—concur that there were scenes during these last years together. However Remarque, always feeling secure about Paulette, was quoted as saying, "She will never leave me. Paulette will stay until the last carpet."

From 1965 until his death, Remarque was in considerable pain. Along with arterial discomfort and alarmingly regular small accidents, his angina was acting up. It is clear from his diary that he felt he was on the verge of having a major heart attack. "With me, everything is a story, even the things that concern me directly," he said in the winter of 1965–66, when an avalanche struck Casa Remarque (while he and Paulette were in it), sparing the house but practically erasing the garage and Remarque's cherished garden. In 1965, he had booked passage to New York on the *Michelangelo*, canceling at the last minute because Paulette wanted to stop and shop in Paris; he later found out that the ship had been hit by a monster wave and had gone under, killing the people who had taken their place in the stateroom. After these events, Remarque attempted to stay more or less sedentary, but to keep Paulette happy, they would winter in Rome. He did not want to contemplate going to New York anymore. Paulette was still determined to make the rounds of restaurants, theater, opera, and shopping in Europe and New York.

In 1965, they went from Rome to Milan to attend performances at La Scala of *Norma* and *La Bohème*, after which Remarque did not feel at all well. He records, "On the morning of the 22nd, I feel pressure on my chest. Feeling of angina pectoris. Took medication, did not help. After an hour, the Dr. Blood pressure lower than usual. Injections, daily visits by Dr. Just missed heavy attack. . . . Thoughts: Two very fast attacks, one after the other. Life expectancy shortened considerably."

Remarque was beginning to worry about Paulette, who felt the strain of living with his restrictions. Back in Porto Ronco, he records, "Still pressure in chest at times. Slight problems with P. It's difficult for her, what shall she do here? Alone, I talk very little, she almost has no acquaintances. Who speaks English here? And, she cannot read the entire time, either. On the 25th, she wants to go to Paris, to do synchronization of her film there [there was dubbing to be done on *Time of Indifference*]. What shall I do? I can't travel yet, the medicine makes me tired. Poor P.! She has so much life, happiness, and natural easy-goingness! But everything here is like lead. And I can't leave with her. Winter was too long for her. We wanted to go to Cairo, but then did not go. It was better that way. The attack caught up with me in Milan all the same."

———

Through the pain and fear of death, through his anxiety about Paulette, he worked on a new novel, with a new intensity and as though he had a score to settle. The novel, *Shadows in Paradise* (*Schatten im Paradies*) was a natural continuation of *The Night in Lisbon*, picking up where the last left off. Always tied to the plight of the émigré, the story in this posthumously published work involves the flight of the émigré to America, something he knew everything about. The ship, still in port at the end of *The Night in Lisbon*, sails the next morning, in the new book, to the promise of a paradise in America. In this novel, his mournful theme plays itself out: of being lost forever in a newfound land.

Barker and Last have titled a chapter in their exploration of the work of Remarque "False Paradise," which encapsulates the results of Remarque's philosophy of the exile arriving anywhere that is a supposed haven. Barker and Last note that Remarque was haunted not only by the German émigré's fleeing the Nazi regime, but by "refugees from other countries, notably from Russia and Spain. He seems to regard the émigré existence as a twentieth-century disease. Schwartz tells Helen in *The Night in Lisbon*: 'There are . . . more emigrants than one thinks. Including some who have never moved from the spot.'"

Remarque was working on the novel as well as on some old problems. He finally succumbed to the pressure of owing money on a 1930 German tax bill. The Germans had been hounding him since 1929 about it. He writes in his diary, "Should not have done it, but paid the small sum. I am still not healthy enough to enter risks."

One of his old problems, that of working slowly and erratically, was being addressed by the feeling that time was no longer on his side: "I always had the worst conscience in the world. If only I had written as regularly as other writers I should have had a much happier life. Only now am I beginning to get some pleasure from my work. Ever since the doctor has tried to prevent me from writing, the whole business has acquired something dangerous and attractive."

Remarque seemed to be hanging on to the thrill of seeing Paulette each time she returned to him: "P. Life and all answers." Yet his work was a more constant life raft. The last entry in his diary is dated March 7, 1965:

Movie version of *Zorba the Greek* is one of those false myths that purport that only irresponsible adventurers know how to live. One should examine all such truths! (Like B. Shaw did.) It would be enough for two writers to live for and on!

Continue to read Berenson diaries. Discover more and more similarities, on the surface as well as in attitude. A Cancer, with all his shortcomings. . . .

Condition now like during the war. One is in position, more dangerous than peace, but not as dangerous as the front. It could happen, more often than during peace, but like a fire attack. One lives and is almost satisfied. This is how it is with people who have heart illnesses. . . .

And the entire world with all justices and injustices, with mass murderers, with crimes and its indescribable beauty. And everything that remains in the end is another hand holding the hand of the dying. . . .

Maybe start the book differently. Pre-spring, evening before on the terrace, tight chest, the feeling of having to breathe quietly so that nothing would burst—and the other, whether one would survive the night. Only a feeling, but the night has become the great uncontrollable, the fabric that chokes and heals. Every morning appears, should appear like Aphrodite from wine-colored, foaming ocean, wind in the hair, the horizon in the background. And every evening is a last one, with moon, the wide, open sky, the transparent green, the white fog.

"I look like an iguana that has leprosy," Paulette wrote cheerfully to Remarque in 1965 after looking at the daily rushes of *Time of Indifference*, not having seen herself on film in ten years. She protests against "re-creating that whole ghastly part," but inserts, "Well, I still just love to act—even the dubbing is great fun." Paulette was used to hearing regularly from Remarque, to reading that she was his "beloved golden panther," his "Angelica," his "Delight of the Millennium," and when she did not hear from him for a time, then she worried.

April 26, 1965: "Here's the latest flash—I haven't had one word by mail from you and I must tell you I feel miserable not to find a letter from you in my postbox. You spoiled me so with lovely letters that now if a few days pass without a word from you, I worry and wonder how you feel and what you are dreaming about and could you ever miss me as terribly as I do you?"

He missed her sorely, as these excerpts of intimacy from his letters convey. Although lonely and in pain, he apologizes for deserting her, he forever reiterates the celebration of their union and reunions, and he offers a curious combination of clinical descriptions of his condition and sexual longing:

I hope to heaven my neuralgia will stop. . . . I had a strange dream: You were sitting on a chair, I was sitting on the floor, my shoulders and neck between your legs and I felt my pain going. In any case, pain or not, I will try it. . . . I am taking since you left daily ten strong anti-pain tablets and on top of it daily four in my behind—suppositories, furthermore, daily, two shots from [the doctor]. Of course, my skin is in rather lousy condition and, since I don't walk (no time, and I shouldn't much, anyhow) I have gained 5 pounds. . . . This is to prepare you for not exactly a Greek god . . . but I will be all right as soon as I am in your paws. It's very tough for me to wait—the moment I heard your voice on the telephone Abraham was standing up and before I put down the phone the bastard was spitting like a fountain. Even now, writing you, my hands are shaking, and yesterday, Sunday, it was rather difficult. . . . I feared I would get another heart attack. For the same reason I better close this letter now, especially since next to me lies a photo of us in Venice, in a Dutch magazine, which has an absolutely nutty effect on me . . . it's two months now! I adore, worship, and love you every day more.

I do really think that you are the utmost of everything which could be combined in a human, a femme, and a phantasmagoria without breaking the seams. Do enjoy your rich, solitary life, you sneaky gorgeous snake, enjoy it to the hilt. You are adorable here in this beautiful petit bourgeois place, made by gods and inhabited by mice and half-finished beings. You did it! Every night I go into your rooms before I go into mine, and they are serene, beautiful, and full of the moon. The stars are all hanging around, the lake is a platter of restless silver . . . the moonlight falling through the French doors . . . the quiet Renoirs and the furniture of the Grand Canal . . . telling silently that there is no difference anywhere, that it is you who makes and gives the enchantment and Polly who makes Abraham work again and keeps things going again.

Both Remarque and Paulette agreed that Porto Ronco was too desolate for her in the winter, and so they were mostly apart for the holidays during the last five years of his life. After the first of the year, from 1965 through 1968, they would spend long winters-into-spring together in Rome, but Paulette tried to be in New York whenever possible. She was at heart a "mama's girl," as Licci Habe called her, and because in 1966 she had moved her mother into 15E, his old apartment at 320 East Fifty-seventh Street, she was happier and busier in New York with her ever-young mama than with her aging, sick husband.

Alone, Remarque on New Year's morning of 1966 sends love and money: "My Gorgeous Darling, it is very early morning . . . and I've crept secretly out of my bed to write you the first letter of the year. . . . I am sitting here contemplating my luck, shaking myself by both hands (an acrobatic little stunt) and thinking of all the things I've wanted to do for you and with you and didn't. Full of remorse I stare out of the window and swear that I will be better this year, healthier, more gay, and a traveler comme il faut. Have a bit of patience with me and I promise you I will just start to bloom like a camellia. . . . I am happy with you and you have made me far, far happier than I ever thought I could be, as such a born worrier of Westphalian origin, Don Quixote of exuberance and misanthropy equally mixed. And to do . . . the first thing of the year let me for once be rather sensible and give you a very small check so that the year is lucky for both of us and is starting right."

Paulette thanked him for the "lovely, fresh money," and issued a heart's desire: that they try, after wintering in Rome, to spend together a couple of months in New York in the spring. Since his physician had forbidden him to fly, they sailed from Genoa on the liner *Raffaelo* at the end of April.

They "played New York," as Paulette put it, going to some of their favorite haunts: Chambord, Pavillon, Sardi's, the Metropolitan Museum, as well as being adventurous and sampling Paulette's "nouvelle theater" by going to *The Birthday Party* and *The Basement* by Harold Pinter. Paulette's comment about what they saw was scribbled on her program: "These plays were so dull, really immature, painfully boring, really agony to sit through."

In New York, Remarque managed to work a bit on the new book— although with this one he kept entirely quiet about its subject matter as well as his struggle in writing it. This was something new for him. Previously, the activity of writing each novel had been, according to his frequent translator and editor, Denver Lindley, "the drama of the century."

Because Remarque had to watch himself so carefully about what he ate, where he went, and how much energy he could exert, both he and Paulette agreed that it was best he return to Porto Ronco in August and not see out the very active "autumn in New York."

It was time for old friends. He heard from Victoria Wolff after many years—she and her husband had relocated in California. In a mellow mood, he wrote to Hanns-Gerd Rabe about his trip to the States and his newly balanced, Paulette Zen-like perspective:

The weather was happy, New York terrific, and it did me good, especially the until-now-unknown fact that New York is the most exciting city I know. I have lived too long in the peacefulness of village life on Lago

Maggiore, and even Rome, Florence, and Venice are mere variations from that life, whereas New York! It is really a city without the melancholy and oppression of the past! It is exciting life! It is the future. It is possible that one could get tired of it and then look forward to cottages and furniture of the 18th century, but I was only there for two exciting months and that was just right.... Now, I should dare to go to Osnabrück! And I hope that I can attempt a visit in September, if all goes well. These attacks, unfortunately, have something very sudden about them. Yesterday still on the high horse, today—But let's hope! It would be nice!

Hope was what he was full of when again he began the New Year alone in his beautiful house on the lake. And again, the first thought on his mind was Paulette, as he writes on January 1, 1967: "My gorgeous and beloved one, it is the time this morning to tell you that without you the last year would have been dark and rather hopeless for me—with you it seems to me like the beginning of a wonderful love—so many new and marvelous qualities sprouted out of you which I would never have expected. You are such a surprise every day that I felt like lying in the cradle of your arms and nothing could happen to me, nothing bad as long as you were there. Thank you, my love, thank you with all my heart—it was a terrible time for you, I know— but it was a secure time full of love for me. Thank you, my love forever!"

In July of 1967, Paulette and Remarque's friend the attorney Robert Kempner was present for a strangely dubious honor that was bestowed upon Remarque in Porto Ronco. The award, given by the Federal Republic of Germany, was the Distinguished Service Cross of the Order of Merit of the Federal Republic of Germany; it was granted by President Heinrich Lubke and presented by the German ambassador. Paulette carried a sheaf of roses and looked uncomfortable, as well she might have from the lukewarm words attached to the award:

The author Erich Maria Remarque, despite the loss of his civil rights at the hands of the national socialist government, his exile fate, and the tragic events in his family—his sister was executed during the Third Reich—has vigorously sought a reconciliation with today's Germany. His attitude has not been without effect on numerous German literary personalities who, like him, chose Switzerland as an exile.

If one takes as a basis the number of copies sold, no German-language author in this century has had a greater success than Remarque with *All*

LEFT: *Remarque is reunited with his wartime friend Hanns-Gerd Rabe for the presentation of the Möser Medal for being an outstanding citizen of Osnabrück, in Ascona, 1964.*

ERICH MARIA REMARQUE

This last book photo of Remarque was taken for his posthumous novel, Shadows in Paradise, *ca. 1970.*

Quiet on the Western Front, and a few others of his novels (estimated total publication—ea. 15 million).

Among the great survivors of German literature of the Exile Period who live in Switzerland today, Remarque, in addition to Zuckmayer, occupies a prominent position.

Remarque was gracious as ever, but also ambivalent. Accepting the award suggested that he was accepting the German government again, yet with this changed and forgiving Germany, renewal of his citizenship was still being withheld.

In August of 1967, Remarque suffered another heart attack, and then a more severe one in mid-November. He recovered in the St. Agnes Clinic in Locarno for six weeks, after which there was more recuperating in bed in Porto Ronco—mostly without Paulette. His New Year's letter of 1968 gently and stirringly apologizes for his condition and forgives her for not physically being with him more:

My gorgeous capitano, thank you for guiding your husband's erratic lifeship over the year 1968. It was a wonderful year, full of quiet surprises and full of the warm feeling of love which you gave me and I couldn't reciprocate as much as I wanted. I would have liked to go everywhere with you, to strange countries and to new adventures. You had to do your traveling by yourself. But believe me, I was all the time with you in spite of sitting in an armchair at home. My fantasies flew with you and each time you came home with your luminous smile and your incredible presence, it lifted me right away to the Himalayas, to Timbuktu, Noa-Noa, to New York, Alaska, and all the South Sea Islands of the world. You were in my heart all the time, that was the secret—in its most precious chamber of jade and gold. All I wish, Capitano, is that you stay there, even if you navigate around through wonders of the world. The heart is a wonder, too.

As Remarque was working through drafts and rewrites of *Shadows in Paradise*, which took him farther away from home than any of his other books, he yearned for Osnabrück and the times he thought he had loved.

Mrs. Karla Henkelmann, née Hoberg, was the daughter of Maria Hoberg, who had rented the top floor of her house to Remarque over thirty years earlier so that he could work in peace on *The Road Back*. While he and Paulette were wintering in Rome at the Hôtel de la Ville, he received a letter and a photograph of the Hoberg house from Karla Henkelmann of Osnabrück, who might have been encouraged to send them by Hanns-Gerd Rabe. Rabe was always imploring Remarque to come to Osnabrück, and was always being rebuffed. Remarque, in his response to Karla Henkelmann, was clearly moved by her approach: "I do remember the time, more than 35 years ago in Osnabrück, with a young Irish terrier, Billy, who has been dead almost 25 years. It was a beautiful time! I hope you are well and I hope we will see each other once more, when I get to Osnabrück."

Hanns-Gerd Rabe, also a writer, whom Remarque seemingly had encouraged, had been working for some time on biographical material of the early Remarque and Osnabrück—hence the accelerated attempt to get Remarque there, who wrote, "Dear Hanns-Gerd, Thank you very much for your letter and your work. It is strange how vivid the pictures of my hometown register in my mind, when you send me these articles. . . . I feel an urgent longing to see everything again, despite the fact that much of it exists probably only in my memory. In the meantime, I have a terrace that is encircled by swallows with a view over all of Rome on the Trinità di Monti—but these are the same swallows that encircle the towers of the cathedral in Osnabrück. . . . These are not the swallows of youth. . . . I asked my doctor about a trip to Osnabrück. Too far, too strenuous, and, he added, that the reunion would be too exciting after such a long time. He put it off until fall. I have to take it in stride. He does not even want me to go to parties, which is not a sacrifice for me. To sit quietly in the streets and watch life float by is something I always loved."

In June of 1968, Remarque, having turned seventy, was made an honorary citizen by the communities of Ronco and Ascona, which, as Remarque reported to Hanns-Gerd, "signals the arrival of old age, but I hope that I can live a few more years before I calcify. Actually, I had planned to come to Osnabrück, but the doctors felt that my 70th would cause enough excitement here. They advised me to stay here. The festivities in Ronco and Ascona were reduced to a minimum and a doctor was present all the time. The gala dinner went on without me. I was already in bed.

"Many thanks for your beautiful article and letter on my birthday. There is an irreplaceable feeling to have spent most of one's life in such a friendship that started in youth and became stronger. I hope that it will continue for many more years. The wine in my basement waits patiently for you to come here. Wine does not get more senile with age, but only more mature. In contrast to many people."

Remarque had held out a bit of hope to go to New York with Paulette in October to celebrate Alta's eightieth birthday, but of course it was impossible—perhaps as much because he was busy writing as because of his weak-ened condition. Determined as he was to finish the work, he was more of a perfectionist with this book than ever before. He just would not let it go, dis-cuss it, or let it be seen by anyone. Perhaps he felt that as long as he was working, he would not die.

The event of Paulette's mother's birthday seemed a bit of a mixed blessing; Alta was anguished about Remarque's not being with them, as was Paulette, who writes to her husband about it with a certain cattiness. (They are dining at a restaurant called Sea-Fare the evening before the birthday.)

"Ma moons all thru the dinner—Erich & I always sat over there—Erich always ordered a simple but delicious dish for me! Erich should come to N.Y. before I am on crutches, while I still look & feel pretty good. Infinitum! So you are never far from my mind. I always feel a bit sad after talking to you on the phone. Makes me realize how much I miss you, and how won-derful & good & sweet & attractive & charming & 'utterly' you are (sounds like a Cole Porter song)."

True to gallant form, Remarque flooded Alta's new apartment (formerly his) with roses and orchids and a letter full of compliments that are typical of Remarque's ability to rise to the occasion even when under extreme duress:

It is not to believe that you are a few years older than I, you look so very young, just like a sister of Paulette.

I wanted to send you a little present, but thinking it over I thought the best would be if you choose it yourself . . . so, I send you here a small check to do with it what you feel [the small check was for $1,000].

I am very sorry not to be with you! But I am still forbidden to use the plane and on top of it I have the gout, like a true old fuddy-duddy from England, so I could not even go with you to the Four Seasons, limping next to two Goddards' pairs of the most gorgeous legs of the century. But we will come again in spring. This time both of us!

In October of 1968, Paulette was ready to return to Remarque, at which time she writes, "every mission will be accomplished—theatres, birthdays, dinners & street-running. This is one wild town. Will try to describe it blow by blow when we are tranquilly together and the excitement of being togeth-er has subsided to a quiet roar," and ever alert, or feeling that she should be alert to politics, she writes, "I want to be here for these crazy elections. I think Johnson will call a bombing halt only if Humphrey needs last-ditch help for votes. Bet you $1.00! After seeing and hearing Wallace on T.V. I am convinced he has colored blood! That would explain his point of view. All 3 candidates are horrifying creatures. A million kisses and all my thoughts until we meet and then—complete joy—for me—I love you so very very much. Moi."

Over the next two years, life was relatively quiet, even for Paulette, because she spent more days with Remarque than she ever had before. The winter of 1968 into 1969, they stayed in Rome. Switzerland had become too cold for Remarque. He was working well—about two hours a day was his maximum—and the doctor was nearby. Paulette was at his side to help him celebrate the news that the city council of Osnabrück had named a street after his sister Elfriede. This fact moved him very much, and again, he considered attempting the trip, accompanied by Paulette. "We both desire to go to Osnabrück to relax, to remember, to say thanks, to see friends, most of all to see you again," he wrote to the intrepid Hanns-Gerd.

But the trip had to be put off, for Paulette decided to go back to New York; he would spend the summer in Porto Ronco, and then they would see.

Before he left Rome, Remarque set one record straight for Rabe, and that was that although he keenly desired to return to his hometown, he did not want to be part of any biography that Rabe was preparing. He issued a most definitive statement regarding the subject of biography:

Regarding the theme of "Remarque and Osnabrück," I cannot help you much, since I am opposed to anything autobiographical and biographical. These to me are always an overestimation of one's own importance and thus indirect egotism, touched by a trace of conceit. I know, I know: Goethe's poetry and truth, the great opposites—but it was (first) poetry and (then) truth, and thus already creative. Every writer has to do it the way he feels about it. Some like to talk about themselves and their life, others would prefer that only their works will be judged. I belong to the latter. Believe me, I've already had dozens of offers, very tempting financially, but I have turned them all down. What I have learned in my life, I have used in my works and the rest is private and does not influence the work and this is how I would like to keep it.

Rabe tried once again, in November of 1969, to persuade Remarque to lend himself to a biography, whereupon Remarque simply dismissed him with "Let us postpone this to a distant future, and instead talk about your beloved France and my beloved Italy." Perhaps with regret at having to dash

Rabe's own hopes for a certain kind of immortality, Remarque wrote to the City Council of Osnabrück, suggesting that it honor Rabe with the same Möser Medal that he had received.

In April of 1969, Remarque sent Rabe twenty bottles of Beaune Burgundy 1961, Curée Maurice de Arouhr, for his seventy-fifth birthday, and a note: "Unfortunately, you can see from my writing that I am pretty sick, fever every day for the last four weeks, otherwise I would have come. I am so weak, but I would try anyway, but the doctor won't even allow me to leave my room to go to another room."

Remarque took Paulette on a "green second honeymoon," as he called it— because it was so expensive—to Venice in the fall of 1969, but he began to hemorrhage there and was forced to return to Porto Ronco.

Through the spring and summer, Paulette remained in New York, "running the streets," as she called it. In September, she went to Paris for shopping and then to Porto Ronco to visit with her husband, who was in a state of great anticipation—as always. Remarque's last letter of record to Paulette was written on November 22, 1969. It was around Thanksgiving and she was in New York, and writes that she hopes "your crazy gout simply fades away, as most problems do." Remarque writes, full of hope, understanding, humor, and patience:

My heart, my life, and you, all the joy of my life—this should be a Thanksgiving Day letter but that is not enough! Every day of my life is a Thanksgiving Day since that wonderful and miraculous day on Fifth Avenue where I found and had the incredible sense not to let you go ever again! My rather empty and hollow life has been fulfilled since you danced into it on that afternoon and has become a series of wonders . . . since you arrived here under thunder, lightning, and storm, a magnum bottle of champagne in your fist and a magic wand hidden under your checkered Balenciaga costume!

I have my Thanksgiving alone, happy because you are happy at *Oh Calcutta* with your mother and at 21. I am sitting with the cats snoozing under my desk, had some potato pancakes with applesauce, and think of happiness of the years past and the years to come. As usual, I hear your trip-trap all the time on the stairs, and at night there is an entertaining ghost sneaking up and down for apples and cheese to the kitchen.

But I, I am pressing my snout into the cushions and I am murmuring without a sound: Thank you, thank you, my love, for being there, for being alive, and for being with me, and bless you for all of it a thousand times. Your eternal troubadour, husband, and admirer.

Paulette was there in August of 1970 when Remarque's health failed to the point where he was admitted to the St. Agnes Hospital in Locarno.

"His cardiac condition had worsened, he suffered from angina with enormous pain and anxiety attacks," remembers his old comrade, the journalist Curt Riess. "I went to visit him in the clinic where he stayed a few years before his death. I came during one of these attacks and heard him screaming, 'Help me, help me, help me!' The nurse explained to me, 'Well, this happens with this particular disease.'"

In late August of 1970, Curt Riess engaged in a startling telephone conversation when he called Remarque's hospital room: "Paulette picked up the telephone. She said, obviously in English, that he was very bad. She said, 'He will die soon,' and then she said, 'Do you want to talk to him?' I couldn't believe it. I couldn't believe that she was in his room and that he had obviously overheard everything she'd said. She could have very easily asked to call me back later, but she had no qualms announcing the death sentence in his presence.

"He picked up the phone, 'Yes, it's very bad. No, you can't help me. No, nobody can help me.' And those were the last words I ever heard from him."

On Friday, September 25, 1970, Erich Maria Remarque died in the hospital in Locarno, not far from his home.

"After his death," Riess recalls, "a few friends came to Locarno and went to Porto Ronco to attend the burial above his house in Ronco. We had counted on very few people. Obviously Paulette and her already quite elderly mother, who insisted on dressing as though she were a teenager, his sister from Osnabrück, and probably a dozen people from Ascona or Locarno. Someone to represent the German government—Berlin—absolutely not. That was all we expected. But instead, we found hundreds of strangers. We later found out that the tour director for a group of German tourists had decided to offer, as one of the attractions, attending the burial of this famous author. And so it came about that a large number of people were at Boni's grave—people who had never known him and probably many who had never read any of his works. He would have probably laughed about this."

Found among Paulette's papers was an old folk poem that she had scribbled in 1971. She had changed its intent by writing in her own last line, which succinctly conveys how haunted she must have felt:

> As I was walking up the stair,
> I saw a man who wasn't there,
> He wasn't there again today,
> I wish to God, he'd go away.

Dietrich, upon hearing of Remarque's death, had sent a coverlet of white roses to encase his coffin. Paulette had refused to allow them on her husband's bier. As the news of Remarque's death sank in, Dietrich wailed to Noël Coward, "Oh, he only left me a jewel and he left all that money to THAT WOMAN!" Coward, unflappable as always, replied, "Now, come, Marlene, that woman was his wife." Dietrich's wail became a snap: "Don't be silly! It WAS THE GODDARD!"

THE WIDOW REMARQUE

1 9 7 0 – 1 9 9 0

FOR A WHILE, the widow Remarque was everything that Marion Goddard
Levy had ever wanted to be, and probably more. She began playing her role
of a lifetime at Remarque's Catholic funeral service. Two men spoke at his
funeral, Hanns-Gerd Rabe, who praised him as a "champion of friendship,"
and the writer and neighbor Robert Neumann. Neumann recalled how he
had changed his mind about Remarque's being an arrogant, less-than-great
writer after he had been invited to Casa Remarque: "Behind all the nabob-
ballyhoo—what a decent man! With what grace he lives in his beautiful
house. He is not a figure on the edge of literature, but rather, literature is a
distant speck on the edge of Remarque."

Remarque was actually a lapsed Catholic, but Paulette wanted a Mass said
for him; she wanted it holy. She was partial to churches, and enjoyed the
dogma, the gestures, covering her head. As Bob Colacello, who edited Andy
Warhol's *Interview* for years and was often with Andy and Paulette in New
York in the seventies, commented, "She did everything but pray." Standing
beside her mother at her late husband's grave site, she could well have been
taken for an Italian Catholic widow in her simple weeds, black veil, dark
glasses, and little if no makeup. She went into seclusion for a week afterward, emerging in dignified anger to chastise the German press—specifically the *Rheinischer Merkur*—for the insensitive, erroneous obituary that

Paulette, on the left, at Remarque's funeral in Ronco, 1970.

Jutta with her friend "Mickey" in St. Moritz, ca. 1971.

stubbornly maintained that "Remarque, who died in Locarno, was really called Kramer."

"Look!" Paulette said as she retold the statement that she issued many times over. "This is a Nazi story! It was started by the Nazis! This is a story that you never want to read or hear again!"

As executor, Paulette had many estate matters to deal with. There was the legacy of the last novel, whose working title, given by the author, was *The New York Story*. Paulette decided to change the title to *Shadows in Paradise* when she delivered a finished manuscript to Harcourt Brace Jovanovich, proclaiming that "Erich finished the book the night before he went to the hospital for the last time." She immediately became the spokeswoman for the new novel and, subsequently, for his career.

There were many harsh opinions of the widow Remarque—especially during the couple of "transition" years. Among the people in her employment, she had a reputation for being autocratic, if not downright ruthless; she would do anything to defend and protect what she saw as her own. While the will was being probated, she took action to ward off financial probes into the manner in which she and Remarque handled their money. She was deeply afraid that because of their complicated tax situation, coupled with their various dodges (that is, moving their valuable acquisitions from household to household, continent to continent), a good part of her money would be confiscated.

Remarque had left three legacies of $50,000 each—to his sister Erna; to his ex-wife, Jutta; and to his devoted housekeeper, Rosa. Paulette wanted to pay them at once—especially Jutta's—in order to dodge any claims that could be made against the estate, because, as she candidly told Pilpel, "The authorities will start looking into the whole situation of what she and Erich had." Her desire was moot, since Jutta had already made a claim listing things in Casa Remarque that she said belonged to her. Pilpel advised Paulette not to pay Jutta her legacy, because it would leave her with no bargaining power, to which Paulette replied, "Tell her it's just fine if she wants to go ahead and sue me."

In October of 1971, there was a letter to Harriet Pilpel from Richard Kay, a young lawyer who worked for Pilpel's firm of Greenbaum, Wolff & Ernst, in which he reluctantly revealed that Paulette had asked him to take over from Pilpel: "Mrs. Remarque is quite upset that we do things without her approval and I promised that this would not happen again. She has asked that I personally take care of anything from now on, which I am reluctant to do."

Without so much as discussing it with Remarque's longtime champion, Harriet Pilpel, Paulette had summarily dismissed her, replacing her with a junior in the firm.

Dismissal was in the air. In order to maintain her Swiss resident status, Paulette was obligated to spend six months—but no more than six months—in Switzerland, which would mean more time at Casa Remarque than she had ever spent. She was the total mistress of the manor now, and as such decided that Rosa Kramer cast a shadow of a threat to her propriety and would have to go. She fired her on the basis of an inheritance-tax technicality—that Rosa was too expensive to keep. And then there was also the slightly trumped-up second reason—that technically, in the Ticino, it was illegal to employ a foreigner as a domestic. Paulette maintained that with the special scrutiny of the tax authorities upon Remarque's death, Rosa Kramer had become a liability. Additional fuel was Paulette's irritation that she was subject to paying a tax on Rosa's inheritance, and so, after almost half a century of the ultimate dedicated service, Rosa Kramer was sent away with $50,000 and a reference.

Paulette kept Marino, the chauffeur, but the new housekeeper, whom she had obtained through the mayor of Ronco, was a Swiss Italian woman named Bellosta, who was given a one-year contract to attend to the house all year round, whether Paulette was there or not. She proved unsatisfactory, Paulette expelled her, but turned around and hired her sister, Antonietta Bellosta, who, as she explained to Alta, was "lovely and kind and a lousy cook, which keeps my weight at 120 lbs. which it was in 1945!"

Antonietta Bellosta had staying power. She learned how to please Paulette. Hired in 1973 and remaining with Paulette until her death in 1990, Antonietta was a walking dossier on the aging movie star, who increasingly lived in her own obscurity. Antonietta, during the time that this book was being researched, was still living in Casa Remarque. The scent of Yves Saint-Laurent's Opium, Paulette's perfume, was still redolent in many of the rooms. Antonietta recalled the details of Paulette:

> She wore an American size 12 and liked lively colors. She was very partial to red and avoided green, blue, and black. She always preferred matching bag and shoes. She owned five fur coats, but wore mainly Yves Saint-Laurent and Valentino clothes.
>
> She was very appreciative of what I cooked for her. She ate lots of vegetables, fruit, and fish, but not much meat. She loved little sweets and home-made pastries. She drank Soave Bolla and a lot of mineral water. She had

her five o'clock glass of champagne every day, alone or in company. She did not drink juice, she did not diet, and she did not drink liquor. She never did any cooking, and we decided the daily menu together.

She had her hair done once or twice a week in Ascona or Locarno. She had no preferred hairdresser. [Sources who prefer anonymity have said that Paulette became so difficult and unpleasant in the various local beauty salons that many of the operators would refuse to do her hair.] She never changed her hair color, which was a dark copper red. She did her own makeup and beauty care at home, sending for her cosmetics from New York. In later years she trained at home with a physical therapist. Paulette never suffered from headaches, rheumatism, or head colds. She was, in fact, rarely ill until the emphysema that killed her. In the morning she swam and took long walks with her dog, Kim. Often in the afternoon she was driven by her chauffeur, Marino, to Ascona, Locarno, or Italy to shop. She went to a restaurant every Sunday evening and sometimes during the week for lunch or dinner. She was occasionally accompanied by my niece, Paola, who was a biology student. [Paola was very pretty and Paulette was drawn to her, giving her discarded clothes and costume jewelry, behaving more like an older sister than a mother. She seemed to identify with Paola as the beauty that she once had been or, perhaps, as the child that she never had. Years later, she paid for Paola's entire college education at New York University.] For entertainment she attended fashion shows and an occasional art exhibition. She never went to the opera or to concerts. As for friends, she had little contact with her neighbors. She hardly ever received friends at home; she invited them to accompany her out to dinner. Occasionally she would travel to Milan or Zurich to see friends. She never celebrated her birthday and would spend Christmas Eve at home.

She subscribed to the *International Herald Tribune* and the Christie's and Sotheby's catalogues, which she would pore over for hours. She loved Italian fashion and "scandal" magazines. She had no television of her own, but would regularly watch the news with me in front of my set in my room downstairs. Occasionally, she would watch an old Chaplin movie, and sometimes we would see one of her old pictures. She never enjoyed it; it was always spoiled for her, because she knew how everything was done. When a man was jumping out of the Empire State Building, she would say, "Oh, he's really just jumping off the couch. Don't believe it." When she saw blood, she would say, "Oh, that's made out of Mott's tomato juice." In the scene in *The Gold Rush* when Charlie Chaplin eats the sole of his shoe, she told me it was ice cream, that they had made an ice-cream sole. Since she knew everything there was to know about pictures, it all meant nothing to her.

Normally, she would go to bed early, and would often sleep for ten or twelve hours. She loved music—particularly Vivaldi. When she was happy, she would hum and dance with the music. That was in the earlier days. Then there was the regular dance boat for tourists that cruised during summer evenings between Ascona and Brissago. The boat used to slow down in front of the house and the local band on board would play "Limelight" in a serenade to her, and she would emerge onto the terrace in thanks for the attention.

"That was also in the earlier days," recalls Bellosta, who watched Paulette's life darken.

For the first five years after Remarque's death, Paulette was an activist executor, taking her job extremely seriously. Her star rubies were locked away, and her desk was full of contracts. She had launched *Shadows in Paradise* with the German publication in 1971, followed by the American publication a year later. In general, the novel was not critically acclaimed, although, as Hans Wagener points out, "it is nevertheless of considerable importance, not only because it documents Remarque's later political views, but also because in it Remarque deals with America for the first time."

The next project Paulette wanted to address was Remarque's play *The Last Station*. Remarque had very much wanted it to have a New York production, and Paulette saw to it that it happened. She ran into Otto Preminger one day on Madison Avenue and then and there secured a commitment for the season of 1973. With Peter Stone's adaptation, a new title, *Full Circle*, and a cast that included Leonard Nimoy, the Swedish actress Bibi Andersson, Joseph Sommer, James Tolkan, David Ackroyd, and Peter Weller, the play premiered at the Eisenhower Theatre of the Kennedy Center in Washington on October 5, 1973, and then, on November 7, at the ANTA Theatre in New York.

Between 1972 and 1975, Paulette began to behave quite differently. She disregarded the opinions, wishes, and feelings of most everybody. She had always been capricious, but now her behavior was beginning to border on the eccentric. Her friend Jean Tailer, who had known her for years, felt she had always been somewhat eccentric. She remembered the days when she used to visit Paulette and Meredith on their farm, and one time in particular when they were keeping a lot of chimpanzees in cages and decided to let them out to scamper all over the house; of course, chimpanzees can't be house trained. Tailer feels that they kept them just to be different.

"She kept her jewelry in a shoe box when she traveled," Tailer recalls. "I mean, who would suspect a shoe box of holding anything but shoes?" Tailer felt Goddard was very good with the quick response: "One time when they went into a restaurant and someone recognized her and said, 'Are you Paulette Goddard?' 'Well, I was when I came in' was her answer."

Tailer liked Paulette because she was amusing and surprising, a tremendous individual who didn't play by the rules. However, she concurs that in later years, after Remarque's death, things began to go wrong. Paulette's sense of fun and occasionally naughty ways turned slightly odd and imperious: "We used to go out for lunch, and she often wanted to go to the wholesale houses afterward to look for bargains. She always carried nothing smaller than a hundred-dollar bill, which in those days guaranteed that she couldn't pay for anything because no one could break a bill that large. She never did pay for anything. 'I'm a pirate,' she would say. Whoever was with her would pay the tab."

There had always been somewhat outrageous stories about Paulette. The British film actress Patricia Roc tells about Paulette at a dinner party in Switzerland given by a mutual friend:

We were eight for dinner. We arrived about seven o'clock for drinks. I must say she looked absolutely beautiful. She had on a thick, creamy white silk suit, upon which she wore one magnificent heart-shaped ruby jewel, about two-and-a-half-inches thick. You couldn't take your eyes off it on this white, heavy silk.

We had drinks and everything was fine. And then round about twenty past seven she said, "I'm going into the kitchen, because it's time we ate." So, our hostess said, "Well, do if you like but don't disturb my cook because she's making something very special." So Paulette went in and came out about ten minutes later and said, "Well, we can eat now." So our hostess said, "All right, we'll go in to dinner. Thank you."

And we had a beautiful dinner, beautifully done, beautifully served, and about a quarter to nine, when we had finished our main course in leisurely style and were chatting a bit, Paulette just stood up and said, "Well, I can't wait any longer. I've got to go home. You know I have to go to bed early."

So our hostess said, "Oh, but we've got a wonderful sweet. It's all done specially for you, Paulette."

"I can't wait, I can't wait. It's too bad," said Paulette. She didn't say good-bye to anybody. Just stood up and walked out. I found it so ill-mannered that it has stuck in my mind ever since.

For the next couple of years—1973 to 1975—she made some plans for immortality. She expanded her financial holdings by beginning to sell off some of Remarque's treasured collection—the paintings through their late dealer Walter Feilchenfeldt's widow, Marianne, who welcomed her into the family business with a sale of a Degas drawing for a net profit of $72,000 less her 10 percent commission. She wrote, "I am including the check on $20,000. This is our first business transaction! Now I still owe you $44,800. This is the way we always did it and I like you to know every detail."

There were those who advised her to hold on to her bounty, that the art, rugs, antiques, and jewelry could only escalate yearly; she thrilled at moving the pieces around, and at her buying and selling power. Warren Alpert, former president of the Ritz Towers, who took her out a bit, remembered that what she wanted was to find out how to get richer, and she used to call him from Switzerland or wherever she was to ask questions about turning over properties. Alpert understood and admired her single track: "She liked to talk about money, and she was informed. She read money magazines and investment guides. You didn't talk about what she didn't want to hear. I made most of Paulette's money for her through buying government bonds. I told her, don't buy gold; you sell gold and buy government bonds."

During a greater part of her life after Remarque, she tried to stimulate Remarque sales outside the United States, because Remarque, having been granted a resident citizenship in 1963, was exempt from paying taxes on earnings made outside the country. Hence, she was particularly interested in optioning *The Black Obelisk* to a German film company, or in the German sales of his last novel, but, contrarily, was not involved in his book sales in the Soviet Union—where he did a tremendous business—because it did not pay royalties. As Alpert put it, "Money guaranteed Paulette that she was somebody."

Anita Loos certainly thought that she was "somebody" enough to enter into a book deal with— a collaborative effort whose working title was "The Perils of Paulette." Loos would write and Paulette would talk loose—or so Harcourt Brace Jovanovich, the publisher, thought. Anita Loos had a backlog of Paulette stories and sayings that she could provide and did, but they were Loos's memories and observations, not Paulette's revelations.

The two women went to Switzerland and Italy together in 1973 so that

Paulette's apartment at the Ritz Towers in New York. Mexican Girl with Sunflowers, *by Diego Rivera, hangs to the right of the fireplace.*

Anita Loos and Paulette at the time they were collaborating on their book, "The Perils of Paulette," and Paulette practicing yoga, ca. 1973.

Loos could get material while Paulette played. It was the beginning of the end of the book and their friendship. According to various sources, because Paulette would not talk, Loos patched together some two hundred pages of fairly weak material. Both women agreed that the material was inadequate and that the contract would have to be canceled. Each "author" had received $30,000 from Harcourt, payable in three installments. Loos returned her share of the first third with a rueful statement indicating that the parts of Paulette equaled an impenetrable sum. "She knew all about authors and books I had only barely heard of," Anita said. "But what went on in her head, I don't know; nobody did. I think that's the reason why she fascinated so many intellectuals—they couldn't figure her out. H. G. Wells was gaga about her. Aldous Huxley adored her."

The underlying reason for Paulette's stalling out on the book was that she had grown tired of Loos's "double-gaited" ways, as she referred to her lesbianism. In a letter to her mother, Paulette mentions that summer of 1973, and a Gladys and a Miss Moore who were keeping company with Loos: "I know she [Loos] will never come up here [Casa Remarque]. She can't bear to leave Gladys & especially Miss Moore for one day. They are her bosses and would never let her come here without them. And they have to be entertained every minute. Can't see myself spending my summer with the 3 of *them*."

In the meantime, Paulette had come by a preferable form of entertainment. Andy Warhol, who rarely missed a party in the seventies and also gave his own celebrated lunches at The Factory in New York, inherited Loos's position of frequently accompanying Paulette, and secured a book contract from none other than Harcourt (Remarque's longtime publisher) to tape and transcribe the definitive life and times of Paulette— to be titled *Her*.

Paulette and Warhol taped for over a year. Mostly she talked like "a personality"—amusing, vain, sometimes silly, sometimes outrageous—but never said much that was wildly revealing. So, the question might be why she agreed to the tapings for so long. Both Bob Colacello and Andy Warhol felt that Paulette was a little sweet on "the white fox," as she called Warhol, and had set her cap for him—assessing that he was as stimulating, modern, and rich as she was—if not richer. "She was the classic coquette," says Colacello; "even when she knew there were no romantic or sexual possibilities, she still kept up that façade. That was her way of relating to men."

Paulette continued to look very good, but the body that had been voted the most beautiful in Hollywood in 1941 underwent a severe punishment in March of 1975. At the same time as her friend Rocky Cooper Converse,

Paulette was diagnosed with cancer—in Paulette's case, breast cancer. Just prior to going into the hospital for a mastectomy, she made an incredible tape with Warhol, which, in its way, is the last of Paulette as the fiercely sunny, funny, outspoken star. This tape perfectly conveys her heretofore attitude about darker topics. Fear was clearly not her style: "Rocky tipped me off. She said, 'Believe me, when you go, pack your ermine coat—give them the full treatment. They go for it.' . . . She said the doctors treat you better. They really do! So I'm packing my little white fox."

Lois Granato was the "new secretary" who went on to stay with Paulette for her last fifteen tormented years. Lois started working for Paulette in 1975, when she was in her early twenties and Paulette was sixty-five. Lois was a graduate student at the Institute of Fine Arts at New York University. She was working in Florence, Italy, for her Ph.D. when she ran low on funds and took what was to be a part-time job working for Paulette so that she could complete her degree. She thought it would be a novelty to work for a movie star of the past. Lois had never heard of Paulette until she went for the interview, nor was she particularly impressed by her or her energy, which right from the beginning she felt was quite destructive.

Her employment began shortly following Paulette's mastectomy. She took a class in arm massage at Sloan-Kettering, where Paulette underwent surgery, because Paulette had a horrible problem with swelling in her arm and hand from the surgery, which was exceedingly brutal. "They really did an incredible butcher job on her," Lois recalls. Not only was the incision deep and wide, but several ribs had been removed. Lois's version, according to what Paulette told her, was that the whole thing was handled in an abrupt and cruel fashion: "She went in one afternoon, and the doctor said, 'You know, you've got cancer,' and the next day they operated."

Psychologically, the aftermath of the surgery was harrowing. There was no consolation for Paulette. Lois felt that "for her, that was it. I think at that point in her life she had been ready for another man, but now she no longer saw herself as beautiful. She became obsessed with her body. She would not buy clothes, she wouldn't let anyone look at her, she thought people stared at her."

The two spent hours stuffing her bras and finding clothes that looked right on her. Awful as it was, Paulette would never go for help; she would not seek anyone out who could fit her for the proper bras and blouses or sweaters; she would not go for massage treatments; she denounced all suggestions of physical or psychological therapy. The way she helped herself was to drink heav-

Paulette with her "White Fox," Andy Warhol, 1974.

*In the garden at Casa Remarque: the German shepherd, Kim,
Antonietta Bellosta and her niece, Alta, and Paulette, ca. 1985.*

ily, proclaiming that Remarque had taught her to drink. She would swig vodka straight from the bottle. She would usually start to drink at three P.M., when Lois came in; she would try to hold herself together until then. But sometimes Lois would find her drunk and abusive.

With few preliminaries, Lois Granato had entered Paulette Goddard's private hell. Paulette would often reflect upon her time with Remarque with pleasure and pride, saying that he always found her extremely amusing no matter what she did. She never spoke a bad word about him in all the time Lois was with her; however, there were some signals that all had not been perfect. According to Paulette, Remarque would worry—to her face—about what would become of her after his death; how would she cope? His worries were grounded. When Lois found her, Paulette was increasingly unable to cope. On her part, however, she would confide in Lois that, in their last years together, Remarque had become "old and smelly," and it was just as well that he died when he did because she didn't want to be stuck taking care of him forever. Apparently, she had urged him to sell the house in Switzerland because she disliked it so, but he had refused, and a wedge was driven between them. It was the only time she did not get her way with Remarque.

As Lois Granato puts it, "I knew from day one that she was crazy." One late afternoon, just before Lois was leaving for the day, Paulette offered her a Mason jar half filled with caviar, saying that it was "left over" and she thought her new secretary and her beau should enjoy it. Lois, never a caviar lover, took it home, had a funny feeling about it, and threw it out. The next day Paulette asked her whether she had eaten it, whereupon Lois confessed that she did not care for caviar and had dispensed with it. Paulette was greatly relieved. She had dropped the caviar in its original glass container, which had broken. She had attempted to separate the fish eggs from the broken glass as she scooped the mass up into another jar. After she had bestowed it upon Lois, she had worried that there might be some shards of glass still left, and now she did not have to worry anymore.

Another time, Lois met Paulette in the airport upon her return from a visit to Switzerland, when she had stayed in the house in Porto Ronco for as long as she could stand it, and then gone to Zurich to attend to her "high finance," as she would call it. Lois was waiting with a chauffeured car, and what followed is another example of the horror that enveloped the two women—one impelled to bestow it upon the other.

"As soon as we got into the car she said, 'I have to go to the bathroom. I have to pee.' She never spoke in euphemisms. 'I have to pee, I have to do it now.' I told her that she couldn't, that we were on the highway, but she said she was going to do it in the car and that the driver wouldn't mind. And there's the driver in the front seat with his eyes in the mirror looking like he was going to die. And then she urinates in the back of the car. The driver and I were horrified. But by the tenth year of working for her, I'd go to the airport assuming that she was going to take her underwear off in the backseat of the car, because she loved to flaunt her private parts. In the tenth year, the driver and I had gone beyond being horrified and beyond embarrassment. During those years, people either had a fairy-tale version of Paulette or they knew the way it really was. All I was able to do was sit back and watch."

Lois describes Paulette's behavior during those final ten years in New York, between 1976 and 1986, as that of a wild little animal's: undomesticated, unpredictable, and sometimes appalling. Lois provides the image of a kitten who can play very nicely sitting on your lap one minute and, in the next, scratch your eyes out. While Paulette always had a kitten's boldness and insouciance, age and sickness exacerbated and distorted the very qualities that had enthralled Remarque.

Having had to deal daily with Paulette, Lois speculates on what bound Remarque to her: "Of course, he was attracted to her at first—this beautiful, young woman who made him feel young again. But at some point, he must have realized that she was attracted by his money and reputation, and that she loved appearances, which were everything to her. She was lousy at reading anyone's personality or anyone's real nature. She just couldn't do it. And at some point, I wonder whether he just accepted her as an incredible entertainment. For someone who watched other people's reactions, who was interested in characterizations and interested in people's relationships—how incredible it must have been to be with a person who's going to stimulate all sorts of odd reactions in others. She made him a voyeur."

It is ironic, then, that Paulette told Lois why Remarque had stopped writing his diaries. He had said soon after they had begun their relationship, "I don't have to write my life anymore now. I live it."

In 1975 Jutta Zambona Remarque died in Monte Carlo, at the age of seventy-four. Paulette wrote cryptically to Alta, "Only one more left." Perhaps she meant Dietrich. Perhaps she meant herself. She began to divest, selling off her things—or planning to—with a certain urgency that was not so much greed as fear of dying poor. If she could bequeath millions, it would have to mean that she was somebody. In 1976, at Sotheby's in London, she auctioned off thirty-two of her Oriental and Persian rugs and carpets, collecting approximately $185,000 for her Ushaks, Isfahans, and Mamluks, among others. In 1977, she had another sale at Sotheby's, of her antiquities and bronzes, and she made out a surprising will, prompting her financial consultant, Maurice Greenbaum, to assess the situation. He understood that Paulette seemed compelled to auction off many of her valuables, although he thought she would probably hang on to the important paintings and jewelry. Greenbaum worried about the will, wondering whether it was rash to leave everything to New York University (except for all her clothes and furs in Porto Ronco, to go to Antonietta Bellosta, and $250,000 to Lois Granato for fifteen years of service added in a codicil shortly before her death). In a memo to her appointed executor, Richard Kay, he pondered the reason: "I have now had calls from the Dean of the School of Arts, the President of the University, and the Senior Vice President of the University in charge of fund-raising. It is clear to me that both her dentist and her dermatologist have promoted NYU to her, but the initial interest in the School of the Arts came from some other source. In any event, we have to be careful what we say to these people and I will make it clear to them that their best interests would be served by not trying to involve her in public affairs, etc., unless she initiates something herself."

The question whether it was altruism or self-interest that propelled the donation could be considered moot, because NYU was indeed a worthy beneficiary. However, Paulette's old friend Jean Tailer was familiar with a pattern of Paulette's that she had first witnessed during Paulette's marriage to Burgess Meredith: "I don't recall any great attraction between Paulette and Buzz. But he was a very big actor then, and she was at the end of her career." Tailer saw the same pattern appear along with Paulette's gift to NYU: "I went down to the Tisch School of the Arts with her when they dedicated a stairwell to her. She gave them $20 million and she got a stairwell. It was kind of sad. But she gave them all that money only for self-aggrandization. She got everything she could out of everybody else. She was never a giver, and if she was, it was for self-adulation. She never did anything for anybody else. It didn't exist."

The words "vague" and "disturbing" were applied to Paulette's monetary decisions, and it could be said that they tended to be progressively more emotional and less businesslike. Her decisions finally were about power and respect in their purest and most alarming form, as in her attitude toward NYU after she had bequeathed it the bulk of Remarque's literary estate as well as $20 million. She made it known that she was angry at NYU because it had named a School of the Arts building after Laurence Tisch, when it should have been named after Remarque. She also felt John Brademas, the president of the university, had romanced her—according to her, had "done a job on her." And then, with a what-can-you-expect shrug, she would say, "It's not too bad for a girl to have twenty million." As far as Lois Granato knows, John Brademas only met Paulette once. Since 1977, she had parceled out donations in the form of scholarships to New York University's Tisch School of the Arts. When Paulette had definitely decided to bestow the gift to NYU, Brademas received the information in her living room and, although stunned, handled the news deftly and graciously. Paulette charmed him, he charmed Paulette, and Lois ushered him out rather quickly before Paulette could change her mind.

In 1979, Paulette sold thirty of her French Impressionist paintings in an auction at Sotheby's, for $3.1 million. Remarque had collected some of the world's most famous paintings—gone in a flash in one auction lot.

Also in 1979, she put up for auction what she called her "important" diamond necklace ("just a bunch of engagement rings"), her diamond dome ring with matching ear clips (given to her by Chaplin), a cabochon ruby and diamond necklace (a gift from Remarque), and a cabochon emerald and diamond bangle (another gift from Remarque), among other items.

Over the next several years, she made some attempts to do business on behalf of the Remarque properties. In 1977, *Heaven Has No Favorites* was made into a Columbia Pictures–Warner Brothers movie under the title *Bobby Deerfield*, directed and produced by Sidney Pollack and starring Al Pacino and Marthe Keller. The year 1979 brought a remake of *All Quiet on the Western Front*, done for television by England's Marble Arch Productions, directed by Delbert Mann and starring Richard Thomas, and in 1985, *Arch of Triumph* was remade—also for television, directed by Waris Hussein, starring Anthony Hopkins and Lesley-Anne Down.

According to Lois Granato, Paulette felt increasingly diminished and demoralized. She was finding it difficult to really function. If someone was paying a visit at three P.M., she could do nothing before that time but prepare herself. It was like a performance, with costume, makeup, and script. She and Lois would write the script beforehand so that nothing would be left to chance. She would look amazingly good in her close-ups; she would act her part well, and then, when the visit was over, she would collapse, be gotten a drink, and put to bed.

Paulette insisted that the past didn't interest her, and methodically went about cutting herself off from it. She had no photographs in her apartment, no memorabilia, no personal objects, no souvenirs, nothing that she loved. The antiques that decorated the apartment had belonged to Remarque, and had been moved from Switzerland. If, as has always been reported, she was an avid reader, it was no longer true. She skimmed fashion magazines, marking for Lois what she wanted ordered, and she read books on homosexuality, which seemed to fascinate her. There was a homosexual couple who lived in the building directly across from Paulette's apartment at the Ritz Towers and often did not draw the drapes. Paulette would sit by the window for hours, watching and waiting for something to happen.

There were times when Paulette could not get herself together because she shook so badly from drinking. She did not sleep at night because she took quantities of pills all through the day, and although she then took quantities of sleeping pills at night, they did no good. She would walk all night, and in contrast to the nights in the house in Porto Ronco when Remarque would find her in the wee hours in the kitchen munching a piece of pancetta, now there was no comfort.

Paulette avoided most of her friends, seeing them rarely or cutting them off entirely. However, in 1977 an old friendship was tentatively renewed. Paulette had not seen Jinx Falkenburg McCrary for fifteen years. Alcohol had been the chief factor in causing their separation. Seemingly out of nowhere, Jinx had developed a drinking problem and had lost touch with many valuable aspects of her life, including Paulette, who had never attempted to contact her. Jinx, a recovered alcoholic, heard that Paulette was at the Ritz Towers in New York and decided to get in touch.

"There are twelve steps in the program [Alcoholics Anonymous]," she explains, "and the ninth step is to make amends, to find relationships that have dissolved. Since I was the one who disappeared because of my drinking, the first amend I made was toward Paulette. I thought I'd love to speak to her and tell her where I'd been. When I called and said, 'Paulette, this is Jinx,' the first thing she said was, 'Where on earth have you been for fifteen years?!?' She asked, but didn't really want to know; she didn't want any sob story. In her welcome of me, she didn't drop a beat. 'Come on, I want to see you this evening. How about dinner and the theater?' It was total acceptance of a friend."

Paulette began to see Jinx and to visit her at Greentree, in Manhasset, where she was staying. She would go to the country estate all dressed up in her white dress and ruby pin, her arms full of tulips. She'd dress for the country as if she were going to Le Cirque. She seemed less vital but accessible. But then she withdrew and Jinx never saw her again.

What followed was a descent of grotesque proportions. The drinking and pill-taking escalated. She made scenes in stores and banks. She made endless demands upon her lawyers, viewing them as in league to do her in. She also ate prodigious amounts in a very messy fashion and was usually unpleasant to those around her.

There were events and decisions in between the pain, degradation, addiction, and five suicide attempts. By the end of the seventies, Paulette was spending six months in Switzerland and six months in New York. There was a three-month period while she was in New York that Lois decided to leave if Paulette did not stop drinking. She and Paulette's doctor hired a nurse who specialized in alcohol abuse, and for twenty-four hours a day for three months, they attempted to wean Paulette off alcohol. Finally, their efforts were rewarded. Paulette stopped drinking vodka. She was miserable. She went to Switzerland, and within six weeks was in the hospital, having tried once again to commit suicide.

Through it all, Paulette took exacting care of her mother, having moved her just down the street into Remarque's old apartment at 320 East Fifty-seventh Street. Although Alta seemed to be the doted-upon mother, and perhaps the subject of a joke or two—for instance, Paulette would say that after Alta died, she didn't want her urn to be next to Remarque's because they would spend the whole time gossiping—Lois Granato saw something else. She saw an old woman, practically abandoned, and totally dependent upon an extremely capricious daughter. Alta seemed to have no friends and saw no one. Paulette would go back to Switzerland and Alta would go into her apartment, close the door, and not see anyone for six months—except Lois, who would visit her once a week. In sixteen years, Paulette had Alta to Switzerland only once for a stay.

The evidence is that Paulette was always very generous to her mother. In fact, Celestine Wallis thought Alta could be quite perverse with her daughter. She was clearly competitive, and there were times during the seventies when Wallis visited Paulette and saw Alta being quite cruel: "Paulette would come out in some new outfit or other, and her mother would always say, 'You look like hell. You look terrible.' Obviously that's why Paulette kept going back to the closet; that's why she was so obsessed with her looks. I mean, what other mother at ninety-three would come in wearing little sparkly dresses with polka dots and try to play the coquette?"

And yet, the letters between the two were warm and caring. Lois remembers that Alta cherished Paulette's letters, and well she must have, because she saved enormous quantities of them in shoe boxes. They represented her loving, devoted daughter. In June 1984, Alta Goddard Levy Fleming Jacobson suffered a stroke. After three weeks of causing the least trouble she possibly could under the circumstances, she died at age ninety-four.

Finally Paulette was drinking so much that Warren Alpert (then owner and manager of the Ritz Towers), in fear that she might be committed, suggested that she move permanently to her house in Switzerland. And that is where she lived out her last five years, in the house and town from which she fought so hard to stay away. There she was surrounded by a devoted group who, along with Lois Granato, did their best to care for her. In addition to the housekeeper, Antonietta Bellosta, there was her secretary, Ruth Fantoni, her chauffeur, Marino de Maria, her physiotherapist, Barbara Wiese, her doctor, Joseph Bissig, and Antonietta's niece, Paola Bellosta. Everyone profited from her; she knew it and kept them all hopping. They still talk about her with relish and anger and awe.

Paulette attempted to keep a regimen. The ravages of alcohol, her many suicide attempts, the mastectomy, melanoma, and encroaching emphysema curtailed most of her favorite activities. Sick, and bored with being sick, she still managed a daily routine: up in the morning around nine, a bath, breakfast, her toilette, which took an hour and a half, and then, by noon—never before— she was ready to receive. Her visitors consisted less of friends than professionals—her doctor, her physical therapist, occasionally an appraiser from Sotheby's or Christie's, or her executor, Richard Kay. She had virtually cut off all of her friends in the States, who at one time had been eager to make the trip but, being constantly rebuffed, had stopped calling.

The dog, Kim, provides an allegory of those final years. Paulette, who had had dogs at various stages of her life—with Chaplin and with Remarque— acquired Kim, raised from a puppy primarily by Antonietta. One day, Kim ran in front of a car, which broke his leg. The leg had to be set and placed in a cast. Paulette was devastated. At one point, she ordered the cast removed, deciding that the leg would heal more naturally without it, that it wasn't good for the dog's activities to be so limited. She was told that there would be a risk of infection. She stuck to her decision. It was the one instance when Antonietta conspired against her. When Paulette went to bed, which was very early, around nine P.M., Antonietta would slip the cast on the dog's leg for the night and into the morning, since Paulette didn't come down until nearly ten A.M. That way the dog would be protected for nearly twelve hours. But during the day, as ordered, the cast was off, so that the dog could run free, which pleased Paulette. Eventually, the dog's leg became infected and it had to be put down.

Dr. Joseph Bissig, who treated Paulette for the emphysema that finally killed her, had the last intense relationship with her. Calling him "my sweet prince," she would insist that with every visit he have a glass of champagne with her, until her system could not tolerate it anymore, and then she would grab his hand and scream and shout at him to help her breathe. "Nobody ever talked back at her," he recalls, "because she was so beautiful and so pitiful."

She called herself Ondine, after the fable of the one who could not breathe on land. She had plenty of fire, but not enough oxygen for the fire, and yet she managed to burn Dr. Bissig's ears with tales of still more lovers in a voice, as Barbara Wiese describes, "like someone who eats a kilo of flames." There was mention of Alexander Haig, and of Alexander Calder, who she said once called for her wearing a tie that was also a mobile; it had a string that you pulled to make it flap. When Bissig said it sounded like it was a phallic symbol, "She doubled over with the most wonderful laughter," he recalls.

Paulette was seventy-nine in 1989, the last year of her life. She was confined to the house, wretched, often making her staff wretched with her demands, barely able to breathe, and yet, still beautiful to behold. Lois Granato provides this amazing description: "Paulette at seventy-nine, lying in bed, oxygen all the time, no makeup, skin gone, her hair washed—we managed to wash her hair—it was like a pouf. Curly out to here. So, she's in bed with pretty bedclothes and we've put a ribbon in her hair and she looks like a Kewpie doll. She's beautiful at seventy-nine. Always the cheekbones underneath the blue-green eyes. I mean she's gorgeous."

Toward the end, Dr. Bissig put Paulette on cortisone and morphine, trying to ease her immense suffering, equaled only by her ferocious will. Three hours before she died, she asked for a Sotheby's catalogue of her jewelry and for a mirror, studied herself, and examined her teeth. That day, April 23, 1990, six hours earlier in New York, Sotheby's had held a major auction of her jewelry, including her most precious signed Van Cleef & Arpels pieces as well as her legendary platinum and diamond necklace. The sale brought in over a million dollars. She died clutching the catalogue in her hands.

There were no survivors other than thirteen novels, three plays, and twelve films to Remarque's credit, forty-five Paulette Goddard movies, twenty-two of her television appearances, and her inimitable voice:

Last night, when I went to see *Gatsby*, I said to the producer, when he was calling for me—because I knew the film would start at eight and we wouldn't be out until eleven—I said, "Please bring me some caviar!" And I don't know him that well but he said, "What a great idea!" Because it's necessary. Sometimes. Because it has the highest food content—protein—and you have a glass of wine with it. I mean, it should be lavish. And the movie was three long hours. So we ate the whole tin! And he was so startled because he's an American from California. He said, "I thought you might keep some for tomorrow." I said, "Tomorrow! I may not be here!"

Nothing is interesting unless it succeeds. Unless it's behind you. Or done. It really isn't. What you're going to do and what you've done. It's how it comes out. The moment. But I don't know why I'm getting so philosophical with you. Suddenly.

The last photograph of Paulette, ca. 1990.

Paulette joins Erich and Alta at Ronco, 1990.

PAULETTE GODDARD:

FILMOGRAPHY

Berth Marks (1929) A Laurel and Hardy sound short subject.

The Locked Door (1929) United Arists. Director, George Fitzmaurice.

The Girl Habit (1931) Paramount Pictures. Director, Edward Cline. Screenplay, Owen Davis and Gertrude Purcell. Starring Charlie Ruggles, Tamara Geva, Margaret Dumont.

The Mouthpiece (1932) Warner Brothers. Directors, James Flood and Elliot Nugent. Based on the play by Frank J. Collins; screenplay, Earl Baldwin. Starring Warren William, Ralph Ince, Aline MacMahon, Guy Kibbee, Jack La Rue, J. Carrol Naish.

The Kid From Spain (1932) United Artists. Director, Leo McCarey. Producer, Samuel Goldwyn. Based on a story by William Anthony McGuire, Bert Kalmer, Harry Ruby; screenplay, McGuire, Kalmer, and Ruby. Starring Eddie Cantor, Lyda Roberti, Robert Young.

Modern Times (1936) United Artists. Director, producer, and screenplay, Charlie Chaplin. Starring Charlie Chaplin, Paulette Goddard, Henry Bergman, Chester Conklin.

The Young in Heart (1938) United Artists. Producer, David O. Selznick. Director, Richard Wallace. Based on the play *The Gay Banditti*, by I.A.R. Wylie; screenplay, Paul Osborne and Charles Bennett. Starring Janet Gaynor, Douglas Fairbanks, Jr., Roland Young, Billie Burke, Richard Carlson, Paulette Goddard, Minnie Dupree.

Dramatic School (1938) Metro-Goldwyn-Mayer. Producer, Mervyn Le Roy. Director, Robert B. Sinclair. Based on the play *School of Drama*, by Hans Szekely and Zoltan Egyed; screenplay, Ernst Vadja and Mary McCall. Starring Luise Rainer, Paulette Goddard, Alan Marshall, Lana Turner.

The Women (1939) Metro-Goldwyn-Mayer. Director, George Cukor. Producer, Hunt Stromberg. Based on the play by Clare Boothe; screenplay, Anita Loos and Jane Murfin. Starring Norma Shearer, Rosalind Russell, Joan Crawford, Paulette Goddard, Mary Boland, Joan Fontaine.

The Cat and the Canary (1939) Paramount Pictures. Producer, Arthur Hornblow, Jr. Director, Elliot Nugent. Based on the play by John Willard; screenplay, Walter De Leon. Starring Bob Hope, Paulette Goddard, John Beal, Gale Sondergaard.

The Ghost Breakers (1940) Paramount Pictures. Producer, Arthur Hornblow, Jr. Director, George Marshall. Story by Charles W. Goddard and Paul Dickey; screenplay, Walter De Leon. Starring Bob Hope, Paulette Goddard, Richard Carlson, Paul Lukas, Willie Best.

The Great Dictator (1940) United Artists. Producer, director, and screenplay, Charlie Chaplin. Starring Charlie Chaplin, Paulette Goddard, Jack Oakie, Reginald Gardiner, Henry Daniell.

Northwest Mounted Police (1940) Paramount Pictures. Producer, Cecil B. DeMille. Director, Cecil B. DeMille. Screenplay, Alan LeMay, Jesse Lasky, Jr., and C. Gardner Sullivan. Starring Gary Cooper, Madeleine Carroll, Paulette Goddard, Robert Preston, Preston Foster.

Second Chorus (1941) Paramount Pictures. Producer, Boris Morros. Director, H. C. Potter. Story by Frank Cavett; screenplay, Elaine Ryan, Ian McClellan Hunter. Songs, Johnny Mercer and Hal Borne; Mercer and Bernie Hanighen; Artie Shaw; Mercer and Shaw. Starring Fred Astaire, Paulette Goddard, Burgess Meredith, Artie Shaw and his band.

Pot O'Gold (1941) United Artists. Producer, James Roosevelt. Director, George Marshall. Story by Monte Brice, Andrew Bennison, Harry Tugend; screenplay, Walter De Leon. Starring James Stewart, Paulette Goddard, Horace Heidt, Charles Winninger.

Nothing But the Truth (1941) Paramount Pictures. Producer, Arthur Hornblow, Jr. Director, Elliott Nugent. Story by James Montgomery, Frederick S. Isham; screenplay, Don Hartman, Ken Englund. Starring Bob Hope, Paulette Goddard, Edward Arnold, Leif Erickson, Willie Best.

Hold Back the Dawn (1941) Paramount Pictures. Producer, Arthur Hornblow, Jr. Director, Mitchell Leisen. Story by Ketti Frings; screenplay, Charles Brackett and Billy Wilder. Starring Charles Boyer, Olivia de Havilland, Paulette Goddard.

The Lady Has Plans (1942) Paramount Pictures. Associate producer, Fred Kohlmar. Director, Sidney Lanfield. Story by Leo Birinski; screenplay, Harry Tugend. Starring Ray Milland, Paulette Goddard, Roland Young, Albert Dekker.

Reap the Wild Wind (1942) Paramount Pictures. Producer and director, Cecil B. DeMille. Story by Thelma Strabel; screenplay, Alan LeMay, Charles Bennett, Jesse Lasky, Jr. Starring Ray Milland, Paulette Goddard, Susan Hayward, John Wayne, Raymond Massey, Robert Preston.

The Forest Rangers (1942) Paramount Pictures. Associate producer, Robert Sisk. Director, George Marshall. Story by Thelma Strabel; screenplay, Harold Shumate. Songs, Frank Loesser and Frederick Hollander. Starring Fred MacMurray, Paulette Goddard, Susan Hayward.

Star Spangled Rhythm (1942) Paramount Pictures. Associate producer, Joseph Sistrom. Director, George Marshall. Screenplay, Harry Tugend. Starring Betty Hutton, Eddie Bracken, Victor Moore, Macdonald Carey, William Bendix, Dorothy Lamour, Paulette Goddard, Veronica Lake, Vera Zorina, Alan Ladd, Bing Crosby, Fred MacMurray, Robert Preston.

The Crystal Ball (1943) United Artists. Producer, Richard Blumenthal. Director, Elliott Nugent. Story by Steven Vas; adaptation, Virginia Van Upp. Starring Ray Milland, Paulette Goddard, Gladys George, Virginia Field, Cecil Kellaway, William Bendix.

So Proudly We Hail (1943) Paramount Pictures. Producer-director, Mark Sandrich. Screenplay by Allan Scott. Starring Claudette Colbert, Paulette Goddard, Veronica Lake, George Reeves, Sonny Tufts.

Standing Room Only (1944) Paramount Pictures. Associate producer, Paul Jones. Director, Sidney Lanfield. Story by Al Martin; screenplay, Darrel Ware. Starring Paulette Goddard, Fred MacMurray, Edward Arnold, Roland Young, Hillary Brooke.

I Love a Soldier (1944) Paramount Pictures. Producer-director, Mark Sandrich. Screenplay, Allan Scott. Starring Paulette Goddard, Sonny Tufts, Beulah Bondi.

Duffy's Tavern (1945) Paramount Pictures. Associate producer, Danny Dare. Director, Hal Walker. Screenplay, Melvin Frank, Norman Panama. Starring Bing Crosby, Betty Hutton, Paulette Goddard, Alan Ladd, Dorothy Lamour, Veronica Lake, Eddie Bracken.

Kitty (1946) Paramount Pictures. Producer, Karl Tunberg. Director, Mitchell Leisen. Based on the novel by Rosamund Marshall; screenplay, Darrell Ware and Karl Tunberg. Starring Paulette Goddard, Ray Milland, Patric Knowles, Reginald Owen, Cecil Kellaway, Constance Collier.

The *Diary of a Chambermaid* (1946) United Artists. Producers, Benedict Bogeaus and Burgess Meredith. Director, Jean Renoir. Based on the novel *Celestine's Diary* by Octave Mirbeau, and the play by Andre Heuse, Andre de Lorde, Thielly Nores. Screenplay, Burgess Meredith. Starring Paulette Goddard, Burgess Meredith, Hurd Hatfield, Francis Lederer, Judith Anderson.

Suddenly It's Spring (1947) Paramount Pictures. Producer, Claude Binyon. Director, Mitchell Leisen. Story by Binyon; screenplay, Binyon. Starring Paulette Goddard, Fred MacMurray, Macdonald Carey, Arleen Whelan.

Variety Girl (1947) Paramount Pictures. Producer, Daniel Dare. Director, George Marshall. Screenplay, Edmund Hartman, Frank Tashlin, Robert Welch, Monte Brice. Starring Olga San Juan, DeForest Kelley, Bing Crosby, Bob Hope, Gary Cooper, Ray Milland, Alan Ladd, Barbara Stanwyck, Paulette Goddard, Dorothy Lamour, Veronica Lake, Sonny Tufts, William Holden.

Unconquered (1947) Paramount Pictures. Producer-director, Cecil B. DeMille. Based on the novel by Neil H. Swanson; screenplay, Charles Bennett, Frederic M. Frank, Jesse Lasky, Jr. Starring Gary Cooper, Paulette Goddard, Howard Da Silva, Boris Karloff, Cecil Kellaway, Ward Bond.

An Ideal Husband (1948) 20th Century-Fox. Producer-director, Alexander Korda. Based on the play by Oscar Wilde; screenplay, Lajos Bir. Starring Paulette Goddard, Michael Wilding, Diana Wynyard, Glynis Johns, Constance Collier.

On Our Merry Way (1948) United Artists. Producers, Benedict Bogeaus and Burgess Meredith. Directors, King Vidor and Leslie Fenton. Story by Arch Oboler; screenplay, Laurence Stallings. Starring Burgess Meredith, Paulette Goddard, Fred MacMurray, James Stewart, Dorothy Lamour.

Hazard (1948) Paramount Pictures. Producer, Mel Epstein. Director, George Marshall. Story by Roy Chanslor; screenplay, Arthur Sheekman and Roy Chanslor. Starring Paulette Goddard, Macdonald Carey, Fred Clark.

Bride of Vengeance (1949) Paramount Pictures. Producer, Richard Maibaum. Director, Mitchell Leisen. Story by Michael Hogan; screenplay, Cyril Hume and Michael Hogan. Starring Paulette Goddard, John Lund, Macdonald Carey.

Anna Lucasta (1949) Columbia Pictures. Producer, Philip Yordan. Director, Irving Rapper. Based on the play by Philip Yordan; screenplay, Yordan, Arthur Laurents. Starring Paulette Goddard, William Bishop, Oscar Homolka, John Ireland, Broderick Crawford, Mary Wickes, Will Geer, Whit Bissell.

The Torch (1950) Eagle Lion. Producer, Bert Granet. Director, Emilio Fernandez. Screenplay, Inigo de Martino and Noriega Fernandez. Starring Paulette Goddard, Pedro Armendarez, Gilbert Roland.

Babes in Bagdad (1952) United Artists. Producers, Edward J. Danziger and Harry Lee Danziger. Director, Edgar G. Ulmer. Screenplay, Felix Feist, Joe Anson. Starring Paulette Goddard, Gypsy Rose Lee.

Vice Squad (1953) United Artists. Producers, Jules V. Levey, Arthur Gardner. Director, Arnold Laven. Based on the novel *Harness Bull* by Leslie T. White. Screenplay, Lawrence Roman. Starring Edward G. Robinson, Paulette Goddard.

Paris Model (1953) Columbia Pictures. Producer, Albert Zugsmith. Director, Alfred E. Green. Story-screenplay, Robert Smith. Starring Eva Gabor, Marilyn Maxwell, Paulette Goddard.

Sins of Jezebel (1953) Lippert. Producer, Sigmund Neufeld. Director, Reginald LeBorg. Screenplay, Richard Landau. Starring Paulette Goddard, George Nader, John Hoyt, Eduard Franz.

Charge of the Lancers (1954) Columbia. Producer, Sam Katzman. Director, William Castle. Story-screenplay, Robert E. Kent. Starring Paulette Goddard, Jean-Pierre Aumont.

The Unholy Four (1954) Lippert. Producer, Michael Carreras. Director, Terence Fisher. Based on the novel by George Sanders; screenplay, Michael Carreras. Starring Paulette Goddard, William Sylvester, Patrick Holt.

Time of Indifference (*Gli indifferenti*) (1966) Continental. Producer, Franco Cristaldi. Director, Francesco Marselli. Based on the novel by Alberto Moravia, adaptation by Suso Cecchi d'Amico; screenplay, Marselli. Starring Rod Steiger, Claudia Cardinale, Shelley Winters, Paulette Goddard, Tomas Milian.

ERICH MARIA REMARQUE:

NOVELS, PLAYS, AND

FILMOGRAPHY

Novels

The Dream Room (*Die Traumbude*). Dresden: Verlag der Schönheit, 1920.

Station on the Horizon (*Station am Horizont*). *Sport im Bild*, 1927, issues 24–26; 1928, issues 1–4.

All Quiet on the Western Front (*Im Westen nichts Neues*). Berlin: Propyläen, 1929. Translated by A. W. Wheen. Boston: Little, Brown, 1929.

The Road Back (*Der Weg zurück*). Berlin: Propyläen, 1931. Translated by A. W. Wheen. Boston: Little, Brown, 1931.

Three Comrades (*Drei Kameraden*). Amsterdam: Querido, 1938. Translated by A. W. Wheen. Boston: Little, Brown, 1937.

Flotsam (*Liebe Deinen Nächsten*). Stockholm: Bermann-Fischer, 1941. Translated by Denver Lindley. Boston: Little, Brown, 1941.

Arch of Triumph (*Arc de Triomphe*). Zürich: Micha, 1946. Translated by Walter Sorell and Denver Lindley. New York: Appleton-Century, 1945.

Spark of Life (*Der Funke Leben*). Cologne: Kiepenheuer und Witsch, 1952. Translated by James Stern. New York: Appleton-Century-Crofts, 1952.

A Time to Love and a Time to Die (*Zeit zu leben und Zeit zu sterben*). Cologne: Kiepenheuer und Witsch, 1954. Translated by Denver Lindley. New York: Harcourt, Brace, 1954.

The Black Obelisk (*Der schwarze Obelisk*). Cologne: Kiepenheuer und Witsch, 1956. Translated by Denver Lindley. New York: Harcourt, Brace, 1957.

Heaven Has No Favorites (*Der Himmel kennt keine Günstlinge*). Cologne: Kiepenheuer und Witsch, 1961. Translated by Richard and Clara Winston. New York: Harcourt, Brace & World, 1961.

The Night In Lisbon (*Die Nacht von Lissabon*). Cologne: Kiepenheuer und Witsch, 1962. Translated by Ralph Manheim. New York: Harcourt, Brace & World, 1964.

Shadows in Paradise (*Schatten im Paradies*). Munich: Droemer, Knaur, 1971. Translated by Ralph Manheim. New York: Harcourt, Brace & World, 1972.

Plays

The Last Station (*Die letzte Station*). Retitled *Berlin, 1945*, premiered on September 20, 1956, at the West Berlin Renaissance Theater.

Full Circle (formerly *Berlin, 1945*). Adapted by Peter Stone; produced and directed by Otto Preminger. Opened in New York on November 7, 1973.

Homecoming of Enoch J. Jones (*Die Heimkehr des Enoch J. Jones*). An amateur production was presented for 12 performances on October 15, 1988, in Osnabrück, Germany.

Brunnenstrasse (*Fountain Street*) An unfinished and unproduced play.

La Barcarolle: A Study in Brown. Notes for a play.

Filmography

All Quiet on the Western Front (1930)

Directed by Lewis Milestone; produced by Carl Laemmle, Jr.; screenplay by Maxwell Anderson, George Abbot, and Dell Andrews. Cast: Lew Ayres (Paul Bäumer), Louis Wolheim (Katczinsky), John Wray (Himmelstoss), Raymond Griffith (Gerard Duval), George "Slim" Summerville (Tjaden), Russell Gleason (Müller), William Bakewell (Albert), Beryl Mercer (Mutter Bäumer). Dubbed in English by ZaSu Pitts. A Universal International Picture, 140 minutes.

The Road Back (1937)

Directed by James Whale; produced by James Whale and Edmund Grainger; screenplay by R. C. Sherriff and Charles Kenyon; music by Dimitri Tiomkin. Cast: John King (Ernst), Richard Cromwell (Ludwig), George "Slim" Summerville (Tjaden), Andy Devine (Willy), Barbara Read (Lucy), Louise Fazenda (Angelina). A Universal International Picture, 103 minutes.

Three Comrades (1938)

Directed by Frank Borzage; produced by Frank Borzage and Joseph L. Mankiewicz; screenplay by F. Scott Fitzgerald and Edward E. Paramore; music by Franz Waxman. Cast: Robert Taylor (Lohkamp), Robert Young (Lenz), Franchot Tone (Koster), Margaret Sullavan (Pat), Guy Kibbee (Alfons), Lionel Atwill (Breuer). Metro-Goldwyn-Mayer, 100 minutes.

So Ends Our Night (1947)

Directed by John Cromwell; produced by David Loew and Albert Lewin; screenplay by Talbot Jennings. Cast: Fredric March (Steiner), Margaret Sullavan (Ruth Holland), Frances Dee (Marie Steiner), Glenn Ford (Kern), Anna Sten (Lilo), Erich von Stroheim (Brenner), Alexander Granach (Der Pole). A Loew-Lewin Film for United Artists, 120 minutes.

The Other Love (1947)

Directed by Andre de Toth; produced by David Lewis; screenplay by Ladislas Fodor and Harry Brown. Cast: Barbara Stanwyck (Karen Duncan), David Niven (Dr. Stanton), Maria Palmer (Huberta), Joan Lorring (Celestine), Richard Conte (Paul Clemont), Richard Hale (Professor Linnaker). An Enterprise Production for United Artists, 95 minutes.

Arch of Triumph (1948)

Directed by Lewis Milestone; produced by David Lewis and Lewis Milestone; screenplay by Lewis Milestone and Harry Brown. Cast: Ingrid Bergman (Joan

Madou), Charles Boyer (Dr. Ravic), Charles Laughton (Haake), Louis
Calhern (Morosow), Curt Bois (Ober). Enterprise Productions for United
Artists, 120 minutes.

Der letzte Akt (The Last Ten Days) (1955)
Directed by Georg Wilhelm Pabst; produced by Carl Szokoll; screenplay by
Fritz Habeck, according to a film story by Erich Maria Remarque based on
the novel *Ten Days to Die* by Michael A. Musmanno. Cast: Albin Skoda (Adolf
Hitler), Oskar Werner (Hauptmann Wurst), Erich Frey (General Burgdorf),
Kurt Eilers (Martin Bormann), Willy Krause (Joseph Goebbels), Otto
Schmole (Alfred Jodl). Cosmopol Productions for Columbia Pictures, 115
minutes.

A Time to Love and a Time to Die (1958)
Directed by Douglas Sirk; produced by Robert Arthur; screenplay by Orin
Jannings. Cast: John Gavin (Ernst Graeber), Liselotte Pulver (Elisabeth
Kruse), Jock Mahoney (Immermann), Don DeFore (Boettcher), Keenan
Wynn (Reuter), Erich Maria Remarque (Prof. Pohlmann), Charles Regnier
(Joseph), Kurt Meisel (Heiner), Agnes Windeck (Frau White), Klaus Kinski
(Untersturmführer). Universal International Pictures, 133 minutes.

The Night in Lisbon (1971)
Directed by Zbynek Brynych; produced by Dieter Nobbe; screenplay by
Zbynek Brynych. Cast: Martin Benrath (Joseph Schwartz), Erika Pluhar
(Helen), Jorst Frank (Georg Jürgens), Vadim Glowna (Der Mann), Hans
Schweikart (Dr. Dubois), Charles Regnier (Lachmann). Produced by ZDF,
110 minutes.

Bobby Deerfield (based on the novel *Heaven Has No Favorites*) (1977)
Directed by Sydney Pollack; produced by John Foreman; screenplay by Alvin
Sargent. Cast: Al Pacino (Bobby Deerfield), Marthe Keller (Lillian), Anny
Duperey (Lydia), Walter McGinn (Leonard Deerfield), Romolo Valli (Uncle
Luigi), Stephen Meldegg (Karl Holtzmann). Columbia Pictures, 124 minutes.

All Quiet on the Western Front, a remake for television (1979)
Directed by Delbert Mann; produced by Norman Rosemont; screenplay by Paul
Monash. Cast: Richard Thomas (Paul Bäumer), Ernest Borgnine (Kat),
Donald Pleasence (Kantorek), Ian Holm (Himmelstoss), Patricia Neal (Frau
Bäumer). Marble Arch Productions, 155 minutes.

Arch of Triumph, a television movie (1985)
Directed by Waris Hussein; produced by Peter Graham Scott. Cast: Anthony
Hopkins (Dr. Ravic), Lesley-Anne Down (Joan Madou). Newland-Raynor
Productions.

The Black Obelisk (1988)
Directed by Peter Deutsch; screenplay by Gerd Angermann. Cast: Udo Schenk
(Ludwig Bodmer), Rainer Hunold (Georg Kroll), Karina Theyenthal
(Isabelle), Marina Krogull (Gerda Schneider), Elfi Eschke (Lisa Watzek),
Heinz Schimmelpfennig (Riesenfeld), Jean-Paul Raths (Heinrich Kroll),

Joachim Bernhard (Willy), Petra Maria Grühn (Renée de la Tour), Werner Eichhorn (Feldwebel Knopf), Karen Grüger (Fritzi), Illo Schneider (Puffmutter), Frauke Jansen (Rosa), Stefan Schwartz (Otto Bambus), Sigfried Grönig (Hungermann), Lutz Reichert (Schneeweib), Gerhard Giesecke (Grund), Rainer Pigulla (Dr. Wernicke). Deutsche Buchgemeinschaft, Berlin, 90 minutes.

BIBLIOGRAPHY

Archival and Estate Sources

The Erich Maria Remarque Collection belongs to New York University and resides in the Fales Library of the Elmer Holmes Bobst Library at New York University.

The Paulette Goddard Collection, which is part of the Paulette Goddard Remarque Estate, belongs to, and is housed at, the Tisch School of the Arts, Film Studies Program, at New York University.

The Paulette Goddard Remarque Estate Collection, some of which has yet to be curated, belongs to New York University.

All letters between Erich Maria Remarque and Paulette Goddard, as well as the diaries (in German) of Erich Maria Remarque, reside in the Fales Library of the Elmer Bobst Library at New York University.

The Erich-Maria-Remarque Archiv/Forschungsstelle Krieg und Literatur at Osnabrück University in Osnabrück, Germany, is also a repository for an Erich Maria Remarque collection; much of the information and materials concerning his early life are to be found in this archive.

The Powell Library at the University of California in Los Angeles, and the Library of Congress in Washington, D.C., house and conserve many of the films of Paulette Goddard and the films, based on the novels, of Erich Maria Remarque.

I have also used the Film Collection and the Film Stills Archive of the Museum of Modern Art, New York; the Conde Nast/Vogue Archive, New York; and the Margaret Herrick Library of the Academy of Motion Picture Arts and Sciences, Los Angeles.

Unpublished Materials

Loos, Anita. "The Perils of Paulette" (1973). This unfinished and unpublished work, originally contracted by Harcourt Brace Jovanovich, resides in the Paulette Goddard Remarque Estate Collection, New York University.

Swaner, Michele, and Tom Vitelli. "A Capsule Biography of Leslie L. Goddard" (1987). This unpublished work was commissioned by Paulette Goddard and is a possession of the Paulette Goddard Remarque Estate Collection, New York University.

The diaries of Erich Maria Remarque have been heretofore unpublished. Excerpts from them appear for the first time in my book. The diary of 1918 as well as the diaries of 1935–1950 have been translated by Monika Anderson, and those translations are owned by me. The diaries of 1950–1965 have been translated by Gerdi Eller, and those translations are also owned by me.

Unpublished tapes and transcriptions of the voice and words of Paulette Goddard are the possession of the Paulette Goddard Remarque Estate, New York University.

Author's Interviews

Warren Alpert: October 9, 1992, New York

Lew Ayres: December 1, 1992, by telephone

Steven Bach: November 4, 1992, New York

Antonietta Bellosta: February 17, 1991, Porto Ronco, Switzerland

Dr. Joseph Bissig: March 12, 1992, Ascona, Switzerland

Macdonald Carey: : December 1, 1992, by telephone

Bob Colacello: June 3, 1994, by telephone

Ellen Janssen Dunham: April 4, 1991, New York

Douglas Fairbanks, Jr.: August 2, 1992, New York

James Frazier: February 19, 1992, by telephone

John Gavin: May 12, 1993, by telephone

Rolf Gerard: March 9, 1992, Ascona, Switzerland

Lois Granato: March 9, 1991, and February 4, 1993, New York; October16, 1994, by telephone

Licci Habe: March 10, 1992, Ascona, Switzerland

Michael Hall: February 22, 1991, New York

Margaret Horlitz: November 19, 1992, by telephone

Robert Lantz: December 6, 1993, New York

Jinx Falkenburg McCrary: July 30, 1994, by telephone

Joseph Mankiewitz: June 9, 1992, by letter

Ruth Marton: November 14, 1991, by telephone, and May 21, 1992, New York

Burgess Meredith: April 15, 1991, Malibu, California

Ruth Albu Morgenroth: April 19, 1991, May 5, 1992, April 29, 1993, Santa Barbara, California

Helen Murray: May 2, 1991, and May 15, 1994, by telephone

Leonard Nimoy: September 25, 1992, by telephone

Harriet Pilpel: November 18, 1990, New York

Luise Rainer: July 28, 1991, Lugano, Switzerland

Patricia Roc Reif: July 27, 1991, Locarno, Switzerland

Dr. Thomas Schneider: June 22, 1992, Osnabrück, Germany

Daniel Selznick: July 31, 1992, New York

Rod Steiger: March 14, 1994, by telephone

Peter Stone: February 13, 1992, New York

Jean Tailer: July 30, 1994, by telephone
Bob Ulman: May 11, 1994, by telephone
Celestine Wallis: January 14, 1991, New York
Mary Wickes: December 1, 1992, by telephone
Billy Wilder: April 11, 1991, Beverly Hills
Victoria Wolff: April 9, 1991, Los Angeles
Charlotte Elk Zernik: January 17, August 10, August 28, 1992, New York

Books

Antkowiak, Alfred. *Ludwig Renn: Erich Maria Remarque, Leben und Werk.* Berlin: Volk und Volkseigener Verlag, 1965.

Avisar, Ilian. *Screening the Holocaust.* Bloomington: Indiana University Press, 1988.

Bach, Steven. *Marlene Dietrich: Life and Legend.* New York: William Morrow, 1992.

Barker, Christine R., and R. W. Last. *Erich Maria Remarque.* London: Osward Wolff; New York: Barnes & Noble (Harper & Row), 1979.

Behlmer, Rudy, editor. *Memo from David O. Selznick.* Hollywood: Samuel French, 1972.

Carey, Gary. *Anita Loos: A Biography.* New York; Alfred A. Knopf, 1988.

Chaplin, Charlie. *My Autobiography.* New York: Penguin, 1992.

Dietrich, Marlene. *Marlene.* Translated by Salvator Attanasio. New York: Avon Books, 1987.

Durgnat, Raymond. *Jean Renoir.* Berkeley: University of California Press, 1974.

Eggebrecht, Axel. *Der halbe Weg: Zwischenbitenz einer Epoche.* Hamburg: Rowohlt, 1975.

Firda, Richard Arthur. *Erich Maria Remarque: A Thematic Analysis of His Novels.* New York: Peter Lang, 1988.

Friedrich, Otto. *City of Nets: A Portrait of Hollywood in the 1940s.* New York: Harper & Row, 1986.

Herrera, Hayden. *Frida: A Biography of Frida Kahlo.* New York: Perennial Library (Harper & Row), 1983.

Howard, Jean. *Jean Howard's Hollywood: A Photo Memoir.* Text by James Watters. New York: Harry N. Abrams, 1989.

Kessler, Harry. *In the Twenties.* London: Weidenfeld & Nicholson, 1971.

Kreuger, Miles, ed. *Souvenir Programs of Twelve Classic Movies, 1927–1941.* New York: Dover Publications, 1977.

Loos, Anita. *Fate Keeps On Happening: Adventures of Lorelei Lee and Other Writings.* Edited by Ray Pierre Corsini. New York: Dodd, Mead, 1984.

Lorant, Stefan. *I Was Hitler's Prisoner.* London: Victor Gollancz, 1935.

Morella, Joe, and Edward Z. Epstein. *Paulette: The Adventurous Life of Paulette Goddard.* New York: St. Martin's Press, 1985. (Author's note; This is an unauthorized biography.)

Parish, Robert James. *The Paramount Pretties.* New York: Castle Books, 1972.

Remarque, Erich Maria. *All Quiet on the Western Front.* Translated by A. W. Wheen. New York: Fawcett Crest (Ballantine Books), 1982.

————. *The Road Back.* Translated by A.W. Wheen. Boston: Little, Brown, 1931.

————. *Three Comrades.* Translated by A. W. Wheen. London: Sphere Books, 1967.

————. *Flotsam.* Translated by Denver Lindley. London: Panther Books, 1961.

————. *Arch of Triumph.* Translated by Walter Sorell and Denver Lindley. New York: Signet Books (New American Library), 1945.

————. *Spark of Life.* Translated by James Stern. London: Arrow Books, 1959.

————. *A Time to Love and a Time to Die.* Translated by Denver Lindley. New York: Popular Library, 1960.

————. *The Black Obelisk.* Translated by Denver Lindley. New York: Harcourt, Brace & World, 1957.

————. *Heaven Has No Favorites.* Translated by Richard and Clara Winston. London: Panther Books, 1961.

————. *The Night in Lisbon.* Translated by Ralph Manheim. London: Panther Books, 1966.

————. *Shadows in Paradise.* Translated by Ralph Manheim. New York: Harcourt Brace Jovanovich, 1972.

Renoir, Jean. *My Life and My Films.* New York: Da Capo, 1974.

Riefenstahl, Leni. *A Memoir.* New York: St. Martin's Press, 1993.

Riess, Curt. *Meine berühmten Freunde (My Famous Friends).* Germany: Herder Taschenbuch Verlag, 1987. The translations used in this book are by Henry Goldsmith and are owned by the author.

Riva, Maria. *Marlene Dietrich.* New York: Alfred A. Knopf, 1993.

Spoto, Donald. *Blue Angel: The Life of Marlene Dietrich.* New York: Doubleday, 1992.

Taylor, Harley U., Jr. *Erich Maria Remarque: A Literary and Film Biography.* New York: Peter Lang, 1989.

Thomson, David. *Showman: The Life of David O. Selznick.* New York: Alfred A. Knopf, 1992.

Wagener, Hans. *Understanding Erich Maria Remarque.* Columbia: University of South Carolina Press, 1991.

Wells, H. G. *H. G. Wells in Love.* Boston: Little, Brown, 1984.

Winters, Shelley. *Shelley II: The Middle of My Century.* New York: Simon & Schuster, 1990.

SOURCE NOTES

One. A German Youth, 1898–1922

6 "The different homes on Jahnstrasse": Hanns-Gerd Rabe, "Remarque und Osnabrück," *Osnabrücker Mitteilungen*, vol. 77, 1970, p. 3; EMR Archiv.

6 "I never felt that anyone": Richard Arthur Firda, *Erich Maria Remarque: A Thematic Analysis of His Novels*, p. 5.

6 "proud and prominent traverses": Quoted in Rabe, p. 4.

7 I shared my schooldays": Kristen Kranzbuehler, quoted in Rabe, pp. 205–10.

7 "He told me his story": Harry Kessler, *In the Twenties*, p. 5.

8 "Kantorek had been": *All Quiet on the Western Front*, pp. 10–11.

8 Information given by Joseph Witt; cited in Firda, p. 9, and in Rabe, p. 28.

10 "Peter Remark liked to": Harley U. Taylor, Jr., *Erich Maria Remarque: A Literary and Film Biography*, p. 9.

11 "The sun appeared": *Heimatfreund,* 1916; in EMR Archiv.

12 "the sad state of parental": Taylor, p. 12.

15 EMR diary entries: EMR Collection, NYU. Translation by Monika Anderson owned by the author.

15 "I went to No. 9": *All Quiet on the Western Front*, p. 23.

16 "One Sunday": Ibid., p. 25.

16 "The going is more": Ibid., p. 288.

18 "I was without aim": Quoted in an article by Vogler, EMR Archiv.

18 "The room is dark": *All Quiet on the Western Front*, p. 185.

18 "Ah! Mother!": Ibid., p. 183.

19 Letters to George Middendorf: EMR Archiv.

19 "It was early evening": Interview with Victoria Wolff.

21 "We, the young, who have served": *The Dream Room*, translation by Monika Anderson; EMR Collection, NYU. Translation owned by EMR Collection.

22 Letter to Ludwig Bate: EMR Archiv.

23 "I had just handed over": Rabe, quoted in Firda, p. 21.

23 "It was to a volatile": Taylor, p. 24.

24 "a badge worn": Ibid., p. 25.

24 Letter to Erika Haase: EMR Archiv.

24 "had to admit": Rabe, p. 218.

24 "The rumors were that": Interview with Dr. Thomas Schneider.

25 "In my next book": "Remark to Flee," *New York Times*, Sept. 7, 1929.

26 "You and I": *Die Schönheit (Beauty)*, vol. 4, 1918, p. 77; EMR Archiv.

26 "There they stand": *The Road Back*, p. 212.

27 Hanns-Gerd Rabe's observations: Christine R. Barker and R. W. Last, *Erich Maria Remarque*, p. 10.

27 Letter to Miss Mimi: EMR Archiv.

29 Letter to Deacon Brand: EMR Archiv.

29 "The information": Ibid.

30 "Evening Song": *Osnabrücker Tageblatt*; EMR Archiv.

31 "The model for Europe": "Art and Nature," *Die Schönheit*, vol. 6, 1920; EMR Archiv.

31 "In the checkroom": "Oooh, la la Theatreballe," EMR Archiv.

31 Letter from Lolott: EMR Archiv.

32 Letter to Stefan Zweig: EMR Archiv. Letter belongs to EMR Archiv; also found in Stefan Zweig Collection, Reed Library, SUNY College at Fredonia.

33 "We shared the dream": Pastor Biedendieck's quotation from Rabe, p. 224.

33 "I ignore the slight": EMR Archiv.

33 "We designed and sold atrocities": *Der Spiegel*, Sept. 1, 1952, p. 23.

34 Discussion of *The Black Obelisk*: Hans Wagener, *Understanding Erich Maria Remarque*, p. 82.

34 Letter to Osnabrück government: EMR Archiv.

36 Episode of the Captain Hein Priemke cartoon: EMR Archiv.

Two. *Marion Goddard Levy, AKA . . . , 1910–1936*

37 Early biographical information: "A Capsule Biography of Leslie L. Goddard," compiled May 1987 by Michele Swaner and Tom Vitelli.

38 "At the time of the divorce": Interview with Helen Murray.

39 Portions of J. R. Levy's testimony: *Los Angeles Herald*, May 8, 1940.

39 "I was about eight or nine": Tape-recorded and transcribed reminiscences of PG, ca. 1973–74; PGR Estate.

40 "Mother and I": Hedda Hopper interview, 1948, quoted in Swaner and Vitelli, p. 48; originally found in Joe Morella and Edward Z. Epstein, *Paulette: The Adventurous Life of Paulette Goddard*, pp. 4–5.

42 "By the time I was thirteen": Reminiscences of PG, PGR Estate.

42 "There was Uncle Charlie": Interview with Helen Murray.

42 "I think a background of poverty": Morella and Epstein, p. 5.

42 Quotations about Leslie and Uncle Charlie: Swaner and Vitelli, p. 51.

43 "At first Mother wouldn't let me come": Interview ca. 1926; clipping in Film Stills Archive, Museum of Modern Art, New York.

44 "The musical numbers were lavish": Morella and Epstein, pp. 6–7.

44 "Just because we are dancing": Interview ca. 1926; clipping in Film Stills Archive, Museum of Modern Art, New York.

45 Quotations regarding strike: Unidentified clipping, Film Stills Archive, Museum of Modern Art, New York.

46 "I thought": Reminiscences of PG, PGR Estate.

48 "Our courtship was": Ibid.

48 "Paulette offered to adopt": Interview with Helen Murray.

49 Quotations from Lois Granato: Interview with Lois Granato.

50 "I am what I am": Reminiscences of PG, PGR Estate.

50 "He was from North Carolina": Ibid.

50 "My husband had given me": Ibid.

50 "Now I can hardly wait": Unidentified interview, ca. 1930; PG Collection, NYU.

51 Information from Morella and Epstein, p. 13.

53 "So I arrived": Reminiscences of PG, PGR Estate.

54 "That he [Chaplin]": Article by Edwin Shallert, 1933; PG Collection, NYU.

55 "The ensuing divorce": Morella and Epstein, p. 17.

55 "Paulette entered the suite": Ibid., p. 32.

56 "There is no biographical data": Unidentified clipping, ca. 1931; PG Collection, NYU.

56 "When she began": Anita Loos, "The Perils of Paulette," unpublished manuscript, PGR Estate.

57 PG quotations on Stewart, jewelry, and early career: Unpublished interview, ca. 1974, PGR Estate.

58 "CHAPLIN KISS NO BETROTHAL": Dorothy Kilgallen's syndicated column, Academy of Motion Picture Arts and Sciences Library, Los Angeles, PG file.

58 "It isn't so much": Unidentified article, PG Collection, NYU.

58 "Paulette struck me as being": Charles Chaplin, *My Autobiography*, p. 377.

59 "He [Chaplin] helped": Morella and Epstein, p. 21.

59 "I saw them all the time": Interview with Daniel Selznick.

59 "He told me": Reminiscences of PG, PGR Estate.

60 "Wanting to act": Ibid.

62 "Paulette Goddard is the most extravagantly gowned": Unidentified clipping, Academy of Motion Picture Arts and Sciences Library, Los Angeles, PG file.

63 "Most people in Hollywood": Loos, "Perils of Paulette."

63 "She . . . told me how she had been educated": Unidentified clipping, PG Collection, NYU.

65 "I never deeply wanted them": Reminiscences of PG, PGR Estate.

65 "I always assumed they were married": Interview with Douglas Fairbanks, Jr.

65 "We had seven servants": Reminiscences of PG, PGR Estate.

66 "Charlie was a great talker": Ibid.

66 "Anarchy was to him": Ibid.

67 "It was the glamour": Ibid.

67 Gertrude Stein's visit to *Modern Times* set: Ibid.

67 "I was about to start": Ibid.

68 Press release by Catherine Hunter: PG Collection, NYU.

68 "was a difficult role": James Robert Parish, *The Paramount Pretties*, p. 376.

70 "Whatever Chaplin touched in her": Interview with Burgess Meredith.

Three. Boni, 1922–1933

72 Letters from EMR to Brigitte Neuner: EMR Archiv.

72 Letters from EMR to Karl Vogt: EMR Archiv.

73 Quotations from *Three Comrades*: A. W. Wheen translation, p. 17.

74 "I dislike everything autobiographical": Hanns-Gerd Rabe, "Erich Maria Remarque und Osnabrück," Preface, EMR Archiv.

74 "It is futile": Hans Wagener, *Understanding Erich Maria Remarque*, p. 48.

74 "typified Remarque's feminine ideal": Harley U. Taylor, Jr., *Erich Maria Remarque: A Literary and Film Biography*, p. 57.

75 "You smile, dear lady": "Decadence of Love," in *Berliner Leben*, vol. 25, no. 19, pp. 20–23; EMR Archiv.

75 "It was apparently a leitmotif": Interview with Charlotte Elk Zernik.

77 "On New Year's Eve": Interview with Dr. Thomas Schneider.

77 Letters from EMR to Edith Doerry Roseveare: EMR Archiv. The Edith Doerry Roseveare Collection was donated by Iris Roseveare.

77 Information on Edith Doerry's articles: Dr. Thomas Schneider, foreword to Erich Maria Remarque Yearbook II, 1992, EMR Archiv.

80 "The experience on Capri": Ibid.

81 "In this situation": Letter from Edith Doerry Roseveare, addressed to the PGR Estate's co-executor, Richard Kay, in connection with a memoir that she wished to write about herself and Remarque.

81 "lots of articles": *Die literarische Welt*, June 14, 1920; EMR Archiv.

81 "wide range of intellectual": Taylor, p. 53.

82 "The judges of the nightly beauty competition": *Die Literatur*, 1928–1929 (October–October), p. 467.

82 "She was a decorative object": Interview with Ruth Albu Morgenroth.

82 "Although I have lived": Unidentified clipping found in the Margaret Herrick Library of the Academy of Motion Picture Arts and Sciences, Los Angeles.

83 "A thousand thunderous screams": *Sport Im Bild*, no. 12, 1924, pp. 684, 712.

84 Information regarding title: Taylor, p. 57.

84 "Germans were riding the crest": Richard Arthur Firda, *Erich Maria Remarque: A Thematic Analysis of His Novels*, pp. 29–30.

84 "Betty Stern was a friend": Steven Bach, *Marlene Dietrich: Life and Legend*, pp. 75–76.

85 "We saw *All Quiet*": Maria Riva, *Marlene Dietrich*, p. 86.

85 "The irony of Remarque's being employed": Firda, p. 32.

86 "The heroes move in a mundane tinsel-world": Alfred Antkowiak, *Ludwig Renn: Erich Maria Remarque, Leben und Werk*, p. 102.

86 "unpretentious novel": Taylor, p. 59.

86 "I had experimented": H. W. Baum, "Remarque und seine Zeit," *Bibliothekar*, vol. 6, 1957.

86 "Formerly, I had never thought of writing": Frédéric Lefevre, "An Hour with Remarque," *The Living Age*, no. 339, 1930, pp. 344–49.

87 "Erich certainly only drank": Interview with Robert Lantz.

87 "Ode to the Cocktail": *Sport im Bild*, 1927; EMR Archiv.

88 "As for what they call fame": Louella Parsons column, *Los Angeles Examiner*, June 12, 1940.

88 "Remarque pleaded innocence": Stefan Napierski, "Ein Gespräch mit Remarque," *Wiadomosci Literarckie*, 1929, EMR Archiv. Translation by Henry Goldsmith owned by the author.

88 "We were always conscious": Curt Riess, *Meine berühmten Freunde* (*My Famous Friends*), p. 179. Translation by Henry Goldsmith owned by the author.

89 "I knew Remarque quite well": Interview with Billy Wilder.

89 "The truth was": *New York Times*, Sept. 22, 1929.

90 Letter from Herbert Read: EMR Collection, NYU.

91 Dr. Thomas Schneider's quotation and information: *Krieg und Literatur*, vol. 1, no. 1, 1989; EMR Archiv.

92 "My husband who had been in the field": Quoted in Dr. Thomas Schneider and Angelika Howind, "The Marketing of *All Quiet on the Western Front*," Erich Maria Remarque Dokumentationsstelle, Osnabrück University.

92 "In 1929 alone": Article by Angelika Howind, "The Marketing of *All Quiet on the Western Front*," *Krieg und Literatur*, vol. 1, no. 1, 1989; EMR Archiv.

95 "I used to hang about at the Toppkeller": From Axel Eggebrecht's autobiography, *Der halbe Weg* (*Halfway*), 1975, cited in Firda, pp. 32–33.

96 Letters from Jutta Remarque to EMR: EMR Collection, NYU.

96 "He [Remarque] was terribly pessimistic": Eggebrecht, pp. 241–44.

97 Quotations from Victoria Wolff: Interview with Victoria Wolff.

98 "She rested her head on my shoulder": *Three Comrades*, p. 400.

98 "Little Kramer": *Die grossen Namen*, Kindler Publishers, Germany, n.d.; cited in Firda, pp. 51–52.

99 "Because I didn't and don't": Axel Eggebrecht, "Gespräch mit Remarque," *Die literarische Welt*, June 14, 1929, p. 1.

100 "That opposition to my works": *London Observer*, Oct. 13, 1929.

101 "In 1933 he didn't want": *Der Spiegel*, Jan. 9, 1952, cited in Taylor, p. 28.

101 Letter to Stefan Zweig: Stefan Zweig Collection, Reed Library, SUNY College at Fredonia.

102 "Remarque is a good amateur": Arnold Zweig, cited in Harry Kessler, *In the Twenties*, p. 367.

102 "no attempt was ever made": Claude Owen, article in *Krieg und Literatur*, vol. 1, no. 1, 1989, pp. 42–43; EMR Archiv.

103 "What created the great success": Riess, p. 181.

103 "A naked soldier": *All Quiet on the Western Front*, pp. 207–8.

104 "A writer's backside": EMR diary entry, EMR Collection, NYU.

104 Letter to Putnam: EMR Archiv.

105 "He worked slowly": Riess, p. 182.

108 "How do you do?": *Time*, Jan. 25, 1931, p. 22.

109 "In my next book": *New York Times*, June 7, 1930.

110 Quotations from Lew Ayres: Interview with Lew Ayres.

110 "Twenty acres were dynamited": Information regarding movie, in Miles Kreuger, ed., *Souvenir Programs of Twelve Classic Movies, 1927–1941*, pp. 72–73.

110 "Battleground realism was achieved": Taylor, p. 79.

111 Information about showing of film in Berlin: Riess, p. 185.

112 Quotations from Ruth Albu: Interviews with Ruth Albu Morgenroth.

118 Information about *The Road Back*: Ibid., p. 100.

119 "We let [Renn] talk": Firda, p. 90.

119 "No desire for war": Lefevre, "An Hour with Remarque."

119 Letters from EMR to Ruth Albu: EMR Collection, NYU.

121 "In the year 1933": *Motion Picture Herald*, Jan. 13, 1949.

Four. The Honey Pot, 1936–1939

127 "Now Charlie": Anita Loos, "The Perils of Paulette," unpublished manuscript, PGR Estate.

127 "a companion from his days of poverty": Anita Loos, *Fate Keeps On Happening*, p. 203.

127 "Both Paulette and I": Loos, "Perils of Paulette."

128 "She was the first person": Jinx Falkenburg, "My Pal Paulette," *Movieland*, ca. 1944; undated clipping in 1944 scrapbook, PG Collection, NYU.

130 "Gentlemen, I have been reading": Letter to *Vogue*, ca. 1938, PG Collection, NYU.

130 Description of furs: Ibid.

130 "We stayed away from Hollywood": Charles Chaplin, *My Autobiography*, p. 38.

132 "The way I learned": Tape-recorded and transcribed reminiscences of PG, ca. 1973–74; PGR Estate.

133 "How else could she have": Anonymous source, author's interview.

133 "Saw Puma Saturday night": EMR diary entries, EMR Collection, NYU.

134 "He stayed at my house": Reminiscences of PG, PGR Estate.

134 "Dear Miss Goddard": Clipping in Film Stills Archive, Museum of Modern Art, New York.

134 "Paulette's secret": Interview with Celestine Wallis.

135 "I built my house": Chaplin, pp. 344–45.

135 "It wasn't a whole sweater": Reminiscences of PG, PGR Estate.

137 "Returned from Palm Springs": PG Collection, NYU. The piece was written by Paulette for the spring 1937 issue of the *Regency*, the newsletter of the Paulette Goddard International Club.

138 "Dietrich did not like": Maria Riva, *Marlene Dietrich*, p. 641.

139 Quotations from Loos, Levant, and Arlen: Joe Morella and Edward Z. Epstein, *Paulette*, pp. 56–57.

140 "I was married to Charlie": Reminiscences of PG, PGR Estate.

141 Constance Collier quotation: Morella and Epstein, p. 56.

142 "Of course Chaplin was a genius": Interview with Daniel Selznick.

143 "I asked her how Chaplin": Jean Renoir, *My Life and My Films*, pp. 224–25.

143 "by 1937–38, Chaplin": David Thomson, *Showman: The Life of David O. Selznick*, p. 269.

144 "very fine looking": Interview with Douglas Fairbanks, Jr.

144 "In the period of the forties": Interview with Daniel Selznick.

145 Luise Rainer quotations and information: Interview with Luise Rainer.

145 Virginia Grey quotation: Unidentified article, perhaps from a movie magazine, PG Collection, NYU.

146 "It has been obvious": Thomson, p. 268.

147 "a symbol of downtrodden humanity": James Robert Parish, *The Paramount Pretties*, p. 379.

147 "I am still hoping": Rudy Behlmer, ed., *Memo from David O. Selznick*, p. 168.

149 "SHE REFUSES": Unidentified article, PG Collection, NYU.

150 "It will throw": Morella and Epstein, p. 70.

150 "I have looked at the new Goddard test": Behler, p. 176.

152 Quotations from Michael Hall: Interview with Michael Hall.

153 "Before my brother, Myron": Behler, p. 180.

153 "Charlie wouldn't release me": Reminiscences of PG, PGR Estate.

154 "predatory chorus girl": Parish, p. 378.

154 "she had all of her close-ups": Reminiscences of PG, PGR Estate.

156 "Kahlo's volatile": George Ptacek, article in *Hollywood Reporter*, Apr. 24, 1991.

156 "When the divorce": Hayden Herrera, *Frida: A Biography of Frida Kahlo*, p. 273.

157 Discussion of bracelet: EMR diary, 1938, EMR Collection, NYU.

157 "I had an amusing time": H. G. Wells, *H. G. Wells in Love*, pp. 219–20.

158 "How could I throw myself": Chaplin, p. 386.

159 Paulette on fathers: Reminiscences of PG, PGR Estate.

161 "Every film I ever made": Article by Elsa Maxwell, Film Stills Archive, Museum of Modern Art, New York.

162 Paulette's recollections about Howard Hughes: Reminiscences of PG, PGR Estate.

Five. *Traveler Without a Country, 1933–1948*

165 "The night of the public burning": *Time*, Oct. 9, 1933.

165 "Against literary betrayal": Stefan Lorant, *I Was Hitler's Prisoner*, p. 193.

166 "Two Storm Troopers": Kyle Crichton's interview with Remarque, *Collier's*, 1939; cited in Harley U. Taylor, Jr., *Erich Maria Remarque: A Literary and Film Biography*, p. 99.

166 "At the reception in Manhattan": *Time*, Oct. 9, 1933.

167 Places visited by Remarque: Described in Taylor, p. 101.

167 Quotations from Victoria Wolff: Interview with Victoria Wolff.

168 Letters from Ruth Albu: EMR Collection, NYU.

169 Letters from Jutta Remarque: EMR Collection, NYU.

169 "Dear, dear Erich": Letter from Lotte Preuss, EMR Collection, NYU.

170 "I have just read": Letter from Hutchinson quoted in EMR diary, June 1936; EMR Collection, NYU.

170 Information and Goebbels's quotation: Richard Arthur Firda, *Erich Maria Remarque: A Thematic Analysis of His Novels*, p. 88.

170 EMR diary entries: EMR Collection, NYU.

171 Correspondence between EMR and Ruth Albu: EMR Collection, NYU.

174 Remarque in Ascona: Firda, p. 89.

176 "The whole thing is a swindle": Firda, p. 94, quoting a serialization of *Three Comrades* in *Good Housekeeping*, January 1937.

176 "I had known women": Ibid.

176 "The girl sat silent": *Three Comrades*, Wheen translation, p. 71.

187 "Herr von Sternberg?": Maria Riva, *Marlene Dietrich*, p. 464.

190 "She was the one": Interview with Douglas Fairbanks, Jr.

192 Gestapo document: Taylor, pp. 121–22.

194 "He was spending": Curt Riess, *My Famous Friends*, p. 186.

195 "My wife and I were invited": Ibid., p. 193.

198 Quotations from Maria Riva: Riva, pp. 466, 468.

218 "a debonair fox": As told to author by Maria Riva.

219 Background for *Flotsam*: Hans Wagener, *Understanding Erich Maria Remarque*, p. 54.

220 Information on Swiss immigration laws: Ibid., p. 56.

220 "Remarque himself": Ibid.

228 Quotations from Maria Riva: Riva, p. 487.

234 Jean Howard's comment on Dorothy di Frasso: *Jean Howard's Hollywood: A Photo Memoir*, p. 12.

235 "Mr. Ravic is": Quoted in Wagener, p. 62.

236 Letters and notes from Dietrich: EMR Collection, NYU.

238 Letter to Franz and Alma Mahler Werfel: EMR Archiv.

239 Discussion of EMR's art collection: Taylor, p. 160.

243 Letters from Lupe Velez: EMR Collection, NYU.

248 Letter to Natasha Paley Wilson: EMR Collection, NYU.

249 Letter from Elfriede Scholz: EMR Collection, NYU.

250 Material concerning the death sentence and execution of Elfriede Remark Scholz: EMR Archiv and EMR Collection, NYU.

253 "Toward the end of 1943" Riess, p. 189.

254 Letter from Claire Lehmkuhl: EMR Archiv; translation by Henry Goldsmith.

258 Orville Prescott's review: *New York Times*, Jan. 21, 1946.

261 "Remarque was a stickler": Interview with Robert Lantz.

262 "I am not German anymore": *New York Times*, Sept. 26, 1970.

263 Robert Lantz's recollections: Interview with Robert Lantz.

265 Letter to Ingrid Bergman: EMR Archiv and EMR Collection, NYU.

Six. Rings on Her Fingers, 1939–1951

268 Paulette's recollections: Tape-recorded and transcribed reminiscences of PG, ca. 1973–74, PGR Estate.

270 " 'Tola' got a mouth infection": In Joe Morella and Edward Z. Epstein, *Paulette*, p. 105.

270 "It makes a girl think": "Paulette Goddard Discovers Mexico," *Look*, May 1940.

272 "amid Aztec and Mayan relics": Ibid.

272 "The real problem": Hayden Herrera, *Frida*, p. 247.

273 "Rivera and Paulette Goddard": Ibid., p. 269.

275 "She conspired with Wally Westmore": Morella and Epstein, pp. 92–93.

276 Federal Bureau of Investigation Freedom of Information letter: File on PG.

277 "It was inevitable that Paulette": Charles Chaplin, *My Autobiography*, p. 400.

277 "Her home is": Jinx Falkenburg, "My Pal Paulette," *Movieland*, ca. 1944; un-dated clipping in 1944 scrapbook, PG Collection, NYU.

279 "What she has": Ibid., p. 121.

279 Quotation from Charles Chaplin, Jr.: Morella and Epstein, p. 182.

281 "I'll never try dancing": Ibid., p. 99.

281 Quotation from Burgess Meredith: Interview with Burgess Meredith.

283 Quotation from Edith Head: Morella and Epstein, p. 84.

284 Document implicating Charlie Chaplin in the paternity suit: Federal Bureau of Investigation, Freedom of Information/Privacy Acts release, file: preprocessed material.

286 "She was in her prime": Ray Milland, in a Paramount press release for *Reap the Wild Wind*, Academy of Motion Pictures Arts and Sciences Library, Los Angeles, PG file.

291 Federal Bureau of Investigation Freedom of Information/Privacy Acts release, file on EMR.

292 Paulette's recollections of "flying the Hump": PG Collection, NYU.

294 Keenan Wynn's published journal: Among clippings in PG Collection, NYU.

295 "Are you the appointed captain": Anita Loos, "Perils of Paulette," unpublished manuscript, PGR Estate.

298 "Paulette has always been": Louella Parsons' column, *Los Angeles Examiner*, ca. 1945; in Film Stills Archive, Museum of Modern Art, New York, PG clipping file.

301 "Paulette Goddard has worked up": Review in *New York Herald Tribune*, April 1, 1946.

303 Quotations from Jean Renoir: Jean Renoir, *My Life and My Films*, pp. 224, 225.

304 "I shot it": Raymond Durgnat, *Jean Renoir*, p. 252.

304 Renoir on Benedict Bogeaus: Ibid., p. 152.

306 "Paulette Goddard alludes": Ibid., pp. 256–57.

307 Samuel A. Tower's article: *New York Times*, 1946; in Academy of Motion Picture Arts and Sciences Library, Los Angeles, PG file.

308 Letter from an American serviceman: PG Collection, NYU.

308 "Maw, I used to call": Interview with Burgess Meredith.

310 "Mr. DeMille wouldn't speak": Morella and Epstein, p. 159.

310 "This was a chicken house": Burgess Meredith quoted in an unidentified article dated Dec. 28, 1947; Film Stills Archive, Museum of Modern Art, New York, PG clipping file.

313 "In one big way": Interview by Louella O. Parsons, Hollywood, June 4, 1948; unidentified clipping, PG Collection, NYU.

313 "It was such a turkey": James Robert Parish, *The Paramount Pretties*, p. 387.

314 Headline of Charles Pool article, unidentified clipping, PG Collection, NYU.

315 "Paulette didn't even know": Interview with Mary Wickes.

316 "A star may have": Leo Rosten, "Hollywood Revisited," *Life*, 1951.

318 "She took all of our collection": Interview with Burgess Meredith.

319 "The movie colony": From Dorothy Kilgallen's column, *Journal-American*, July 18, 1949.

319 "She appreciated": Quotation from Celestine Wallis in an article by Brooks Peters in *Quest* magazine, March 1993.

320 "One night I was": Unidentified clipping, PG Collection, NYU.

321 "I told Jinx": Tex McCrary, "New York Close-Up," *New York Herald Tribune*, April 23, 1950.

322 "Dear C. B.": Morella and Epstein, p. 177.

322 "I've wanted to do this": Ibid., p. 179.

322 "The audiences were thrilled!": Interview with Bob Ulman.

323 "Certainly I didn't": Unidentified clipping, PG Scrapbook, PG Collection, NYU.

323 Unidentified 1950 Ohio newspaper article, in Academy of Motion Picture Arts and Sciences Library, Los Angeles, PG file.

Seven. New Moon, 1948–1958

324 "Remarque uses grotesque contrasts": Hans Wagener, *Understanding Erich Maria Remarque*, p. 71.

326 "The subject was considered": Ibid., p. 68.

326 "at one point Remarque": Ibid., p. 69.

326 Letters to Harriet Pilpel: EMR Collection, NYU. Remarque sometimes signs these letters with his name spelled in the American way, "Eric."

328 EMR diary entries: EMR Collection, NYU.

329 Quotations from Ellen Janssen Dunham: Interview with Ellen Janssen Dunham.

330 Quotations from David Niven: From press release clipping for his autobiography, *The Moon Is a Balloon*; in Academy of Motion Picture Arts and Sciences Library, Los Angeles, PG file.

331 "Probably neither one": Wagener, p. 129.

348 "In the 1930s": Richard Arthur Firda, *Erich Maria Remarque: A Thematic Analysis of His Novels*, p. 161.

356 Licci Habe's recollections: Interview with Licci Habe.

357 Robert Lantz's recollections: Interview with Robert Lantz.

358 "If I were sick": Interview with Victoria Wolff.

358 "Perhaps what I should have": In Joe Morella and Edward Z. Epstein, *Paulette*, p. 172.

358 Quotations from Ellen Janssen Dunham: Interview with Ellen Janssen Dunham.

361 Letter from Denver Lindley: EMR Collection, NYU.

362 "There are several": Wagener, p. 76.

368 "The film followed": Ibid., pp. 115–16.

369 Letter from Walter Rudolf: EMR Collection, NYU.

370 "Be Vigilant!" piece: EMR Archiv.

370 "The combination of": Wagener, pp. 117–18.

371 Quotations from Peter Stone: Interview with Peter Stone.

372 Letter to Alma Mahler Werfel: EMR Collection, NYU.

373 Maurice Greenbaum's memo to Harriet Pilpel: EMR Collection, NYU.

374 "First of all": Interview with Harriet Pilpel.

374 "Remarque wanted to meet": Leni Riefenstahl, *A Memoir*, pp. 64–65.

376 "During the first weeks": *The Black Obelisk*, pp. 39–40.

376 "I had been thinking": From a *Newsweek* interview; in Firda, p. 186.

376 "I never saw any of them": *The Black Obelisk*, p. 432.

377 Jutta Remarque's letter to EMR: EMR Collection, NYU.

380 "The less things change": *New York Times*, April 2, 1957.

381 "Usually I'm so tired": In Firda, p. 175.

381 "It is very interesting": *New York Times* interview, ca. 1958; in Academy of Motion Picture Arts and Sciences Library, Los Angeles, PG file.

382 Letters from EMR to PG: EMR Collection, NYU.

383 Quotations from John Gavin: Interview with John Gavin.

Eight. Fourth Chorus, 1951–1958

385 Letters from PG to EMR: EMR Collection, NYU.

388 Michael Hall's recollections: Interview with Michael Hall.

397 "It's just as if": PG Scrapbook, PG Collection, NYU.

397 Edward G. Robinson quotation: PG Scrapbook, PG Collection, NYU.

397 "Could the fact": Vincent Rodgers, unidentified clipping in PG Scrapbook, PG Collection, NYU.

398 "Saw Cy Howard": Letter from PG to Alta Goddard Jacobson, PGR Estate.

398 "Actors and actresses": Unidentified clipping in PG Scrapbook, PG Collection, NYU.

400 "If you feel": Letter from PG to Alta Goddard Jacobson, PG Collection, NYU.

401 "Jezebel is a Biblical story": Unidentified clipping, PG Scrapbook, PG Collection, NYU.

401 "But this much is true": Elsa Maxwell's column in the *Hollywood Reporter*, quoted in Joe Morella and Edward Z. Epstein, *Paulette*, p. 45.

401 "We missed you": Cole Porter's letter to PG: PG Collection, NYU.

404 "I love doing TV": Unidentified clipping, PG Scrapbook, PG Collection, NYU.

405 "My poor little baby": Letter from EMR to Alta Goddard Jacobson; EMR Collection, NYU.

405 "Erich and I will marry": Sheila Graham's interview with PG, in *Hollywood Today*, 1957.

408 "For the ceremony": *Daily News*, Feb. 26, 1958.

409 "But at long last": Anita Loos, "The Perils of Paulette," unpublished manuscript, PGR Estate.

409 "What insanity!" Maria Riva, *Marlene Dietrich*, p. 629.

410 "These actresses": Steven Bach, *Marlene Dietrich: Life and Legend*, pp. 275–76.

410 Letters from EMR to PG: EMR Collection, NYU.

Nine. Mr. and Mrs. Erich Maria Remarque, 1958–1970

411 Letters from Alta Goddard Jacobson to EMR: EMR Collection, NYU.

411 Letters from PG to EMR: EMR Collection, NYU.

413 "Stumbling around": Bosley Crowther review, *New York Times*, July 10, 1958.

414 "Perhaps because": Christine R. Barker and R. W. Last, *Erich Maria Remarque*, pp. 27–28.

417 "They were the early years": Letter to author from Gardner McKay.

418 PG letters to Alta Goddard Jacobson: PG Collection, NYU.

419 EMR letters and telegrams to PG: EMR Collection, NYU.

426 Letters from EMR to Hanns-Gerd Rabe: EMR Archiv.

427 "The aging race car driver": In Hans Wagener, *Understanding Erich Maria Remarque*, pp. 92–93.

428 "is thus kin to Remarque's": Richard Arthur Firda, *Erich Maria Remarque: A Thematic Analysis of His Novels*, p. 235.

428 "She felt she was breathing light": *Heaven Has No Favorites* as serialized in *Good Housekeeping*, Feb. 1961, p. 67.

428 "The vehicle for this experience": Firda, p. 235.

429 "When the first things arrived": *Heaven Has No Favorites*, pp. 104–105.

429 Maxwell Geismar's review: "Terror Marched with a Goose Step," *New York Times Book Review*, March 22, 1964.

430 "I am sure she": Letter from Harriet Pilpel to Paul Lazarus, PG Collection, NYU.

435 "started in chaos": Shelley Winters, *Shelley II: The Middle of My Century*, pp. 523, 525.

435 "I think my scenes": Ibid., p. 528.

436 "*Time of Indifference* was": Interview with Rod Steiger.

436 "Paulette Goddard probably walks": Harold Cornsweet's review in *Variety*, 1964.

437 "PAULETTE GODDARD, whom we never": *Lo specchio*, Oct. 18, 1964.

437 Remarque's letters to Alta Goddard Jacobson: EMR Collection, NYU.

439 "Yesterday morning": EMR diary entries, EMR Collection, NYU.

441 "Please send my greetings": Letter from EMR to Hanns-Gerd Rabe, in Barker and Last, p. 29.

441 "Nothing will come": Ibid.

441 "It is almost a manual": Geismar, "Terror Marched with a Goose Step."

442 Quotations from Licci Habe: Interview with Licci Habe.

445 "refugees from other countries": Barker and Last, p. 122.

445 "I always had": Quoted in Barker and Last, p. 30.

449 "The author Erich Maria Remarque": In Harley U. Taylor, Jr., *Erich Maria Remarque: A Literary and Film Biography*, p. 250.

452 "I do remember": Letter from EMR to Karla Henkelmann, EMR Archiv.

456 Quotations from Curt Riess: Curt Riess, *My Famous Friends*, p. 194.

Epilogue: The Widow Remarque, 1970–1990

458 "Behind all the nabob-ballyhoo": Robert Neumann, in a clipping sent to the author by Victoria Wolff, who also translated it.

460 "Mrs. Remarque is quite": Letter from Richard Kay to Harriet Pilpel, PGR Estate.

461 "She wore an American size 12": Interview, through the translator Regina Gfeller, with Antonietta Bellosta.

463 "it is nevertheless": Hans Wagener, *Understanding Erich Maria Remarque*, p. 106.

464 Recollection and quotations from Jean Tailer. Interview with Jean Tailer.

464 "We were eight": Interview with Patricia Roc Reif.

465 Warren Alpert's recollections and quotations: Interview with Warren Alpert.

467 Letters from PG to Alta Goddard Jacobson: PG Collection, NYU.

467 "She was the classic coquette": Interview with Bob Colacello.

468 "Rocky tipped me off": Tape-recorded and transcribed reminiscences of PG, ca. 1973–74, PGR Estate.

468 Recollections and quotations from Lois Granato: Interviews with Lois Granato.

472 "I have now had calls": Memo from Maurice Greenbaum to Richard Kay, PG legal files, PG Collection, NYU.

474 "There are twelve steps": Interview with Jinx Falkenburg McCrary.

475 "Paulette would come out": Interview with Celestine Wallis.

477 "Nobody ever talked back": Interview with Dr. Joseph Bissig.

477 "Last night, when I went": Reminiscences of PG, PGR Estate.

CREDITS

PERMISSIONS ACKNOWLEDGMENTS

Grateful acknowledgment is made to the following for permission to reprint previously published and unpublished material:

Arbeiterwohlfahrt Landesverband Hamburg e.V.: Excerpt from an interview with Axel Eggebrecht and Erich Maria Remarque (*Literarische Welt*, June 14, 1929), copyright Axel Eggebrecht/Arbeiterwohlfahrt. Reprinted by permission of Arbeiterwohlfahrt Landesverband Hamburg e.V.

Berg Publishers: Excerpts from *Erich Maria Remarque* by Christine R. Baker and R. W. Last, copyright (c) 1979 by Christine R. Barker and R. W. Last. Reprinted by permission of Berg Publishers, Oxford, England.

The Bodley Head: Excerpts from *My Autobiography* by Charles Chaplin, copyright (c) 1988 by the Estate of Charles Chaplin. Reprinted by permission of The Bodley Head, London.

Ray Pierre Corsini: Excerpts from "Anatomy of a Siren" from *Fate Keeps on Happening* by Anita Loos (Dodd, Mead & Co., New York, 1984), copyright (c) 1984 by The Anita Loos Trusts; excerpt from, *Anita Loos* by Gary Carey (Alfred A. Knopf, Inc., New York, 1988), copyright (c) 1988 by Gary Carey. Reprinted by permission of Ray Pierre Corsini.

Marlies d'Heureuse: Excerpts from letters from Jutta Remarque to Erich Maria Remarque. Reprinted by permission of Marlies d'Heureuse.

Edward Z. Epstein and Joe Morella: Excerpts from *Paulette: The Adventurous Life of Paulette Goddard* by Edward Epstein and Joseph Morella (St. Martin's, New York, 1985). Reprinted by permission of Edward Z. Epstein and Joe Morella.

The Estate of Marlene Dietrich: Excerpts from letters of Marlene Dietrich, copyright (c) Marlene Dietrich Collection. Reprinted by permission of the Estate of Marlene Dietrich, Maria Riva, executor.

The Estate of Harriet F. Pilpel: Excerpts from letters of Harriet F. Pilpel. Reprinted by permission of the Estate of Harriet F. Pilpel.

The Estate of Paulette Goddard Remarque: Excerpts from *Spark of Life* by Erich Maria Remarque, copyright (c) 1952 by Erich Maria Remarque, copyright renewed 1980 by Paulette Goddard Remarque; excerpts from *The Black Obelisk* by Erich Maria Remarque, copyright (c) 1957 by Erich Maria Remarque, copyright renewed 1985 by Paulette Goddard Remarque; excerpts from *Heaven Has No Favorites* by Erich Maria Remarque, copyright (c) 1961 by Erich Maria Remarque, copyright renewed 1989 by Paulette Goddard Remarque; excerpts from *All Quiet on the Western Front* by Erich Maria Remarque, copyright (c) 1929, 1930 by Little, Brown and Company, copyright renewed 1957, 1958 by Erich Maria Remarque. Reprinted by permission of the Estate of Paulette Goddard Remarque.

by The New York Times Company; excerpt from book review by Orville Prescott of *Arch of Triumph* (1945), copyright (c) 1945 by The New York Times Company; excerpt from an article about House Committee on Un-American Activities by Sam Tower (November 24, 1946), copyright (c) 1946 by The New York Times Company; excerpt from book review by Charles Poore of *Black Obelisk* (April 2, 1957), copyright (c) 1957 by The New York Times Company; excerpt from "Erich Maria Remarque Happily Returns to Filmland" by Thomas Pryor (July 7, 1957), copyright (c) 1957 by The New York Times Company; excerpt from film review of *A Time to Love and a Time to Die* by Bosley Crowther (July 10, 1958), copyright (c) 1958 by The New York Times Company. Reprinted by permission of The New York Times Company.

Michael Romanoff: Excerpt from letter of Natasha Paley Wilson. Reprinted by permission of Michael Romanoff.

I. Roseveare and Professor Dr. H. G. Roseveare: Excerpt from letter from Edith Doerry Roseveare, 1983. Reprinted by permission of I. Roseveare and Professor Dr. H. G. Roseveare.

Klaus Rudolph: Excerpts from letters of Walter Rudolf and Elfriede Remark Scholz, copyright (c) by Klaus Rudolph, Dissen, Germany. Reprinted by permission of Klaus Rudolph.

Regents of the University of California and the University of California Press: Excerpts from *Jean Renoir* by Raymond Durgnat, copyright (c) 1974 by Raymond Durgnat. Reprinted by permission of the Regents of the University of California and the University of California Press.

Rowohlt Verlag GmbH: Excerpt from *Der Halbe Weg [Halfway]* by Axel Eggebrecht, copyright (c) 1975 by Rowohlt Verlag GmbH, Reinbek bei Hamburg. Reprinted by permission of Rowohlt Verlag GmbH.

Selznick Properties, Ltd.: Excerpt from *Memo from David O. Selznick*, edited by Rudy Behlmer (Samuel French Trade Inc., NY, 1988). Reprinted by permission of Selznick Properties, Ltd.

Der Spiegel: Excerpt from an article about Paulette Goddard Remarque. Reprinted by permission of Der Spiegel.

St. Martin's Press, Inc., and Quartet Books Ltd.: Excerpt from *Leni Riefenstahl: A Memoir* by Leni Riefenstahl, copyright (c) 1992 by Leni Riefenstahl. Rights outside the United States for *The Sieve of Time: A Memoir by Leni Riefenstahl* administered by Quartet Books Limited, London. Reprinted by permission of St. Martin's Press, Inc., and Quartet Books Limited.

University of South Carolina Press: Excerpts from *Understanding Erich Maria Remarque* by Hans Wagener, copyright (c) 1991 by Hans Wagener. Reprinted by permission of the University of South Carolina Press.

Verein für Geschichte und Landeskunde von Osnabrück: Excerpts from "Remarque und Osnabrück" by Hanns-Gerd Rabe (*Osnabrücker Mitteilungen*, vol. 77,

1979). Reprinted by permission of Verein für Geschichte und Landeskunde von Osnabrück.

Verlag Herder GmbH & Co. KG: Excerpt from *Meine berühmten Freunde* by Curt Riess, translated by Henry Goldsmith (Freiburg: Verlag Herder, 1987). Reprinted by permission of Verlag Herder GmbH & Co. KG.

ILLUSTRATION CREDITS

Page v (left)   Courtesy of the Estate of Paulette Goddard Remarque.

Page v (right)   Photograph by Marianne Breslauer, courtesy of M. Feilchenfeldt.

Page 5   All photographs courtesy of the Erich Maria Remarque Papers, Fales Library, New York University.

Page 9 (top)   Courtesy of Rud Lichtenberg, Fotografisches Atelier.

Page 9 (bottom)   Courtesy of Niedersächsisches Staatsarchiv Osnabrück Erw A 23 Nr. 17.

Page 13   Both photographs courtesy of Fam. Henrichvark, Osnabrück.

Page 17 (left)   Courtesy of Niedersächsisches Staatsarchiv Osnabrück Erw A 23 Nr. 17.

Page 17 (right)   Courtesy of Heinrich Koopman.

Page 17 (bottom)   Courtesy of the Erich Maria Remarque Papers, Fales Library, New York University.

Page 35 (top)   Courtesy of the Erich Maria Remarque Papers, Fales Library, New York University.

Page 35 (bottom)   Courtesy of Continental Aktiengesellschaft, Hannover, Germany.

Page 41   All photographs courtesy of the Paulette Goddard Archive, Tisch School of the Arts, Cinema Studies Department, New York University.

Page 47   All photographs courtesy of the Paulette Goddard Archive, Tisch School of the Arts, Cinema Studies Department, New York University.

Page 52 (top and bottom)   Courtesy of Photofest.

Page 52 (center)   Photograph by Clarence Sinclair Bull. Courtesy of the Estate of Paulette Goddard Remarque.

Page 61 (left)   Courtesy of the Erich Maria Remarque Papers, Fales Library, New York University.

Page 61 (right)   Courtesy of the Estate of Paulette Goddard Remarque.

Page 61 (bottom)   Courtesy of Lois Granato.

Page 64 (top)   Courtesy of Photofest.

Page 64 (bottom)   Courtesy of the Everett Collection.

Page 69 (top)   Courtesy of the Everett Collection.

Page 69 (bottom)   Courtesy of the Estate of Paulette Goddard Remarque.

Page 76 (top and center)   Courtesy of the Erich Maria Remarque Papers, Fales Library, New York University.

Page 76 (bottom) Courtesy of Miss I. Roseveare and Professor H. G. Roseveare.

Page 94 All photographs courtesy of the Erich Maria Remarque Papers, Fales Library, New York University.

Page 107 (top) Photograph by Marianne Breslauer, courtesy of M. Feilchenfeldt.

Page 107 (bottom) Courtesy of the Erich Maria Remarque Papers, Fales Library, New York University.

Page 115 (top) Courtesy of Lois Granato.

Page 115 (bottom) Courtesy of the Erich Maria Remarque Papers, Fales Library, New York University.

Page 122 (top) Photograph by Hedda Walther. Courtesy of Bildarchiv Preussischer Kulturbesitz, Berlin, and Lois Granato.

Page 122 (bottom) Courtesy of the Erich Maria Remarque Papers, Fales Library, New York University.

Page 124 Both photographs courtesy of the Erich Maria Remarque Papers, Fales Library, New York University.

Page 126 (left) Courtesy of Photofest.

Page 126 (right) Courtesy of Jinx Falkenburg McCrary.

Page 126 (bottom) Courtesy of the Museum of Modern Art, Film Stills Archive.

Page 129 Courtesy of the Everett Collection.

Page 131 (top and bottom) Courtesy of the Erich Maria Remarque Papers, Fales Library, New York University.

Page 131 (center) Courtesy of the Museum of Modern Art, Film Stills Archive.

Page 136 (top) Courtesy of Culver Pictures, Inc.

Page 136 (bottom) Courtesy of the Kobal Collection.

Page 139 (top) Courtesy of the Museum of Modern Art, Film Stills Archive.

Page 139 (bottom) Courtesy of Lester Glassner Collection/Neal Peters.

Page 148 (top) Courtesy of Lester Glassner Collection/Neal Peters.

Page 148 (bottom) Courtesy of the Kobal Collection.

Page 151 Courtesy of Archive Photos.

Page 186 Courtesy of the Kobal Collection.

Page 188 Both photographs courtesy of the Erich Maria Remarque Papers, Fales Library, New York University.

Page 222 (left) Courtesy of the Erich Maria Remarque Papers, Fales Library, New York University.

Page 222 (right) Courtesy of the Estate of Harriet F. Pilpil.

Page 222 (bottom) Courtesy of Photofest.

Page 231 (left) Copyright © by Universal City Studios, Inc. Courtesy of MCA Publishing Rights, a Division of MCA Inc.

Page 231 (right and bottom)   Courtesy of Photofest.

Page 245 (left and bottom)   Courtesy of the Erich Maria Remarque Papers, Fales Library, New York University.

Page 245 (right)   Courtesy *Vogue*. Copyright 1933 (renewed 1961) by the Condé Nast Publications, Inc.

Page 255 (left)   Courtesy of the Erich Maria Remarque Papers, Fales Library, New York University and the Ingrid Bergman Estate.

Page 255 (right and bottom)   Courtesy of the Erich Maria Remarque Papers, Fales Library, New York University.

Page 271 (top)   Courtesy of Lois Granato.

Page 271 (bottom)   Photo by Earl Thiessen, *Look* magazine.

Page 274 (top)   Courtesy of Lois Granato.

Page 274 (bottom)   Courtesy of Sotheby's New York.

Page 278 (top)   Courtesy of Culver Pictures, Inc.

Page 278 (center)   Courtesy of the Estate of Paulette Goddard Remarque.

Page 278 (bottom)   Courtesy of the Kobal Collection.

Page 280 (top)   Courtesy of the Estate of Paulette Goddard Remarque.

Page 280 (bottom)   Courtesy of Photofest.

Page 288 (top)   Courtesy of the Everett Collection.

Page 288 (bottom)   Courtesy of the Museum of Modern Art, Film Stills Archive.

Page 296 (top)   Courtesy of Lois Granato.

Page 296 (center)   Courtesy of The Academy of Motion Picture Arts and Sciences.

Page 296 (bottom)   Courtesy of Culver Pictures, Inc.

Page 300 (top and center)   Courtesy of Jean Tailer.

Page 300 (bottom)   Courtesy of Photofest.

Page 305 (top)   Courtesy of UPI/Bettmann.

Page 305 (center)   Courtesy of Jean Tailer.

Page 305 (bottom)   Courtesy of the Erich Maria Remarque Papers, Fales Library, New York University.

Page 325   All photographs courtesy of the Erich Maria Remarque Papers, Fales Library, New York University.

Page 327 (left and right)   Courtesy of the Erich Maria Remarque Papers, Fales Library, New York University.

Page 327 (bottom)   Courtesy of the Kobal Collection.

Page 352   Both photographs courtesy of the Erich Maria Remarque Papers, Fales Library, New York University.

Page 366 (left)   Photograph by Karl-Hans Plilfer. Courtesy of the Erich Maria Remarque Papers, Fales Library, New York University.

Page 366 (right)   Courtesy of the Estate of Paulette Goddard Remarque.

Page 366 (bottom)   Courtesy of the Erich Maria Remarque Papers, Fales Library, New York University.

Page 394 (top)   Courtesy of the Kobal Collection.

Page 394 (bottom)   Courtesy of Photofest.

Page 402   Both photographs courtesy of the Estate of Paulette Goddard Remarque.

Page 412 (top)   Courtesy of Lois Granato.

Page 412 (bottom)   Courtesy of the Erich Maria Remarque Papers, Fales Library, New York University.

Page 416 (top)   Courtesy of the Erich Maria Remarque Papers, Fales Library, New York University.

Page 416 (bottom)   Courtesy of Photofest.

Page 440   Both photographs courtesy of the Erich Maria Remarque Papers, Fales Library, New York University.

Page 450 (top)   Courtesy of *Neue Osnabrücker Zeitung.*

Page 450 (bottom)   Courtesy of the Erich Maria Remarque Papers, Fales Library, New York University.

Page 459 (top)   Courtesy of Lois Granato.

Page 459 (bottom)   Courtesy of the Erich Maria Remarque Papers, Fales Library, New York University.

Page 466 (top and left)   Courtesy of Lois Granato.

Page 466 (right)   Courtesy of the Estate of Paulette Goddard Remarque.

Page 469   Both photographs courtesy of Lois Granato.

Page 479   Both photographs courtesy of Lois Granato.

INDEX

ABOUT THE AUTHOR

Julie Gilbert is the author of *Umbrella Steps*, a novel, and *Ferber: The Biography of Edna Ferber and Her Circle*, which was nominated for the National Book Critics' Circle Award. Gilbert lives in New York with her husband and teaches fiction writing at New York University.